# 1998

# Russia, Eurasia, and Eastern Europe 1998

### 29TH EDITION

DISCARD

## M. Wesley Shoemaker, Ph.D.

STRYKER–POST

PUBLICATIONS

HARPERS FERRY

WEST VIRGINIA

Next Edition—AUGUST 1999

*M. Wesley Shoemaker . . .*

Associate Dean, Lynchburg College, Lynchburg, Va. B.A *Magna Cum Laude,* Waynesburg College (History); M.A. and Ph.D., Syracuse University (Russian History). Before he entered the teaching profession, he served for a number of years as a Foreign Service Officer with the Department of State. He had assignments in the European Bureau of the Department and abroad at the American Embassy in Kingston, Jamaica, the American Embassy in Bonn, Germany, and the American Consulate General in Stuttgart, Germany. He travels extensively in Eastern Europe.

Photographs used to illustrate *The World Today Series* come from many sources, a great number from friends who travel worldwide. If you have taken any which you believe would enhance the visual impact and attractiveness of our books, do let us hear from you.

First appearing as a book entitled *The Soviet Union and Eastern Europe 1970,* revised annually, published in 1970 and succeeding years by

**Stryker–Post Publications**
P.O. Drawer 1200
Harpers Ferry, WV. 25425
Telephones: 1–800–995–1400
   From outside U.S.A.: 1–304–535–2593
   Fax: 1–304–535–6513
VISA–MASTERCARD

International Standard Book Number: 1–887985–15–8

International Standard Serial Number: 1062–3574

Library of Congress Catalog Number 67–11537

Cover design by Susan Bodde

Historical Research: Robert V. Gross

Cartography by William L. Nelson

Typography by Maryland Composition Company, Inc. Glen Burnie, MD 21060

Printed in the United States of America by United Book Press, Inc. Baltimore, MD 21207

18th century Russian wedding feast. The new husband lifts the bride's veil.

# contents

Political and economic conditions in the republics of the former Soviet Union are in a state of flux. The **Commonwealth of Independent States (CIS)** is probably just a transitional arrangement designed to manage the emergence of these new nations. Boundaries of some of the republics which seceded from the now defunct Socialist Federal Republic of Yugoslavia are in doubt, especially with the attempted dismemberment by its neighbors of multi-ethnic Bosnia-Herzegovina.

# Russia, Eurasian States, and Eastern Europe 1998

Seven years after the collapse of communism and the breakup of the old Union of Soviet Socialist Republics, the newly independent Russian Federation is finally coming into its own. According to the latest available statistics, the Russian economy began growing again some time in 1997 and will grow at a somewhat faster rate in 1998. The rate of growth is not impressive, but it is does indicate that Russia has finally turned the corner economically.

Russia's transition to a market economy is still not complete, however. Although the percentage of GDP tracable to enterprises operating on the new market principles is probably close to seventy percent and growing, there is still a great deal of loss–making industry around that continues to survive only because the state provides subsidies so that people may have jobs. Much of the coal–mining industry fits into this category, though most of heavy industry, including what is left of the old military–industrial complex, fits here as well. Sadly, it also includes almost all agriculture.

It should also be added that the transition would have been further along except for the consistent opposition to reform of the leadership of the State Duma, which has made it impossible, for example, to pass legislation legalizing the private ownership of land. One should recognize that Russia finds itself in a "Catch 22" situation in this regard. Prosperity will only come when Russia has completed its transition to a market economy, a transition that will require new legislation enshrining the principles of a market economy; but Russian voters will continue to elect significant numbers of anti–reformers to the State Duma until they personally begin to benefit from the new economic system. Is there any way to break this impasse?

President Yeltsin's dismissal of Prime Minister Chernomyrdin in March 1998, and his appointment of Sergei Kiriyenko, a 35–year old technocrat, as his new Prime Minister, may be just such an attempt. According to this interpretation, Yeltsin decided in March that Chernomyrdin and reformers such as Anatoly Chubais had accomplished all that they were capable of accomplishing, and it was time to bring in a new team to try a new approach. We should, therefore, expect the Kiriyenko government to abandon some of the tactics and programs of the previous government and to initiate new programs aimed, first, at bringing some immediate benefits to ordinary Russians and, second, to build support for needed legislation in the State Duma. Certain statements that Yeltsin and Kiriyenko have made with regard to the energy sector indicate that this process is already underway. The fact that the State Duma was persuaded to confirm Kiriyenko against its own better judgment is also an indication that it may be brought to support government policies, provided the right "incentives" are used.

If this reading is correct, the government's emphasis will be on programs "that work," i.e. produce some immediate, beneficial result. New programs will require new revenues, however, and Russia currently collects only about ten percent of GDP in taxes. The need for a new tax code is pressing, so also expect extensive discussions with leaders in the State Duma aimed at creating majority support for a new tax code which will raise the revenues needed to support the new programs.

Now a word about the other republics that emerged from the collapse of the old Soviet Union. The surprising thing is that, except for the three Baltic republics, none has done better, either politically or economically, than Russia—and most have done worse. We need say little about the three Baltic republics. All are fully functioning democracies and Estonia has already made sufficient economic progress to merit an invitation to join the European Union. The records of Latvia and Lithuania are not as impressive, though they have both made significant economic progress. Latvia needs to come to terms with its non–Lett residents before it will deserve a clean bill of health, but the necessary political decisions are likely to come sometime this spring or summer.

Of Russia's western neighbors, Ukraine has been pursuing a policy of reform for the past three years with some promising results, while Belarus exists in a sort of time warp. President Lukashenko dreams of a Belarus as it was under communism. This is also the reason why he pushes for a union with Russia. The problem is that he wants the economic benefits that will flow from access to the reformed Russian economy while rejecting the democratic elements that have helped to bring that greater prosperity about. In addition, he is trying to maintain important elements of the command economy at home in Belarus. That's unlikely to work in the long run. Moldova, the last of Russia's western neighbors, has made excellent progress in recent years and that appears likely to continue, in spite of communist gains in the recent parliamentary elections.

The Caucasus has been an area of instability since 1991 and that situation remains largely unchanged. Attempted political assassinations, disaffected populations seeking independence, poorly performing economies—this area has them all. Georgia, in particular, has had all of the above in recent years, while Armenia and Azerbaijan still face off in a war over the ethnic–Armenian enclave of Nagorno–Karabakh. While a truce has held since 1994, neither side is talking, and meanwhile Azerbaijan maintains an energy embargo against Armenia that has left its economy operating at an extremely low level. Azerbaijan, of course, has oil, so its future looks much brighter.

That leaves the Central Asian republics plus Kazakhstan. In addition to Islam, what these republics have in common is that they are primarily agriculturally–based economies with industrial enclaves created during Soviet times. Kazakhstan and Turkmenistan have oil and gas and they have begun to open their economies to outside investment, so they can boast some progress. The other republics have changed little since 1991. Tajikistan, perhaps the worst off, is currently attempting to put a continuing civil war behind it, though not with complete success.

Eastern Europe, on the other hand, is the success story. All of Eastern Europe has made some progress, and countries such as Poland, Hungary, the Czech Republic and Slovenia—all of which recently received invitations to join the European Union—have essentially completed the transition to democratic, market economies. Romania and Bulgaria have also made significant progress in the past two years and are on track to continue to do so. Croatia has made economic progess, but democratic forces are weak there. Macedonia, a poor republic, was badly hurt economically by the war in Bosnia, then by a Greek embargo imposed when it refused to stop calling itself *Macedonia*, but its democracy is intact. The laggards are Slovakia and rump Yugoslavia, or at least the Serbian portion of it. Anti-democratic forces are powerful in both countries and the leaders in both countries have resisted economic reforms. New elections in Slovakia in September 1998 may bring a change, but there is no such hope for Serbia. That leaves Albania. The poorest country in Europe, Albania is still suffering the after effects of a civil war brought on by the collapse of pyramid schemes there. Dependent on foreign assistance for a large part of its national budget, Albania strives to rebuild itself, but progress is slow. In addition, it must struggle against being drawn into what appears to be the beginning of a new political fight next door in Kosovo.

A mixed bag, to be sure, but, overall, clear signs of progress.

M. Wesley Shoemaker
Lynchburg, VA
May 1998

# The Russian Federation

**Area:** 6,592,692 sq. mi. (17,075,000 sq. km.).

**Population:** 149,299,000.

**Capital City:** Moscow (Met. Pop. 9 million).

**Other Major Cities:** St. Petersburg (5.1 million), Nizhny Novgorod—formerly Gorky (1.5 million), Ekaterinburg—formerly Sverdlovsk (1.4 million), Samara—formerly Kuibyshev (1.3 million), Omsk (1.2 million), Kazan, Perm (1.1 million each).

**Climate:** Russia lies within the temperate sub–arctic, and arctic zones. Most of European Russia is within the temperate zone, while most of Siberia lies in the arctic zone.

**Neighboring Countries:** (counter–clockwise from the northwest) Norway, Finland, Estonia, Latvia, Belarus, Ukraine, Georgia, Azerbaijan, Kazakstan, Mongolia, China, North Korea, Japan. Kaliningrad (separated from the rest of the nation) is lodged between Lithuania (north and east) and Poland (south).

**Official Language:** Russian.

**Ethnic Composition:** Russian (83%), other (17%).

**Principal Religions:** Russian Orthodox and Protestant Christianity, Islam, Judaism. Until recently, religious worship was officially discouraged.

**Chief Commercial Products:** Russia is a major industrial power, albeit highly polluted, largely self–sufficient insofar as the domestic economy is concerned. Exports consist of petroleum and natural gas, many commercial and precious metals, including manganese, nickel, chromium, copper and lead, gold, silver and platinum, diamonds, furs, and, almost alone among processed goods, military equipment. Imports include grains, tropical produce, manufactured goods, including consumer goods and machinery. Russia has more than 90% of the former U.S.S.R.'s oil reserves.

**Currency:** Ruble.

**Per Capita Annual Income:** About U.S. $2,500. Inflation makes this figure difficult to determine.

**Former Political Status:** Core of the Russian Empire for centuries to November 7, 1917. Russian Soviet Federative Socialist Republic, member of the Union of Soviet Socialist Republics from 1922 to 1991.

**Federal Structure:** Under the new constitution, Russia is defined as a Federative Republic consisting of republics, provinces, autonomous provinces, districts, autonomous districts and territories. Republics enjoy greater rights of self–government than other subdivisions and some of the republics have negotiated separate agreements with the national government. For example, the Russian Government signed a treaty with Tatarstan in February 1994 under which Tatarstan acknowledged that it was "united" with Russia but retained its own constitution. Chechnya declared its "independence" in 1991. When it refused to recognize the 1993 constitution, Russian troops invaded and occupied it in early 1995.

**National Day:** June 12.

**Chief of State:** Boris N. Yeltsin, President.

**Head of Government:** Sergei Kiriyenko, Prime Minister (since April 1998).

**National Flag:** Three equal horizontal stripes of white, pale blue, and red (the same as used by the Russian Imperial Empire).

## THE LAND AND THE PEOPLE

The Russian Federation, which became a separate, independent nation in December 1991 after the collapse of the Union of Soviet Socialist Republics, consists of the Russian–speaking core of that former union. Still the largest country in the world, it stretches 5,500 miles (9,200 km.) from the Kaliningrad enclave in the west to the Kamchatka Peninsula in the east, encompassing not only the lands of historic Russia west of the Ural Mountains, but all of Siberia. Expressed another way, the Russian Federation reaches 172 degrees around the globe (from longitude 19°39'E to 169° W).

Eleven time zones separate the Kaliningrad Region in the West from the Chukotka Peninsula in the East. Thus, even though fourteen republics broke away and established themselves as independent nations in 1991, the Russian Federation continues as one of the great nations of the world.

The heart of this enormous land is a seemingly endless plain that stretches from the Polish border in the west to beyond the Yenisei River in the east and into Central Asia in the south. This Eurasian plain, actually three interconnected plains partially separated by the low–lying Ural Mountains, is known as the Russian Plain west of the Ural Mountains. East of the Urals, it becomes the Western Siberian Lowlands. That part of the plain that extends across Kazakhstan and into Central Asia is known as the Turan Lowland.

The Russian Plain is part of the even larger East European Plain. It begins at the Baltic Sea in the North and extends to the Black Sea and the Caucasus Mountains in the South. Not totally flat, it is broken up by a series of higher elevations, the most significant of which is the Valdai Hills (also known as the Central Russian Upland), located in the northwest.

These somewhat higher elevations give rise to several large rivers which, flowing outward to the seas, connect most parts of the Russian Plain. Although the Valdai Hills only cover an area of approximately 100 square miles, they are the birthplace of four rivers, including the two largest rivers of the Russian Plain, the Dnieper and the Volga. The other two rivers are the Western Dvina (known in Latvia as the Daugava) and the Lovat.

Today, the Valdai Hills form part of the

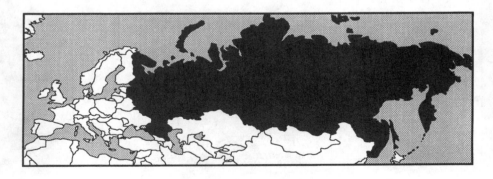

1

border between the Russian Federation and the Republic of Belarus (formerly Byelorussia). However, this area, and the area of the Pripet Swamps to the southwest, is usually accepted as the birthplace of all the Eastern Slavs which include Russians. The Dnieper River flows west, then south, crossing the border into Belarus. It then continues southward, passing through the Republic of Ukraine before entering the Black Sea.

The Volga flows eastward, then southward, finally emptying into the Caspian Sea. The Western Dvina flows northward into Latvia, where it undergoes a name change and becomes the Daugava. It flows through Latvia into the Gulf of Riga, an arm of the Baltic Sea. The Lovat flows north into Lake Ilmen. When its waters leave the lake, they become the Volkhov, on which the historic city of Novgorod is located. The Volkhov, in turn, flows into Lake Ladoga. As they go from the lake, they become the Neva River. The Neva, on which St. Petersburg is located, flows into the Gulf of Finland, another arm of the Baltic Sea.

The origins of the Russian state are associated with a north–south water trade route that arose in the ninth century using the western part of this river system. The major river involved was the Dnieper, along whose middle reaches the city of Kiev is located. Kiev, capital of the Republic of Ukraine, was also the capital of Kievan Rus, the first Russian state. The other river system was the Lovat–Volkhov–Neva, and here the other important Russian city was Novgorod, located on the Volkhov at the northern edge of Lake Ilmen. These two cities guarded the trade route, and their unification under a single ruler marked the beginning of the then small Russian state.

There is one other river of the Russian Plain that needs to be mentioned, though its significance is more recent. The Don River lies between the Dnieper and Volga Rivers in the South. It flows into the Sea of Azov, an arm of the Black Sea. Because it is connected to the Volga by the Volga–Don canal, it provides a link between the Caspian and Black Seas.

The Western Siberian Lowlands, though nearly as large as the Russian Plain, have little of its importance, largely because of the climate. All of Russia lies quite far to the north, but most of European Russia benefits from weather patterns that give it a milder climate than its northern location would indicate. The warm waters of the Gulf Stream, pushing up through the English Channel and into the Baltic Sea, greatly modify the climate of northern Russia. Other weather patterns associated with the Mediterranean Sea have a similar effect on the southern part of Russia.

The influence of these weather patterns are not found east of the Ural Mountains. Moreover, they are replaced by countervailing weather patterns whose effect is to make the climate even more severe than would be expected at similar latitudes. In addition, much of Siberia lies further north than the European part of the Russian Federation.

Nearly half of Siberia is situated north of the 60° parallel, the same parallel as St. Petersburg, and perhaps one–fifth of it lies north of the Arctic Circle. Another influence is that the land tends to slope downward from south to north, meaning that Arctic fronts can sweep unhindered southward across the landscape. This means also that Siberia's rivers flow from south to north—and their mouths in the north freeze earlier in the fall and thaw later in the spring than their more southerly upstream sections. The northern two–thirds of the Western Siberian Lowlands are, accordingly, a land of mixed evergreen forest and swamp.

This is the western third of that broad

**To keep the map simplified, names of the former, now independent, Soviet republics, are not shown.**

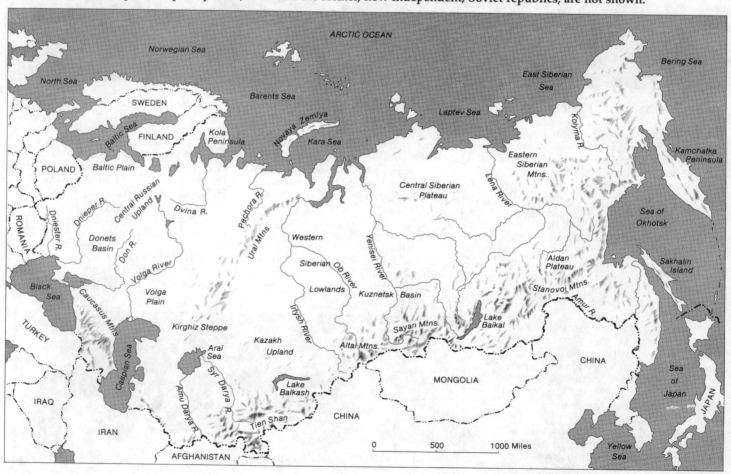

The first helicopter tour by an American journalist of the main harbor of Vladivostok (eastern coast of Siberia facing on the Sea of Japan) produced this aerial view. In the foreground is a naval shipyard now serving the Russian Pacific fleet, with the aircraft carrier Minsk (center) undergoing maintenance.
Photo by Bryan Hodgson © 1990 National Geographic Society

band of forest stretching from the Ural Mountains to the Pacific Ocean known as the Taiga. Agriculture is possible only in the south, in a fairly wide band just east of the Ural Mountains, but sharply narrowing as one travels eastward, ending west of Irkutsk. It is easy to locate this fertile band on a map for here are found all of the major cities of western Siberia, connected by the Trans–Siberian Railway, which passes through the region.

The Western Siberian Lowlands are dominated by two great river systems, the Ob–Irtysh and the Yenisei. The Ob–Irtysh drains the western and central part of the plain; the Yenisei drains the eastern part plus the western edges of the Central Siberian Plateau. Because they both flow northward, their economic usefulness is very limited.

To the east of the Western Siberian Lowlands, the land rises and becomes known as the Central Siberian Plateau. Here the land is still mostly flat or slightly rolling, but the climate is also much harsher, partly because of the higher elevation. In the North, the area is all treeless tundra, while the rest of the land is covered by evergreen forests, a continuation of the taiga. All of the plateau is classified as an area

of permafrost—the land is permanently frozen to a depth of 50–60 feet and in the short Siberian summers only the top 3–4 feet thaw. Subsistence agriculture is carried on in openings in the forests in the south, but this is generally not an area suitable for agriculture.

The Lena River, mightiest of Siberia's rivers, divides the Central Siberian Plateau from the Eastern Siberian Mountains. The southern, upstream portion of the Lena River Valley has been developed somewhat more because of extensive mineral deposits that have been found in the area. Yakutsk, capital of the Republic of Yakutsk–Sakha, which is located on the banks of the Lena River, boasts a population of over 200,000 inhabitants.

The Eastern Siberian Mountains are a series of ranges that run for 1,500 miles from west to east, up to the Bering Strait and the Pacific Ocean. Like the Central Siberian Plateau, this is an area of permafrost, with tundra in the north and taiga in the south. The tallest of these mountains is only about 10,000 feet in height, but the area is largely uninhabited except for wandering tribes of reindeer herders because of the extreme climate. Temperatures average above freezing for

only about two months out of the year, partly because of the northern location, but also because of the effect of cold Arctic ocean currents just offshore.

South of the Eastern Siberian Mountains, the Amur River forms the boundary between the Russian Federation and the People's Republic of China for a distance of about 700 miles before it turns northeastward and eventually empties into the Sea of Okhotsk. The Amur is the only major Siberian river to flow from west to east and the Amur River Valley is the only area of extensive cultivation in the eastern part of Siberia. The amounts produced are insufficient to supply the population, however, so this, like the rest of Siberia, is a net food–importing area.

The last major feature of the Siberian landscape is a series of very high mountain chains that stretch all along the southern border. These are, starting from the west, the Altai, Sayan and Yablonoi, plus the Stanovoi Mountains. The latter, which begin north of the Amur River, are separated from the Eastern Siberian Highlands by the Aldan Plateau. These are mostly high, rugged mountains that hem in the land and isolate Russian Siberia from its neighbors.

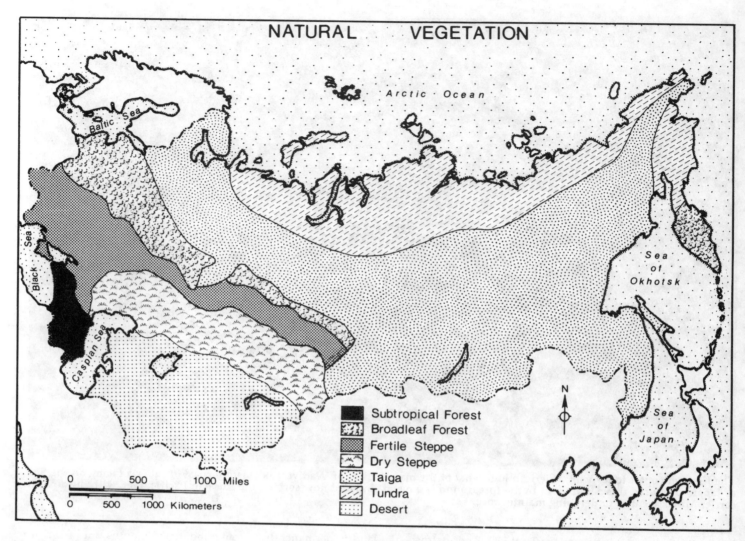

## NATURAL VEGETATION

**Legend:**
- ■ Subtropical Forest
- Broadleaf Forest
- Fertile Steppe
- Dry Steppe
- Taiga
- Tundra
- Desert

### Natural Regions

The Russian Federation includes within its limits climatic belts varying from the temperate to the Arctic, stretching from west to east in wide bands across the country. Two of these, the tundra and the taiga, are found primarily in Siberia. The tundra stretches across the northern part of the land that borders on the Arctic Ocean from the Ural Mountains in the west to the tip of the Chukotka Peninsula in the east. It is almost entirely uninhabited and nothing but moss and swamp shrubs grow there. Migratory herds of reindeer graze briefly in the southernmost part of the tundra during the brief summer.

Immediately south of the tundra is the taiga, a zone of evergreen forest that begins at about Archangel in the west and gradually widens toward the east until it takes in an area as far south as Lake Baikal. The belt then bends somewhat northward before continuing on to the Sea of Othotsk.

To the south of the taiga is a zone of mixed forest which stretches from west to east across the entire country. West of the Urals, this takes in about two–thirds of the Russian Plain, reaching as far south as Kiev, capital of the Republic of Ukraine.

On its southern edge, it gradually thins out, becoming mixed wooded steppe and grassy meadow. The northern slope of the Caucasus Mountains also belongs in this climatic zone.

The last vegetation zone is the steppe, or prairie area. The steppe begins as a 150–mile band north of the Black Sea and stretches eastward into Central Asia. It was originally a natural grassland, but today this area is mostly cultivated land. The chief city of the Russian steppe is Stavropol, the main city of the region where Mikhail Gorbachëv grew up.

### Ethnic Diversity: The Symbol of Chechnya

The Russian Federation, with 83% of the population ethnic Russians, is relatively homogeneous. Nevertheless, it is home to numerous non–Russian ethnic groups and this is reflected in its federal structure—which divides the country into 21 Republics, forty–nine Regions, six Territories, ten Autonomous Areas, two cities of federal importance—Moscow and St. Petersburg, plus the Jewish Autonomous Region. After the collapse of communism in 1991, a number of the republics declared

their "sovereignty" vis–à–vis the Russian Federation and several modified their names. For example, the Tatar Autonomous Republic became the Republic of Tatarstan, while the Yakutsk Autonomous Republic, changed its name to the Republic of Sakha (Yakutia). In the area of the northern Caucasus, one group, the Chechens seceded from the Chechen–Ingush Autonomous Republic to establish their own Republic of Chechnya. Under the leadership of Dzhokhar Dudayev, a former Soviet Air Force general, Chechnya then declared its independence.

President Yeltsin attempted to reassert Russian authority over the Republic of Chechnya in November 1991, but discovered he had neither the force nor the political support to carry it out. He backed down when the Russian Supreme Soviet refused to endorse his policy. Over the next three years, a series of attempts were made to get Chechnya to drop its independence bid, but without success. Chechnya also refused to sign the general Federation treaty which Yeltsin negotiated with the various republics in 1992. And General Dudayev refused to accede to the new constitution of the Russian Federa-

4

tion, approved in December 1993, even though, under its terms, Chechnya would have had extensive autonomy, including its own constitution.

It has been suggested that one reason why the Chechens continued to hold out for independence is that most of the republic's 1.3 million inhabitants are Muslims who want to separate from Russia for religious reasons. It is true that General Dudayev did, at times, make references to the creation of an Islamic nation. Yet that is not the only reason, for other Muslim–majority areas have accepted the new constitution. In any case, President Yeltsin's patience was exhausted by December 1994 and he then authorized the use of military force against the Republic of Chechnya.

Although greatly outnumbered, the Chechnyan defenders resisted strenuously and even managed to create a temporary stalemate. It took the Russian army approximately three months to capture Grozny, the capital and, even so, additional units had to be brought in to accomplish this. By April 1995, most of Chechnya had been brought under Russian control and a new Chechen government, headed by Salambek Khadjiev, a longtime opponent of General Dudayev, had been installed. General Dudayev and his embattled forces retreated into the mountains in the south. They had not been finally defeated, however, so guerrilla fighting continued, with occasional Chechnyan forays even into nearby parts of Russia. Though Russian forces managed to kill General Dudayev in early 1996, anti–war sentiment continued to grow in Russia, eventually forcing President Yeltsin to begin seeking a way out of the impasse. After his reelection, therefore, Yeltsin named General Lebed as his new security adviser and gave him responsibility for Chechnya. Using his new authority, Lebed negotiated a settlement with the new Chechnyan leadership, agreeing to a withdrawal of all Russian forces from the republic in return for a Chechnyan pledge not to press for formal independence for five years. Although Lebed later lost his job, the agreement has held, partly because no one on the Russian side wants to restart the war. As for the Chechnyans, they selected Aslan Maskhadov, the man who negotiated the agreement with Lebed, as their new president in January 1997.

President Yeltsin's resort to use force against the Chechnyans must be viewed as something of an aberration, however. He has been a consistent advocate of local sovereignty for the republics and other autonomous political subdivisions and this position was essentially enshrined in the December 1993 constitution. If he felt he had to take action in Chechnya, it was because of his concern that, if Chechnya were permitted to secede, some of the other republics might try to break away as well. There is at least some basis for this

fear. There are still separatist tendencies in several of the republics, in particular Tatarstan and Bashkortostan, both of whom have large Muslim populations and occupy a strategic location along the Volga River. Any movement toward independence in these republics would have to be viewed extremely seriously, for they are situated astride all the major railroad lines and oil pipelines connecting Siberia to European Russia. Thus the war in Chechnya is essentially a war on behalf of Russia's territorial integrity.

## History

The origins of both the Russian state and nation are found in the area north of the Black Sea and in the steppe lands to the north and east of that strategic body of water. Although there is evidence of human settlement in the area dating back to the neolithic period of the Stone Age,

European Russia's Heartland
showing principal cities

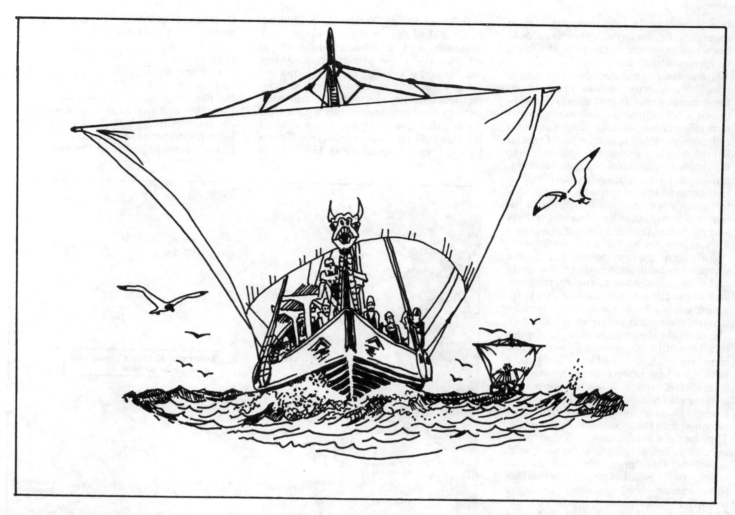

significant history begins with the Slavs. These people were and are identified by a common or similar language rather than by any other common features. The Russians are part of an Eastern Slav group, the other members of which speak Ukrainian and Byelorussian.

The Poles, Czechs and Slovaks belong to a second major group, the West Slavs. There is also a South Slav branch represented by the Bulgarians and the ethnic groups of Yugoslavia.

Little is known about the original home of the early Slavs and many theories have been developed and discarded by scholars. As early as the beginning of the Christian era, however, Slavic people were found throughout most of the Russian Plain west of the Dnieper River and in Eastern Europe as far west as the Vistula River in what is now central Poland. References to the Slavs are also found in the writings of the Greek and Roman historians of the early Christian era, but very little is known about them in this time period. Essentially, they were cut off from classical civilization by the fact that they occupied only the center of the Russian Plain, the more southern part bordering the Black Sea not being suitable for medieval agriculture. The Slavs were traditionally agricultural people and left the grassy steppe of southern Russia to others.

The early political organization of the Slavs was basically tribal, with groups of self–governing villages cooperating in such areas as defense. By the 7th century, towns had begun to develop and trade between the tribes became more important. Kiev, later the capital, was founded at about this time and probably owed its existence to the trade that had started along the Dnieper River. Located high on the bluffs that overlook the western shore of the river, Kiev was ideally located to dominate all such trade.

Novgorod, located at the northern edge of Lake Ilmen, was established somewhat later. Begun as a trading post for amber and other products of the Baltic Sea area, it soon developed as a manufacturing center for jewelry, metals and wood products. Its chief significance, however, was as the northern terminus of the trade route known as the "Road from the Varangians to the Greeks." It was the existence of the trade route that led to the creation of the first organized Russian state.

"Varangian" was the old Slavonic word for a Norseman or Viking. Ancestors of today's Scandinavians, the Vikings were great seamen and from about the seventh century onward, they had been pushing out of Scandinavia, carrying out raids and explorations in all directions. Eventually they established settlements in eastern England, northern France and along the southern coastline of the Baltic Sea. This brought them into contact with Novgorod. According to tradition, Rurik, leader of one of these Viking bands, established himself at Novgorod in 862.

The story of the coming of the Vikings is told in *The Primary Chronicle*, a 12th century compilation of history from unknown earlier sources. According to the *Chronicle*, Rurik and his band of Varangians were invited to set themselves up as the local rulers—"Our land is great and abundant, but there is no order in it; come rule and reign over us." It is more likely that the Novgorodian merchants hired Varangians as mercenaries and then Rurik decided to take complete control himself. Twenty years later, Oleg the Norwegian, Rurik's successor, "set himself up as prince in Kiev." Since he retained control in Novgorod, he then controlled the two chief cities of the "Road from the Varangians to the Greeks."

**Kievan Russia:** This was the beginning of "Kievan Rus," the first organized Rus-

6

sian state. Oleg lived until 913 and he spent the rest of his life extending his control over neighboring Slavic tribes and building up the trade route upon which the prosperity of the new state was based. His most spectacular gesture, according to Russian sources, was an attack on Constantinople which he launched in 907. Byzantine sources make no reference to such an attack but they do record that in 907 the Byzantine Emperor signed a treaty with Oleg which granted access to Byzantine markets on very favorable terms. Oleg was succeeded by Igor in 913; the latter was either the son or grandson of Rurik and from that time onward the descendants of Rurik sat on the throne of Kievan Rus. This Rurikovichi ("sons of Rurik") dynasty later made the transfer when the capital was moved to Vladimir and, later to Moscow, so that it remained the ruling dynasty of Russia until 1598, when Fedor, son of Ivan the Terrible, died without an heir.

The first ruling family of Russia was thus Varangian in origin, but it must be emphasized that they became rulers of a land that had already developed an extensive "slavic" culture. The Varangians were fine warriors and good leaders, but the Viking culture did not replace the native Slav culture. In fact, the opposite happened—the Varangian rulers were soon enveloped by Slavic culture.

This can be seen in the names of subsequent rulers. Igor was killed in 945 while on an expedition to collect tribute from a neighboring Slavic tribe. He was succeeded by his wife, Olga, because his son was still only a child. But that son, who succeeded to the throne in 962, was named Sviatoslav—the third generation of Varangian rulers already had Slavic names and, one can reasonably assume, were speaking the local Slavic language.

The subject of early Slavic culture is complex; by this time it was indeed fairly well developed, but was centered around a belief in pagan Slavic deities. The trade connection between Kievan Rus and Constantinople meant that the Russians were exposed to Byzantine culture and religion.

Constantinople was the leading city of Europe, the capital of the Byzantine Empire and the home of the Patriarch of Constantinople, leader of Greek Orthodox Christianity. It was a center of wealth, power and culture. Further, the Orthodox Church was actively committed to a policy of conversion of the Slavs; its missions had been active among the Bulgarians for some time. Two Orthodox monks, Cyril and Methodius, had translated the *Bible* into Old Slavonic and in the process, created the Cyrillic alphabet designed to portray the *sounds* of Slavonic in characters different from the Roman alphabet. There thus was created the first written Slavic language.

Oleg permitted an Orthodox mission to

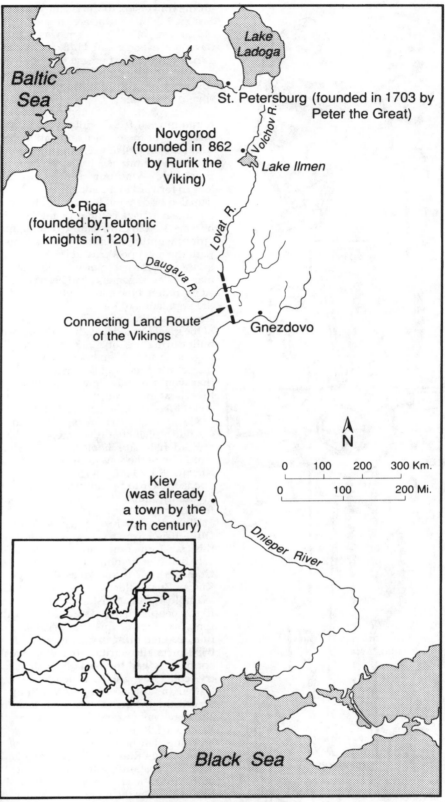

**ROAD FROM THE VARANGIANS TO THE GREEKS**

open in Kiev, but the first breakthrough did not occur until 955 when Olga underwent Christian baptism by missionaries from Constantinople. But her son, Sviatoslav, never converted, and Christianity remained a minority belief. The largest conversion to Orthodox Christianity occurred during the reign of Sviatoslav's son, Vladimir (978–1015). It was somewhat ironic that Vladimir was responsible

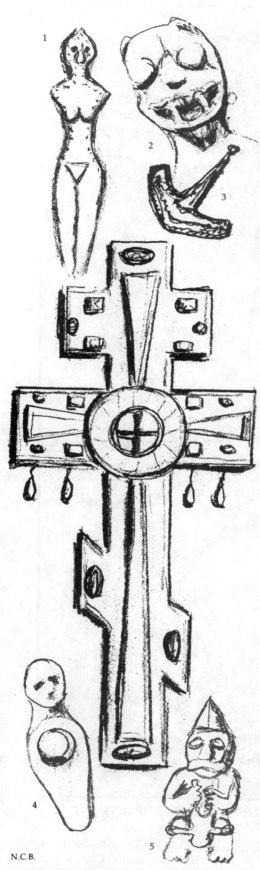

**Christian Orthodox (Byzantine) cross
and pagan symbols**

1. Goddess
2. God of the Under–World
3. Hammer of a God
4. Sky God
5. Male God

for the conversion to Christianity, since he assumed the throne as a champion of the old Slavic gods. Paganism was a dying force, however. Poland, Hungary and Bulgaria had already become Christian and the kings of Denmark and Norway were converted shortly after Vladimir's accession to the throne.

Thus, when the Byzantine Emperor found himself faced with revolts in various parts of the empire and called upon Vladimir for assistance, offering his own sister to Vladimir as a bride, the offer was irresistible—Vladimir sent help and looked forward to the added power his anticipated bride would bring. But he found that the marriage could only take place if he converted to Christianity. Without hesitation, with the intent of allying himself with the most powerful state of that age, he underwent baptism in 988. After the marriage arrangements had been completed, he ordered the mass baptism of the entire population of Kiev and began the construction of St. Sophia Cathedral, the first of the great Orthodox cathedrals that were built during the time of Kievan Rus. The Byzantine style of architecture was introduced into Russia in this manner, a style that would remain dominant until Peter the Great introduced the neo–classical style at the beginning of the 18th century.

Kievan Rus also officially adopted the Cyrillic alphabet at this time, and Vladimir ordered that schools be set up for the education of the sons of the upper classes. Kievan Rus had, in fact, completely opened itself to Byzantine influence and gradually, much of its culture was transformed.

Vladimir and his successor, Yaroslav (1019–1054), were responsible for much of this transformation, and it is for this reason that the combined reigns of these Grand Princes is known as the height of Kievan Rus. Influenced by the Byzantine example, the relationship of Grand Prince to the people changed and it was at this time that Kievan Rus first became a nation. Earlier princes had merely levied tribute on the various tribes and each spring they had traveled about the country, collecting goods which were then traded in Constantinople. Vladimir replaced the tribute system with taxation. Yaroslav was responsible for having the Bishop of Kiev named a *Metropolitan*, meaning that he became the head of an autonomous Russian Church. The Patriarch of Constantinople still retained the authority to *name* the Metropolitan, but this made Kiev the religious as well as political capital of the state. Yaroslav's other important achievement is that he was re-

sponsible for the first Russian law code, the *Russkaya Pravda*.

After the death of Yaroslav there was a period of decline partly because of a system of inheritance which tended to break up the kingdom into separate principalities, and encouraged competition for the throne among brothers and cousins. Occasionally uncles and nephews entered the contest for the dominant throne of Kiev. New Asian invaders, the *Polovtsy*, appeared on the scene, contributing to the decline of Kiev. The city was attacked in 1169 by a contender for the throne and lost its position as capital of the Russian states for a time. It was almost completely destroyed in 1240 by a massive invasion of Mongols (Tartars) let by Batu, grandson of the renowned Ghengis Khan, founder of the empire of the "Golden Horde."

What came to be called the "Mongol Yoke" had to be endured by the Russians until it was finally overthrown in 1480 by Ivan III, Prince of Moscow. An earlier attempt in 1380 ended in failure, despite the dashing military exploits of the Russian forces led by Dmitri, also a Prince of Moscow.

**The Effects of Mongol Occupation**

Historians are in dispute concerning the exact significance of the period of Mongol (Tartar) occupation. Generally speaking, the division is between those who point to the catastrophic result of the Tartar rule, those who felt it was beneficial and scholars who feel that the importance of the occupation is exaggerated. In the view of the so-called Eurasian school, the Tartars contributed to the transformation of a number of small and disjointed states into a strong, centralized and autocratic unit, launching it on the way toward becoming a powerful, modern state. Some specific developments, such as the legal system, military organization, taxation and tax collection are listed (sometimes incorrectly) as positive results. Some scholars argue that the contemporary Russian style of behavior and other psychological attitudes are to be attributed to evil Mongol influence. They stress the bad aspects, such as the fearful destruction of cities and the wholesale murder of populations as well as forced migrations of people from the fertile plains to the dense woodlands of the northeast. Of greatest importance, according to this group, is the disruption of contact between the Russian people and important centers of culture such as Byzantium and the developing European states to the west. One of the results of this isolation was the lack of beneficial influences provided by the European Renaissance and the Reformation.

The necessity of resisting the greedy Tartars affected the style of government life in Russia, encouraging cheating, evasion, corruption and violence. A lasting element of the modern Russian outlook is the sense

**19th century drawing of a
Mongol general**

of being threatened and exploited; some scholars charge that this attitude was founded in the harsh period of Tartar rule.

Regardless of what judgment is placed on the effect of Tartar rule, there is agreement on one incidental result: the growth and rise to power of a new center of leadership in the Russian lands: the state of Moscow. The emergence of this area as a leader compensated for the destruction of Kiev and the breaking away of other states which remained detached from Russia for centuries.

To understand the contribution of the Tartars to the growth of Moscow, it is necessary to know of the way the Mongols exercised their power over the conquered Russian lands. With few exceptions, the Tartars usually left the native princes on their thrones and converted them into collectors of tribute and taxes and also used them as law enforcement officials of their territories. First as pagans and later as Moslems, the Tartars also left the Orthodox Church alone, and in fact increased its authority and power. Working for the Tartars was one of the many factors that helped to transform the insignificant village of Moscow, first mentioned in the year 1147, into the center of a future empire.

**The Rise of Moscow**

Moscow profited from its location close to frequently traveled river routes. Called *Moskva* in Russian, the city is located on a river of the same name that flows to the Oka River, the most important western tributary of the mighty Volga. The rise of

the small principality of Moscow was helped by the traditional battles to determine the successor to the throne, as well as by the expansion through purchase and conquest, service agreements with lesser princes and, finally, clever dealings with the Tartar leaders that appeared to be part of a pattern of obedient behavior. Occasional military help was provided to the Tartars in their battles to suppress rebellious princes and populations.

According to one prominent historian, Moscow was the more or less deliberate choice for a grand–ducal position because of support from the large landowners, called *boyars* in Russian, and from the Church. The boyars suffered from the constant damage resulting from feuds among the lesser princes—they were looking for a suitable state that could enforce its authority and thus bring greater law and order to Russia. The Orthodox Church had transferred the seat of the head of the Russian Church, known as the Metropolitan, from devastated Kiev. During the reign of the Grand Prince Ivan Kalita (whose name literally means "John Moneybags") the Metropolitan Theognostus settled in Moscow, making it the new spiritual capital of "all Russia."

The Prince of Moscow thus acquired the status of a national leader and was looked upon to protect the Russian lands against the Mongols.

As the power of the *Golden Horde* began to wane, the leading position of Moscow became more of less uncontested. The amount of territorial gain was tremendous—from the time of Ivan Kalita to the

second half of the 15th century, the area of Moscow control expanded from about 600 to 15,000 square miles. In still further expansion, the ruler Ivan III ("The Great") added another 40,000 square miles by a combination of purchases, inheritance and conquest.

**Ivan "The Great"**

Ivan's most important military effort resulted in the capture of the powerful city of Novgorod, referred to in its own official title as "Lord Novgorod the Great." This was the most significant trading place in western Russia. It possessed a unique form of government. Although a prince was the head of state, he was required to keep his throne outside the city walls; the internal affairs of the city were managed by the *Veche*, a representative city council which could be summoned into session when any citizen rang the town bell. This early experiment in democracy came to an end when Novgorod was absorbed by autocratic Moscow.

Ivan III further achieved prestige in 1472 when he married Zoë, niece of the last of the Byzantine emperors who was killed when the Turks conquered Constantinople in 1453. The Moscow prince adopted the term *Tsar*, a Slavic contraction of the word *Caesar*, to refer to himself. Ivan started to behave like a direct heir to the Byzantine throne, adding also the titles *Autokrat* (Greek for "absolute ruler") and *Gosudar* ("sovereign") to *Tsar*. About this time, a scholarly Russian monk developed in his writings the concept of a "Third Rome," which identified Moscow as the

**An Italian map (1560) of the Principality of Moscow**

**Ivan IV—the boy and the man**

Nell Cooke Byers

true capital of Christendom, in a line of succession through Rome and the recently fallen Constantinople. In later centuries, this doctrine was interpreted as a call for imperial expansion, although it had only a religious significance when first expounded.

### Ivan "The Terrible"

The "ingathering of lands" was continued by Ivan's successors. His grandson, Ivan IV (1533–1584) came to be known as "The Terrible." Actually the English word "terrible" is not an entirely accurate translation of the Russian word *grozny,* which is better described by the term "awe–inspiring." There is much to justify Ivan's nickname—he was a ruler impressive enough to inspire awe and he was undoubtedly cruel and unpredictable enough to be called "terrible."

Well–educated by comparison with other princes of his time, this shrewd man with a deep interest in theology was given to uncontrolled outbreaks of violence and cruelty. His pattern alternated between exaggerated acts of pious behavior and periods of unrestrained viciousness.

Ivan was a child of three in 1533 when his father died and he became the titular ruler of Russia. When his mother, Elena Glinskaya, died mysteriously five years later, Ivan found himself at the mercy of two competing *boyar* families: the Belskys and the Shuiskys. In their struggle for power, the two families paid public homage to Ivan, but ignored him in private. They exploited the state and pillaged the treasury. Ivan put an end to the situation in 1543 when, as a 13–year–old boy, he turned to his guards and ordered them to take Prince Andrew Shuisky away and kill him. A 13–year–old boy can't rule a state, but from that day onward, no one dared to oppose his will.

Ivan was crowned "Tsar of All the Russias" in 1547, the first ruler to assume the title at the time of his coronation. In this same year, he married Anastasia Romanova, daughter of a minor *boyar* family. Ivan proved to be an energetic Tsar and the next years were full of his reforms and military conquests. The changes were intended to reduce the traditional powers of the *boyars,* but they also included a new code of laws, the *Sudebnik,* which was issued in 1550, and an attempt to reform the Church through the calling of a church council in 1551.

Ivan was also responsible for creation of Russia's first parliament, the *Zemskii Sobor* ("Assembly of the Land"), which he convened in 1550 and again in 1566.

Ivan also defeated and annexed the Khanate of Kazan in 1552, thus giving him control over the middle Volga. Four years later, he attacked and defeated the Khanate of Astrakhan, adding those domains to his realm. This gave him control of the entire course of the Volga River and access to the Caspian Sea. To celebrate his victory over the Tatars (Tartars), Ivan ordered the construction of St. Basil's Cathedral in what is now Red Square in Moscow.

Problems began in 1558 when he decided to launch an invasion of Livonia—modern Estonia and Latvia—in an attempt to gain access to the Baltic Sea. When Livonia disintegrated, Poland–Lithuania and Sweden moved in to pick up the pieces and Ivan found himself at war with both of these nations plus Denmark. The war dragged on until 1582 and left Russia all but depleted.

The war also was at least partly responsible for Ivan's creation of the *Oprichnina,* a separate administration which was intended to finally destroy the traditionally separate power of the *boyars.* During the Livonian war, some of the *boyars* engaged in open treason and joined the side of Poland–Lithuania. One of the most distinguished of the *boyars* was Prince Andrei Kurbsky, one of Ivan's army commanders. He defected to the enemy side in 1564 after having been defeated by Lithuanian forces. The event is remembered through a fascinating exchange of correspondence between the Tsar and the prince; the Tsar called the prince a traitor, while Kurbsky maintained that he "chose freedom."

Ivan became determined to deal with all "traitors" and he threatened to abdicate as Tsar unless he was given a free hand to deal with his enemies, both real and imagined, as he wished. His terms were spelled out in two letters he had delivered to the Metropolitan of Moscow. What Ivan proposed was to set up half of the realm as a personal domain, free from normal governmental administration and supervision by the "Chosen Council." In effect, half of Russia was to become Ivan's private property, and he would be free to take the lands of all the *boyars* located within the *Oprichnina*—"area set apart."

To enforce his will, he set up an *oprichnik* army of 6,000 men. Black–robed and riding black horses, each *oprichnik* had a dog's head fixed to his saddle and carried a broom, all to symbolize the Tsar's determination to hound traitors and to sweep corruption from the land.

As Ivan obviously intended, the *oprichniki* struck terror throughout the land and the operation was successful from his viewpoint. The ability of the *boyars* to oppose the Tsar was destroyed completely. The purges lasted seven years and, its purpose accomplished, Ivan dissolved the *Oprichnina* in 1572, after executing some of the chief executioners.

### The Time of Troubles

Two years before his death in 1584, Ivan quarreled with his eldest son and namesake and, in a fit of passion, struck and killed him. He was succeeded, therefore, by his second son, Fedor, who was mentally retarded. Under Fedor, actual power was exercised by a regency council headed by Boris Godunov. Fedor had no children, so the Rurikovichi dynasty came to an end when he died in 1598.

This left the throne vacant and meant that the Russian people had to choose a new tsar. There were a number of candidates but three men eventually emerged as serious contenders—Boris Godunov, Fedor Romanov and Basil Shuisky. Each had some connection to the previous ruling family. Boris Godunov was married to the sister of Fedor, Fedor Romanov was the son of Nikita Romanov, brother of Anastasia, Ivan IV's first wife; and Basil Shuisky was descended from the elder branch of the Rurikovichi line.

To give legitimacy to the choice, the Patriarch proposed calling a *Zemskii Sobor* and allowing this popular assembly to select the new tsar. It chose Boris Godunov, who took the throne as Boris I (1598–1605).

Boris's reign started out well but, when a combination of early frosts and droughts produced widespread crop failures, the superstitious Russian people began to believe that they had made a mistake in choosing Boris, and opposition mounted to his rule. He managed to hold on to power during his lifetime but things be-

gan to fall apart when he died suddenly in April 1605. Within a month, his son, who had succeeded him, was overthrown by the first would–be Dmitri, an impostor who claimed to be the youngest son of Ivan IV.

This marked the beginning of a period of great turmoil in Russian history known as the "Time of Troubles." Dmitri (1605-1606) survived for approximately a year before he was murdered by Basil Shuisky, who then ascended the throne as Basil I (1606–1610). Basil, who represented the interests of the old *Boyar* class, was unable to consolidate his control and was overthrown in 1610. Russia was once again without a tsar. In addition, a Polish army occupied Moscow while a Swedish army occupied parts of northern Russia. A number of Russian nobles proposed to offer the throne to Wladyslaw, the 15-year old son of Sigismund, the Polish king. Sigismund rejected the offer and claimed the throne himself.

This posed a basic threat to a major power: the Russian Orthodox Church. Sigismund was a Roman Catholic and probably would have tried to force a union of the Church with the Roman Church. The Patriarch of Moscow, Hermogen, called urgently for the Russian peo-

ple to drive out the Poles. A national revival to save "Mother Russia" began, led by Kuzma Minin, a wealthy commoner from Nizhni Novgorod. Minin assembled an army representing all classes of Russian society from *boyar* to serf and the Polish army was driven out of Moscow. A *Zemskii Sober* was summoned and proceeded to choose Michael Romanov as the new tsar.

### The First Romanovs

Michael Romanov (1613–1645) was a boy of sixteen when he was elevated to the throne of Russia. The *Zemskii Sobor* wanted Michael's father, Fedor Romanov, as tsar, but that proved impossible for two reasons. The first was that Boris Godunov, after his own election as tsar, had forced Fedor to become a monk. He did this in order to remove a potential rival to the throne since Fedor, as a monk, would be ineligible for the throne. The second reason was that Fedor, now the Metropolitan Filaret, was in prison in Poland.

He had gone to Poland in 1610 as a member of the Russian delegation sent to negotiate with the Polish king with regard to his son Wladyslaw's accession to the Russian throne. When Sigismund decided to claim the throne for himself, he threw

**From Act I of Musorgski's opera Boris Godunov.**

Courtesy of OPERA NEWS

Michael

Alexis

Fedor

the entire Russian delegation into prison. When Filaret was finally permitted to return to Moscow in 1619, he was named Patriarch of the Russian Church and made co–ruler with Michael. He effectively ruled Russia until his death in 1633. Thus Michael remained in the shadow of his father most of his life.

Michael was succeeded by his son, Alexis (1645–1676) who also was sixteen when his father died. Like his father, he was a gentle person easily dominated by those about him. Dominated in his youth by his tutor Morozov, he later fell under the influence of the Patriarch Nikon and, still later, by his last favorite, Artamon Matveev. Most of the accomplishments of his reign are more the product of these men than of Alexis.

Fedor III was the third Romanov Tsar (1676–1682), son of Alexis who came to the throne as a boy of fourteen. An invalid, Fedor left most of the decision-making of the state to his advisors; he died after six years on the throne.

The first Romanovs were thus not very impressive, either as individuals or as rulers. Cautious and conservative, always looking to the past rather than the present or future, manipulated by those around them, their greatest contribution was that they survived. Yet this was a significant period since a number of things occurred during the reigns of these three tsars that would have an important bearing on subsequent Russian history.

The first thing is that the Russian state had to recover from the effect of the Time of Troubles and the Livonian War. The situation in 1613 was less than positive. The economy was in a shambles with large parts of the countryside going untilled

and whole villages abandoned. Rebellious peasants and gangs of soldiers from the various disbanded armies roamed the countryside, robbing civilians and looting property. Novgorod was under Swedish occupation and Russia was still at war with Poland. Prince Wladyslaw of Poland continued to press his claim to the Russian throne.

Sweden agreed to return Novgorod in 1617 but, in that same year, Prince Wladyslaw invaded Russia at the head of a Polish army and laid siege to Moscow. The invasion actually helped Michael to establish his authority since he became identified with defense of the Russian homeland against the foreign invader. Wladyslaw's forces were driven out and a truce was signed between the two sides in 1618.

To further bolster his authority, Michael kept the *Zemskii Sobor* in more or less continuous session in Moscow and all important decrees were issued under the joint authority of the Tsar and that body. This might have led to the creation of a permanent representative institution in Russia, but as he became more firmly established, Michael made less use of the *Zemskii Sobor*. A policy emerged whereby sessions were called only to discuss unusually important issues, such as whether Russia should go to war against Poland in the 1630's. A new *Zemskii Sobor* was also called to confirm Alexis' succession to the throne in 1645.

Alexis called two further sessions—in 1649 to issue a new law code and in 1651–1653 to address the question of war with Poland. It did not meet thereafter. The *Zemskii Sobor* was thus used to create and reinforce the authority of the Tsar at a

time when that authority was not firmly established. When this purpose was fulfilled, it was allowed to evaporate.

Another major development had to do with the revolt of the Ukraine against Polish rule and its acquisition by Russia. The area of the Ukraine had originally become part of the Principality of Lith uania in the 14th century. Subsequently, a dynastic marriage brought Poland and Lithuania together under a single monarch and in 1569 they merged into a single state.

Poland was Roman Catholic and the Ukrainians were Russian Orthodox. Efforts to catholicize the Ukrainians were intermittent until 1589, when the Metropolitan of Moscow was raised to the rank of Patriarch and given authority over all Russian Orthodox believers. Poland refused to recognize the authority of the Patriarch within any of its territories and attempted to force all its Orthodox subjects to join a new "Uniate" church that recognized the authority of Rome.

In addition, economic pressure was applied as the estates of upper class Orthodox were seized and redistributed to Polish nobles while attempts were made to turn the mass of Ukrainian peasants into serfs.

Bogdan Khmelnitsky, who had himself lost lands to a Polish nobleman, was elected *Hetman* (chief) of the Zaporozhian Cossacks, a group of adventurous independent soldiers and mercenaries. He became the leader for Ukrainian autonomy. Khmelnitsky was successful initially, but a defeat at the hands of Polishforces convinced him that the Ukrainians could not hope to maintain their independence for long. Believing that a victory by Poland would mean the end of the Orthodox

Church and the enslavement of the people, Khmelnitsky offered to bring the Ukraine under Russian rule.

Tsar Alexis and his advisers discussed the matter for two years before accepting the offer because they recognized that if they did so, it would mean war with Poland. The *Zemskii Sobor* finally in 1653 decided to incorporate the Ukraine into Russia and declare war on Poland. The war lasted until 1667, ending with the Truce of Androsovo under the terms of which Russia obtained all of the Ukraine east of the Dnieper and was permitted to occupy the city of Kiev for two years. Russia never gave back Kiev, however, and in 1686 the terms of the truce were made permanent by a treaty of peace.

Another important territorial addition that occurred in the 17th century was the extension of Russian control over Siberia. The penetration of Western Siberia first occurred in the 16th century during the reign of Ivan IV when the famous merchant family of the Stroganovs became interested in Siberian furs. It was this family that hired Yermak, an *ataman* of the Volga Cossacks, to explore east of the Ural Mountains. He led an expedition to the Irtysh River, defeated the Siberian ruler and claimed Siberia west of the Ob and Irtysh rivers for Russia.

Territorial acquisition was resumed in the 17th century. The Stroganovs continued to be involved, but now they were joined by other enterprising types; these merchant traders and explorers advanced from the Ob to the Yenisei, then from the Yenisei to the Lena. As they advanced, they left fortified trading posts behind them. By the middle of the century, they had reached the Amur River and had come into contact with the Chinese. The Chinese attempted to starve out the Russians by withdrawing the entire population from the Amur River valley. The matter was resolved in 1689 by the Treaty of Nerchinsk whereby Russia gave up all claims to the area of the Amur River Valley, but was conceded the rest of Siberia north of the Amur. Thus, by the end of the 17th century, Russian territory in the east extended to the sea.

The last development associated with the first Romanovs had to do with a church reform carried out by the Patriarch Nikon. Russian church books contained many errors that had crept in over the centuries as a result of mistakes of copyists. Nikon was determined to correct them according to the Greek originals. The changes were not very significant—correcting the spelling of the name Jesus, making the sign of the cross with three fingers instead of two, three Hallelujahs instead of two at a certain time during the worship service—but the old ways had been entrenched by tradition. Nikon found himself opposed by a significant el-

ement among the clergy who resisted the changes. Avvakum, the chief spokesman for the "Old Believers," called Nikon "a mocker of God and a heretic." Nikon retaliated by banishing the supporters of the old order.

A church council eventually approved Nikon's changes and Avvakum was sentenced to be burned at the stake. That, however, only resulted in a division in the church as the Old Believers continued to oppose the reforms. Since Tsar Alexis supported the measures, he became the "Anti–Christ" as far as the Old Believers were concerned, a term they applied to subsequent tsars as well. The government outlawed them as heretics but there were too many of them for this to be effective. Overall, the effect of the schism was to weaken the power of the church and to make it more dependent on the government for support. That soon became an important consideration, for it is unlikely that Peter the Great could have carried out many of his reforms against the united opposition of the church.

## Peter "The Great"

This man (1682–1725) is usually conceded to have been the greatest of Russia's rulers and to have had a greater impact on the Russian land and people than any of his predecessors or successors. Yet, his was a disputed succession to the throne and for seven years after he became co–tsar in 1682, there was a serious question whether he would be permitted to rule in his own right.

The problem was that his father, Alexis, had married twice and Peter was born of the second marriage. Alexis' first wife, Maria Miloslavska, had given him two sons, Fedor and Ivan, as well as several daughters, including the ambitious and strong–willed Sophia. When Fedor came to the throne in 1676, he chose his advisors from among the Miloslavsky family and shunted the relatives of his step–mother, Natalia Narishkina, aside. When Fedor died in 1682, the next in line for the throne was Ivan, Fedor's younger brother. Ivan, however, was mentally retarded, subject to fits and nearly blind.

**Nikon, Patriarch of Moscow**

Peter I

The Narishkin clan proposed that the ten–year–old Peter become the next tsar. Sophia, recognizing that this would mean her total exclusion from power, appealed to the *streltsy*, the hereditary tsarist guard, to intervene on behalf of the weak Ivan, suggesting that his life was in danger. She promised pay increases to the *streltsy* to encourage their support. They invaded the Kremlin, killed a number of Peter's relatives and demanded a reordering of the succession to the throne. As a result, Peter and Ivan were named "co-tsars" and Sophia became regent and the real ruler of Russia. Peter and his mother were permitted to take up residence in a palace in the village of Preobrazhenskoe outside Moscow, and it was here that he spent the next seven years.

Moscow's "foreign quarter" was located in a suburb near Preobrazhenskoe, and Peter, bored with life in the village, soon made the acquaintanceship of a number of foreigners who had come to Russia to take service with the Russian government. These included a Swiss, Franz Lefort, a Scot, Patrick Gordon and a Dutchman, Franz Timmerman.

Another of Peter's diversions was to organize the young nobles assigned to him as playmates into opposing "toy regiments" and to have mock battles. He also

discovered that a note dispatched to the Royal armory would bring him any piece of military equipment he asked for. So, he combined his two diversions, using Lefort, Gordon and Timmerman, who were all military men, as advisors.

Gradually Peter learned military engineering, artillery and even geometry as part of these war games, and the "toy regiments" became more and more proficient. Eventually the two regiments were given the names of Preobrazhensky and Semenovsky and became the nucleus of a new army that Peter later created.

When Peter was fourteen, he found an old English sailboat that was in storage. He had it brought out and launched on a nearby lake. Soon he found a Dutch shipmaster to instruct him, and he began building other boats, working alongside Dutch carpenters from the foreign quarter. Peter also liked to sit in the foreign quarter drinking with his friends, so it is not surprising that his first mistress was the daughter of the Dutch innkeeper Mons.

Peter's mother disapproved of Peter's choice of pastimes and decided that he needed a wife to settle him down. He was therefore married at the age of sixteen to Eudoxia Lopukhina, a rather pious and uninteresting young woman. Peter was

distracted long enough for her to become pregnant, but within a few weeks he returned to his military games and his boats. Some years later, Peter banished Eudoxia to a convent. His son, Alexis, was partly raised in that convent, and he grew up hating his father and all he stood for.

When Peter was seventeen in 1689, Sophia decided that she should become ruler of Russia in her own right and began making plans to dethrone both Ivan and Peter. Peter, learning of the plot, fled to the Trinity Monastery and called his "toy regiments" to his side. Sophia's support began melting away and she was forced to surrender power. Peter banished her to a nunnery.

Never particularly interested in the more ordinary aspects of governing, he turned the day–to–day control of Russia to his wife's relatives and returned to his military training. He participated in his first military campaign in 1695–1696 which resulted in the capture of a Turkish fortress at Azov, at the mouth of the Don River. It was to seek allies for a general war against Turkey that Peter next organized a "Grand Embassy" to travel to western Europe. Peter accompanied the embassy in the guise of an apprentice shipbuilder, Peter Mikhailov. He went to Brandenburg–Prussia, Holland, England and Vienna, capital of the Holy Roman Empire. He spent six months in Holland working as an ordinary shipbuilder. Although he learned a great deal, he found no potential ally for a war against Turkey. Charles XI of Sweden had recently died, however, and several countries—Poland, Brandenburg–Prussia and Denmark— were eager to go to war to despoil Sweden of territories won during the 17th century in the Baltic Sea area. This offered Peter an even better chance to gain a seaport, so he agreed to go to war against Sweden as soon as he could bring the war against Turkey to an end.

Peter was in Vienna when he learned of another revolt by the *streltsy*. Although the revolt had been quashed by the time he got back to Moscow, Peter took terrible revenge upon the mutineers. The leaders were beheaded and hundreds of others were tortured or killed and their bodies left to lie out on display as an object lesson for others. Sixteen *streltsy* regiments were ultimately disbanded; Peter had managed to destroy the political power of the *streltsy* but he also had left himself without an army.

Peter is remembered as the "Great Westernizer" and it is true that he introduced many things into Russia from the west, particularly dealing with culture and manners. Peter was not an uncritical admirer of the west, however, and his primary motivation for introducing western styles was to make Russians more acceptable to Europeans. Thus beards, which were out of style in the west, were forbidden at court and Peter personally took a pair of shears and cut the hair of his chief courtiers. Nobles who chose to keep a beard were required to pay a tax of 100 rubles and to wear a badge indicating that they had paid it. Peasants were permitted to keep their beards, but had to pay a fine of 1 kopeck each time they entered Moscow. Western–style clothing became mandatory for members of the upper classes. Women, previously kept in isolation, were now invited to public entertainments and dinners, and court balls were organized where men and women danced in the western manner.

Peter kept changing Russian ways of doing things all the rest of his life, but most of the other changes which he introduced might more properly be characterized as modernizations. He simplified the Russian alphabet, eliminating what he considered useless letters, and ordered that the new characters be used in all lay books. Church books continued to use the old style, which came to be known as Old Slavonic.

He also set up the first newspaper in Russia in 1703, established all sorts of technical institutes, laid the foundations for the Universities of Moscow and St. Petersburg, created the Russian Academy of Sciences, sponsored expeditions to explore the Kamchatka Peninsula, the Kuril Islands and the Bering Strait, carried out extensive administrative reforms, reorganized the government of the Orthodox Church, established an iron industry, a munitions industry, textile factories, and in general encouraged the development of trade.

Peter also built a modern army and navy and he fought a long, 21–year war with Sweden for control of the southern shores of the Baltic Sea. The war was ultimately successful, and Russia became established as one of the "great powers" of Europe as a result, but it was extremely costly. Taxes had to be increased on the peasantry and other commoner classes, while a lifetime service obligation beginning at age 15 was instituted for the nobility. Peasants were also drafted into the military for the first time. Although military service became a lifetime obligation for them, it did have the advantage that they ceased to be serfs upon taking the military oath.

After Peter's death, the term of military service for both nobility and commoners was reduced to 25 years. His proudest achievement was the city he built at the mouth of the Neva River on land newly liberated from the Swedes. St. Petersburg, whose foundations were laid in 1703, was to be his capital, his chief seaport on the Baltic and his "window to the west." It was here—and at Tsarskoe Selo ("the Tsar's village"), twelve miles away—that he began the magnificent palaces which

were to signify Russia's new great power status. His new capital was partly responsible for his death, however, for St. Petersburg was built on a swamp and was subject to periodic flooding. Peter died in early 1725 as the result of a chill he caught while helping to rescue victims of such a flood.

## An Era of Palace Revolutions

One of Peter's greater disappointments was his son, Alexis, who in the normal course of events would have succeeded him. Alexis opposed everything that Peter stood for, however, and he made no secret of the fact that he planned to undo all of Peter's reforms if he came to power. He embarrassed his father further in 1716 by fleeing abroad and requesting sanctuary from the Holy Roman Emperor. Two years later, he returned home at his father's urging, where Peter forced him to renounce his claim to the throne, then had him put on trial for treason. He was found guilty and sentenced to death, but it was later announced that he had died while under interrogation.

Peter issued a decree abolishing succession of the oldest son or child of the tsar, which stated that the tsar would name his successor. He never got around to designating his own, however, and his sudden death left the succession unsettled. It was resolved by Prince Alexander Menshikov, one of Peter's close associates, who called upon the Guards regiments to support Catherine, Peter's second wife, as his successor. The Guards regiments, descendants of Peter's original "toy regiments," thus set a tradition of intervention which would continue throughout the 18th century. It was not until 1796 when the Emperor Paul came to the throne that Peter's succession decree was finally repealed

and primogeniture was reinstituted as the method of succession.

The weird succession to the throne of Russia following the death of Peter the Great at the age of 53 is best understood with the help of a diagram. The rulers between Peter the Great and Catherine the Great were as follows:

CATHERINE I, a peasant woman, Peter's second wife (two years)

PETER II, son of the dead Prince Alexis (three years)

ANNE, Duchess of Courland, half-niece of Peter I (ten years)

IVAN VI, half great–great nephew of Peter I (one year)

ELIZABETH, younger daughter of Peter I by his second wife (twenty–one years)

PETER III, son of Elizabeth's older sister Anna and the Duke of Holstein, grandson of Peter I. (Less than one year; deposed)

This peculiar succession reflects the sequence of intrigues, plots and *coups* by a series of advisers, court favorites and lovers. The amazing thing is that during this period Russia's international position did not decline because other powers failed to take advantage of the internal upheaval.

Of these rulers, only one, Elizabeth, made any important contribution to Russian development. She consciously took up Peter's reforms where they had been left hanging in 1725 and carried them forward. It was Elizabeth who completed the Winter Palace in St. Petersburg, who hired the famous Italian architect, Rastrelli, to rebuild the Peterhof at Tsarskoe Selo and who established Moscow University. She also emulated Peter's foreign policy by signing alliances with Paris and Vienna and by intervening in the Seven Years War

**The Winter Palace of the Tsars in St. Petersburg**

against Frederick the Great of Prussia. She partially neutralized that accomplishment, however, when she named Peter III as her successor to the throne.

When he succeeded her at the beginning of 1762 he immediately set out to undo nearly everything she had accomplished. Although a grandson of Peter the Great, Peter III was completely German by upbringing and was Lutheran in religion. He was not at all happy about becoming Tsar of Russia, a position for which he was totally unfit, both physically and mentally. His marriage to the daughter of a minor German princely family, Sophie of Anhalt–Zerbst, had been arranged by his aunt, the Empress Elizabeth. It had been Peter the Great who had begun the practice of "arranged marriages" for political purposes (a pattern followed by German and other western European dynastic alliances) and she continued the policy. But the 1745 marriage remained "in name only" for nine years because the young Grand Duke had a physical disability which made it impossible for him to consummate the relationship. Peter eventually had an operation to cure his disability, but Catherine, as the young Grand Duchess, was known after her conversion to Russian Orthodoxy, had already been urged by Empress Elizabeth to take a lover in order to assure an heir to the throne. In her memoirs, Catherine identified the young lover, Sergei Saltykov, as the father of her son, Paul. Whether true or not, Peter III evidently believed it because, when he became Tsar in 1762, he decided to disinherit Paul and send Catherine to a convent. This led to his overthrow and to his death in a *coup d'etat* which installed Catherine as Empress of Russia.

## Catherine "The Great"

Catherine had no personal claim to the Russian throne, but she did win the support of the Guards regiments—partly because her latest lover, Gregory Orlov, was an officer of the Guards. For thirty–four years the growing Russian Empire was governed by a woman of great talent and even greater determination to excel in everything and to control all things. She was hard–working and devoted to matters of state. She saw herself as both a figure of the Enlightenment and as Peter the Great's successor. She had a lively correspondence with Voltaire and Frederick the Great of Prussia and at one point she invited Diderot, the French Encyclopedist, to St. Petersburg and set aside an hour each evening for conversation with him.

When she first came to the throne, she had great hopes for further reforms and she did a great deal to encourage culture and learning. At one point, she spent two years drafting instructions for a Legislative Conference which she called to draw up a new code of law. The instructions, heavily based on the writings of Montesquieu and other Enlightenment thinkers, were considered so radical that they were banned in France. The instructions were apparently also too radical for members of the Legislative Conference; they were unable to draft a new code based on them.

When Catherine first came to the throne, she expressed her dislike for serfdom. But she ultimately found that she could do nothing about it, for serfdom formed the economic basis of the nobility, the class that staffed the army and civil administration. In her role as an enlightened despot, therefore, Catherine didn't accomplish very much. On the other

**ROMANOV DYNASTY**

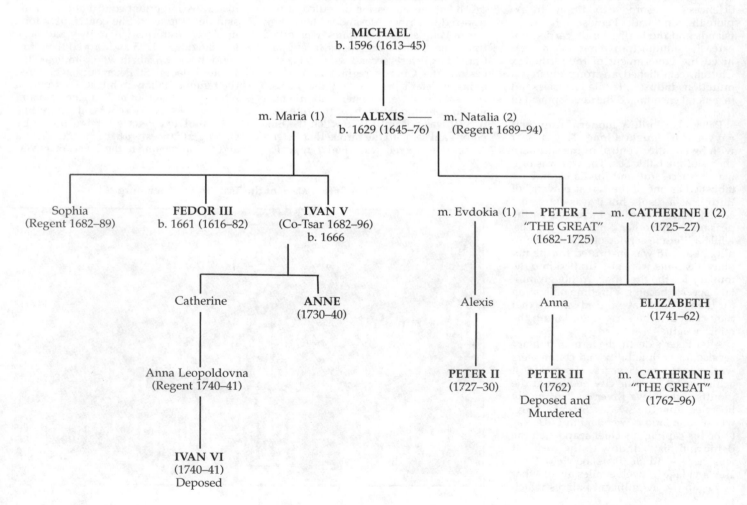

hand, she proved to be a good publicist whose writings and correspondence created a good impression of Russia in the West.

Something more should perhaps be said about her lovers. It is a matter of record that she had, over a period of many years, at least 21 lovers. In this regard, Catherine was not greatly different from other 18th century monarchs. The Empress Elizabeth, at whose court she grew up, had a succession of lovers who were given the official title of "Gentleman of the Bedchamber." Louis XIV of France was famous for his succession of official mistresses, known as "Ladies of the Bedchamber." The practice was so well accepted that one Prussian monarch had an officially appointed Lady of the Bedchamber even though he personally preferred men.

Catherine had more lovers than most, but only four had any significance insofar as Russian history is concerned. Two of these, the presumed father of Paul and the officer who helped her come to power, have already been mentioned. A third was Stanislaw Poniatowski, a handsome Polish nobleman whom she later made King of Poland. The fourth was Gregory Potemkin (Poh–*tyom*–kin), who was responsible for a number of Russia's military victories during her reign, including the conquest and annexation of the Crimea. Potemkin became her lover and chief adviser—and there may even have been a private marriage ceremony. But when the two functions conflicted, he chose to remain her chief adviser—and over the next several years personally selected the young Guardsmen who became Catherine's "Gentleman of the Bedchamber."

Catherine deserves to be called "the Great" primarily because of her successful wars and because of Russia's extensive territorial expansion during her reign. Perhaps the most important of her territorial expansions is associated with her participation with Prussia and Austria in the partitions of Poland that resulted in an end of the Polish–Lithuanian state.

The liquidation of Poland brought into the Russian empire all the lands which had been claimed as "Russian" during earlier history. This was not the only success of Catherine—under her leadership the first major victory was scored against the Ottoman Turkish empire to the south, hastening the decline of a once–powerful foe. Russia obtained access to a considerable portion of the Black Sea in 1774 and secured the right of passage through the Turkish Straits into the Mediterranean. It was also recognized as the official protector of Orthodox Christians living under Turkish rule. Further expansion led to the acquisition in 1792 of a little–known fortress called Ochakov and the right to control the Crimean Peninsula. These events

Catherine II

caused the first alarm in England over the possibility of Russian expansion into areas of interest to the British.

During the struggle between England and the American colonies, Russia played an important role in the League of Armed Neutrality. This was a group of nations that insisted on the right of passage of neutral ships across the Atlantic Ocean and other bodies of water in spite of British objections. Catherine followed with interest the developments in Western Europe and broke off relations with France after revolutionaries executed King Louis XVI. She apparently intended that Russia would be part of an armed intervention in France. She also entertained a greater scheme for the creation of a Christian empire out of Greece and other Turkish possessions, but nothing came of this.

**The French Revolution and Russia**

For a century prior to the French Revolution, Russia had been governed by a series of rulers committed to the concept of a "revolution from above." In the process, the nobility and urban classes had been transformed, but the peasantry—90% of the people—remained the same. It was this obstacle that Catherine was unable to

overcome and when the French Revolution popularized the ideas of "liberty, equality and fraternity" and announced the end of serfdom and legal distinctions based on class, this made the ideas of the French Revolution subversive within the Russian part of Europe.

An even greater difficulty was that Russian rulers from Catherine onward, educated in the Enlightenment traditions, agreed with many of the ideals of the French Revolution, but could not see how to achieve them in Russia without completely disrupting the very fabric of Russian society. All agreed, for example, that serfdom was a clearly seen evil and ought to be abolished, but none before Alexander II could bring himself to do so. As a result, the distance between convictions and actions widened, and the actions of Russian rulers became more and more conservative as the 19th century progressed. Half–hearted and partial reforms were still proposed and sometimes implemented, but they were never sufficient to transform the basic organization of the Russian society; the ideals of the French Revolution continued to be regarded as suspect and unworthy in Russia.

Further change was afoot in Western

Europe—the Industrial Revolution—transforming social and economic relationships. As England, France and Germany industrialized, Russia, with a social and economic system incompatible with capitalism, fell further behind. In spite of all of its efforts, therefore, Russia's system of government and its role as a great power were both in decline throughout most of the 19th century, even as its rulers attempted to catch up. Russia remained "on hold."

## Romanov Monarchs After Catherine

We continue to refer to monarchs after Catherine the Great as Romanovs even though she was a German, and if her memoirs are correct, they are all descendants of Catherine and Sergei Saltykov. Before the Romanov dynasty ended its historical role, a sprawling and multi–national Russia was ruled by six tsars—Catherine's son, Paul, his two sons, Alexander I and Nicholas I, Nicholas I's son, grandson and great–grandson—Alexander II, Alexander III and Nicholas II.

Paul, who succeeded his mother in 1796, had been alienated from her because he believed that she had usurped his rightful throne. He therefore spent the first part of his reign attempting to undo his mother's accomplishments. Possessing a military mentality and a foul temper, his was an unstable reign that ended after five years in a *coup d'etat* made on behalf of his son, who gave his advance approval. Paul was murdered during the *coup*, a fact that was said to prey on Alexander's conscience and may explain some of his otherwise unexplainable actions. As one historian has pointed out, this was the last "indoor" assassination—the Tsar was killed in his bedroom by an "inside" group of conspirators and officers of the Guards regiments. In the next century, "assassinations were to take place in the open street." With this last palace revolution, Russia drifted into the 19th century, loaded down with traditions of the past, with autocratic rule, a privileged upper class and with serfdom weighing as heavily as ever on the shoulders of the Russian people.

The first Alexander has presented a puzzle to both historians and psychologists. At first, he was inclined toward liberal ideas and was determined to continue efforts to westernize Russia. He ended up in a fanatically conservative and mystical stupor, dying in southern Russia apparently during an attempt to run away from it all. Typical for Russia, there was a legend that he didn't really die, but chose the life of a saintly hermit to ask forgiveness for his sins. His knowledge of the plot to kill his father may have been the sin that really bothered him.

At the beginning of his rule, Alexander asked the outstanding statesman, Michael Speransky, to plan basic reforms, including a constitution, a modern code of laws and an educational system. He even gave half–hearted consideration to abolishing serfdom, but the only result of this was a law of 1803 that permitted the voluntary emancipation of serfs by landlords. Needless to say, few were inclined to make use of this opportunity. On Alexander's orders, Speransky drew up a constitution which would have created a national legislature and guaranteed various civil rights. Most of the nobility opposed the plan, however, and Alexander, needing the nobility's support in his confrontation with France, was forced to dismiss Speransky. Alexander did carry out an administrative reorganization, turning the Colleges he had inherited from Peter the Great into Ministries and organizing them into something analogous to a cabinet, called the Committee of Ministers. In addition, he created an appointed legislature called the Council of State, to draw up legislation for the Tsar's approval and increased the authority of the Senate. None of these changes or new institutions actually restricted the Tsar's authority, but they did regularize procedures and increase the size of the circle of advisers.

## The War of 1812

The most famous achievement of Russia in this period was the spectacular defeat of Napoleon I of France when he tried to invade the endless land mass of Russia.

Russia had joined in the so–called Third Coalition to fight against Napoleon in 1805. It and its allies, Prussia and Austria, were beaten and had to submit to rather harsh conditions of the Treaty of Tilsit. A period of relative peace and cooperation with Napoleon, then the master of the European continent, followed. Russia profited from it by securing areas remote from Napoleon's control at the expense of Persia and Turkey. Georgia was annexed in the south; to the southwest, Bessarabia was added, giving rise to a greater Russian influence on the neighboring Balkan area of Eastern Europe. At the same time, Russia also seized Finland from Sweden, converting it into a Grand Duchy with the Tsar as ruler. It was also during this period that forts were established in "Russian America"—first in Alaska and then close to what is now San Francisco.

Mutual jealousy between France and Russia emerged in 1811–1812. Napoleon, swayed by his past successes, decided to invade Russia and did so on June 21, 1812, with an army of almost one–half million; the French constituted only about half of this force. A great number of Poles joined the effort, expecting Napoleon to liberate and restore to them all or most of the territory of the defunct Polish–Lithuanian commonwealth.

As in the past, the peasant masses, in spite of their grievances, rallied to the support of "Mother Russia." Another significant factor in turning Napoleon's invasion into a major defeat was the well-known Russian winter, which in 1812–1813 was unusually severe. This completely disrupted the extremely long supply lines of the French.

Hoping for a speedy surrender of the Tsar's forces, Napoleon rejected the advice to retreat to winter quarters and before long his glorious army was in tatters and without food. "Scorched earth" tactics and roaming bands of guerrillas were used against the invader by the Russian general, Mikhail Kutuzov. The departure of Napoleon's forces was not just a retreat—it was a rout.

Russia played a major role at the Congress of Vienna which was convened to settle the affairs of Europe. The supposed allies of Russia had some success in trying to contain the "undue" expansion of Russian political power in Europe. Great Britain and Austria in particular opposed the demands of Alexander I for reestablishment of a large Kingdom of Poland with himself as king under a constitutional government with an independent Polish army.

Although such a kingdom was created, it was much smaller than desired by the Russians, and substantial portions of what used to be Poland were kept until after World War I by Austria and Prussia. While haggling over the boundaries of Europe in Vienna, the Russian Tsar tried to promote a scheme for a "Holy Alliance" of monarchs. This was to bind the rulers of Europe in a spirit of Christian brotherhood. It was a rather unclear plan that had no important practical results in the field of international relations. Of greater significance was the Quadruple Alliance, signed by Russia, Great Britain, Austria and Prussia, which made provision for periodic conferences to review matters of common interest and to assure continued peace. The consensus about what it meant to maintain the peace settlement did not last very long, however. The British wished to limit international cooperation to international attempts to overthrow the *status quo*, while Russia, Prussia and Austria argued for international cooperation to put down revolutionary movements within individual states. Great Britain broke with the other three nations on this issue in 1820, but Russia, Prussia and Austria continued to cooperate.

Alexander I put domestic policies on hold during the War of 1812. After Napoleon's defeat he turned his attention back to domestic affairs, but a large foreign debt and a budget deficit precluded major new programs such as had marked the earlier part of his reign. His antipathy toward serfdom continued, however, and in 1816 he abolished serfdom in Estonia. An-

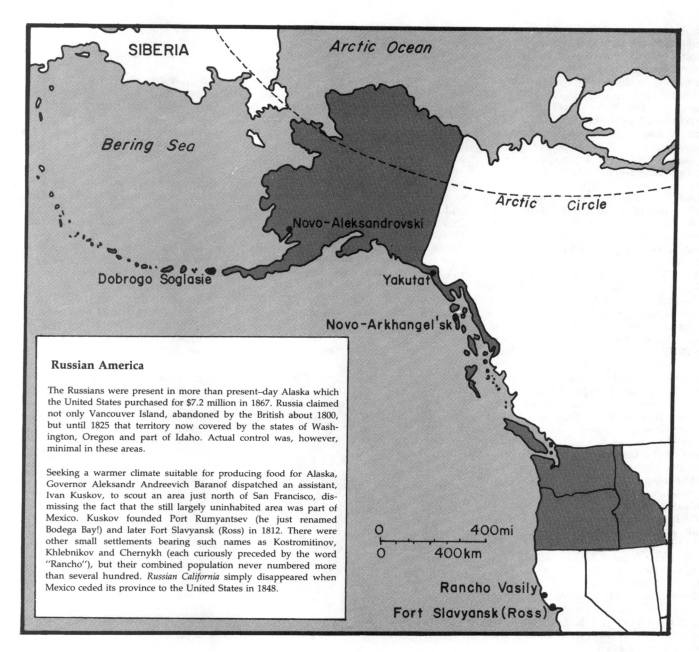

SIBERIA

Arctic Ocean

Bering Sea

Arctic Circle

Novo-Aleksandrovski

Dobrogo Soglasie

Yakutaf

Novo-Arkhangel'sk

### Russian America

The Russians were present in more than present–day Alaska which the United States purchased for $7.2 million in 1867. Russia claimed not only Vancouver Island, abandoned by the British about 1800, but until 1825 that territory now covered by the states of Washington, Oregon and part of Idaho. Actual control was, however, minimal in these areas.

Seeking a warmer climate suitable for producing food for Alaska, Governor Aleksandr Andreevich Baranof dispatched an assistant, Ivan Kuskov, to scout an area just north of San Francisco, dismissing the fact that the still largely uninhabited area was part of Mexico. Kuskov founded Port Rumyantsev (he just renamed Bodega Bay!) and later Fort Slavyansk (Ross) in 1812. There were other small settlements bearing such names as Kostromitinov, Khlebnikov and Chernykh (each curiously preceded by the word "Rancho"), but their combined population never numbered more than several hundred. *Russian California* simply disappeared when Mexico ceded its province to the United States in 1848.

0          400mi

0          400km

Rancho Vasily

Fort Slavyansk (Ross)

other decree the next year ended serfdom in Courland, while a third decree abolished it in Livonia in 1819.

But Alexander I began to lose interest in secular change after he fell under the influence of a Russian monk known for his piety during the Napoleonic Wars. Another influence on him was Prince Metternich, chief minister of the Austrian Empire, who persuaded Alexander that revolutionary forces threatened the political stability of Europe. Alexander began to collect more conservative advisers about him and, increasingly, to act on their advice. The most influential of these was General Alexis Arakcheev, who drew up and implemented plans for "military colonies" in the western part of Russia. Recruits assigned to the military colonies helped to support themselves by growing most of their food. Hated by both soldiers

and officers, the military colonies were abolished by Nicholas I after Alexander's death.

Alexander also appointed religious conservatives to major posts such as the Ministry of Education with predictable results. A new regime of censorship was imposed and religious instruction was given a more prominent place in the curriculum.

### The Decembrists

The end of Alexander's reign in 1825 is associated with the first Russian revolution—that of the Decembrists. Although this was exclusively a revolt by army officers and lasted only one day, it is labeled a revolution because the leaders had specific plans about changing the nature of the Russian state and society and did not merely wish to change rulers. The Decem-

brists were all nobles who had served in western Europe and who wished to rid Russia of its backwardness. Their specific goals included the abolition of serfdom and the creation of a constitutional government. They were particularly aggrieved that Alexander I had granted a constitution to Poland and had permitted Finland to retain a constitution it had when it was annexed in 1809, but one was refused in Russia.

Organized into secret societies, they carried on discussions for a number of years, but were unable to agree on any specific action to take. They were galvanized into action by Alexander I's death, when no new Tsar was immediately sworn in as his successor. The confusion about the succession arose because Constantine, the nominal heir, had married a Polish countess and relinquished his claim to the throne—

but this was not known. It was compounded by the fact that Constantine was in Warsaw, where he was regent and all communications were by mail.

By the time the matter was sorted out and Nicholas was ready to officially take over as Tsar, the Decembrists had decided "to refuse to take the oath of allegiance to Nicholas and . . ." But it seems that they had gotten no further than that for, on the appointed day, 3,000 troops, assembled on the Senate Square, refused to take the oath to Nicholas, but then did nothing further. Nicholas surrounded the square with 10,000 loyal troops and demanded their surrender. When they refused, he ordered the artillery to fire on the insurgents, who then broke and ran. The revolt was over.

The Decembrist revolt was therefore only a minor affair. Five of the top leaders were executed, while approximately a hundred others were imprisoned and later exiled to Siberia. But what made it important was the myth that grew up about the Decembrists. Alexander Herzen, Russian revolutionary publicist, later took up the cause of the Decembrists and made them heroes to subsequent generations. Another importance of the Decembrist revolt was the breach it opened between the government and Russian liberals, who never forgave Nicholas for his harsh treatment of the Decembrists and remained alienated throughout his reign. Conversely, Nicholas was never able to overcome his suspicion that all liberals were potentially disloyal.

Nicholas was 29 years old when he became Tsar and ruled Russia for 30 years until his death in 1855. He was not particularly well educated and he had no practical experience in administration before he succeeded to the throne. His background was entirely in the military, where he held the rank of brigade general. He liked the military and during his lifetime he surrounded himself with soldiers, preferring them as advisers and chief administrators.

He distrusted public opinion and did not believe that solutions could arise from among the people. He therefore prohibited public discussion of current problems, and books, journals and newspapers were censored. Since he also distrusted the bureaucracy but needed sources of information, he created "His Majesty's Third Section" as his eyes and ears; this organization was no more than a secret police organization.

However, he kept a report of the testimony of the Decembrists on his desk and conscientiously attempted to meet some of the criticism contained in their statements. One of his early successes was the new code of laws which was issued in 1833—the first new code since 1649. He was also deeply concerned about serfdom and appointed a series of committees to

work on the problem, but he could not bring himself to the point of abolishing the system. He did, however, improve the lot of the State Peasants by commuting all labor service into taxes and by setting up local government for them. Just over 50% of all peasants were State Peasants—people who lived on state land rather than on the land of individual nobles.

Nicholas I's reign has also been referred to as "the reign of outer repression and inner liberation" since it was during his tsardom that Russian literature and culture first attained international stature and recognition. Great Russian writers of this period included the poet Alexander Pushkin, the author of the first great Russian Novel *A Hero of Our Time*, Mikhail Lermontov and Nicholas Gogol, famous for novels, plays and short stories. Nicholas I, who attended the premiere of Gogol's play *The Inspector General*, a biting satire on Russian officialdom, afterwards

**Nicholas I**

commented "Everybody got what was coming to him and I got more than anyone."

Other Russian creative artists who began their work during the reign of Nicholas I included Ivan Turgenev, (*A Sportsman's Sketches*), and Mikhail Glinka, founder of Russian classical music and famous for his operas. The Bolshoi Theater, constructed in 1824, also provided a showcase for Russian ballet, comparable to that of France from where it came.

There were economic changes of some note as well, though the prohibitive tariff system adopted at the close of the Napoleonic Wars tended to isolate Russia from the momentous changes in Western Europe as a result of the spread of the Industrial Revolution. The continued existence of serfdom was another factor hindering change.

In spite of that, there was a dramatic growth in textile manufacturing in the province of Moscow and in and around the city of Lodz, in Russian Poland during the reign of Nicholas I. Most of the factories were primitive. Powered machinery only began to be introduced toward the end of his reign. This new industry was significant, however, because it was the first to make widespread use of free wage labor in Russia.

What made it even more interesting is that most of the workers were serfs who also compensated a master for labor services not performed in return for permission to take an outside job. The success of the new factories using wage labor foreshadowed the end of serfdom in Russia, for they established that free labor was more efficient than serf labor.

Nicholas I was also responsible for construction of the first railways in Russia, against the advice of his ministers. The first line, between St. Petersburg and Tsarskoe Selo, the royal palace complex located 12 miles away on the Baltic, was constructed as an experiment. The second line connected St. Petersburg with Moscow. Nicholas I authorized a third line linking St. Petersburg and Warsaw, but the Crimean War intervened and the project was put on hold.

In foreign affairs, Nicholas carried out a mainly peaceful policy, though he did fight a war against Turkey in 1828–29 which gave Russia the mouth of the Danube River and the eastern coast of the Black Sea. His troops were used again in 1830–31 to put down a Polish insurrection. The Poles were punished when Nicholas abolished their constitution and declared Poland an integral part of the Russian Empire. Troops were dispatched to Hungary in 1849 to end a revolt there and force the Hungarians back within the Austrian Empire.

Two years before his death, Nicholas involved the Russians in his first major war, the Crimean War. The basis of the original quarrel with Turkey—Russia's claim to be the protector of all Orthodox Christians under Turkish rule—would not have justified a war involving three great powers, but England and France intervened because England believed that Russia was attempting to partition Turkey. The war began with naval attacks against coastal Russian towns on the Baltic Sea, the White Sea and the Pacific Ocean, but the main attack came in 1854 when 60,000 allied troops began a siege of the Russian naval base at Sevastopol on the Crimean Peninsula.

Although faced with superior forces, the siege of the Russians lasted almost a year. One episode of the senseless loss of many lives is known to most pupils from Alfred Tennyson's "Charge of the Light Brigade." Tsar Nicholas died in the midst of the war, which was brought to an end

**St. Isaac's Orthodox Cathedral in St. Petersburg was commissioned by Tsar Nicholas I. It was designed by French architect Auguste Montferrand and under construction from 1818–1858. The workers who applied the magnificent gold–mercury amalgam knew when they breathed the toxic fumes that they would die, often within 2 years.** Photo by Miller B. Spangler

by the Treaty of Paris in 1856. Russia had to surrender some territory, including Bessarabia, and give up the right to have naval forces or fortifications on the Black Sea.

## The Tsar Emancipator

Alexander II (1855–1881), who succeeded to the throne upon the death of his father, Nicholas I, went down in history as the "Tsar Emancipator," the greatest westernizer since Peter the Great. Yet, he was not particularly well-liked during his reign, and he died the victim of a terrorist's bomb. The problem was that, though he saw the need for reforms, he wished to implement them in the form of another "revolution from above," in the manner of previous tsars. Perhaps that was inevitable, but the result was that, first, his reforms were modified in their application by a conservative bureaucracy and, second, his unwillingness to involve the newly educated elites created by his reforms meant that he lost a chance to develop a popular constituency to support his measures.

Alexander II came to the throne much better prepared than his father, for Nicholas had appointed him to the State Council (the appointed legislative assembly created by Alexander I) and the Committee of Ministers (the Tsar's cabinet, also created by his predecessor). He held a series of military commands and had also sat on a committee on serfdom appointed by Nicholas. At the conclusion of one session, Alexander petitioned his father to abolish serfdom. Nicholas said he recognized that serfdom was a present, existing evil, but to touch it might perhaps create greater evils.

Russia's defeat in the Crimean War convinced Alexander that Russia could no longer afford to do nothing; its continued existence as a great power was now at stake. The industrialization that had spread across Europe in the first half of the nineteenth century had largely left Russia untouched. Serfdom, with its mass of peasant workers tied to the soil, was incompatible with industrialization. Russia stood still while Europe progressed.

Moreover, serfdom, which had been abolished everywhere else in Europe, had come to be viewed as a moral evil whose continued presence in Russia excluded it from the company of civilized Europe. This moral revulsion toward serfdom had been an important factor in the harsh terms applied to Russia in the Treaty of Paris. Alexander II thus had two important reasons to move for the abolition of serfdom.

Alexander appointed his first committee to consider ways to abolish serfdom in 1857. Four years later, in 1861, he gave his approval to the emancipation manifesto which immediately freed all serfs from personal bondage. Since Russia had an overwhelmingly agricultural economy, it was decided to free the serfs with a type of land tenure. Since the land legally was the property of the nobles, however, the law stipulated that the ex–serfs would get the amount of land they had worked for themselves before emancipation, but they would have to pay for it. Since the ex–serfs had no money, the government arranged to pay the nobles for the land and to have the ex–serfs pay off their debt to the government over a period of 49 years.

Direct and personal ownership of the land was not given to the peasants; the so–called peasant commune was to be collectively responsible for the payments of its members and had the right to allot the land to peasant families. This was to be done according to the size of the family, and the allotments were open to revision every few years. Because of the financial responsibility, the commune hindered the attempts of the peasants to move away,

**Alexander II**

causing overpopulation and land hunger in some areas.

Emancipation ended the control of the nobility over the serfs and necessitated the creation of local government and judicial institutions for the newly–freed peasants. Both of these reforms were carried out in 1864. The *Zemstvo* reform created elective councils at the district and provincial level and gave them responsibility for the local economy, health protection and education. Although voters were organized into three classes—nobles, townsmen and peasants—and voted separately, the *Zemstvo* assemblies were genuinely democratic institutions in which all classes participated. They became an important voice for rural interests.

The judicial reform was even more radical, because it abolished traditional Russian judicial practices and created an entirely new system that introduced trial by jury, public trials, defense attorneys and an independent judiciary, none of which had hitherto existed in Russia.

Cities were granted local government in 1870 along the lines of the *Zemstvo* reform. Elected city councils were created and an executive board was headed by a mayor. Although weighted voting systems meant that a relatively few large taxpayers could control the city council, the effect of the overall reform was positive.

An army reform, introduced in 1874, initiated the principle that every man, regardless of class, was liable for military service. The ordinary term of service was reduced to six years, schools for officers were modernized and specific provisions were made to ensure that all enlisted men were taught how to read and write. Since illiteracy was quite high in Russia, the army thus became a significant adjunct to the nation's educational system.

Alexander also reorganized the secondary school system, granted autonomy to the universities and waived university fees for those too poor to pay. The *Zemstvos* had been given responsibility for primary education, but Alexander did approve a law calling for the establishment of a system of primary education throughout Russia. Many *Zemstvos* were slow to follow through on the Tsar's orders, but primary schools slowly came into existence; by 1914, *Zemstvos* were spending approximately one–third of their budget on primary education.

Alexander's economic reforms were—aside from serf emancipation—his most important measures, but they were more long–term and so took longer to show an effect. In addition, Alexander's commitment to industrialization was closely connected to his desire that Russia remain a great power. One of the major reasons for Russia's defeat in the Crimean War was the inability of the Russian government quickly to move men and supplies to the Crimean area. Because of the nature of the climate and the soil, getting about on land was nearly impossible for several months every year—roads turned into quagmires in the spring and fall. Russia's rivers were important transport links, but they were frozen during six winter months.

Alexander, whose mother and wife were both German and who visited Germany regularly, had been impressed by the extensive railway building in Germany in the 1840's and 1850's and the thrust this had given to German industrialization. The Tsar conceived of a similar program for Russia. But since there was little capital in Russia for investment and even fewer entrepreneurs—and the Russian government had no funds adequate for such railway construction—Alexander and his advisers set out to encourage the creation of private railway companies in Russia financed by foreign private capital investment.

Railway companies were permitted to

# THE GROWTH OF RUSSIA

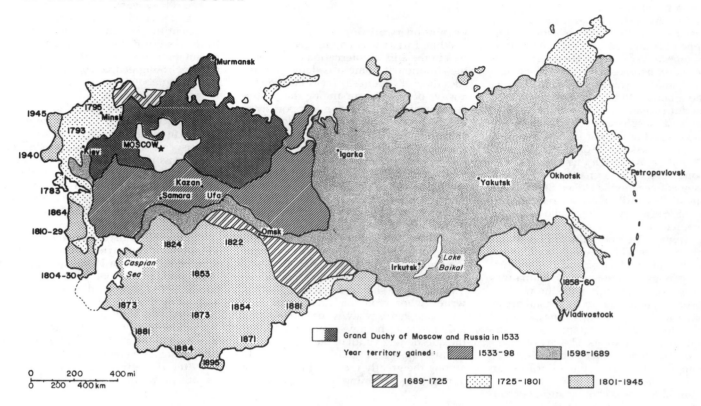

Grand Duchy of Moscow and Russia in 1533
Year territory gained : 1533-98  1598-1689
1689-1725  1725-1801  1801-1945

bring in duty–free all equipment and material needed to construct a railroad; in addition, dividends and interest on stocks and bonds issued by the railway companies were guaranteed by the Russian government. Investors were, in effect, guaranteed against all losses.

The plan worked. By 1881, the time of Alexander II's death, approximately 7,500 kilometers of railroad had been constructed, metal–working and machine–building companies had sprung into existence and the beginnings of a modern iron and steel industry had been laid. It was still only a beginning, but railroad construction continued in the 1880's and 1890's and, after a financial and political crisis that lasted for several years, again began between 1907 and 1914. By 1914, European Russia was covered by an extensive network of railways and the Trans–Siberian Railway had been built across Siberia down to Vladivostok.

Alexander II was obsessed with Russia's defeat in the Crimean War and was determined to undo at least the more onerous clauses of the 1856 treaty. This became the main thrust of his foreign policy; his efforts to win over the French resulted in a friendship treaty between the two nations in 1857, but the Polish uprising six years later disrupted this relationship, since the French were sympathetic to the Poles. Alexander next turned to Prussia as a potential ally and this led to Russian support for German unification and a growing economic relationship between the two.

When the Franco–Prussian War broke out in 1870, the Russian government took advantage of the situation by denouncing the Black Sea clauses of the earlier treaty. England protested, but agreed to drop the offending clauses when it became clear that the new German government supported Russia.

Russia and the Austro–Hungarian Empire tended to be rivals in the Balkan area and their relations had been strained since the Crimean War. However, Russia, Germany and Austria signed an agreement in 1873—The Three Emperor's League—which brought them together in a quasi–alliance. It was Bismarck, the German Chancellor, who sponsored the agreement; he hoped to end the Russo-Austrian rivalry in the Balkans. Russia and Austria could, however, only agree to maintain the *status quo*, so when an uprising began in Bosnia in 1875 and quickly spread to Serbia and Bulgaria, relations between the two countries soured.

Russia and Austria signed the Reichstadt Agreement in 1876 whereby Austria agreed to remain neutral in case of war, while Russia agreed to a suitable territorial compensation for Austria and promised that it would not sponsor the creation of a single large Slavic nation. War broke out between Russia and Turkey in 1877; Russian armies were victorious. In the ensuing treaty, Russia got back southern Bessarabia plus three small towns east of the Black Sea; Turkey agreed to recognize the independence of Serbia, Romania and

Montenegro. The remaining Slavic territories in the eastern Balkans would be organized into a single, autonomous state with an elected Christian Prince. No mention was made of any territorial compensation for Austria.

A bitter Austria threatened to go to war and England also objected to the terms of the treaty, sending its fleet into the eastern Mediterranean. War appeared imminent and Bismarck quickly agreed to host a conference of the powers in Berlin.

At the Congress of Berlin, the powers modified the terms of the treaty as follows: Bulgaria was reduced to one–third of its former size; another third was set up as the autonomous region of Eastern Rumelia and the final third, Macedonia, was returned to Turkey. Austria received the right to administer Bosnia and Herzegovina and was allowed to station troops in the Sanjak of Novibazar. England got Cyprus. Even as modified, the Treaty of Berlin was a triumph for Russia, for with the return of Bessarabia the last of the offending clauses of the 1856 treaty had been overturned. But instead, the Congress of Berlin was considered to be a humiliation for Russia and Alexander's foreign policy was judged to be a failure. The Three Emperors' League was dead; relations between Russia and Germany cooled and for three years Russia drew more and more into self–isolation.

Although at odds with most European powers, Russia was quite friendly with the United States of America. During the

Civil War, the North was pleased to see squadrons of the Russian fleet appear both in New York and San Francisco. The Russians actually came to avoid being trapped inside their bases in the event of a European war—they were not really interested in helping the North. The abolition of serfdom was greeted in the U.S. as a move similar to the emancipation of the American slaves.

In the atmosphere of mutual friendship, it was possible for the United States to purchase Alaska in 1867 for the sum of $7.2 million. Although this turned out to be one of America's greatest bargains, it was denounced in the United States at the time as "Seward's Folly," a reference to the U.S. Secretary of State who arranged the purchase.

In spite of Alexander II's preoccupation with relations with the West, the Russian nation continued to expand in Asia during his reign. In the Far East, China was involved in a struggle with the western powers encroaching on its coastal areas. Taking advantage of this, Russia forced China to cede the regions around the Amur and Usuri Rivers. The city of Vladivostok, meaning "Ruler of the East," was founded in 1860 as a symbol of Russian power on the Pacific shores.

Central Asia was another area of expansion for Russia in the 19th century. This was Russia's southern frontier and as settlers pushed southward, they came increasingly into contact with central Asian peoples who resented their presence and showed this by carrying out periodic raids against Russian settlements. This would be followed in turn by punitive forays by the Russian army against central Asian settlements. As the raids continued, the army would begin building a new line of forts along the frontier and a new piece of territory would be added to the Russian empire.

By 1846, when a large part of Kazakhstan was incorporated into Russia, central Asia had been reduced to three independent Islamic khanates, Bokhara, Khiva and Kokand. Great centers of trade and export in the middle ages which had made them legends of wealth and power, all three khanates had subsequently declined in importance. By the middle of the 19th century, their main cities had been reduced to regional trading centers and the khanates were pale shadows of their former selves. Moreover, the writ of their rulers extended mainly to the larger settlements and they made no significant attempt to control the undisciplined tribesmen of the countryside or to stop them from carrying out raids on Russian settlements across the border.

In the 1860's, the Russian armies began a final conquest of the area. Kokand, with its ancient cities of Tashkent and Samarkand took three years to subdue. Its final conquest came in 1868. Bokhara fell the same year and Khiva was conquered in 1873.

## Revolutionary Stirrings

While Russia was having general success in the area of international relations, the situation at home was deteriorating. Alexander II's promise of reforms brought a wave of enthusiasm among the people at the beginning, and even support from old revolutionaries such as Alexander Herzen in his exile in London. But disillusionment set in as implementation of the reforms began, for it became clear that, first, from the point of view of liberals, there were flaws in the legislation itself and, second, that a conservative bureaucracy would do its best to limit even further the benefits to come from the new legislation. Moreover, the very fact of reform from above brought a questioning of the *status quo* among educated Russians because it legitimated the question— "what further should be changed?" One writer who wrote on this theme was Nicholas Chernaevsky, whose novel, *What Is To Be Done?* became almost a bible for the questioning youth of the 1860's.

This questioning occurred mainly among the greatly increased numbers of young men streaming into the universities—as yet young women had to go abroad if they wanted a university education. Exposed for the first time to the latest scientific and philosophical theories from western Europe—revolution, positivism, French Utopian Socialism—many of these young people began questioning everything about Russian culture and the Russian way of life. Although women were denied access to the universities, some of them soon became important leaders in this new movement.

We speak of this movement as *nihilism* and it was perhaps best summed up by the great Russian novelist Turgenev in his novel *Fathers and Sons.* Turgenev saw the development as a kind of generation gap, a clash between the ideas of the "fathers and sons."

The *nihilists* of the 1860's were in general not revolutionaries, but there were some exceptions. In 1866, one such "student" decided to shoot the tsar and he actually went to the garden of the palace, walked up to Alexander II, pulled out his revolver and shot at him. What saved Alexander II's life at that moment is that a worker in the gardens, seeing what was happening, grabbed his arm.

By the 1870's the vague and somewhat negative revolutionary stirring of the pre-

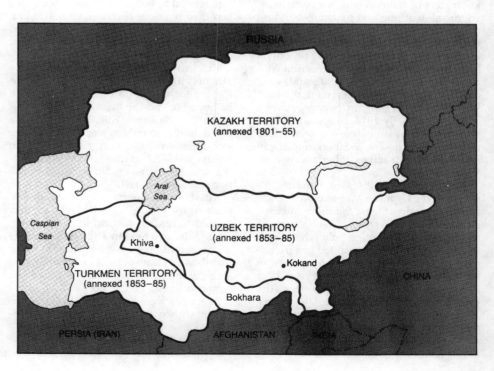

vious decades merged into the so-called *Narodnik* (populist) movement.

The *Narodniki* were heavily influenced by the writing of the French Utopian Socialists. Appalled by what they thought of as the evils of industrialism, they advocated a kind of agrarian socialism based on the traditional Russian peasant commune. The leadership expected to stir the Russian masses by going among the simple people, teaching them, but also learning from their supposedly pure and simple outlook which they allegedly had because they had not been "contaminated" by urban life. It became fashionable to "go to the people" to bring education and sanitary habits to the primitive, rural folk. Often the peasants repaid this by denouncing the uninvited tutors to the police.

Some of the populist leaders concluded that someone else would have to work for the peasants, because the masses were not mature and thinking enough to stage a

Alexander III

general uprising against the Russian system. A decision was made to engage in acts of terrorism, the most spectacular of which was the attempt to kill the military governor of St. Petersburg. By the end of the 1870's, the revolutionary organization *Zemlya i Volya* (Land and Freedom) split into two major groups, one of which favored gradual change. The other, *Narodnaya Volya* (Will of the People) chose more terror in the somewhat questionable belief that removal of a few high personalities would change things in Russia. The Tsar was selected as the chief target for assassination. After several unsuccessful attempts, Alexander II was killed by terrorists in 1881. This apparently came on the very day when he was about to sign a new decree granting more political freedom to the people.

**An Age of Reaction**

The death of Alexander II brought to an end the age of reforms that originally began with Peter the Great. "Western" and "liberal" took on sinister meanings in the eyes of the government and upper classes. Alexander III (1881–1894), who was in narrow political terms a reactionary, believed that it was impossible to come to terms with the liberals and that his father's assassination had partly resulted from his attempts to do so. He made it clear that liberals could expect nothing from him when, in his accession address, he declared his "complete faith in the strength and truth of autocracy" and that "for the good of the people" he would "maintain and defend the autocratic power from attack."

He was 36 when he came to the throne. A great bear of a man, he referred to himself as the "peasant Tsar," and he was very proud of the fact that he could straighten horseshoes with his bare hands. He was honest and hard-working, but intellectually somewhat dull. He recognized his limitations, however, and left many decisions to his ministers, supporting them and keeping them in office even when he didn't understand what they were trying to do.

His most important political advisers were Constantine Pobedonostsev, Michael Katkov and Dmitri Tolstoy. Curiously enough, all had been supporters of Alexander II's reforms. Pobedonostsev had helped to draft the judicial reforms, for example, and Tolstoy had been Minister of Education in the previous regime. Katkov had been a well-known westernizer and liberal.

By 1881, however, they rejected their earlier admiration for foreign ideas and sought Russia's salvation in its own past. Alexander III, strongly nationalistic with Pan-Slav leanings, accepted their advice about the need to Russify the minorities and to bring the entire population into the Russian Orthodox Church. In Poland and in the Baltic provinces, Russian was made the language of instruction in the schools. Catholics, Protestants and Old Believers found themselves affected by government policies aimed at the conversion of these groups to Russian Orthodoxy. More affected were the Jews, for even more restrictive policies were applied to them. Laws forbidding their settlement in central Russia were tightened, and they were confined to an area called the "Pale of Settlement." Limitations were placed on the entry of Jews to universities; they were excluded from most government service and forbidden to acquire land in rural areas. In addition, agencies of the government were frequently engaged in stirring up violent outbreaks *(pogroms)* of the people against their Jewish countrymen. Repeated outbreaks caused a massive migration of Jews from the lands of the Russian empire. Many came to America.

The nature of Alexander III's reign was thus quite different from that of his father. Yet, though he disagreed with his father politically, he was loath to undo the work which his predecessor had begun. The substance of reform survived, although the new Tsar did approve some amendments aimed at reducing popular participation. Provincial governors were, for example, given greater control over the *Zemstvo* assemblies and the franchise was changed to increase the representation of the nobility. The government also increased its administrative powers over the judiciary.

Alexander III shared his father's commitment to industrialization, so there was no essential change in economic policy. Government policy continued to encourage the construction of railroads, though more state–owned railroads were built in this period. Tariffs were also raised several times in order to encourage "infant industries." The policy worked in the sense that there was a good deal of foreign investment in Russia in the 1880's, but it also led to a tariff war with Germany from 1887 to 1893.

The policy of Alexander III toward the peasantry was probably his most important personal contribution toward the economic policy of his reign. Genuinely interested in the welfare of the peasantry, the Tsar set out to do what he could to improve their lot—at least insofar as that could be done within the framework of Russia at that time. The redemption debt was reduced in 1881 and again in 1884. Two taxes that weighed heavily on the lower class, the salt tax and the poll tax, were repealed. They were replaced by two taxes which applied mainly to the upper and middle classes: an inheritance tax and a tax on bonds.

The increase in population since emancipation had also reduced the average size of peasant allotments. To remedy this, the government set up a Peasant Land Bank to lend money. It also made loans to those who were willing to move to Siberia. In spite of these measures, the true state of Russia became evident in 1891 when crop failures led to famine in the countryside.

Although Russia remained at peace during the 13 years that Alexander III was on the throne, Russia's foreign relations were often abrasive, for, as one historian says of him, Alexander III attempted to obtain peacefully objectives that are usually obtained only as the result of a successful war. Russia's quarrels were primarily with Austria–Hungary and Germany and led to Alexander's decision to sign an alliance with France in 1892.

Alexander III's quarrels with Germany were of a two–fold nature, but they were exacerbated by his pan–Slav leanings. In the 1870's, Alexander III, then the heir to the throne, had supported pan–Slav aspirations in the Balkans and was deeply angered when Austria refused to accept the Treaty of San Stefano, negotiated at the close of Russia's victorious war against the Ottoman Empire in 1878. He favored a connection with Germany, however, and, in 1881, accepted his foreign minister's advice that a renewal of the Three Emperors' League was the only way this could be arranged.

Things went smoothly until 1885, when the Bulgarians, at that time proteges of the Russians, decided to carry through a union with East Rumelia without consulting their Russian overseers. Alexander III "punished" the Bulgarians by withdrawing all Russian military advisers. When Austria took advantage of the situation to increase its own influence in Bulgaria, Alexander III felt betrayed and denounced the Three Emperors' League. His real quarrel, therefore, was with Austria. Alexander III still wanted a connection with Germany, however, and suggested a bilateral alliance with Germany in 1887, "not against Austria, but without Austria." This became the Re–insurance Treaty, which existed for three years, until 1890.

Alexander III also had a grievance with Germany having to do with economic relations between the two countries. In the 1880's, Germany was Russia's chief trading partner and the source of most foreign capital investment in the Russian economy. Russia had an adverse trade balance with Germany, which it attempted to solve by raising tariffs on the main goods coming in from Germany. This led a good number of German firms to open affiliates in Russian Poland as a way to retain the Russian market. However this large German commercial presence in Russian Poland became another problem, because Russian nationalists felt it threatened Russian political control in this borderland area. In 1887, the Russian Government issued a decree prohibiting foreigners from owning land in border areas such as Russian Poland, and Germany retaliated by an attack on Russian securities, known as the *Lombard Verbot.* Thus began an economic war that lasted until 1894 and brought the two nations as close to war as they were to come in the 19th century. It was these poor economic–political relations with Germany which led Alexander III to sign an alliance with France in 1892. That alliance, still in force in 1914, would bring Russia and France into World War I as allies against Germany and Austria.

## The Last Tsar

Alexander III has sometimes been referred to as the last Russian autocrat; whatever else can be said of him, it is generally agreed that he personified the policy of his reign. Nicholas II (1894–1914), by contrast, was a weak– willed individual who all his life was dominated by those about him. Moreover, he hated confrontations and got around them by seeming to agree with whomever he was talking. This made it extremely difficult for government ministers, for they never knew whether his approval of one of their suggestions was apparent or real. This also inclined him against strong–willed ministers, for that increased the possibility of disagreement. This trait became even more noticeable as he grew older, probably the result of the influence of his wife, Alexandra.

Alexandra, who also attempted to dominate him, called him weak–willed to his face and demanded that he stand up to his ministers. Other examples of her advice follow. Her baleful influence came primarily toward the end of his reign, however, as she undoubtedly saw the future crumbling.

Nicholas II was 26 years old when he succeeded to the throne. Professing his admiration for his father, he retained his father's ministers and promised to continue his policies. Meeting with representatives of the *Zemstvo* of Tver, for example, Nicholas told them that:

"It has come to my knowledge that . . . there have been heard in some *Zemstvos* the voices of those who have indulged in senseless dreams that the *Zemstvos* might participate in the direction of the internal affairs of the state. Let all know that I shall devote my energy to the service of the people, but that I shall maintain the principle of autocracy as firmly . . . as did my father."

In spite of his promise, Nicholas did modify his father's policies in one area. He did not share his father's dislike for German culture and this showed up domestically in his reversal of his father's Russification policy as it applied to the Baltic Germans. It showed up internationally in the much better relations that developed with both Austria and Germany after 1894.

Russia was already in the midst of an economic boom when Nicholas came to the throne. The Minister of Finance was Sergei Witte (*Vit*–ay), a strong proponent of industrialization. Witte put the country on the gold standard, encouraged the inflow of foreign investment and pushed the construction of railroads. The boom lasted until 1899; by that time, the production of large–scale industry as a whole had doubled.

One ominous sign on the horizon was

Nicholas II and Alexandra

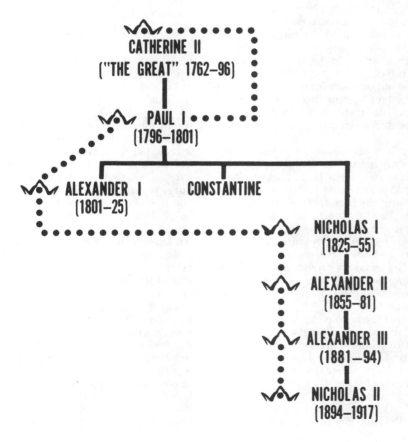

CATHERINE II
("THE GREAT" 1762–96)

PAUL I
(1796–1801)

ALEXANDER I          CONSTANTINE
(1801–25)

NICHOLAS I
(1825–55)

ALEXANDER II
(1855–81)

ALEXANDER III
(1881–94)

NICHOLAS II
(1894–1917)

the lack of domestic entrepreneurs, however. Of 14 new steel mills built during the 1890's, only one was Russian. The other 13 were foreign–owned and had foreign management. Other branches of industry dominated by foreign capital included the electric and electro–technical industry, the gas industry, chemicals and dyes. Many metal–working and machine building companies were also foreign–owned and run. Using the terminology of Karl Marx, whose economic theories were to have such a dynamic impact on Russia, it was *creating* capitalism *but very few capitalists.*

## The Revolution of 1905

The flow of new foreign capital into Russia was halted by a world–wide financial crisis in 1899, and brought about a wave of bankruptcies and mounting unemployment. Just as business was starting to recover, the economy was set back by crop failures in the countryside. A period of unrest followed, with strikes in the cities and peasant demonstrations in the villages. Illegal political parties began to appear and agitation for basic reforms increased.

Then came the Russo–Japanese War of 1904. It was badly fought, and the defeat of Russian forces at Port Arthur swelled the numbers of those who had come to believe that the government was unfit to rule.

In this tense atmosphere, the government made yet another blunder and set off the Revolution of 1905. Father Gabon, a Russian Orthodox priest who had started an organization for workers, was asked by them to lead them in a march to the Winter Palace to present a petition for redress of grievances to the Tsar. The peaceful crowd of workers, accompanied by their wives and children, were fired upon by the police as they approached the Winter Palace. Approximately a hundred people were killed and another hundred wounded. Although it had been one of the Russian Grand Dukes who had given orders to fire on the crowd—Nicholas II was not in residence at the Winter Palace at the time—Nicholas was blamed for what happened. Thus this event, which has gone down in history as "Bloody Sunday," had a significance beyond the immediate deaths and injuries. On that day, a myth died. The peasants had always thought of the Tsar as the "Little Father" who cared for his people. With the events of Bloody Sunday, that myth could no longer be sustained.

It triggered a wave of resentment and protests that continued throughout the spring and summer of 1905 and led, then, to a general strike that began in early fall. The general strike established that Nicholas II's government had lost the confidence of all Russian society, with the possible exception of the nobility and some of the military.

On the advice of Sergei Witte, Nicholas issued a manifesto promising constitutional government, civil liberties to all citizens and a national legislature (Duma). This was termed the "October Manifesto;" Nicholas also named Witte as his new chief minister.

Elections to the first Duma took place in March 1906. Nicholas showed his pettiness and lack of foresight by dismissing Witte as chief minister just before the legislature convened. The first Duma was dominated by a liberal group supported by Russia's professional classes, the Constitutional Democrats (Kadets). They clashed with the executive branch of government and when this division deepened, the Duma was dissolved. A second Duma was even more radical and it also was dissolved.

In calling for elections to a third Duma, Nicholas changed voting regulations to reduce the representation of troublemakers that had been voting for more radical candidates. He also appointed Peter Stolypin as his new Chief Minister.

The change in voting made the new Duma less representative, but it also produced a body willing to work with the Tsar and his ministers. Stolypin turned out to be a strong individual who managed for several years to save the Tsar from himself. Stolypin's name is particularly associated with a land reform which broke up the peasant communes and redistributed the land to the peasants as their private property. He hoped that, by giving the peasants something to lose, he would wean them away from their support of the radicals. But the reforms came too late and took too much time; by 1914 only about 25% of the peasants had managed to exchange their scattered strips for a single, contiguous plot of land. Stolypin was himself assassinated by revolutionaries in 1911 and with his strong presence gone, Nicholas II again began to exercise a greater say in the government.

**World War I**
The good relations which Nicholas had cultivated with Germany and Austria came to an end in 1908 when a new quarrel erupted between Russia and Austria over events in the Balkans. Austria's annexation of Bosnia began the dispute, but it soon spread and involved Germany—because of its support of Austria. Russia then became a patron of Serbia, which was anti–Austrian. The assassination of Archduke Francis Ferdinand, heir to the Austrian throne by a Serbian nationalist led Austria to declare war on Serbia. The general system of alliances transformed this Balkan war into World War I.

It was not long before the continent of Europe was aflame. At first the Russian people responded to the call to arms with patriotic fervor, but this cooled considerably when the tides of battle turned. The Germans were pressing forward in France and soon threatened Paris; in order to take the pressure off, Russia invaded East Prussia. The army turned out to be ill–prepared and poorly equipped for a lengthy war, and Russia suffered a humiliating defeat. The government was incapable of enlisting the help of social organizations that were willing to assist in the war effort. Attention was focused mainly on the prospects of a glorious post–war seizure of coveted lands; especially attractive was the idea of taking Constantinople from the Turks, who had entered the war on the side of Germany. A victory would also have meant a Russian control over the straits that separate the Black Sea from the Mediterranean. However, while the government engaged in these dreams, German and Austrian forces actually occupied parts of Russian territory.

Tsar Nicholas made things worse for himself by assuming direct command of the armed forces. This kept him away from the capital and the result was that crucial matters of government were left in the hands of his German–born wife, the Empress Alexandra. She was extremely conservative, ambitious, hysterical and surrounded by advisers, some of whom may have been German spies. There also was another unbelievable influence in the palace—that of an illiterate, immoral and filthy peasant "Holy Man" named Rasputin who had wormed his way into the highest social circles of St. Petersburg. Empress Alexandra turned to Rasputin because of a tragic family problem, the incurable bleeding disease hemophilia. Her only son and heir to the throne, Alexis, suffered from this illness, inherited through his mother. Rasputin became a powerful figure at the palace, and extremely important matters of state were soon "solved" according to his advice. Tsar Nicholas had become weak and sentimental and offered no opposition to his wife.

The effects of the war at first caused unrest mainly among the city dwellers who were suffering from fuel shortages and high food prices caused by disrupted supplies. Soon the countryside also became restive. The army command lacked skill— it tried to remedy Russia's lack of modern weapons by pouring seemingly endless millions of human bodies into the battle lines. The peasants provided the bulk of the manpower sent into what became a senseless slaughter; desertions became frequent.

The first move to remedy the alarming situation was a revolt from above; members of the highest aristocracy murdered Rasputin in December 1916. As the supplies of food decreased, food riots occurred more frequently in the cities, and workers went on strike. Troops summoned to restore law and order tended to side with the angry people. A half–heart-

ed attempt was made to save the monarchy by having Nicholas abdicate in favor of his son, an incurably ill boy. However, the Tsar's brother, the Grand Duke Mikhail (Michael), refused to accept a regency under the circumstances, and overnight the Romanov dynasty ceased to govern Russia. The royal family was later put under arrest and finally gunned down by a gang of Bolsheviks in a cellar in Ekaterinburg, together with the family pet dog and the court doctor on the night of July 16–17, 1918.

**An Experiment With Democracy**
During the war years the Duma had been totally ignored by the Tsar. As the end of the monarchy approached, it began to show signs of activity. When the tsarist regime "evaporated," the Duma organized a Temporary Committee. This contained all political groups except the extreme right and the extreme left; the Bolshevik representatives in the Duma were in jail or in Siberian exile. The Committee in turn produced a Provisional Government under the chairmanship of a liberal aristocrat, Prince George Lvov. It was intended that the Provisional Gov-

Nicholas II: A Prisoner at Tsarskoe Selo, 1917

ernment would run the affairs of Russia until a Constituent Assembly could be elected by the people and write a constitution. The leadership of the Provisional Government later passed to a moderate socialist, Alexander Kerensky, who held power until overthrown by the Bolsheviks in October (November) of the same year—1917. In order to understand what happened in Russia after the Romanovs were deposed, it is important to know that on the very day that the *Duma* organized its Temporary Committee, there also came into existence the *Soviet* (Council) *of Worker's Deputies*. This was actually a revival of the institution that briefly functioned during the unsuccessful revolution of 1905. The Soviet was soon enlarged by adding representatives of the soldiers in

**Grigori Efimovich Rasputin**

revolt, and was led by moderate socialist members. These men believed that Russia, a rather backward country in terms of industrial development, would first have to "catch up" by going through a *bourgeois democratic* stage which would sweep away the remnants of the old feudal system. It was thought that the *bourgeois–democratic* administration would bring Russia to the level of a mature, capitalist nation which would then, and only then, be ripe for a socialist revolution. The workers, or *proletariat*, would grow in numbers in the democratic capitalist period and would become aware of their power and historical role and be the basis for another revolution that would usher in socialism.

The leftist parties, including the Bolsheviks prior to Lenin's return to Russia, gave their support to the Provisional Government, although at first refusing to serve in it. A peculiar pattern of power emerged; the Soviet enjoyed substantial support from the workers and soldiers, but refused to govern directly. It reserved for itself the position of being a critic and "watchdog" of the revolution. While the Provisional Government was the official governing body, it had no mass following and was forced to rely on the Soviet for support. This was particularly true in matters involving the army—the Provisional Government had nominal control of the armed forces, but the Soviet had ordered enlisted personnel to keep arms out of the reach of officers in order to prevent a counter–revolution.

### Lenin's Return

Events took a decisively new turn when Vladimir Illich Ulianov (Lenin), the lead-er of the Bolshevik faction of the *Social Democratic Party*, returned to Russia on April 3, 1917. A natural politician, Lenin understood how to appear faithful to Marxist ideals and at the same time to be flexible enough to deal with unexpected situations not covered by Marx. Lenin saw through the confused situation and brilliantly analyzed it as being one of "dual government." The Provisional Government held nominal authority but the *Soviet* enjoyed the support of the people. The way to eliminate this duality was to dominate the *Soviet* and then eliminate the "official" government.

Lenin was aware that at the moment his own group, the Bolsheviks, were a minority in the Soviet. It took him some time to win over the leadership of his own group. He added a new direction of thinking to the Bolsheviks—seizure of power. The Bolsheviks were able to win additional support because of the insistence of the Provisional Government that Russia had an obligation to continue to fight Germany, an idea that was becoming increasingly unpopular. Another factor was the failure of moderate elements to deal with pressing internal problems such as distribution of land to peasants and creating an orderly supply of food.

Propelled by Lenin's determined will and by simplified slogans directed to the people, such as "Peace, Bread and Land," the Bolsheviks began their quest for power. Because of his more flexible leadership they were not saddled with burdensomely rigid theories of government that handicapped the other socialist groups.

In July 1917, there was a Bolshevik–inspired uprising in Petrograd (the Russian version of St. Petersburg adopted in 1914) which was suppressed, and Lenin was forced to flee across the border to Finland. In spite of this temporary setback, the influence of the Bolsheviks grew steadily, particularly among the soldiers and sailors. The determined attitude of the Bolsheviks against continuing the war with Germany was especially helpful. The Provisional Government, besides failing to solve internal problems, seemed to make no real effort to get out of the unpopular war because it felt bound by an agreement with Russia's allies not to make a separate peace.

An unfortunate decision to mount one more military offensive in the summer of 1917 contributed to the near collapse of army organization and morale. This played right into the hands of the Bolsheviks. The government, by this time quite desperate, tried to turn the anger of the people against Lenin and his followers, stating that the instigators of the July uprising were German agents.

Lenin was not widely popular throughout Russia nor within his own party organization. It was charged that he had spent the war years away from Russia, mainly in neutral Switzerland; that he was an "internationalist" who had opposed the war from its very beginning in 1914; that he had returned to Russia with the assistance of the German army's High Command, who arranged for his travel through Germany in a sealed railway car, and that he had been the recipient of sums of money from Germany since his arrival in Russia. Lenin never denied the first three charges and there is some evidence that the fourth accusation was true as well. But Lenin was never a German agent. The German army High Command helped Lenin to get back to Russia because he was a known opponent of the war and they hoped his presence in Russia would weaken the Russian resolve to continue the war. Any financial assistance they may have given Lenin was for the same reason. And Lenin was willing to take assistance from any source, provided it promoted his own particular goals.

Lenin was forced to remain in hiding because of these charges against him, but the Bolsheviks continued to grow in popularity, primarily because of bumbling and failures on the part of the Provisional Government and the other political parties. One such case of bumbling was the "Kornilov Affair."

Alexander Kerensky, who had been head of the Provisional Government since July 20, 1917, entered into negotiations with the recently-appointed commander-in-chief of the armed forces, General Lavr Kornilov. The exact nature of their understanding remains a matter of contro-

---

### FROM LENIN'S "APRIL THESES"

(A few days after his return to Russia, Lenin published on April 7, 1917, a set of brief "theses" stating his view of the situation in the war-torn country. He outlined a program for the "second stage" of the revolution. Below are some excerpts.)

1. In our attitude toward the war, which unquestionably remains on Russia's part a predatory imperialist war under the new government of Lvov Company because of the capitalist nature of that government, not the slightest concession to "revolutionary defencism" is permissible.

The class-conscious proletariat can give its consent to a revolutionary war which would really justify "revolutionary defencism" only if (a) the power passes to the proletariat, (b) all foreign annexations be renounced in fact and not just in word, and (c)

that a complete break be made in fact with all capitalist interests . . .

5. There should not be a parliamentary republic—to return to a parliamentary republic from the Soviets of Workers' Deputies would be a step backwards—there must be a republic of Soviets of Workers', Agricultural Laborers' and Peasants' Deputies throughout the country, from top to bottom.

There also must be abolition of the police, the army and the bureaucracy . . .

9. (c) (We must) change the Party's name. Instead of "Social Democracy," the world leaders of which have betrayed Socialism and deserted to the bourgeoisie . . . we must call ourselves a Communist Party.

10. There must be a new International. We must take the initiative in creating a new revolutionary International . . .

---

versy to this day, but it appears that Kerensky turned to the general, a believer in "law and order," to obtain military assistance against the growing influence of the Bolsheviks. However, when Kerensky thought the general and his troops were marching on Petrograd to stage a *coup* and possibly restore the old regime, he turned on Kornilov.

When the general refused to give up his post and issued a statement directed against the Provisional Government, Kerensky sought the help of the workers of the threatened capital, including groups that were known to be under Bol-

shevik influence. The end of the "Kornilov Affair" with the arrest of the general and his leading staff officer seemed for a while to strengthen Kerensky's position. In reality, the prestige of the Provisional Government had all but vanished.

Lenin's attitude at the time of the "Kornilov Affair" is reflected in his response to Kerensky's plea for support against Kornilov—"We will support him the way a noose supports a hanged man." Lenin apparently liked analogies about ropes and nooses, for on another occasion he characterized capitalists as being willing to "sell you the rope with which to hang them."

**Demonstration against the Provisional Government, July 1917**

Lenin

The Kornilov affair actually rehabilitated the Bolsheviks and prepared the way for their eventual seizure of power. In September, the Petrograd Soviet returned a Bolshevik majority; a week later, the Moscow Soviet did likewise. The new chairman of the Petrograd Soviet was Lev D. Bronstein, better known by his revolutionary name, Trotsky. Although a longtime revolutionary and radical ideologist, he had only joined the Bolshevik faction in the summer of 1917. With Lenin still in hiding, however, it was Trotsky who took charge and actually carried out the *coup d'etat* against the Provisional Government which was to go down in history as the "Great October Socialist Revolution."

Very little is heard about Trotsky in the Soviet Union today. This is because, after Lenin's death, there was a struggle for power between him and Josef Stalin and he came out the loser. Forced into exile, he became a bitter opponent of Stalin and his policies in the 1930's. He was eventually killed on Stalin's orders. But no amount of falsification of history can erase the key role Trotsky played in organizing the workers and winning over the soldiers and sailors to the side of the Bolsheviks. Trotsky was a fiery orator who could sway masses of workers and peasants to follow his advice. His leadership in the brief military operations which resulted in the overthrow of the Provisional Government was brilliant.

However, even Trotsky later conceded that Lenin was the one indispensable individual in the Russian Revolution. It was Lenin who was convinced that the time was ripe to move against the Provisional Government and who persuaded the Central Committee of the Bolsheviks to begin preparations for the seizure of power.

Trotsky accepted that decision and set about to implement it. He persuaded the Executive Committee of the Petrograd Soviet that a Military Revolutionary Committee needed to be created for the de-fense of the revolution. This Military Revolutionary Committee then sent "political commissars" to each of the military units stationed in Petrograd. Their instructions were to persuade the soldiers and sailors to accept no orders from their officers unless they were countersigned by the political commissar of the Petrograd Soviet. In this manner, Trotsky managed to neutralize the entire Petrograd Garrison.

After many hesitations, the attempt to seize power was timed to coincide with the sessions of the All–Russian Congress of Soviets called for November 7, 1917 (October 25 by the old calendar). However, events came to a head a day earlier—the government had been tipped off about the impending *coup* and began to move some loyal troops into position. It also ordered the soldiers to occupy the premises where the Bolshevik newspaper *Pravda* (Truth) was printed.

By this time the Bolsheviks were in control of the major military unit of the Petrograd garrison, and easily secured a number of important points. The seat of government in the Winter Palace was defended briefly by a detachment of military cadets and a women's battalion, but when the guns of the cruiser Aurora were trained on the palace, resistance ceased. Most members of the Provisional Government were put under arrest. Kerensky escaped in disguise in a car flying the U.S. flag. He died in New York in 1970; his writings blame everyone but himself for the events of 1917.

The Bolsheviks march into Moscow

# THE COMMUNIST ERA (November 1917–August 1991)

## Soviet Russia

### Creation of the New Soviet Regime

Although the *coup d'etat* that brought the Bolsheviks to power was made in the name of the Second Congress of Soviets, it was actually carried out by the Military Revolutionary Committee of the Petrograd Soviet, and the Bolsheviks announced the overthrow of the Provisional Government before the Congress of Soviets convened on the evening of October 25/November 7. The Congress was dominated by the Bolsheviks and their allies, the Left Socialist Revolutionaries, however, so they accepted their new role and passed a resolution written by Lenin proclaiming the transfer of all power to the Soviets. Executive power was vested in a Soviet of People's Commissars (SOVNARKOM).

Lenin became chairman, and he filled the other positions on the *SOVNARKOM* (equivalent to a cabinet) with Bolsheviks. Thus the Bolsheviks managed to clothe themselves in the legitimacy of the Soviet movement and to use it to gain political power in Russia. The Congress of Soviets, having installed the Bolsheviks in power, had completed its usefulness. A Central Executive Committee was therefore elected, composed of 2/3 Bolsheviks and 1/3 Left Socialist Revolutionaries, and given full authority to pass legislation in the name of the Congress, which now adjourned. Just in case that wasn't sufficient, the *SOVNARKOM* was authorized to issue decrees which would have the force of law.

Soviets had sprung up spontaneously over all Russia after the February Revolution, but they only existed at the local level and were not universal. In December 1917, a decree of the *SOVNARKOM* called for the creation of Soviets at the local, district, regional and provincial level, these Soviets to replace the *Zemstvos* as organs of government. Soviet officials were in theory to be elected, but only workers and peasants had the right to vote.

Since the Soviets only recognized socialist political parties, all others had become illegal as of the creation of the new Soviet government. Mensheviks and Socialist Revolutionaries lost their representation when the Congress of Soviets adjourned and they soon found themselves subject to some repression as well. Menshevik newspapers were closed first, but this ban was soon extended to all opposition newspapers, By the spring of 1918, all opposition political parties had been outlawed and the *Communist Party* (the new name the Bolsheviks had adopted in March 1918) had become the sole legal party in Soviet Russia.

### War Communism

The period of Soviet history down to March 1921 is usually referred to as the period of *War Communism*. Once it got itself organized, the new regime set out to communize the country—or at least those parts that recognized its authority, since at this time the various minority nationalities had broken away and were in the process of establishing separate governments.

First priority was given to the nationalization of the means of production. A decree on land, issued immediately after the takeover, abolished private property in land but permitted the peasants to continue to use the land, provided they did not make use of hired labor. Banks, railroads, shipping and foreign trade were nationalized almost immediately, and the Supreme Economic Council was set up to begin state planning. Another decree established worker control over production and distribution of industrial output. Lenin would probably have preferred to move more slowly with nationalization of the rest of the economy, but he found his pace forced by so–called "nationalizations from below" as individual workers expelled owners and seized control of factories on their own. By the spring of 1918, all industry had been nationalized and the government had taken control over all internal trade as well.

## The Treaty of Brest–Litovsk

Of all the things Bolshevik propaganda had promised the people, peace had perhaps been the most significant. But the Bolsheviks also needed peace in order to have time to consolidate their government. They attempted a "Decree on Peace" on the very first day after seizing power, but that had no more than a propaganda effect. For real peace, they had to find a way to negotiate with those making war on Russia—the German Imperial General Staff. Preliminary negotiations resulted in the signing of a temporary truce in December. But when peace negotiations began in January, the German terms were so harsh that Trotsky, in charge of the negotiations, rejected them out of hand. Lenin argued that there was no alternative to acceptance of the German terms, but it was not until the Germans began a new advance that he could get his associates to agree. The Treaty of Brest–Litovsk on March 3, 1918, ended the state of war between Russia and the Central Powers, Germany and Austria.

By the terms of the treaty, the Soviet government obligated itself to recognize that Georgia (in southern Russia), the Ukraine (between Russia and Poland and Finland (to the northwest) were no longer parts of Russia. Poland and three small Baltic states, Lithuania, Latvia and Estonia, were conceded to be in Germany's sphere and control. The Aaland Islands in the Baltic Sea were evacuated, and the Turks, then allied with Germany, were given land in and near the cities of Kars, Ardahan and Batum.

Profiting from Russia's weakness, the Romanians occupied the province of Bessarabia which had been a part of southwestern Russia. Altogether, the terms of the treaty meant a loss of 1.3 million square miles of Russian territory. This represented about 32% of the agricultural land, about one–third of the factories and approximately 75% of the coal and iron mines of Russia.

Harsh as the terms of the Treaty of Brest–Litovsk were, they gave the hard-pressed Bolsheviks an opportunity to consolidate their power in areas outside the two main cities of the country. Trotsky undertook the gigantic task of building an army. The name of this new force was *Workers and Peasants Red Army*. The name "Red Army" continued to be used by some in the western world although the name had been changed to the more respectable *Armed Forces of the USSR*.

# What is Communism?

Every human society claims to be guided by some basic set of rules—a philosophy, theory or ideology. With the Age of Enlightenment, there was an attempt to substitute for the traditional religious explanations for the origin and behavior of man a more "modern" description of (1) what man was, (2) why he was here and (3) where he was going. Further, there was an effort to explain why mankind thought the way it did.

This philosophic effort occupied several centuries and still persists, although now at a lower degree. The study of philosophy reached its heights in the 17th and 18th centuries in Europe—England, France, Germany, Switzerland and Rome, not necessarily in that order. The effort of philosophers was to discover, through the processes of science and thought, the reason, origin and destiny of mankind, independent of the teachings of religion.

The ideas and ideals of modern communism had their birth in the writings of Karl Marx (1818–1883), a German–born philosopher, social critic and revolutionary, who spent almost 35 years in England. His residency there was contemporary with the life styles described in the writings of Charles Dickens, which heavily influenced his thinking. His original work, *Das Kapital* (referring to capital) of which only the first volume was published during Marx's lifetime, was supplemented by others edited from his notes by his closest colleague, Friedrich Engels. The latter was a wealthy capitalist who had turned radical. The two founding fathers of communism are even better known for the *Communist Manifesto*, made public in 1847.

The theory (if a legitimate one ever actually existed) has undergone so much change that it is difficult to explain to the world today.

The first consideration was Marx's belief as to the origin of ideas. Borrowing heavily from the ideas of others, particularly the philosophers Hegel and John Locke, Marx accepted the idea of Hegel that human ideas—thought—arose from the interplay of two forces. A theory (idea) always had an opposite: the antithesis. From the two, there was a combination of the best features of both into a *synthesis*. But Marx went further—he rejected the proposition that man could think independently of things he had experienced with his five senses. All thought, he urged, was nothing more than a mirror of material things which had been experienced. This borrowed

from the so–called "blank tablet" theory of John Locke. It is demonstrably wrong as has been repeatedly proved during the decades following Marx. Chemical elements of the *periodic table* were predicted far in advance of any opportunity to *see, hear, feel, touch or smell them*. Many of Einstein's theories of relativity remained to be experienced or proven until after his death.

But Marx doggedly persisted in his advancement of the "blank tablet" idea of Locke, and went further: he said in effect that human ideas, insofar as they would effect history, were determined by the *changes in the modes of production*. He further proclaimed that the "modes of production" had made people wealthy or poor. Applying his ideas to 19th century England, he labeled the times as "capitalistic" and proclaimed that the ruling class was the "bourgoisie" (boor-zwah–see). It was fashionable toe borrow terms from other languages, particularly French, at the time he wrote.

Marx correctly observed that capitalists were identified with the economic idea of "free competition" and that they had "historically played a most revolutionary part" and could not, in fact, "exist without constantly revolutionizing" (i.e. improving) the instruments of production.

But he then denounced the capitalist "class" as evil. He said that as a result Marx saw three sinister laws associated with capitalism: capitalist accumulation, concentration of capital and increasing misery (of the lower classes). His laws were based on the conclusion that *human labor alone creates value*, and, accordingly, the profits of capitalists *are derived from unpaid labor time*.

Marx urged that competition results in

more labor–saving machinery (or bankruptcy) and therefore increased unemployment and a general lowering of employee wages. The end result is monopoly capitalism—whereby all wealth is in the hands of a few capitalists and a countless mass of the people have been driven down into the ranks of "the proletariat."

The ultimate result, according to Marx, was "the more or less veiled civil war . . . break(ing) out into open revolution," overthrowing the bourgeoisie and raising the proletariat to the position of the ruling class. Once in power, the proletariat would nationalize all means of production and institute state planning to replace the discarded schemes of competition. The state—"nothing more than a machine for the oppression of one class by another"—will wither away and mankind will have entered the highest and last stage of development: Communism.

Marx claimed his to be a scientific doctrine which, having mastered the general laws that govern human society, could apply them to understand the future. The logical test of Marxism, of course, is whether his "laws" subsequently came true.

In fact, none came true. The total number of capitalists continued to grow throughout the remainder of the 19th and 20th centuries as inventions such as the electric dynamo, the internal combustion engine, the light bulb, the telephone, the aerosol valve, the silicone chip, radar, the computer (which is setting this typography) and a multitude of whole new industries came into being. As for Marx's "proletariat," living standards improved as wages began an upward spiral, the union movement took hold and living standards steadily improved. By 1900, it was generally conceded that Marx's law of "increasing misery" was not in opera-

Karl Marx

tion and his followers made efforts to update and correct him.

Vladimir I. Lenin was not actually one of these "revisionists." He thought of himself as primarily a revolutionary, not a theoretician, but it was precisely for this reason that he wanted to know *why* the revolution had not yet occurred and what could be done to bring it about. He set forth his conclusions in *What Is To Be Done?*, a book he wrote in 1902. In essence, he argued that the revolution hadn't occurred because the proletariat wasn't capable of carrying out a socialist revolution—that, left to itself, it was only "able to develop trade union consciousness."

The revolution would be made by "a revolutionary youth, armed with Social–Democratic theory." What was needed, therefore, was an organization of fulltime professional revolutionaries who, acting as "the vanguard of all the revolutionary forces," would bring about the revolution in the name of the proletariat.

Lenin thus presented an "organizational solution" to the question "what could be done to bring the revolution?" This "organizational solution" had additional implications, however, for it effectively excluded the proletariat (which it intended to benefit) from control of the revolutionary party. Only individuals trained in Marxist ideology would have the necessary "socialist consciousness" to be able to provide proper guidance to the proletariat.

Lenin's position on the nature of the party became the chief issue at the Second Congress of the Russian Social Democratic Labor Party when it met in 1903.

Lenin's supporters became known as Bolsheviks, while his opponents became known as Mensheviks. There was, in effect, a split in the party.

The Bolsheviks became a small band of professional revolutionaries, whose chief common characteristic was their personal loyalty to Lenin. Lenin's control was further reinforced in July 1917 when a Bolshevik party congress adopted the principle of *democratic centralism* as the basis of party organization. This is still the basis of Communist Party organization and it has meant in practice that subordinate party units are mere agents of the party leadership, bound to follow all instructions from above. When this is contrasted with Jefferson's ideals of democracy, one can see how it has been possible for the proletariat—anyone not in a position of leadership—to be subjected to almost anything.

Lenin made a somewhat broader contribution to Marxist theory in 1916 when he wrote *Imperialism, The Highest Stage of Capitalism*. Most of the thought of the book is not original, but it does contain an argument which tends to modify Marx's theory that the socialist revolution occurs

in a country only after capitalism has been fully developed. According to Marx, According to Lenin, however, imperialism created a new situation which called for a modification of Marx's statement insofar as colonial or semi–colonial people were concerned. Under imperialism, monopoly capitalists exploit "backward, colonial peoples," first as markets and, second, as a cheap source of raw materials. This exploitation permits the capitalists to pay their own workers higher wages than they would otherwise be able to pay, and accounts for the improvement in the lot of the workers, contrary to Marx's theory. At the same time, it gave a new form to the *proletariat*—which came to include the "toiling masses of the backward countries."

Accordingly, every country that was subject to capitalistic exploitation was a suitable target for revolution *regardless of the extent of its industrial development.* Russia thus became a proper target for revolution although it had not entered the industrial stage required for revolution. The Russian Revolution of February 1917 further reinforced Lenin's conviction that Russia was ready for a socialist revolution. He returned to Russia in April 1917 to fulfill his fate with destiny.

**Intervention and Civil War**

Russia's departure from the war with Germany led to military intervention from the outside and to a civil war within Russia waged by elements opposed to the new regime. These anti–Bolshevik groups received some, but not enough outside support—"a wretched half–measure" as the late Sir Winston Churchill called it. The intervention was due to a number of reasons. There was fear that Germany, freed from the need to fight on the eastern front, would be able to move large numbers of troops to the western front. This would permit Germany to score a decisive victory before the impact of America's entry into the war would be felt. There were also arguments that large stores of military supplies in the far north of European Russia would fall into the hands of the Germans.

In France there was an outcry to protect the money of many investors who were holding tsarist Russian loan bonds. The Japanese were looking for an opportunity to establish themselves on the Asian mainland at the expense of a weakened Russia. This, in turn, stimulated U.S. participation in the intervention because the American leadership did not care for the idea of Japanese expansion in the Far East.

Technically, American intervention was also on behalf of the *Czechoslovak Legion*, a group of about 100,000 troops of the Austro–Hungarian army who had deserted or had been captured on the Russian front during the war. While moving across Russia to form a fighting force that was to as-

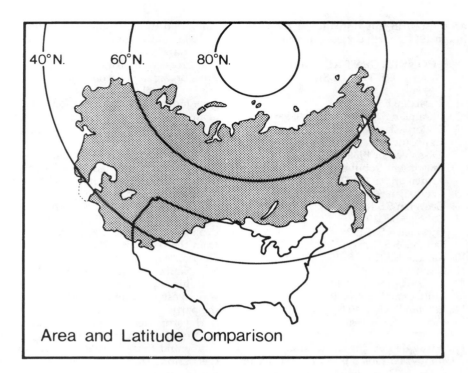

**40°N.    60°N.    80°N.**

Area and Latitude Comparison

sist on the western front, they clashed with the Bolsheviks.

The intervention was a series of badly coordinated military efforts. The foreign forces became tied in with the attempts of opposition groups to hold parts of the vast Russian territory and to form counter–governments in attempts to overthrow the Bolshevik regime. Various groups were sponsored and supported by foreign powers. There was a period of short–lived resistance by former tsarist generals in the winter of 1918, followed by a major effort of General Anton Den ikin to deny the Soviet government access to the food and oil producing regions of the south.

Elsewhere, an uprising against the Bolsheviks was staged by the right wing of the *Social Revolutionaries* who were in favor of rejoining the war on the side of the Allies. They engineered the murder of the first German ambassador to Soviet Russia, Count Wilhelm von Mirbach. An anti–Bolshevik counter–government was established in the Siberian city of Omsk by socialist elements. This was quickly taken over by Admiral Alexander Kolchak, who proclaimed himself "Supreme Ruler" of Russia. In still another area in the Caucasus, General Peter Wrangel was fighting the Bolsheviks, largely with French support. The British were lending their support to General Denikin and Admiral Kolchak.

The civil war was marked by much heroism and cruelty on both sides, and dragged on until 1920. By that time, the allied intervention had come to an end and most of the anti–Bolshevik armies had been defeated. During the year, Russia signed peace treaties with Estonia,

Latvia, Lithuania and Finland, recognizing their independence and establishing their boundaries.

Poland was another problem, however, for the Pilsudski government which was in control claimed Poland's "historic" boundaries and insisted that the Soviet government surrender all land west of the 1772 border—in other words, prior to the first partition of Poland. This included areas with significant Byelorussian and Ukrainian populations and the Soviets therefore refused this demand.

Pilsudski launched an invasion into the area of the Ukraine in the spring of 1920. He captured Kiev, but was unable to hold it. A Soviet counterattack then drove the Poles back into Poland and shortly thereafter a Soviet army was threatening Warsaw. But the tide of battled turned once again, and the Russian troops found themselves retreating and on the defensive. A compromise territorial settlement was then reached giving Poland part of what it wanted—though not the 1772 boundaries—and the Peace of Riga was signed in October 1920. The settlement left about 4.5 million Byelorussians and Ukrainians inside Poland, however, a factor that continued to influence Soviet–Polish relations until 1939.

In the autumn of 1920, the Soviets drove the last of the anti–Bolshevik armies out of western Russia. This led to the collapse of anti–Bolshevik governments in Georgia, Azerbaijan and Armenia and their replacement with socialist governments allied with Soviet Russia. Shortly therafter, the Central Asian provinces came back under Russian rule. This effectively brought peace to Russia. Only the area

east of Lake Baikal remained outside of Soviet control—organized as a separate Far Eastern Republic. And, in late 1922, that territory also decided to rejoin Russia.

### New Economic Policy

With the end of the civil war and the war with Poland, a new situation existed. The economy had deteriorated over the preceding three years to such an extent as to make a mockery of the Bolshevik claims to have improved the lot of the worker. Industrial output had fallen to 20% of its 1914 level and half of all industrial jobs had evaporated. Cities were being deserted as people fled to the countryside to find food. The population of Petrograd had declined from a pre–war total of 2.3 million to 900,000. Agricultural output had also declined significantly, partly because of the ravages of the civil wars, but also in response to the government's food requisition policy.

Neither the workers nor the peasants had supported the anti–Bolsheviks, but many were also unhappy with Bolshevik policies. They now felt free to put pressure on the government to change its policies. The result was peasant unrest, strikes by workers and, finally, a revolt of sailors at Kronstadt in early 1921. Lenin now recognized that some compromises were necessary and he announced a *New Economic Policy (NEP)* in March 1921.

The *NEP*, as it came to be called, reestablished a market economy in Russia. Food requisitions were to cease, to be replaced by a tax on agriculture to be paid with produce. After the peasant had paid the tax, he could dispose of the remainder of his crops as he saw fit. That meant that internal trade had to be within the private sector, otherwise the peasant would not have been able to dispose of his crops. An important feature of this era was the *NEP–Man*, the private trader who bought the peasant's produce and furnished him with the products he wanted to buy. In the cities, private ownership of the shops and factories employing fewer than 20 workers was to be permitted. Money, which had largely lost its value, came back into use and a new currency was issued with gold backing.

The "commanding heights"—all large factories, mines, steel mills, transportation, banking and foreign trade—remained in government hands. Eighty-five per cent of all industrial workers, therefore, continued to work in nationalized industry. Even the government plants were reorganized into separate combines or trusts, and ordered to operate on the basis of market principles. The government also invited foreign capital to invest in Russia and offered contracts to foreign technicians to come to Russia to teach their skillls to Soviet workers. The Ford Motor Company opened a tractor factory in Russia at this time, but in general, the attempt to secure foreign capital investment was unsuccessful.

The *NEP* brought new life to Soviet Russia. By 1927, agricultural production had surpassed the levels of 1913 and consumer goods were again in ample supply. Only the large nationalized plants had not regained their pre–war levels—but even they had made great progress.

The *NEP* was never intended to exist for any given length of time, however, and Soviet state planning for industrialization continued throughout the period of the NEP. The State Planning Commission *(GOSPLAN)*, which subsequently became responsible for the *Five Year Plans*, was actually set up on February 22, 1921, that is, immediately prior to the adoption of the *NEP*. Thus, one might say that Lenin ordered that planning would begin which would make it possible to eliminate the *NEP*, at the very same time he was approving the new program.

## Constitutional Arrangements

It was also during the period of the *NEP* that the Union of Soviet Socialist Republics (USSR) came into being—though nearly all the territories included in the new USSR had been under Communist control since 1920. The first piece in the new constitutional structure was the *Russian Soviet Federated Socialist Republic (RSFSR)*, created in July 1918 when the Communists adopted the first Soviet constitution. As they extended their control to Byelorussia, the Ukraine and the Caucasus, these areas were given similar constitutions and the designation of Soviet Socialist Republic. Although they had signed treaties with the RSFSR, they remained technically independent republics. That situation created all kinds of legal and bureaucratic problems, so these four republics were brought together as the USSR in December 1922. The RSFSR institutions were then enlarged and somewhat modified to become "union" institutions. A new constitution for the USSR was drawn up and adopted in 1924. It was essentially a copy of the 1918 RSFSR constitution. These constitutional arrangements were extended to Central Asia in 1924 with the admission of the Turkmen and Uzbek Republics to the USSR. By 1936, five more republics had been created, raising the number of union republics to eleven.

In spite of these developments, it was interesting in 1945, when the United Nations was formed, the USSR insisted that Ukraine and Byelorussia were separate, sovereign nations, deserving a separate vote in the organization. The rationale given was that the Latin American nations were U.S.–"allied" (i.e. "puppet states") and the USSR should be allowed to balance this by espousing the theory that its areas were independent. Unwise minds acquiesced in this unreality at the time, but in 1991 it virtually became true.

## CONSTITUENT REPUBLICS OF THE USSR

1. Russian S.F.S.R.1922
2. Ukrainian S.S.R.1922
3. Byelorussian S.S.R.1922
   Transcaucasian S.S.R.1922
   (Dissolved in 1936 into three
   constituent Republics, 4–6):
4. Armenian S.S.R.1936
5. Azerbaijan S.S.R.1936
6. Georgian S.S.R.1936
7. Uzbek S.S.R.1924
8. Turkmen S.S.R.1924
9. Tadzhik S.S.R.1929
10. Kazakh S.S.R.1936
11. Kirghiz S.S.R.1936
12. Moldavian S.S.R.1940
13. Lithuanian S.S.R.1940
14. Latvian S.S.R.1940
15. Estonian S.S.R.1940

### The Struggle For The Succession

Lenin was disabled by a major stroke in the fall of 1922, but lived on until January 1924, even returning briefly to his desk. The struggle for succession, however, began with his first stroke. The problem with succession in the Soviet Union was never (as some scholars insisted) certain. Rather, all power resided with the Communist Party, with all power concentrated at the top. The struggle was over who, if anyone or group, controlled the party.

Once Lenin's stroke removed him from the active leadership of the party, a struggle broke out among Lenin's chief lieutenants to determine who would succeed him. Lenin himself identified four possible successors—Trotsky, Kamenev, Zinoviev and Stalin. Trotsky appeared to be the most logical choice, for he was the only one of Lenin's associates whose contributions to the revolution rivaled those of Lenin. In fact, according to a document reported on by a Soviet historian, Lenin offered Trotsky the number two position in the government in 1922 but he turned it down. His reason, according to what he told the Central Committee in 1923, was that "we should not give our enemies the opportunity to say that our country was being ruled by a Jew."

As Lenin's deputy, Trotsky would have been in a good position to outmaneuver Stalin when Lenin's stroke set off a struggle for the succession. Instead, it was Stalin, Kamenev and Zinoviev who formed a *troika* (a three–member team) with the express purpose of excluding Trotsky from the leadership.

Trotsky had his own levers of power—he was Commissar for War and a member of the Politburo—and he decided to carry the battle to the Party Congress. As has been said, he was a great orator, and he expected to win over the delegates to his side. Two things made that impossible. First, Lenin had gotten the Party Congress to outlaw factions in 1921. This meant that Trotsky could not do any pre–Congress organizing. Second, Stalin had been made General Secretary in 1922, and this gave him control over selection of the delegates to the Party Congress. Trotsky found the battle had been lost before it had begun.

Stalin later fell out with Kamenev and Zinoviev and this led them in turn to form a "United Opposition" with Trotsky against Stalin. But Stalin's control over the administrative levers of the party allowed him to defeat all three. Trotsky was expelled from the Politburo and then from the party; in 1928 he was exiled to Siberia, then a year later deported to Turkey. Stalin rapidly filled the Politburo with his supporters and was well on his way to establishing his "dictatorship over the party."

The struggles between Stalin and Trotsky involved apparent differences over policy and these were also aired during the period. Trotsky was an advocate of world revolution and he also wanted to end the *NEP* and embark on a rapid, large–scale industrialization of Russia. Stalin developed a theory of "socialism in one country" and defended the *NEP*. These turned out to be differences without a difference, however, for Stalin adopted Trotsky's policy on industrialization immediately after eliminating Trotsky as a source of competition.

### Foreign Policy During the NEP

When the communists first came to power in November 1917, their first consideration, as stated, was to end the war with Germany. They considered it an "imperialistic" war that they had opposed from the beginning, but mainly because Lenin recognized the need for peace in order to firm up his control over Russia. Because of Russia's withdrawal from the war under the Bolsheviks, France and England excluded Russia from the peacemaking at Versailles. Russia reciprocated by condemning the Treaty of Versailles and the League of Nations. Russia was thus hostile to the postwar settlement and the allies responded by attempting to isolate the new government of Russia, and all that it stood for, diplomatically.

This didn't bother the Russian communists too much, for it essentially coincided with their own perception that the capitalistic countries would inevitably be hostile to the new Soviet government. Further, Lenin was convinced that the world socialist revolution predicted by Marx would break out at any moment; he was primarily concerned with what the Russian communists could do to bring it about.

This led to the creation of the Communist International *(COMINTERN)* in

March 1919 as a sort of coordinating body for the coming world revolution. Efforts such as these only convinced the British and French in their opinion that Soviet Russia was a radical nation that had to be quarantined internationally.

With the adoption of the *NEP* in 1921, however, the Russian policy began to change. The revolutionary tide in Europe had begun to ebb and Lenin opted for a policy which he called "peaceful coexistence." His emphasis was now on rebuilding the Russian economy and for that he wanted outside assistance. He therefore called for the establishment of trade and diplomatic relations with all countries willing to live in peace and offered to reopen the country to foreign capital investment.

The free market aspects of the NEP convinced many people that Russia was moving away from communism and that, too, had a good effect abroad. Trade talks took place with England and Germany in 1921, but neither nation wanted to be the first to open diplomatic relations with Russia.

The breakthrough came in 1922 when the allies called for an international conference to discuss reparations. The Soviets had to be invited because, according to the Treaty of Versailles, they were also entitled to reparations from Germany. The Genoa Conference failed to resolve the reparations issue, and this convinced the German delegates that they had nothing to lose by signing an agreement with Russia—particularly since the Soviets were willing to give up any claim to reparations from Germany. Over the weekend, the Russian and German delegates got together in the nearby town of Rapallo and signed an agreement reestablishing diplomatic relations between the two countries.

The Rapallo Agreement became the basis for a Russo–German relationship that was to continue throughout the 1920's and to serve the interests of both countries. What they had in common is that both were outcast nations who opposed the post–World War I settlement. Germany used the Russian connection to obtain concessions from England and France; for Russia, it served the purpose of ending its diplomatic exile. A major British trade delegation led by ex–Prime Minister Baldwin visited Russia in 1923, and this was followed by the resumption of diplomatic relations between the two countries in 1924. Italy, Austria, Greece, Norway and Sweden followed almost immediately thereafter and before the year was out they had been joined by China, Denmark, Mexico and France. Of the major countries, only the United States continued to withhold diplomatic recognition. Although there were fairly extensive trade relations between the two countries, formal recognition did not come until 1933.

**Leon Trotsky**

### Building Socialism—The Five–Year Plans

Marx had written that "new, higher productive relationships never come into being before the material conditions for their existence have been brought to maturity within the womb of the old society itself." Lenin's revolution had brought the communists to power in an, at best, imperfectly industrialized country, one that obviously lacked the material conditions for communism, however. There could be no real guidance in Marx as how to remedy the lack, for he had never anticipated that this situation would arise. Lenin, guided by a reference in the *Communist Manifesto* to increasing "the total of productive forces as rapidly as possible" and, elsewhere, by references to **state planning** as the mechanism that would replace free competition as the driving force within a society under communism, did create the *Supreme Economic Council* in 1917 and the *State Planning Commission (GOSPLAN)* in 1921; he also linked the creation of large–scale industry with the electrification of the country. But he favored government efforts in this direction within the context of the *NEP*.

The policy of "socialist" industrialization was first proclaimed at the 14th Party Congress in late 1925 and was the first victory for Stalin's "socialism in one country." The measure did not come into effect immediately, however, for there were serious disagreements at the time as to how

the industrialization was to be carried out. Two years later, the Party Congress ordered *GOSPLAN* to prepare a Five–Year Plan for expansion of the national economy. This first Five–Year Plan went into operation in 1928.

The purpose of the plan was to carry out a large–scale, state–directed rapid industrialization. The priority was on heavy industry. Specifically, the government embarked on the construction of steel mills, the opening of coal mines, building dams for production of hydro–electricity, building plants for the manufacture of tractors, agricultural machinery, automobiles, chemicals and a host of other products. The goals for increased production were impressive: steel production was to go from 4.2 million tons to 10 million tons; coal from 35 million to 150 million tons; electric power from 5 million to 22 million kilowatt–hours. Some of these higher levels were to come from increased production at already existing plants, but it mostly involved new productive capacity.

In all, the plan called for the creation of 1,500 new enterprises and a capital construction budget of 64.5 billion rubles. Such funds were not available to the state under the conditions of the the *NEP* market economy. Stalin's solution was to phase out the NEP and to replace it with a "Command Model" which gave the state direct control over all economic activity. For the urban sector, this meant a return to the situation as it had existed

**Stalin: Ruler of Russia**

wages. The object was to turn the peasants into proletariat in line with Lenin's theory, expressed in *The Agrarian Program of Russian Social Democracy*, that hired agricultural workers belonged to the "working class." The communists also had in mind to create examples of good farming methods which the peasants could follow.

The *sovkhozy* represented—and until Gorbachëv's agricultural reforms continued to represent—the communist ideal for organization of the countryside, but the obligation to pay year–around wages means that they are expensive to run. The communists therefore developed a second type of farm organization which they called the *kolkhoz*. This, in theory, is a co-operative organization formed on a voluntary basis by a group of peasants. Land, livestock and farm machinery are pooled and then become the property of the *kolkhoz*.

The unit is farmed collectively by the group of peasants, and all income after expenses and taxes is shared on the basis of the total number of workdays performed by each member of the collective. The farmers were permitted an individual "private plot" of not more than an acre for use as a garden. They also could keep a cow, pigs and chickens.

In the 1920's, the government offered special subsidies and favorable tax treatment to those who would join a *kolkhoz*, but they were not popular with the peasants and, by 1928, only about one peasant in 60 had joined.

The first Five Year Plan called for 17.5% of the cultivated land to be organized into *kolkhozy*, which would have entailed persuading between 4 and 5 million peasants to join collective farms. There was strong resistance to the collectivization, however, and even the offer of seed, credit and the use of state–owned machinery brought a meager response, primarily among poorer peasants having little to lose. The communists, recalling how the peasants had frustrated them during the period of War Communism, decided to force the issue. Peasants opposing collectivization were labeled *kulaks* and were declared to be class enemies. Communist squads from the cities were sent into the countryside to seize the grain of the *kulaks*. Committees of poor peasants were also set up to cooperate with the government and report on their wealthier neighbors. In effect, the communists deliberately promoted class warfare in the countryside. At first, Stalin made it look as if the new measures of the government and party were only directed against the *kulaks* who were said to constitute less than 1 million out of a total of over 25 million peasant families. It was not long, however, before the bulk of the peasant population was involved. The progress of collectivization is shown by the following figures:

under War Communism; for the villages it meant an end to individual agriculture and the forcible creation of collective farms.

**The Collectivization of Agriculture**

Although collectivized agriculture eventually came to be an integral part of the economic system of nearly every communist country, Marx had, in fact, little to say about the organization of agriculture under communism. Some of the more pertinent references are found in the *Communist Manifesto*, where he referred to

*the bringing into cultivation of wastelands, and the improvement of the soil generally in accordance with a common plan . . .*

*Establishment of industrial armies, especially for agriculture [and] . . .*

*Combination of agriculture with manufacturing industries; gradual abolition of the distinction between town and country, by a more equitable distribution of the population over the country.*

After the revolution, the communists took over the estates formerly owned by the Imperial family and organized them into state farms *(sovkhozy)*.

These units, owned and operated by the state, were run like "factories in the field," with the peasants receiving daily

| Year | Per Cent Collectivized |
|------|------------------------|
| 1928 | 1.7 |
| Oct. 1929 | 4.1 |
| Jan. 1930 | 21.0 |
| Mar. 1930 | 58.0 |

A temporary halt was called in early 1930. Collectivization was slowed down and many *kolkhozy* were dissolved and the land was returned to individuals. This was done on Stalin's order after he criticized in a famous article the "dizziness with success" of those carrying out the forced collectivization. But the program was soon fully resumed and by the end of 1932, the percent collectivized had grown to 61.5. By the end of 1938, the 25 million peasant households were almost completely gathered into some 240,000 collective farms.

Because of extensive resistance, the former voluntary nature of the *kolkhoz* ceased and the farm manager, formerly elected by the membership, was selected by and subordinate to the higher Communist Party authorities. In addition, Machine–Tractors Stations (MTS's) directly controlled by the state, were set up in the countryside. The MTS got all the new farm machinery that was being manufactured and, using its own crews, it performed all of the mechanical labor on the collectives. It usually also contained the local Communist Party cell, so it exercised a control function in rural areas.

At the end of the harvest, each collective farm first delivered a set amount of its total production to the state at a controlled price, then paid off the MTS. Any remaining production was divided among the peasants. In many years, the amount remaining to be divided was relatively small and the peasants had to rely on produce raised on the garden plots to feed themselves.

There were several important reasons for the collectivization of agriculture, but the most important was that it allowed the Communist Party to gain control of the countryside in a predominantly rural nation and to force the peasantry to serve the interests of the Communist State. In one of his moments of candor, Stalin explained that since Russia had no colonies to exploit, it could only find the funds for industrialization by taking them from its own people. And, this is what was done.

During the period of the first Five–Year Plan, overall living standards diminished by an estimated 35%, with the peasantry suffering a greater drop than the urban population. But by pouring 35% of the gross national product into new productive facilities, the government managed to more or less meet the goals of the plan.

Second and third Five–Year Plans followed and continued the process of industrialization. Nearly all of the investment continued to be in heavy industry,

however, so the Soviet people saw very little change in their standard of living. But the heavy pace wore out the country, and criticism of Stalin's harsh policies increased even among his supporters. His reaction was to launch a purge—massacre—that eventually enveloped all parts of Russian society.

## Terror and Purges

Stalin resorted to terror not only to deal with temporary emergencies; terror became a permanent and prominent feature of his style of governing. Lenin and other Bolshevik leaders had used terror on a smaller scale, and they had employed a special organization to combat "counter–revolution"—the Cheka. It came into existence soon after the Bolsheviks seized power. The name of the organization was changed several times; known by its Russian initials, it has been the GPU, OGPU, NKVD, MVD, MGB and KGB. Its function was always the same—a highly secret police snooping into the private lives of the people and looking everywhere for saboteurs, spies and counter–revolutionaries. Abroad, it came to be used as a highly active espionage organization; more often than not, members of the Russian diplomatic corps were members of the organization. In this sphere of operations, agents had been "cultivated" for years to gain positions of prominence enabling them to spy on virtually every government in the world, particularly the U.S. and western powers. Bribes were commonplace, and the organization systematically tried (frequently with great success) to obtain technological advances of western nations through this method.

Stalin made the secret police a major instrument of ruthless purges. These mass "liquidations" of people were calculated to uproot every possible source of opposition to him and his dream of transforming Russia's social, economic and political structure.

The first targets of a systematic series of purges were the non–communist technicians and specialists, both Russian and foreign, who had been enlisted to help in the first Five–Year Plan. They were convicted with the help of manufactured evidence and forced confessions. This had the effect of terrorizing the people into redoubled efforts and at the same time provided an excuse for failure to achieve some of the goals of the plan. Another group subjected to terror and liquidation were those peasants who were accused of sabotaging the collectivization drive. The action was officially known as the "liquidation of the *kulaks* as a class," but it actually affected millions who could by no stretch of the imagination be called "rich" peasants. Besides the million or so who suffered death, there were others who filled forced–labor camps and were used in digging canals, mining gold and other

enterprises under unbelievably inhuman conditions.

What is known as the *Great Purge* lasted from 1934 to 1938 and differed from earlier periods of Stalinist terror. This time it was directed against the leaders of the Communist Party. In Soviet terms, "purge" technically means removal from the party, not necessarily followed by criminal prosecution, exile or death. In reality, these severe consequences followed, especially in the *Great Purge*. The orgy of purges was triggered by the assassination of Sergei M. Kirov, a rising star in the party leadership and boss of the Leningrad (formerly Petrograd) party organization. It is now known that Stalin probably engineered the murder because Kirov was questioning the wisdom of continuing the break–neck tempo of change in Russia. He also was seen as a possible leader in a move to unseat Stalin, whom many were beginning to suspect of having lost his mind.

### Purge at the Top

Although Stalin professed grief at Kirov's death, he used the occasion to unleash a vicious purge of party members, and particularly, party leaders. Most significantly, the Society of Old Bolsheviks, whose members had worked closely with Lenin, was dissolved in mid–1935. A "verification" of party membership cards was ordered, and some 10% were expelled; by 1936 at least one–quarter of the membership had been dropped from the party. A series of trials was held, and in 1936 sixteen Old Bolsheviks, including Zinoviev and Kamenev, were convicted and executed. Michael P. Tomsky, leader of the trade unions, committed suicide. In early 1937, seventeen prominent communists, diplomats, economists and writers, including Karl Radek, who had closely collaborated with Lenin, were tried as alleged German and Japanese spies. They were also charged with other crimes that were ridiculous and most unlikely. At the trials, an attempt was made to "expose" Trotsky and to condemn his activities abroad as being directed against the USSR. Thirteen of the accused were shot and the other four sentenced to long prison terms—they were never heard from again. There was a brief press announcement in mid–1937 which told of the secret trial and execution of Army Marshal Michael Tukhachevsky and seven other leading generals of the Red Army. This was followed by a mass purge of officers which undoubtedly contributed to the poor showing of the Russian forces during the first part of Russia's involvement in World War II.

The climax of the purge trials came in 1938 when several former Politburo members, Nikolai Bukharin, Alexei Rykov and N.M. Krestinsky and distinguished provincial party leaders were liquidated. For good measure, Stalin included Yagoda, former head of the secret police and himself a major purger; he was executed as a spy. The period known as the *Yezhovschina,* after Yezhov, the new head of the secret police, lasted until late 1938, when Lavrenti Beria was named in turn to replace Yezhov (who simply disappeared).

One observer has aptly called this period "a reign of terror without parallel in Soviet history" in which "no sphere of Soviet life, however lofty, was left untouched." The destructive madness can only be explained by the assumption that Stalin was determined to eliminate once and for all any possible challenge to his personal power within the party leadership. He evidently believed that terror was a most useful instrument of power because it made sure that there were no entrenched or safe positions and therefore discouraged organized opposition to the will of the leader.

Many westerners, while accepting the fact of the purges, have been loath to believe that Stalin was directly responsible for them. They argued that the purges must have been the product of overzealous subordinates who carried out the executions on their own. A new book published in the Soviet Union in 1989, *Stalin: Triumph and Tragedy,* answers those doubts. According to a review in the *Economist,* the author, Dmitri Volkogonov, "examined Stalin's personal papers and found his marginal comments or initials on thousands of execution lists and reports of mass repressions. His scribbled remarks invariably call for harsher measures."

**Forced Movements**

Stalin, however, had a great talent for calling a sudden halt to the orgies of brutality unleashed by himself, to blame and liquidate his own agents and pose as a man of moderation, justice and mercy—a sort of father–protector. The start of World War II also made it possible for him to whip up patriotic fervor and to divert attention from his grisly pursuits.

During the second World War, the security organization was busy uprooting whole groups of the population whose loyalty to the Soviet regime was in question. Thus, the Crimean Tatars and the Volga Germans were forced to abandon their homes and move to Siberia. As the war progressed, other ethnic groups that had shown a willingness to collaborate with the Germans, or to engage in massive desertions from the Red Army, were also affected.

After the war, the main task of the NKVD, as it was then called, was to screen and "brainwash" Soviet citizens who had spent some time in Germany as prisoners of war or as forced labor. Many people also were deported from the areas acquired by the Soviet Union during and after the war.

Renewed watchfulness, rather than relaxation became the policy of Stalin as the memory of the war began to recede into the background and the "Cold War" became a reality. Following the death of A.A. Zhdanov, a close collaborator of Stalin, in 1948, a new purge was launched, particularly in Leningrad. A vicious campaign was launched against intellectuals, especially those of Jewish origin who were accused of being unpatriotic, "rootless cosmopolitans." Several Jewish writers were executed without a trial in 1952. Toward the end of Stalin's life, a monstrous general purge was apparently in the making. It began with the ominous "discovery" of a "Doctors' Plot" allegedly aimed at killing or undermining the health of leading Soviet officials.

In a "secret" speech in 1956, the Soviet leader Nikita Khrushchev stated that the doctors' plot was fabricated from beginning to end. Apparently it was part of a major scheme to eliminate the entire top rank of the party leadership, including such old faithfuls as V.M. Molotov and Marshal Klementi Voroshilov. As Khrushchev put it so dramatically, whenever he was summoned by phone to the Kremlin, he wasn't sure whether this meant promotion or death. This simple statement revealed the main purpose of Stalin's terror: to implant uncertainty.

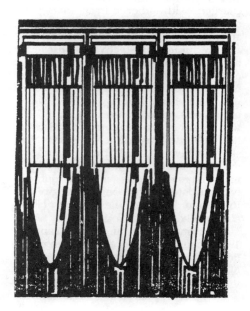

*Death of a Commissar* (1928)                                                                                K. S. Petrov–Vodkin

# Stalin's Cultural Counter–Revolution of the 1930's

Marx had very little to say about the implications of his philosophical system insofar as the performing and creative arts were concerned, though it follows that, since the creative arts must be part of the superstructure of society, they must, according to Marx's general theory, reflect the social and economic environment in which they appear. Marx did indicate that the proletariat would take over that which was good in the previous bourgeois society, but he also stipulated that much would be discarded—and he made a specific attack on the bourgeois family. In most respects, however, Marx had conventional tastes in art and literature.

Lenin was also rather ordinary in his tastes, but he never attempted to enforce his personal viewpoint on the new communist state and his first Commissar for Education specifically proclaimed the right of individual creation. Lenin never permitted the printing of anything anti–revolutionary or anti–communist, but with that limitation, there was considerable artistic freedom in Russia under Lenin. Among the excellent works produced in the 1920's were Alexander Blok's

*The Twelve*, Mikhail Bulgatov's *The Master and Margarita*, Mikhail Sholokov's *Quiet Flows the Don*, poems by Boris Pasternak and Vladimir Mayakovsky and, finally the music of Dimitri Shostakovich.

In the schools, all sorts of experimental ideas were tried out—such as abolishing discipline—and courses in mathematics and chemistry, geography and physics were phased out in favor of vocational education. Traditional family values also came under attack as divorce became a mere registration process and the emancipation of women from home life was stressed. Religious training, traditionally also a function of the family, came under attack.

All of this came to an end in 1929 when Stalin, launching his Five–Year Plan, decided that the creative arts had to be mobilized in support of the industrialization program of the Communist Party. Publishers were instructed on the types of books they were to publish. Specific "proletarian" goals were announced for art, music and literature. Experiments in style were condemned and creative workers were informed that what they produced

had to be intelligible to the masses. Themes suggested to the creative artists included industrial construction, the fight against external aggression and internal subversion and the glory of life on collective farms.

Schools were reorganized and traditional courses reinstated. Examinations were reintroduced, and teachers were again given control in the classroom. Family life was again emphasized and the parents were instructed that they were responsible for training and disciplining their children.

### Socialist Realism

Stalin also developed a specific theory for the arts which he called Socialist Realism—in his definition, a portrayal of reality in its revolutionary development in order to remake and re–educate the workers in the spirit of socialism was the goal of the state. What this meant in practice is that artists were to depict Soviet reality *as it would be, or should be*, rather than as it was. As one historian has expressed it, it was Communism with a smiling face. No morbid or pessimistic themes were allowed;

41

*Militarized Communist Youth* (1933)                                              A. N. Samokhvalov

music was to be melodic and life was to be portrayed as good and getting better.

The effect of these restrictions was predictable. Soviet paintings tended to be either poster art in the revolutionary style or Soviet versions of *Saturday Evening Post* covers. Favorite themes were portraits of Lenin and Stalin; scenes from the Russian Revolution and Civil War; and landscapes that included factories or glamorized collective farms. Modern dance and jazz were outlawed and Soviet ballet returned to classical style. Composers such as Shostakovich and Prokofiev began to base their compositions on folk music. Abstract and semi–abstract art were out, and this led to a purge of paintings in Russian museums. Artists whose works were now labeled decadent included Vincent Van Gogh, Paul Gauguin, Georges Seurat, Henri Matisse, Pablo Picasso, Marc Chagall and Vasili Kandinsky. Their paintings were taken down from display and locked away in storerooms.

*Kolhkoz Festival* (1937)                                                        S. V. Gerasimov

## Soviet Foreign Policy In The 1930's

The Soviet Union established friendly relations with Germany as a result of the Rapallo Pact in 1922 and those relations continued after Stalin came to power. Trade between the two countries actually increased after 1928 as the Soviet Union began its Five–Year Plan. Political relations also remained good and in 1931 the two nations signed an agreement prolonging the Berlin Treaty on neutrality which the two nations had signed in 1926. The Soviet Union was willing to continue good relations even after Adolf Hitler came to power in 1933; it was Hitler's decision, not Stalin's, that changed the course of German–Soviet relations—and eventually led to a change in overall Soviet foreign policy.

The change of course by Hitler and his extreme anti–communist speeches convinced the Soviet Union that it would have to seek new friends. Russia had always been an opponent of the League of Nations, but when Nazi Germany left the League, the Soviets decided to join. Stalin appointed Maxim Litvinov, a Jew, as the new Soviet Foreign Minister—a move that must have been intended to irritate Hitler. Litvinov became a familiar figure at Geneva and the Soviet Union became a leading advocate of "collective security."

Although it appeared that the Soviet Union was interested in active opposition to Nazism and Fascism, Stalin's actual policies at the time can best be described as isolationism with a substantial amount of appeasement. This reflected his caution and his obsessive fear of having to fight alone against a united capitalist world. Appeasement was also shown towards Japan when it decided to assert its strength on the Asian mainland. Although Stalin encouraged the Chinese nationalists and communists alike to resist the Japanese, he was unwilling to expose the USSR to direct Japanese attack. To lessen the threat of conflict, he agreed to sell the Russian share in the Chinese Eastern Railway to the Japanese conquerors of Manchuria (technically to the puppet state of Manchukuo set up by the Japanese).

Although Stalin was determined to find allies in the West to oppose the growing menace of Nazi Germany, he proceeded here, too, with caution, to avoid involving the USSR too early in a conflict with Hitler. Attempts to enter into mutual assistance treaties to protect eastern Europe against German aggression failed mainly because of the objection of the independent–minded and then excessively self–assured Poles.

Stalin then turned to more distant potential allies. He signed agreements with France and Czechoslovakia in 1935. In the Spanish Civil War (1936–1939), the Soviet Union supported the loyalist side against the insurgents led by General Francisco Franco. At the same time, pressure was

Lenin's Tomb, Red Square, Moscow

brought to bear on the Spanish communists not to adopt a radical program of reforms in order to avoid discouraging public opinion in the West, especially in France.

When Germany demanded that it be given a part of Czechoslovakia in 1938, France, following the appeasement–minded lead of England, made no move to assist the Czechs in spite of treaty obligations. The treaty between Russia and Czechoslovakia was worded in a way that obligated the USSR to give assistance only if France did likewise. In a meeting at Munich, the Western Powers yielded to Hitler's demands.

Attempts at closer and friendlier relations turned out, from Stalin's viewpoint, to be frustrating and unproductive. The leading Western governments were turning away from the League of Nations and the policy of collective security. They were tolerating one violation after another committed by Hitler, such as the reintroduction of the military draft and occupation of the Rhineland Province which was supposed to remain demilitarized. The willingness of Great Britain and France to deal with Hitler at Munich, and their willingness to exclude the Soviet Union from those discussions, showed that the Western Powers were not taking Russia's power or its interests seriously. In addition, there was an extremely negative reaction in the West to the gruesome purges that Stalin was then conducting in the Soviet Union. Stalin probably realized that this Western revulsion would make any close cooperation between the Soviet Union and the Western democracies extremely difficult.

The actions of the Western Powers may have also led Stalin to suspect that they

were hoping to encourage Hitler to attack the Soviet Union and thereby remove the threat from themselves. Some groups in the West did indeed nourish such hopes, although it was a crude falsification when Soviet propaganda claimed that this was the official and deliberate policy of the Western governments.

The seizure of the rest of Czechoslovakia by Germany in March 1939 created a serious crisis. Neither Great Britain nor France took any action, even though both had guaranteed Czechoslovakia's remaining territories. On the other hand, Britain's Prime Minister Chamberlain did make it clear in his Birmingham speech of March 17 that his country would resist any further act of aggression by Germany. The position of the Soviet Union was spelled out by Stalin in a famous speech to the 18th Party Congress in which the Soviet dictator declared that the Soviet Union was not willing to "pull the chestnuts out of the fire" for the benefit of others.

Hitler could expect war with Great Britain, and possibly France, if he pursued his objectives on Poland, but this did not deter him. On the other hand, the position of the Soviet Union now became all important. Germany would need to come to an understanding with the Soviet Union before it could invade Poland.

As the crisis deepened, the Soviet Union became involved in two sets of negotiations: with the French and British on one hand and with Nazi Germany on the other. Stalin had to ask himself whether an alliance with Great Britain and France would deter Hitler—or whether it would only mean that the Soviet forces would be exposed to the fury of a German attack from the very beginning of an armed conflict.

Legend:
- Hitler's Germany
- Under German rule
- Axis military occupation
- Axis satellites

0  150  300  450 mi
0  200  400  600 km

NORWAY
FINLAND
SWEDEN
DEN.
MOSCOW
Minsk
U. S. S. R.
GERMANY
Warsaw
Kiev
Stalingrad
SWITZ.
SLOVAKIA
HUNGARY
ITALY
CROATIA
ROMANIA
SERBIA
MON.
BLACK SEA
ALB.
BULGARIA
GREECE
TURKEY
IRAN
SYRIA
IRAQ

Jan 85

make peace with the Soviet Union and to submit to some of its demands.

The use of military force by the biggest country in the world against the proud and popular Finns added to the bad reputation the Soviet Union had in the West, where resentment had been aroused by the Soviet deal with Hitler. Unrealistic ideas of coming to the assistance of Finland almost resulted in the involvement of France and England in war *against the Soviet Union*, which was then looked upon as an "ally" of Adolf Hitler. Actually, Stalin was fighting his own war, with an eye toward the future, taking up military positions directed against possible German aggression.

German troops swept across France, Belgium and the Netherlands in record time in the spring of 1940. This swift military success in the West disturbed Stalin, who would have preferred to see a long involvement of German troops on the Western front. He began nervously to tighten his hold on the areas gained in 1939. The Baltic republics were forced to join the Soviet Union. Romania was asked to cede the province of Bessarabia, taken from Russia during World War I, and parts of Bukovina, about which there had been no clear arrangement with the Germans in 1939. The Russians protested the entry of German troops into Finland and domination of the remaining Romanian territory. Hitler, flushed with success, began to feel that he had paid too high a price in 1939 for Stalin's neutrality.

## The Nazi–Soviet Non–Aggression Pact

An offer from the German side looked much more interesting: the division of Poland between Germany and Russia. From Stalin's selfish point of view, this offered the opportunity to stay out of the war and to be rewarded by Hitler with part of soon–to–be defeated Poland. The Germans were also willing to recognize the Baltic area as belonging to the Soviet Union's "sphere of influence."

The agreement between the Soviet Union and Germany was announced on August 23, 1939, and came as a shock and surprise to the world. It was, however, the most logical choice among the alternatives facing Stalin at the time. Soviet–Polish relations had never been particularly good, and the Soviet Union had no substantial reason to come to Poland's assistance. Moreover, what Stalin feared most of all was to be dragged into a war against Germany by Great Britain and France, and then be forced to bear the brunt of that war while those countries sat on the sidelines. Hitler's invasion of Poland came on September 1, 1939, its purpose, in the language of the war order, "to destroy Polish military strength and create, in the East, a situation which satisfies the requirements of defense." The end was not long in coming. The Polish forces collapsed under the

onslaught of the first German *Blitzkrieg*. The fighting was mostly over by September 17 when Soviet troops entered from the east to claim the Soviet share of the spoils. The last member of the Polish Government had already left the country to seek refuge abroad. Stalin then claimed that his troops were entering a no–man's land and even had the nerve to suggest to Hitler that he be permitted to state that Soviet troops were entering the former Polish territory in order to save the largely Ukrainian and Byelorussian population of the area *from the Germans!*

The Soviet side also suggested a change in the terms of the secret agreement. They wanted less of the territory of Poland than originally was given them in the deal, and asked instead to have Lithuania included in the Soviet "sphere" along with the other Baltic republics, Latvia and Estonia. They soon imposed agreements on the three providing for the stationing of Soviet troops on their terri tory.

Similar pressure was exerted on Finland, but here the Russians encountered determined opposition to their demands and had to resort to war in the winter of 1939–1940. Although the Finns first managed to stop the Soviet offensive and in doing so inflict embarrassing losses, the small country was eventually forced to

## Soviet Entry Into World War II

In late 1940 and early 1941, relations between the Soviet Union and Germany acquired an air of unreality. Stalin, frozen with fear, was alternately appeasing and teasing Hitler, while the *Führer*, already scheming to crush the Soviet Union, tried to lull the latter into believing that he was willing to share the spoils of the British Empire, soon to become available. The Soviet Foreign Minister, V.M. Molotov, was presented with such a proposal during a visit to Berlin in late 1940, but the Soviets took the position that it was too early to discuss the cutting up of the hide of the British lion.

By the autumn of 1940, Hitler was in a quandary. His invasion of England, Operation Sea Lion, had to be aborted when his air force was unable to gain control of the air over England. Now America was throwing its support behind England, and that support was sure to grow. There was no immediate threat in the west but also no chance to bring the British to the negotiating table. Was this the time to turn on the Soviet Union and, in another lightning onslaught, destroy his long–term foe in the east? On December 18 he answered that question by signing Operation Barbarossa "to crush Soviet Russia in a quick campaign even before the end of the war against England." This was contrary to the advice of his top military advisors, who foresaw that Germany would be stretched too thinly to be successful on *all* fronts.

It mattered very little what the Russians did at that point. However, Stalin's behavior immediately prior to the German attack was erratic, alternating between appeasement and provocation. It has been said that Stalin refused to believe the reports of an impending German invasion supposedly because he "liked" and "trusted" Hitler. This cannot be taken seriously because Stalin neither liked nor trusted *anyone*. His problem was serious—the Soviet Union had damaged its reputation in the deal with Hitler in 1939. It could now be accepted as an ally of the West only if it became the victim of unprovoked aggression by Hitler. Therefore, Stalin was forced to let the Germans fire the first shot. Nevertheless, his unwillingness to prepare for battle later caused millions of unnecessary Russian deaths.

His failure to improve the combat readiness of the Soviet armed forces exposed millions of soldiers to slaughter and capture in the very first weeks of the war launched by Hitler on June 22, 1941. Even Soviet sources now admit that Stalin "failed to take full advantage" of the time gained by the Soviet Union as a result of the 1939 agreement.

## Ally of the West

Hitler's fateful decision to attack the Soviet Union changed Russia's international position literally overnight. England's Winston Churchill, though a life–long enemy of communism, welcomed the Soviet Union as an ally of isolated and threatened England. With admirable precision and honesty, he stated "If I heard that Hitler invaded Hell, the least I could do would be to say a few nice words about the Devil." The United States, not yet engaged in the war, also promised aid to the Soviet Union. However, there were serious doubts in the West about Russia's ability to resist Hitler's offensive for a very long time. The speedy advance of German troops seemed to justify gloomy predictions. Although it was felt that Russia should be supported in its struggle against Germany because it was tying down masses of German troops, the Soviet Union appeared not to be an important factor to reckon with at the time.

In this period the Russians yielded to British pressure to reestablish relations with the Polish government–in–exile located in London. However, even at the darkest time of their military fortunes, the Russians made it clear that their postwar plans included retention of all the territorial gains made during the period of "friendship" with Hitler from 1939 to 1941.

The German offensive consisted of three attacking forces whose destinations were Leningrad, Moscow and the Caucasus. It achieved tremendous successes at the beginning as Soviet defense units at the border disintegrated and German mechanized armies swept into Russia, surrounding and conquering whole Russian armies. Stubborn Russian defenses temporarily halted the German armies at Pskov and Smolensk, but reinforced German armies eventually overcame the Soviet defenders and continued their advance eastward. In the meanwhile, Kiev was captured on September 19th. In the north, the siege of Leningrad also began in September; but the Germans were not able to cut off the city entirely, so that it continued to be reprovisioned from outside. The siege eventually lasted for 600 days before it was broken by a German retreat.

The 1941 offensive ended with the German Central Front just 35 miles west of Moscow, while in the south, the German armies had overrun the entire Ukraine and reached as far east as the Donets River. Hitler was not satisfied with the extent of the advance, however. Enraged that neither Leningrad nor Moscow had been captured, he dismissed his chief generals and assumed personal command himself.

This was a gift for the Russians—Hitler, although occasionally capable of brilliant insights, was not a military strategist. In 1942, for example, he held his forces on the north and center on the defensive while he attempted to make a breakthrough in the south. His original goal was the oil of the Caucasus, an entirely logical one under the circumstances. But in June he turned his armies directly east and opened a drive toward Stalingrad (since renamed Volgograd), a city of no particular strategic significance. Stalingrad was reached in September 1942, after slow progress in the face of heavy Russian resistance.

In late 1942 a new offensive began. It brought disaster to the German forces apparently made worse by panic among Hungarian, Romanian and Italian troops fighting alongside Hitler's armies. The German Sixth Army was soon encircled, but Hitler ordered the 285,000 men trapped by the Soviets not to retreat. Attempts to relieve the army failed and the 90,000 survivors of the battle of Stalingrad finally surrendered to the Russians on January 30, 1943. This was one of the major turning points of the war.

Hitler did not realize or didn't care that he had fallen into the same trap as did Napoleon when he attempted to take Russia. The faithful ally of the Northern slavs had again come to the rescue—"Mother Winter." Not only did this friend cause countless deaths by freezing among the German troops, few of whom had buildings in which to take refuge, when the spring thaw came, the whole land turned to a sea of mud in which a mechanized army could only become bogged down.

## After Stalingrad

The reversal of Soviet military fortunes created an entirely new political situation. Stalin made the utmost use of the delays in Anglo–American plans to open a western front in Europe. A promise had been made to Stalin that this would happen in 1942, but he was soon informed that there would be no second front during that year or the next. Lend–lease supplies began to flow into Russia in very large amounts from the United States at the cost of many lives lost to German submarines. However, the Russians developed the feeling that they had managed to live through the darkest moments of the war largely by their own efforts and that their Western allies were deliberately dragging their feet.

As soon as the military situation eased, Stalin began to test the intentions of his allies. The question of the status of Poland was used for this purpose and the Polish government–in–exile actually played into Stalin's hands.

The Germans announced the discovery of a mass grave in the Katyn Forest in the spring of 1943, containing the bodies of thousands of Polish army officers who had fallen into the hands of the Russians in September 1939. They had been shot in the back of the head, a standard method of execution practiced by the Soviet secret police. Alarmed by the discovery, the Poles in London asked for an investigation by the International Red Cross. Stalin accused the Polish government–in–exile of aiding German propaganda and broke off diplomatic relations. Soon a new organization, the Union of Polish Patriots, was formed from among Polish refugees in the Soviet Union. This became the nucleus of the Soviet–sponsored Lublin Government, which was installed in power by the Soviet army after the liberation of Poland.

## Wartime Conferences and the Occupation of Eastern Europe

The Soviet military occupation of Eastern Europe and the Soviet decision to set up communist governments in the area are usually considered to be important factors in the origins of the Cold War that developed between the Soviet Union and its western allies after World War II. The matter is somewhat more complex, however.

First of all, there were always differences between the Soviet Union and its allies over Soviet territories obtained as a result of the Non–Aggression Pact which Stalin signed with Hitler in 1939. In particular, neither the United States nor Great Britain ever recognized the incorporation of Latvia, Estonia, Lithuania and Bessarabia into the Soviet Union.

When the United States and Great

"The Big Three:" Stalin, Roosevelt and Churchill at Tehran

Britain drew up the Atlantic Charter in 1941, setting forth their wartime goals, they stipulated there were to be no territorial changes without the freely registered approval of the people involved.

They also promised to respect the right of all peoples to determine the form of government under which they would live. When, six weeks later, the Soviet Union gave its approval of the Atlantic Charter, American policymakers accepted that as a basis for cooperation. Toward the end of 1941, although the United States was not yet at war, it extended a billion dollar "lend–lease" grant to the Soviet Union for the purchase of supplies in the United States. By the end of the war, the United States had shipped to the Soviet Union approximately $11 billion worth of equipment and supplies.

Presumably the Soviet Union signed the Atlantic Charter because it wanted the "lend–lease" agreement with the United States and it would have been for the same reason that it agreed to the incorporation of the Atlantic Charter into the Declaration of the United Nations which the U.S., Great Britain, the U.S.S.R. and 23 other nations signed on January 1, 1942. That it never intended to apply the terms of the Atlantic Charter to territories annexed in 1939–1940 can be seen by the fact that it continued to pressure the U.S. and England to recognize the incorporation of these territories into the U.S.S.R. after signing the Atlantic Charter.

Another factor was Franklin D. Roosevelt's opposition to balance of power politics and spheres of influence. The United States was committed to allowing the peoples of Eastern Europe to set up their own freely elected government and FDR attempted to bind his allies to a similar position. What he forgot, however, is that Nazi Germany's defeat would bring about a power vacuum in Eastern Europe and, *one way or the other*, that power vacuum would be filled. But perhaps the most important factor influencing American foreign policy at this juncture was FDR's belief that Stalin didn't want anything for himself in Eastern Europe. As he commented to Ambassador Bullitt just prior to the Tehran Conference, "I have just a hunch that Stalin doesn't want anything but security for his country, and I think that if I give him everything I possibly can and ask nothing in return, *noblesse oblige* he won't try to annex anything and will work for a world of democracy and peace."

Roosevelt's "hunch" seemed to be confirmed when he, Churchill, and Stalin met in Tehran in November 1943, for it was here that the "Big Three," in a general declaration which they drew up, promised an enduring peace in which "all the peoples of the world may live free lives untouched by tyranny and according to their varying desires and their consciences."

In delineating spheres of military operations, however, Romania, Bulgaria, Hun-

gary, Yugoslavia, Czechoslovakia, Poland and Finland were designated areas of Soviet operations. If Roosevelt was right about Stalin, it wouldn't matter; but if he was not, he was putting his stamp of approval on whatever policy Stalin chose to carry out in Eastern Europe. Churchill, recognizing the potential danger in such an arrangement, pushed for an allied invasion up through the Balkans, but he was overruled.

Soviet troops began entering Eastern Europe in August 1944; by the time of the Yalta Conference in early 1945, Soviet armies occupied Romania, Bulgaria, Poland and parts of Hungary and Czechoslovakia. The Yalta Conference was primarily concerned with the problem of Germany, and it was at this time allied zones of occupation were established. The Soviet Zone would eventually become the German Democratic Republic.

Poland was also considered. Its eastern and western borders were established; the Communist Provisional Government was to be enlarged by the inclusion of democratic leaders from abroad, and the broadened Provisional Government was to hold "free and unfettered elections as soon as possible on the basis of universal suffrage and secret ballot. The rest of Eastern Europe was covered by a general declaration that other people of the region would be encouraged to  It has often been charged that the United States essentially yielded to Soviet demands concerning territorial

46

matters and the composition of the government of postwar Poland because it was eager for Soviet military assistance in the Far East. It is true that Stalin agreed at Yalta to enter the war against Japan within 90 days of victory in Europe. It is also true that an American military study had estimated that, without Soviet assistance, the war against Japan would last until 1947 and might mean another million American lives. The study obviously did not take the atomic bomb development into consideration, and it is possible that Roosevelt didn't either. On the other hand, the essential fact is that the American armies were only approaching the Rhine River at the time when Soviet troops were in western Poland and approaching the German border at a point much closer to the main prize: Berlin. Political and strategic decisions made much earlier meant that the United States could only hope that the Soviet Union shared American perceptions about the future of Eastern Europe.

## The Cold War

The Cold War essentially began when the Soviet Union, in occupation of Eastern Europe, began to implement its intentional misunderstanding of the various wartime agreements. The problem arose over the differing Soviet and western Allied understandings of such terms as "democratic," "free elections" and "governments friendly to the Soviet Union." The United States, recognizing the Soviet Union's concern for its security, agreed that the Russians could demand governments "friendly to the Soviet Union" in Eastern Europe. The problem was that Stalin believed that any non–communist government would be *hostile* to the Soviet Union. The same thing applied to such terms as "democratic" and "free elections." According to communist dogma, both terms applied only to states in which communism prevailed.

Stalin was probably not certain that his Western Allies would permit him to communize Eastern Europe. He also recognized that it was necessary to mobilize as much popular support as possible for the new regimes he was installing. That is why "Popular Front" governments were installed nearly everywhere in Eastern Europe in the beginning and why they were normally headed by a non–communist. This transition phase lasted approximately three years. In the meantime, Soviet–Allied relations worsened as it became clear just what Stalin was doing.

It is difficult to pinpoint an exact date for the beginning of the Cold War, but revisionist historians who suggest that President Truman's suspension of "lend–lease" assistance to the Soviet Union in May 1945 was motivated by anti–Soviet feelings place it too early. Actually, Truman was merely following the mandate of Congress, which in passing the original

legislation, specified that it would continue only for the duration of the war. Moreover, a quarrel over the political make–up of the new Polish Government was resolved just prior to the Potsdam Conference (July 1945) when the U.S. and Great Britain extended diplomatic recognition in return for Stalin's promise to add non–communist elements to it.

At Potsdam (a suburb of Berlin), the U.S. and Great Britain threatened to withhold recognition from the communist–dominated governments of Romania and Bulgaria unless they were enlarged to include a broader political spectrum. But on the major topic, Germany, the Big Three were in general agreement on policies of disarmament and de–Nazification. The U.S. and Great Britain also agreed that the Soviets were entitled to reparations from Germany, although they insisted that the Soviets extract them primarily from their own zone of occupation. That may have been hard on the East Germans, but did not affect the Soviets unduly.

Averill Harriman, who was U.S. Ambassador to Russia at the time, dates the beginning of the Cold War to a conversation he had with Stalin in the fall of 1945. Stalin had apparently just come from a meeting of the Politburo, and he told Harriman that "we have decided to go it alone." Stalin expanded on this theme in a speech which he gave in early 1946, just prior to new elections to the Supreme Soviet. It was a long speech, but its essence was that the alliance between the Soviet Union and the western democracies had been for limited purposes—to defeat fascism—and now that the purpose had been accomplished there was no longer any basis for cooperation. From now on, the emphasis would be on strengthening the "Soviet social order," which had established its superiority over any non–Soviet form of social organization.

If we place Stalin's comments into the context of the widespread destruction that occurred in the Soviet Union during World War II, they take on a more specific meaning. Large parts of the country had been occupied by foreign troops, and the effects of the actual fighting plus the Soviets' *scorched earth* policy during the retreat of 1941 and the willful destruction of the Germans as they retreated in 1943–44, left very little intact in the western part of Russia. In addition, an estimated 20 million Soviet citizens had died during the war—seven million of them in action. Even though the blame for much of this destruction is historically that of Stalin, it was realized that the rebuilding of Russia would require tremendous sacrifices on the part of the Soviet people. Some who lacked a sufficient "proletarian consciousness" might be *seduced* by capitalist promises of a better life. This explains why, as Alexander Solzhenitsyn has documented, hundreds of thousands of Soviet soldiers

and prisoners of war were shipped off to labor camps in the GULAG Archipelago rather than being treated as heroes. They had become ideologically contaminated because they had seen and might bear witness to what Soviet propaganda endlessly continued to deny—*that even in devastated Germany the people were better off than those living in the land of the victorious proletariat.*

It also helps to explain Stalin's policy toward Eastern Europe. If these economies could be tied to the Soviet economy, exploitation would make the rebuilding much easier. To accomplish this, trade agreements and mutual friendship and alliance treaties with the Eastern European countries were forged as soon as new governments were formed, with the purpose of reorienting their trade toward the Soviet Union. By 1947, a third of Russia's imports were coming from Eastern Europe, and the figure continued to grow thereafter. Slowly, Eastern Europe was being cut off and isolated from Western Europe. When Winston Churchill made his famous speech stating that a curtain of iron had been erected between East and West by Stalin in 1946, he was partly referring to this occurrence.

Though disturbed by developments in Eastern Europe, the United States continued to maintain an ambivalent attitude toward the Soviet Union. Something of a break in that pattern came in March 1947 when President Truman, in a speech to Congress, enunciated a policy toward Greece and Turkey that subsequently became known as the "Truman Doctrine." The Greek government was fighting a communist insurgency supported by Bulgaria and Yugoslavia, while Turkey was under pressure from the Soviet Union to cede certain frontier districts. In Truman's words, it was to be "the policy of the United States to support free people who are resisting attempted subjugation by armed minorities or by outside pressure." Neither communism nor the Soviet Union was mentioned, but the meaning was clear.

Three months later, Secretary of State George Marshall, speaking at the Harvard commencement, offered a broader response, insisting that: He thus spelled out a policy which later became known as the "Marshall Plan." The purpose of this was to assist Europe in the restoration of its destroyed economies, and it was to be open to all European nations. For a short while, it appeared that the Soviet Union was interested in the American offer, and Foreign Minister Molotov even attended a preliminary meeting in Paris to discuss details. Czechoslovakia and Poland also expressed their interest. Then Molotov abruptly denounced the Marshall Plan as an attack on the sovereignty of Europe and announced that the Soviets would not participate after all. Czechoslovakia and

Poland withdrew their applications as well. As American economic assistance began to pour into Western Europe, the gulf between East and West widened even further.

The Soviet Union, recognizing that a resurgent Western Europe might prove such an attraction that it would weaken the Soviet hold over Eastern Europe, decided to tighten its controls by organizing the Council for Mutual Economic Assistance (CMEA). While Stalin was alive, the CMEA was used primarily as a tool to exploit the Eastern European economies. After 1953, however, it became more of a coordinating body to facilitate economic planning and effort.

A second reaction to the Marshall Plan was the creation of a successor organization to the COMINTERN, which had been dissolved in 1943. The Communist Information Bureau (COMINFORM) came into being in the fall of 1947 with its headquarters in Belgrade, Yugoslavia. This turned out to be a poor choice—a scant year later, Yugoslavia was expelled from the COMINFORM upon Stalin's orders. Its offense: Marshal Tito's objection to Moscow's intermeddling in Yugoslavia's domestic economic affairs.

Stalin would have driven Tito from power had he been able to. But Stalin had no Soviet troops stationed in Yugoslavia and the Yugoslavian Communist Party remained loyal to Tito. And, compounding his treason, Tito turned to the United States for support; Stalin did not dare risk sending in his armies. Concerned that there might be other Titos, Stalin ordered a purge of other communist parties of Eastern Europe. Individuals suspected of "national deviationism"—putting the interests of one's own country above the interests of the Soviet Union—were removed from office and sometimes put on trial and executed. As the number of executions grew, the American distaste for what was going on inevitably also grew, and so American–Soviet relations deteriorated even further.

The year 1948 also brought a direct Western–Soviet confrontation over Berlin, when Stalin cut off all land access routes between West Germany and Berlin. The Western response was an "airlift" that kept West Berlin supplied with food and fuel for nearly a year until Stalin lifted the blockade.

The Berlin Blockade was a double failure, for it, plus the communist *coup d'etat* in Czechoslovakia, convinced the West that a more long–term response was needed. The North Atlantic Treaty Organization (NATO) came into being in April 1949 with General Dwight D. Eisenhower as Supreme Commander of the Allied Forces in Europe. Agreement was also reached on merging of the three western zones of occupation of Germany, and in May 1949 the Federal Republic of Germany came

into being. Conceding defeat, the Soviet Union ended the Berlin Blockade in May 1949. Five months later, it organized a separate government for its own zone of occupation, which became the German Democratic Republic.

As the European situation turned into a stalemate, Soviet interest began to turn to the Far East. Here, the victory of Mao Zedong's communists and the establishment of the People's Republic of China seemed to open new vistas for communist expansion. In mid–1949, *Pravda*, the Soviet Communist Party newspaper, carried a long article by Liu Shaoqi, one of the main leaders of the Chinese revolution, reporting on Asian communist parties. The article explicitly endorsed armed struggle as the primary tactic to be pursued by them. Since the article was followed by several similar articles, it was evident that the party line on armed struggle had changed. Thus, when the communist government of North Korea launched an invasion of the south in June 1950, the United States assumed that it was operating under Soviet direction. The United States, therefore, brought the matter before the Security Council of the United Nations, which declared the North Korean invasion to be an act of aggression and called upon all members of the United Nations to join in a united "police action" to defend South Korea. This action was possible because the Soviet delegate had been boycotting meetings of the Security Council since January 1950 in protest of the failure to seat communist China.

The Korean "police action" turned into a full–scale war that lasted until after Stalin's death in March 1953. It soon became obvious that neither side would be permitted to resolve the issue by force, but too much prestige had been invested on both sides to allow for a compromise. News of the gray–haired old dictator's death was therefore greeted with relief, for it was hoped that a compromise now might be reached. The armistice came approximately four months later—on July 27, 1953.

# The Post–Stalin Era

## The Struggle for Succession

The announcement of Stalin's death came on March 5, 1953. It was a strange announcement, for it spoke of the need to prevent "any kind of disorder and panic." The disarray in the leadership which this indicates derived from the fact that Stalin had never permitted his lieutenants any independent authority and squelched any discussion of who his successor would be; now, for the first time, they were on their own. In his memoirs, Nikita Khrushchëv reminisced about this period: The disorder did not last very long, but it did result in some policy reversals in the first few days. Georgi Malenkov, who was silently looked upon as Stalin's logical successor, was permitted to succeed to both of Stalin's positions—General Secretary of the Central Committee of the Communist Party and Chairman of the Council of Ministers—but after one day he gave up the position of General Secretary for unexplained reasons. Nikita Khrushchëv unofficially got the top party position. It was obvious that the *Presidium* (the new name for the Politburo, adopted at the 19th Party Congress in 1952), was attempting to end the rise of a new "sole leader," and had decided to split the top party and state offices. Malenkov chose to remain as Chairman of the Council of Ministers—apparently because he believed that the more immediate power position lay with that title. For awhile, it appeared that he had made the correct choice, for in the party, collective leadership of the entire Presidium was stressed while Malenkov was treated in the Soviet press as spokesman for the regime.

A recent Soviet history characterizes this period as one of "restoration of Leninist norms and the collective principle in the work of the Party and state." There was actually a great deal of agreement in the Presidium about the need for modifications in the system. Some of these changes were inevitable. Stalin had concentrated all decision–making in his own hands—now, some decentralization was in order. The Central Committee, which had fallen into disuse, was revived and regular meetings scheduled. The various ministries were given a greater say in decision–making and there was a great deal of talk about streamlining and rationalizing the ministerial and planning bureaucracies.

In foreign affairs, the turn away from confrontation that led to an armistice in Korea also had an effect on Eastern Europe. In East Germany, the political leadership, concerned about the lack of domestic support, announced a "New Course" aimed at reducing popular dissatisfaction. But before the "New Course" could be put into action, worker demonstrations and strikes broke out in East Berlin and in other cities. When Soviet tanks were brought in to quell the demonstrations, the workers rebelled and had to be put down with force. June 17th, the date of the workers' rebellion in East Berlin, is still commemorated as a legal holiday in the Federal Republic of Germany.

In July 1953 the Central Committee met in a plenary session to hear that Lavrenti Beria, head of the Secret Police and a top member of the party leadership since 1939, had been arrested and subsequently executed. The charge was that he had been attempting a bid for total power based on his control of the Secret Police. To forestall such an attempt in the future, the Secret Police were brought firmly under party control by taking them out of the Ministry of the Interior and creating a separate Committee for State Security (KGB) directly accountable to the Presidium. The powers of the KGB were also somewhat restricted by the issuance of new regulations specifying when arrests could be made. Beria was to be the last leading communist to be physically eliminated after losing in a struggle for power. From 1953 until the collapse of communism in 1991, the maximum penalty was expulsion from the party. Ironically, following his execution, Beria, a well–known ruthless. cold-blooded killer, was lamented by some of the more naïve U.S. press as a "good guy" who was an innocent victim of ruthless communism.

## The Beginning of the Khrushchëv Era

In September, the first indication that Khrushchëv might be a claimant for power came when it was announced that the title of the chief party post had been changed from *General* Secretary to *First* Secretary and that Khrushchëv had been confirmed in this office. He now became a vigorous advocate of strength ening the party after years of Stalin's neglect.

The first sign that there were policy differences between Malenkov and Khrushchëv also appeared in September—though in the carefully phrased way in which Party speeches are made, but this was easy to see only in retrospect. In August, Malenkov had addressed the Supreme Soviet setting forth the future direction of the regime. Bidding to reverse Stalin's traditional emphasis on heavy industry, Malenkov set forth a program calling for additional investment in the areas of consumer goods and agriculture. His theme was that people had a "right to demand consumer goods of high quality."

Khrushchëv, addressing a plenum of the Central Committee of the party after having been installed as First Secretary, argued that something had to be done for agriculture, but rejected a change in investment priorities to finance it.

The battle continued in 1954 and, in fact, became clearer. Khrushchëv wanted to retain the priority of heavy industry and wanted to pour additional funds into modernizing defense—while greatly increasing agricultural production. He pro-

Nikita Khrushchëv

49

posed to accomplish this through what later became known as the "virgin lands" program. This involved opening up for cultivation huge quantities of steppeland in Kazakhstan in Central Asia that had traditionally been considered too dry for normal agriculture. Khrushchëv's program was approved by a Central Committee plenum in March 1954; it was started in that year, but primarily was carried forward in 1955.

In the meantime, Khrushchëv had continued his attacks against Malenkov and managed to get him removed as Chairman of the Council of Ministers in early 1955. His replacement was Marshal Nikolai Bulganin. Khrushchëv had won a victory, but it was only partial. Bulganin belonged to the same faction on the Presidium as Malenkov.

Although it is largely coincidental, the period of joint leadership by Bulganin and Khrushchëv is associated with a number of breakthroughs in the foreign policy area. Calling for a resurrection of the old Leninist doctrine of "peaceful coexistence," the team of "B and K," as they became known to the West, engaged in a number of spectacular trips abroad, the most notable of which was a trip to Belgrade, Yugoslavia, to heal the breach with Marshal Tito. In a gesture to the West, the Soviet Union also agreed to end the joint military occupation of Austria, which regained its independance in 1955. This was the first withdrawal of Soviet troops without leaving a communist regime behind since World War II.

The good feeling engendered by the Soviet action in Austria was an important factor in producing the first meeting of major heads of government since the Potsdam Conference in 1945. This was the Geneva Summit of 1955. No specific agreements were reached but there was an exchange of views on German rearmament and reunification, European security, disarmament and the improvement of East–West contacts. The major Soviet proposal dealt with the opposing military alliances. It offered to disband the newly created (in May 1955) Warsaw Pact in return for the disbanding of NATO and the withdrawal of all "foreign troops" from the European continent. The proposal was so obviously one-sided that the West was unwilling to even consider it seriously. The summit was valuable from the Soviet point of view, however, for it signified that the West was willing to accept the Soviet Union as an equal in diplomatic discussions.

The 20th Party Congress, which met in February 1956, represented a new high for Khrushchëv, for it confirmed that he had taken control of the party apparatus. It also represented a new foreign policy departure, for it was here that Khrushchëv first articulated the view that war between capitalism and communism was no longer "fatalistically inevitable"—the view *always* held by Stalin. Khrushchëv justified his position on the basis of the emergence of socialism into a world system which made possible a world–wide peaceful transition to communism.

It appears, however, that the real basis for the change was Khrushchëv's recognition that the existence of nuclear weapons had changed the basic nature of war and rendered it no longer "thinkable."

### De–Stalinization

Khrushchëv's most important speech at this Congress did not take place in the public session, however. In a separate "secret" session of the Congress, Khrushchëv launched a major attack on the record of Stalin and what he called the "cult of personality." The speech set forth in great detail the many crimes of Stalin. Its content soon became known in the Soviet Union, however, and the actual text, first available in the West, has since been made public.

Khrushchëv gave the speech to smash the "Stalin myth" and so to free himself to carry out wider changes in the system than conservatives favored. Khrushchëv and his supporters apparently believed that it was possible to condemn Stalin's "errors" and at the same time maintain and even strengthen their own position. This was an effort to make communist rule more respectable by moving back toward older, "Leninist" norms. It signaled no basic change in the nature of communist rule, but it did suggest an end to harsh, terrorist tactics.

The impact of Khrushchëv's speech went far beyond what he had obviously intended. Stalin had defined the nature of communism for so long that the move to repudiate him unleashed forces which threatened the very foundations of Soviet power. Only weeks after the Congress, riots in Tbilisi, the capital of Soviet Georgia, resulted in the deaths of over a hundred persons.

The most serious and direct consequences of de–Stalinization occurred in Eastern Europe, however. In the Polish cities of Poznan and Warsaw, armed clashes occurred between the workers and police. In Hungary, university students demanded, and obtained, an end to compulsory Russian language instruction.

The situation continued to build in both countries. In October, a Polish Party plenum elected Wladislaw Gomulka as First Secretary and called for internal reforms. In Hungary, the clash between university students and the Hungarian secret police led to large–scale fighting and, when it was ordered to intervene, to the disintegration of the Hungarian army. The Soviet Ambassador to Hungary, Yuri Andropov, met with the new Hungarian Government and arranged for the withdrawal of Soviet troops from Bu-

dapest on October 28. One week later, on November 4, they returned and put down the uprising. The Soviet intervention in Hungary brought revulsion abroad and a wave of resignations among prominent foreign communists. Jean– Paul Sartre of France and Howard Fast of the United States were among those who turned in their party cards at this time.

Khrushchëv began now to downplay de–Stalinization, but he had lost the confidence of a number of the leading members of his own party. In June 1957 the Presidium voted seven to four to dismiss him as First Party Secretary. Khrushchëv refused to accept the decision of the Presidium, however, and demanded that the full Central Committee be convened to vote on the matter. Khrushchëv won in the larger forum and managed to obtain the removal of his opponents from full membership on the Presidium. Malenkov was sent to manage a remote installation in Central Asia while Molotov was named Soviet Ambassador to Mongolia. Nine months later, in March 1958, Khrushchëv assumed the additional office of Chairman of the Council of Ministers (head of government).

One of those who benefited from Khrushchëv's victory was Leonid Brezhnev, who became a full member of the Presidium in June 1957. Three years later, in May 1960, Brezhnev became Chairman of the Presidium of the Supreme Soviet (titular head of state). That same month, Alexei Kosygin and Nikolai Podgorny were promoted to full membership in the Presidium.

The 22nd Party Congress met in Moscow in October 1961. Its major theme was de–Stalinization. Following the Congress, Stalin's body was removed from alongside Lenin in the mausoleum on Red Square and buried outside the Kremlin wall. The city of Stalingrad had its name changed and became Volgograd, and other cities named after Stalin had their names changed as well. Yevgeni Yevtushenko, already well-known because of his poem about Babi Yar (where the Nazis carried out a massacre of Soviet Jews during World War II), now produced his poem entitled "The Heirs of Stalin" in which he spoke of those who

"from rostrums, even heap abuse on Stalin
but, at night, hanker after the good old days"

and warned that

"As long as the heirs of Stalin walk this earth
Stalin, I fancy, still lurks in the mausoleum."

This was followed in November 1962 by the publication of *One Day in the Life of*

*Ivan Denisovich,* Alexander Solzhenitsyn's bold novel about life in Stalin's concentration camps.

Writings with a specific political content were not published in the Soviet Union except with approval from high up, and it was said that Khrushchëv authorized publication of Solzhenitsyn's book. But this was the surface reality. None of the "heirs of Stalin" denounced as criminals at the 22nd Party Congress suffered anything more than verbal abuse. They kept their jobs and bided their time. And in October 1964 they took their revenge by casting their votes for Khrushchëv's ouster from power.

De–Stalinization was only one of several factors involved in Khrushchëv's dismissal from power, however. Foreign policy was an issue and in particular, the Cuban missile crisis. It was an American who characterized Khrushchëv's foreign policy as one of "overextension followed by capitulation" but this appears to have been the opinion of some of those on the Presidium itself. One of the few specific charges brought against Khrushchëv in October 1964 was that he had caused a Soviet defeat at the time of the Cuban missile crisis. The theme of overextension was specifically taken up by Brezhnev the following month when he asserted that, in the future, Soviet foreign policy would take into consideration the "military power of the countries of the socialist camp."

The other chief issue was domestic. Khrushchëv had staked a great deal on economic development and he had promised the Soviet people that the U.S.S.R. would catch up with the United States economically by 1980. He had carried through a partial economic decentralization in 1957 when he created 105 new regional Economic Councils *(sovnarkhozy).* In November 1962 he announced a division of the party into separate industrial and agricultural sections, the object to turn the party into an economic administrative apparatus. This move threatened the power position of the regional first party secretaries and created a great deal of dissatisfaction throughout the party.

In the end, it was probably the failure of Khrushchëv's agricultural policies that did him in. After the initial success of his "virgin lands" program, agricultural production stagnated and the country began to suffer chronic food shortages. The 1962 division of the party was an attempt to deal with the problem administratively, but it was a failure. In August 1964, Khrushchëv announced yet another reorganization of agriculture which he intended to submit to a November party plenum. But by this time the other members of the Presidium had had enough. On October 15, 1964, Moscow's TASS (the official news "wire") announced that Khrushchëv had been relieved of his duties as First Party Secretary and Chairman of the Council of Ministers, and that Leonid Brezhnev had been elected First Party Secretary in his place. Alexei Kosygin became Chairman of the Council of Ministers. Anastas Mikoyan, who had succeeded Brezhnev as Chairman of the Presidium of the Supreme Soviet (titular head of state) in July 1964, retained that position until his retirement in December 1965; he was succeeded by Nikolai Podgorny, who continued to serve in that position.

## Soviet Foreign Policy under Khrushchëv

Of key importance to the leadership of the Soviet Union was the problem of relations with the United States, the country which, after World War II, was the leader of the Western alliance. Stalin, knowing that he could not both keep control over Eastern Europe and continue good relations with the United States, chose confrontation. His successors, perhaps frightened at the turn that confrontation had taken and more aware of the threat that nuclear weapons represented, attempted to reach an accommodation with the West while retaining Stalin's empire. This led to some easing of tensions and to increased diplomatic contacts. A Geneva Summit Conference in 1955 after Stalin's death represented the culmination of this trend. No significant agreements were reached, but the "spirit of Geneva" continued to influence relations between the two powers for about five years.

The United States' refusal to accept Soviet domination of Eastern Europe always remained a factor in U.S.–Soviet relations, however, and when, as in 1956, the Soviet Union resorted to the use of force to retain its control, bilateral relations suffered. Not all of the Soviet Union's problems with regard to maintaining control were amenable to the use of force, however. One such case was Berlin, established under separate four–power occupation in 1945. In the 1950's, West Berlin (representing a union of the three western zones of occupation) was a free enterprise, democratic island in the middle of a communized East Germany and it had become a place of refuge for East Germans fleeing communism. Determined to put an end to the constant drain of manpower, Khrushchëv demanded in November 1958 that the occupation of West Berlin be terminated and that it be turned into a "free city" within the territory of the communist German Democratic Republic. Khrushchëv's position, put in the form of an ultimatum, created the Berlin Crisis of 1958.

It is difficult to determine whether Khrushchëv expected his viewpoint to prevail, but it did result in a four–power Foreign Ministers' conference in Geneva in May 1959 and an invitation to Khrushchëv to visit the United States in September. Khrushchëv stayed for 18 days, which included three days spent at Camp David in private conversation with President Eisenhower.

Though the talks produced only an agreement for additional summit level negotiations, the Soviets subsequently referred to them as having created the "spirit of Camp David." When Khrushchëv returned to Moscow, he publicly characterized Eisenhower as a man who "sincerely wants to liquidate the cold war and improve relations between our two great countries." That also led Khrushchëv to suggest, in early 1960, that the Soviet armed forces would be reduced by about one–third.

This was the high–water mark in U.S.-Soviet relations under Khrushchëv. But in May, the Soviets shot down an American U–2 photo–reconnaissance plane that had penetrated Soviet air space. Khrushchëv demanded an apology from Eisenhower and, when it was not forthcoming, he torpedoed a Summit Meeting scheduled to take place in Paris in mid-May. This also was one of the factors that explains Khru-

**First Secretary Khrushchëv and President Kennedy, Vienna, 1961**

shchëv's extraordinary performance at the United Nations General Assembly in September when he took off his shoe and banged it on his desk to show his disapproval of one of the speeches.

A meeting between Khrushchëv and President Kennedy in May 1961 proved to be unproductive and, in fact, Khrushchëv resurrected the Berlin Crisis by demanding a settlement by the end of the year. Further, he coupled this with a statement that the Soviet defense budget would be *increased* by one–third. Then, on August 13, 1961, the Soviet Union instituted a unilateral solution to the Berlin Crisis by beginning to build a wall between West and East Berlin. Since the wall was being built on the territory of East Berlin, there was little that the United States and its allies could do other than to issue a diplomatic protest—but it obviously had a negative effect on U.S.-Soviet relations. Barriers were later placed to totally divide East Germany from West Berlin. This was the first time in history that a fortified wall had been erected to keep people *in* instead of *out*.

The next test of wills came in October 1962—the Cuban missile crisis. In his memoirs, Khrushchëv relates that: But the United States found out what the Soviet Union was up to as the missiles were being installed and demanded their removal. Khrushchëv had to acquiesce, but he attempted to save face by claiming that he had preserved world peace and obtained (an oral) guarantee for Cuba's Fidel Castro against any future attempts to overthrow him by troops launched from the U.S. In fact, he did have some gains to show. In the final settlement, the United States confined its objective to the withdrawal of Soviet missiles, thereby conceding Castro's right to remain a Soviet ally and to retain a communist form of government if he wished. This was a tacit repeal of the Monroe Doctrine. In addition, the U.S. soon afterwards began removing its intermediate range ballistic missiles from Turkey, which Khrushchëv could claim as an additional victory on his part.

Moreover, in retrospect, the United States was as appalled as the Soviet Union at how close the two nations had come to all–out war and the result was further steps toward *détente*. This led to the installation of a Washington–Moscow "hot line" and the signing of a limited test ban treaty in 1963.

Domestically, however, Khrushchëv drew different conclusions from the Cuban missile crisis and in March 1963 he pushed through a revision of the last two years of the Seventh Five Year Plan to allow for a large–scale deployment of Soviet ICBMs. As he records in his memoirs, "the experience of the Caribbean crisis also convinced us that we were right to concentrate on the manufacture of nuclear missiles."

# The Brezhnev Era

During the years that followed Khrushchëv's ouster, the Soviet Union was governed by a relatively stable coalition of leaders that included Brezhnev, Kosygin and Podgorny, but also included Michael Suslov, the party's chief ideologist, as well. Brezhnev gradually consolidated his position as first among equals, however, and, starting in the late 1960's, he became the dominant figure in foreign policy. Brezhnev's style of leadership was undramatic, however, and both his successes and his failures tended to be associated more with the system than with the man.

The immediate period following Khrushchëv's departure was characterized by a reversal of many of his policies. Most importantly, the November 1962 division of the party into separate industrial and agricultural units was reversed and a unitary party structure was recreated. The regional Economic Councils created in 1957 were also gradually phased out and replaced by centralized ministries.

In 1965 at a Central Committee plenum, Brezhnev announced a change in agricultural policy which, he said, would place the emphasis on farm autonomy. The real thrust of the new program was *not* farm autonomy, however, but increased incentives—diffused in such a way that they probably had little economic effect. Ever since their creation in the 1930's, collective

farms had been required to deliver a set quota of grain to the government at artificially low prices. Brezhnev now lowered that quota by 11 million tons and increased the price that the government would pay for above-quota deliveries. The price of various types of agricultural equipment was also lowered at this time. These changes increased retained earnings for the collective farm administrations, but they did not filter down in a meaningful way to the individual peasant. Two other reforms did, however; peasants for the first time became eligible for old age pensions and were guaranteed a minimum monthly income. In addition, there was an attempt to encourage the production of more fruit, vegetables and meat for sale in the free peasant markets of the big cities by easing restrictions and reducing taxes on small private plots. All of these changes under Brezhnev had the effect of blurring the distinction between state and collective farms.

Major changes in the industrial sector were also experimented with at this time. These experiments, collectively known as the *Liberman Plan*, were actually suggested in 1962 when a Kharkov (Ukraine) University professor by the name of Yevsei Liberman wrote an article for *Pravda* setting forth general principles for economic reform. Under the Soviet economic system, manufacturing enterprises operated on the basis of detailed instructions drawn up by planning experts in centralized ministries. Liberman proposed that much

**Leonid Brezhnev**

View of Moscow and the Moscow River

of this planning be dismantled and that individual plant managers be given authority to run their enterprises themselves, subject only to overall production figures and fulfillment of delivery dates. Profitability, rather than the meeting of production norms, would be the new test of the efficiency of an enterprise, and supply and demand would replace the exchange of goods on the basis of pre–planned indexes. Wages and salaries would also be tied to the profitability of individual enterprises.

The Liberman article in *Pravda* had been personally approved and endorsed by Khrushchëv, and in August 1964 the first test of the *Liberman* ideas began with an experimental tryout of the system in two textile plants. After Khrushchëv's fall, Alexei Kosygin made the Liberman Plan his own and ordered that a reform program be drawn up for the entire economy. The new program was put into effect beginning in September 1965.There was considerable opposition from among those who believed that it would tend to decrease the role of the party in the economy, however, and Brezhnev apparently aligned himself eventually with this group. As a result, the Central Committee plenum that instituted the reform also re-instituted central industrial and technical ministries, at least partially negating the reform from the very beginning. *Liberman-ism* was subsequently adopted by many Eastern European regimes, most notably Hungary, but in the Soviet Union it was phased out beginning in 1970.

Another program reversal that followed

the ouster of Khrushchëv was the gradual end of de–Stalinization, accompanied by a generally harder line on the cultural front. A *Pravda* article in 1965 by Professor Sergei Trapeznikov, chief of the Central Committee's department of science and education, characterized the Stalin era as "one of the most brilliant in the history of the Party and the Soviet State" and suggested it as a pattern for the theoretical and practical activity of the Party.

A month earlier, in September 1965, A.M. Rumiantsev, editor of *Pravda*, had been dismissed after he came to the defense of Andrei Voznesensky, a Soviet writer who had been accused of nihilism. In that same month, Andrei Sinyavsky and Yuri Daniel were arrested and tried for publishing abroad works critical of the Soviet Union. They were sentenced to 7 and 5 years at hard labor.

The 23rd Party Congress of 1966 appeared to confirm the trend toward re–Stalinization. The Presidium again became known as the Politburo while the First Party Secretary resumed the title of General Secretary. Both names dated from the Stalinist era and had been dropped by Khrushchëv.

## The Dissident Movement

De–Stalinization was accompanied by the rise of a dissident movement that grew in numbers and in significance in the late 1960's. In 1966, an underground journal, *Phoenix 61*, began to appear. Four writers associated with the journal were arrested at the beginning of 1967 and later sentenced. This, in turn, led to several

public and private petitions of protest, signed by increased numbers of distinguished Soviet intellectuals. The situation was further worsened when Stalin's daughter, Svetlana Allilueva, defected in April 1967 and in a subsequent book, *Twenty Letters to a Friend*, expressed her solidarity with the Soviet intellectuals in their struggle for intellectual freedom. Also, about this time, two of Alexander Solzhenitsyn's novels, *First Circle* and *Cancer Ward*, were published abroad—without Solzhenitsyn's permission, to be sure, but the mere fact of publication abroad was considered to be an act of dissidence *by him*.

As the dissident movement continued to grow, it gained a widening circle of recruits. In July 1968, Andrei Sakharov, a distinguished physicist and father of the Soviet Union's hydrogen bomb, allowed a manuscript of his entitled *Thoughts on Progress, Peaceful Coexistence and Intellectual Freedom*, to be published abroad. Sakharov had joined the ranks of active dissidents two years earlier when he wrote a letter to Brezhnev protesting the arrest of four persons whose crime was that they had protested against the trial of Sinyavsky and Daniel. Since Sakharov was a prominent member of the Soviet Academy of Sciences and a recipient of both the Stalin Prize and the Lenin Prize, nothing had happened then or subsequently when he signed a letter to the Party warning against a resurgence of Stalinism. In August 1968, however, Sakharov was removed from all secret work and transferred to another academic institute

in Moscow; he and his wife were later sent to the official detention city, formerly named Gorky.

The Soviet invasion of Czechoslovakia in 1968 brought both renewed protests and a harsher crackdown on dissidents. One of the seven individuals who staged a brief demonstration in Red Square against the invasion was Pavel Litvinov, grandson of Maxim Litvinov, Stalin's Foreign Minister in the 1930's. Litvinov was sentenced to five years internal exile in a Siberian village. After his return to Moscow in 1973, Litvinov and his wife applied for exit visas as Jews and shortly afterwards emigrated.

One of the more interesting developments of the Brezhnev era was the adoption of a policy of allowing Jewish emigration. There are a little over two million Jews in the Soviet Union and the large majority of them consider themselves to be assimilated and at home. In 1970 for example, only 17.7% of all Jews listed either Hebrew or Yiddish as their mother tongue. There has always been some anti–Semitism in Russia, but the Soviet Union, to its credit, has seldom encouraged the attitude. In 1967, however, following Israel's defeat of the Soviet Union's Arab clients, Egypt and Syria, the Soviet Union unleashed a violent anti–Zionist campaign. For some of the Russian public, the distinction between anti–Zionism and anti–Semitism was too fine a difference to draw. As a result, an increasing number of Jews began applying for visas to emigrate to Israel; eventually over 100,000 Jews applied to emigrate. In 1968, the Ministry of Interior notified a few Jewish families that, if they still wanted to leave, they could. The flow of Jewish emigrants grew steadily thereafter, and by

1973 an average of 30,000 Jews were leaving every year. This abated by the end of 1975, but since 1988 the pace has quickened with the encouragement of Israel. Actually their preferred destination is the U.S.

The question of Jewish emigration became a foreign policy matter in 1974 when the U.S. Congress, following the leadership of Senator Henry Jackson of Washington State, approved an amendment to the 1972 trade agreement on "most–favored–nation" status for the Soviet Union which made approval contingent on increased Jewish emigration from the Soviet Union. The Soviets, calling the Jackson Amendment an interference in their domestic affairs, rejected the trade agreement in 1975.

Jewish emigration continued at a decreased level for awhile after 1975, but then began growing again. By 1979, an average of 4,000 Jews were departing monthly. Then came a policy reversal. From a peak of 51,320 in 1979, the number of emigrants declined to 2,688 in 1982, the last year of Brezhnev's regime.

Non–Jewish dissidents did not, in general, have the right to apply for emigration but the Brezhnev regime rediscovered, in the period of the 1970s, that emigration or expulsion sometimes provided a suitable alternative to imprisonment for individuals too prominent to treat as ordinary criminals. Alexander Solzhenitsyn, expelled in February 1974, remains the most famous of these, but the list of those given permission to go abroad temporarily who thereafter had their Soviet citizenship withdrawn is much longer. Thus by the end of the Brezhnev regime in 1982, most individuals who had joined the ranks of the dissidents in the

1960s or early 1970s were either living abroad, in prison, a psychiatric hospital, or in internal exile.

A few new dissidents did appear in the late 1970's, particularly in association with attempts to demand implementation of the human rights provision of the Helsinki Accord, signed in 1975. They were small in number, however, and quickly rounded up. There was also some dissident activity in connection with the 1980 Summer Olympics and again at the time of the 1980–81 Madrid follow–up conference to the Helsinki Conference on Security and Cooperation in Europe.

Yet the movement, although troublesome because of its international ramifications, was never more than an annoyance to the regime. The actual number of dissidents was always quite small. A recent Western study which attempted to identify all those who were in any way involved in the dissident movement was able to come up with names of only 3,400 persons for the period 1956 to 1975. The disturbing element from the point of view of the regime was that the dissidents originated in a social base that consisted essentially of the scientific–cultural intellentsia. Their significance was that they *said* aloud what other intelligent people could only think.

### A Regime In Crisis

A more serious problem in the long run was that the Soviet economy, which began a slowdown by 1970, continued in that pattern to the end of the Brezhnev era and, in fact, the pattern is yet to be reversed. Moreover, wage increases granted to the workers after 1965 exacerbated the situation for they had not been accompanied by an equivalent increase in consumer goods.

The Five Year Plan for 1971–1975 attempted to deal with this situation by calling for vast investment in agriculture and increased investments in consumer industry. For the first time in Soviet history, consumer goods were to be favored over heavy industry. But by the end of 1972, the planners had to admit that their priorities did not permit the planned investments in consumer goods and the plan was revised to renew the emphasis on heavy industry. The Tenth Five Year Plan (1976–1980) continued the revised priorities of the preceding plan. These targets were also not met.

The 11th Five Year Plan (1981–1985) called for a slightly larger growth in consumer industry than heavy industry. Some of its goals, particularly those with regard to agriculture were unrealistic, however, and were never met. The essential problem—and it is one that the Soviets never solved—is that Soviet productivity slowed to a negligible rate in the 1960's and all the tinkering with the economy after that time did nothing to reverse that trend. Any effective economic reform would have had to decrease the role of the cadre of the Communist Party in the economy. Under Brezhnev, this was always unacceptable.

The Brezhnev era has one last characteristic worth mentioning. The Soviet Union had a huge bureaucracy which ran all things under the guidance of the Party. Khrushchëv had feared that the bureaucracy was becoming ingrown (which it was) and in 1961 he had sponsored a new Party statute which attempted to deal with the problem. Under the terms of the statute, there was to be a normal turnover of personnel on each of the Party committees, with a certain percentage of the membership to be replaced at each election. There was considerable opposition to this policy among Party bureaucrats and, at the 23rd Party Congress in 1966, the policy was reversed. Although a general clause was added stressing the intention of the Party to promote "energetic and competent young cadres," this was generally ignored in the period of the 1970's.

The result was an unparalleled continuity in office at all levels of government, and an aging Party and government elite. One can see how this operated with regard to membership on the Central Committee. In 1966, 76% of those elected at the 24th Party Congress were already full members. The percentage of full members reelected subsequently remained at this level. In fact at the 26th Party Congress in 1981, the figure was actually 75%; it would have been much higher, but the Central Committee was also growing during these years, having increased by 44 since the previous Congress.

### Soviet Foreign Policy under Brezhnev

When Brezhnev replaced Khrushchëv as Party chief in October 1964, a subtle change occurred. Without repudiating *détente*, Brezhnev began to speak about the necessity of maintaining Soviet defense potential at the highest possible levels. In July 1965, he spoke of a five–year defense plan to "increase the defensive might of the U.S.S.R." The subsequent 1966–1970 Soviet defense budget nearly doubled defense spending; it continued to grow in the period of the 1970's, though a CIA report issued in the middle 1980s indicated that the annual growth rate may have dropped somewhat for the period 1979–1982.

Brezhnev's push for increased defense expenditures was, from the Soviet point of view, entirely compatible with a policy of *détente* and, in some respects, a precondition for it. Cooperation between the two super powers was made somewhat more difficult because of the United States' increasing involvement in Vietnam but, in spite of this, a treaty to ban nuclear weapons in outer space was negotiated in 1967.

This was followed in 1968 by a treaty on the non–proliferation of nuclear weapons.

Negotiations to limit the size of both countries' strategic nuclear forces were to begin in 1968, but were canceled by President Johnson after a Soviet invasion of Czechoslovakia. The Strategic Arms Limitation Talks (SALT) concept was revived by President Nixon, however, and this led to a visit by President Nixon to Moscow in May 1972 and the signing of the SALT–1 accords. SALT–1 primarily limited the deployment of antiballistic missiles (ABMs) but it also contained a five-year interim agreement freezing the number of land and sea–based missiles. In late 1974, President Ford met with Brezhnev in Vladivostok and there the two leaders agreed on general guidelines for a SALT–2 pact which would deal with strategic nuclear missiles. SALT–2 was finally initialed in 1979, but President Carter later withdrew the treaty from consideration by the United States Senate after a Soviet invasion of Afghanistan.

### Military Intervention in Afghanistan

A group openly claiming to be Marxist-Leninist came to power in Afghanistan in a bloody *coup.* in late 1978. The U.S. government recognized the new regime, but became more and more disquieted by subsequent events. A large number of "advisers" were imported from the Soviet Union and the regime began an attempt to bring about a social revolution within the country. This produced strong resistance among the Afghan population, however, and it wasn't long before armed uprisings throughout the country threatened the very existence of the regime. In late 1979

therefore, the Soviet Union intervened with 80,000 Soviet troops to prop up the faltering Afghan communist regime. But Afghanistan is mostly rugged mountain country with a population of about 20 million people; the Soviet troops were only sufficient to keep the communist regime from being overthrown, but not enough to put down the rebellion.

Soviet intervention in Afghanistan had an adverse effect on the Soviet Union's relations with most of the rest of the world, however. A number of countries, including the United States, boycotted the 1980 Moscow Olympics.

President Carter also announced a partial embargo on the sale of grain to the Soviet Union and began negotiating an agreement with Pakistan to provide military support to the *mujahidin,* the Afghan resistance. In addition, the Carter Administration reversed its earlier position on the adequacy of American military power and began a new buildup of U.S. forces. Further, it sponsored resolutions in the United Nations condemning the Soviet military presence in Afghanistan.

The Reagan Administration continued and intensified most of these policies. Agreement with Pakistan was reached and significant aid began flowing to the *mujahidin..* Military budgets were greatly enlarged and the administration openly boasted about beginning a new arms race which they expected to win. The B–1 bomber aircraft, canceled by the Carter Administration, was reinstated and a number of new weapons systems, including the multiple–warhead MX and the Trident submarine, were proposed.

This was the stick. At the same time, the

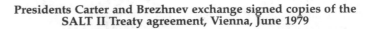

**Presidents Carter and Brezhnev exchange signed copies of the SALT II Treaty agreement, Vienna, June 1979**

*Mujahidin* resistance fighters look down on a village after a Soviet aerial attack. At left are terraced crop fields.

AP/World Wide Photos

Reagan Administration stipulated its willingness to negotiate arms reductions and symbolized this by changing the name of the arms negotiations process from SALT—Strategic Arms Limitation Talks—to START—Strategic Arms Reduction Talks.

The START negotiations began in June 1982. The American position, set forth by President Reagan, called for a reduction of missile launchers to 850 each (down from 2,000 for the USA and 2,700 for the USSR) and a reduction of nuclear warheads by about a third. No more than half of the missile launchers could be land-based. Agreement on these points would lead to a second round of talks aimed at reducing other elements of the two nations' "balance of terror."

Brezhnev rejected Reagan's proposal in May 1982, apparently disturbed by its proposed limits on land–based ICBMs. His own proposal called for a two–thirds reduction in nuclear warheads, a ban on the development of new types of strategic weapons, and a freeze on strategic weapons at current levels, to begin concurrently with the negotiations. The United States rejected the freeze on the basis that it would codify existing Soviet advantages, but welcomed Brezhnev's willingness to negotiate.

The USA and USSR were at least talking with each other in the area of strategic weapons. One other area of American concern, that of theater nuclear weapons in Europe, remained totally stalemated. The problem dated from 1977, when the Soviet Union began installing SS–20 missiles in Eastern Europe. A mobile missile with three warheads, the SS–20 caused great concern among Western European leaders and they began pushing for NATO to match these missiles.

In 1979, therefore, NATO voted for the emplacement of American Pershing II and Cruise missiles in Europe, if talks with the Soviet Union did not produce another solution. The Soviets refused to discuss the removal of their missiles, however, so President Reagan offered his Zero Option—if the Soviet Union would pull its SS–20s out of Eastern Europe, then the USA would refrain from installing Pershing IIs and Cruise missiles in Western Europe—in a public speech in September 1981. The Soviet Union had not yet responded as of November 1982, when Brezhnev died.

# Government Transition

### November 1982–March 1985

Prior to Brezhnev's death in November 1982, there was a widespread feeling that the last years of his regime had been ones of stagnation and even decline. Many felt that what was needed was a strong, vigorous, but tested leader who could get the country going again.

Konstantin Chernenko was Brezhnev's protégé and therefore represented continuity; Yuri Andropov, who had been head of the KGB for 15 years, was a man from outside Brezhnev's inner circle, and therefore represented change. The choice fell to Andropov. It turned out, however, that Andropov was a frail reed on which to lean. He was personally honest and hard–working, and he had attached to himself a number of younger individuals committed to change. But he was also suffering from a heart condition and diabetes, and was temporarily incapacitated only five months after becoming General Secretary. Moreover, although a majority

of the Politburo had chosen him over Chernenko, it soon became clear that there was no firm majority for reform. As a result, there were only three major policies associated with Andropov's name. The first of these was his campaign against corruption and slack labor discipline. There was undoubtedly corruption and slack discipline, but if western observers were correct that these things were only symptoms and that the major problems were systemic—arising from or pertaining to the system *itself*, then Andropov's campaign was relatively meaningless.

Andropov was also interested in renewing the leadership of the Party by retiring older individuals and promoting younger men in their places. He succeeded to a cer-

*Pravda* announces Brezhnev's death

56

tain extent at secondary levels, but the average age of the Politburo was well past the usual age of retirement.

He also introduced two economic "reforms," a system of brigades for farm workers that permitted some wage differentiation based on actual production, and an experiment, limited to five ministries, in which work teams were set up in factories and encouraged to compete with each other. The factory reform was begun as of January 1, 1984. Both reforms constituted "tinkering with the system" and therefore made no significant contribution to higher productivity. They did represent Andropov's commitment to economic reform, however, and provided a beginning upon which Gorbachëv could later build.

Foreign relations under Andropov deserve comment. He essentially represented a hard–line faction in this area, but he was extremely vigorous in his negotiating stance. Thus it was Andropov who issued the first formal reply to President Reagan's "Zero Option" speech of September 1981. In November 1982, shortly after becoming General Secretary, Andropov gave a speech in which he proposed to reduce the number of SS–20s in Eastern Europe to the same number of missiles held by Great Britain and France if, in return, NATO would cancel deployment of Pershing IIs and Cruise missiles in Western Europe. The offer was unacceptable because the British and French missiles, being part of their "national" arsenals, were not under NATO control. It did open the way for formal negotiations to begin, however.

The United States continued to push its Zero Option until March 1983. Then President Reagan gave another speech in which he introduced his "Interim Proposal." He proposed that the USA and the USSR agree to an equal number of theater nuclear warheads on each side, with the expectation that talks on an eventual Zero Option would continue. The Soviets rejected this proposal.

Negotiations nevertheless continued and there was at least the possibility that an agreement would have been reached, except for the unfortunate circumstances of the Soviet shooting down of a commercial airliner, South Korean Flight 007, in September 1983. The mutual recriminations that followed that event doomed the Theater Nuclear Weapons discussions.

In order to preserve their real or imaginary advantage, the Soviets embarked on a vigorous campaign to drive a wedge between the USA and its Western European NATO allies through mountains of propaganda describing the horrors of nuclear war. This did, in fact, succeed in attracting the sympathies of a substantial number of people in Western Europe and led to numerous anti-nuclear demonstrations. However, in November 1983, with no agreement in sight, the United States began delivering the first of the Pershing II and Cruise missiles to Western Europe. The Theater Nuclear Force discussions were then abruptly recessed by the Soviets in December 1983. They announced that they would not return to the negotiating table unless the United States agreed to withdraw all nuclear missiles emplaced in Western Europe.

Andropov fell ill at just about this point. He was last seen in public shortly before the downing of the airliner, and it is not known what role, if any, he had in foreign affairs during those last five months when he remained sequestered from the world.

This is the record which the members of the Politburo had to evaluate when they met to choose Andropov's successor in February 1984. The promise he represented had been largely unfulfilled, but even the pallid reforms instituted had been negatively received by a large part of the bureaucracy. In particular, Andropov's attempts to weed out incompetents and to promote younger persons to positions of higher responsibility threatened the security of the tenure of the "old guard" Party cadre, and they mobilized their forces accordingly. Chernenko, passed over once precisely because he represented the politics of the waning years of the Brezhnev era, became their candidate.

The other two candidates were Mikhail Gorbachëv and Grigori Romanov. Gorbachëv and Romanov represented the younger generation of the Politburo and tended to be classified as economic specialists because both probably favored greater experimentation in the area of the economy. The Politburo chose Chernenko—although it appeared that Gorbachëv moved into a clear number two position and was the heir apparent.

And how did Chernenko change things after becoming General Secretary? Serge Schmemann, Moscow correspondent for The New York Times, wrote, quoting from an interview he had with a knowledgeable figure in Moscow: Chernenko was a transitional figure, chosen to hold the fort a little longer before transferring power to a new generation. As such, his initiatives, or lack of them, reflected the will of a majority of the Politburo. When he first took over, there apparently were high–level disagreements on a number of policy issues, most importantly, on foreign policy. The result was several months of hibernation, exemplified by a Soviet boycott of the 1984 Summer Olympics in Los Angeles and a cancellation of a visit to China by Ivan V. Arkhipov, Vice Chairman of the U.S.S.R. Council of Ministers.

But Chernenko, who suffered from emphysema and a weak heart, disappeared from view for two months in mid–1984 and reportedly was brought back to Mos-

*Izvestia* announces Andropov's death

cow in a wheelchair. It was shortly afterwards that Foreign Minister Gromyko agreed to a meeting with President Reagan. The seriousness of Chernenko's illness had apparently broken the stalemate in the Kremlin and a new majority favoring negotiations with the U.S. had emerged. At the beginning of November, it was announced that new high–level economic talks would be held in Moscow in January 1985. Two weeks later, Gromyko and Secretary of State George Shultz agreed to meet in Geneva in early January to discuss resumption of arms talks. It was also at about this time that Moscow announced that Arkhipov's delayed visit to China would take place in December.

The Moscow talks were inconclusive, but there was agreement to resume arms talks in Geneva beginning March 12, 1985. Arkhipov's visit to China also resulted in some improvement in Soviet–Chinese relations.

These events occurred in Chernenko's absence, for he had disappeared from sight on December 27 and had not been seen again in public. In February it was officially confirmed that he was ill. A short television clip showed him voting in the Republic elections on February 24th, but it appeared to have been "doctored," since its background matched another clip reported to be at another time and place. Fifteen days later his death was announced. According to the official medical report, his death resulted from a combination of factors which included emphysema, a heart condition and chronic hepatitis which had developed into cirrhosis. Evidently his death was quite expected, for the Central Committee had already met and decided on his successor.

General Secretary Konstantin Chernenko of the U.S.S.R.

# THE GORBACHEV ERA

### A new General Secretary

The story of Gorbachëv's formal installation as General Secretary is well-known—how Gromyko made the nominating speech at the meeting of the Central Committee and how he concluded his remarks with the observation that "Comrades, he has a nice smile, but he has iron teeth." No other candidates were presented to the Central Committee and acceptance was therefore assured.

In March 1987, however, a somewhat different report surfaced about a secret Politburo meeting which took place prior to the Central Committee meeting that installed Gorbachëv as General Secretary. This report, which appeared in a Finnish newspaper, *Svomen Kuvalehti,* was based on an interview with Mikhail Shatrov, a Soviet playwright and Gorbachëv adviser. According to Shatrov, nine persons were present at the Politburo meeting. With Gromyko as chairman and abstaining, the vote was tied four to four between Gorbachëv and Viktor Grishin, Moscow party leader. Gromyko then intervened to cast the deciding vote.

The story can't be directly confirmed, but Gromyko was later named Chairman of the Presidium of the Supreme Soviet (head of state) and Grishin and three other members of the Politburo did shortly afterwards lose their seats on the Politburo. Moreover, the story has a plausibility in that Grishin was logically the leader

of what was left of Brezhnev's faction after the death of Chernenko.

Born on March 2, 1931, Gorbachëv was at the time the youngest man on the Politburo. He was also the best educated, having graduated from Moscow University in 1955 with a degree in law. He later would add a second degree when he earned the qualification of "agronomist–economist" from the Stavropol Agricultural Institute in 1967.

It was at Moscow University that Gorbachëv first began to take an active interest in politics. He became the head of the Moscow University branch of the *Komsomols* (Young Communists) and it was at this time that he joined the Communist Party. After graduation, Gorbachëv joined the Stavropol Agricultural Institute. East of the Black Sea, this is an important agricultural district in southern Russia. It was also Gorbachëv's home region, so he probably had political contacts there. He began work as a researcher, agronomist and economist, but he soon moved over into full–time party work. By his thirty–fifth birthday, he was Stavropol party chief; four years later, he had become the party chief of the entire region.

Gorbachëv was brought to Moscow in 1978 to become a member of the Central Committee Secretariat with responsibility for agriculture. A year later, he was made a candidate member of the Politburo; in 1980 he became a full member.

When Andropov became General Secretary in 1982, he apparently began grooming Gorbachëv as a possible successor. The first evidence of this came in May 1983 when Gorbachëv made a visit to

Canada. This was his first official trip outside the Communist Bloc and he acquitted himself very well. A trip to England in December 1984 was equally successful. Domestically, Gorbachëv had been in charge of the Secretariat since at least October 1984. By March 1985, it was clear that Gorbachëv was well-qualified to handle the General Secretary position.

In making his acceptance speech at the CPSU Central Committee meeting on March 11, 1985, Gorbachëv broke no new ground but he did make a number of points which gave some indication of his thinking. First of all, he referred to "enhancing the independence of enterprises, raising their interest in the end product of their work." This implied a commitment to greater economic reform. Second, he made the assertion "we want a real and major reduction of the arms stockpiles." Although again somewhat vague, it appeared to be a commitment to pursue arms reductions talks with the United States with a definite goal in mind rather than simply exploring areas of disagreement.

### Manipulation of the Politburo

The first order of business of the new leader was to consolidate his power base. He began the process a little over a month later, on April 23, at a special session of the Central Committee. Three men, all obviously Gorbachëv allies, were promoted to full membership on the Politburo and one other individual was made a candidate member. The elevation of Viktor Chebrikov, the KGB chairman—who was already a candidate member—came as no surprise. But the promotions of Yegor Ligachëv and Nikolai Ryzhkov were different, because both were elevated to full membership without having to go through the intermediate step of candidate member. Moreover, both worked in the Secretariat under Gorbachëv and were closely tied to him personally. The other promotion, that of Minister of War Sokolov to non–voting candidate membership, was probably an effort to appease the "old guard" and military at the same time. Sokolov, already 74, was viewed at the time as an interim appointee.

The April 1985 changes gave Gorbachëv a firm majority and he used it to begin remaking the Politburo and the government. At the regular plenary session of the Central Committee on July 1, 1985, Georgi Romanov—another of Gorbachëv's rivals for the position of General Secretary—was retired from the Politburo "on health grounds." His Politburo seat went to Eduard Shevardnadze, First Secretary for the Georgian Republic. Gorbachëv's promotion and Romanov's retirement had also created two vacancies in the Secretariat and these were filled by Boris Yeltsin and Lev Zaikov.

Some additional reasons for the changes

became evident the next day when the Supreme Soviet met. One of its tasks was the selection of a new Chairman of the Presidium (often referred to in the West as the Soviet President), vacant since the death of Chernenko. It had been thought that Gorbachëv would assume this position but, in a switch, he announced that, having been requested to devote all of his time to Party affairs, he was nominating Andrei Gromyko to the position. He then added that Eduard Shevardnadze would replace Gromyko as Minister of Foreign Affairs. Gromyko thus got the honor of becoming head of state, while Gorbachëv got a new Minister of Foreign Affairs, untainted by any connection with previous Soviet foreign policies.

When he took over his new job, Shevardnadze was totally without experience in foreign affairs. He did have a reputation for being honest and hard–working, however, and had, it was said, waged an energetic and effective campaign against corruption and laziness in his native Georgia. Shevardnadze's appointment suggested that Gorbachëv intended to have the principal voice in foreign affairs. That indeed proved to be the case, although Shevardnadze earned high marks during his tenure as Foreign Minister.

Gorbachëv continued his rebuilding in the fall of 1985. In September, Nikolai Tikhonov stepped down as Chairman of the Council of Ministers and was replaced by Nikolai Ryzhkov. A Gorbachëv ally now occupied the office responsible for implementing economic reforms approved by the Politburo.

Additional changes occurred in October when Tikhonov retired from the Politburo and Nikolai Talyzin became a candidate member. Talyzin, a telecommunications specialist, became head of GOSPLAN at the same time. Now an individual closely associated with Gorbachëv was also in charge of economic planning. The move was particularly significant, since Gorbachëv had already rejected the draft Five Year Plan drawn up by Nikolai Baibakov, the man whom Talyzin replaced at GOSPLAN. But Talyzin proved to be the wrong choice. At the mid–1987 meeting of the Central Committee, he was singled out for criticism by Gorbachëv for failure to embark upon economic change with sufficient rapidity. Somewhat later, he was replaced at GOSPLAN and named Permanent Representative to the Council for Mutual Economic Assistance.

Economic leadership changes were particularly important to Gorbachëv. As he made clear at the 27th Party Congress in February 1986, the Soviet leader intended an economic transformation of his country and was well aware of the human factor in any such transformation. This almost certainly is why he forced the resignation of the relatively young Georgi Romanov, an economic specialist, but also

a conservative on programs of economic reform. Tikhonov, 81, and Baibakov, 75, on the other hand, were probably replaced primarily because of advanced age.

Having promoted four of his allies to the Politburo within six months of becoming General Secretary and accepted the resignation of two others, it is clear that Gorbachëv had carried out a rapid transformation of this ruling body. As it turned out, however, the transformation was not complete. In January 1986, Viktor Grishin resigned his Politburo seat and simultaneously turned over his position as Moscow City First Secretary to Boris Yeltsin. One

month later, a number of other personnel changes were announced. Lev Zaikov became a full member of the Politburo while Boris Yeltsin and Nikolai Slyunkov became candidate members. Two candidate members, Boris Ponomarev, 81, and Vasily Kuznetsov, 85, were edged into retirement.

There were also two interesting additions to the Secretariat at this time. The first of these was Anatoli Dobrynin, who had served as Soviet Ambassador to the United States since 1962. Gorbachëv, probably hoping to make use of his extensive personal knowledge of the United States,

**Gorbachëv speaks at the Kremlin's Palace of Congresses**

appointed a new ambassador to replace him in Washington and added him to the Secretariat. The second addition was Alexandra Biryukova, who thus became the highest ranking woman in the Soviet Communist Party. Biryukova, whose background was that of a national trade union leader, had been a member of the Central Committee since the early 1970's, but this marked her transition to full–time party work.

Gorbachëv's extensive changes since becoming General Secretary placed a new generation of leadership in power in the Soviet Union. At the 27th Party Congress in February 1986, this new leadership committed the Soviet Union to a Five Year and a Fifteen Year Plan whose goal was to triple the rate of productivity growth by the year 2000 and at the same time double living standards. The goals for the five years 1986–91 were less ambitious—basically an increased growth of approximately one percent over what had taken place during the previous five years. As the end of that plan came, it became clear that it had not been achieved.

Gorbachëv's greatest problem was that while the top leadership favored reform, the working level bureaucrats who had to implement any reform remained unconvinced, particularly when it involved the potential loss of their jobs. It was this opposition in both the party and administrative bureaucracy that explained why Gorbachëv began waging a major public relations campaign following the 27th Party Congress designed to generate support for reform, going over the "heads" of the bureaucracy with a direct appeal to the people.

## Glasnost, Perestroika and Democracy

In the process, Gorbachëv introduced three slogans, *glasnost*, *perestroika*, and *democracy*, which came to symbolize for the West what he wanted to accomplish in the Soviet Union. However, none of these words has the same meaning in Russian that they have in the West. For example, we have translated *glasnost* as "openness." The actual root of the word is "voice," thus a more appropriate translation might be "speaking out." That was what Gorbachëv was stating when he used the term—that people who support what he was trying to do should speak out to make their support known. His campaign resulted in a greater openness within Soviet society, but that was a by–product of what he sought to accomplish.

Gorbachëv's second key word, *perestroika*, is usually translated as "restructuring." Again, the translation here is adequate, but also does not really reflect what is understood by the term within the Soviet Union. When Gorbachëv first used the term, he meant it in the purely economic sense of reorganizing economic activity to make it more productive. At that point, the principles associated with it were "socialist" and "self–financing." But later people began applying it to all aspects of the society, speaking of the restructuring of science, the media or even politics. Thus it became a synonym for general societal change.

*Democracy*, Gorbachëv's third slogan, is perhaps the most difficult word to explain in the Soviet context. At least in the beginning, it did not mean democracy in the sense of political democracy and it was not meant to challenge the monopoly of the *Communist Party of the Soviet Union* as the directing agent of Soviet society. Yet Gorbachëv did mean greater popular participation in decision making at the local and possibly even up to the Republic level. Partly, this was once again an attempt to mobilize popular support behind his reform program, but it was also an attempt to give the people a feeling that they had a real stake in their country's future. Because more than one candidate was to be nominated for each position, it also gave the people somewhat more control at the local level and moved toward something like genuine democracy.

## Additional Politburo and Leadership Changes

This campaign was accompanied by changes in the Politburo related to Gorbachëv's campaign for reform. The first such change came in December 1986, when Dinmukhamed Kunaev was dismissed as First Secretary for Kazakhstan. Accused of corruption, he lost his Politburo seat in January 1987. Kunaev may have been corrupt for it was the policy of the Brezhnev regime to co–opt non–Slavic leaders by not paying too much attention to what they did within their own jurisdictions (including thievery) so long as they remained loyal supporters of Mos-

**The legendary summer palace—*Tsarskoe Selo* ("The Tsar's Village"), 15 miles south of Leningrad**

cow's policies nationally. On the other hand, he was dismissed primarily because he was an oldline conservative unable to adjust to Gorbachëv's new technocratic vision.

But Gorbachëv's decision to put his own man in charge backfired in this case. When word reached Alma Ata, the Kazakh capital, that Kunaev had been dismissed and that he was being replaced by Gennady Kolbin, an ethnic Russian, violent rioting broke out and several persons were killed. Kolbin's appointment violated a long–standing tradition that the first secretary of a republic always represented the dominant ethnic group (i.e., in this case, the Kazakhs). Kolbin was later reassigned and a Kazakh was appointed First Secretary in his place.

The next changes came at a plenary session of the Central Committee on June 26, 1987. Three men, Aleksandr N. Yakovlev, Nikolai Slyunkov and Victor Nikonov, were added to the Politburo, while Dmitri Yazov, the new Defense Minister, became a candidate member. Yakovlev, who had served for a number of years as Ambassador to Canada, quickly established himself as a strong voice for reform. Nikonov, a member of the Secretariat, had picked up the agriculture portfolio from Gorbachëv when he became General Secretary. Slyunkov, who had been First Secretary of the Republic of Byelorussia, was considered to be a protege of Ryzhkov's.

These additions to the Politburo must have strengthened Gorbachëv politically, even though two stalwarts of the Brezhnev era, Geidar Aliyev and Vladimir Shcherbitsky, retained their positions.

Geidar Aliyev announced his resignation three months later, in October, ostensibly because of ill health. Although there were some rumors earlier that Aliyev had suffered a heart attack, it is still not clear whether Aliyev left voluntarily or was pushed out. What was significant, however, is that Aliyev was the last Central Asian on the Politburo and his departure left Foreign Minister Shevardnadze as the sole non–Slav on the ruling body.

If Aliyev's departure may have been voluntary, the dismissal, in the same month, of Boris Yeltsin as First Secretary for Moscow was clearly not. His dismissal, after a speech criticizing the pace of reform, came as something of a shock because he had been closely associated with Gorbachëv up to that time. His "crime" was apparently that he favored a more confrontational approach with the bureaucracy than Gorbachëv and wanted to force the pace of reform even against growing opposition. He was subsequently accused of holding the "political illusion" that reform "could be achieved through vigorous and honest guidance from above alone, that is, by using 'purified' but still high–handed methods."

It appears that Yeltsin fell victim to an emerging split in the top leadership ranks over the issue of how quickly economic reform should be implemented. Everyone in the top leadership accepted the necessity of economic reform but several wanted the reform to be as narrow and technical as possible. At this time, Ligachëv, Chebrikov and Yazov were the most outspoken exponents of this point of view. All three publicly criticized aspects of the reform. Gorbachëv obviously felt that he needed their general support, however, and when Yeltsin took a confrontational position and attacked Ligachëv and others, Gorbachëv abandoned him and he lost his leadership position in the party.

Even though Yeltsin was subsequently made First Deputy Chairman of the State Construction Committee, meaning that he was not totally disgraced, his dismissal had a chilling effect on the more outspoken reformers. In February 1988, Yeltsin lost his seat as an alternate member of the Politburo, though he retained his membership on the Central Committee.

However, the same Central Committee meeting that dropped Yeltsin also added two persons as alternate members of the Politburo. They were Yuri Maslyukov, 50, a defense expert, and Georgi Razumovsky, 52, an agricultural expert. Maslyukov subsequently replaced Nikolai Talyzin as head of GOSPLAN. Razumovsky, who was supposed to have close ties to Gorbachëv, became a member of the Secretariat with responsibility for personnel.

### And a New Definition of Democracy

The next event of significance in 1988 was the 19th All–Union CPSU Conference, which met in Moscow on June 28–July 1. Gorbachëv, who presided over the conference, encouraged an atmosphere of open expression and, occasionally, debate among the delegates. The delegates eventually voted to accept six resolutions, the most important of which called for "Democratization of Soviet Society and the Reform of the Political System."

The resolution provided only a bare outline of a new political system, but it did put the party on record as favoring a restructuring of the political system. Not everyone was happy with the resolutions, however. In August, two Politburo members, Yegor Ligachëv and Viktor Chebrikov, gave speeches critical of the direction Gorbachëv was taking the party.

Gorbachëv responded by calling a meeting of the Central Committee which met at the end of September. The meeting led to a major reshuffle within the top leadership, several retirements, and some promotions. Among those retired were Andrei Gromyko, who also stepped down as Chairman of the Presidium of the Supreme Soviet (informally, President), and Mikhail Solomentsev. Vladimir Dolgikh, and Pyotr Demichev, who had been alternate members of the Politburo, were retired at the

Boris Yeltsin

same time. The meeting also nominated Gorbachëv as Gromyko's successor as Chairman of the Presidium of the Supreme Soviet, and this was subsequently confirmed by the Supreme Soviet.

Yegor Ligachëv retained his seat on the Politburo, but he lost his position as chief ideologist and his informal position as Second Secretary, by virtue of which he had chaired meetings of the Secretariat. He gained the title of Chairman of the Agricultural Commission. Chebrikov was removed as head of the KGB and made Chairman of the Legal Affairs Commission. Both moves were considered to be demotions.

Vadim Medvedev, considered to be an ally of Gorbachëv, was added to the Politburo and made chief ideologist. His official title was Chairman of the Ideological Commission. In addition, Alexandra Biryukova, Aleksandr Vlasov, and Anatoly Lukyanov were made alternate members of the Politburo. Biryukova thus became the first woman on the Politburo since the Khrushchev era.

In yet another change, Anatoli Dobrynin was relieved of his duties as secretary of the Central Committee and sent into honorable retirement. Increasingly, Gorbachëv's chief adviser on relations with the United States would be Aleksandr Yakovlev.

Although these personnel shifts helped Gorbachëv to further consolidate his power, structural changes adopted at the same time may have an even more important long–term significance. Essentially, the Central Committee voted to abolish the old Secretariat in the form in which it had previously existed—that is, as a body charged with implementing Politburo de-

The *das* have it: Gromyko is voted out as Chairman of the Presidium of the Supreme Soviet. He sits dejected while Ryzhkov and Gorbachev vote "yes".

cisions. Instead, secretaries of the Central Committee were appointed as chairmen of six newly created commissions. In addition to those mentioned above, commissions were created for Party Building and Cadre Policy (Razumovsky), Socioeconomic Policy (Slyunkov), and International Policy (Yakovlev).

The secretaries thus became responsible for longer–term policy planning, while shorter–term decisions became the prerogative of persons occupying state positions. The obvious purpose of the change was to remove the party from the day–to–day supervision of affairs and to have it concentrate on matters of broad policy. Similar instructions—that is, to stop interfering in the day–to–day affairs of the Soviets and the economy—were sent out to party secretaries at subordinate levels at this same time. The continuing evidence indicated that it had little effect on how party secretaries operated, however.

### A Legislature?

The party had, in fact, long decided everything. If it were to be restricted to long–term planning, then a power vacuum would be created unless the governmental institutions were strengthened. This was the thrust of the reorganization plan which Gorbachëv submitted to the Supreme Soviet in late November. An elaboration of the outline approved by the party conference in June, it created a 2,250-member Congress of People's Deputies, to be elected on the basis of a competitive ballot. The new Congress, when it met, would elect a Chairman of the U.S.S.R. Supreme Soviet (informally, President), plus a two chamber standing legislature, the U.S.S.R. Supreme Soviet.

In effect, Gorbachëv had redesigned the political system to allow for at least a partial transfer of power from the *Communist Party* to popularly elected legislative bodies. In addition, by creating strong executive ties to the new legislative bodies, he had partially freed himself from having to consult constantly with other members of the Politburo.

Elections to the Congress of People's Deputies took place on March 26, 1989, with the most interesting part being the campaign that preceded the actual election. Every candidate had to present an election platform, so the voters were able to choose between candidates based on issues. Most seats were contested. Of 1500 seats, only 384 had a single candidate; the rest had two or more. Seven hundred and fifty other seats were filled by various officially recognized organizations, including 100 filled by the *Communist Party*. But, although only this small number were elected directly by the *Communist Party*, it is significant that 82% of all the candidates were members of the *Communist Party* and the party endorsed candidates in most of the districts.

Approximately 80% of those endorsed by the party won. The party was, therefore, in no way repudiated. However, a number of individuals who, a few years ago, were considered to be dissidents were among the winners. These included Andrei Sakharov and historian and writer Roy Medvedev. A third individual who won running against a candidate endorsed by the party was none other than Boris Yeltsin, who got almost 90% of the vote in a Moscow at–large seat. There were also some prominent losers. The highest ranking of those was Yuri Solovyev, First Secretary for the Leningrad area, who failed to muster 50% of the vote, even though he was running unopposed. As a result, he eventually lost both his position as First Secretary and his seat on the Politburo.

The new Congress was scheduled to convene at the end of May but, before that occurred, Gorbachëv called a meeting of the Central Committee at the end of April and asked for the retirement of 110 people, or approximately one–third of the membership of that body. In turn, 24 persons were added to the Central Committee. In one sense, this was not a purge, however, as most of those who were retired from the Committee had already retired from the jobs that had earned them entry to the Central Committee in the first place. As one official associated with Gorbachëv expressed it, since there was to be a genuine working legislative body for the first time, Gorbachëv needed a Central Committee which was also made up of currently active individuals.

The Congress, when it did meet, proved to be lively but, ultimately, Gorbachëv dominated the session. The Congress first grilled Gorbachëv, then proceeded to elect him Chairman of the U.S.S.R. Supreme Soviet (informally, President). The new U.S.S.R. Supreme Soviet, the smaller, standing legislature, was then elected, and remained in session over the summer.

Although Gorbachëv set the agenda and tended to dominate discussions, it established itself as a genuine independent voice and a valuable forum. The second session showed itself to be even more independent and less subject to Gorbachëv's control.

Gorbachëv's greatest problem was to find groups who were not only loyal but were also committed to his programs. Again and again he made it clear that commitment to his goals came even before loyalty. This was shown once again in 1989, when he directed another major reshuffle. Three members of the Politburo, Viktor Nikonov, Viktor Chebrikov and Vladimir Scherbitsky, were "relieved of their duties" as Politburo members. They were joined in retirement by two alternate members, Yuriy Solovyev and Nikolay Talyzin.

Shcherbitsky was the last remaining member of the old Brezhnev Politburo (except for Gorbachëv) and his dismissal had been long predicted. Chebrikov, Nikonov, Solovyev and Talyzin, on the other hand, were early allies of Gorbachëv who had shown a general lack of commitment to reform.

The additions were equally telling. Vladimir Kryuchkov, head of the KGB, and Yuriy Maslyukov, head of GOSPLAN, had both been early Gorbechëv supporters. Their promotion to full membership appeared to give Gorbachëv two strong allies on the Politburo. The two new alternate members, Yevgeniy Primakov and Boris Pugo, were also viewed as Gorbachëv loyalists though they later would turn on him. Primakov, chairman of the Council of the Union of the U.S.S.R. Supreme Soviet, was also an academician of the U.S.S.R. Academy of Sciences with a doctorate in economics. Pugo, chairman of the Party Control Commission, and a former head of the Latvian Communist Party, was also a deputy of Latvia's Supreme Soviet.

## Nationality Problems

The major agenda topic at the Central Committee Plenum at which these political changes were made was nationality policy. The *Communist Party* had always boasted that it had solved the nationality problems in the U.S.S.R. but, in fact, the problems were merely suppressed.

Gorbachëv's policies, which among other things encouraged people to get involved and to demand reform, and which also tolerated the creation of unofficial groups and promised economic autonomy to the individual republics, had led to the creation of national fronts in nearly every republic and other groups organized along ethnic or nationality lines whose function was to air grievances and demand redress. In the Caucasus region, this had eventually led to a state of virtual war between Armenia and Azeribaijan over the mixed area called Nagorno–Karabakh and autonomy movements in the Baltic republics, in Moldavia, and within Western Ukraine (where the Ukrainian Catholic Church is predominant).

At the Central Committee Plenum, Gorbachëv, arguing that "the need for profound changes is long overdue in ethnic relations," promised a new federation under which "the right of each ethnic group to enjoy all the fruits of sovereignty and to decide all issues of its development—economic, political, and cultural," would be guaranteed.

Although Gorbachëv's position was endorsed by the Central Committee Plenum, the subsequent collapse of communist governments throughout Eastern Europe in the last three months of 1989—even though in one sense orchestrated by Gorbachëv—changed the equation and brought calls for greater change.

## A Distressed Economy

In addition, the domestic economic situation had been deteriorating for some time and this added to the pressures as shortages of consumer goods continued to grow worse, producing greater public dissatisfaction. Reform–spirited communists, now organized into the *Democratic* Platform, threatened to split the party unless they got their way. Conservatives, on the other hand, reacted by urging a slowing down in the pace of reform.

In December, Nikolai Ryzhkov, Chairman of the USSR Council of Ministers, brought in a new draft five–year plan that represented a clear retreat from economic change. It looked like the planners would remain in charge for another five years.

As had become his practice, it was at this moment that Gorbachëv opted for more political reform. First of all, he accepted the idea of a multi–party system and formally proposed that the constitutioin be changed to delete the *Communist Party's* leading position. This was accomplished in January–March 1990.

Next he proposed that, under the new circumstances, what the Soviet Union needed was an executive President, able to take action in an emergency without consultations with other bodies such as the Presidium of the Supreme Soviet.

This led, in March, to creation of the office of President of the U.S.S.R., to which Gorbachëv was subsequently elected. It also led to creation of a Presidential Council, which appears to have been an attempt to create a Soviet version of a National Security Council or, possibly, a "super cabinet." Its membership, originally 16, included the foreign, interior, and defense ministers, the head of the KGB, other government and party officials, plus two prominent writers, Valentin Rasputin and Chingiz Aitmatov. In addition, the Chairman of the Council of Ministers sat as an ex–officio member. It didn't work out and was later disbanded.

The first challenge which the new President had to handle came from Lithuania. Following multiparty elections which were won by *Sajudis*, the Lithuanian national front, the Lithuanian legislature installed Vytautas Landsbergis as President and passed a declaration of independence. Similar declarations were adopted by Latvia and Estonia, although in a somewhat different form. Gorbachëv condemned all three as illegal and initiated a partial economic blockade of Lithuania. He then offered that, if the three republics suspended their declarations, talks leading to independence within two years could begin.

Gorbachëv also said that he would not use force against the would–be breakaway republics. Since he was scheduled to meet with President Bush on May 30, that obviously acted as a restraint on his actions. Although President Bush raised the subject, he apparently did not press it with vigor. The United States found itself in an awkward position at this time. The three republics had been incorporated into the Soviet Union as a result of the Nazi–Soviet Non–Aggression Pact signed in August 1939. In the Pact, Hitler had recognized these nations as being in the Soviet sphere of influence in return for a Soviet promise of neutrality when Hitler invaded Poland.

The United States had never recognized the incorporation of the three republics into the U.S.S.R. and its legal position was that they were still sovereign nations. In fact, embassies of the three republics were still to be found in Washington, D.C. At the same time, the United States favored closer relations with the Soviet Union.

However, the Soviet position articulated by Gorbachëv was even more awkward. Although the Soviet Government had repudiated the Nazi–Soviet Non–Aggression Pact and considered it invalid, it continued to maintain that the three republics were factually a part of the

U.S.S.R. and therefore had to apply for and receive permission to leave.

## Rumblings of Change

Gorbachëv also had other concerns. In the spring of 1990, elections in the Russian, Byelorussian, and Ukrainian republics produced a strong showing for the radical reformers, who won majorities in the largest cities, including Moscow and Leningrad. In Moscow, Gavriil Popov, a member of the Congress of People's Deputies and one of the leaders of the radical inter-regional group in the USSR Supreme Soviet, was elected mayor on the promise to move Moscow quickly toward a market economy.

Perhaps more important, Boris Yeltsin, was elected Chairman of the RSFSR Supreme Soviet (popularly, Russian President) on the third ballot in May. Gorbachëv thus lost control of the all-important Russian Republic.

Essentially, all of this happened because the party had split into three factions, conservatives, Gorbachëv supporters and democrats. The democrats wanted to move more quickly on reforms than Gorbachëv did, and threatened to leave the party and form a new political party if Gorbachëv didn't go along. Gorbachëv, citing the need for party unity, urged them

to stay. The conservatives, on the other hand, urged the democrats to leave.

This was the background to Gorbachëv's other concern, the party congress which was scheduled to take place in late June/early July 1990. Gorbachëv decided to use the party congress to remake the party, getting rid of the Politburo and replacing it with a larger, less powerful Presidium, the majority of whose members would be ex officio—the party chairman and his deputies plus the 15 republic party secretaries. Gorbachëv intended the new Presidium to concentrate on coordinating the activities of the party. Broad policy functions would then become the prerogative of the Soviet Government.

The draft made no mention of the office of General Secretary but it did specify that there would continue to be a secretariat. The leader of the party would be the "chairman," and he was to be elected by the party congress as was the case under Lenin.

The draft was modified at the Party Congress but Gorbachëv got most of what he wanted. The office of General Secretary was retained, but he was elected by the party congress. The Politburo was retained, but its membership and function were modified as Gorbachëv desired.

The delegates also adopted a document

called "Toward Humane, Democratic Socialism." Although the word socialism is in its title, the document actually moved the party a long way toward a rejection of what traditionally has been understood as Marxism–Leninism. Instead, the document spoke of the ideology of the party being based on "the legacy of Marx, Engels and Lenin, freed from dogmatic interpretation."

This document broke with traditional ideology in two basic ways. Socialism, it declared, should be based on individual, not collective, interests; and "private ownership . . . must have a place in the system of forms of ownership" of equal validity with collective ownership. What this meant is that the *Communist Party* was now claiming to represent the interests of Soviet citizens as individuals, not as members of a class or socio-economic grouping. Thus Marx's entire class-based analysis was discarded. And granting private property equal status with collective property flaunted Marx's premise that ownership of the means of production provided the basis for exploitation of man by man. In ideological terms, this programmatic statement moved the *Communist Party* a long distance from Marxist-Leninist orthodoxy. It could still claim to be a socialist party, of course.

**Just weeks before his dream collapses, a giant portrait of Lenin, father of modern communism, rises in front of KGB headquarters in Moscow.**
Photo by Steve Raymer © National Geographic Society

Two other issues preoccupied Gorbachëv in 1990–91, the economy and the negotiation of a new union treaty. The two issues were intricately linked to each other, since one of the demands of the republics was control over economic activity and natural resources. An economic plan that would devolve authority to the republics would go a long way toward meeting this demand.

That is why the Shatalin Plan, which proposed transforming the Soviet Union to a market economy in 500 days, had the support of fourteen of the fifteen republics. Proposed in August 1990 as an alternative to the government's plan to retain the old system of state orders for

**Gavriil Popov**

another 18 months, it even got Gorbachëv's backing for a short while.

But Gorbachëv backed down when Ryzhkov, Chairman of the Council of Ministers, threatened to resign rather than take responsibility for implementing a plan he disagreed with. Gorbachëv then proposed that Ryzhkov take the two approaches and combine them. The result, which turned out to be mainly the Ryzhkov plan, was accepted by the Supreme Soviet in November. As a result, however, nearly every one of Gorbachëv's economic advisers left to work for Boris Yeltsin and the Russian Government.

Gorbachëv did get one good bit of news in October when he learned that he had been awarded the Nobel Peace Prize. Even that could not distract from worry about the economy, however. As Georgi Arbatov, the traditionalist director of the U.S.A. and Canada Institute, commented at the time, "I am sure that he deserves the Peace Prize. I wouldn't think he has deserved the Nobel Prize for economics."

In late 1990, under prodding from the

Supreme Soviet, Gorbachëv changed the organizational structure once more. The Presidential Council and Council of Ministers were abolished and their place was taken by a strengthened Council of the Federation (created in March 1990) and a streamlined Cabinet of Ministers. There continued to be a Chairman who headed up the Cabinet, but he was made directly subordinate to Gorbachëv. These provisions were more or less implemented while some other provisions, such as Gorbachëv's suggestion that the Congress of People's Deputies be replaced by a directly elected Supreme Soviet, were not.

Gorbachëv lost his most valuable ally in December 1990 when Foreign Minister Eduard Shevardnadze resigned after charging that the Soviet Union was headed toward a dictatorship. He was replaced by Alexandr Bessmertnykh, whose previous position had been Soviet ambassador to Washington. After his resignation, Shevardnadze became head of a new independent foreign policy research institute, the Soviet Foreign Policy Association.

Gorbachëv lost a second adviser in December when Nikolai Ryzhkov suffered a heart attack and resigned as Chairman of the newly created Cabinet of Ministers. He was replaced by Valentin Pavlov, who had been Ryzhkov's Finance Minister. A conservative, Pavlov's first major action was to attempt to reduce the money overhang by a partial repudiation of the currency. All 50 and 100 ruble notes were withdrawn from circulation, with individuals given three days to redeem a limited amount related to monthly salary. Pavlov's overall economic program was a continuation of the Ryzhkov program. Gorbachëv also dismayed many people when he appointed Gennadi Yanayev, a Communist Party bureaucrat, as his Vice President.

The Baltic Republics became the center of attention once again in January 1991, when Ministry of the Interior troops stormed the Lithuanian press center and a building occupied by the Lithuanian civilian militia on January 13, killing 14 persons. Gorbachëv's role in all this was ambivalent. He did not repudiate the attack, but claimed to have found out about it only after it happened. The following weekend, five more persons were killed when Ministry of Interior troops seized the Latvian Ministry of Interior building.

The European Parliament then moved to block $1 billion in food aid to the Soviet Union, and a number of European nations began threatening other sanctions. In Washington, the Bush administration began discussing postponement of an upcoming summit meeting, which was in fact postponed, though publicly it was because of the Iraq conflict. Responding to this international pressure, Gorbachëv backed down in early February and

agreed to appoint a commission to consult with the Baltic Republics about their demands for independence.

Gorbachëv's great concern was the national referendum on the question of the future of the USSR which was scheduled for March 17, 1991. The question asked of the Soviet people was whether they considered it "necessary to preserve the Union of Soviet Socialist Republics as a renewed federation of equal sovereign republics, in which human rights and the freedoms of all nationalities will be fully guaranteed?"

Six republics refused to participate in the referendum, and four other republics modified the question in some way. Gorbachëv nevertheless claimed a victory on the basis of the 76% who voted "yes" among those who participated.

The next month, Gorbachëv and the heads of the nine republics who had participated in the referendum announced their agreement on an outline for a new union treaty that would create a Union of Sovereign Soviet Republics. The draft called for a great deal of decentralization, particularly in the economic area, plus a remaking of the national government, including new elections for a national legislature and President. In early May, Gorbachëv agreed to turn coal mines over to the Russian Government as part of a deal to end a miners' strike.

Later in the month, Gorbachëv also endorsed a new plan for economic reform drawn up by Grigory Yavlinsky, who had also contributed to the Shatalin Plan. This new plan called for significant international economic assistance to act as a "shock absorber of social costs and shocks" as the Soviet Union moved to a market economy.

Events tumbled on at a faster and faster rate. In May–June there was a resolution of differences over the CFE Treaty and a new immigration law was passed by the Supreme Soviet. It was announced that President Bush would travel to Moscow for a Summit meeting sometime during the summer. And, in a new test of public opinion, Boris Yeltsin won 60% of the popular vote in his run for the newly created office of President of the Russian Federation. The official communist candidate came in a dismal third. Gorbachëv, reversing his previous position, warmly embraced Yeltsin's victory.

Communist conservatives, evidently alarmed by this development, began to plot a "constitutional *coup*" against Gorbachëv in late June. It took the form of a request by Premier Pavlov that the Supreme Soviet transfer from Gorbachëv to him the power to rule by decree. The President, Pavlov explained, was "overworked." Pavlov's request was supported by Defense Minister Yazov, KGB Chairman Vladimir Kryuchkov and Minister of Interior Boris Pugo.

**The Supreme Soviet of the USSR discussing problems of stabilizing the national economy and transition to a market system, October 1990.**

The attempt failed. Forewarned of Pavlov's attempt to strip away some of his powers, Gorbachëv counterattacked and defeated the move. In the process, however, Gorbachëv did two things that he would later rue. He permitted all four of his treasonous subordinates to retain their positions of power, while he attacked their political arguments. He told these four representatives of the military–industrial complex that the Soviet Union was over-militarized and that "we have to remove this burden and turn the economy over to the people. Otherwise my mission will be useless and I will have to resign."

Gorbachëv had a busy summer. In July, he traveled to London to meet with the "Group of Seven" (USA, Great Britain, Canada, Germany, France, Italy and Japan). His purpose in requesting the meeting was to try to get a promise of economic assistance. He basically used the Yavlinsky Plan as the basis of his discussions. He got no promises of cash, though the Group did offer the Soviet Union some technical assistance and a "special associate status" with the IMF and World Bank.

President Bush came to Moscow at the end of July. The summit meeting included two days of discussions and a ceremonial signing of the completed START agreement. Gorbachëv then left for a vacation in the Crimea with his family.

He planned to return to Moscow on August 19 since, the following day, he and the leaders of nine of the republics were to sign a new union treaty that conceded significant powers to the individual republics. Instead, Gorbachëv was placed under house arrest on the evening of August 18. The next day, the world learned that a *coup d'etat* had been launched by conservative communists in the top echelons of government—their goal to preserve the Soviet Union and the communist system. Among the top leaders were Pavlov, Yazov, Kryuchkov, and Pugo, the four participants in the attempted "constitutional *coup*" against Gorbachëv in late June. They were joined this time by Vice President Gennadi Yanayev. These five, plus three other conservatives, took control as the "State Committee for the State of Emergency."

The *coup* lasted approximately 60 hours and eventually failed, thanks primarily to Boris Yeltsin and supporters of reform and democracy throughout the country. But the complicity of the Communist Party in the *coup* was so great that there were few objections when Boris Yeltsin, on the morning after the *coup* was defeated, banned Communist Party activities in the Russian Republic. Two days later, Gorbachëv resigned as General Secretary and called upon the Central Committee to dissolve itself. He then issued a decree suspending the activities of the party and seizing all party property. After 74 years, the Communist Era had come to an end.

## FOREIGN POLICY UNDER GORBACHËV

Soviet foreign policy had been changing since 1985, not only with regard to the United States, but also with regard to the Third World and Eastern Europe. Soviet support for a settlement in southern Africa led to an agreement to pull Cuban troops out of Angola. It was also Soviet pressure on Vietnam that caused that country to pull its troops out of Cambodia. It also eventually halted the shipment of military equipment to Nicaragua and then tacitly supported the free elections that resulted in a non–Communist government coming to power there in April 1990.

When Iraq invaded Kuwait, Gorbachëv gave his support to the various UN Security Council resolutions demanding that Iraq pull out of Kuwait and then those authorizing the use of force against Iraq, even though Iraq had been a long–time ally of the Soviet Union. Gorbachëv also presided over the demise of the CMEA and the Warsaw Pact, thus formally dissolving the ties that bound the various countries of Eastern Europe to the Soviet Union. And, of course, he presided over a series of military negotiations that helped to bring an end to the Cold War.

## Changing Relations with Eastern Europe under Gorbachëv

The pattern of foreign relations established by Stalin with Eastern Europe after World War II was one of almost total subordination on the part of the communist leaderships of those countries, exemplified after 1948 by Stalin's campaign to remove from office those communist leaders who showed any independence whatsoever. During this period, Soviet ambassadors acted as virtual proconsuls, whose orders had the force of law.

Poland's Wladyslaw Gomulka, one of those who resisted and, as a result, was purged, described this phenomenon:

"In this bloc of socialist states, it was Stalin who stood at the apex of this hierarchic ladder of cults. All those who stood on lower rungs of the ladder bowed their heads before him. . . . The first secretaries of the central committees of the parties of the various countries who sat on the second rung of the ladder of the cult of personality, in turn donned the robes of infallibility and wisdom."

**Soviet–East European relations were thus, for Stalin, an extension of domestic Soviet politics.**

All of that began to change after Stalin's death. The new Soviet leadership, which had been subject to the same treatment during Stalin's lifetime, committed itself to a "New Course" in intrabloc relations. Modifying the previous relationship, they allowed Eastern European leaders greater independence and encouraged them to develop policies designed to win them

greater popularity among their people. This was, they concluded, the best way to ensure the long-term success of communism in Eastern Europe.

There were limitations to this independence, of course. All were required to join the Warsaw Pact when it was established in 1955 and even Khrushchëv, chief spokesman for this viewpoint, didn't hesitate to intervene militarily in Hungary in 1956, when the communist leadership there began to lose control. Khrushchëv's decision to allow Gomulka to take power in Poland in 1956 was another part of this loosening of control.

Khrushchëv sought to further integrate the Soviet and East European economies, but he permitted Romania to opt out when that country opposed the international division of labor proposed by the Soviet Union. Khrushchëv also did nothing when, in April 1964, Romania claimed

Soviet President Mikhail Gorbachëv joins the Group of Seven leaders in London. First row (l. to r.) President Bush, Gorbachëv, British Prime Minister Major, French President Mitterrand, German Chancellor Kohl. Second row: EC President Jacques Delors, Italian Prime Minister Andreotti, Canadian Prime Minister Mulroney, Japanese Prime Minister Kaifu, Dutch Prime Minister Lubbers.

Reuters/Bettmann

**President–Elect Bush, President Reagan and General Secretary Gorbachëv check out their "where to stand" marks for a photo–taking session at Governor's Island, NY., December 7, 1988.**

AP/Wide World Photo

the right to develop its own policies. Romania would later go on to develop its own, independent foreign policy, though it always remained an orthodox communist society domestically.

Brezhnev intervened in Czechoslovakia in 1968 when that country's communist party moved to give up its monopoly of political power. He also put strong pressure on the Polish communist leadership to reverse its decision legalizing the independent trade union *Solidarity* in 1981. But he quietly permitted Hungary to implement ever more far–reaching economic reforms without interference. Gorbachëv's attitude toward Eastern Europe when he became General Secretary in 1985 appeared to be relatively orthodox, though from the beginning he tended to treat individual communist leaders as though he considered them partners in a common enterprise. His first plans for economic re-

form relied heavily on Eastern Europe as a source of new technology and he confidently expected them to join him in implementing similar reforms in their own countries. The Soviet Union already got many of the more sophisticated products that it imported, such as computers, computer software and machine tools, from Eastern Europe, and he expected that they would want to upgrade their technology and become a source of ever more sophisticated technology.

He was disappointed by the first response to his reform ideas. Only Hungary, already well along in its own reform program, was enthusiastic. For a while, he attempted to lead by example and by persuasion, speaking of his economic reform and pointing out its advantages on visits to Eastern Europe, but making no effort to coerce communist leaders into adopting the same approach. On the other hand, the

Soviet Union did chide Eastern European leaders for the poor quality of their exports and it put behind the scenes pressure on them to upgrade the quality and technological level of their products, though with little success. Czechoslovakia and the German Democratic Republic, the Eastern European countries with the most developed economies, were both led by conservative leaders who believed that a program of economic reform would undermine their own legitimacy.

Gorbachëv slowly came to realize that the Eastern European countries weren't going to provide the significant assistance in the area of technology that he had been counting on to help him with his own *perestroika*. Their unreformed economies simply weren't up to it. Finland, the only non–communist neighbor, proved to be much more valuable as a source of technology than any of the communist countries of Eastern Europe.

Meanwhile, the Soviet Union was providing Eastern Europe with energy supplies and raw materials below world prices, while receiving shoddy consumer goods and old technology in return. The question Gorbachëv had to ask himself was whether the conservative and unreformed communist leaderships were more of a burden than an asset. Was Finland a better model? A number of articles appeared in the Soviet press at about this time discussing the merits of a "Finlandization" of Eastern Europe.

**The 1989 Revolutions**

Thus we come to the events and decisions of 1989, when communism collapsed nearly everywhere in Eastern Europe. In country after country, ruling communist parties were first forced to compromise with their opponents and then, in most cases, to relinquish part or all of their power to them. Communism, a doctrine imposed from the outside by Soviet armies after the defeat of Nazi Germany, never was popular among the people of Eastern Europe. Yet the communist elites remained in power, partly because they controlled a monopoly of power and partly because they could always count on the support and backing of the Soviet Union, spelled out after 1968 in the "Brezhnev Doctrine."

So no one predicted the events of 1989, precisely because no one expected that the Soviet Union would permit such changes to occur in Eastern Europe. And that points out the most important difference about 1989—that the Soviet Union did not merely acquiesce in these changes; it was, in fact, an active agent in bringing them about. In hindsight, it was predictable. The Soviets had become economically exhausted and their only choice to continue control in Eastern Europe was military, which would have enraged world opinion.

Gorbachëv had several times said things that sounded like a repudiation of the Brezhnev Doctrine after becoming General Secretary, but no one was certain whether he meant it. It was his intervention in Poland in the latter part of 1988 that gave the first indication that he meant what he had said.

After outlawing *Solidarity* in December 1981, General Jaruzelski and the ruling *Polish United Workers' Party* introduced a program of economic reform to remake the Polish economy and to deal with the conditions that had brought *Solidarity* into existence in the first place. That attempt at economic reform from above was unsuccessful and the government, under challenge from the official trade unions, collapsed in September 1988.

It was at this moment that the first indication of a reversal of Soviet policy occurred, in the form of a series of articles in the Soviet press portraying Lech Walesa and *Solidarity* in a favorable manner. This led to formal talks between the Polish Government and *Solidarity* and the now famous April 1989 agreement relegalizing *Solidarity* and setting new elections for June 4.

Those elections provided for only 35% of the seats in the *Sejm* (lower house of parliament) to be freely contested, but did include elections to a new Senate, all of whose seats were competitive. *Solidarity* took 99 out of 100 seats in the Senate, plus all of the open seats in the *Sejm*. In addition, most of the top communist leadership, running unopposed for *Sejm* seats, were rejected because they failed to get 50% of the valid votes. These seats, reserved for communists, were filled in a second round of voting only because *Solidarity* instructed its supporters to endorse the new candidates.

The failure of the communists at the polls meant that they were in practice unable to form a government. Their allies, the *United Peasants' Party* and the *Democratic Party*, refused to support the communist candidate for Chairman of the Council of Ministers and opened discussions with *Solidarity*. This led Lech Walesa to propose a *Solidarity*–led coalition government which would include communists. Now came a second decisive Soviet intervention. After Mieczyslaw Rakowski, the new head of the *Polish United Workers' Party*, announced his opposition to such a coalition, he got a 40 minute telephone call from Gorbachëv, the essence of which was that Gorbachëv expected the Polish party to accept a *Solidarity*–led coalition government.

The psychological effect on the rest of Eastern Europe of the installation of a non–communist government in Poland was enormous; and even more important, it was known that Gorbachëv not only gave his support to the change but actually intervened to help bring it about. This

was seen as making change possible all over Eastern Europe. Surprisingly, Gorbachëv continued to support change in Eastern Europe, even as those changes led to the collapse of communist governments throughout the region.

After Poland, the next development occurred in Hungary, where a reform communist leadership had been installed in May 1988. Over the next year, opposition political parties were legalized and free elections were scheduled. New laws were also passed guaranteeing Hungarians the right to travel abroad and to emigrate. And in March 1989, Hungary signed a United Nations protocol on refugees in which it obligated itself not to force refugees to go back home. In signing the protocol, the Hungarian Government obvi-

ously had in mind Hungarian–speaking Romanians who were infiltrating across the border from Romania. By August 1989, however, tens of thousands of East German citizens had gathered in Hungary, drawn there by Hungary's decision to begin dismantling the barbed wire on its border with Austria. Refusing to return to East Germany, they wanted to go west.

The problem was a treaty that Hungary had signed with the German Democratic Republic in 1968 under which the Hungarian Government promised to obtain clearance from the GDR before permitting GDR citizens to travel from it to a third country, a permission that was not forthcoming. The Hungarian Government now decided to let the East Germans go, but there was some concern about the Soviet

**October 1989: On a stone lion in front of parliament a Hungarian youth hoists the flag of his country—with the hammer and sickle surgically removed.** AP/Wide World Photos

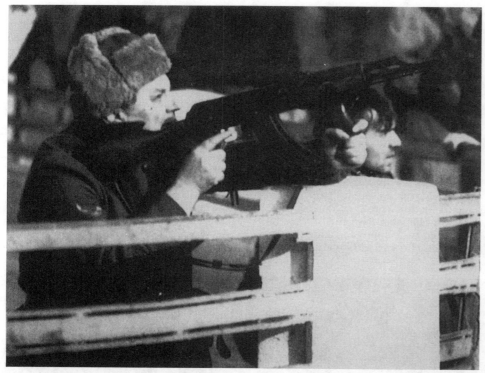

Bucharest, Romania, Christmas Eve 1989. A Romanian soldier points his rifle at enemy positions during street fighting.

AP/Wide World Photos

reaction. When informal sounding established *that the Soviet Government would not object*, Hungary opened the border for the East Germans on September 10.

The third break occurred in the German Democratic Republic, largely as a result of the decision of the Hungarian Government to allow East Germans to depart for the west. After the Hungarian action, other East Germans, unable to obtain visas to Hungary, began traveling in large numbers to Czechoslovakia, where no visa was required. Gathering in Prague, they began to inundate the grounds of the West German Embassy. Here they were given West German passports, but they still needed permission to depart Czechoslovakia for the west. The Czechoslovakian Government, not wanting to be caught in the middle, requested clearance from the GDR Government. The GDR eventually gave in and began arranging for trains to carry its citizens directly to West Germany.

The flight of hundreds of thousands of East Germans began to have repercussions at home, however. Protest demonstrations which were already occurring in a number of East German cities grew in size and number. The most organized of the demonstrations occurred in Leipzig. At first, the regime tried to handle the situation through the use of force. In addition to its usual riot police, it called out special "battle groups" of its party militia and fighting teams of the state security police, equipped with water cannons and armored cars. And on October 3, the East German Government closed its borders with Czechoslovakia.

The matter came to a head on October 9 in Leipzig, when the local party leadership rejected orders from East Berlin to put down demonstrations scheduled for that day and instead called for a dialogue, promising to "use our full power and authority to ensure that this dialogue will occur, not only in the Leipzig area but with our national government."

At the Politburo meeting called to discuss the Leipzig decision, Egon Krenz, the number two man in the party, supported the Leipzig leaders over Erich Honecker's objections. This led to a Central Committee meeting eight days later and to Honecker's ouster as General Secretary on October 18.

Egon Krenz took over as General Secretary and promised reforms. He reopened the borders with Czechoslovakia and promised East Germans 30 days a year travel abroad. The flight through Czechoslovakia immediately resumed. Krenz next gambled that he could stabilize the situation by granting all citizens the right of unrestricted travel to the west, symbolized by the opening of the Berlin Wall on November 9, 1989. He accompanied this with promises of freer elections, economic liberalization, and power–sharing with other parties. Within a week, an estimated one–third of all East Germans had visited either West Berlin or West Germany.

After the initial euphoria, however, the pressure for change continued. On November 17, Hans Modrow, Dresden party chief, who had a reputation as a reformer, became the new head of government. Modrow proposed roundtable discussions with the opposition and these began on December 7.

In the meanwhile, Egon Krenz and the other members of the Politburo submitted their resignations and a caretaker committee was appointed to run the party. At a special party congress that began five days later, Gregor Gysi, an attorney who had made his reputation as a defender of critics of the state and people caught fleeing the country, was appointed the new party leader. The delegates also voted to change the name of the party and to set the goal of the party as "democratic socialism."

At the congress, Hans Modrow spoke in favor of a confederation between the two Germanys. Helmut Kohl, the West German Chancellor, had proposed a ten–point plan for unification in November, but this was the first time that any East German leader had endorsed the concept. Unification received another boost when Chancellor Kohl paid an official visit to East Germany on December 19. Kohl spoke in Dresden to cheering crowds and then he and Modrow joined the mayors of West and East Berlin in a ceremony opening a pedestrian crossing at the Brandenburg Gate.

Reunification was the big issue in the elections on March 18 and they were won by the conservative "Alliance for Germany," led by the GDR *Christian Democratic Union*. On April 12, Lothar de Maizere, leader of the *Christian Democratic Union*, became the first non–communist head of government, leading a "Grand Coalition" of the main non–communist parties, including the *Social Democrats*.

The new government immediately began preparing for German reunification. For a while, Gorbachëv maintained that the Soviet Union would not agree to German unification, unless Germany either suspended its membership in NATO or maintained its membership in the Warsaw Pact as well. After negotiations with the Federal Republic, however, he accepted continued German membership in NATO. An economic, social and currency union went into effect on July 1 and final unification took place on October 3, 1990.

Czechoslovakians had not reacted to the large numbers of East Germans fleeing west by way of their country, but subsequent events in East Germany did lead to the beginning of massive demonstrations in Prague. On November 17, three thousand young people gathered near Wenceslas Square in Central Prague and began demanding free elections. The Government reacted by ordering the police to put down the demonstration by force. It was a fatal mistake. The Czechoslovak people, aroused by the government's brutality, went into the streets in great numbers, singing, chanting, and demanding the ouster of Milos Jakes, the party General Secretary who had approved the police action. It was at this moment that Michael Gorbachëv intervened by sending a message that the Soviet Government would not tolerate violence.

As the demonstrations continued and grew in size, a Central Committee meeting was called for November 24 and Milos Jakes and his entire Presidium resigned. The party had begun to crumble. Prime Minister Ladislav Adamec opened negotiations with the opposition, now organized as the *Civic Forum*. But Adamec, who wanted to retain a communist–dominated government, was forced to resign on December 6. His replacement, Marian Calfa, organized a new government in which the communists were in a minority.

The Czechoslovak parliament was subsequently purged and on December 28 Alexander Dubcek, leader of the 1968 Prague Spring, was elected chairman. The next day, Vaclav Haval, the Czech playwright whose opposition to the previous regime had landed him repeatedly in

prison, was elected President. Czechoslovakia thus had its first non–communist president since 1948. *Civic Forum* won the multiparty elections that took place on June 6, 1990 while the communists were reduced to a tiny remnant.

Change also came to Bulgaria, though in the beginning at least it was engineered to a greater extent from above. On November 9, Todor Zhivkov was forced out as communist party leader and replaced by Petar Mladenov. Zhivkov had been in power for 36 years. Mladenov, who had served as Bulgarian foreign minister for the previous 19 years, immediately instituted a policy of liberalization that soon led to legalization of opposition groups and the beginning of demonstrations in the streets. Broad–based talks began in January between the party and the opposition and a few days later the parliament voted to end the party's monopoly of power. At a hastily called party congress, the party voted to change its name and to become the *Bulgarian Socialist Party*. Mladenov also stepped down as party leader in April, after he had been elected to a new executive Presidency.

Multi–party elections that took place in

June were won by the ex–communists, but they had lost in the cities and the opposition, emboldened by this, continued their attacks on the government. In July, Mladenov was replaced by Zhelyu Zhelev, a leader of the opposition. After continued demonstrations, Dimitar Popov, a non–communist, was appointed Prime Minister. There was never any direct Gorbachëv intervention in the political events occurring in Bulgaria in 1989–90. However, Gorbachëv's responses with regard to events in other parts of Eastern Europe were well known in Bulgaria and undoubtedly were a factor influencing events in Bulgaria as well.

Romania experienced perhaps the greatest change of any country in Eastern Europe in 1989 when Nicolae Ceaucescu, who had ruled the country since 1965, was overthrown in a violent uprising that ended in Ceaucescu's death by firing-squad on December 25. Ceaucescu, who was proud of his independence from Moscow, had rejected Gorbachëv's policy of reform and made every effort to isolate his countrymen from events going on elsewhere in Eastern Europe. In November 1989, he had reaffirmed his policies at a party con-

**November 11, 1989: With the Reichstag in the background, young Germans sit on the Berlin Wall in its final hours.**

Foreign ministers meet in Bonn, West Germany, May 1990. Third from left is Foreign Minister Shevardnadze

gress and had been reelected head of the party for a further five–year term. It was probably this reaffirmation of policies that was responsible for his downfall, for they had been responsible for a significant decline in the standard of living of Romanians over the previous nine years.

The revolt, which actually began as an ethnic dispute in the city of Timisoara, in the western part of Romania, spread to Bucharest, the capital, when Ceausescu called a mass meeting for December 21 to denounce the events in Timisoara. Instead, the people began shouting "freedom" and "democracy" and Ceausescu stalked off. That afternoon, the streets were full of people demonstrating against Ceausescu. That evening, Ceausescu ordered the secret police to begin firing on the people. A similar order to the army brought a refusal from General Milea, the Defense Minister. General Milea was executed the next morning, but the army now joined the revolution. Ceausescu and his wife fled the capital, but they were captured, brought back to Bucharest, and summarily tried and executed.

The *Securitate*, Ceausescu's secret police, fought on for a few days more but the army gradually managed to restore order. In the meantime, a group calling itself the *National Salvation Front* emerged as the new political leadership in the country. The *Front*, at first made up almost exclusively of former establishment figures who had fallen out with Ceausescu, was enlarged within a few days to take in various non–communist elements. It then began referring to itself as the *Council of National Salvation*. In the third week of January, the *Council* announced that multi–party elections would take place in May

and that it intended to run its own candidates. This brought a condemnation from the leaders of the three largest opposition parties. After a series of negotiations, the *Council* agreed to make room for representatives of other parties. On February 1, the *Council* brought the representatives of 29 other political parties into the government coalition.

By this time, it had grown to approximately 180 members. It also underwent a name change and became the *Provisional Council for National Unity*. A new ten member Executive Committee, headed by Acting President Ion Iliescu, also came into existence now. Meanwhile, the original *National Salvation Front* reorganized itself as a political party and announced that it, not the *Council*, would field candidates in the upcoming May 20 elections. As its candidate for President, it nominated Ion Iliescu. Most of the leadership of the *Front* had been members of the old *Romanian Communist Party* and the local branches of the *National Salvation Front*, set up at the time of the revolution, were largely made up of ex–officials. Thus, while the old communist party structure had collapsed, a large percentage of its membership transferred their loyalties to the *National Salvation Front*.

Eventually, some 80 political parties came into existence, though only three of them had any significant political support in the country. Two of these, both parties that were outlawed when the communists took over, are the *Liberals* and the *Peasant Party*. The third, the *Hungarian Democratic Union*, represents the interests of ethnic Hungarians. Although the opposition attacked the *National Salvation Front* because of its high component of ex–communists,

there was, in fact, little to differentiate between them as far as programs were concerned. All were committed to the creation of a multi–party democracy and a market economy.

In the May elections, Ion Iliescu was elected President with approximately 83% of the vote while the *National Salvation Front* took 66% of the seats in the National Assembly. Election observers announced that there had been some irregularities in the voting but that, overall, the election was free.

**An Overview**

The events of 1989 and 1990 transformed eastern Europe and laid the basis for a new relationship with the Soviet Union. In the beginning, all of the new governments promised to remain in the Warsaw Pact and the Council for Mutual Economic Assistance, but the basis for those organizations no longer existed. The CMEA was changing in any case, having agreed to carry on all trade in dollars as of January 1, 1991. This turned out to be so destabilizing that the CMEA effectively ceased to exist after the changeover and was formally dissolved on July 1, 1991. The military aspects of the Warsaw Pact were phased out in April after Hungary had announced that it intended to resign its membership; on July 1, 1991, the Warsaw Pact was also dissolved.

The Soviet Union pulled the last of its troops out of Hungary and Czechoslovakia in June 1991. It also signed an agreement with Germany to withdraw all Soviet troops by 1994 and gave a similar promise to Poland.

The various East European countries had begun to reorient their exports toward hard currency areas and away from the Soviet Union, a process that speeded up after the Soviet Union canceled standing orders with eastern European companies because of an inability to pay for the products in the now required hard currency. In a curious twist, the Economic Community actually helped to recreate some of those ties in 1991 as part of an agreement giving Hungary, Czechoslovakia and Poland associate membership status in the EC. France, concerned about agricultural imports from eastern Europe, persuaded the EC to buy a part of the production from these countries for delivery to the Soviet Union.

**U.S.–Soviet Relations Under Gorbachëv**

In 1985, the overriding factor in U.S.-Soviet relations was the military rivalry between the two superpowers and how it was managed. Arms negotiations had occurred at intervals since the 1960s. There had been the occasional, successful negotiations, but the period 1979–85 was basically one of stalemate. The two sides had continued to talk, but no agreements were reached. Meanwhile, the size of the arsenals continued to grow on both sides. Gorbachёv's first policy speech after becoming General Secretary outlined a traditional Soviet position, but even that speech contained the phrase, "we want a real and major reduction of the arms stockpiles." The sticking point was President Reagan's Strategic Defense Initiative, launched in March 1983.

The SDI was a proposal to use emergent technology to develop a shield to stop incoming missiles, using a combination of laser beams, computers, satellites and radar. SDI promised to reduce the threat of Soviet missiles to the United States. The failure of international negotiations gave it much of its political support, for it promised to achieve unilaterally what could otherwise be achieved only by successful negotiations.

The threat of having its missile force neutralized alarmed the Soviet leadership, and led to a Soviet proposal for talks on space weapons in mid–1984. The first discussions actually took place on March 12, 1985, one day after Gorbachёv succeeded Chernenko as General Secretary. The beginning Soviet position was that the USA cease *research* on development of a SDI system.

Officially, the Soviet opposition to American development of an SDI system was based on the premise that a successful one would give the United States a first strike capability *since it would not have to worry about retaliatory Soviet missiles.* The actual reasons for this opposition were far more complex, but were associated with Soviet weakness in the area of technological innovation and a Soviet recognition that the western world was experiencing a technological revolution in the areas of computers and automation that was leaving the Soviet further and further behind.

This new computer technology had significant military applications and constituted, in fact, the heart of any successful SDI system. The Soviets thus feared SDI for the emerging technology it could produce. There was also the possibility of SDI "spin-offs" which could revolutionize conventional warfare, thus reducing Moscow's huge advantage in this area. (Consider, for example, the effect of a lethal beam effective at a distance of five miles on the vast Soviet tank fleet.) It is no coincidence that Gorbachёv's opposition to SDI internationally was coupled with a domestic program aimed at giving the Soviet Union mastery of advanced technology.

Although arms negotiations talks continued in Geneva, no progress was possible because of the deadlock over SDI. To break this, Reagan and Gorbachёv decided to hold a summit conference in Geneva in November 1985. The talks were relatively cordial, and the two spoke privately for about five hours. There was no breakthrough on SDI, but Gorbachёv did accept an invitation extended by Reagan to visit the United States in 1986.

Negotiations at Geneva continued in 1986. They were serious, and differences were narrowed, but a final agreement still remained beyond their grasp—because of SDI differences. When Gorbachёv, as a consequence, postponed his visit to the United States, it was decided to hold a "pre–summit" in Reykjavik, Iceland. The two leaders met on October 11–12, 1986 for what turned out to be wide–ranging discussion of the entire field of arms control.

No accord was reached, but the astonishing thing is how close they came, considering the topics discussed during that historic weekend. Insofar as intermediate range ballistic missiles stationed in Europe, Gorbachёv agreed to the U.S.-proposed "zero option." On strategic offensive weapons, the two sides agreed to 50% cuts in five years and elimination of *all* such weapons in ten years.

Negotiations with regard to SDI proved to be most intractable, but even here progress in resolving differences was made. Thus, the Soviet position was that each side agree to adhere to the ABM Treaty for ten years; that during this time all SDI testing be confined to the laboratory, and that the two sides negotiate about SDI stationing at the end of ten years. Prior to the summit, the United States had been offering not to withdraw from the ABM Treaty for a term of 7-1/2 years. At Reykjavik the U.S. agreed to adhere to the ABM Treaty for ten years if, during that same time period, strategic nuclear ballistic missiles were reduced to zero.

The two sticking points were the question of confining SDI testing to the laboratory and the question of whether the United States could begin deploying SDI at the end of ten years without further negotiations with the Soviet Union. When agreement could not be reached on these two points, the negotiations fell through, because the Soviet position was that the arms talks proposals were a single package, and agreement on any part of the package depended on acceptance by both sides of the *entire* package.

The first reaction to the Reykjavik summit was one of disappointment, but as both sides began looking back at what *had been accomplished,* the many areas of agreement became clear. In January 1987 the Soviet Union indicated its desire to continue discussions by naming a new chief Soviet negotiator at Vienna, Yuli Vorontsov, who held the rank of First Deputy Foreign Minister.

Because of the lack of breakthrough, Gorbachёv launched a new initiative on February 28. Reversing his position at Reykjavik, he called for urgent negotiation of a separate agreement on intermediate–range nuclear missiles. He accompanied this with the promise that once agreement on intermediate–range missiles was reached, the Soviet Union would withdraw its shorter–range missiles from East Germany and Czechoslovakia. In April, he further modified his proposal by indicating that the Soviet Union would eliminate all shorter–range missiles from Europe as part of an agreement on intermediate–range missiles. He was also quoted by TASS at this time as saying that he was ready to meet Reagan in order to "conclude" a treaty on intermediate–range missiles and to reach agreement on "key provisions" regarding strategic offensive arms, space defense, arms and nuclear tests. Negotiations between the two countries continued over the summer of 1987 but became stalled when the Soviet

**Presidents Gorbachёv and Bush at dinner aboard the Soviet Ship *Gorky*, off Malta, December 1989**

side insisted that West Germany's 72 Pershing 1A missiles (with U.S.–controlled warheads) had to be included in the deal. This obstacle was removed in August when West German Chancellor Kohl agreed conditionally to dismantle the Pershing 1A missiles. It took a visit to Washington by Foreign Minister Shevardnadze in September and a visit of Secretary of State Shultz to Moscow in October, but the result was a draft agreement banning intermediate-range (and Soviet shorter-range) missiles, known as the INF agreement. It was this INF agreement that General Secretary Gorbachëv signed when he made his first visit to the United States on December 8–11, 1987.

The successful conclusion of the INF treaty did not, as it turned out, provide enough momentum for agreement on strategic arms in time for President Reagan's visit to the USSR on May 29–June 2, 1988. As a result, the Moscow summit was largely ceremonial, though not less important for that reason.

Negotiations on strategic arms continued, but no agreement was reached, partly because of the change of American administrations and partly because of the complexity of the subject. There were other major developments in this area, however. The most important of these came in December 1988, when Gorbachëv, during an address to the United Nations General Assembly, announced that the U.S.S.R. would make unilateral cuts of 500,000 troops and 10,000 tanks, with 50,000 troops and 5,000 tanks to be pulled out of Eastern Europe. He also promised that, in addition to the tanks, other equipment used in an attack, including river–bridging equipment would also be withdrawn.

The new Conventional Forces in Europe (CFE) talks—the enlarged version of the old MBFR talks—also began in Vienna in March 1989. The talks went very well from the beginning for it was the Soviet Union which proposed eliminating "imbalances and asymmetries" over a period of two years. Since they had an overwhelming advantage in ground equipment, their proposal meant that the Soviet Union would have to eliminate about 10 tanks for each tank eliminated by NATO.

The Soviet plan also suggested "equal collective ceilings which would be 10 to 15 percent lower than the lowest level possessed by either of the politico–military alliances." The ceiling proposed by NATO had been only slightly higher than this.

Finally, the Soviets also acknowledged the need for "the most stringent and rigorous verification, including inspections without right of refusal," thus meeting yet another of NATO's concerns.

A further significant breakthrough came in May 1989 when Gorbachëv announced that the Warsaw Pact was pre-

pared to withdraw from Eastern Europe 40,000 of 58,470 tanks, 42,000 out of 70,330 armored vehicles and 47,000 out of 71,500 artillery pieces, and finally that it was willing to "make similar reductions in manpower and other types of weaponry." This was precisely the area of NATO's greatest concern and, therefore, Gorbachëv's offer was accepted with enthusiasm.

Two weeks later, President Bush, at a NATO summit in Brussels, proposed an equal ceiling of 275,000 troops which the two super–powers would be permitted to station in Europe outside their own territory and suggested that the CFE talks be expanded to include helicopters and land–based combat planes. He further called for demobilization of all troops to be withdrawn and for destruction of all equipment thus removed. Bush also suggested that it would "be possible to reach agreement in six months or even a year." Since the Soviets had earlier suggested troop reductions and had wanted to include combat aircraft in the discussions all along, they welcomed President Bush's proposals. The CFE talks subsequently became stalled, however, partly because of

the political changes that occurred in Eastern Europe in 1989. With non–communist leaderships in power throughout the region and with the German Democratic Republic moving toward unification with the Federal Republic of Germany, the old political basis of the Warsaw Pact no longer existed. In addition, the Soviet Union had agreed to withdraw its troops from Hungary and Czechoslovakia by the end of 1991 and those in Germany and Poland by 1994.

The CFE Treaty was initialled in November 1990 at a meeting of the CSCE. Shortly afterwards, the Soviet armed forces leadership reclassified three divisions as naval forces and claimed that these divisions were not covered by the CFE, since naval forces had not been included in the discussions. The United States and other western nations objected and the treaty was put on hold. The disagreement was resolved in May 1991 when Gorbachëv sent General Moiseyev, the chief of the Soviet Staff, to Washington, D.C. to work out a compromise. The compromise stipulated that the three divisions could be excluded from overall figures, provided commensurate reduc-

**President Reagan and General Secretary Gorbachëv, Reykjavik, Iceland, October 11, 1986**

tions were made in forces not originally covered by the agreement.

Two months later, the USA and the Soviet Union announced that they had reached agreement on a START Agreement and that it would be signed at the end of July when President Bush traveled to Moscow for a Summit Conference with President Gorbachëv. The agreement, signed on July 31, 1991, required the two signatories to reduce the number of nuclear warheads to 6,000 each, though an involved method of counting raised this figure by about one–third. Nevertheless, it was the first treaty to achieve actual reductions in the number of nuclear weapons on each side. This was, it turned out, Gorbachëv's swansong. Less than three weeks later, conservative communists tried to oust him in an attempted *coup*. Although the *coup* was defeated, it discredited the Communist Party and led to the collapse of the Soviet Union.

# An Independent Russia is Reborn

Gorbachëv still thought to save the union, even if under another name and with reduced powers, but it was not to be. By the end of August, nine of the fifteen republics were committed to independence. With the three Baltic Republics already receiving international recognition, Gorbachëv called a special session of the Congress of People's Deputies for September 2. After three days of debate, the Congress accepted Gorbachëv's proposal for the creation of a new interim government whose chief purpose would be to negotiate a new union treaty.

Gorbachëv remained president of this new interim government, but final executive authority was lodged in a State Council made up of Gorbachëv and the leaders of the participating republics. A separate Interrepublic Economic Committee, appointed by the State Council, assumed the economic functions of the former Council of Ministers. Finally, a two chamber legislature was established, the membership of the second chamber to be appointed by and represent the governments of the individual republics. In this chamber, voting would be by delegation, with each republic having one vote.

From the beginning, only ten of the republics participated in the interim government. The first act of the State Council was to recognize the independence of the Baltic Republics. Moldova refused to participate at all and Georgia sent only observers. In addition, over the next several days, all of the remaining republics other than the Russian Federation, Kazakhstan and Turkmenistan declared their independence. Later, even Kazakhstan and Turkmenistan would join the list.

Gorbachëv knew that his new interim government existed on sufferance and that Boris Yeltsin's support was the first requisite. Gorbachëv therefore dismissed all of his former advisers and accepted Yeltsin's advice on the make–up of his new government. He thus surrounded himself with liberals. He even appointed Ivan Silayev, Prime Minister of the Russian Federation, as Chairman of the Interrepublic Economic Committee, a post that effectively made him the caretaker Prime Minister of the union government.

Determined to save some form of union, he asked the reform economist Grigori Yavlinsky to draw up a plan for economic union and he and the State Council began working on a plan for a new political union. Yavlinsky's draft for a new economic union was submitted to the State Council in late September and won general approval. It was then submitted to the individual republics in October.

Most of the republics accepted the language of the economic union treaty, but the big exception was the Republic of Ukraine. Opposition was centered in the Ukrainian parliament, which drew up two pages of objections. The parliament demanded the right to set up an independent Ukrainian national bank, to issue a separate Ukrainian currency and, in general, to control its own fiscal policy. Later that same month, the Ukrainian parliament withdrew the mandate from its delegates to the USSR Council of the Republic and instructed them to participate as observers.

It came as no surprise, then, when the Republic of Ukraine decided to boycott the November 14 session of the State Council, called to consider Gorbachëv's draft for a new union treaty. In the event, only seven republics gave their preliminary approval to a new treaty creating a "Union of Sovereign States." Two weeks later, the State Council met again, supposedly to initial the draft agreement. Instead, they voted to submit it to the individual republic legislatures for approval, a process that put the proposed treaty into severe jeopardy.

Up to this point, Boris Yeltsin had consistently maintained that he favored a continuation of the union. But he had also said that he could not envisage a union without the Ukraine. Yet Leonid Kravchuk, the Ukrainian leader, said on November 12 that he would "never sign" a treaty which contained "even the slightest hint of certain governing central bodies" and he had refused to participate in discussions in the State Council on the new union treaty.

Yeltsin's own actions during this time indicate that he was also having second thoughts about the advisability of maintaining a strong center. At the end of October, he took over as his own Prime Minister and then announced that Russia would unilaterally begin a sweeping pro-gram of economic reform that included freeing prices, privatizing industry and land, and creating a strong Russian currency. He requested the Russian parliament to grant him the power to suspend Soviet laws that "hamper economic reforms." He also announced that, effective November 15, the Russian Government would no longer finance union ministries which it did not utilize. Yeltsin's program got the Russian parliament's endorsement on November 1. Two weeks later, he assumed control of Soviet diamonds and gold production and took charge of issuing oil export licenses. He followed this up with another decree taking over the remaining structures of the Soviet finance ministry, including its controls over foreign currency. This was accompanied by an announcement that Russia would no longer be responsible for any new debts incurred by the union government.

In effect, Yeltsin had begun a unilateral dismantling of the central government. This was carried a step further at the end of the month when Yeltsin stepped in and offered to finance the Soviet payroll after the central government had run out of funds. An integral part of the agreement was that Yeltsin henceforth controlled the union budget. He used his new power to order most central ministries to be closed.

Very little of the central government remained on December 1 when the Ukrainian people went to the polls to elect a new president and to vote on a referendum on independence. Leonid Kravchuk won the presidential race with 61.5 percent of the vote. Nearly 90 percent of all Ukrainians voted yes on independence.

"The independence of the Ukraine is a new political reality," commented Boris Yeltsin upon receiving the results of the Ukrainian vote. Yeltsin recognized that the draft union treaty drawn up by Gorbachëv was dead, but he still felt that some kind of coordinating mechanism was necessary to handle the many problems of the now–separating republics. He therefore contacted President Kravchuk and Stanislav Shushkevich, President of Belarus, and suggested that the three presidents meet the following weekend to discuss the future. Shushkevich agreed to host the meeting and offered the use of a hunting lodge located not far from the Belarusian city of Brest. "We came to the conclusion," Shushkevich commented after the meeting, "that we had to sort out the concept of the kind of union we are capable of building."

The three leaders talked for two days, December 7–8. At the end of the second day, they returned to Minsk, where they signed an agreement creating a "Commonwealth of Independent States." Its most significant clause stated that "the USSR has ceased to exist as a subject of international law and as a geopolitical reality." This was, in effect, the Russian Federation's declaration of independence. Eight other republics—the sole holdout was Georgia—joined the CIS at a conference in Alma Ata on December 21. Gorbachëv resigned as President of the U.S.S.R. on December 25, turning the Kremlin and authority over the Soviet Union's nuclear arsenal to Boris Yeltsin. The Russian Federation succeeded to the Soviet Union's membership in the United Nations and its seat on the security council.

### Economic Reform

Boris Yeltsin launched his economic reform on January 2, 1992. Over the next several months, his government was mainly occupied with the implementation of that program, assuming the Soviet Union's international obligations, including its various diplomatic missions abroad, and carrying on negotiations with the other members of the CIS over economic relations and the future of the Soviet military forces. The republics had agreed to maintain strategic and nuclear forces under a single command, but three republics, Ukraine, Moldova and Azerbaijan, opted from the beginning to establish their own national armies. Plans for a unified command under the CIS for the remaining forces were gradually discarded as the remaining republics moved toward creating their own national armies.

The original CIS agreement called for the republics to maintain a single economic space, but that has proved impossible in practice. One problem is that the other republics would like to buy more from Russia than it needs to buy from them. As a result, Russia had built up a positive balance of 1.2 trillion rubles with the other republics by the end of 1992. The Russian Government abandoned its commitment to maintaining a single ruble zone for the CIS about the middle of 1992.

In view of the growing trade imbalance coupled with Moscow's perception that the governments of the other republics were not doing enough to control spending, the Russian Government began limiting the amount of rubles they were willing to make available to the other republics and it began encouraging the other republics to develop their own currencies. Most eventually moved to do so, though in a number of cases "coupons" rather than a new currency were authorized.

A number of the other republics complained about the speed of Russia's economic reform, particularly the wide-ranging freeing of prices, but most grudgingly went along with it. At home, however, Yeltsin soon found that a majority of the members of the Supreme Soviet were also appalled at the speed of the reform. Even though they had, in December 1991, granted Yeltsin the right to rule by decree for the period of one year, by June 1992 they were strongly attacking his program and doing what they could to frustrate it or slow it down. Between June and December, they undermined his economic reform mainly through an enormous increase in credit, accomplished through taking control of the Russian State Bank. And in those same months, Speaker Khasbulatov emerged as the chief spokesman for the anti–reform majority in the Supreme Soviet.

This raises an important question, for Khasbulatov had been elected Chairman in 1991 with the support of reformers associated with Yeltsin; further, he had stood at Yeltsin's side in August 1991 in opposition to the attempted coup. Why did he now abandon his former allies and throw in his lot with many of the same individuals he had opposed in August 1991? It appears clear that he did it, not primar-

ily for ideological reasons, but because his own position was threatened. Khasbulatov was elected in 1990 to represent the autonomous republic of Chechyna. Since that time, Chechyna had declared its independence and was attempting to secede from Russia. An extremely ambitious individual, Khasbulatov's one chance for continued power on the national level was if secessionist movements were put down resolutely.

Thus he made common cause with a coalition of ex–Communists and Russian nationalists dreaming about a restoration of the old Soviet Empire. Because he is an able man and a facile speaker, his joining the parliamentary opposition to President Yeltsin gave that grouping more success than it would have been able to achieve on its own.

That became clear in December 1992, when the Congress of People's Deputies met to decide what policy to take toward President Yeltsin and his reforms. At issue was whether to extend President Yeltsin's power to name his own government ministers and to issue decrees with the force of law. Under the leadership of Speaker Khasbulatov, the Congress failed by a narrow four votes to pass a constitutional amendment that would have stripped President Yeltsin of most of his powers. The Congress then voted a resolution condemning Acting Prime Minister Yegor Gaidar's reform program and calling his methods of work unsatisfactory. They subsequently rejected Yegor Gaidar as Prime Minister.

President Yeltsin then stalked out of the Congress and threatened to organize a referendum on his policy of economic reform. Apparently frightened by the possibilities inherent in such a referendum, the Congress leadership proposed additional talks with Yeltsin. Valeri Zorkin, chairman of Russia's constitutional court, also intervened at this time, offering his services as an honest broker during any talks. The result was a compromise whereby Yeltsin would retain his decree–issuing powers for another four months while a nation–wide referendum on a new constitution would be scheduled for April. In return, President Yeltsin agreed to nominate as Prime Minister a person acceptable to the Congress. The Congress's choice fell on Viktor Chernomyrdin, a centrist who had been vice prime minister for oil and gas production since July. Chernomyrdin was undoubtedly a disappointment to the Congressional majority, however, for he continued the basic thrust of Gaidar's economic program.

Frustrated in its attempts to put an end to economic reform, the Supreme Soviet continued its attacks on Yeltsin and his government. In addition, a majority of the Supreme Soviet began having second thoughts about a referendum which might lead to a new constitution and new

**Inside St. Petersburg's nuclear power plant**     Courtesy: NOVOSTI

elections which might see them removed from office. Things came to a head in February 1993 when Speaker Khasbulatov denounced the idea of a referendum. A few days later, Valeri Zorkin added his voice in opposition to a referendum. In addition, the leaders of Russia's regional governments, meeting with Yeltsin on February 9, told him that a referendum might lead to an explosion in the country. Faced with this wide–spread opposition, Yeltsin backed down and agreed to postpone the referendum indefinitely, provided a power–sharing arrangement could be reached with Khasbulatov and the Supreme Soviet. Yeltsin and Khasbulatov finally reached an agreement of sorts, subject to approval by the Congress of People's Deputies, which was reconvened on March 10.

But the full Congress was not in a mood to compromise. Rejecting Khasbulatov's efforts, the Congress voted to severely limit Yeltsin's right to rule by decree and canceled the referendum scheduled for April. Yeltsin temporized for seven days, then went on national television on March 20 to announce that he would organize his own referendum to take place on April 25. The Russian people would be asked to cast a vote of confidence on his presidency and to approve a new constitution that would serve as a basis for new elections. In the meantime, Yeltsin added, he planned to ignore the Supreme Soviet and rule by decree.

Vice President Rutskoi and Valeri Zorkin, Chairman of Russia's constitutional court, immediately denounced Yeltsin's plan as unconstitutional. On the other hand, at an emergency meeting of the Supreme Soviet the next day, the prime minister and the defense, security and interior ministers all threw their support behind Yeltsin. The Supreme Soviet then requested the Constitutional Court to rule on Yeltsin's plan. The Court declared Yeltsin's decree to be unlawful on the basis of his television speech, since it had not yet received a copy of the decree itself. On that basis, Khasbulatov called for Yeltsin's impeachment and the Supreme Soviet voted to convene the Congress of People's Deputies on March 26.

A motion to impeach was supported by a majority of the Congress members voting, but fell 72 votes short of the two–thirds vote necessary to convict. Having failed to impeach Yeltsin, the Congress agreed to the idea of an April 25 referendum, but demanded that four questions be submitted to the people instead of Yeltsin's two: "Do you have confidence in the president? Do you approve of the socioeconomic policy carried out by president and government in 1992? Do you think early presidential elections are necessary? And do you think early parliamentary elections are necessary?"

The Congress further stipulated that

Yeltsin would have to win the votes of a majority of all registered voters on the first two questions in order to claim a popular mandate. Such a stipulation would have been almost impossible to obtain. In 1991, Yeltsin won 57 percent of all votes cast but that constituted only 42 percent of registered voters. The Constitutional Court subsequently ruled that Yeltsin could claim a victory on the first two questions if he won a majority of votes cast, but that the last two questions were constitutional and required the support of a majority of all registered voters to be binding.

In the event, Yeltsin won a 57.4 percent approval on the first question and 53.7 percent on the second. On the third question, 49.1 percent favored immediate presidential elections; however, 70.6 percent voted in favor of immediate parliamentary elections. Nevertheless, this constituted only 44.8 percent of the registered electorate, so was not legally binding.

But Yeltsin had won only a battle, not the war. Speaker Khasbulatov dismissed the voting results as meaningless and divisive and announced that neither he nor the Congress of People's Deputies were prepared to accept the results as decisive. Vice President Rutskoi, for his part, argued that:

"there can be no talk of overall popular support. Those who said 'no' or remained silent are also Russian citizens, and we have to ask ourselves why they did so."

Rutskoi later added:

"There is no popular support. That is why all these reform policies should be changed."

Yeltsin's reaction to his victory was predictably different. Saying that the referendum had created "a fundamentally new political situation" which required a new constitution, he summoned the political leaders from Russia's regions and republics to Moscow in April. Here he presented them with copies of a new draft constitution dating from the Brezhnev era. Yeltsin proposed that each region and republic examine the draft and submit comments to him within a month. He asked them also to appoint two delegates to a constituest assembly which would convene to complete work on the document.

This procedure, not specified anywhere in the old Soviet constitution—which gave the power to amend to the Congress of People's Deputies—was Yeltsin's attempt to circumvent the opposition of the Congress of People's Deputies. The 585 member constituent assembly met for about a month. After closely examining and modifying the constitution, they approved it by a better than two–thirds ma-

jority and sent it on to President Yeltsin. He then submitted it to the 88 republics and regions for their approval.

As this was going on, the Supreme Soviet took up the government's draft budget and proceeded to gut it. Declaring that the budget was "anti–social," they increased spending to 40 trillion rubles ($40 billion), which according to the chairman of the Supreme Soviet's own budget committee would have meant a budget deficit of 25% of GDP. That would have destroyed the government's reform program entirely and unleashed hyperinflation. Not content with that, the Supreme Soviet tried to sabotage the privatization program of the government by voting to cancel a presidential decree requiring state-owned firms to swap at least 20% of their shares for privatization vouchers. Instead, it announced that from October these vouchers could be replaced by "privatization accounts" at the government-owned savings bank. Cutting short his holiday, President Yeltsin returned to Moscow and issued a new decree guaranteeing that privatization would continue. There was little he could legally do about the budget, however. He could veto it, but his veto could be overruled by a two–thirds vote in the Supreme Soviet.

President Yeltsin did, in fact, veto the budget twice over the next month and a half, but the Supreme Soviet was preparing to pass it for a third time on September 22. It was this which finally caused President Yeltsin, on the evening of September 21, to go on television to announce that the Russian parliament had been disbanded and that elections to a new parliament would take place on December 11–12. Within an hour, the rump Supreme Soviet, under Ruslan Khasbulatov's leadership, voted to strip Yeltsin of his powers, then installed Alexander Rutskoi, the vice–president, as a rival president.

In the succeeding confrontation, Prime Minister Chernomyrdin and his cabinet, plus the police and the army, remained loyal to Yeltsin. The stand–off continued for nearly two weeks. The parliamentary forces, refusing to disband, barricaded themselves in the parliament building and began to collect arms. Yeltsin surrounded the building with a cordon of police, then ordered that electricity, heat and water be cut off from the building.

Things turned violent on the night of October 3, when a mob broke through the police cordon and entered the parliament building. Urged on by Vice–President Rutskoi, the mob attempted to seize Ostankino, the main television building. A number of television channels were knocked off the air, but the mob never managed to gain control of the entire building.

President Yeltsin then called on the army to restore order and after some hesitation they agreed to do so. The first tanks

**President Boris Yeltsin shares microphones with Chairman Ruslan Khasbulatov**

Courtesy: NOVOSTI

arrived at the parliament building at 5:20 the next morning. Systematically firing into the building, then beginning a room by room movement through the building, the army rounded up the last of the defenders that afternoon. Kasbulatov and Rutskoi were arrested and imprisoned. That cleared the way for the December parliamentary elections. President Yeltsin set them for December 12 and enlarged the scope of the vote by specifying that the Russian people would also vote in a referendum on a new constitution and elect new regional and local councils.

The results of the elections were a disappointment for the reformers, however. Although the people approved the new constitution, that was the last good news. It was the elections to the State Duma, the lower house of the Federal Assembly, that were the most disappointing. There were 450 seats to be filled, half by proportional representation and half by first–past–the–post voting. The largest vote getter for the proportional seats was the badly misnamed *Liberal Democratic Party* of Vladimir Zhirinovsky, the ultranationalist leader, which got 22% of the vote. The reform party of Yegor Gaidar, *Russia's Choice* came in second with 20%.

Because Zhirinovsky's party did poorly in the first–past–the–post voting, however, *Russia's Choice* was the largest party in the State Duma with 76 seats. The *New Regional Policy* faction, formed after the election by individuals who had run without a party label, was second with 65 seats. The third largest faction was Zhirinovsky's *Liberal Democratic Party* with 63 seats. Other parties included the *Agrarian*

*Party* (53 seats), the *Communist Party* (45 seats), the *Party of Russian Unity and Accord* (30 seats), *Yabloko* (25 seats), *Women of Russia* (23 seats), and the *Democratic Party of Russia* (15 seats). The remaining 35 seats were held by independents not affiliated with any party.

That makes the result sound better than it actually was, however. Except for *Yabloko*, the party of reform economist Gregory Yavlinsky, nearly every one of the remaining parties was cool to reform; together they controlled a majority of the seats in the State Duma. Reflecting this fact, the man they selected as their Speaker was Ivan Rybkin, a member of the *Agrarian Party*.

The situation in the Federation Council, the upper house of the Federal Assembly, was more positive. Here a majority of the members supported reform. Vladimir Shumeiko, the Speaker, was a former Deputy Chairman of the Russian Council of Ministers.

One of the powers given to the State Duma in the new constitution is the right to grant amnesty. One of the first things the State Duma did after it met was to declare an amnesty to all those involved in the August 1991 and October 1993 attempted *coups*. This was widely seen as a rebuke to President Yeltsin, though it did have the advantage of cutting short what was turning into a long political trial.

Despite a stormy beginning, relations between the government and the legislature subsequently settled down into a form of cohabitation that occasionally became even cooperation. The best sign of this was the peace accord which President

Yeltsin managed to get most of the factions in the State Duma to sign in the spring of 1994 giving the government two years of calm to focus on economic recovery.

That truce largely came to an end in December 1994 after President Yeltsin authorized the military to send troops into Chechnya to put down a separatist movement there. Curiously, however, it was his former supporters among the reformers who led the attack against the intervention. In January, the State Duma passed a resolution supporting a political solution in Chechnya and calling on the government to "take all necessary measures" to bring an end to the fighting. The resolution was in the form of a recommendation to the President, however, and lacked the force of law. Only 172 out of 450 members voted for a separate resolution which would have barred the army from fighting in domestic conflicts. Yet even those who objected to the use of force in Chechnya made it clear that they considered Chechnya to be an integral part of Russia.

Much the same was true of international opinion. Although the U.S. Government accused Russia of violating international agreements by failing to notify other countries about large–scale troop movements into Chechnya, it was also clear that it considered Chechnya to be strictly an internal affair. Senator Jesse Helms was more critical, commenting that he would oppose aid to President Yeltsin's government "if he can't control his people in terms of killing women and children and other innocent people."

The drop in domestic and international popularity was not surprising. Most people were appalled by the news stories coming out of Chechnya and reacted accordingly. The decline would undoubtedly have been temporary had the Russian military been able to restore order in Chechnya and bring all fighting to an end. Unfortunately, this has not been the case. In fact, General Dudayev had managed to maintain a guerilla force in the mountainous areas of southern Chechnya and had twice shown—through terrorist raids on Russian hospitals in Budyonnovsk in June 1995 and in Kizlyar in January 1996—that he could make the Russian occupation of Chechnya costly.

Yet the results of the legislative elections which took place in December 1995, though clearly not favorable to either President Yeltsin or his government, indicate that political opinion has changed very little since the previous elections in December 1993. The first thing about these most recent elections was the extreme political fragmentation as each ambitious politician, it seemed, founded his own political party as a vehicle for his pretensions. Ultimately, forty–three parties, blocs and movements contested them. This proved to be self–defeating for a party needing a minimum showing of 5% of the national vote to enter the Duma on a party list. Since it was the reformers who had splintered the most—often concentrating their venom on other reformers during the campaign—their final representation showed the greatest drop. The more disciplined *Communist Party of Russia* was the runaway winner with 22.3% of the vote—up ten percentage points from 1993. Vladimir Zhirinovsky's ultranationalist *Liberal Democratic Party* came in second with 11%—though that was only half what the party had gotten in 1993. The only other parties to surmount the 5% barrier were two reform parties, *Our Home is Russia*, the party of Prime Minister Viktor Chernomyrdin, which came in third with 10%, followed by *Yabloko*, the party of Grigory Yavlinsky with 7%. Since only these four parties entered parliament on a party list, that meant that almost 50% of the votes were wasted because they had been cast for parties that failed to enter parliament on party lists.

Since only half of the seats are filled by party vote, the remainder being single-seat constituencies, there are several additional parties represented in the Duma. These include the *Agrarians* (21 seats), *Power to the People* (10 seats), *Russia's Democratic Choice* (10 seats), *Congress of Russian Communists* (5 seats) and *Women of Russia* (3 seats). A number of additional parties won one or two seats, and 76 individuals won as independents. Finally, the *Communist Party of Russia* won 58 single–constituency seats, *Our Home is Russia* won ten seats, *Yabloko* won 14 seats, and the *Liberal Democrats* won one single–constituency seat.

When parliament convened in January, it proved to be dominated by the *Communists*. Although they hold only 149 out of the 450 seats themselves, they have a voting strength of 212 seats because of the support of a large number of individuals who ran and won as independents, meaning that they are just 14 seats short of a majority. After a stiff fight, they managed to elect one of their own, Gennadi Seleznyov, a former editor of *Pravda*, as the new Speaker of the Duma. They also obtained the chairmanships of more than a third of the committees, including almost half of the major committees.

Although the position of the *Communists* was that economic reform has been a failure and should be ended, they were able, in fact, to find a lot of common ground with the government following the elections. One reason for this is that President Yeltsin also drew his own conclusions from the election results and essentially put economic reform on hold. Even more important, he got rid of the remaining reformers in his administration, replacing them with individuals more acceptable to the new majority in the Duma. Those departing included Anatoly Chu-

bais, who as first deputy prime minister in charge of economic policy had been in charge of privatization, Sergei Shakrai, also a deputy prime minister, and Andrei Kozyrev, Foreign Minister. But these dismissals were probably more symbolic than anything else, since all were ultimately implementers of Yeltsin policies rather than independent figures in their own right. More importantly, everyone understood that Yeltsin's term of office would expire in less than six months and that it would be the winner of the June 1996 elections who would determine the future course of government policy.

The major candidates in the presidential race were President Yeltsin himself, Gennady Zyuganov, the *Communist* leader, Grigory Yavlinsky, founder of the reform party *Yabloko*, Vladimir Zhirinovsky, leader of the *Liberal Democrats*, and General Alexander Lebed, a Russian nationalist considered to be somewhat more moderate than Zhirinovsky.

From the beginning, Zyuganov was the favorite in the polls, first of all because the *Communists* had the best party organization and, secondly, because of the *Communist Party's* victory in the December 1995 Duma elections. Yeltsin, technically not a member of any party, had the additional disability of being the incumbent responsible both for the economic situation and the continuing Chechen conflict. Even he admitted that he could not be elected if the Chechen conflict were not settled by June. Another factor arguing for a Zyu-

ganov win was that the *Communists* had no competitors on the left, while Zhirinovsky and Lebed were competing for the nationalist vote and Yeltsin and Yavlinsky were dividing the reform vote. Zyuganov was not expected to win more than 30–35 percent of the vote in the first round of voting, however, so the most important question was who would come in second and so survive to stand against Zyuganov in the second round.

From the beginning, Yeltsin's strategy was to win enough votes to come in second. Sensing that most Russian voters wanted stability most of all, he told the electorate that the reforms had accomplished their purpose and now it was time for consolidation, not change. To make this point even clearer, he dismissed all of the reformers in the government and promised new, costly social programs that would benefit pensioners and others hurt by the collapse of the old command system. Reformers were extremely critical of him in the beginning, but he picked up the endorsement of a number of prominent reformers after they had pondered the various alternatives. He also picked up a surprise endorsement from the *Women of Russia* party. He also had the support of *Our Home is Russia*, the party founded by Prime Minister Chernomyrdin.

Yeltsin's chances improved in March when the *Communists* pushed through a resolution in the Duma declaring the 1991 dissolution of the Soviet Union to be illegal. They almost certainly hurt their case

The Russian weekly, *Arguments and Facts*, predicts the outcome of the April 1993 referendum. Pictured are President Yeltsin and Ruslan Khasbulatov, Chairman of the Russian Federation's Supreme Soviet.

Russia's parliament building—The White House

Courtesy: NOVOSTI

also when they promised that a *Communist* victory would lead to extensive re–nationalizations and a rebuilding of state control over the economy.

The Russian public were well aware that any attempt to reestablish the Soviet Union was likely to result in many more Chechnyas. Except for Belarus, a *Communist* victory would have been viewed with dismay throughout the region and any attempt to recreate the Soviet Union would have been opposed. Even the various Central Asian republics, though they had rebuilt some of the military and economic connections with Russia that existed prior to 1991, made it clear that they wished to retain their political independence and would react negatively to any attempt to bring them under Moscow's control. All of the Caucasus republics felt the same way.

As for the Republic of Ukraine, largest of the republics after Russia, its greatest fear all along had been domination by Russia and this was the reason it had kept its participation in the CIS at a minimal level. As for *Communist* threats to renationalize important segments of the economy, that promised continued instability, precisely the opposite of what most people wanted.

Yeltsin evidently read the Russian populace correctly because he continued to pick up support between March and June and, when the election finally took place, Yeltsin came in first with 35 percent of the vote to Zyuganov's 32 percent. The Russian people obviously decided to opt for the devil they knew rather than take a chance on the unknown. The third place winner was General Alexander Lebed, with 15 percent of the vote. Zhirinovsky and Yavlinsky trailed much further behind.

Lebed was now courted by both sides, but Lebed decided to throw his support to Yeltsin. Since the vote was now either Yeltsin or the *Communists*, the rest of the

reformers came aboard as well. Yeltsin won in the second round with approximately 54% of the vote to Zyuganov's 40%. The remaining ballots were cast "against" both candidates.

Almost immediately after the election, however, Yeltsin went into seclusion, and it was announced that he would need a heart bypass operation. Yeltsin did appoint General Lebed as his security adviser immediately after the election, however, and Lebed negotiated an end to the war in Chechnya before he was sacked in October. This was about the only positive development during those months. Yeltsin had a successful heart bypass operation on November 5, receiving five arterial grafts. Almost immediately after returning to work in January 1997, however, he developed pneumonia. Though this was apparently not directly connected to his heart bypass operation, it incapacitated him for a further six weeks.

During the several months that he was ill, little got done in the government. Prime Minister Chernomyrdin, supposedly in charge, continued to run the day–to–day affairs of government but showed himself to be no leader. Meanwhile the Duma, dominated by *Communists* and nationalists, attempted to take control of the country's agenda, and there were repeated calls for Yeltsin's resignation.

The calls ceased soon after Yeltsin's return in March, however, for he soon made it clear who was in charge. Moreover, Yeltsin had clearly decided that further reform was needed to deal with such continuing economic problems as the widespread failure of employees to be paid on time, he brought Anatoly Chubais back into the government as First Deputy Prime Minister, even though he was aware that Chubais had few friends in the Duma. Also significant but symbolic as well, he appointed Boris Nemtsov as the other First Deputy Prime Minister. Nemtsov, Governor of Nizhny Novgorod

Province for the previous five years, had been among the first regional leaders to privatize small business enterprises and to promote land reform. As a result, Nizhny Novgorod, a closed city under the Soviets, had come to boast a fashionable pedestrian shopping mall, a glittery trade fair, a Coca-Cola bottling plant, a branch office of the accounting firm Price Waterhouse, and regular service by Lufthansa Airlines. Yeltsin was obviously hoping that Nemtsov could do something similar for the country. In any case, Yeltsin's selection of Nemtsov was undoubtedly a good political move, for the youthful Nemtsov was quite popular with the Russian people and provided a good "public face" for reform.

Over the summer, Chubais and Nemtsov pushed policies designed to lower the rate of inflation, pay off pension arrears, and carry out the sale of Svyazinvest, Russia's large telecommunications company. Their policies had some positive effect, but it became increasingly clear as time went by that some larger measures would be necessary to get the Russian economy growing again.

Yeltsin sought to spell out just what was still needed in an address to the Federation Council, the Russian parliament's upper house, in September 1997. The message was an interesting one, for Yeltsin essentially pledged to put an end to the era of free–wheeling crony capitalism that had come in with the fall of communism in 1991. What was needed, Yeltsin said, was a "new economic order" in which government, not big business, made the rules. The speech, in other words, was an explicit attack on the new industrial barons and bankers who had bankrolled his reelection campaign. However, now these same men were attempting to extend their economic power even further and refusing to pay taxes to the state. This was, undoubtedly, their chief "crime," for the government had recently been able to collect only about ten percent of GDP in taxes, which provided an insufficient amount of money to pay back wages and pensions and meet the government's pressing current needs. That same week, Boris Nemtsov reinforced Yeltsin's message when he warned the bosses of Avtovaz, a car–maker, that they had until October 1 to pay their back taxes or see themselves forced into bankruptcy.

Two things now occurred that largely derailed reform, however. First, the economic crisis in Asia led to a world–wide decrease in investor confidence that resulted in some significant disinvestment in Russia in the fall of 1997. Second, Anatoly Chubais found himself caught up in a scandal when he and a team of colleagues agreed to accept a "publisher's advance" worth $450,000 for a book on privatization from a publishing firm

**Anatoly Chubais**

linked to a bank that had made significant profits from participating in a number of privatizations overseen by Mr. Chubais. To his enemies, the "publisher's advance" looked like a bribe or a payoff. Chubais offered his resignation as First Deputy Prime Minister and Minister of Finance on November 15, but Yeltsin refused it, though he subsequently downgraded Chubais's position in the administration by stripping him of the Minister of Finance title.

Although President Yeltsin's administration had a few accomplishments over the next three months that he could point to—most salary and pension arrears were paid off by the end of the year and the 1998 budget was finally approved by the Duma in February 1998—this was essentially a period of drift. That came to an end toward the end of March when Yeltsin dismissed Prime Minister Chernomyrdin and his cabinet and appointed Sergei Kiriyenko, a 35–year old junior minister, in his place. This also set up a confrontation with the opposition–controlled Duma, which had to confirm Kiriyenko before he could actually assume the job.

The only explanation that Yeltsin gave for his firing of Chernomyrdin—that he wanted the Prime Minister to "concentrate on political preparations for the forthcoming election," which would "decide the future of Russia"—didn't satisfy most people, so there were numerous speculations as to the "real" reasons. These ranged from speculations about Yeltsin's failing health to his anger at

Chernomyrdin for moving too quickly to establish himself as a candidate for election to the presidency in 2000. None seemed adequate, particularly since they all had in common that they ignored the increasing drift of the previous three months. It appears more likely that Yeltsin, recognizing that this drift was discrediting reform in the minds of Russian voters, decided that some decisive action would have to be taken to get Russia back on track. His gamble was an extremely large one, but he has won round one. The Duma, after rejecting Kiriyenko twice, finally confirmed him as Prime Minister by a vote of 251 to 25 on April 24. Kiriyenko needed 226 votes to win.

It is interesting to see which political parties voted for and against him. Gen-

**Victor Chernomyrdin**          NOVOSTI

nady Zyuganov, the Communist Party leader, urged his followers to vote against Kiriyenko—and they did so during the first two rounds of voting. In the third round of voting, however, a significant number voted to confirm Kiriyenko. It helped that Duma Speaker Gennady Seleznev, a member of the Communist Party, threw his support to Kiriyenko in the third round, arguing that "Russia will not forgive us if we sacrifice the State Duma over a nomination for the Prime Minster." Seleznev was referring to the fact that, had Kiriyenko been defeated in the third round of voting, President Yeltsin would have been required by the constitution to dissolve the Duma and call for new elections.

Most members of Our Home is Russia, the party led by Chernomyrdin, voted for Kiriyenko, even though a successful Kiriyenko might threaten Chernomyrdin's own run for the presidency in 2000. Kiriyenko had the support of Vladimir Zhirinovsky and his Liberal Democrats, though Zhirinovsky also publicly negotiated for seats in the cabinet in return for his support. No public promises were made to him, though that is not to say that he will have no influence in the new government.

Curiously, perhaps the most consistent opponent was Grigory Yavlinsky, along with his Yabloko party. Yavlinsky bills himself as a reformer but, in fact, he has been a consistent opponent of the government since 1993. However, the real reason for his refusal of support is that Yavlinsky has presidential ambitions for 2000 and a successful reform government would diminish his chances of winning. Yavlinsky and Yabloko ostentatiously refrained from taking part during the third round of voting to make clear their united opposition to Kiriyenko. Of course, if Kiriyenko stumbles, that action will stand Yavlinsky in good stead.

Kiriyenko has said that he wants to put together a cabinet of technicians who will push through necessary reforms and get Russian growing again economically. On the other hand, he has already promised not to break up the "natural monopolies" in the energy and transportation sectors or to sell controlling interests in these monopolies. He has also said that his govern-

**Gennady Zyuganov**          NOVOSTI

Prime Minister Sergei Kirivenko

NOVOSTI

ment will enact measures to help oil companies hurt by the recent drop in world oil prices, and he has promised to provide regular financing to coal companies and to help coal miners. Finally, Kiriyenko is expected to provide adequate financing for salaries and pensions and increase social spending. It appears, therefore, that President Yeltsin has decided on a change of direction aimed at winning support for government policies. Perhaps he will also attempt further reforms, but he has apparently decided that policies aimed at building popular support for the government come first.

### Foreign Policy of the Russian Federation

After independence, the various ex–Soviet republics agreed to honor the various arms agreements signed by the now defunct Soviet Union. President Yeltsin, who took control of the Soviet Union's nuclear missiles after Gorbachёv resigned, ordered that ICBMs be targeted away from American cities.

In his State of the Union speech in January 1992, President Bush proposed that the USA and the former republics of the Soviet Union eliminate all multiple–warhead missiles and reduce the number of permitted nuclear warheads to 4,500. President Yeltsin countered with an offer to end production of all new nuclear warheads and reduce the total number of long–range warheads to 2,500 on each side. In a speech at the United Nations a few days later, he suggested that the USA

and Russia jointly construct a global anti-missile shield. In that same speech, Yeltsin proclaimed that he considered "the United States and the West not as mere partners but as allies."

This major change in foreign policy probably came about because Yeltsin recognized that the collapse of the Soviet Union threatened the unified Soviet armed forces, and might make them vulnerable to attack. Since that time, most of the republics have indeed opted for separate armed forces. In most cases, the new armed forces are only lightly armed and there is a real question whether they would be able to defend their borders if attacked. In 1992, however, the Russian Government was probably thinking about its long border with the People's Republic of China and so wanted the assurance of American and Western support should such a threat arise.

The United States Government also announced in early 1992 that the Peace Corps would begin operating in the area of the former Soviet Union. Peace Corpsmen were to be sent to Russia, Ukraine, Armenia and one Central Asian country. A separate program applied to the three Baltic republics. Those various programs are now in place.

Yeltsin paid an official visit to the United States in June 1992. The highlight was the signing of an agreement in principle setting a new limit of 3,000–3,500 nuclear warheads on each side. This agreement was then codified into the START–2 agreement, which the United States and Russia signed in Moscow in December 1992. START–2 remained in a state of limbo for the next three years, however, because of a problem with the Government of Ukraine over START–1. Although the United States and Russia had ratified START–1 and had begun implementing it, certain parts needed the cooperation of the Government of Ukraine. But the Ukrainian legislature refused to support implementation of the agreement, because, it was argued, there were no funds to commit to the cost of dismantling the nuclear missiles, estimated to cost at least $1.5 billion. The American Congress had already authorized $800 million to help defray the cost of dismantling nuclear missiles in the four ex–Soviet Republics that had them. Eventually the Ukrainian Government received a promise of an additional sum of money and then signed off on the agreement. With START–1 finally on its way, START–2 was ratified by the U.S. Congress in January 1966. President Yeltsin then committed himself to seek Russian ratification of START–2 by April. It is not clear whether the Duma will react favorably or not.

Also during the Yeltsin visit in 1992, the U.S. and Russia worked out the broad outlines for an agreement for joint space

flight beginning in 1993. Since then, a Russian cosmonaut participated in a U.S. shuttle flight in 1993 and a U.S. astronaut began a lengthy stay aboard the Russian space station *MIR* in March 1995. In January 1996, the U.S. Government announced that cooperation was continuing on a planned international space station. To facilitate cooperation and reduce Russian costs, NASA had agreed to add three space shuttle missions, two to ferry supplies to the existing space station Mir and one to place in orbit a Russian science module. These will bring the number of joint missions to nine through 1998, when the first astronauts are expected to occupy the new space station.

Another area of Russian–American cooperation is that of ex–Yugoslavia. Russia originally supported sanctions against Serbia after war broke out in Bosnia, then adopted a rather ambivalent policy, sometimes refusing to support further actions against the Serbs. On the other hand, Russia played an important role in getting the Serbs to withdraw from the vicinity of Sarajevo in the spring of 1994 and it supported the effort that led to the agreement on Bosnia in December 1995. In addition, the Russian troops sent to Bosnia as a part of the implementation force take their operational orders from General Joulwan, the American general who is the senior NATO military commander in Europe. The quirk is that the Russian troops will come under his operational command as part of the American forces serving under him, not in his role as NATO commander.

Russia's relations with Japan remain somewhat cool. The issue between the

**Foreign Minister Yevgeny Primakov**

NOVOSTI

two countries remains the four islands taken by the Soviet Union at the end of World War II which Japan insists on getting back.

An important part of Russia's foreign policy is concerned with that area which they refer to as the "near abroad," a term they apply to the ex–Soviet republics other than the three Baltic nations. Russia had negotiated individual agreements with a number of republics, but it became clear in 1993 that the Russian Government's policy toward these republics had changed. Essentially, Russia began placing its emphasis on the Commonwealth of Independent States, demanding that relations between the various republics take place within that context. Since that time, Georgia has joined the CIS, Azerbaijan has reactivated its membership, and a number of general agreements have been negotiated dealing with a customs union, currencies, and military assistance. A number of the ex–Soviet republics, in particular Kazakstan and Belarus, but most of the Central Asian republics as well, favor a much closer working relationship with Russia. These republics actively participate in the CIS's Inter–governmental Assembly and have also signed agreements establishing an economic union, a payments union, a customs union and CIS peacekeeping forces. Russia favors the CIS because it provides, in the Russian view, a framework for Russia's relations with the "near abroad".

Although CIS relations continue to develop, the chief frustration is with Ukraine, which, although a founding member of the CIS, has opposed a further elaboration of CIS institutions out of a fear of Russian domination. Ukraine remains only an "observer" at the Inter-governmental Assembly, an associate member of the economic union, and has refused to sign any of the other separate agreements. Russia will undoubtedly continue to use the CIS as a focus for its relations with the "near abroad," but its relations with Ukraine are likely to remain bilateral for the foreseeable future.

The impressive showing of the *Communist Party of Russia* in the December 1995 Duma elections had some effect on Russian foreign policy, though it has been less than many feared. Its chief effect was to bring about the resignation of Foreign Minister Andrei Kozyrev, disliked by both the *Communists* and the nationalists. He was replaced by Yevgeny M. Primakov, whose previous job was director of Russia's foreign intelligence service. A foreign policy adviser to President Gorbachëv until 1991, Primakov is an Arab expert who served for a number of years as head of the Moscow Institute of Oriental Studies. In his rare public statements prior to becoming foreign minister, Primakov had been critical of any expansion of NATO

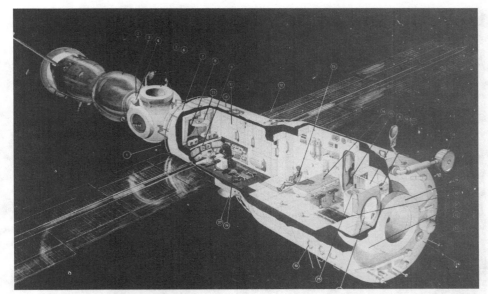

Sketch of the MIR space station                                        NOVOSTI

eastward and he urged that Russia take a tougher stance to defend its national interests.

A longtime *Communist Party* member before 1991, Primakov was clearly more acceptable to the new majority in the Duma than his predecessor. Yet he has worked very well with Yeltsin since his appointment, and has also been able to establish good working relations with the U.S. Government as well. As a result, Russia effectively withdrew its objections to NATO expansion in May 1997 when Yeltsin, joining the sixteen NATO members in a ceremony in Paris, signed a pact for mutual cooperation and security which established a new NATO–Russia council for consultation on security issues. In return, Russia got a public assurance from NATO that it had no plans to deploy nuclear weapons on the territory of new members.

It should be emphasized that Russia still has an independent foreign policy that sometimes puts it into competition with the United States on specific foreign

policy issues. Two issues over the past year illustrate this point. In the case of Iraq, Russia objected to American threats to launch retaliatory bomb attacks against Iraq after Saddam Hussain blocked United Nations inspections. It then supported the Kofi Annan mission to Iraq, which defused the situation, and promised to act as an advocate for Iraq in the future. Russia is owed several billions dollars by Iraq and cannot hope to be repaid until United Nations sanctions are lifted. The second case has to do with Serbia's recent actions in its province of Kosovo. The United States threatened additional sanctions against Serbia after Serbian paramilitary units carried out attacks on Kosovan villages in an effort to put down an independence movement in the province. Russia condemned the killings of Kosovan villagers, but opposed additional sanctions. Such differences of opinion between the United States and Russia on foreign policy issues are, of course, normal and will continue.

Outside of the MIR                                                     NOVOSTI

83

# Government of the Russian Federation

A presidential bodyguard salutes Russian President Boris Yeltsin and Italian President Francesco Cossiga at the Quirinale Presidential Palace on December 19, 1991.

Reuters/Bettmann

Under the new constitution approved in December 1993, Russia is a federation with a division of powers between the central government and the local governments. The Federal Government is delegated certain exclusive powers. Those powers which can be exercised concurrently by the federal government and the member units are specifically enumerated. The constitution then stipulates that the member units may exercise powers not mentioned in the constitution. The constitution has thus achieved Yeltsin's intention to devolve considerable authority on the republics and regions.

The President of the Russian Federation, directly elected by popular vote, is the head of state and the guarantor of the constitution. He is commander–in–chief of the armed forces. He conducts foreign policy and provides the general guidelines for domestic policy. He also has wide powers of appointment. In addition to the prime minister (technically, Chairman of the Government of the Russian Federation), he appoints and dismisses members of the cabinet, judges, the Prosecutor–General of the Russian Federation, top commanders of the armed forces and diplomatic representatives. He has the power to call elections and dissolve the State Duma (as specified in the constitution), submit bills to the State Duma, and sign federal laws. He decides questions of Russian citizenship and may grant political asylum.

The prime minister proposes the members of his cabinet to the President and presides over meetings of his cabinet. Neither the prime minister nor members of his cabinet may be members of the State Duma. In case of a vote of no confidence in the prime minister, the President decides whether to dismiss the government or dissolve the State Duma and call for new elections.

## The Court System

The new constitution creates a court system modeled on western democracies. There is a Constitutional Court which reviews laws when requested to do so by the President of the Federation, the Supreme Court of the Russian Federation, the Supreme Arbitration Court of the Russian Federation and local legislative and executive bodies. The Constitutional Court will also accept original jurisdiction over cases of individuals who feel that their constitutional rights and freedoms have been violated.

## What is Being Changed

One of the first things that Lenin did after coming to power in 1917 was to abolish the old Russian court system and create new people's courts staffed by communists and other revolutionaries. The Russian court system, created by Alexander II in the 1860s, was modeled on western judicial practices. It incorporated the concept of "equal justice under the law" and included an independent judiciary, trial by jury, public trials, and defense attorneys.

The Soviet court system was specifically created to defend the revolution. Judges and prosecutors were required to be members of the Communist Party and to be loyal implementers of the party line. Trials by jury were abolished. Guilt or innocence was determined by a judge, assisted by two ordinary citizens who were referred to as lay assessors. Their function was to support the prosecution. Defense attorneys existed, though their role differed from that of attorneys in western countries. With no presumption of innocence, a long legal tradition developed against an acquittal–oriented defense. The function of the defense attorney was therefore to negotiate for the most lenient sentence rather than to get the client off. This was reinforced by the fact that, under the law, defense attorneys had a lesser status than representatives of the state. Acquittals were almost unknown.

Attitudes toward the law began to change after Gorbachёv came to power in 1985, particularly after he endorsed the concept of a "nation of laws." The first practical manifestation of this changed thinking came in December 1989, when a law on judicial procedure went into effect giving individual republics the authority to increase the number of lay assessors on the bench. This was viewed by some as a move toward creation of a jury system. Defense attorneys were also permitted to establish a national Union of Advocates and the number of acquittals began growing slightly.

Gorbachëv's main goal was to free the legal system from outside political interference. He wanted to create courts where fairness and objectivity were the rule and cases were decided exclusively on the basis of evidence presented in court. He made some progress, but most of the authoritarian system originally created in the 1920's and 1930's continued to exist even after his reforms.

The repudiation of communism and the emergence of an independent Russian Government created a new situation, however. Moscow was full of talk about reforming the entire legal system in 1992–93, but the quarrel between President Yeltsin and the Russian Supreme Soviet meant that little was resolved. The new Russian constitution approved in December 1993 did make major modifications in the legal system, however. Under Article 120, judges are "independent and subject only to the Constitution of the Russian Federation and federal law." Article 121 makes them irremovable, while article 122 guarantees their inviolability. Article 123 reintroduces the concept of trial by jury—now being slowly implemented. In addition, Chapter 2 of the constitution contains numerous individual legal rights, including "the right to have a case heard by a court with the participation of jurors in the cases provided for by federal law (Art. 47);" the right to receive qualified legal assistance (Art. 48); presumption of innocence (Art. 49); guarantees against double jeopardy (Art 50); and protection against self–incrimination (Art. 51).

The first trial by jury since 1917 occurred in December 1993. Thus far, however, only nine of 89 regional courts have gone over to the new procedure. In the first eight months of 1994, something over 5,000 trials were held in regional courts; of that number, 99 were trials by jury. Trial by jury has not yet been introduced into the local "people's courts." There is apparent reluctance to depart from the communist idea that the state is a party in every trial and that courts should use trials to teach current doctrine.

### Criminality in the Russian Federation

Over the past few years, American newspapers have been full of stories about rising crime in Russia and the private security forces that have become necessary to cope with it. Many journalists seem to be at a loss to explain this new phenomenon, though they clearly tie it to the economic transformation currently underway there. There is no question but that crime has been increasing in Russia over the past several years. On the other hand, it should be remembered that the Soviet Union never permitted any reporting on crime until the last years of the Gorbachëv regime and the very existence of adequate reporting creates an image of a greater increase in crime than has been the case. Moscow is still, for most people, one of the safer cities of the world.

Another problem is that the police had been until recently responsible for suppressing the very sort of "economic crimes" which now constitute the emerging market system. Since many of those

**Midnight, with the Russian tri–color floating over the Kremlin after 74 years. St. Basil's Church is in the foreground.**
Courtesy: NOVOSTI

who arrested such "criminals" remain on the police force, it should not be surprising that they have been less than vigorous in enforcing the new legality.

A more serious problem is that corruption became endemic in the last years of the Brezhnev Era with many officials taking bribes to overlook black market activity. Payoffs became an important way to supplement salaries and the corruption reached high into the government and party. The Minister of the Interior, Shelokov, and his deputy, Chubanov, who also happened to be the son–in–law of Brezhnev, were eventually accused of illegal transactions. Shelokov committed suicide before being brought to trial, but Chubanov was found guilty and sentenced to several years in prison. But the corruption was too pervasive for the arrests of these top people to put a stop to it. When, with the fall of communism, private economic activity became legal, many of these officials and ex–officials continued to demand protection money from the new capitalists in much the same way they had milked black marketeers earlier. For example, *Izvestia* reported on May 6, 1994 that a group of senior Ministry of Interior officials had been charged with operating a protection ring for well–connected gangsters (i.e. ex–black marketeers) which included intervening to help killers, kidnappers and thieves stay out of jail.

As a result of widespread police corruption or even, in some cases, antipathy to developing capitalism, most businessmen feel that they cannot depend on the police for protection. This has spawned a whole new industry, private security companies, most of them started by retired Soviet soldiers, former members of *spetsnaz*, i.e., special Interior Ministry troops, or ex–policemen. The size of these security forces is sometimes enormous. Moreover, foreign businessmen wanting to establish a presence in Moscow often find that one of the first things they have to deal with is the matter of security. One such American businessman reported that he had been accosted by five men with pistols and a print–out of his firm's worth. They demanded 7% of future earnings. In this case, the businessman took the first flight back to New York. It is estimated that three–fourths of all private firms are paying 10% or more of their earnings in protection money.

This is obviously a heavy tax on the new market system, but the extent of this phenomenon can be and often is exaggerated. For example, *Izvestia* made the claim in July 1994 that more than half of all capital and 80% of voting shares in privatized enterprises "pass into the possession of criminal structures." There is no evidence to support such an enormous role for organized crime. There is, in fact, some evidence that some individuals opposed to

reform are publicizing rising crime figures as a means of discrediting the government and the idea of reform.

The rising level of crime is causing a political backpedaling of sorts, however. Reformers have, in general, stressed the rights of individuals and argued for limitations on the power of government. In July 1994, however, President Yeltsin issued a strong anti–crime decree which gave the police tough new powers. Acting under the new authority, the police seized some nine tons of weapons from suspected organized crime members in July. Demands for even more drastic action continue, however. As one complaint from the general directors of nine Moscow companies put it, the police are "doing nothing to put a stop to criminal activity, displaying indecisiveness and indifference toward the appeals of private entrepreneurs."

A number of Russian legislators, journalists and businessmen were killed in the period 1992–95, but the killing that brought the public to a frenzy of rage was

that of Vladislav Listyev, the head of Russia's public television network, gunned down in his apartment stairwell on March 1, 1995. In the resulting political firestorm, President Yeltsin himself went on television to express his sorrow at the killing and to apologize for allowing crime to spiral out of control. In the end, of course, the things that President Yeltsin can do about crime are all long–term.

Rising crime is, in fact, largely a symptom of the disruptions and discontinuities arising out of Russia's transformation from a command system to a market economy. Contributing to the problem is the fact that the government has not yet managed to establish clear and easily enforceable property rights, nor has the Federal Assembly been willing to pass a land code resolving, once and for all, who owns the land on which privatized enterprises and buildings are located. The government did manage to put a new civil code into effect in January 1995 which includes a section on entrepreneurial property rights.

**Hon. Yuri M. Luzhkov, Mayor of Moscow**

# THE NEW CONSTITUTION

**Article 1**

1. The Russian Federation—Russia shall be a democratic, federative, law–based state with a republican form of government.

**Article 3**

1. The multi–ethnic people of the Russian Federation shall be the bearers of its sovereignty and the sole source of authority in the Russian Federation.

**Article 5**

1. The Russian Federation shall be made up of republics, territories, regions, cities with federal status, the autonomous regions and autonomous areas, all of which are equal members of the Russian Federation.

**Article 8**

1. A unified economic space, the free movement of commodities, services and finances, and support for competition and freedom of economic activity shall be guaranteed in the Russian Federation.

2. Private, state, municipal and other forms of property shall be equally recognized and protected in the Russian Federation.

**Article 12**

Local self–government shall be recognized and guaranteed in the Russian Federation. Local self–government shall be independent within the limits of its powers. The bodies of local self–government shall not be part of the system of the bodies of state authority.

**Article 13**

1. Ideological pluralism shall be recognized in the Russian Federation.

2. No ideology shall be established as a state or compulsory ideology.

**Article 15**

4. Universally acknowledged principles and standards of international law and international treaties of the Russian Federation shall be a part of its legal system. Should an international treaty of the Russian Federation establish rules other than those established by law, the rules of the international treaty shall be applied.

**Article 27**

1. Each person who is legitimately within the territory of the Russian Federation shall have the right to move freely and to choose where to live temporarily or permanently.

**Article 35**

1. The right of private ownership shall be protected by law.

**Article 38**

3. Able–bodied children who have reached the age of eighteen years shall take care of parents who are unable to work.

**Article 40**

1. Each person shall have the right to housing. No person may be arbitrarily deprived of housing.

**Article 41**

1. Each person shall have the right to health protection and medical assistance.

**Article 43**

3. Each person shall be entitled on a competitive basis and free of charge to receive a higher education in a state or municipal educational institution or at an enterprise.

**Article 47**

1. 2. A person accused of committing a crime shall have the right to have a case heard by a court with the participation of jurors in the cases provided for by federal law.

**Article 49**

1. Each person accused of committing a crime shall be presumed innocent until his/her culpability is proved in the manner specified by federal law and established by a court sentence which has become effective.

2. Defendants shall not be obliged to prove their innocence.

**Article 59**

3. In cases where the performance of military service runs counter to a citizen's persuasions of religion, and also in other cases specified by federal law, a citizen of the Russian Federation shall have the right to replace military service with alternative civilian service.

**Article 81**

1. The President of the Russian Federation shall be elected to office for a term of four years by the citizens of the Russian Federation on the basis of universal, direct and equal suffrage by secret ballot.

3. The same individual shall not be elected to the office of President of the Russian Federation for more than two consecutive terms.

**Article 83**

The President of the Russian Federation shall:

a) appoint, with the consent of the State Duma, the Chairman of the Government of the Russian Federation;

b) be entitled to preside over sessions of the Government of the Russian Federation;

d) nominate for approval by the State Duma the Chairman of the Central Bank of the Russian Federation and bring before the State Duma the issue of removing the Chairman of the Central Bank of the Russian Federation from office;

f) nominate judges to the Constitutional Court, Supreme Court and Court of Arbitration of the Russian Federation and the Prosecutor-General of the Russian Federation; and appoint judges to other federal courts;

g) organize and chair the Security Council of the Russian Federation, the status of which shall be defined by federal legislation;

k) appoint and dismiss the top commanders of the Armed Forces of the Russian Federation;

**Article 86**

1. The President of the Russian Federation shall:

a) be in charge of the foreign policy of the Russian Federation;

**Article 87**

1. The President of the Russian Federation shall be Commander–in–Chief of the Armed Forces of the Russian Federation.

**Article 90**

1. The President of the Russian Federation shall issue decrees and directives.

2. Decrees and directives of the President of the Russian Federation shall be binding for execution throughout the territory of the Russian Federation.

**Article 95**

1. The Federal Assembly shall consist of two houses—a Federal Council and a State Duma.

**Article 103**

1. The State Duma shall have the power:

a) to approve the nominee of the President of the Russian Federation to the office of the Chairman of the Government of the Russian Federation;

c) to appoint the Chairman of the Central Bank of the Russian Federation and to remove him from office;

f) to declare amnesty;

g) to lodge accusations against the President of the Russian Federation for the purpose of removing him from office by impeachment;

**Article 105**

1. The federal laws shall be adopted by the State Duma.

3. The federal laws adopted by the State Duma shall be submitted for consideration by the Federation Council within a period of five days.

5. In case of the disagreement of the State Duma with the decision of the Federation Council, a federal law shall be considered adopted if in the repeat voting at least two-thirds of the total number of the State Duma deputies have voted for it.

**Article 117**

3. The State Duma may give the government of the Russian Federation a vote of no confidence . . . by majority vote of the total number of the State Duma deputies. . . . The President of the Russian Federation may announce the resignation of the government of the Russian Federation or reject the decision of the State Duma. If within the next three months the State Duma again gives the government a vote of no confidence, the President of the Russian Federation shall announce the resignation of the government of the Russian Federation or dissolve the State Duma.

**Article 120**

1. Judges shall be independent and subject only to the Constitution of the Russian Federation and federal law.

**Article 121**

1. Judges shall be irremovable.

**Article 123**

4. Judicial proceedings shall be conducted with the participation of a jury in cases provided for by federal law.

**Article 132**

1. The bodies of local self–government shall independently manage municipal property; prepare, approve and execute the local budget; establish local taxes and levies; maintain public order; and decide other questions of local importance.

The grand staircase in the Winter Palace (now part of the Hermitage Museum in St. Petersburg.) In 1732 Tsarina Anna commanded Italian architect Bartolomeo Rastrelli to build a four–storied Winter Palace of extravagant design and furnishings; it was built during the reign of Tsarina Elizabeth (1741–62).

Photo by Miller B. Spangler

# Culture

The failure of the August 1991 *coup* led to the repudiation of communism and the subsequent collapse of the Soviet Union, thereby giving birth to an independent Russian Federation committed to the goals of pluralism, democracy, privatization and a market economy. These events marked the end of an era of official culture, but seventy years of sloganistic indoctrination of the people with the philosophy of Marxism–Leninism cannot be overcome overnight. Proletarianism and socialism remain defining ideas for many people, and even terms like "socialist realism" have their supporters among conservatives. The old ideas live on, particularly among the old, among the peasants of the countryside, and among all segments of the population in the old industrial towns.

The greatest transformation has occurred in St. Petersburg and Moscow. Even in large cities, however, change is often resisted. In St. Petersburg, for example, the Kirov Ballet, which resumed the name of Marinsky in 1992, as it was known prior to the revolution, is once again known as the Kirov Ballet, though it has retained the name Marinsky for the theater. Even today, the battle continues over just how commercial the new Kirov needs to become to survive as a great ballet company.

That probably should not be surprising. Throughout the Soviet era, at least two other cultures co–existed with the official version of Soviet culture. The first of these was pre–revolutionary Russian culture; the second was non–official culture. To these must be added religious culture, which survived in spite of official disparagement by the state, and today again flourishes. The meaning of the repudiation of communism is that these cultures have, once again, assumed their traditional role in defining Russian culture; now it is Soviet culture that is tolerated and lingers on.

How much of Soviet culture will persist? Some "proletarian" authors and artists will undoubtedly continue to write or paint, although the Russian people have very little taste for political art after a steady diet of it for 70 years. But the fact is that there never was very much purely "Soviet" art and what there was of it was usually tied to specific political campaigns that became outdated. Such art has a historical interest, of course, but it was by definition not made to transcend the age in which it was produced, and so it now lacks artistic interest.

Some of the work by revolutionary artists and novelists in the 1920s was an exception to this, but even that period had its darker aspects. Many artists, stifled in the new conformity, fled abroad. Others, like the poets Vladimir Maiakovsky and Sergei Yessenin, committed suicide.

The Association of Proletarian Writers was an annoyance in the late 1920's because of its intolerant attitude toward those who did not share its "proletarian" outlook, but that period appeared mild in retrospect after Stalin had instituted his authoritarian cultural controls and enforced his "socialist realism." Most of the great works of the 1920s were banned as unproletarian in the 1930s. These included the novels of Mikhail Bulgakov, author of *The Master and Margarita* and *Heart of a Dog*, and the paintings of Andrei Malevich, who even in the 1920s had been forced to give up his earlier, abstract style.

Dmitri Shostakovich, the composer, and Sergei Eisenstein, the film producer, were two exceptions who managed to produce great works in the 1930s, but both of them came under criticism in the periods of the 1940s and either had to revise their works or couldn't get them released at all.

But the fact is that most "Soviet" culture was actually pre–Soviet culture. There never were that many revolutionary artists, and most of these eventually found themselves stifled by the regime's tight controls. So the great novels that people continued to read or the great artists that they admired were mostly pre–revolutionary. In effect, except for elements considered anti–revolutionary, the regime appropriated Russian culture to itself. Thus poets like Alexander Pushkin and Michael Lermontov continued to be published throughout the Soviet period, along with short story writers like Nikolai Gogol, novelists like Ivan Turgenev, Fedor Dostoyevsky, Leo Tolstoy and Maxim Gorky, and playwrights such as Anton Chekhov.

Russian ballet, one of the "glories" of Soviet culture, continued to be dominated by classical French choreography. There were some experiments with modern dance after Stalin's death but, because they usually expressed revolutionary themes, they seldom rose to the level of art. Most Russian operas performed throughout the Soviet era were pre–revolutionary. All of this gave Russian culture the eerie aspect of being a museum of the past.

Things did get better after Stalin's death, but artists had been repressed so long by that time that very few of them were capable of great art. Still, some of these works are interesting for historical purposes. Ilya Ehrenburg's novel, *The Thaw*, is not a very good book, but everyone read it because of its message of hope. To a certain extent, this period of liberalization was associated with the personal fortunes of Nikita Khrushchev. Although vocal in his own dislike for modern, especially abstract, painting, he encouraged writers who wrote works critical of the "distortions" of the Stalin era. He personally defended the book *Not By Bread Alone* by Vladimir Dudintsev. It was also he who authorized the publication of Alexander Solzhenitsyn's *A Day in the Life of Ivan Denisovich*.

Cultural controls were tightened again after Khrushchev's departure. This produced a great outpouring of unofficial Soviet culture. Some painters had always found their art to be unacceptable to the regime, so they had to find ways of supporting themselves by other means. The number of individuals able to afford paintings increased considerably after the death of Stalin, however, so artists, though shut out of official exhibits, were able to find customers for their unofficial art.

The situation for writers was somewhat different. Unable to get works published, some resorted to circulating them in manuscript form. This was referred to in Russian as *samizdat*—literally, self–publication. Others, seeking a wider circulation, contrived to have a manuscript smuggled abroad, where it would be published, usually in translation. Having an unapproved manuscript published abroad was legally an anti–Soviet act, however, and a number of writers were imprisoned for this offense. Because of the Soviet Union's policy of "socialist realism," nearly every great work of Soviet literature written after 1930 had to be published abroad and almost every Soviet Nobel Prize winner for literature was labeled a dissident.

In the early 1970s, the Brezhnev regime added a refinement when it began expelling Soviet artists or stripping them of their citizenship while abroad. The most famous of those was Alexander Solzhenitsyn, expelled from the Soviet Union in 1974. A number of other artists who had

*"Family":*——D.D. Zhilinsky (Grand themes tended to give way to scenes of daily life in the 1960s)

been given permission to travel chose to live and work abroad. The pianist Vladimir Ashkenazy chose to live in England. The renowned cellist–conductor Mstislav Rostropovich and his talented wife settled in the United States. Several top ballet performers defected while touring abroad, while others, like the Panovs, emigrated after long delays in waiting for permission to leave Russia.

The beginning of the Gorbachëv era, with its emphasis on *glasnost,* widened the area of the permissible and brought the publication of previously banned works. Thus writings of Anna Akhmatova, Boris Pasternak, Alexander Solzhenitsyn, Mikhail Bulgakov, Vladimir Nabokov, Osip Mandelshtam and Marina Tsvetaeva were all published. A selection of Akhmatova's poems was put out by the journal *Oktyabr.* Moscow's Taganka Theater brought a play about Pasternak and his novel, *Dr. Zhivago,* to the Soviet stage, and the novel itself, for which Pasternak received the 1958 Nobel Prize for literature, was published beginning in January 1988 by the journal *Novy Mir.*

Another example of greater freedom for the arts under Gorbachëv was the new play by Mikhail Shatrov, *The Brest Peace.* Shatrov's play gives a detailed and fairly sympathetic treatment of Lev Trotsky and Nikolai Bukharin. Trotsky's name had been anathema in the USSR ever since his expulsion by Stalin in 1929; Bukharin was executed in 1938 as part of the Stalinist purges. What is perhaps most interesting about the play is that it was written in 1962, but the author had previously been unable to get it performed or published. Gorbachëv eventually put his personal stamp of approval on this new trend:

"There should be no forgotten names or blanks. We must not forget names and it is all the more immoral to forget or pass over in silence large periods in the life of the people."

As Gorbachëv apparently intended, part of this new "openness" turned into an attack on Stalin. Thus a novel by Anatoly Rybakov published in 1986, *Children of the Arbat,* depicts Stalin as pathologically suspicious and politically obtuse. Like Shatrov's play, *The Brest Peace,* Rybakov's novel was written in the 1960's but he was not able to get it published earlier.

New plays with similar themes also began to appear by 1988. The best known was another play by Mikhail Shatrov, entitled "On, On, On," which was published in the January 1988 issue of the literary monthly *Znamya.* A controversial play, it is full of suppressed details of Soviet history and is harshly anti-Stalinist. Interviewed about the play, Shatrov commented that "If you read my plays you will see that all of them are in essence about one thing: Stalin is not Lenin's heir. Stalin is a

criminal of the kind the world has never had. He is not a Communist for me, because if he is a Communist, I have to leave the party immediately."

Many Soviet intellectuals who shared Shatrov's point of view began pressing the party for a total repudiation of Stalin and a rehabilitation of his victims. Gorbachëv was, in general, sympathetic but other members of the leadership, including Ligachev, Chebrikov and Yazov, spoke out against what they termed the "one–sided" evaluation of Stalin. While willing to condemn such things as the 1930s purges, they argued that Stalin should be given credit for such things as industrialization and collectivization and the USSR's victory in World War II. In essence, their view of Stalin was that he was a good Communist who had made mistakes.

The resulting division led to a battle in the Soviet media in which Shatrov, in particular, was accused of "inaccuracies," "juggling with the facts," and "departure from the truth." What more conservative reformers like Ligachev apparently feared is that excessive criticism of the past would weaken popular faith in the party. In the summer of 1990, after the final defeat of Ligachev at the 28th Party Congress, Gorbachëv ended the controversy by issuing a decree rehabilitating Stalin's victims.

After 1990, artists were basically free to write or compose or paint what they wanted, free of party tutelage. Thus, with few exceptions, Gorbachëv had brought an end to the long period of official supervision of the arts by the cultural affairs section of the Communist Party. These last few exceptions ended in August 1991 with the failure of the *coup* to unseat Gorbachëv and reinstate a new orthodoxy. The complicity of the Communist Party in the *coup* led to its repudiation and Boris Yeltsin subsequently issued a decree in effect banning the party.

The collapse of the Soviet Union and the emergence of an independent Russian Federation with Boris Yeltsin as President marked the beginning of a new era in which Russian culture, free finally of all state controls, was free to develop as Russians wished it. This has already brought changes, not all of them laudable, to be sure. Culture now has to be much more "commercial," since it needs customers to survive. As some artists are beginning to recall with nostalgia, the old Soviet regime subsidized art as well as controlled it.

**Religion in the Russian Federation**
Religion had a peculiar status in the now defunct Soviet Union. There was an officially declared separation of church and state, and Soviet citizens had a constitutionally guaranteed freedom of worship. But communism, the ideology of the only legal political party, was militantly

**His Holiness Patriarch Aleksiy of Moscow and All Russia**

atheistic, so the constitution guaranteed the right of anti–religious propaganda as well.

Official opposition to religion had its roots in the basic materialistic philosophy of Marxism, which held that spiritual matters were merely a reflection of material things and conditions. Karl Marx, in a famous phrase, stated that religion was being used by the ruling classes as an opiate, or drug, which dulled the ability of the masses to know their real problems and find the solution for them. Claiming to derive their views from scientific knowledge, communists saw themselves as secular and "this world" minded and opposed religion as "unscientific" and false. Since communists held that their value system represented "truth," they were extremely intolerant of all religious teachings, because of their competing claims to truth. In fact, communism had a comprehensive world outlook and set of beliefs which made it a sort of "religion" itself. It even promised paradise, though it was to be here on earth rather than in another world.

Communist theory held that communism represented a new "consciousness" on the part of mankind. To reach the stage of communism, therefore, it was necessary to "transform" the thinking of the people through a process of consciousness–raising or indoctrination. This process was to result in the emergence of a "New Man," conditioned to living in a communist society.

Communists attached particular importance to the "educational" functions of the party. They were especially concerned with shaping the basic beliefs of the younger generation, since young people were still untainted with the corruptions of the previous system. Religious bodies, since they represented the values of the previous system, were forbidden to proselytize or to carry on any public functions other than the worship service itself. Churches, synagogues, and mosques were barred from all areas of education, including Sunday schools and catechism classes. Organized acts of charity were also forbidden and religious marriage ceremonies were banned. For a time, even the ringing of bells was forbidden.

Beyond that, the regime tended to differentiate in its treatment of individual religions depending on the total number of adherents and the role accorded it in pre–revolutionary Russia. The Orthodox Church, to which most Russians, Ukrainians and Byelorussians belonged, had been one of the mainstays of the old system and a loyal tool of the tsarist governments. Moreover, the Orthodox Church adopted a strongly anti–Bolshevik position during the revolutionary upheaval of 1917 and the civil war that followed. Thus the Orthodox Church became a particular target. During the civil war, many members of the clergy, including the Patriarch, were arrested and quite a number were executed. All church buildings were nationalized and many were closed. In the 1920s, the party created an organization known as the *League of Militant Atheists* to carry on the battle against religion. Members of the league, lavishly supported by the regime, engaged in all sorts of anti-religious propaganda. One of the things they did was to turn Kazan Cathedral in St. Peters-burg, a beautiful, neoclassical church built in the 18th century, into the Museum of Atheism.

Islam came under similar restrictions. Islam was considered to be even more dangerous than Christianity in some respects, since it recognized no distinction between the secular and the religious. In addition, the Moslem clergy were strong defenders of the traditional way of life, and so opposed most of what the communists were trying to do. Communists therefore did their best to stamp out Islam in Central Asia. Religious schools and mosques were closed and many of the Islamic clergy were imprisoned.

Nor did this cease after the regime had consolidated its power. In the 1930s, Stalin ordered churches, synagogues and mosques closed all over the country and he had a number of Moscow's historic churches torn down as a part of his rebuilding of the center of the city. Most of the remainder were turned into museums or converted to other secular uses.

As conditions became stabilized in the late 1930's, the Stalin regime adopted a somewhat less militant position toward religion. A dramatic turn occurred after the German invasion of the country in June 1941. The *League of Militant Atheists* was dissolved and its printing facilities were actually turned over to the Russian Orthodox Church. Stalin had come to the conclusion that, in a crisis, the communist regime could make use of the support of the Church with its deep roots among the masses.

The regime tightened its control again after the end of the war, but this was mainly to guarantee that the church continued to serve the goals of the state. Internationally, members of the higher Orthodox clergy were frequently used as delegates to various international peace congresses. Domestically, the Patriarch and other members of the hierarchy were expected periodically to speak out in support of Soviet policy. The Islamic clergy, by this time tamed, was also used occasionally for diplomatic missions, mainly to the Middle East.

Even so, about 10,000 additional churches were closed between 1959 and 1964—about half the remaining total in the Soviet Union. In 1960, the Archbishop of Kazan was tried and sentenced to prison. That same year, the Metropolitan Nicholas of Krutitsy was deprived of his offices. And in Central Asia, historic mosques, sitting unused, fell further into disrepair. This policy of repression, associated mainly with the regime of Nikita Khrushchev, came to a partial end in 1964. The Brezhnev regime later permitted 500 of the closed churches to be reopened. Mosques were not reopened, but the most historic ones were given the classification of national treasures and the first efforts at restoration were begun.

Faithful Moslems gather for Friday prayer at the central mosque in Kazan, capital of the Tatar autonomous region on the Volga River.

Photo by Steve Raymer © 1991 National Geographic Society

The Brezhnev regime remained officially atheist, but it was a conservative regime that tended to accept religion as part of the status quo. Russian nationalism enjoyed something of a revival at this time as well, and that was often extended to include the Orthodox Church. As a result, it was the best–treated of all the organized religious groupings in the U.S.S.R. under Brezhnev and saw even a modest growth in its nominal membership to more than 30 million. In the last years of the Brezhnev regime, church services were overflowing and, in a change from the past, many young people began attending services. Since most of this growth occurred in the period now known as "the era of stagnation," it was partly a symptom of the loss of faith in communism that was then only beginning to manifest itself.

Brezhnev died in November 1982, but the era of stagnation really lasted until March 1985, when Mikhail Gorbachëv was appointed General Secretary. Although it was not immediately apparent, Gorbachëv had an entirely different attitude toward religion than his predecessors as leader of the Communist Party of the Soviet Union. Although not a believer, his attitude may have been influenced by the fact that his mother is. But whatever the reason, Gorbachëv set out rather systematically to end the party's traditional hostility toward religion. One of the points he made in justifying this change of position was that people needed moral values and that religion had an important contribution to make in this area. In 1988, official celebrations marking the millennium of Russia's conversion to Christianity symbolized this changed attitude on the part of regime.

In September 1990, the USSR Supreme Soviet passed new legislation prohibiting the government from interfering in religious activities. Another law required the state to reopen a place of worship on receipt of a petition signed by at least 20 believers. Some 4,000 new parishes opened between 1985 and 1991.

In another indication of this change, when Patriarch Pimen died in May 1990, one of those who spoke a eulogy at his funeral service was Anatoliy Lukyanov, Chairman of the USSR Supreme Soviet. And in 1991, Boris Yeltsin, the President of the Russian Federation, and Valentin Pavlov, the Soviet Chairman of the Cabinet of Ministers, were among those attending Easter services at Epiphany Cathedral in Moscow. Easter services were also held at St. Basil's Cathedral on Red Square, even though it was still officially a museum.

Gorbachëv's changed policy eventually came to be applied to Moslem areas as well, though somewhat later because the Iranian revolution and the war in Afghanistan had created fears of an Islamic fundamentalism sweeping through Central Asia. The Soviet troop pullout from Afghanistan and the death of Iran's Khomeini reduced that threat, and paved the way for a changed policy toward Islam.

This brought the beginnings of a religious revival. Mosques were reopened all over Central Asia. In 1990, fourteen new mosques were opened for services in Kokand, some while still under construction. For decades, a single mosque had served a Moslem population of 150,000 in that city. Elsewhere, mosques were being opened at the rate of almost one a day. In Uzbekistan, over 200 new mosques were opened in 1989–90. Hundreds of students were enrolled in theological colleges and millions of copies of the Koran were distributed. And more than 1,500 Soviet Moslems made the pilgrimage to Mecca in 1990, the largest number in recent memory. As Muhammad Yusuf, the grand mufti of Tashkent and Central Asia's senior Moslem leader said, "at first Moslems were rather passive and did not react quickly to what was happening elsewhere in the country. Now we are demanding the same privileges accorded to other religions."

Judaism represented a somewhat different situation because, under Soviet law, Jews were viewed as both a religious group and a nationality. Various factors made the situation complex, including a pre–revolutionary tradition of anti–Semitism which Lenin combated as being a tool of reaction. Stalin reversed this position in the late 1940s with his campaigns against "rootless cosmopolitan writers," and his later "Doctors' Plot." Anti–Zionism survived Stalin and continued to justify anti–Semitism under his successors.

In the past, religious practices of Soviet Jews were limited by the government, but the Gorbachëv regime's changed attitude toward religion brought about a basic change of attitude toward Jews as well. In general, the restrictions on the practice of Judaism were abolished. Jews were authorized to set up religious schools and seminaries and to begin giving religious instruction to young people. One problem was the lack of trained rabbis. That was partially solved by bringing in rabbis from abroad. Hasidic organizations from the United States and Israel have also been actively providing assistance of all sorts.

The failed *coup* of August 1991 created a new situation by bringing a repudiation of the Communist Party and a break up of the Soviet Union. The newly independent Russian Federation closed down the Communist Party and rejected its ideology. Religion is now considered to be a matter of conscience and as such beyond the purview of the state. In December 1991, President Yeltsin symbolized this new approach by issuing an appeal to heads of religious faiths and believers in which he condemned "the policy of spiritual genocide" of the previous regime and promised to "eliminate the consequences of the profoundly unjust policy of the many–year–long communist dictatorship with regard to believers [and] to hand over religious shrines, churches, and cloisters to those to whom they should rightly belong."

Christian churches still have a job of rebuilding after the years of repression, but they have already begun the task. The Moslems of the Soviet Union, located mainly in the six republics of Central Asia, now have their own independent governments to look after their interests. Moslems living in the Russian Federation constitute a tiny percentage of the population. They have been guaranteed the same rights as other believers, but they have another guarantee as well, since they are mainly to be found in the autonomous republics or other autonomous regions and so have their own governments to represent their interests. They are mainly found in the Volga River Valley and in the area of the north Caucasus.

The greatest current threat to Jewish culture in the Russian Federation today is probably the large emigration currently going on, approximately 400,000 in the period 1990–91. If that rate of emigration continues, there will soon be few Jews left in Russia. That would be unfortunate, since the Jews have made many great contributions to Russian culture in the past. In fact, emigration seems to be declining somewhat following the collapse of the Soviet Union and there are increasing indications that Jews are reconsidering leaving. A number of new Jewish high schools, newspapers and theaters have been opened in the past two years, and an increasing number of individual Jews are speaking about the newly independent Russian Federation as a place that offers bright prospects for Jewish life.

### Education

Russian education, like almost everything else in Russian society, is currently in a state of transition. The failure of the August 1991 *coup* has brought about a repudiation of Communism and the subsequent collapse of the Soviet Union itself. As a result, the regimentation in the area of education enforced by that old system has also disappeared. The Government of the Russian Federation has not rushed in to assume the authority of the old center, so individual school districts find themselves very much on their own. The result is that individual schools are beginning to make changes and institute programs that, increasingly, set them off from other schools. Some school authorities fear that this is producing a fragmented, localized system, but others see this as another example of increasing pluralism in the society.

**Religious procession in Moscow**

Photo by Miller B. Spangler

One of the changes already evident is an abandonment of the school uniforms worn by all school children under the old system. Most children continue to wear the uniforms, or parts of them, but they now also wear a variety of sweaters and jackets. Some schools have also begun offering classes in religious education. In other schools, educational reformers are asking how school systems can be changed to make them better able to serve the needs of a market economy.

Education in Russia saw many changes in the 74 years following the Russian Revolution of 1917. In the first years after the revolution, "Progressive" methods were tried on all levels, with an almost total elimination of classroom discipline. Teachers were subjected to the rule of committees of pupils; there was much noisy activity and very little learning.

When the revolutionary fervor faded, education was reestablished along traditional lines, with uniform studies for all schools of the huge country and a strong emphasis on the sciences and mathematics. Elective courses were abolished in favor of a standard curriculum throughout the Soviet Union. Teaching was conducted in the native languages of the various Union Republics, but the content was centrally determined in Moscow.

A major problem of pre–revolutionary Russia was that more than 60% of the people could not read and write. This high illiteracy rate was vigorously attacked by the Soviet government and as a result, by 1928, more than half of the citizens were literate. The figure rose to 81% in 1939 and is now almost 100%.

For a while, the state–controlled school was looked upon as a counter–balance to the "reactionary" influences of traditional family ties; at the height of the purges, children were encouraged to report "subversive" activities of their own parents and other relatives. In the late 1930s, this approach was abandoned in favor of an emphasis on the Soviet family as the source of "correct" values. The events of August 1991 have reinforced this approach.

Because increasing numbers of Russian women were drawn into the work force in the 1930s, a wide network of nurseries and kindergartens—usually run by individual factories—was created to take care of children of working mothers. These facilities have often been crowded and not particularly well run, and in recent years privately–operated day care centers have come into existence. That trend is expected to increase as the Russian privatization program progresses over the next several years. In addition, many factories will begin running their day care centers as commercial ventures, making them available to anyone who wants to use them, not just their own factory employees. The Russian Supreme Soviet has already set fees at "20 percent of the cost of maintaining the child" as of April 1, 1992.

Regular schooling lasts for 8, 10 or 11 years, depending on where the student lives and his or her academic achievement. Children attend school six days a week, though the school day for primary students is relatively short, consisting of four 45–minute lessons. Additional after-school supervision is offered to children of working mothers. Such children are organized into "extended–day" groups and they remain at school until their parents come to take them home. After-school supervision is an area that is likely to feel the pinch of tight budgets which are scaling back the amount of money going into education.

There are basically two types of secondary schools—general and technical— but a movement began in the late 1970s to merge the two. In 1978, for instance, the time reserved in the school curriculum for machine–shop practice was doubled. Senior pupils were also required to spend four hours a week at a factory or on a farm, receiving on–the–job training.

A new reform decree, issued in early 1984, carried this evolution further. Beginning in 1986, children started school at age 6, one year earlier than previously, and they began to receive greater vocational training as an integral part of their schooling. Each student was now expected to master at least one basic mechanical skill before graduating, even though enrolled in an "academic course." Compulsory vocation courses will probably disappear under the new system that is beginning to evolve, though vocational education for those who opt for it is likely to become more available in the future.

There were great fears even before August 1991 that Gorbachëv's move to a market economy would have an adverse effect on the university system. Thus far, the collapse of the union government has had no such effect, because the Russian Government has taken over responsibility for institutions of higher education and has continued to fund them.

The likely scarcity of funds over the next several years and the policy of the Russian Government that societal institutions should, to the maximum extent possible, be self–supporting will undoubtedly bring about changes. Most universities will probably have to institute tuition fees to cover part of the cost of education. The Russian Government has also authorized the creation of new schools and universities and some non-state educational institutions, including church schools and private schools, have already come into being. Some of the current state universities have raised the possibility of turning themselves into private institutions. A distinct growth of pluralism is thus beginning within the system, though the process will continue to be gradual.

The area of culture most favored under the old system was that of the natural sciences, mainly because the regime came to the conclusion that keeping scientists in a strait–jacket in harmony with official dogma hampered Russia's ability to compete with nations with superior technology. Scientists were some of the most independent people in the Soviet Union and some of them spoke out courageously against the official pressures and Party–imposed limitations. One has only to think of Andrei Sakharov as an example.

The life sciences such as biology always had to put up with greater tutelage than the natural sciences, but even here the party eventually withdrew as an arbiter. The social sciences remained under official tutelage until 1985, but gained almost total freedom under Gorbachëv. Sociolo-

gy, not even recognized as a separate discipline until recently, was also freed by Gorbachëv.

Opinion polls began to play an increasing role in the society. Even history, always the most controlled of the social sciences, underwent the beginnings of a renaissance when Gorbachëv called for new histories of the Communist Party and new school books that would restore names and historical periods that had been cloaked in official silence. "There should be no forgotten names or blanks either in history or literature," he said, adding that "history must be seen for what it is." In fact, Gorbachëv's policy of *glasnost* had brought about so many changes in this area by 1988 that the history exams had to be canceled that year, since all of the history books were completely out of date.

Thus the older system of control was

greatly weakened even before the attempted *coup* of August 1991 brought that whole system down completely. Still, it had a major effect for the Communist Party apparachniks were expelled from their previous positions of power, and centralized controls disappeared. Much that existed down to August 1991 had nothing to do with Communist ideology as such, however, but rather reflected traditional Russian cultural mores. The new leaders of Russian society have now had four years to purge remnants of communist ideology from the system, but a great deal continues to look and operate the way it always did. The difference is that there is a great deal more pluralism in the new system being created than the one that is being replaced.

**A St. Petersburg school specializing in English. Russian students present Tom Sawyer, Becky Thatcher, and the fence painted white—with the dialogue all in English!**

Photo by Miller B. Spangler

Democratic groups march through Moscow in September 1990 to demand immediate steps towards a market economy

# The Changing Economy

The old command economy created by Stalin in the 1930s had already been seriously undermined—though not eradicated—by Gorbachëv's policy of *perestroika* even before the failed *coup* in August 1991 brought about a repudiation of communism and a collapse of the Soviet Union. The end of the Union and the emergence of an independent Russian state have transformed the situation completely. With the Union abolished, the old centralized bureaucracy, which had dominated the economy for so long, came under the control of the Russian Federation, which gradually phased it out. The Government of the Russian Federation did retain some instruments of economic control, but President Yeltsin's government has gone a long way toward eradication of the command system and replacing it with a market economy based on private enterprise.

This process of transformation has not been smooth, however. The last two years of Gorbachëv's *perestroika* were a disaster insofar as the economy was concerned, so the Russian Federation inherited a system that was in collapse. Some of the symptoms were a hyperinflation in which the ruble, officially valued at about $1.75, actually traded at about one cent; a state trading system which was unable to provide the public with any goods because they could obtain almost no goods at the low, fixed prices they were authorized to pay—and much of what they did obtain was siphoned off for sale at a large mark–up on the black market; and a budget deficit that was over half the size of the overall budget. Industrial production was also down, approximately 10% over the preceding year as individual enterprises found it more and more difficult to obtain raw materials and component parts.

President Yeltsin launched his program to begin the transformation to a market economy and private enterprise on January 2, 1992. His first step was to abolish state–set prices for most goods. Prices jumped an average of 300–350% percent, reflecting the hyperinflation of the preceding months but, by the end of January, more goods began to appear in the shops and prices started to drift downward, reflecting the increased supply and resistance among consumers to the higher prices. In the cities and towns, lively street vending also made more consumer goods available. The increase in prices permitted the government to begin phasing out subsidies

The price increases permitted the government to begin phasing out subsidies to industry and agriculture, and allowed it to draw up a budget for the first three months of 1992 with a deficit reduced to 4.4% of the Gross Domestic Product. The government later lowered the Value Added Tax, which the Yeltsin Government had instituted to replace the old turnover and sales taxes, from 28 percent to 15 percent as a way to lower costs to consumers. The ruble continued to stabilize, however, then actually began to increase in value as demand for the ruble grew—in effect a vote of confidence in the government's program.

Freeing prices and moving toward a balanced budget were necessary first steps. President Yeltsin's government was also committed to achieving ruble convertibility as soon as possible and had negotiated with the International Monetary Fund for a ruble stabilization fund, like the one created in 1990 to support the Polish currency. As an interim step, he announced that the Russian Central Bank would set a single official value for the ruble based on the results of weekly currency auctions. Yeltsin hoped that the stabilization process could begin in the summer of 1992, after Russia was admitted to the IMF and World Bank.

Yeltsin also moved forward on other aspects of his economic reform. In February 1992, he announced plans to privatize 25% of state property by the end of the year. Under the plan, 25% ownership in state firms would be turned over to current employees, while the remaining 75% would be sold at auction.

The government also decided that, in order to maintain a tightened fiscal policy, it would have to phase out most remaining subsidies. Even in this first stage of reform, however, approximately 90% of consumer goods and 80% of industrial goods were freed of direct administrative regulation. Controls were maintained over twelve basic food products, certain communal services, certain fuels and some semi-finished products. The government also announced that it would begin a liberalization of fuel prices after the winter heating season was over. Fuel prices were then to begin rising in steps until they reached world prices at the end of 1993. The government predicted that the economy would continue to decline until sometime in 1993, when a turnabout was expected.

In retrospect, the government's predictions on the amount of inflation that would be unleashed with the freeing of prices turned out to be unduly optimistic. By June 1992, the exchange rate for the ruble had declined to about 100+ to the dollar, there were money shortages throughout the country and many individuals had not been paid for weeks. Other disruptions were occurring as well. Many of the state stores had closed down, while others had almost nothing to sell. Overall, more goods were available, but they were mainly sold from kiosks erected along the sidewalks, since most of these new, private entrepreneurs operated on a small-scale and, in any case, the state-owned buildings were still not available for private entrepreneurs to rent. Many of the items sold were imported also, since the state companies continued to deal only with other state companies. Some private shops did manage to find local suppliers, but it wasn't easy. The result was that ordinary individuals were ambivalent in their attitudes. There was still support for Yeltsin, but almost everybody had their complaints.

In this atmosphere, the Supreme Soviet, which five months earlier had granted President Yeltsin the power to rule by decree for one year, emerged as a center of opposition to Yeltsin's reforms. Under the leadership of Arkady Volsky, Chairman of the Union of Entrepreneurs of Russia, and with the cooperation of Vice President Rutskoi and Ruslan Khasbulatov, Chairman of the Supreme Soviet, the Supreme Soviet became the forum for blistering attacks on President Yeltsin's economic policies.

In a series of measures taken during the month of June, the Supreme Soviet voted down two separate attempts to pass a bankruptcy law, rejected a land reform law which would have permitted greater private ownership, then refused to consider the draft constitution submitted by President Yeltsin. It also began putting extreme pressure on the government to loosen up on credit to state enterprises. About 25% of the members of the Supreme Soviet and the larger parent body, the Congress of People's Deputies, were managers of state enterprises, but this was not viewed as a conflict of interest. In their rhetoric, in fact, the enterprise managers portrayed themselves as protectors of the workers' livelihoods.

Industrial production had dropped by about 15 percent over the preceding year and President Yeltsin now recognized that something would have to be done to prevent further declines. Accordingly, the government promised to provide industry with an extra 320 billion rubles in credit. In addition, President Yeltsin issued a decree at the beginning of July canceling the accumulated debts of all state enterprises, a sum amounting to approximately 1.9 trillion rubles. The government also agreed to postpone scheduled increases in energy prices.

The conservative majority in the Supreme Soviet was not satisfied with these governmental actions, however. Yeltsin was still committed to his program of economic reform and other decrees had continued that process. For example, a decree issued at the beginning of July established a process for bankruptcy for enterprises defaulting on debts incurred after July 1. Yet another decree ordered the privatization of all state-owned enterprises, except state farms and certain defense and energy firms deemed vital to the country, by July 1, 1995.

Coincidentally, the Supreme Soviet was presented with an opportunity to further undermine economic reform when Georgy Matyukhin, head of the Russian State Bank, resigned toward the end of June. Taking advantage of the fact that the old Communist Era constitution designated the parent Congress of People's Deputies as the highest authority within the system and made the State Bank Chairman accountable to the Supreme Soviet, Speaker Kasbulatov and the Congress appointed Viktor Gerashchenko, former head of the USSR State Bank, as the new Russian State Bank Chairman.

Gerashchenko immediately began issuing large amounts of credit to state enterprises. This policy, which Gerashchenko later said he had instituted at the behest of the Supreme Soviet leadership, had the full and vocal support of the members of the Supreme Soviet. The alternate, argued individual speakers, was massive layoffs of workers. Over the next five months, the State Bank Chairman flooded the country with massive new credits, setting off an inflation that dropped the value of the ruble from about 100+ to the dollar to about 750 to the dollar.

**President Yeltsin with alert bodyguards**

Courtesy: NOVOSTI

Then in December the leaders of the Supreme Soviet convened the parent Congress of People's Deputies and used this forum to challenge Yeltsin directly. Here they attempted to strip him of most of his powers; though they failed, they did manage to oust Yegor Gaidar as Deputy Prime Minister and to force Yeltsin to accept a man of their choice, Viktor Chernomyrdin, as Prime Minister. Prime Minister Chernomyrdin turned out to be a disappointment to the parliamentary leadership, however, for he shortly became a convert to Yeltsin's overall economic reform.

Parliamentary opposition to Yeltsin and economic reform continued, however. In March 1993, the Congress of People's Delegates narrowly failed to impeach Yeltsin, then structured the referendum he had requested into a four question query designed to undermine him. In that they were to be disappointed, however, for the referendum, held on April 25, actually provided a vote of confidence in Yeltsin and his economic program. Meanwhile, the parliamentary attacks continued.

Yeltsin's political struggle with the legislature undoubtedly consumed a great deal of his time but, surprisingly, his overall reform remained more or less on track. Much of the credit for this properly goes to Anatoly Chubais, the minister in charge of privatization, who announced in March 1993 that his ministry had managed to privatize 46,815 firms in 1992. The 1992 privatizations were largely limited to small firms, mostly retail shops, however. The first privatizations of large industrial firms occurred in December 1992 when the government transformed 18 large firms into joint–stock companies, then began exchanging shares of stock for some of the 144 million privatization vouchers which had been issued earlier to the general public.

This became the new pattern. In March 1993, another 249 large firms were privatized using this method, among them the automobile manufacturing company Zil. This industry, with 103,000 workers, was important not only because of it size, but because the privatization was supported by the management and employees. The voucher system of privatization continued over the next fifteen months. When it finally ended in July 1994, more than 100,000 state companies had been transformed. These included 15,779 medium-sized and large enterprises, representing 62% of gross domestic production and employing 60% of the industrial work force. In addition, the 85,000 shops represented 70% of the national total. Approximately 50,000–70,000 kiosks continued to operate in the major cities, but the more successful ones are now beginning to buy or lease permanent shops. Perhaps the most interesting statistic of all is that approximately 40 million people had become shareholders in operating companies.

Privatization has continued since July 1994, but remaining enterprises are now being sold for cash, not vouchers. More recently, this has led to significant infusions of foreign capital as investment firms have begun to pump money into the newly privatized Russian firms. Some 500–600 American firms have set up shop in Moscow, sometimes alone and sometimes in joint ventures with Russian companies. The total amount of private American investment has been relatively small, however.

Although the program has been a success, general economic statistics have been more mixed. Overall production declined drastically in the first half of 1992, then leveled out in August 1992. Overall production began growing again after that, but sharp contractions in the military sector and a downturn in textile production, the latter caused mainly by a sharp increase in the cost of cotton imported from Central Asia, kept overall production figures below the December 1991 level. Subsequent government statistics have seemed to indicate that the economy had taken a turn for the worse and that what was left of the state–run economy was collapsing. That is probably misleading, however.

First of all, as privatization has been implemented, government statistics have become less and less meaningful. As an article in *The New York Times* put it in August 1994, "Russian figures barely touch the growing private economy." A second point to take into consideration is that official retail trade turnover figures for this same period were actually stable. Finally, many of the remaining state–run firms, refusing to adjust or change, continued to turn out products during this period that no one wanted to buy. Cutting out such production would actually be a help for the economy.

Still, statistics suggesting many firms in deep financial trouble was obviously a matter of concern for the government. President Yeltsin's response came in August 1994 when he signed a decree making available approximately $2 billion in state credits to firms, to use either for investment projects or to help them convert to other activities. Under the terms of the decree, enterprises were required to provide one–third of the money for conversion projects and half of the money for investment projects. Concurrently, the government announced that debts between companies totalled about $45 billion, and that a commission had been set up to deal with that problem.

### The Russian Economy and Inflation

Inflation has been the Russian economy's most persistent problem since prices were freed in January 1992. The problem has been that, although the government has been committed to a policy of relative fiscal austerity, political forces representing sectors of the economy hurt by the policy have periodically managed to get the government to grant huge new credits to their ailing sectors. The argument used has always been that such credits protect jobs which would be lost if the firms were forced out of business. Separate subsidies have also been voted for agriculture each fall in response to threats by collective farmers that otherwise they would not harvest the crops.

The first such flood of state credits began in June 1992, ordered by the Supreme Soviet and provided by the Russian State Bank. This brought a quick jump in inflation and a corresponding drop in the value of the ruble. By January 1993, inflation was running at 27% a month. A renewed restraint on credit then caused it to drop

**The ice cream vendor in St. Petersburg is a highly popular figure even in winter.**

Photo by Miller B. Spangler

to 21% by March, and it then continued downward throughout the summer. The Russian Government also got greater control over credit creation in April 1993 when the Russian State Bank agreed to work within restraints set by the government—though Gerashchenko, head of the State Bank, said that he agreed to the restraints because he believed that the government would find itself unable to live within them.

The government also received some psychological help when the industrial nations promised an additional $43 billion in the run-up to the April 25 referendum—even though a large part of that package included things such as loan facilities conditional on further reform, debt relief that would provide no new cash, and aid promised earlier and not yet delivered.

By September, however, the battle between reformers and conservatives had been renewed in full vigor. After rejecting the government's budget, the Supreme Soviet attempted to force a budget on the government which would have destroyed the government's program of reform. This brought on the confrontation between the Supreme Soviet and President Yeltsin that ended with the legislature being disbanded with new elections set for December 1993.

Although inflation had dropped to 12% a month by December, reformers did badly in that month's elections to the new Federal Assembly. By January 1994, most reformers had withdrawn from or been forced out of the cabinet, with only Anatoly Chubais remaining on as Minister for Privatization. Although Chernomyrdin continued as Prime Minister, the policy statement of the new government stressed a need for cushions against market forces and for investment in export industries, while downgrading the fight against inflation.

When the new budget was presented in March 1994, however, it appeared that the fight against inflation was not dead after all. In his budget message, Chernomyrdin warned that hyperinflation "means death" and announced that he had trimmed the budget from an estimated 17% of GDP to just over 10% of GDP. Why the reason for the change of emphasis? As it happened, the Russian Government was in the middle of negotiations with the IMF for a $1.5 billion loan to help finance the continued transformation to a market economy. Following publication of the 1994 budget and inflation figures for March indicating that inflation was running at 7.8%, the IMF agreed to release the requested funds.

Inflation dropped further to 6.4% in May, then to about 4% in June, and it began to appear that Russia was close to establishing a stable economy. In fact, however, the government was once again under extreme pressure from conserva-

For a century (in importance, if not quality), the GUM Department Store flanking Red Square has been the Macy's of Moscow.                    Photo by Miller B. Spangler

tives to come to the aid of the ailing defense industries and agriculture. Thus, beginning in July and continuing through September, the government made available an estimated 10 trillion rubles to these two sectors of the economy. Such a large influx of new money into the economy would normally have been accompanied by a downward drift in the value of the ruble. To counteract this trend, the Russian Central Bank spent some $2 billion between August and October to support and stabilize the ruble.

But the central bank's foreign reserves were not unlimited and it could not afford to dissipate all of its reserves. When it was forced to stop its support of the ruble in October 1994, the ruble all but collapsed, dropping in a single morning from 3,081 to the dollar to 3,926 to the dollar. Heavy intervention on the part of the Russian Central Bank brought the exchange rate down to 2,988 to the dollar, but Viktor Gerashchenko, President of the bank, coming under extreme criticism, submitted his resignation after President Yeltsin demanded his dismissal.

Following the events of October 1994, the government instituted a new stabilization policy. Furthermore, when it submitted its 1995 budget to the Federal Assembly, it indicated that it intended to utilize

a new mechanism for financing the deficit. Instead of requesting credits from the central bank, the government indicated that it would finance the deficit through the issuance of government securities and/or external loans from the West. The government also announced at this time that it had managed to reach an agreement with its 600 foreign bank creditors for the refinancing of $26 billion in loans. Finally, the Ministry for Privatization announced in October that foreign investment coming into Russia had quadrupled since the beginning of 1994 and was running at $400 million a month.

The Russian Government had hoped to obtain loans totalling $6.2 billion from the IMF, but discussions held in February 1995 failed to produce an agreement. One factor, undoubtedly, was that monthly inflation for the month of January reached 17.8%, a 12–month high. Another factor was the military campaign in Chechnya starting in December and was still continuing at the time of the meeting. Everyone recognized that the cost of the campaign, estimated to have already cost $1 billion, would inevitably increase the size of the budget deficit. The Russian-IMF talks continued, but the IMF took the position that the Russian Government would have to make a much greater effort to rein in inflation if it wanted any further credits. Perhaps in response, President Yeltsin signed several decrees giving him unprecedented control over government spending. Meanwhile, inflation dropped in March to 9.9%, an encouraging sign.

Reacting to the government's newfound will to control its money supply, the IMF announced on March 10 that it would make $6.4 billion available to the Russian Government, with the restriction that the monies would be advanced on a monthly basis and would be subject to greater controls than previous loans. The new IMF controls were undoubtedly a factor but, more importantly, the Russian Government seems to have finally become convinced that it was in the country's best interest to follow the IMF guidelines. As a result, inflation fell steadily throughout the year and had fallen to 3.2% per month by December 1995. Partly based on these results, economists predicted in early 1996 that the Russian economy would begin growing again for the first time since 1989.

The predictions, which were based on a continuation of the government's economic program, proved to be premature, for subsequent events changed the political, and therefore the economic, situation. First of all, the December 1995 Duma elections gave the Communist Party of Russia a plurality of the seats, and they and their allies were just 12 seats short of an absolute majority. Gennady Zyuganov, leader of the party, makes the point when talking with non–Russians that his party is not the old Communist Party of the Soviet Union—that it was, in fact, founded during the last years of the Gorbachëv era as a reform party. He then says that the party accepts a market economy and private property.

But some of Zyuganov's other position statements, while vague, are less reassuring. Thus he described the situation in Russia in January 1996—"in our country, it's the mafia and corrupt bureaucrats who have power," then suggested renationalization of major companies—"We believe in a regulated market where every type of ownership—state, collective, partial, private—is allowed to have its place in the sun." To make the point clear, he added that privatized companies could stay in private hands "if they work well and are being run properly."

The relatively weak Duma could not, of course, unilaterally force a change of economic policy. But President Yeltsin, a candidate for reelection in the June 1996 presidential race, began desperately trying to reposition himself to increase his chances of winning. First, he dismissed the remaining reformers in the cabinet, replacing them with individuals more acceptable to the new majority in the Duma. Then he gave a speech in which he blamed the cabinet for everything that people thought was wrong with the country. Finally, he began making pledges for additional spending which by February had become the equivalent of three-quarters of the government's entire budgeted borrowing for 1996. Meanwhile, Vladimir Kadannikov, Anatoly Chubais's successor as First Deputy Prime Minister for economic policy, began pushing for additional subsidies for industry. As he put it, "Directors of state enterprises have exhausted all inner resources that could help enterprises survive. Now the only thing left to do is deal with the financial and political environment." Still, because most western economists continued to believe that Yeltsin's reelection would be preferable to a victory by Gennady Zyuganov, the IMF signed an agreement with Russia in February 1996 making available $10.2 billion in loans linked to a sweeping plan to proceed with privatization and trade liberalization, in the words of Michel Camdessus, the IMF's managing director, to make the economic reforms "truly irreversible."

Yeltsin did win reelection in 1996, but this was followed by a period of almost six months when he was incapacitated, first by a heart bypass operation, then by a bout of pneumonia. Then, in March 1997, Yeltsin took charge again and appointed Anatoly Chubais and Boris Nemtsov as First Deputy Prime Ministers. These two reformers managed to carry out a series of reforms in 1997, but Chubais then discredited himself by agreeing to take a large advance from a book company for a book on privatization. Chubais is now scheduled to leave government, possibly taking a major job in industry. Yeltsin also got a new Prime Minister, Sergei Kirienko, in April 1998. If he proves to be a strong Prime Minister and adopts a workable program, Russia may finally turn the corner and join the ranks of those countries who have successfully made the transition from a communist command economy to a market economy. He does have a fairly solid basis on which to build. After at least six years of decline, Russia apparently grew at a 0.4 percent rate last year and predictions for 1998 range from one percent to four percent.

### What is Being Changed

The most distinctive feature of the now defunct Soviet economic organization was the reliance on a rigid central plan for the national economy. This is in contrast to a *market* economy, which relies on the independent, or semi–independent decisions of many producers. In theory, a rigidly planned economy was supposed to avoid the ups and downs—inflation and depression—of a free market economy. Marx and Engels charged that a market economy amounted to "anarchy of production."

In practice, centralized planning proved to be difficult. For many years, economic targets and goals were met by lavish investments of capital and labor. Progress was identified with the rate of growth of specific key industries—coal, steel and heavy industry in general—and a high percentage growth rate for overall industrial production. Quantity was stressed over quality.

Such a growth strategy produced an economy that led the world in the production of a long list of industrial products, including coal, steel, cement, manganese and chrome ores, locomotives, metal–cutting lathes and mineral fertilizer. Yet it also produced an economy that, from the point of view of the consumer, was an economy of scarcities. Some consumer goods were not manufactured at all while others were obtainable only after a long waiting period. Still, there were important improvements in the availability of consumer goods over the years. By the time Gorbachëv became General Secretary in 1985, for example, most Russian families had a color television set.

Although the Soviet standard of living improved between 1960 and 1985, it was

**On Moscow's Arabat Street, models pose in some of the latest fashions**

still only about 37% of the level of the United States—and probably falling. Moreover, it was even below the level of the neighboring countries of Eastern Europe. From the point of view of the consumer, an even more important problem was that Soviet goods were of such poor quality that they could not be sold abroad.

Gorbachëv was already aware of the weaknesses in the system when he came to power in 1985. During his first year as General Secretary, he put together a team of younger and better–educated individuals and, at the 27th Party Congress in February 1986, he put the party on record as favoring economic reform. He then began to give substance to this commitment.

It soon became clear that many party members objected to any major modification of the economic system on ideological grounds, however. As Gorbachëv pointed out at the 27th Party Congress:

*Unfortunately, there is a widespread view that any change in the economic mechanism is to be regarded as virtually a retreat from the principles of socialism.*

Gorbachëv was faced with a major contradiction. Gorbachëv's own chief source of authority was his leadership of the party. Moreover, since the party controlled the levers of power, economic reform was possible only with the party's support. Yet how could he use the party to direct his program of economic reform if the party was itself the chief opponent of that reform? Gorbachëv's twofold answer was to remake the party in terms of personnel, organization and ideology while, at the same time, restructuring the system so that the party was no longer in direct control.

The process began in 1987 with the introduction of three slogans which came to symbolize his campaign for reform—openness (*glasnost*), restructuring (*perestroika*), and democracy. Unfortunately, his successes in political reform were not matched in the economic area.

In June 1987, Gorbachëv outlined future economic plans to a Central Committee Plenum. Here he called for "cardinal reform" in the *financing and credit systems*. He also spoke of the need for "development of self–management," and "fundamental change in the style and methods of work." Factories should, he urged, be "self–financing" and more efficient so as to reduce their work force.

That same Central Committee session approved a "Law on the Socialist Enterprise" which went into effect on January 1, 1988. Under the terms of the law, 60 percent of Soviet industrial and agricultural production began working under a new system of "economic accountability" in which individual enterprises became responsible for obtaining their own raw ma-

George A. Cohon, Vice Chairman of Moscow–McDonald's and President/CEO of McDonald's Restaurants of Canada Ltd., with Russian crew members at McDonald's on Pushkin Square.

terials and fuel and were expected to compete with other enterprises for business.

While they now had the right to dispose of any profits earned by the enterprise, they also became responsible for replacing obsolete machinery and paying the wages of their employees. Subsidies to money–losing enterprises were supposed to be phased out and such enterprises were to be permitted to go bankrupt, if they could not begin turning a profit. Companies were also to be able to get rid of surplus workers, so unemployment became another possibility. All of this was supposed to be in effect by the end of the 1986–90 Five Year Plan.

The system was never fully implemented, however. In 1988, 90 percent of the output of factories was still produced for "state orders." Two years later, state orders still controlled nearly 90% of industrial production. The state was also supposed to gradually withdraw from direct control of most economic activity with GOSPLAN relinquishing its control over individual enterprises and concentrating on long–term planning. Some of that happened. In 1987, for example, the number of centrally planned indicators was reduced from 46,000 to 22,000. It was supposed to be further reduced to 3,500 indicators in 1988, though it cannot be verified that this second reduction took place. Ministries and departments were supposed to be reduced by approximately one–third and there was supposed to be a drop of approximately 100,000 in personnel. Again, reductions occurred but not in those magnitudes.

One problem was that the economic program had two major goals—a short-term goal of accelerating the growth rate of national income and a long–term one of promoting innovation and reconstruction—and they were in basic conflict with

each other. The first goal required all out production, while the second goal could only be met by things like closing down assembly lines while obsolete machinery was being replaced by modern technology and enforcing higher quality standards by rejecting goods that failed to meet the new standards. That conflict, obvious by 1989, got considerably worse in 1990–91, with the result that neither goal was met.

A second problem had to do with decentralization of decision–making authority within the system. Essentially, enterprises were given authority to set wages but no responsibility for paying them. As a result, they granted wage increases far in excess of increases in productivity, and the state had to make good the difference. It did this through the expedient of printing additional money. The increase in money in circulation first produced shortages as individuals used their higher wages to buy more goods. In a capitalist system, that would have led to inflation as prices increased to reflect additional demand. But all prices were controlled, and so could not increase. What happened instead was a loss of faith in the banking system and the currency itself.

The result was well summed up in February 1990 by N. N. Slyunkov, a member of the Politburo, in remarks he made at the Central Committee Plenum:

"The situation has deteriorated especially in the consumer market as regards both food and essential goods over the past two years."

A similar picture of the state of the Soviet economy is to be found in a poll published in the Moscow *Ogonek*, also in February 1990. Seventy–three percent of all respondents said that they "constantly or quite often" experienced difficulty in locating food that they needed, while 60% reported that they spent over half of their income on food.

All of this economic distress put the government under extreme pressure. Everybody agreed that *something* had to be done but there was no consensus on what that something should be. The radical reformers wanted to push forward rapidly, while conservatives urged pulling back. Gorbachëv fell somewhere in the middle. The draft Five Year Plan submitted in December 1989 by Nikolai Ryzhkov, Chairman of the Council of Ministers, represented a distinct pulling back, but there continued to be strong pressures to move more quickly.

Ryzhkov submitted a later version of his plan in May 1990. Saying that the state of the economy and the mood of the people did not permit any immediate changes, he proposed a continuation of the policy of state orders for another 18 months coupled with what he called price reform. They were, in fact, just price increases, since prices were not to be freed but simply raised. He characterized his program as "a transition to a regulated market economy." Radicals attacked his proposals and Gorbachëv called them absurd, though he added that people were unprepared for market economics.

Economic reform was on the agenda at the 28th Party Congress in July 1990. After heated discussions, the party adopted a document called "Toward humane, democratic socialism," one of whose major points was that private property did not contradict communist ideology. Reflecting this change, Ryzhkov, in a speech given on July 20, spoke of moving toward a market economy. All references to the word "regulated" were dropped.

Then in August came the Shatalin Plan for a 500 day transition to a market economy. It had the support of Boris Yeltsin and the other radicals and was actually accepted by the Russian Supreme Soviet in early September. Gorbachëv rather reluctantly endorsed the plan, but it came under attack by conservatives and Ryzhkov threatened to resign if the plan were adopted. Eventually the USSR Supreme Soviet turned it down. Essentially the Soviet Union had no plan for economic reform.

Ryzhkov suffered a heart attack at the end of December and was replaced by Valentin Pavlov in January 1991. Pavlov, who had been Finance Minister under Ryzhkov, was a conservative. One of his more notorious "reforms" was to attempt to reduce the fiscal overhang by withdrawing 50 and 100 ruble notes from circulation. Since individuals were limited in the amount of bills they could redeem, Pavlov in effect reduced the overhang by expropriating a portion of the public's wealth. Its most important effect was to further reduce faith in the currency.

GROW!

GORBACHEV

SOVIET AGRICULTURE

DANZIGER
The Christian Science Monitor

Real GNP fell by ten percent in 1990 and shortages were even more pervasive than they were in 1989. Yet the stalemate continued. Conservatives were convinced that further moves in the direction of a market economy would disrupt the economy even more, while reform advocates argued that any action was better than no action. Gorbachëv, no economist, didn't know what to believe. A joke he told reporters in November 1990 illustrated his position.

"They say that Mitterrand has 100 lovers. One has AIDS, but he doesn't know which one. Bush has 100 bodyguards. One is a terrorist, but he doesn't know which one. Gorbachëv has 100 economic advisers. One is smart, but he doesn't know which one."

By May 1991, Gorbachëv had lost confidence in Pavlov's economic program and he began seeking outside advice. Grigory A. Yavlinsky, who had helped draw up the Shatalin Plan, now proposed a new plan whereby the western nations would provide substantial aid to the Soviet Union to help in its economic transition. Gorbachëv endorsed this plan and used it as a basis for his meeting with the "Group of Seven" nations in July 1991. Though no specific overall sums were mentioned, Soviet economists talked about the need for $30 billion a year in grants and loans. The G–7 nations gave a cool reception to the general idea, though they promised assistance once transition to a market economy had begun. Before any further progress could happen, the August 1991 failed *coup* brought an end both to the Soviet Union and Gorbachëv's leadership.

### Agriculture

The failure of the August 1991 *coup*, although it gave Mikhail Gorbachëv four more months as President, actually marked the beginning of the breakup of the Soviet Union and the emergence of Boris Yeltsin as head of an independent Russian Federation. What this meant insofar as agriculture was concerned is that the reforms that Yeltsin had been demanding for two years could finally be implemented.

This had a two-fold significance. First of all, the demise of the Soviet Union definitively ended the various central control mechanisms of the old regime. For the first time since the early 1930s, Russian peasants were on their own. Amazingly, they managed to plant even more winter wheat following the collapse of the Ministry of Agriculture than they had when it was telling them what to plant and when.

Yet while the peasants welcomed the end of bureaucratic control, they very quickly realized that being on their own meant an end to supports, credits, loans and guidance. Moreover, although the reformers said that they wanted to break up the collective and state farms and create a private agriculture, the government offered almost no assistance to peasants who wanted to leave the collective and start on their own. It was in fact, another two years before President Yeltsin finally issued a historic decree granting Russians the right to buy and sell private land.

The reform of prices also turned out to be a negative factor insofar as agriculture was concerned. Two examples will illustrate this point. In 1991, one pound of wheat would buy two pounds of diesel fuel or fertilizer. By 1994, that same two pounds of fuel cost the equivalent of nine pounds of wheat, while a single pound of fertilizer sold for the equivalent of eight pounds of grain.

Although the government has been, on paper, largely successful in its campaign to break up the collective/state farm system—94% of the agrarian sector was officially classified as private by the end of 1994—the real situation is that, while collective/state farms are now "joint stock companies," they continue to operate in much the same way they always have. Moreover, the state continues to set the prices of many grains through Agroprom, its state buying agency, which still collects grain from the farms and delivers goods in return.

Farms are, to be sure, not obligated to sell to Agroprom, but the lack of alternative purchasing agents means that farms that do not want to sell to Agroprom have to find a way to market their goods on their own. At the Koltsovo joint agricultural enterprise, formerly the Suvorov Collective Farm, for example, all milk is still sold at fixed prices to the state. To the question, why not sell it elsewhere, the reply was: "Where will we get the fuel, the trucks? We did try once, but these thugs met us and 'suggested' we go home."

According to the most recent figures, there are about 350,000 private farms in Russia—out of 30 million people who depend on the land. Many of these private farms are, moreover, extremely small, and most lack adequate machinery to work their land. Most do not have access to credit, so they are unable to improve their holdings. They also control only about 4% of the agricultural land in the country.

The transition to a genuinely privatized agriculture is likely to be long and arduous. As the strong support for the anti-reform *Agrarian Party* in the December 1993 elections indicated, most ordinary peasants oppose change, fearing apparently that they will lose what they already have. Many are also older—the average age for collective farmers is over 50—and they don't want to start over. Thus real change may have to wait until the next generation of farmers takes over. In the meantime, most economists argue that the current emphasis should be to turn the ex-collective farms into competitive enterprises. All also agree that the process will take years.

## What is Being Changed

When the Soviet Union introduced the collectivization of agriculture as part of its first Five Year Plan, it was considered to be the first step in the creation of a modern, scientifically-organized, mechanized agricultural system. Distinctions between city and the countryside were to be abolished and peasants were to become "proletarians in the fields." Until 1953, this remained largely a dream, although Khrushchev's plan for the creation of *agrogoroda*—loosely, "agricultural cities"—which he first put forward in 1950, showed that the dream had only been postponed, not abandoned.

Khrushchev, as he consolidated his power after 1953, gave a great deal more emphasis to agriculture than had Stalin. Agriculture was placed much higher on the Soviet list of priorities and additional investments were directed into this area.

In addition, a program of consolidation of the collective farms, actually begun in 1950, continued under Khrushchev and, in the process, many were transformed into state farms (*sovkhozy*). The Machine Tractor Stations were also phased out beginning in 1958 and their agricultural equipment was sold to the *sovkhozy* and *kolkhozy*. As the process of transformation and consolidation continued over the next two decades, the number of agricultural units shrank until, by 1987, the number had dwindled to 22,900 *sovkhozy* and 26,300 *kolkhozy*, with slightly over half of the land being organized as *sovkhozy*.

Another innovation in agricultural organization, introduced in the early 1970s, was the "agro-industrial complex." Always considered experimental, their numbers nevertheless increased over the next decade until there were more than 9,000 of them in existence. Most tended to specialize in the production of a single crop—for example, grapes, which they also further processed into wine or raisins.

One Khrushchev policy innovation that was to have great consequences in later

**Russians line up in front of McDonald's in Moscow for a "Beeg Mak."**

**Performance of the Kuban Cossack Choir in Kranodar**  Courtesy: NOVOSTI

None of this did any good. Grain harvests from 1979–1985 were uniformly dismal, averaging between 40 and 50 million tons below annual targets specified in the Five Year Plan. As a result, the Soviet government stopped publishing overall grain production figures in 1980. No overall figures were published again until October 1986, when it was announced that the grain harvest for 1985 totaled 191.5 million tons. Although this figure was 47.4 million tons less than the target, it actually was an improvement over the trend for the period 1981–1985, when production averaged only 179.5 million tons.

Grain figures for 1987 and 1988 were higher, at 210 and 211.3 million tons, but dropped in 1989 to 195 million tons. The 1990 harvest, on the other hand, was magnificent, reaching 247 million tons, though a significant amount was lost before reaching the Soviet public. The 1991 grain harvest was a disappointing 180–185 million tons.

The important thing, however, is that the Soviet Union, year after year, imported an average of 40 million tons of grain because Soviet collective and state farms fell that much short in meeting the demands of the economy. Even in the bumper year of 1991, the government imported approximately 28 million tons of grain.

Western agricultural experts have believed for a long time that the basic problem was in the system itself, that a basic conflict existed "between a centrally planned and controlled agriculture and the evolution of a modern, highly productive agriculture." Before Gorbachёv, Soviet planners always rejected this point of view and tended to blame it on Russian weather.

Western experts also point out three other problems which they feel contributed to the failure of Soviet agriculture. The first is that Soviet farm equipment was always breaking down. This is partly because Soviet tractors didn't last very long and partly because there was never a sufficient supply of spare parts for them. This is still an unsolved problem. A February 1992 report indicated that 200,000 tractors were standing idle because of a lack of spare parts.

The second problem is the lack of adequately trained and motivated labor in the countryside. Young, better educated individuals have been leaving the collective and state farms and seeking work in the cities for a long time. In the 1970s, 15 million workers left for the cities and that trend, though diminished, continued in the 1980s. The reason is that young people see no opportunity for advancement on the collective or state farm. A large number of persons are still employed in agriculture, but many of these persons are women and lesser educated, older men, precisely those elements which are least productive and least amenable to change.

years was his decision, made in the late 1950's, to commit the country to a great increase in meat production. The large increases in the numbers of livestock and poultry that resulted from this policy led to a greatly increased demand for grain for use as animal feed. Between 1960 and 1980, the amount of feed grains used for livestock and poultry tripled, going from 40 million tons to 120 million tons.

Grain production also increased during this period, but it could not keep up with the constantly growing demand. In 1963, after a relatively poor harvest, the Soviet Union imported its first grain. It imported grain only intermittently during the remainder of the 1960's, but after 1972 it become a regular customer on the world grain market.

This concerned the Soviet leadership and under Brezhnev huge sums of money were poured into the agricultural sector. Capital investment in the 1970's was over 300 billion rubles, which was 2.3 times what had been invested in agriculture in the previous decade. Most of the investment went into creation of a large artificial fertilizer industry.

The third problem is related: there is a terrible shortage of food–carrying railroad cars and storage facilities. Because of this a substantial part of annual production fails to reach city markets, but simply rots. When properly used, food–carrying cars, refrigerated and unrefrigerated, properly become a place of storage as they move over large distances.

Gorbachëv had held the agriculture portfolio in the secretariat for a number of years before becoming General Secretary. There were some reforms he had been urging for a number of years, and he began implementing them after 1985. In his keynote speech to the 27th Party Congress, Gorbachëv spoke of the need to significantly extend "the independence of collective and state farms," and he proposed a two–fold plan for agriculture. State and collective farms would be assigned fixed annual quotas that would not be altered. All production in excess of the quotas could be used as the farms saw fit, including selling it "in fresh or processed form at the collective farm market or through cooperative trade."

Gorbachëv described his proposal as "the creative use of the Leninist idea of a tax in kind"—a reference to Lenin's *New Economic Policy*. The idea had great potential, for it could have been manipulated to create a major free market for agricultural produce if the level of fixed deliveries were set low enough. In addition, 100% of the production of state farms has traditionally gone to the state. Including them in the proposal was a departure from past practice and a genuine decentralization as far as state farms were concerned. Including them was also important because slightly over 50% of all agricultural land belonged to state farms. The potential was never reached, however, largely because so many people were opposed to any general loosening of control, and they managed to sabotage the reform.

Another of Gorbachëv's innovations was to suggest that the "brigade" or "team" system in agriculture might be extended by making them available at the level of families. Under this setup, a group of workers "contracted" to perform certain agricultural tasks as, for example, to cultivate a specified acreage or run a dairy. Remuneration, divided according to the individual contributions of the members of the brigade or team, was based on the productivity of the unit. Gorbachëv's innovation was approved, but the problem was in the implementation. Some family contracts were certainly written, but anecdotal reports indicate that the idea was not widely implemented.

This is the background that produced a Central Committee Plenum on Agriculture that took place in March 1989. In his speech to the Plenum, Gorbachëv argued that "the essence of economic change in the countryside should be in granting farmers broad opportunities for displaying independence, enterprise and initiative." To accomplish this, he proposed turning collective and state farms into "a supreme type of cooperative."

To accomplish this, he proposed that land, equipment and buildings be leased out to individual farmers for periods up to 50 years. The state and collective farms would continue to exist as some sort of co-ordinating agency, but would not directly control production.

Although conservatives such as Ligachev spoke up for lesser reforms, Gorbachëv's plan was approved in principle. The Plenum also voted, once again on Gorbachëv's initiative, to abolish *Gosagroprom*, the super–ministry for Agriculture that Gorbachëv had created in 1985.

In April 1990, the Supreme Soviet actually passed a new law allowing the leasing of land, equipment, buildings and other property for 50 years. Private farms were now a possibility. A few braver peasants moved to take advantage of it. They often had difficulty with the management of their collective or state farm, but there were an estimated 100,000 private farmers in Russia by the beginning of 1992.

## Natural Resources

The Russian Federation is well supplied with most of the raw materials necessary for industrial production, although the major source of minerals is Siberia. European Russia is less well supplied. The area of the Russian Plain has bauxite and lignite deposits, while anthracite and iron ore are found mainly along the western slopes of the Ural Mountains. The northern Caucasus has a petroleum field, an extension of the famous petroleum field centered on the city of Baku, in the Republic of Azerbaijan. Oil is also produced in the area between the Volga River and the Ural Mountains.

In Siberia, on the other hand, there are found some of the largest reserves of coal, petroleum and natural gas in the entire world, plus gold, silver, diamonds, platinum, copper, lead, zinc, chromium, cobalt, tungsten, manganese, and uranium. Beginning in the west, there are the iron ore and anthracite coal deposits of the eastern Urals that are exploited by the cities of Magnitogorsk and Yekaterinburg (Sverdlovsk).

To the northeast is Russia's largest oil field, centered on the city of Raduzhny, in Tyumen Province. The Tyumen Field, located in the southern part of the West Siberian Plain, produced 6.1 million barrels a day in 1992, more than any country other than the United States and Saudi Arabia. Small fields are found in the vicinity of Pechora, far to the north on the Barents Sea, and further to the east in an area known as the East Siberian Lowland. Both are extremely isolated areas and production costs are thus higher.

The rest of the Russian Federation produces another 2.13 million barrels a day, making current Russian production 9.23 million barrels a day. That is down approximately 1.3 million barrels a day over 1990.

The rest of the Russian Federation produced another 2.13 million barrels a day in 1992, making Russian production 9.23

**Patrons buying drinking water at dispensers in St. Petersburg**  Photo by Miller B. Spangler

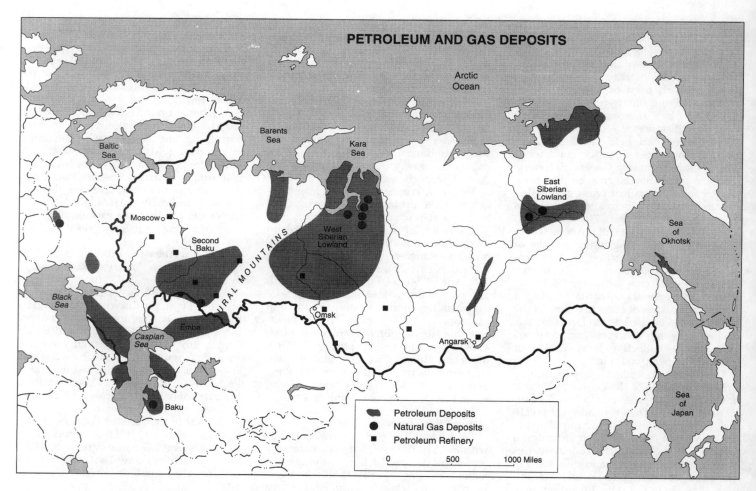

## PETROLEUM AND GAS DEPOSITS

Petroleum Deposits
Natural Gas Deposits
Petroleum Refinery

0        500        1000 Miles

million barrels a day at that time. Daily production was approximately 1.3 million barrels a day higher in 1990. Production has continued to decline since that time, dropping 11% in 1994 alone. A large part of the problem has been Russian Government policy. Until March 1992, the government continued to sell petroleum for the equivalent of a dollar a barrel, not only domestically but to the former Soviet republics as well. Oil exported to Europe brought $18 a barrel, but oil companies got only 25% of the resulting revenues, the rest going to the government as a royalty.

At those prices, particularly with the virulent inflation raging in the country, the state companies producing the oil were not getting a sufficient return to replace worn out or broken equipment. Domestic petroleum prices were subsequently allowed to rise to 40% of world levels, but a new 50% royalty tax acted as a negative incentive.

Another disincentive was Russia's system of oil–export quotas, which required oil producers to sell 65% of their output at home, at prices 70% less than the world price. In an attempt to raise its own revenues, the government also instituted a $5 a barrel tax on oil exports. After strong pressure from the IMF and the World Bank, Russia ended quotas on oil exports

as of January 1, 1995, though the new export tax of $3.75 a barrel instituted as an alternative depressed oil exports even further. On the positive side, domestic oil prices are scheduled to rise gradually to world levels. That promise of future profits may attract sufficient new investment to reverse the trend and get oil production growing again.

There are large reserves of natural gas, also located in Siberia. Most of the natural gas is found in West Siberia, in the northern part of Tyumen Province. These are the Urengoi Fields. Some natural gas also comes from the area of the East Siberian Lowland. The production of natural gas has grown greatly in importance in recent years as new fields have been found and exploited. Production is down from a daily output in the 1980s of 1,000 million cubic meters—equivalent to 29% of total world output in 1981—but Russia remains the world's leading exporter of natural gas. Most of Eastern Europe is almost totally dependent on this supply and Western Europe is becoming increasingly dependent.

One of the Soviet Union's larger and more controversial industrial projects in the 1980s was a 3,400 mile pipeline constructed from the Urengoi fields of Siberia to Western Europe. The pipeline was largely constructed with Western technol-

ogy and credits, with the Western European countries that have financed it— Great Britain, France, Germany and Italy—receiving payment in future gas deliveries. The first gas began to flow to Western Europe in December 1983. The collapse of the Soviet Union has brought no change in this arrangement.

The Russian Federation, and the Republics of Kazakhstan and Ukraine together contain almost 20% of the world's known reserves of coal and lignite and the three republics today account for nearly a quarter of all coal mined in the world. The Ukraine's main coal field is in the Donbas region, while Kazakhstan's coal is found in the region surrounding the city of Karaganda. Russia's two largest coal fields are located in Siberia. Both were developed by the Soviet Government after 1917. Pechora, the first Siberian field developed, is in the far north at the beginning of the Ural Mountains, along the Barents Sea. More interesting—and more challenging—is a major new coal field located in the southern part of the Republic of Yakutsk–Sakha (formerly the Yakutsk Autonomous Republic), which the Soviet Union began developing in 1974 in a joint project with Japan.

The Republic of Yakutsk–Sakha in eastern Siberia has large deposits of gold, diamonds, gas and tin, in addition to coal.

But it is also one of the coldest inhabited places on earth, with temperatures known to plunge to –60°C (–108°F.). It is also extremely remote from the major populated areas of Russia.

This provides a problem for any form of development, but presents a specially difficult one in the case of a low value, bulk item like coal. As early as the 1930s, Soviet scientists had identified deposits of high grade coking coal in the vicinity of the city of Neryungri, estimated to be as large as 300 million tons. It is an isolated area, however, and the Soviet government poured its limited development funds into more accessible areas. Then, in 1974, the Soviet Government negotiated a joint project with a number of Japanese companies to develop the coal field. The Japanese companies provided the necessary technology and equipment, while the Soviet Union built a spur rail line to connect Neryungri with the Baikal–Amur Railway (BAM), a new railway completed in the 1980s that runs parallel but to the north of the Trans–Siberian Railway. The Japanese payment was in the form of deliveries of coal.

The project went forward and was eventually completed, though capital costs turned out to be four times the level of European Russia, and the project took several years more to complete than originally planned. As a result of the development, however, Yakutsk, the regional capital, has grown from a small settlement to 200,000 people. The potential for further development in this area is very great, but most projects are on hold at the moment.

Russian deposits of iron ore are found, first of all, in the Ural Mountains and, secondly, in the mountains that form the southern border of Siberia, particularly in the area around Lake Baikal. There are vast deposits around Lake Baikal, but the iron mines of the Urals are extremely old and largely worked out, having been originally developed in the 18th century. But Russian iron ore deposits are lower in ore content than those of the Republic of Ukraine, particularly those of Krivoy Rog, where the pure iron content runs as high as 68 percent. Russia will continue to get much of its iron from the Ukraine for the next several years, but development of the iron deposits of the Lake Baikal area is a good possibility for the future.

With respect to other ferrous metals, the Russian Federation is remarkably endowed; it is the world's largest producer of manganese and chromium and has substantial reserves of nickel, titanium and vanadium. On the other hand, there is a relative shortage of such important metals as cobalt, molybdenum and tungsten, all of great importance in steel production.

Insofar as non–ferrous metals are concerned, copper mining resources, developed primarily since World War II, now produce about 12% of the world total. Tin is in relatively short supply; lead and zinc are available in relatively large quantities. Russia is the world's second–largest producer of gold, though production is down and the mines, at the moment still all state owned, have been having labor problems. The production of light metals such as aluminum is steadily growing; the known deposits of aluminum ore are estimated to be adequate for at least forty years.

In discussing the natural resources of this country, mention must be made of the extensive system of waterways. Because of the difficulty in building roads in some areas, waterways played an important role in past centuries. The network of navigable inland waterways, totaling some 75,000 miles, is still of importance in reaching certain otherwise almost inaccessible areas, but the total volume of goods now carried by water is no more than 10% of the total. Practically no rivers remain open all year, and those that do suffer from seasonal shortages of rainfall which makes them too shallow.

The water resources of the Russian Federation have been used to construct hydroelectric power stations, including some of the largest in the world. An intri-

**Times are changing! Baskin Robbin's offers Moscovites a "List of Ice Cream Flavors"— "The most popular ice cream in America" . . . beginning with Vanilla, Strawberry, Chocolate, Chocolate Almond, Chocolate Chip, etc.**
(Courtesy of David Hertzberg)

**View of Lake Baikal**

cate system of canals, developed in the past, is still maintained and continues to play a significant economic role.

Paved roads continue to be scarce and the number of all–weather roads suitable for trucks is limited, so people and goods are still carried primarily by railroad. The Soviet Union was the first country to use jet airplanes for passenger traffic and certain remote areas can still be reached only by air; thus the network of air routes gets much use. Flights tend to be irregular and many times are simply cancelled. Railroads have been designated a "Commonwealth" interest, and the newly independent republics are committed to maintaining the integrated network that had existed under the now defunct Soviet Union.

### Nuclear Power

Until the nuclear accident at Chernobyl in April 1986, the Soviet Union had been committed to nuclear power as a major source of electric power. At that time, the USSR had a capacity of 17.5 million kilowatts generated from this source and it had 18 more nuclear power stations under construction. In addition, Russia had produced two prototype industrial fast breeder–reactors, plus two nuclear heat supply stations, each of which was designed to produce enough heat for a city with a population of about 400,000. The most important reason for this ambitious program was the severe lack of alternate energy sources in the area of European Russia.

The nuclear accident at Chernobyl changed all that. Under growing public pressure, most of the nuclear power stations under construction were put on hold, then canceled entirely.

Chernobyl is a small town about 60 miles north of Kiev, in the now independent Republic of Ukraine. The plant had four reactors, two with "containment" buildings and two without. An experiment was underway using one of the unprotected devices when a sudden burst of power surged through the reactor, causing a steam leak. This led to the formation of hydrogen gas, which then exploded, demolishing the roof of the plant and killing two workers. Unrestrained by containment, the released radioactive gases quickly spread into the atmosphere, leading to widespread contamination not only of Soviet territory, but of neighboring nations as well.

The world found out about the accident two days later when the Swedes, detecting increased radiation in the atmosphere, began making inquiries. After first denying that anything untoward had occurred, the Soviets finally admitted the fact of the accident. It is now known that the reactor which got out of control was an unusual type that made use of graphite in its core. The graphite caught fire when overheating occurred. There was at least a partial "meltdown" and the reactor continued to spew out radiation for about two and a half weeks before it began to be controlled.

About 300 radiation victims were

brought to Moscow hospitals; thirty five of these had suffered severe radiation exposure. Emergency bone marrow transplants were performed under the direction of an American surgeon. The death toll from radiation quickly reached 19 out of the 35; *The Times* of London reported that the figure had grown to 31 and that 209 others "remained in hospitals or sanatoria suffering from various degrees of radiation sickness." Dr. Gale, the American surgeon who performed the emergency bone marrow transplants gave as his own estimates that there were "about 50,000 to 100,000 individuals who have received at least some dose [of radiation] that may be of long–term concern. Soviet delay in the matter and failure of communication was, at best, shabby. Primary blame was placed on local officials who "didn't have a true assessment of the accident."

The Soviet Union did carry out major modifications of the 14 other graphite-core nuclear reactors which it operated. It also announced that future reactors would have containment buildings and would be pressurized. That was not enough for an increasing number of Soviet citizens, however. Protests grew around the Soviet Union and, increasingly, republic governments began putting pressure on the central government to cancel nuclear reactor building programs in their republics. The Soviet Government canceled the two reactors it had been planning to build at Chernobyl, and later stopped construction on a number of other plants in southern Russia, Armenia, and elsewhere, but it never abandoned its commitment to nuclear power. In particular, it continued to discuss construction of at least three more reactors in the northeast by the year 2000. This area produces gold, and other minerals and new sources of energy will be required in the future to exploit this mineral wealth.

The Russian people were not among the major protesters against nuclear power in the past, but there is an increasing movement in Russia urging that the government phase out nuclear energy. The government has already drawn up plans to convert one of the nuclear heat supply stations to alternate fuels. There are, on the other hand, the continuing energy shortages in the area of European Russia which the government has to take into consideration.

The Russian Government also has its privatization program and its conversion to a market economy to keep it busy, plus the problem of disposing of tons of ra-dioactive plutonium and enriched uranium from warheads now being disabled because of the CFE and START agreements. Disposing of the warheads alone is estimated to cost billions of dollars, money the Russian Government doesn't have. The U.S. Congress has authorized $400 million to help pay the cost of dismantling the missiles, but much more will be needed. In view of these problems, it is likely the Russian Government will put the entire nuclear energy problem on hold for the next several years. So this may be one decision that is made by inaction. Current nuclear plants will continue to be used, but no new ones will be constructed.

## THE FUTURE

The good news is that President Yeltsin managed to get Sergei Kiriyenko confirmed as his new Prime Minister in April 1998 and the Russian economy has finally stopped contracting and began growing again. The bad news is that Yeltsin and Kiriyenko still have to work with a Duma dominated by a coalition of Communists and nationalists who will do what they can to thwart any governmental program of reform. Some additional bad news is that the government is still collecting only about ten percent of GDP in tax revenues, which means that the government is unable to finance everything it believes it has to do.

It is clear that much will depend on the specific economic policies that Yeltsin and Kiriyenko decide to implement over the next year or two. If they are successful, a reformer will presumably have a good chance to win the presidential elections in 2000. If not, the electorate will probably elect a rightist, possibly someone with a military background. The big question then is whether democracy could survive that shock.

**Moscow's Arbat Street in summer**

Courtesy: NOVOSTI

# The Commonwealth of Independent States

Five of the plotters: Interior Minister Pugo and Vice President Yanayev
(third and fourth from left)

## THE COLLAPSE OF THE SOVIET UNION

It was early in the morning in Moscow on Monday, August 19, 1991, when Soviet television issued its news bulletin. Mikhail Gorbachëv, alleged to be unable for health reasons to perform his duties, had been relieved as President. His powers had been transferred to his vice president, Gennadi Yanayev, who was to exercise them in consultation with an eight–member *State Committee for the State of Emergency*, composed of himself, the Prime Minister, the Ministers of Defense and Interior, head of the KGB, two individuals representing the military–industrial complex, and the chairman of the Farmers' Union of the USSR.

A state of emergency was announced throughout in the country, demonstrations and protest meetings were banned and independent newspapers were closed. Subsequently it was revealed that Gorbachëv had actually been in military custody since the preceding evening.

Although portrayed as an ordinary transfer of power resulting from the inability of the Soviet President to fulfill his duties, this was actually the beginning of an attempted *coup d'état*, a fact that became clear as soon as one looked more closely at what was happening. First of all, if Gorbachëv had really been ill, his vice president could have temporarily as-

sumed his duties without further ado. It was not necessary either to declare a state of emergency or create a "State Committee for the State of Emergency" to supervise it.

Secondly, not only was every member of the State Committee for the State of Emergency a prominent conservative, this was the second attempt by four of them to assume Gorbachëv's powers. Two months earlier, the Prime Minister, Valentin Pavlov had asked the Supreme Soviet to give him the right to issue decrees that would not require Gorbachëv's signature; his request had been supported by the Ministers of Defense and Interior plus the head of the KGB. Gorbachëv had to personally and energetically intervene to defeat this first maneuver of the conservatives. In retrospect, Gorbachëv should have dismissed Pavlov and the other plotters at that time, but he evidently thought he could continue to control them and he desired to rule by consensus without breaking with the more conservative members of his government.

Now the plotters were trying again. They decided to make their move because Gorbachëv, vacationing in the Crimea with his family, was due to return to Moscow that morning. A second consideration was that Gorbachëv was scheduled to

sign a new union treaty the next day that would transfer considerable powers to the republics. Communist traditionalists opposed the new union treaty and were determined to stop it.

That the pending union treaty was a major factor in the timing of the *coup* was made clear by the plotters when they issued their first statement announcing the removal of Gorbachëv. Here they listed their aims as "overcoming the profound and comprehensive crisis, political, ethnic and civil strife, chaos and anarchy that threaten the . . . territorial integrity, freedom and independence of our fatherland" and referred specifically to the March 1991 "referendum on the preservation of the Union of Soviet Socialist Republics." Further, Yanayev's first action after assuming power was to cancel the treaty–signing ceremony. The question was, could the *coup* succeed?

In theory, it should have. The leaders controlled all of the traditional instruments of force within the country. Marshal Dmitri Yazov controlled the military as Minister of Defense; Vladimir Kryuchkov was head of the KGB and Boris K. Pugo controlled both security troops and the police as Minister of the Interior. They demonstrated this control by ordering tanks, troops and armored vehicles into the major cities at the beginning of the attempted *coup*, ringing republic government buildings with troops and tanks, and seizing control of television and radio facilities.

Moreover, the *coup* leaders included, in addition to the Prime Minister, the First Deputy Chairman of the Defense Council (Oleg Baklanov), the president of the Association of State Enterprises and Industrial, Construction, Transport and Communications Facilities of the USSR (V. A. Staradubtsev) and the chairman of the Farmers' Union of the USSR (A. I. Tizyakov). Further, they had the support of the *Communist Party* and a significant percentage of officials throughout the country.

It must be noted that the *coup* would probably have succeeded two or three years earlier. What the leaders overlooked, however, was the significant democratization, coupled with extremely damaging revelations of past history and mismanagement, that had taken place over the preceding years. These moves had produced new leaders such as Boris Yeltsin, elected President of the Russian Federation in June 1991, and Anatoly Sobchok, Mayor of Leningrad. An order was actually issued for the arrest of Yeltsin, but no attempt was made to take other democratic leaders into custody or even to dismiss them from their positions.

The attempt to arrest Yeltsin was bungled. Eluding his would–be captors, Yeltsin made it to the Russian Republic Parliament building by 10:00 a.m. and immediately began organizing opposition to the *coup*. His first step was to call a press conference to question the authority of the "State Committee for the State of Emergency." He followed this up with a decree ordering all Russian Republic citizens to obey the orders of the Russian Republic Government, rather than the orders of the unconstitutional "Committee."

In perhaps his grandest gesture, he then went outside where tanks ringed the parliament building, climbed up on top of one of the them, and called for an "unlimited general strike" and mass civil disobedience. The soldiers, apparently devoid of orders about what to do in case of opposition, allowed Yeltsin to then climb down and go back into the Parliament building. Subsequently, thousands of Yeltsin supporters gathered around the structure and, forming a human shield, made it impossible for the *coup* leaders to move against Yeltsin and his democratic supporters without inflicting major casualties.

The *coup* leaders overlooked many things, but perhaps their greatest failure was in communications. They took the traditional action of seizing control of the radio and television stations (which abruptly acquired an air of unreality). They did close down opposition newspapers, but they never gained control of tele-

phone lines or stopped foreign reporter's from filing their dispatches with their home organizations.

As a result, the democrats built up their own internal communications using computers and modems (a means for communication by telephone line from one computer to another). News of the *coup* and growing opposition to it was broadcast to the Soviet Union by the BBC, Voice of America, and the rest of the international media. The Soviet people also learned thereby of the nearly universal condemnation of the attempted *coup* by world leaders. Western nations suspended aid programs and otherwise made it clear that its leaders would find themselves isolated internationally if they won.

What the leaders also forgot to take into account was the possibility that parts of the military and the KGB might be weaned away from loyalty to the attempted *coup*. In fact, however, as popular demonstrations grew, many individual commanders adopted a passive stance or actively threw their support to Yeltsin and the forces of democracy. In Leningrad, 200,000 demonstrators gathered in the square outside the Winter Palace, while in Siberia coal miners an nounced a protest strike. Gradually, one after another of almost all of the Republic leaders came out against the *coup*.

When it became clear to the *coup* leaders that the Soviet people (1) would not accept their rule peacefully and (2) that

**August 20: A heavily–armed bodyguard watches over Russian President Boris Yeltsin inside the Russian parliament.** Reuters/Bettmann

they could win only through a ruthless use of force and (3) a continuing regime of oppression that would leave the Soviet Union isolated internationally, one after another of the *coup* leaders lost his nerve and the move began to collapse. After approximately 60 hours, Gorbachëv was freed, the troops were ordered out of Moscow, and an order went out for the arrest of the *coup* leaders.

Boris Pugo, Minister of the Interior, committed suicide as later also did Marshal Sergei Akhromeyev, Gorbachev's chief military adviser, who was implicated in the attempted *coup*. Aleksandr Bessmyrtnikh, the Foreign Minister, was fired because of questionable loyalty despite his protests of innocence which were even expressed by live satellite TV in the United States.

### The Return of Gorbachëv and Collapse of the Union

Gorbachëv arrived back in Moscow Thursday morning to loud cheers but, though he claimed to be in complete control of the Soviet Union, it soon became clear that the three–day attempted *coup* had rung a death knell to the old system. Even as Gorbachëv defended the *Communist Party* and promised to work for its renewal, Yeltsin issued a decree banning party activities in the Russian Republic and specifically prohibited party cells in military units, police units of the Ministry of Interior and in the KGB.

Abruptly, on Friday, Gorbachëv, speaking to the Russian Parliament, abandoned his earlier defense of the party and referred to the Central Committee as "traitors." On Saturday, he followed this up by resigning as General Secretary and calling on the Central Committee to dissolve itself. He then issued a decree suspending the activities of the party and seizing all its property. This about–face created a serious problem of credibility.

The Soviet Union, which Gorbachëv still hoped to save, was crumbling around him. Estonia had declared itself independent on August 19 and Latvia followed the next day. In the week following the defeat of the *coup,* four more republics followed with their declarations of independence: the Ukraine on August 25, Byelorussia (now Belarus) on August 25, Uzbekistan on August 26 and Moldavia (now Moldova) on August 27. Armenia set a referendum for a vote on independence for September 16.

Several of the other republics also promised to hold plebiscites to confirm their declarations. The most important of those was the Ukraine, which set its referendum for December 1. Thus the situation was that, including Lithuania and Georgia which had declared their independence even before the attempted *coup,* nine of the fifteen republics were committed to independence. If the republics real-

ly meant their declarations of independence, no viable union was possible. It was unclear whether their declarations of independence were real or only bargaining tools in preparation for negotiations on a new union treaty.

### The Rise of Boris Yeltsin and Attempts Toward Union

Crucially, Boris Yeltsin, President of the Russian Federation, still favored some form of union, and on August 28 he sent a delegation to the Ukraine to see what could be worked out. What he got was a provisional economic and military alliance which, the Russian and Ukrainian Governments announced, other "former subjects of the U.S.S.R." were welcome to join.

The next step came on September 2 when a special session of the Congress of People's Deputies met in Moscow, with the leaders of ten of the republics in attendance. Here Gorbachëv proposed the creation of a new interim government to replace the discredited one over which he presided. After three days of debate, the Congress voted, in effect, to dissolve itself and transfer authority to a new executive council and legislature controlled by the participating republics.

Gorbachëv remained President, but final executive authority was lodged in a State Council made up of Gorbachëv and the leaders of the participating republics. A separate Inter–republic Economic Committee, appointed by the State Council, assumed the functions of the former Council of Ministers. Finally, a two chamber legislature was established, the membership of the second chamber to be appointed by and represent the governments of the individual republics. In this chamber, voting would be by delegation, with each republic having one vote. This clearly interim government was to govern until a new union treaty could be signed by the individual republics bringing into being a proposed "Union of Sovereign States."

The first act of the State Council was to recognize the independence of Lithuania, Latvia and Estonia. It can be argued that recognition had become inevitable by this time, since most of the world, including the United States, had already recognized the independence of the Baltic Republics. Nevertheless, this was the first formal step in the breakup of the Soviet Empire. Even at this time, only ten of the twelve remaining republics were supporting the interim government. Moldavia refused to participate at all and Georgia sent only observers. Neither appeared likely to sign a new union treaty. In addition, over the next several days, all of the remaining republics other than the Russian Federation, Kazakhstan and Turkmenistan declared their independence. Later, even Kazakhstan and Turkmenistan would join the list.

The next three months were to prove decisive. Gorbachëv, determined to save some form of union and, recognizing that Boris Yeltsin's support was absolutely vital, dismissed all of his former advisers and accepted Yeltsin's advice on the make–up of his new government, surrounding himself with liberals and even appointing Ivan Silayev, Prime Minister of the Russian Federation (i.e. the Russian state), as Chairman of the Inter-republic Economic Committee, a post which effectively made him the caretaker Prime Minister of the union government. He then asked the reform economist Grigory Yavlinski to draw up a plan for economic union which he presented in draft form to the State Council in September.

The leaders of ten of the republics attended the meeting and gave their general approval to the plan. The two missing republics were Moldova (formerly Moldavia) and Georgia. Zviad Gamsakhurdia, then President of Georgia, had made it clear that his government was pursuring a policy of complete independence and wanted nothing to do, even economically, with a union. The Moldovan Government was undecided whether to participate in an economic union and so chose to abstain.

The other key republic was the Ukraine, led by Leonid Kravchuk, the former head of the Ukrainian *Communist Party,* who had repudiated the party and become a convert to democratization and a market economy. Kravchuk himself supported the idea of some form of continued union at first, but he came under increasing pressure from the Ukrainian parliament, which opposed supranational ties as a limitation on Ukrainian independence. In October 1991, the Ukrainian parliament drew up two pages of objections to the pending economic treaty, after which the Ukrainian Government announced that it would not sign the agreement without significant changes in the language. Among the changes that the parliament was demanding was the right for the Ukraine to set up its own national bank, issue its own currency and, in general, to control its fiscal policy.

The Ukrainian parliament then decided that the deputies selected to represent the Ukraine in the Union Supreme Soviet would participate only in the Council of the Republic and only as observers. It came as no surprise, therefore, when the Ukraine joined Georgia and Moldova in boycotting sessions of the State Council called to talk about a new union treaty.

Thus, only seven republics agreed, on November 14, to establish a new "Union of Sovereign States." The additional two republics not signing were Uzbekistan and Armenia. Two weeks later, when the State Council met again, supposedly to initial the draft agreement, seven republics were again present but, this time

The presidents of Ukraine, Belarus, and Russia: (l. to r.) Leonid Kravchuk, Stanislav Shushkevich, and Boris Yeltsin in Minsk, Belarus, December 8, 1991.

Reuters/Bettmann

Uzbekistan was represented while Azerbaijan was missing. And instead of initialling the treaty, they decided to submit it to their republic parliaments for approval, a process that put the proposed treaty into severe jeopardy.

By this time, Leonid Kravchuk had dropped his earlier general support for some continuation of the union. Having said on November 12 that the Ukraine would "never sign" a treaty which would contain "even the slightest hint of certain governing central bodies," because "the center has fully exhausted itself," he added two weeks later that he would "take no part in the . . . talks on signing a new Union Treaty" and "all allegations that I meant to join the treaty later are nothing but fiction."

All of that might have become more or less academic, had the December 1 referandum on Ukrainian independence gone differently. In fact, nearly 90 percent of all Ukrainians voted *yes* for independence. At the same time, Kravchuk proved himself to be in line with Ukrainian thinking and a popular politician by winning 61.5 percent of the vote in the concurrent race for the newly created office of Ukrainian President.

"The independence of the Ukraine is a new political reality," commented Boris Yeltsin upon receiving the results of the Ukrainian vote. And what Yeltsin meant when he used the phrase "new political reality" was that Gorbachëv's draft for a political union was now dead. The Ukraine would not join and, as Yeltsin had already said, he could not conceive of a political union that did not include the Ukraine. As far as that goes, Gorbachëv had said much the same thing, although he apparently still hoped that the Ukraine

might still be persuaded to reverse its stand. Yeltsin had no such hopes.

Yet Kravchuk had said on a number of occasions that he favored some kind of coordinating mechanism to handle the many problems of the now–separating republics. The question was what sort of political structure the Ukraine was willing to accept to achieve that coordination. Yeltsin decided to find out. He contacted Kravchuk and Stanislav Shushkevich, President of Belarus, and suggested that the three presidents meet the following weekend to discuss the future of the union. Shushkevich agreed to host the meeting and offered the use of a hunting lodge located not far from the Belarus city of Brest. "We came to the conclusion," Shushkevich commented after the meeting, "that we had to sort out the concept of the kind of union we are capable of building."

So the three leaders talked for two days and, in the end, they produced the agreement, which they signed late in the day on December 8, 1991, in the Belarusian capital of Minsk, calling into being the "Commonwealth of Independent States."

## COMMONWEALTH OF INDEPENDENT STATES

The suddenness of the December 8th agreement probably shocked a lot of people, but two aspects of the agreement caused some disquiet in the beginning. The first was that the three signatories were the heads of the three Slavic republics of the old union, suggesting to some that they were creating a "Slavic Commonwealth," even though the agree-

ment specified that membership was open to "all member states of the former U.S.S.R.," plus "other states that share the goals and principles of the present agreement." The second cause for concern was that the agreement also specified that "the USSR has ceased to exist as a subject of international law and as a geopolitical reality."

The first issue was defused rather quickly when the leaders of the five Central Asian Republics met in Ashkhabad, Turkmenistan, and there signed an agreement to become co–founders of the Commonwealth of Independent States. This led to a conference in Alma Ata, Kazakhstan, on December 21, 1991 which was attended by the presidents of eleven of the republics, with President Gamsakhurdia of Georgia the sole hold out. Even Georgia sent an observer, however, The three Baltic Republics were not represented, have made it clear earlier that they would not join any new political union.

At Alma Ata, the eleven presidents signed a protocol making all eleven republics co–founders of the Commonwealth of Independent States. An additional protocol and two accords were also signed dealing with subsidiary matters. They also signed a resolution supporting Russia's claim to the USSR's United Nations membership, including its permanent membership in the Security Council. They further agreed to meet again in Minsk on December 30.

The December 30 meeting was actually the first "session" of the executive bodies of the Commonwealth of Independent States and included separate meetings of the heads of state and heads of government. A total of 15 documents was negotiated and signed at these meetings, flesh-

Air Marshal Shaposhnikov arrives in Alma Ata, Kazakhstan, December 20, 1991

Reuters/Bettmann

ing out the structures of the CIS and establishing certain forms of cooperation. Since the CIS was seen as a coordinating body, there was to be no "center" as such—no president or prime minister, no ministries and no legislature. Instead, using to some extent the structure of the European Community (EC), the leaders drew up documents creating a Council of the Heads of States and a Council of Heads of Government.

Another agreement created a "working group" as a sort of secretariat to "prepare organically and technically the holding" of the meetings of the two councils. Unlike the EC, however, they did not create the presidential commission and cadre of bureaucrats that plays such an important role in Brussels. In fact, possibly to underline that point, the CIS Heads of State agreed that the the job of drawing up proposals on how this working group should be structured would be handled by a conference of CIS foreign ministers meeting in Minsk in early January.

Perhaps the most important topic discussed at the Minsk meeting was the future status of the armed forces. Immediately prior to the meeting, the defense ministers and chairmen of the committees for defense questions of the 11 member states had met in Moscow with Air Marshal Yevgeniy Shaposhnikov, named Soviet Defense Minister following the August attempted *coup* and designated temporary commander of the union forces at the Alma Ata meeting.

An earlier proposal to maintain a uni-

fied armed force became moot when it became clear that the Ukraine, Azerbaijan and Moldova wanted to have their own armies. Thus the agreement that actually came before the CIS heads of state was based on the concept of joint CIS armed forces. The signed agreement stipulated that each republic had the right to establish its own army; but it also provided for continuation of a unified army under CIS command which republics could participate in if they wished. National armies were to be limited to conventional forces, however; all 11 republic heads of state agreed that nuclear forces would remain under unified command. Nuclear weapons were at that time based in four different republics—the Russian Federation, Ukraine, Belarus and Kazakhstan. All except for the Russian Federation had stated that they intended to go "non–nuclear"—that is, eventually to get rid of all nuclear weapons on their soil. In the meanwhile, it was agreed that the President of the Russian Federation would have primary authority over nuclear weapons with the other three republican presidents having a veto power on their use.

The Ukrainian Government immediately set about creating its own armed forces, and also moved to extend its control over the Black Sea fleet as well. Azerbaijan also moved to take control of the Caspian Sea fleet.

Marshall Shaposhnikov, who also participated in the military discussions at the Minsk meeting, was named commander-

in–chief of the CIS armed forces. A council of republic defense ministers was also created and charged with elaborating a common defense policy.

The CIS Heads of States also touched on the subject of foreign policy. In addition to a general commitment to coordinate policy, they signed an agreement which provided for the division of the former USSR's property held abroad, including embassy and consulate buildings.

Other agreements signed in Minsk included one that called for joint activities in the exploration and use of space, plus several that dealt with a number of regional issues which the various heads of state agreed to treat as matters requiring CIS cooperation. These included the problems of the Aral Sea, the consequences of the Spital earthquake [centering in Armenia], preservation of fish stocks in the Caspian Sea, and elimination of the consequences of the Chernobyl nuclear power station disaster.

Though he had very little in the viability of the Commonwealth of Independent States, President Gorbachëv recognized it as a *fait accompli*. He therefore agreed to a wind up of the old union by December 31 and the transfer of the Kremlin and the state bank to Russian control. Yeltsin, meanwhile, issued a series of decrees taking control of all union ministries other than defense and atomic energy. Gorbachëv himself resigned as President of the USSR on December 25. Separately the USSR Supreme Soviet held its own last session on December 26. The handful of

114

deputies present, far less than a quorum since most of the republics had already withdrawn their deputies, recognized the Commonwealth of Independent States before voting itself out of existence.

Thus the Union of Soviet Socialist Republics officially disappeared and the Commonwealth of Independent States came into being. The CIS did not, if fact, replace the USSR, since the individual independent republics see themselves as the collective heirs to the USSR. The CIS is not even a sovereign entity, but rather a coordinating body for the independent republics which make up its membership. Its significance, and even its viability, remain matters of conjecture. In addition to Gorbachëv, among those who publicly questioned whether the CIS had any chance for long–time survival were Edward Shevardnazde, then a former Soviet Foreign Minister and currently President of Georgia, James Baker and Henry Kissinger.

Their criticisms were to the point. The CIS had then, and still has, a weak structure. It is also true that the newly independent republics, faced with mammoth tasks, have not found the CIS able to contribute much toward the solving of those problems.

On the other hand, the CIS came into existence precisely because the apparachniks of the old center acted as a major force holding back and frustrating necessary reforms. Creation of the CIS got rid of most of that particular countervailing force. More recently, the CIS has provided a structure that has facilitated the negotiation of a number of multilateral agreements among individual members of the CIS.

Perhaps the greatest weakness of the CIS is that some of its members, Ukraine in particular, fear continued domination by Moscow. As this fear recedes in the future and as the republics see the need for greater coordination, they can begin to strengthen the institutions of the CIS and to bestow on them additional responsibilities. What is clear in any case is that the most important problems facing the republics over the next several years are economic and they are best solved at the lowest level possible. The commitment of the members of the CIS to a market economy, private enterprise and to popular participation in government represents the best long–term guarantee that they will be able to solve their problems.

# ECONOMY UNDER THE CIS

The economy of the old USSR was designed and built as a single economy, with all important decisions coming out of Moscow. In addition, the first principle of the planners was economies of scale which translated into "bigger is better." Since all enterprises were owned and run by the Soviet state, they deliberately set out to create monopoly situations in every part of the economy, since these were considered to be more efficient. Accordingly, all over the Soviet Union, single, large factories were built, designed to serve the needs of a large part of the country or even, sometimes, the entire Soviet economy.

Such factories, being part of the "union" economy, took their orders from their supervising ministry in Moscow; the republic government exercised no control whatsoever. This made for a highly integrated economic system, though it also made it highly vulnerable, since a single, badly–run factory could disrupt a complete sector by failing to deliver acceptable products in good time. Two further factors were possible time delays and added transportation costs.

All of these factors were magnified tremendously in 1991 in the situation of a collapsing Soviet Union. As the individual republics moved to establish their political independence, they also moved to take control of their own economies. But when they tried to do so, they found that, in many cases, a significant part of their industry was totally dependent on deliveries of raw materials and parts from other republics and could not operate without these continued deliveries. Moreover, the same was true with regard to factory output. Worst of all, in many cases, too, the customers were factories located in other republics.

Just how complicated this could get was explained in November 1991 by V. Razumov, Deputy Minister of the former U.S.S.R. Ministry of the Chemical and Petroleum Refining Industry, just after the ministry had been abolished on November 15. Razumov used the example of the plastic that goes into making refrigerators. "One of the many things that could make our life a little easier today," commented Razumov, is refrigerators. But you can't make them in, say, Belarus, if you have no polystyrene, which is made in Kazakhstan. Kazakhstan cannot produce polystyrene unless ethylbenzene is supplied from Tataria. They cannot make ethylbenzene in Tataria if they have no benzene. And benzene is made from petroleum, which is extracted mainly in [the] Tyumen [region].

That is roughly the system that is currently just [barely] managing to supply plastic for refrigerators. It could easily be destroyed. The people of Tyumen will sell independently a little more of their petroleum, the refinery workers a little more of the benzene produced from their supply of petroleum, and so on, with the quantities being reduced at each stage of the production of plastic. And it could easily turn out that the end result is that we get no refrigerators."

Razumov was speaking as a planner worried about the collapse of a system that, with all of its faults, managed to produce refrigerators. In the short run, his criticism has some validity, because it will take some time to create the market links necessary to replace the collapsing command economy.

Razumov was dealing with a single example. Just how serious is this problem for the overall CIS economy? A Moscow Interfax "Soviet Business Report," issued on October 31, 1991, looked at the overall problem based on 1989 data, the latest obtainable. What the report established was that 20.3 percent of all domestic trade was inter–republic in 1989. What the report also pointed out, however, is that the smaller republics were most closely bound into the old command economic system, while larger republics like Russia and Ukraine were far less dependent on inter–republic trade.

# Soviet Republics' Individual Share in Inter–Republic Trade (from 1989 data)

| | Imports | Exports | Average |
|---|---|---|---|
| Russia | 12.2% | 13.0% | 12.6% |
| Ukraine | 26.2% | 26.6% | 26.4% |
| Kazakhstan | 36.6% | 20.6% | 28.6% |
| Azerbaijan | 23.6% | 41.6% | 32.6% |
| Uzbekistan | 40.5% | 28.8% | 34.5% |
| Georgia | 34.4% | 40.3% | 37.4% |
| Kyrgyzstan | 42.8% | 32.5% | 37.7% |
| Turkmenia | 40.2% | 35.5% | 37.9% |
| Armenia | 39.7% | 37.2% | 38.5% |
| Tajikistan | 48.9% | 32.8% | 40.9% |
| Belarus | 37.5% | 46.3% | 41.9% |
| Moldova | 43.3% | 43.3% | 43.3% |

There was clearly some deterioration in inter–republic trade in 1991, but the number of alternate producers in the USSR/CIS is so limited that there is almost no likelihood that these figures had changed significantly by that time. What they make clear is that, except for the Russian Federation, there was a high level of mutual economic dependence among the republics which would lead to an almost total disruption if they were unable to work out some form of continued economic cooperation. A number of republics did negotiate bilateral trade agreements, but these did not work out very well, since suppliers and customers were seldom from a single republic or even from the *same* republic. An even more important problem was the matter of prices.

In the old Soviet Union, prices were largely symbolic, set by the state for reasons such as to subsidize development of individual industries or to discourage consumption, and having little or nothing to do with the international value of the articles. All of this was possible because it was then a closed system. In general, the prices of food, fuel and raw materials were kept low, while the prices of most consumer goods were above world prices. The movement to world prices after 1992 tended to disrupt inter-republic trade, since some of the poorer republics were unable to pay the greatly increased prices for food and fuel, while other republics did not want to pay world prices for merchandise that did not meet world standards.

An even more important factor was the failure of the plan for all of the republics to continue using the ruble as their own currency. The former union–wide banking system having collapsed, the individual republics were unable to come to an agreement at the CIS level on the transfer of funds between the republics. The result was a rapidly growing mountain of debt until the Russian Government restricted credit to the other republics, then effectively forced them off the ruble standard. Most republics later developed their own currencies, but the CIS continued to lack adequate mechanisms for the transferral of funds between republics. As a result, inter–republic trade dropped by as much as 70 percent in the period 1992–94.

This was a transitional problem, of course, related to the fact that most economic activity in the CIS was still state–run. The real, long–term solutions were to be found in privatization and movement to a market economy. The various republican leaders were theoretically committed to move in this direction but, with the exception of Russia and, recently, Ukraine, the movement has been extremely slow. It now appears that it will take most of the other republics another five to ten years to make the transition.

### Developments Since 1992

The CIS heads of state and heads of government have continued to meet on a regular basis since 1992 and a number of agreements have been negotiated, though in some cases a minority of republics have participated in such talks. In 1993–94, the Russian Government began pushing for greater military cooperation at the CIS level, particularly with regard to guarding the old borders of the USSR, and it has been successful in encouraging cooperation in this limited area. By the beginning of 1995, all of the CIS members except Azerbaijan had negotiated agreements authorizing the use of Russian troops along the frontier. And even in Azerbaijan, where Soviet troops were withdrawn after the collapse of the Soviet Union, Russian troops have since returned to police the truce line between Nagorno–Karabakh and Azerbaijan proper.

Russian forces are, in fact, still quite active in the ex–Soviet republics. Russian troops prop up the Tajik government and they run Turkmenistan's army and frontier forces. The Russian Government was also responsible for negotiating the cease fire in Abkhazia, the price of which was Georgian entry into the CIS. Georgia also subsequently signed an agreement authorizing the stationing of Russian troops within its borders. In Armenia, a similar agreement exists, and Russian troops now guard the Armenian border with Turkey. In the case of Belarus and Kazakhstan, although separate armies exist, they are closely associated with Russia. One Russian colonel commented that "the Belarusian army is virtually an adjunct of the Russian army." In the case of Kazakhstan, almost all officers are ethnic Russians and Russian the language of command. It is probably wiser to think in terms of "influence" rather than "control," however. Such officers would undoubtedly support and even advise close cooperation with Russia, but there is no reason to believe they would disobey contrary orders deriving from the political leadership of their republics.

The chief holdout has been Ukraine, which has kept its participation in the CIS to a minimum and so far has wanted nothing to do with "jointly" monitoring of CIS borders or CIS peacekeeping forces. But even the Ukrainian Government dropped its claim to most of the Black Sea fleet in early 1995, and agreed in principle to share the Sevastopol naval base with Russia.

There have been a few successes in the economic arena. Among recent agreements, Russia, Kazakhstan, and Belarus agreed to form a customs union in January 1995. Separately, Russia and Kazakhstan signed a separate agreement calling for increased economic and military links. Belarus has openly favored closer economic cooperation with Russia and has expressed a desire to replace its coupons with Russian rubles. The Russian Government agreed in principle, but as of March 1995 no final agreements had been signed.

Uralmach, the biggest Russian machine–building plant, which makes equipment for both Russian and foreign nations. The plant is located in the city of Ekaterinburg.

# WESTERN REPUBLICS (of the former Soviet Union)

Due to their shared histories as well as frequent geographical and cultural similarities, there is necessarily some repetition from one entry to the other.

Showing principal cities

# The Republic of Belarus

**Area:** 80,150 sq. mi. (207,600 sq. km., about the size of Minnesota).

**Population:** 10.4 million.

**Capital City:** Minsk (Pop. 1,589,000).

**Climate:** Temperate.

**Neighboring States:** Russia (east), Latvia, Lithuania (northeast), Poland (west), Ukraine (south).

**Languages:** Belarusian, Russian.

**Ethnic Composition:** Belarusian (78%), Russian (13%), other (9%).

**Principal Religions:** Orthodox Christianity, Roman Catholicism. Until recently religious worship was officially discouraged.

**Chief Commercial Products:** Grain, potatoes, cattle, agricultural machinery, motor vehicles, machine tools, oil, electricity, steel, coal and metal production.

**Currency:** Belarusian ruble. The union agreement signed with Russia in May 1997 provided for an eventual common currency, but it's unlikely that the agreement will be implemented.

**Per Capita Annual Income:** About U.S. $1,600.

**Recent Political Status:** Part of the Russian Empire until 1917, became the Byelorussian SSR in 1919, part of the USSR (1922–1991).

**Chief of State:** Alexander Lukashenko, President (elected July 10, 1994).

**National Flag:** In May 1995, the post–Soviet flag consisting of three equal bars white–red–white was replaced by a flag similar to the old flag of the Belarussian SSR. On the left, there is a white–on–red vertical embroidery pattern. A broad red stripe then fills the upper two-thirds of the field, with a second, green stripe across the bottom.

## The Land

The Republic of Belarus is the ultimate independent successor state to the Byelorussian Soviet Socialist Republic, established on January 1, 1919. It is located in the northwestern portion of the Russian Plain, just southwest of the Valdai Hills. The northern part of the republic is made up mostly of low, rolling hills. Dzyarzhynskaya Mountain, the loftiest point in the republic, is only 1,135 feet high. Most of the southern part of the republic is covered by a lowland area known as the Prypyats (Pripet) Swamp. Much of this area is a mixture of swamp and forest with a very low population density.

Four major rivers flow through Belarus. In the north the Western Dvina River, which begins in the Valdai Hills, enters from the east and then flows in a mainly northwestern direction until it crosses into Latvia, there becoming the Daugava. The Dnieper River also enters Belarus from the east, then flows in a southern direction a short distance west of the eastern border. It actually forms the eastern border for a short stretch before entering Ukraine. The third of the rivers is the Prypyats, which enters from the south from Ukraine, then flows eastward just north of the southern border. It crosses into Ukraine shortly before emptying into the Dnieper.

The last of the rivers is the Nyoman [Nemunas], which begins in northwestern Belarus, a short distance west of the capital city of Minsk, and flows west and then north before crossing the border into Lithuania. A tributary of the Nyoman, the Neris (Villia), starts in northwestern Belarus just north of Minsk. It flows in a meandering northwestern direction before crossing the border into Lithuania. Originally covered in forests and fens, today Belarus is a mixture of forests and fields. Reclamation projects in the south have reclaimed about 6.25 million acres of swampland, thereby increasing the agricultural potential of this area, particularly for pasturage, although hemp is another major crop. The south also has over six thousand peat deposits.

# Belarus

## The People

The population of the Republic of Belarus was 10,200,000 as of the 1989 census. Belarusians constitute about 78 percent of this total. Russians, the largest minority group, are around 13 percent of the population. Other minorities include Poles (4.2%), Ukrainians (2.4%), Jews (1.4%), and Lithuanians. Belarusian belongs to the eastern Slavic family of languages. It is fairly modern in origin and arose primarily for historical reasons. Its ancestor is Slavonic, which had been spoken by all eastern Slavs as late as the thirteenth century. This area became part of the Grand Principality of Lithuania in the fourteenth century. After the Lithuanian Union with Poland in 1569, the upper classes became heavily Polonized and this, plus the several centuries of separation, eventually produced a language that was different from either Russian or Ukrainian. As a result of the industrialization of the twentieth century, about half the population now lives in urban areas.

## History

The area of the Pripet Swamp, in southern Belarus, is believed to be the original home of the eastern Slavic peoples. Spreading out from that point, they eventually occupied most of the Russian Plain. The first organized Slavic state, Kievan Rus, came into existence as a trading state which controlled the "road from the Varangians (Vikings) to the Greeks." That "road" was the water system that permitted travel from the Baltic Sea in the north to the Black Sea and Constantinople in the south. The most important of those rivers was the Dnieper, which flows south through the eastern part of Belarus.

Kievan Rus was destroyed by an invasion of the Mongols in 1238–41. The collapse of that first Slavic state left the northwest in a state of anarchy which ended in the first half of the fourteenth century when Gedaminas founded the Grand Principality of Lithuania. It had its capital at Vilnius but the state extended southward as far as the Black Sea, including all of present–day Belarus. The majority of the people living in this state were Slavs and the language used at the court was old Slavonic, the language of Kievan Rus.

This situation continued until 1569 when Lithuania became part of the Polish Kingdom as a result of the Union of Lublin. From that time onward, the upper classes became increasingly Polonized. When an independent Patriarchate was established at Moscow a few years later, the Polish King separated the Orthodox Church in Lithuania from Moscow and forced it to recognize the Pope as the head of the church, thereby creating the Uniate Rite of the Church. That situation continued for over thirty years before the Orthodox Church was again allowed to begin operating again. After about 1625, therefore, you had a situation where the upper classes were Polonized and increasingly Roman Catholic and the peasants were Orthodox and enserfed.

The southern portion of the Orthodox lands broke away in 1654 and joined Russia; this became the Ukraine. But the northern Orthodox lands remained part of the Polish Kingdom until the three partitions of Poland in 1772, 1793 and 1795. These gave the area of present day Belarus to Russia. From 1795 to 1918, therefore, these lands were part of the Russian Empire. Russia did not recognize Belarusian as a separate language, however, so Russian became the language of government while Belarusian was merely the local dialect of the peasantry.

The Russian Revolution brought about a collapse of the old Imperial Government and the various parts of the empire began to set up autonomous governments. On March 25, 1918, anti–communist leftists established the independent Belarusian Democratic Republic. Lenin and his Bolsheviks in Moscow refused to recognize the new republic and it was later overthrown by the Red Army. On January 1, 1919, the communist victors set up the Byelorussian Soviet Socialist Republic.

The then Byelorussians accepted their inclusion in the new Soviet regime and

**One of the few buildings to survive World War II when most of the city of Minsk was destroyed, an Orthodox Church holds a lonely vigil as it stands surrounded by modern office and apartment buildings.** Photo by Miller B. Spangler

119

# Belarus

they remained loyal and subservient citizens throughout the Soviet era. In return, Moscow transformed the country industrially over the years. In addition, the republic was greatly enlarged in November 1939 when significant territories taken from Poland as a result of the Nazi–Soviet Non–Aggression Pact were added to the republic.

Gorbachëv's program of *glasnost* and *perestroika* brought some changes in Byelorussia, but the majority of the communist leadership was conservative. A *Byelorussian Popular Front* was established but, harassed by the leadership of the republic, it found it difficult to build up support and it remained a minority movement. The infamous Chernobyl nuclear accident in April 1986 created great fear throughout the republic, but the accident had actually occurred across the border in the Ukraine, so Belarusian officials were only blamed for not doing enough. They, in turn, blamed Moscow and otherwise helped keep a tight lid on news of the event.

When the attempted *coup* against Gorbachëv began in August 1991, Nikolas Dementei, the first secretary of the *Byelorussian Communist Party,* made the mistake of supporting the *coup* leaders. When the attempt collapsed, therefore, Dementei was ousted from his position as Chairman of the Supreme Soviet. On August 25, the Byelorussian Supreme Soviet also declared the republic's independence, adopting the name *Belarus* (initially spelled Belorus). It then suspended the activities of the communist party.

Stanislav Shushkevich was elected chairman of the Belarus Supreme Soviet on September 20, 1991. He previously had held the position of first deputy chairman of the Supreme Soviet. He is a nuclear physicist by training, however, and "headed laboratories and departments of nuclear physics in various Minsk higher educational institutions." He was also a member of the USSR Supreme Soviet where he was a member of the liberal Interregional Deputies Group.

Shushkevich supported a continuation of some form of union as long as that appeared a viable option. After the December 1 referendum and elections in the Republic of Ukraine, however, Shushkevich joined with Presidents Yeltsin and Kravchuk in creation of the Commonwealth of Independent States on December 8. Shushkevich had hosted the meeting at his hunting lodge and the agreement was signed in Minsk, the capital of Belarus.

Once Belarus had opted for independence, Shushkevich pushed for "the speediest introduction of market relations and private ownership." However, the Belarus Supreme Soviet, still filled with ex–communists, was really controlled by Vyacheslav Kebich, who held the position

**Hon. Stanislav Shushkevich**

of prime minister. Kebich, much more conservative, advocated a "go slow" policy. Because Shushkevich attempted to govern by consensus, he was never able to bring about very much economic change. Over time, however, his relations with Kebich grew worse. In January 1994, Shushkevich informally supported an attempt to oust Kebich. Kebich won the vote of confidence 175 to 101. The legislature then voted 209 to 36 to dismiss Shushkevich as Chairman of the Supreme Soviet. Although Shushkevich had been an advocate of the need for economic reforms, the most important reason for his ouster was his nationalism. Kebich, feeling that the situation in Belarus had deteriorated after the collapse of the Soviet Union, wanted to rebuild economic ties to Russia. Shushkevich favored good political relations with Russia but opposed closer economic ties because he thought they would compromise Belarus's independence.

Following Shushkevich's ouster, the Supreme Soviet elected Myechyslaw Hryb as its new Chairman in 1994. Under Hryb's leadership, the Supreme Soviet voted to adopt a presidential republic, then voted approval of a new constitution on March 4. This paved the way for new presidential elections in June. These elections were won by Alexander Lukashenko, a former collective farm director without previous political experience. Lukashenko's winning platform called for rebuilding ties with Russia with the ultimate goal of merging the two economies.

Three months earlier, in fact, Prime Minister Kebish had negotiated an agreement with Viktor Chernomyrdin, the Russian prime minister, under which Belarus would begin reintegrating itself into the Russian economy. Belarus was to lift all customs barriers with Russia, while Belarusian "coupons" were to be replaced by Russian rubles. Military bases in Belarus still being used by Russian troops were to be leased to Russia free of charge. As the July elections would later confirm, the

majority of the Belarusian population favored a policy of reintegration with Russia, particularly in light of its dismal experience running its own economy.

President Lukashenko continued to push the policy of reintegration with Russia after his election but, in fact, almost nothing changed because of second thoughts on the Russian side. In particular, the Russian Government decided that it would be too expensive for Russia to exchange Belarusian coupons for rubles, and backed out of the deal.

According to official Belarusian statistics, the economy grew by several percentage points in 1996 and 1997. In fact, the Belarus economy has continued to decline with no sign of a reversal in sight. A $300 million standby loan from the International Monetary Fund was approved in July 1995, based on a government promise to begin a program of reform. When the government did nothing, however, the loan was eventually suspended. Almost alone among the ex–Soviet republics, Belarus continues to oppose any movement toward privatizing its massive state sector.

Part of the problem is the lackluster attitude of the people of Belarus themselves. In the May 1995 elections, for example, a majority of eligible voters turned out to vote in only 119 out of the 260 electoral districts, thus invalidating the results in the remaining districts. Since the new constitution specified that 179 delegates constituted a quorum, the new parliament was unable to meet. The crisis continued until new elections took place in November, with President Lukashenko meanwhile ruling by decree. The electorate did manage to vote in a new parliament the second time around, but they gave a majority of the seats to communists and agrarians, who oppose reform.

Curiously, however, Mr. Lukashenko proved himself unable to work with this

**President Lukaschenko**

"ideal" parliament, the reason being his authoritarian manner; in essence, Lukashenko was unwilling to consult even with people who agreed with him. In August 1996, therefore, Lukashenko called for a "vote of confidence" in his policies in the form of a constitutional referendum to take place on November 7 (not coincidently the anniversary of the November Revolution). Under the terms of the referendum, Lukashenko was to be given a fresh five year term of office, additional powers to rule by decree, authority to create an upper house of parliament appointed directly or indirectly by himself, and authority to appoint half of the members of the constitutional court.

Parliament opposed the referendum and attempted to stop it, but failed. When the vote finally took place, it did so under a general presumption that the outcome was rigged. When Lukashenko claimed a landslide victory, therefore, people were inclined to take it with a grain of salt. Moreover, Mr. Lukashenko's Prime Minister, Mikhail Chigir, resigned after the result had been announced, adding credence to the charge of vote rigging. Public opinion polls consistently show that Lukashenko is the most popular political figure in Belarus, however, so he may have won legitimately. If that is the case, it is because the people of Belarus remain convinced that his policy of reintegration with Russia is the best policy.

Few foreign observers are optimistic about Belarus's future. Internationally, the IMF has halted lending to Belarus and the World Bank has frozen new projects. Switzerland and Austria froze credit lines to Belarus in July 1997, following the lead of Germany. The reason for these actions is that these countries are convinced that foreign credits were being wasted because the country had been unwilling to introduce any real economic reforms. In response to these actions, President Lukashenko announced that Belarus did not need foreign credits.

Even Russia, Lukashenko's supposed savior, continues to have doubts that it wants the full political and economic integration that Lukashenko has been pushing. President Yeltsin may have supported the idea as a candidate for reelection, but that was almost certainly a sop to nationalist sentiment at home. When Russia and Belarus got around to negotiating the union treaty that went into effect on June 11, 1997, the terms were much watered down from earlier expectations. Moreover, it appears that little has changed since the union treaty went into effect. In fact, even President Lukashenko told an assembly at Almaty State University in September 1997 that "speculation on the full merger of Belarus and Russia was dreamed up by politicos who have nothing better to do" and he also stressed that

The House of Government, Minsk

Belarus would never give up its sovereignty. He then added, however, that any slowdown in the rapprochement between Belarus and Russia was not the fault of Belarus.

## Foreign Policy

The Government of Belarus adopted an official stance of international neutrality upon independence. To that end, it signed the Nuclear Non–Proliferation Treaty and, in February 1993, its legislature ratified the START–1 agreement. At that time, there were 81 nuclear–armed SS–25 missiles stationed in Belarus. Over the next two years, all but 18 mobile launchers were shipped to Russia for dismantling. President Lukashenko then cancelled the remaining redeployments in July 1995, saying that the decision to withdraw the missiles had been a "major political mistake." Belarus remained in technical violation of the START–1 agreement for the next two years before finally arranging for a transfer of the remaining missiles to Russia.

In general, Belarus has played a rather reticent role internationally, although it did negotiate agreements with the three Baltic Republics shortly after independence and made a point of establishing good relations with its western neighbors. All of that began to change after President Lukashenko was elected and began to reverse the reforms initiated by his predecessors. Things came to a head in September 1997 when the presidents of ten countries in the region sharply criticized Belarus for its retreat from democratic reforms. The meeting, hosted by the presidents of Poland and Lithuania and held in Vilnius, attracted the presidents of Belarus, Bulgaria, Estonia, Hungary, Latvia, Moldova, Romania and Ukraine, plus Prime Minister Chernomyrdin of Russia. The meeting underlined President Lukashenko's isolation, for virtually everyone present was outspokenly critical of Belarus's policies under his leadership, both

in its retreat from a market economy and its abandonment of democracy.

Belarus's relations with his eastern neighbors are somewhat better. An active supporter of the Commonwealth of Independent States from the beginning, Belarus adopted a policy of favoring closer relations with Russia even before Lukashenko was elected president. For example, Belarus signed an agreement subordinating its military policy to that of Russia in December 1993. In 1994, it signed a second agreement with Russia which was supposed to result in a common customs and currency zone, though it was never implemented. President Lukashenko then negotiated an agreement for full economic and political union in the spring of 1996, during the Russian presidential campaign, but this was never implemented either. Finally, Russia and Belarus exchanged ratifications for a union treaty in June 1997 which once again called for the unification of the two peoples. Little changed after that time and relations between the two countries actually appeared to deteriorate afterwards when Belarus detained several TV journalists working for Russian Public Television (ORT) and charged them with entering the country illegally. Three of the journalists were released after Russia protested, but a fourth was detained for several months longer. In addition, two Belarusians working for ORT were arrested and put on trial. Relations turned even colder in October when Russia barred President Lukashenko from visiting two Russian regional cities. When Lukashenko protested, President Yeltsin replied that he would be happy to have Lukashenko visit—but only when the fourth Russian journalist was released.

Belarus's relations with the United States, which had been fairly good between 1991 and 1994, suffered a severe setback in September 1995 when border guards shot down a hot air balloon, killing its two American pilots. President Luka-

# Belarus

**A folk music ensemble of the Belarus Conservatory**

shenko made the situation even worse when he absolved the military from any wrongdoing. Relations with the United States suffered a further setback in the spring of 1997 when Belarus accused an American diplomat of spying and expelled him. The United States subsequently withdrew its ambassador for consultations.

### Nature of the Regime

The Supreme Soviet adopted a new constitution in March 1994 which established Belarus as a presidential republic. Under the new constitution, the head of state is the President of the Republic. The President, the major political figure within the new system, was charged with determining general policy, though his Prime Minister was directly in charge of the government. Under a constitutional referendum approved in November 1996, however, the President's powers were greatly increased. This referendum extended the current President's term of office to the year 2001, increased his power to issue decrees, permitted him to create an upper house of parliament to be appointed directly or indirectly by him, and gave him the right to appoint half of the members of the constitutional court.

The Prime Minister, appointed by the President and confirmed by the legislature, presides over the cabinet and oversees day–to–day operations of the government. He is also responsible for maintaining good relations with the legislature. The legislature, called the Supreme Soviet, currently consists of 260 members, though the President has been authorized

to set up an upper house, which will presumably reduce the power of the Supreme Soviet somewhat. Of the political parties, the two strongest are the *Belarus Communist Party* and the *Agrarian Party*. The *Belarus Popular Front* and the *United Democratic Party*, which have stood for reform, appear to have very little popular support any longer.

### Culture

Belarus has one prominent architectural monument from the period of Kievan Rus, the Cathedral of St. Sophia in Polotsk, which dates from the eleventh century. There are also two church–fortresses dating from the period of the Lithuanian Grand Principality, Maloye Mazheykava and Synkavichy. The seventeenth century saw the introduction of the Baroque style. The Jesuit church at Grodno exemplies this new style and also the growing presence of Roman Catholicism, officially fostered by the Polish Government at this particular juncture in time.

Polotsk was long a center of learning and there are a number of names associated with it. Frantsyk Skaryna produced the first Belarusian translation of the Bible in the first quarter of the sixteenth century. The two editions of the Bible were actually printed in Prague and Vilnius. Symeon of Polotsk was a seventeenth century poet who wrote in Belarusian.

Maksim Bahdanovich was an important poet of the late nineteenth century. Three poets of the early Soviet period are Ales Harun, Yanka Kupala, and Yakub Kolas. Kupala also produced a play, *Natives,*

which was first produced in 1924. Kolas also produced a three volume novel, *On the Crossroads*. Maksim Haretski was a novelist who wrote *The Quiet* Current. His diary was also published under the title of *On the Imperialist War.*

There was, in fact, a great outpouring of literature in the period of the 1920s. These included poets (Uladzimir Dubouka and Yazep Pushcha) and writers of fiction (Kuzma Chorny and Kandrat Krapiva). Stalin's introduction of socialist realism in 1930 brought a decline in the level of Belarusian writing, although some writers continued to be published. After World War II, a number of good composers appeared in Belarus. Dzmitry Lukas produced his first opera, *Kastus Kalinouski,* in 1947. Ryhor Pukst produced three operas between 1947 and 1955. Yauhen Hlebau produced an opera, *Your Spring* in 1963 and a ballet, *Alpine Ballad* in 1967. Yauhen Tsikotski and Yury Semyanyaka also wrote operas at this time. Belarus has both a conservatory of music and a philharmonic society. There is, in addition, the Belarusian State Theater of Opera and Ballet in Minsk, plus a state dramatic theater.

Belarus has a well–developed system of higher education. There are 33 institutes of higher education scattered throughout the republic, plus another 138 technical colleges. The Belarusian Academy of Sciences also has 32 scientific institutes in various parts of the republic. There is a comprehensive system of primary and secondary schools. In 1989, 71 percent of all eligible children were in preschool institutions.

# Belarus

The republic also publishes approximately two hundred daily newspapers, 130 of which are in Belarusian and the rest in other languages.

## Economy

Belarus has a fairly well balanced economy, with an agriculture capable, in general, of feeding its population and a well developed industrial base. The problem with its agriculture is that about two-thirds of the peasants are still organized into collective farms, with most of the remainder in state farms. A few private farms were set up after that became possible, but the treatment they received from the state sector has discouraged others from trying. The new Belarusian Government originally favored a changeover to private agriculture, but that policy was repudiated by President Lukashenko after his election in July 1994.

Agriculture in the northern part of the republic concentrates on cattle raising, both beef and dairy cattle. The farms produce their own fodder and hay and otherwise, except for those set aside for growing flax, the land is in pasturage. In the center of the republic, the farms concentrate on pig breeding. The most important crop grown in this area is potatoes. In the south, there are once again many farms that specialize in cattle raising, either for milk or beef. Hemp is also grown in this area. Grain is grown throughout the republic with 6.9 million tons produced in 1988. Some grain is imported into the republic, but mainly to be used as cattle feed.

It is capable of producing about 1.1 million tons of steel a year and it manufactures machine tools, agricultural machinery and motor vehicles. It also manufactures chemicals, paper and bricks. There is also a branch of industry that manufactures consumer goods such as watches, radios, televisions and bicycles. Most of the rest of industry is associated either with textiles or processing of agricultural products. It manufactures artificial fibers as well as natural ones. There is a flax-spinning industry and another that manufactures artificial silk. Shoes and boots are also made. Agricultural end products include sugar and preserves. Domestic energy supplies are limited mainly to peat, which is widely used in industry.

The weakness of Belarusian industry is two-fold. It has to import most of its raw materials from other republics and it imports most of its energy. As a result, industry came under severe economic pressure soon after independence and this so frightened the political leadership that economic reform never really got off the ground. Only about 5 percent of enterprises had been denationalized by July 1994 when President Lukashenko took office and halted the process completely. Today, the Belarus economy is struggling for survival, with industrial enterprises operating at approximately 30 percent of capacity with production continuing to fall.

In November 1997, President Lukashenko issued a decree giving the government the right to intervene in the affairs of private joint-stock companies, including forcing them to remain open even if they were unprofitable. In January 1998, the government moved against what little private enterprise continued to exist by announcing that it was reestablishing state monopolies on oil, tobacco, and car businesses. Prime Minister Sergei Ling announced that the government would not go back to "totalitarian planning" but that it did support "indicative planning." The government also decided to turn to the printing presses to cover the shortfall in the budget. If these moves were intended to shore up the failing economy, they did not work. By March 16, 1998, the Belarusian ruble was trading at 59,000 to the U.S. dollar, down some 25 percent from the previous week. At this point, First Deputy Prime Minister Chubais announced that the Russian Government was considering giving financial aid to stop the currency from collapsing completely, though Chubais added that Belarus's disastrous economy was the result of poor policies and lack of reform.

One drag on the economy is the continuing cost associated with the 1986 Chernobyl nuclear disaster, estimated by a Belarus cabinet minister in September 1995 at a quarter of the national economy. The southern part of Belarus was badly hit by nuclear fallout and many of the estimated 2 million victims live in Belarus. This was listed as a continuing problem to be handled by the Commonwealth of Independent States, but so far, only Russia has confirmed its intention to pay a share of the expenses. In the meantime, the Belarus government instituted an 18% wage tax in early 1992 to help raise the necessary money to pay for medical treatments and scientific research.

## The Future

The independence bestowed on Belarus as a result of the collapse of the Union of Soviet Socialist Republics in 1991 turns out to have been an unhappy experience for most Belarusians. The reason for this is not difficult to see, for Belarus's economy consisted largely of secondary industry, dependent on Russia and other Soviet republics for both raw materials and markets. The second problem is that it inherited a weak political leadership at independence that never managed to even begin the process of economic reform. The sharp decline that occurred everywhere in the former Soviet Union led, in Belarus, to an ousting of the post-independence political leadership in early 1994. President Lukashenko, elected later in that same year, argued during the campaign that the answer to Belarus's economic problems lay in a program of reintegrating Belarus with the Russian economy and he has continued to pursue that policy ever since. Meanwhile, the economy of Belarus continues to drift downward, even as President Lukashenko presses Russia for full political and economic integration. Russia is flattered at the attention, but it has its own problems and cannot afford to shore up an unreformed Belarusian economy. At the moment, therefore, Belarus's future looks bleak.

*Zaichik* (actual size)

123

# The Republic of Ukraine

**Kiev, capital of Ukraine, on the Dneiper River on a cold, damp February morning**

**Area:** 232,046 sq. mi. (601,000 sq. km.), twice the size of New Mexico.

**Population:** 50.5 million (December 1997).

**Capital City:** Kiev (Pop. 2.6 million, estimated).

**Climate:** Temperate.

**Neighboring States:** Russia (east), Belarus (north), Poland (northwest), Slovakia, Hungary (west), Romania, Moldova (west).

**Languages:** Ukrainian, Russian.

**Ethnic Composition:** Ukrainian (74%), Russian (21%), others 5%.

**Principal Religions:** Ukrainian Orthodox and Ukrainian Catholic.

**Chief Commercial Products:** Grain, potatoes, fruit, vegetables. Ukraine has some of the richest land in the former USSR. Highly developed fuel and power resources, iron and manganese ore, metal production, engineering, chemical production, gas, processed food, building materials. The nation has 60% of the former USSR's coal reserves.

**Currency:** hryvna (issued summer of 1996).

**Per Capita Annual Income:** About U.S. $2,000.

**Recent Political Status:** Part of the Russian Empire until 1917, Ukrainian Republic (1917–1922), Ukrainian Soviet Socialist Republic (1922–1991).

**Chief of State:** Leonid Kuchma, President (elected July 10, 1994).

**Head of Government:** Valery Pustovoitenko, Prime Minister (August 1997).

**National Flag:** Two horizontal stripes, the top a light blue, the bottom yellow.

### The Land

The Republic of Ukraine is the independent successor to the Ukrainian Soviet Socialist Republic, a constituent republic of the Union of Soviet Socialist Republics. Ukraine declared its independence on August 24, 1991 and this was confirmed by a popular referendum that took place on December 1, 1991. The Republic of Ukraine also has included the Crimean Autonomous Republic (created in 1991), which in early May declared *its* own independence from Ukraine. The matter basically involves control of the former USSR Black Sea naval fleet.

The Republic of Ukraine lies in the southwestern part of the Russian Plain. The chief feature of the landscape is the Dnieper River, which flows down through the center of the republic. There are two upland regions, a series of rolling hills in the southeast and the Volyn–Podol Plateau, which stretches from the Polish to Moldovan border in the west. The only large mountainous area is along the western border, where the northern ridges of the Carpathian Mountains cross the republic. The southern tip of the Crimean Peninsula (the status of which is now open to question) also has a small mountainous area, a western extension of the Caucasus Mountains. Mountains make up only about five percent of the total land surface of the republic.

Because so much of the republic con-

sists of a level plain, the differentiation between the various parts is based on the amount of rainfall that each gets. The most rainfall occurs in the north and diminishes to the south. The northern part of Ukraine is actually a large swampland, called the Pripet Marsh, the major part of which lies across the border in Belarus. The Dnieper Lowland dominates the central part of the republic. It is flat in the west and gently rolling in the east. Its chief feature is the Dnieper River and its tributaries. This is the traditional grain basket of the republic, which extends as far south as the city of Dniepropetrovsk, on the Dnieper River. Here the rainfall is adequate to support wheat and other grains without irrigation. In the area south of Dniepropetrovsk, on the other hand, irrigation becomes necessary.

The area immediately north of the Crimean Peninsula is known as the Nogai Steppe. This, plus the northern part of the Crimean Peninsula, referred to as the Crimean Lowland, were once grassy steppes, homelands of the Nogai and Crimean Tatars and pasturelands for their animals. Today a huge artificial lake on the Dnieper provides water for irrigation.

The southern shore of the Crimean Peninsula has a mild Mediterranean–type climate, with average January temperatures of 39°F. Summers are hot and dry. The northern shore of the Black Sea is much colder, with average January temperatures of 26°F. Spring comes early, however, usually at the end of January. Average January temperatures in Kiev are 18°F. Temperatures are also lower in winter and higher in summer in the eastern part of the republic.

Soils vary somewhat throughout the republic, but rich *chernozems* (black earth soils), which cover the entire central part of the republic, make up about 65% of the total. To the north of the *chernozems* area are found mixed gray *podsol* and black earth soils, and eventually pure, gray *podsol* soils, which are less fertile and also acidic. South of the *chernozems* belt is an area of chestnut soils, not as rich as *chernozems* and tending to be saline as one nears the Black Sea. The vegetation also reflects this soil division. Forests are found only in the north, in the area of the gray *podsols*. Mixed forest and grassy steppe cover the *chernozems* area. Desert and semidesert plants grow in the chestnut soils of the south.

### The People

The population of the Republic of Ukraine was 50.48 million as of December 1997, down approximately 3 percent from 1991. The decline in 1997 alone was 400,000. The drop has been occurring because of rising death rates and falling birth rates. Experts believe that a major causative factor derives from the Cher-

nobyl nuclear accident of 1986, which has contributed to male fertility problems. Approximately 74 percent of the population speak Ukrainian as their first language. Russians constitute the largest minority and they are actually a majority in eastern Ukraine and the Crimea. They make up approximately 21 percent of the overall population. There are nearly a hundred other ethnic groups, but the only two larger groups are Jews (1%) and Belorusians (.8%). Ukrainian belongs to the eastern Slavic family languages, the other two of which are Russian and Belarusian. Ukrainian is derived from Old Slavonic, the language spoken by all eastern Slavs during the period of Kievan Russian history from the 10th century or before. Ukrainian evolved after the split caused by the Mongol invasion in 1240. After 1240, the area of the Ukraine was ruled directly by the Mongol Empire for a hundred years, then was incorporated into the Grand Principality of Lithuania. The area east of the Dnieper River merged with Russia in 1654 and the rest of the Ukraine was added in the eighteenth century. It was this historic separation, and the connection with Lithuania and Poland between 1341 and the end of the eighteenth century, that resulted in the Ukrainian language. The word Ukraine means "the border" and describes Ukraine's position *vis–à–vis* Moscow. Historically, the Ukrainians have spoken of their land as *Malaya Russiya*, or "Little Russia."

### History

Archaeological evidence indicates that the first settlement at the city of Kiev, capital of modern–day Ukraine, was made in the seventh century. Kiev, built on the bluffs overlooking the western bank of the Dnieper River, commanded traffic on the river and soon became a regional trading center. At the end of the ninth century, then, it became the capital of the first organized Russian state when Olaf the Norwegian conquered it and moved his headquarters here from Novgorod. Kiev remained the capital of this first Russian state until 1169, when Iuri Dolgaruki, Prince of Vladimir, became Grand Prince but decided to move the capital to his own city of Riazan. Although Kiev lost its political preeminence at this time, it remained an important trading center until 1240, when it was sacked and virtually destroyed by the Mongols. All of southern Kievan Rus was then incorporated into the new Mongol Empire and ruled from its regional capital of Sarai, located on the eastern bank of the Volga River, just north of the Caspian Sea. Kiev itself became a ghost city when the craftsmen who had not been killed in the sack of the city in 1240 were rounded up and sent to Sarai.

The Golden Horde, as the Russians

called the Mongol Government, appointed new Grand Princes to govern in the north, but the weight of the Mongol yoke brought a collapse of this line by the early fourteenth century. Slowly, then, Moscow rose in the northeast and built its leadership, all the time acting as agent for the Golden Horde.

In the northwest, however, a new leadership rose, based on freeing as much of the area as possible from the Mongol yoke. The leader of this new state was the Lithuanian Prince Gediminas (Gedymin in Russian), founder of the Jagellon dynasty, but the majority of the subjects of this new Grand Principality of Lithuania were eastern Slavs and their language, Old Slavonic, became the official language of the court. Gediminas extended his control southward and in the process freed Kiev and the western territories as far south as the Black Sea from Mongol control.

One effect of the Mongol control had been that most of the area of southwestern Kievan Rus was virtually depopulated. Since this area remained subject to periodic attack from the Mongols, for another two hundred years it remained a borderland where only the brave or the desperate dared to live. Increasingly, however, communities of Slavic speakers fleeing from oppression in either Lithuania or the Moscow area settled this area, adopting many of the habits of nomadic neighbors, particularly the use of the horse and methods of fighting.

These became the Cossack communities of the southern steppe, one of the most important of which was the Zaporozhian Cossacks, with their settlements south of the cataracts on the Dnieper River.

These Cossacks had to fight constantly for their freedom, against nomads to the east and against encroachments from governments to the north. After the Grand Principality of Lithuania was merged with the Kingdom of Poland in the Union of Lublin in 1569, the combined Kingdom of Poland–Lithuania attempted to control this southern borderland area. The fighting prowess of the Cossacks was such, however, that the government was often willing to sign a treaty recognizing their status as Cossacks in return for military service to the Polish–Lithuanian state. At the same time, however, the government was giving out land to Polish noblemen and encouraging their settlement in this borderland area. These Polish noblemen brought the institution of serfdom with them—and there were constant efforts to enserf individual free peasants of the steppe.

A second issue, religion, arose at the end of the sixteenth century. The Cossacks were Russian Orthodox, while the Polish nobility moving into the area were Roman Catholic. When the Patriarch of Constan-

# Ukraine

tinople recognized Moscow (Muscovy) as a separate Patriarchate at the end of the sixteenth century, he recognized the Russian Patriarch's jurisdiction over all Russian Orthodox, including those of the southwest under Polish–Lithuanian control. For political reasons, the Government of Poland–Lithuania refused to recognize this jurisdiction and outlawed the Russian Orthodox Church within the area of its jurisdiction. Instead, it created the Uniate or Eastern Catholic Church, which used the traditional Orthodox service and the Old Slavonic language but recognized the spiritual leadership of the Pope.

Thus the free peasants of the Ukraine found themselves under a three–pronged attack in the first half of the seventeenth century—encroaching serfdom, Polonization pushed by the increasing numbers of Polish nobility establishing estates in the area, and attempts to destroy the independent Orthodox Church. The man who now rose to the leadership of the Ukrainian forces was Bodgan Khmelnitsky, a Ukrainian landowner elected Hetman (head) of the Zaporozhian Cossacks. Khmelnitsky defeated the Polish forces a number of times and for a while apparently dreamt of creating an independent Ukraine. But it soon became apparent to him that the Ukrainian forces were not strong enough to sustain an independent Ukraine. Believing that a victory by Poland would mean the end of the Orthodox Church and the enserfment of the free peasants of the Ukraine, he turned to Muscovy and offered to bring the Ukraine under Russian control.

Tsar Alexis, then ruler of Muscovy, hesitated for some time before accepting the offer because he recognized that it would mean war with Poland. He finally accepted in 1653, however. This led to a war between Poland and Muscovy that began in 1654 and ended with the Truce of Andrusovo in 1667. Under the terms of the truce, Poland recognized Muscovite control over all lands east of the Dnieper River, plus temporary control of the city of Kiev. Russia never gave Kiev back, however, and the terms of the truce were confirmed by a peace treaty signed in 1686. Russia got the remaining parts of the Ukraine during the partitions of Poland in 1772 and 1793. Thus the destinies were tied with those of Russia primarily over the issue of religion, i.e., loyalty to the Orthodox Church. Cossacks also retained their freedom from serfdom, though there was some encroachment in this area in the eighteenth century.

Russian–Ukrainian relations were not always smooth, however. For example, Ivan Mazepa, who was elected Hetman of the Zaporozhian Cossacks in 1687, concluded an alliance with Charles XII of Sweden in 1708 under which the Ukraine was to become an independent nation un-

der Mazepa's leadership. It was only Peter the Great's victory over Sweden at the battle of Poltova that put an end to that dream. There were three further Hetmans in the eighteenth century, all Russian nominees. The last Hetman was Kyrylo Razumovsky, younger brother of Empress Elizabeth's "Gentleman of the Bedchamber." Catherine the Great accepted his resignation in 1764.

Catherine the Great incorporated the Ukraine directly into Russia by dissolving separate Cossack bodies and dividing the area into *guberniyi*. In 1793, when the remaining territories occupied by Ukraini-

ans were taken from Poland in the second partition, the name Ukraine was dropped and all of the territory simply became part of Russia.

Ukrainian nationalism resurfaced in the nineteenth century when the secret Brotherhood of Saints Cyril and Methodius was founded in Kiev in 1846. The membership of the Brotherhood included two historians, Mykola Kostomariv and Panteleimon Kulish, plus the Ukrainian poet Taras Shevchenko. It was suppressed in 1847 and its thirty members were exiled to other parts of the empire.

Tsar Alexander II authorized the publi-

**Cossacks of yesteryear hunt on the open Ukrainian plains**

# Ukraine

cation of a journal, *Osnova* (The Outset) in Ukrainian in 1861. In 1876, however, Alexander II prohibited the publication of journals or books in the Ukrainian language and closed all Ukrainian language schools. Thereafter, Ukrainian nationalists migrated abroad, either to Lvov in Austrian Galicia or to Switzerland. The Austrian Government permitted a Shevchenko Scientific Society to be founded there in 1872 and in 1890 a chair in southeastern European history was established at the University of Lvov.

The first man appointed to fill the position was Myhailo Hrushevsky, a Ukrainian historian. Hrushevsky eventually published a ten–volume *History of Ukraine-Rus,* whose major thesis was the continuation of Kievan Rus–Ukrainian history and the separate development of the history of Muscovy–Russia. After the Revolution of 1905, when the Russian Government lifted its ban against the publication of journals and books in Ukrainian, Hrushevsky moved back to Kiev.

After the Russian Revolution of 1917, Ukrainian nationalists held a National Ukrainian Congress in Kiev in April and elected a Rada (Council) headed by Hrushevsky. The Ukrainian Rada proclaimed an autonomous Ukrainian republic on June 23 with Hrushevsky as President, and within days Volodymir Vinnichenko as premier and Symon Petlyura as minister of war.

After the Bolshevik *coup d'etat* in November, the Ukrainian Rada called for convocation of a freely elected Ukrainian Constituent Assembly. Opposing this, the Bolsheviks announced formation of a Ukrainian Soviet Government on December 26. On January 22, 1918, the Ukrainian Rada proclaimed a "free and sovereign" Ukrainian Republic. The Central Powers signed a separate peace treaty with this government at Brest–Litovsk on February 9, but the Bolsheviks managed to seize Kiev on February 8. The Rada fled to Zhitomir and German and Austrian troops moved in and occupied most of the Ukraine. The Rada and the Central Powers now came into conflict, whereupon the Central Powers overthrew the Ukrainian Rada on April 24 and appointed Pavlo Skoropadsky as Hetman of the Ukraine.

After the collapse of Germany in November 1918, a five–man directorate took over in the Ukraine, with Volodymir Vinnichenko as chairman and Symon Petlyura as commander in chief. A separate Republic of the Western Ukraine was proclaimed in Lvov. Lvov was occupied by the Poles about three weeks later, however, so this government fled to Ivano–Frankovsk. In January 1919, a union of the two Ukraines was proclaimed, but a Red Army occupied Kiev the same day. On March 14, 1919, a Ukrainian Soviet Socialist Republic was formed under the lead-

ership of Khristian Rakovsky. The whole of Galicia remained in Polish hands and the Bolsheviks lost control of Kiev to the anti–Bolshevik forces under General Denikin in September 1919. However, Denikin and the Ukrainian nationalists fell out over the issue of a separate Ukraine. Denikin was defeated in December and most of the Ukraine fell under communist control.

**Communist Control**

In December 1919, Lenin recognized the equality of the Russian and Ukrainian peoples and proposed an alliance. The Ukrainian nationalists couldn't bring themselves to come to terms with the Bolsheviks, however. Instead, Petlyura allied himself with Pilsudski, the Polish leader, which led to a Polish invasion of the Ukraine in April 1920. The Poles occupied Kiev on May 7. Pilsudski now began dreaming of a reconstructed Polish–Lithuanian–Ukrainian Commonwealth. But that vision was not acceptable to Ukrainian nationalists and the Polish forces were soon forced out of the Ukraine. In December 1920, Lenin and Rakovsky, head of the Ukrainian Soviet Socialist Republic, signed an alliance uniting Soviet Russia and the Ukraine. A peace treaty with Poland was signed on March 18, 1921. Under the terms of the treaty, Poland got to keep Eastern Galicia and Volhynia.

In December 1922, an All–Union Congress of Soviets representing the Russian, Ukrainian, Byelorussian and Transcaucasian Soviet Socialist Republics agreed to form the Union of Soviet Socialist Republics. A constitution for the new union was adopted in July 1923.

In the Ukraine, a Language Act of August 1, 1923 established the priority of Ukrainian over Russian. Hrushevsky was appointed president of the Ukrainian Academy of Science, founded in 1918. This period of Ukrainization came to an end in 1928 when Stalin forced the government to introduce Russian as the second official language. Two years later, "nationalist deviation" became a crime punishable by death when 45 intellectual leaders were put on trial and charged with treason. Thirteen were sentenced to death and the rest were deported. Hrushevsky, though not one of the 45 accused, was also deported. As part of Stalin's grisly purges, additional trials were held in 1931 and 1933. Being a member of the *Communist Party* was no defense. Yury Kotsiubinsky, deputy premier, was shot in 1933; in 1937, Panas Lyubchenko, an ex–premier, was also shot; and in 1939, yet another premier, Vlas Chubar, was shot.

Ironically, an undetermined but substantial number of Ukrainians were willing to join Hitler in his invasion directed against the Russians in World War II, but the deranged German simply ignored

them. When the outcome of the campaign in Russia is considered, his actions may have affected it.

The territory of the Ukraine was considerably enlarged as a result of World War II. Those parts of Poland where Ukrainians lived, essentially eastern Galicia and Volhynia, were occupied by the Red Army beginning in September 17, 1939 and incorporated into the Ukraine later that year. Romania ceded Bessarabia and northern Bukovina to the Union of Soviet Socialist Republics in June 1940. Northern Bukovina and the Bessarabian districts of Hotin and Izmail went to the Ukraine. On June 29, 1945, Czechoslovakia ceded Sub–Carpathian Ruthenia to the USSR, and this area was also incorporated into the Ukraine.

The last addition to the Ukraine came in February 1954 when Nikita Khrushchev marked the 300th anniversary of the Russo–Ukraine union by transferring the Crimea to the Ukraine. In 1991, the Ukrainian Government decided to grant the Crimea the status of an autonomous republic. But in early May, it declared, through its parliament, its own independence.

The Gorbachëv program of reform instituted after 1985 found no immediate response in the Ukraine, for Vladimir Shcherbitsky, first secretary of the *Ukrainian Communist Party,* was a Brezhnev stalwart who was quick to slap down any signs of dissent. He was removed in September 1989 and died soon afterwards. His successor, Leonid Kravchuk, although he had come up through the party apparatus, quickly established himself as more "liberal" than his predecessor and more willing to make concessions on nationalism.

This made good political sense, since the Ukraine had by this time a national front movement, *Rukh,* that was challenging the communists for the political leadership of the republic. Kravchuk managed to turn back the *Rukh* challenge in the March 1990 elections by stealing a number of their positions. After the communists had managed to hold on to 239 out of the 450 seats in the legislature, Kravchuk sponsored a declaration of republican sovereignty, which was adopted in July 1990.

In March 1991, Kravchuk agreed to hold a referendum on a new union treaty, but insisted on rewording it to make it clear that the Ukraine was unwilling to give up its claim to sovereignty. As Gorbachëv negotiated for a new union treaty in the summer of 1991, Kravchuk worked to insulate the Ukraine from Gorbachëv's economic policies, suggesting in July, for example, that the Ukraine intended to issue its own currency. The Ukrainian legislature also began taking more nationalistic

127

# Ukraine

**President Leonid Kuchma**

stances, for example repealing a series of Soviet tax and foreign–trade laws.

When conservatives launched their *coup d'etat* to overthrow Gorbachëv in August 1991, Kravchuk compromised by refusing to recognize the authority of the leaders while, at the same time, not condemning them publicly. After it collapsed, he resigned as first secretary of the *Ukrainian Communist Party* and banned the party from the republic. On August 24, he got the Ukrainian legislature to declare the Ukraine independent, subject to a popular referendum to take place on December 1, 1991.

At this point, it was believed that Kravchuk favored some form of continued union, and Ukrainian delegates cooperated in creating the new interim government that the Supreme Soviet approved on September 5. Nationalist pressures continued to grow, however, and by October Kravchuk was beginning to sound as though he wanted a completely independent Ukrainian state. By November, the Ukrainian legislature voted to "decertify" the Ukrainian deputies to the USSR Supreme Soviet; henceforth they were to participate as observers only. Meanwhile, Kravchuk had stated that the Ukraine also intended to create its own national army.

The December 1 referendum and popular election for the office of President of Ukraine became the culmination of this increasing trend. Over 90% of all voters cast their ballots in favor of Ukrainian independence, at the same time giving 61% of their votes to Kravchuk to make him the first president of an independent Ukraine. Eight days later, Kravchuk met with the presidents of Russia and Belarus to declare the Union of Soviet Socialist Republics dead and create the Common-

wealth of Independent States. Eight other republics joined the CIS on December 21, and Gorbachëv resigned as President of the USSR on December 25.

The history of the CIS has been extremely uneven since its creation in December 1991 and Ukraine has contributed to that unevenness. Essentially, Ukraine, fearing a new domination by Russia, has been only a half–hearted participant in CIS efforts to create independent structures that would permit continued cooperation between the ex–Soviet republics. For example, the Republic of Ukraine made it clear from the beginning that it intended to take control of all conventional forces stationed in Ukraine, including naval forces. There were no problems with the army, including nuclear forces, but a quarrel did arise with Russia over the Black Sea Fleet, headquartered in the Crimea. Ukraine first claimed the entire Black Sea Fleet, then only the conventional portion of it, while Russia took the position that dividing it would destroy it. The two countries worked out an arrangement for joint supervision of the Black Sea Fleet in 1992, but it wasn't until 1997 that they were able to reach an arrangement acceptable to both sides.

Another problem has been the status of the Autonomous Republic of Crimea. Crimea, which has a population of about 2.5 million, is about 67 percent Russian and 26 percent Crimean Tatar. Ukrainians actually make up only 26 percent of the population. A majority of the Crimea population voted for Ukrainian independence in December 1991, but Russian nationalists in the Crimean legislature subsequently pushed for a vote of independence from Ukraine, with the real aim of joining Russia. The Crimean legislature has actually been ambivalent on the issue, voting for independence and then modifying the vote to indicate that Crimea was a part of Ukraine. The issue has also been fueled by Russian nationalists in Russia, who argue that Crimea ought to be returned to Russia, to which it belonged until 1954. In May 1992, the Russian Supreme Soviet actually passed a resolution declaring the 1954 transfer to be invalid. The Yeltsin Government repudiated the resolution, but the Supreme Soviet's vote was seen by Ukrainian nationalists as another example of Russia's traditional tendency to bully and dominate. The Friendship Treaty between Russia and Ukraine, signed in May 1997, presumably put an end to this problem because it includes an explicit Russian recognition of Ukraine's borders.

Ukraine's main problems since independence have been economic, however, and this derived partly from the fact that the leadership of the country remained in the hands of ex–communists opposed to significant economic change until 1994. President Kravchuk was, of course, first

secretary of the Ukrainian Communist Party before 1991. His first Prime Minister, Vitold Fokin, was another old–line communist bureaucrat who found himself beyond his depth in the new circumstances of a collapse of the old communist system. Even as Ukraine's economic circumstances continued to grow worse over the next several months, the government did nothing to tackle the problems. By September 1992, inflation was outpacing even the Russian rate so Ukrainian coupons were trading at a ratio of 3 coupons to 2 rubles and, in spite of seemingly unlimited easy credit to industry, economic activity was down 18 percent over the preceding year. Faced with that situation, even the Supreme Soviet, dominated though it was by ex–communists, was unwilling to continue to put up with Fokin's policies. On September 30, he and his cabinet were forced to resign.

President Kravchuk's first choice as his successor was another former communist boss, Valentin Simonenko, but he was unacceptable to the Supreme Soviet. President Kravchuk then settled on Leonid Kuchma, a member of the Supreme Soviet who had also been Director of *Yuzhmash*, Ukraine's largest producer of nuclear missiles, since 1986. Although a long–time member of the *nomenklatera*, Kuchma had a reputation for being hard-driving and competent. Moreover, he took office with a mandate to step up the pace of economic reform if he so wished. In confirming him, the Supreme Soviet also gave him the power to rule by decree until May 1993.

Over the next year, Kuchma pushed a major economic reform that was supposed to address most of Ukraine's problems and move the country toward a market economy. His decrees on privatizing land, reforming income tax and commercializing state–owned enterprises brought loud objections from the legislature, however, and attempts to revoke his right to rule by decree. Over the next several months, therefore, Kuchma spent his time quarreling with parliament and getting very little accomplished. Parliament then refused to renew his right to rule by decree in May 1993. Kuchma remained on as prime minister until September, apparently hoping to work out some accommodation with parliament. He then resigned and was replaced by Youhym Zviahilsky. Zviahilsky, who is an ex–Soviet enterprise director from the Donbass, never claimed to be a reformer and the policies he implemented as prime minister were in line with the hardliners in parliament. Not surprisingly, prices increased 30–fold in 1993 and the government's budget was almost 90% of GDP. Having a large budget deficit to contend with, the government also instituted punitive taxes which suppressed economic activity. With company taxes levied on gross revenues instead of profits, it was not uncommon for companies to hand over more than 100% of their official profits as tax. This had the effect of driving most private economic activity underground. By the end of 1993, the "underground" category was estimated to encompass 60% of the economy.

The Government of Ukraine withdrew from the ruble block in November 1992, at the prompting of Russia. From that time until the summer of 1996, its currency consisted of "coupons" that the government had began issuing in the spring of 1992. The government had a new currency, the *hryvna*, already printed up but, because of a virulent inflation, did not dare to release it.

New parliamentary elections took place in March 1994. 338 out of the 450 seats were filled, with the remainder to be filled in a second round of voting. Of the 338 seats filled, 163 were won by persons running without a party label. Most of these are prominent local people, usually ex-communists. Among parties, those associated with the old communist regime made the best showing. The *Ukrainian Communist Party* came in first with 86, followed by the *Peasant Party*, with 18 seats and the *Ukrainian Socialist Party* with 14 seats. *Rukh*, largest of the nationalist parties, won 20 seats while five other nationalist parties garnered 20 more seats among them. Six centrist parties won 17 seats. In general, communists and their allies did best in eastern Ukraine, while nationalists did best in western Ukraine. While most Ukrainians thus voted against change, Leonid Kuchma, leader of the centrist *Interregional Reform Bloc* won over 52% of the vote for president on July 10, 1994, defeating incumbent Leonid Kravchuk.

Kuchma had run as a reformer and he signaled this by meeting with Michel Camdessus, managing director of the IMF on July 28, ten days after taking office. This was, in effect, a follow-up of a meeting that Kuchma had with Camdessus in Washington in the spring. At the time, Kuchma, still only a candidate, had challenged Camdessus to come to Kiev if he won the election and had concrete economic proposals ready. After the meeting, Camdessus promised that the IMF would work with Kuchma to develop an economic program for the Ukraine aimed at keeping monthly inflation to single digits, reducing the budget deficit, and freeing prices.

This, in turn, would permit a start on implementation of the $4 billion aid package promised at the economic summit meeting in Naples earlier in the month. That promise had been conditioned on the Ukrainian Government's moving forward on programs such as land redistribution, privatization of state enterprises, elimination of price controls, and drastic cuts in the budget. Kuchma subsequently pushed a far-reaching economic reform program through the legislature which promised large-scale privatization of state companies, cuts in the national budget and the removal of price controls on many goods.

Ukraine received its first IMF loan, for $371 million, in October 1994 and agreement was reached for a second loan for $1.5 billion in March 1995. With the payments deficit for 1995 expected to be $5.5 billion, however, the Ukrainian Government requested an additional $900 million from individual Western countries as well. The U.S. Government pledged $100 million, while additional funds eventually came from the members of the European Union. After some Western arm twisting, Russia also agreed to reschedule $2.5 billion in Ukrainian debts, and Turkmenistan took similar action on monies owed it for deliveries of natural gas.

Economic reform has continued since that time, with the government gradually selling off state assets. With inflation slowly being brought under control, the Ukrainian Government was finally able to begin issuing its new currency, the hryvna, in the summer of 1996. However, the economy remained stagnant, the 1996 budget continued to run a large deficit, and the gross foreign debt at the end of 1996 stood $8.5 billion.

The Ukrainian Government did have

**A country wedding day—complete with troubadours**

129

# Ukraine

**St. Sofia Cathedral, Kiev, the city's oldest structure dating back to the times of the Kievan Rus**
Courtesy: NOVOSTI

mer state–farm boss from the Dnepropetrovsk region of eastern Ukraine. Lazarenko served from July 1995 to July 1997, then was replaced after a period of illness. The present prime minister is Valery Pustovoitenko, a former Mayor of Dnepropetrovsk. A leading member of President Kuchma's People's Democratic Party, Pustovoitenko was head of Kuchma's election team in the presidential campaign of 1994. He is as committed to radical economic reform as President Kuchma. He was confirmed as prime minister in August 1997. Pustovoitenko has attempted to win support for his policies from members of parliament by involving them earlier in the process as the new policies are being developed. This technique has allowed him to get somewhat more through the legislature.

One example is the new election law which parliament approved in September 1997. With new parliamentary elections scheduled for March 1998, Kuchma attempted to get a new electoral law which would establish single member constituencies. In a compromise, the legislature approved a new electoral law whereby half of the seats in the 450–seat legislature are filled by ballots cast in single–member constituencies, while the other half are elected by party lists.

The stakes in those elections were raised in November 1997 when the parliament passed a resolution suspending privatization. Although the government argued that privatization was already the law of the land and the parliamentary vote was, therefore, not binding, this was still a serious setback. Although the chief reason for the vote is that the parliament was controlled by individuals hostile to economic reform, it is also true that the situation of the economy gave them an excuse. For example, GDP fell by 4 percent in 1997. This was an improvement over 1996, when the drop was 10 percent, but it still presented a negative picture. Moreover, the currency came under international pressure at this time and began dropping in value. This was primarily a reaction to the economic collapse in Thailand, Korea and Indonesia, but it was easy for opponents to blame it on economic reform. But the government made the argument that parliament's opposition was responsible for the continued fall of the currency. This argument, plus negotiations between the government and the legislature over the government's 1998 budget, persuaded the parliament to approve the budget and lift its ban on privatization in February 1998.

The results of the new parliamentary elections, which took place on March 29, 1998, are not encouraging for the government, however, for the Communist Party of Ukraine (CPU) and its left–wing allies increased their representation in the par-

promises of loans totaling approximately $4 billion from the West, including the IMF, if it carried through with a promised structural reform. President Kuchma has worked hard to do so, though he has not always been able to get his proposals through the legislature. A particular example of this occurred in 1997 when the legislature delayed passage of the budget for over six months, threatening up to $3 billion in credits from the IMF.

Kuchma's policies have considerable support within the country but they are by no means universally liked. Another problem is that, until 1997, Kuchma was unable to get parliament to accept a prime minister who was in agreement with his

economic policies. His first prime minister, Vitaly Masol, was inherited from his predecessor as president, having been appointed in June 1994 by Leonid Kravchuk. Masol, an old communist bureaucrat, often opposed specific elements of Kuchma's policy of economic reform. Kuchma retained him as prime minister because it would have been difficult to get any more liberal successor approved by the communist–dominated parliament.

Masol stepped down in March 1995 and he was replaced by Yevhen Marchuk, Masol's first deputy prime minister. Marchuk was unable to win a vote of confidence in the Ukrainian legislature, however, so he was replaced by Pavlo Lazarenko, a for-

liament, and can now claim a clear plurality of the seats. The CPU has 121 seats in the 450–seat parliament while its left–wing allies, the Socialist/Peasants' Bloc and the Progressive Socialist Party, have an additional 73 seats. Other parties in the parliament include nationalist Rukh party with 32 seats; the Greens with 19; the Popular Democratic Party, led by Prime Minister Valery Pustovoitenko, with 17 seats; the Hromada party, led by former Prime Minister Pavlo Lazarenko, with 16 seats; and the United Social Democrats, led by former President Leonid Kravchuk, with 14 seats. Independent candidates hold 114 seats.

## Foreign Policy

When it declared its independence at the end of 1991, the Ukrainian Government expressed the idea that it wanted to become part of Central Europe, and to that end expressed an interest in joining NATO and the European Union. Although it was one of the founding members of the Commonwealth of Independent States, it was extremely fearful of a continued Russian domination. As a result, its participation in the CIS has often been nominal, and it has several times refused to support CIS initiatives, even when it would have been in its economic interest to do so. Thus Ukraine is only an "associate" member of the CIS economic union, and has failed to sign agreements on payments and a customs union. It is also only an "observer" at the CIS's Intergovernmental Assembly. Ukraine has also refused to provide troops for CIS peacekeeping.

This fear of Russian domination has also affected Ukraine's ability to develop ties with the west. For example, the Ukrainian Government first agreed to foreswear nuclear weapons, then balked at turning the weapons over to Russia while the legislature refused to ratify the Nonproliferation Treaty, apparently because of a fear that Ukraine might become subject to Russian nuclear blackmail at some time in the future. The first breakthrough came in January 1994 when the Ukrainian Government signed a trilateral agreement with the United States and Russia, under which it stipulated that it would dismantle all missiles on its territory and deliver the warheads to the Russian Government for destruction. But it was not until November 1994 that Ukraine legislators finally put aside their reservations and voted to ratify the Nonproliferation Treaty (NPT). Even then, the legislature coupled the ratification with a stipulation that it would go into effect only after the United States, Russia, and Great Britain had provided assurances that they would respect Ukraine's borders and never use nuclear weapons against it. Since Ukraine was the last of the ex-Soviet republics to ratify the NPT, Kazakhstan and Belarus having already done so, this removed the last obstacle to implementation of Start One and brought a pledge from Russia that it would now also ratify Start Two.

Most of the recent movement in foreign policy is the result of the election of Leonid Kuchma in July 1994. Kuchma personally lobbied the Ukrainian legislature for several weeks before the vote, insisting that the legislature's attempt to use the nuclear warheads as a bargaining chip was counterproductive and that Ukraine would get nothing from the west until it had foresworn nuclear weapons. As Kuchma told the legislature, "Ukraine today has no choice between being nuclear or nonnuclear. The process of world disarmament depends on our decision today." Ultimately his argument prevailed, with the final vote being a lopsided 301 to 8.

Almost immediately after his election, the U.S. Government signaled its support for Kuchma by announcing that Vice President Gore had accepted an invitation to Kiev following a visit to Poland to commemorate the 50th anniversary of the Warsaw uprising. When he visited the United States in November 1994, Kuchma received a warm welcome and a promise of $200 million in addition to the $700 million that the United States had promised earlier. One half of this would be in the form of an emergency grant for importing food and fuel. The other $100 million was designated for student exchanges and to provide assistance in the areas of privatization and small business.

At the same time, President Clinton also extended the security assurances that the Ukrainian legislature had asked for in ratifying the NPT. Essentially, the United States Government considers that political stability in Ukraine is a critical element for peace in Europe and that economic aid is essential for the success of President Kuchma and his program of reform. This position has strong support in Congress from both Republicans and Democrats. In May 1995, President Clinton paid an official visit to Ukraine after participating in ceremonies in Moscow commemorating the end of World War II in Europe, partly as a reward to Ukraine for signing the NPT.

The United States and Ukraine did find themselves at odds for a while in 1997–98 when the United States objected to the sale of special turbines for nuclear power plants being built in Iran by Russia and threatened to deny Ukraine access to American nuclear technology and fuel if it didn't cancel the sale. Ukraine agreed after the United States offered to compensate Ukraine for the loss of the turbine sale by providing small business loans, Export–Import Bank credits, and the like.

Prime Minister Lazarenko, who visited the United States in September 1996, was quoted as saying that "integration with the West is the main thrust of our foreign policy." President Kuchma has been putting that policy into practice with regard to Western Europe as well. In 1996, Ukraine was admitted to both the Council of Europe and the Central European Initiative, a regional trade forum. Ukraine wants "associate partner" status with the Western European Union and wants eventually to join the European Union. It is already a member of NATO's Partners for Peace, though Russia's sensitivities on the subject means that it will probably never apply for full NATO membership.

Meanwhile, Ukraine cultivates relations with neighbors to the west such as Poland, Germany and Greece. Ukraine signed a five–year military cooperation agreement with Germany in December 1997. That same day, Greece pledged its support to Ukraine for eventual entry into the European Union.

As it built up these relations with the West, Ukraine began to allow its relations with Russia to become warmer as well. Perhaps this reflects an increased sense of self–confidence in its own ability to deal on a level of equality with its much larger Slavic neighbor. In any case, this culminated in a visit by President Yeltsin to Kiev and the signing, on May 31, 1997, of a Ukrainian–Russian Friendship Treaty plus an agreement on the disposition of the Black Sea Fleet. The Friendship Treaty included a mutual recognition of borders, thus affirming that the Crimea, with its large Russian population, was an integral part of Ukraine. Russia also agreed to can-

**A young Ukrainian economist**
Courtesy: NOVOSTI

# Ukraine

**A family dance group in Ukraine**

Courtesy: NOVOSTI

cel part of the debt that Ukraine owed to Russia for past oil deliveries. In turn, Ukraine ceded most of the Black Sea Fleet to Russia and also gave Russia a long-term lease on the naval base at Sevastopol. Both agreed that neither could reach an accord with a third party that would threaten the other. The Friendship Treaty and agreement on the fate of the Black Sea Fleet contain provisions that are beneficial to both sides. Of greater long-term significance for Ukraine is the fact that Russia has recognized its borders; of perhaps even greater importance is the fact that Russia treated Ukraine as a sovereign equal.

### Nature of the Regime

The Republic of Ukraine has a presidential-parliamentary system with a popularly elected president who acts as spokesman for the nation and sets general policy. He also appoints a prime minister who handles day-to-day activities of the government and presides over the cabinet. The Ukrainian Supreme Soviet has its own internal organization which is inde-

pendent of either the president or the prime minister. Political parties are permitted, but have tended to play a relatively small role.

In the latest parliamentary elections, which took place on March 29, 1998, half of the 450-member parliament were elected on party-list mandates and half were elected by direct vote. The largest party is the Communist Party of Ukraine (CPU), which won 121 seats, up from 86 seats in 1994. It is allied with two left-wing parties, the Socialist/Peasant Bloc and the Progressive Socialist Party, and the three together control 194 seats. That is 29 seats short of a majority, but they will clearly be the loudest voice in the new parliament.

Independents come next with 114 seats, followed by the Ukrainian popular front organization Rukh, which also increased its representation in the parliament, going from 20 to 32 seats. Other parties include the Greens, with 19 seats, the Popular Democratic Party, led by Prime Minister Valery Pustovoitenko, with 17 seats, the Hromada party, headed by former Prime Minister Pavlo Lazarenko, with 16 seats, and the United Social Democrats, led by

former President Leonid Kravchuk with 14 seats.

### Culture

There is a rich cultural life in the Republic of Ukraine, but most of it belongs to a larger Slavic culture, except for a traditional Ukrainian folk culture. Ukrainians are different from Russians, but it is a matter of degree. Ukrainian houses tend to be painted or whitewashed with traditional decorations worked into the wood trim and around the windows. Ukrainians plant many more flowers in their yards. The Ukrainian folk costume is often highly embroidered, with bright colors worked over white or black. Ukrainian villages also tend to be more prosperous looking and better cared for, reflecting the richer soil found in most of the Ukraine. Historically, the Ukrainian Orthodox clergy has had greater contacts with the Greek Orthodox Church and so is closer to the Greek original. Church music of the Ukraine was patterned on Byzantine and Bulgarian models, which set it off from the music of Russia. The Ukraine also developed its own distinct choral music, which also

132

came to influence Russian music in the seventeenth century.

The Ukraine has produced many writers, poets and historians over the years, a number of whom were mentioned in the historical section above. On the other hand, Ukrainian intellectuals were always getting into trouble because of their Ukrainian nationalism, and often found themselves unable to get their works published. This has been true in the Soviet period as well.

The Ukraine began to develop a secular music in the nineteenth century. There are a number of nineteenth century operas with specific Ukrainian themes, such as Semen Hulak–Artemovsky's *A Cossack Beyond the Danube*. Mykola Lysenko was an early twentieth century composer who wrote the opera *Taras Bulba*. Two other composers of this period were Kyrylo Stetsenko and Mykola Leontovych. Lev Revutsky and Borys Lyatoshynsky were two composers of the early Soviet period. The cultural regimentation of the 1930s led to a cultural decline, but there was a revival of sorts after Stalin's death. Contemporary composers include Kostyantyn Dankevych, Yuliy Meytus, and the brothers Yuriy and Platon Maiboroda.

The Ukrainian theater is primarily a twentieth century phenomenon, primarily because censorship laws would not allow works in the Ukrainian language before 1905. Three pre–Soviet Ukrainian playwrights are Lesya Ukrainka, Volodymyr Vynnychenko and Oleksandr Oles. All wrote before 1905, but their works were not available in the Ukraine until after that time.

There was a flowering of Ukrainian theater in the period of the 1920s, the so–called period of Ukrainization. Mykola Kulish, who used expressionist techniques, was perhaps the most famous. As in opera, the introduction of socialist realism led to a decline in drama. A contemporary Ukrainian playwright of some fame is Oleksandr Korniychuk.

The Ukraine has great cultural potential for the future, however, since the Soviet era left it with plenty of facilities. There are currently six opera theaters, numerous symphony orchestras, 60 professional theaters, plus a Ukrainian motion picture industry.

## Economy

The Ukraine has been the historical "bread basket" of Russia and, although industry today plays a larger role in the economy, agriculture continues to play an extremely important role. In recent years, the Ukraine produced about 20 percent of all Soviet food. Grain, in the form of wheat and corn, is the most important crop, but others include potatoes, vegetables, fodder crops, fruits and grapes. Sugar beets are the most important industrial crop.

Cattle are raised for both milk and meat. Other important animals raised include pigs, sheep and goats. Honey is another important product, as are silkworms. All of this was, of course, disrupted by the Chernobyl nuclear explosion, the effects of which will remain for years.

Most of the land is controlled by joint–stock cooperative farms, the successor organizations to the collective farms of the Soviet era. A 1993 government decree aimed at breaking up the collective farms and turning the land over to private farmers created such a storm of protest in the legislature that the government re-treated and took this step instead. The government still exercises a great deal of control over the cooperative farms, however.

The government did manage to implement one aspect of its agricultural reform which has had an important economic significance, however. In 1992, it distributed 11 million garden plots among approximately two–thirds of the population. Although these garden–plots constitute only 14 percent of farmland, they accounted for 95 percent of the potato crop in 1996 and

# УРЯДОВИЙ КУР'ЄР

Газета органів державної виконавчої влади України

четвер, 15 червня 1995 року
№ 87-88 (584-585)

ЗАСНОВАНА В 1990 РОЦІ ◆ ЦІНА ДОГОВІРНА

## ПЕРЕГОВОРНИЙ ПРОЦЕС ДАЄ РЕЗУЛЬТАТИ

### УКРАЇНСЬКО-РОСІЙСЬКЕ КОМЮНІКЕ

9 червня 1995 року в Сочі відбулась зустріч Президента України Л.Д.Кучми та Президента Російської Федерації Б.М.Єльцина, яка пройшла конструктивно, в дусі відвертості та взаєморозуміння.

Президенти поінформували один одного про розвиток внутрішньополітичної ситуації в обох країнах, про хід політичних перетворень та реформування економік. Л.Д.Кучма та Б.М.Єльцин провели поглиблене обговорення поглядів на актуальні проблеми, що являють життєвий інтерес для народів двох дружніх держав.

Було констатовано, що за останні місяці здійснені суттєві кроки, спрямовані на зміцнення плідних українсько-російських зв'язків. Націлений на це переговорний процес дає свої результати. Вдалося або знайти розв'язку, або досягнути помітного прогресу у вирішенні низки непростих проблем двосторонніх відносин. Погоджений і готовий до підписання проект Договору про дружбу, співробітництво і партнерство між Україною та Росією.

Президенти висловили обопільну рішучість зробити все, щоб і надалі настійливо поглиблювати і розширювати відносини дружби, зосередивши спільні зусилля передовсім на врегулюванні ще невирішених проблем. При цьому в основі підходів обох сторін має бути готовність враховувати однаковою мірою інтереси один одного, дбати передовсім про добробут обох народів. Була висловлена впевненість, що такий підхід дозволить знайти вирішення всіх наявних проблем, хоч би якими складними вони були.

Президенти домовилися, що Україна та Росія будуть прагнути до більш тісної та глибокої взаємодії на основі стратегічного партнерства, взаємної поваги та довіри.

Глибокому і всебічному розгляду був підданий весь комплекс питань, що стосується врегулювання проблеми Чорноморського флоту. З цього питання підписаний відповідний документ, згідно з яким основна база Чорноморського флоту Росії розташовуватиметься в м.Севастополі, а також будуть практично вирішені деякі інші питання розподілу Чорноморського флоту. За дорученням Президентів переговори з цієї проблеми будуть продовжені.

Була підкреслена важливість продовження активного політичного діалогу між двома країнами як на найвищому, так і на інших рівнях, розвитку безпосередніх робочих контактів між міністерствами і відомствами двох країн, розширення міжпарламентських зв'язків.

Л.Д.Кучма і Б.М.Єльцин дали доручення урядам двох країн активізувати роботу щодо розширення співробітництва в економічній галузі.
м.Сочі

## ПРЕЗИДЕНТ УКРАЇНИ ПРЕДСТАВИВ УРЯДУ НОВОГО ПРЕМ'ЄР-МІНІСТРА

Президент України Леонід Кучма представив 13 червня членам Кабінету міністрів новопризначеного Прем'єр-міністра України Євгена Марчука. Він тепло поздоровив нового главу уряду з значною подією, побажав йому плідної роботи, щастя, добра й успіхів.

Євген Марчук висловив подяку за виявлене йому довір'я і окреслив уряду в такий складний час. Він запевнив, що зробить максимум можливого для того, щоб виправдати це довір'я. Євген Марчук сказав, що очолюваний ним уряд рішуче проводитиме в життя економічні реформи, не забуваючи про соціальний захист населення.

Потім виступив Леонід Кучма, який окреслив першочергові завдання, що стоять перед Кабінетом міністрів на нинішньому етапі реформування економіки України.

## З ДРУЖНІМ ВІЗИТОМ

Учора розпочався перший офіційний візит в Україну голови уряду Словацької Республіки Владимира Мечіара. Разом з ним у складі делегації прибули міністри економіки, фінансів, транспорту, земельного господарства, будівництва, голова Національного банку Словаччини та інші офіційні особи. Одночасно до Києва прибула група представників виробничих і підприємницьких кіл Словацької Республіки.

Прем'єр-міністра Мечіара прийняв Президент України Леонід Кучма. Високий гість зі Словаччини поклав вінок до пам'ятника Невідомому солдату у Парку Слави.

Відбулися переговори пана Мечіара з главою українського уряду Євгеном Марчуком. Одночасно міністр російського уряду вели переговори зі своїми українськими колегами.

Під час візиту підписано пакет двосторонніх документів, які стануть важливими доповненнями до вже створеної договірної бази між Україною і Словацькою Республікою. Серед них, зокрема, Угода про співробітництво в галузі транспорту, прикордонних переходів і сполучень, Угода про співробітництво між Міністерством економіки Словаччини і Міністерством зовнішньоекономічних зв'язків України, інші документи. Сьогодні прем'єр-міністри обох держав підпишуть Спільну Заяву.

Докладніше про візит урядової делегації Словацької Республіки читайте в наступному номері газети.

## Леонід Кучма на Кіровоградщині

Вчора у другій половині дня Президент України Леонід Кучма прибув до Кіровоградської області.

Як стало відомо кореспонденту Укрінформу з компетентних джерел, Леонід Кучма відвідав під Кіровоградом. Сьогодні в обласній Раді народних депутатів відбудеться нарада з керівництвом області, прес-конференція для журналістів. Того ж дня планується поїздка Президента України

## ВРУЧЕНА ЕКЗИКВАТУРА

10 червня міністр закордонних справ України Геннадій Удовенко вручив екзикватуру нещодавно призначеному урядом Росії генеральному консулу в Одесі Володимиру Немцову. Вручаючи йому екзикватуру, міністр підкреслив, що діяльність генерального консула розповсюджуватиметься на

## РОТАЦІЯ УКРАЇНСЬКИХ МИРОТВОРЦІВ

Як стало відомо кореспонденту Укрінформу, розпочалася ротація особового складу 60-го окремого спеціального батальйону, який входить до складу операції ООН по встановленню миру у Хорватії.

Першим літаком Іл-76 Військово-Повітряних Сил України до Загреба доставлено 150 офіцерів прапорщиків і солдатів.

**A Kiev newspaper (June 9, 1995) reports on Presidents Kuchma and Yeltsin signing the treaty which permits the Russian Black Sea fleet to berth at Sevastopol on the Crimean peninsula.**

# Ukraine

82 percent of all vegetables. They also produced more than one-half of the country's meat and milk and two–thirds of its eggs.

The large, poorly managed cooperatives are in decline, however, today producing even less than they did under communism. Grain production in 1997 was approximately 37 million tons, lower than any year since 1985. Sugar beet production in 1997 was the smallest in 30 years. There have also been declines in livestock and large decreases in milk and egg production. These decreases are blamed on a number of causes, but the most important factor is that few cooperatives have changed their managers, production choices, or methods of resource allocation since 1991. Now farm machinery is wearing out and there is no money for replacement equipment. Although the government continues to favor farm privatization, this will not occur for years in view of the improved showing of the Communist Party and the Socialist/Peasants' Bloc in the March 29, 1998 parliamentary elections.

The development of industry in the Ukraine goes back to the end of the nineteenth century when fourteen steel mills were built on the steppe north of the Black Sea. Even today, the center of Ukraine's heavy industry is a belt that stretches from Krivoi Rog in the west to the border of the republic in the east. Here the republic produces cast iron, steel and rolled steel, and steel pipe. Other allied manufactures include diesel locomotives, freight cars, automobiles, giant airliners, seagoing vessels, electric generators, thermal and gas turbines, metallurgical equipment, and tractors.

Iron ore reserves are found in the Krivoi Rog, Kerch, Belozyorka, Kremenchug and Mariupol regions. Some of the richest manganese–bearing ores in the world are also found in Ukraine. The Donets Basin has huge reserves of anthracite and bituminous coal, while brown coal is found in the Dnieper Basin. Some petroleum is produced in the Ciscarpathian, Dnieper–Donets, and Crimean regions, but the republic imports most of its petroleum from Russia. Ukraine also produces titanium, bauxite, cinnabar, nephelites, ozokerite, potassium salt, rock salt, phosphates, and sulphur. There is a chemical industry that produces mineral fertilizers, coke products, synthetic fibers, caustic soda, petrochemicals, photographic chemicals, pesticides, and sulfuric acid.

The Ukrainian food–processing industry includes the processing of granulated sugar, vegetable oils, and wine. Light industry includes textiles, the manufacture of ready–to–wear garments, and shoes. The preponderant weight of heavy industry in the Ukraine has meant that a large percentage of its production was shipped to other republics—amounting to approximately 25 percent of the republic's gross domestic product. In return, it imported natural gas, some raw materials, and a good percentage of its consumer goods. It has been unable to maintain many of those markets since independence and lost, in fact, a fifth of its export market in the first year.

For the first ten months after achieving its independence, very little was done about the economy and the result was a disaster. By October 1992, inflation was running at 30 percent monthly, economic activity was down 18 percent over the preceding year, and the budget deficit was running at 44 percent of GDP. Prime Minister Fokin was forced out at the end of September and replaced by Leonid Kuchma.

Kuchma turned out to be a reformer. One of his first acts was to raise the central bank lending rate to 80 percent and to announce that the government would no longer provide inefficient state enterprises with soft credit. In November, he submitted an ambitious, market–oriented reform program to the Supreme Soviet which called for a tight budget, a temporary wage freeze in state–owned enterprises, cuts in social welfare payments, a law forbidding the government to finance the budget deficit by printing money, and a commitment to begin large–scale privatization. Kuchma also wanted to break up inefficient enterprises and sell their pieces on the auction block.

Kuchma's plans brought a sharp reaction from the Supreme Soviet, however, which began passing legislation negating what he was trying to do. It also reimposed controls over wages and prices. Kuchma lost his power to rule by decree in May 1993 and resigned in September. After that, everything was put on hold.

New parliamentary elections in March 1994 reconfirmed communist control of the legislature, but Kuchma's victory in the July 1994 presidential elections brought in a whole new equation. Kuchma quickly announced concrete proposals for reform and arranged a quick meeting with Michael Camdessus, head of the IMF, to win the support of that organization. Kuchma subsequently pushed a far reaching economic reform program through the legislature which promised large–scale privatization of state companies, cuts in the national budget and the removal of price controls on many goods.

As a result, Ukraine got its first IMF loan in October 1994 and began receiving loans from individual western countries as well. As economic reform continued, some 11,000 state–owned enterprises were privatized through March 1995 and a further 8,000 large and medium–sized firms privatized in 1996 and 1997. Inflation was brought under control and this allowed the issuance of a new currency, the hryvna, in the summer of 1996. Although the overall economy had not yet achieved positive growth by the end of 1997, but the government is predicting a 0.5 percent growth rate in 1998. Foreign investment is also up, though the amounts are still minimal. Ukraine received $335.5 million in foreign investment during the first half of 1997. The United States is the largest foreign investor (with $315 million), followed by Germany ($165.9 million), the Netherlands ($160.2 million), Great Britain ($130.9 million), Cyprus ($116.4 million), Russia ($114.2 million) and Liechtenstein ($103.1 million). Investments are mainly in the food industry, machine building, metal processing, finance and insurance, construction and construction materials, and the chemical and petrochemical industries.

## The Future

Ukraine has a good political leader in President Kuchma, and he has brought the country a good distance since 1994. This has not been true of the legislature, but the March 1998 elections have, at least, brought in some new members, even if it is too early to see whether this will mean greater support for Kuchma's policies of reform. The Ukrainian economy is still in poor shape, but it is expected to turn the corner in 1998 and began to grow again. The treaty of Friendship signed by Russia and Ukraine in May 1997 also resolved most outstanding differences between the two countries and included a specific Russian recognition of Ukraine's borders. All things considered, things are looking up for Ukraine.

Ukraine's industrial potential is reflected by this 250,000-kilometer transportation network connected with 106 developed oil deposits.

# The Republic of Moldova

**A wheat–growing area of Moldova**

Courtesy: NOVOSTI

**Area:** 13,000 sq. mi. (33.700 sq. km., a little larger than Maryland).

**Population:** 4.5 million (estimated).

**Capital City:** Chisinau (pronounced *Kee-sih–now*, Pop. 700,000).

**Climate:** Moderate winters, warm summers.

**Neighboring States:** Romania (west). Ukraine surrounds the country on the other sides.

**Official Language:** Moldavian (Romanian).

**Ethnic Composition:** Moldavian (64.5%), Ukrainian (13.8%), Russian (13%), Gagauz (3.5%), Bulgarian (2%), others (3.2%).

**Principal Religion:** Eastern Orthodox Christianity.

**Chief Commercial Products:** Grain, livestock, silk, honey, processed foods, wine and cognac. Over 70% of exports still go to other members of the Commonwealth of Independent States and Moldova is heavily dependent on energy supplies from these same republics.

**Currency** Leu/Lei (singular/plural). Adopted in December 1993.

**Recent Political Status:** Formed in 1940 by union of the Moldavian SSR, previously only an autonomous republic within the Ukrainian SSR, and most of Bessarabia, transferred to the USSR by Romania in 1940.

**National Day:** August 27 (Independence Day 1991).

**Chief of State:** Petru Lucinschi, President (inaugurated on January 15, 1997).

**National Flag:** three vertical stripes, sky blue, yellow and red. A right–facing golden Roman eagle, outlined in black with a red beak, is centered on the yellow. The eagle holds a yellow cross in its beak, in its right claw a green olive branch and in its left claw a yellow scepter. A heraldic device forming the body of the eagle pictures a bullhead, star, rose and crescent, all in yellow outlined in black.

## The Land

The Republic of Moldova is the independent successor state to the Moldavian Soviet Socialist Republic. The Moldavian SSR was created in August 1940 when Stalin merged Bessarabia, which he had forced the Romanian Government to cede to the Soviet Union in June 1940, with the autonomous republic of Moldavia, which was then part of the Ukrainian SSR. He gave it constituent republic status. In 1941, after Nazi Germany invaded the Soviet Union, Romania (then an ally of Nazi Germany) reclaimed Bessarabia. Soviet troops retook the territory in 1944 and the Moldavian SSR was reestablished.

The republic was renamed Moldova in 1990. Moldova declared its independence on August 27, 1991.

The Prut River, a tributary of the Danube, forms the western border with Romania. The area immediately east of the Prut is somewhat elevated, with a flat highland in the north and rolling hills interspersed with deep flat valleys further south. The highest elevations are about 1400 feet. The southern part of the republic is a low plain. The chief feature of the eastern part of the republic is the Dnestr River, which originates in the Carpathian Mountains to the northwest and flows southward across western Ukraine, then forms the border between Moldova and Ukraine for some distance. At this point, the border shifts eastward, while the Dnestr continues south and into Moldova. A major feature of the river is the 60–mile–long Lake Dubossary, created when a dam for producing hydroelectric power was built on the Dnestr. The Dnestr crosses back into Ukraine again shortly before it empties into the Black Sea. On its western side, the Dnestr has a high bank, formed by the eastern slope of the Dnestr uplands. Trans–Dnestr, the small strip of territory east of the Dnestr, is a low plain.

Rainfall in the republic varies considerably but averages between 18 and 22 inches. Most of it falls in summer. Moldovan soils are mostly rich, black *chernozem* soils. About 40% of the land is covered by forest, most of it in the uplands.

## The People

The population of Moldova as of the 1989 census was 4,341,000. About 64% of those speak Romanian. Ukrainians, the largest minority, are about 14% of the population. Russians come next with 13%. Most Russians live in the Trans–Dnestr region. Other minorities include Gagauzi (4%) and Jews (2%). The Gagauz are a non–Moslem, Turkic speaking people. Both they and the population of Trans–Dnestr threatened to secede from Moldova.

## History

Moldova's history is really the history of Bessarabia, the historic name for the area between the Prut and Dnestr Rivers. In the first century B.C., this area, and the area of present–day Romania formed the Roman province of Dacia. Rome soon lost control, however, and the area knew many masters over the following centuries. The eastern part of the area was incorporated into Kievan Rus in the tenth century. Later, independent Galician princes ruled. After 1240, it became part of the Mongol Empire for about one hundred years. The Genoese built fortified commercial outposts on the Dnestr in the fourteenth century, though they never attempted to rule the area.

In the fifteenth century, an independent Principality of Moldavia came into existence which included the northern part of present–day Romania and all of Bessarabia. The Ottoman Empire soon extended its control over most of the area, however, along with the second Romanian Principality of Wallachia. In 1711, Peter the Great occupied part of Bessarabia during a short war with Turkey. He was forced to abandon the territory after his army fell into an ambush, however. Russia occupied the territory three more times in the eighteenth century, each time relinquishing it to the Turks. In 1812, however, Russia occupied Moldavia and Wallachia when war broke out between the two countries. This time, Russia forced Turkey to cede Bessarabia to it in the Treaty of Bucharest.

As a result of Russia's defeat in the Crimean War, it was forced to cede Bessarabia to Moldavia, at that time an autonomous principality under the Ottoman Empire, in 1856. After its victory in the Turkish War of 1877–78, Russia took Bessarabia back and kept it until 1918. After the overthrow of the Tsar in 1917, a National Moldavian Committee was organized in Bessarabia in April. Its program included autonomy, use of the Romanian language, and land reform. After the Bolshevik *coup d'etat* in November, a government was established in Bessarabia, called the *Sfatul Tarei*. On December 2, 1917, the government proclaimed Bessarabia to be an autonomous constituent republic of the Federation of Russian Republics. The Bolsheviks occupied the capital, Chisinau (Kishinev) on January 5, 1918. Two weeks later, they were driven out and the Bessarabian Government then proclaimed itself an independent Moldavian Republic. Two months later, it voted for a conditional union with Romania. Unconditional union was voted on December 9, 1918. The Union of Bessarabia with Romania was recognized by the Treaty of Paris, signed by Great Britain, France, Italy, and Japan, on October 28, 1920.

The Union of Soviet Socialist Republics never recognized Romania's right to the province and refused to establish diplomatic relations with Romania until 1934. In the meantime, the frontier along the Dnestr was closed.

Under the terms of the Nazi–Soviet Non–Aggression Pact of August 23, 1939, Hitler recognized Bessarabia as being in the Soviet sphere of influence. The Soviet Union revived its claim to Bessarabia, but Romania rejected the claim until after the fall of France in June 1940. On June 27, the Soviet Union demanded the immediate cession of Bessarabia, plus the additional territory of northern Bukovina as "compensation for Romanian misrule in Bessarabia." Without an ally, Romania had to submit. Troops of the Red Army entered Bessarabia on June 28.

The central districts of Bessarabia were merged with part of the Moldavian Autonomous Republic and in August it became the Moldavian Soviet Socialist Republic. Ukraine was compensated for the loss of the Trans–Dnestr territory by receiving the Khotin district in the north and the Cetatea Alba and Izmail districts in the south.

Romania declared war against the Soviet Union in July 1941. Its war goal was to reclaim Bessarabia and to reincorporate it back into Romania. This was accomplished by December 1942. Soviet forces reentered Bessarabia in 1944 and its forces occupied all of Romania as well. Bessarabia was formally ceded back to the Soviet Union by the peace treaty signed between the two countries on February 10, 1947.

After Gorbachëv launched his programs of *glasnost* and *perestroika*, a nationalist movement arose, which called itself the *Popular Front of Moldavia*. The ultimate goal of the front was union with Romania. In 1989, the legislature abolished use of the Cyrillic alphabet (see Russia), and restored the Roman alphabet which had been used prior to the republic's incorporation into the Soviet Union. On July 29, 1989, Mircea Snegur was elected president of the presidium of the Moldavian Supreme Soviet. Snegur was at that time first secretary of the *Moldavian Communist Party*, but he represented the democratic–nationalist faction of the party. In June 1990, the legislature adopted a declaration of republic sovereignty and changed the name of the republic to Moldova.

In March 1991, the Government of Moldova refused to participate in a referendum on continuation of the Soviet Union. It also refused to take part in subsequent discussions on a new union treaty. When conservatives launched their attempted *coup* against Gorbachëv in August 1991, Moldova became a target also. The local military commander surrounded the capital of Chisinau (Kishinev) with troops and threatened to use them against the republic government. President Mircea Snegur refused to recognize the *coup* committee, however, and called on the people of Moldova to demonstrate in support of democracy and freedom; over 100,000 persons demonstrated in the capital. Following the collapse of the Russian *coup*, Moldova declared its independence on August 27. It also formally outlawed the *Communist Party*.

Moldova now began to have its problems with the Trans–Dnestr region, an area with a population of about 600,000, only a third of whom are Romanian speakers. This area rejected Moldovan independence because it felt it was merely the first step to merging with Romania. As far back as 1989, a separatist movement had been organized in this area after the republic government had declared its intention to move toward independence. In

# Moldova

**Hon. Mircea Snegur**

August, the "Dniester Moldavian Republic" declared its independence. A referendum on independence on September 2 showed that a majority of people of the area supported the policies of the breakaway republic. Igor Smirnov was elected head of the new republic. Its capital was established at Dubossary.

Some violence occurred when the Moldovan Government tried to reestablish its control east of the Dnestr. The situation calmed down after President Snegur threatened to resign if the Moldova Supreme Soviet insisted on using force to restore control. The government also repudiated the idea of immediate union with Romania. This led to the opening of talks between the two sides. In October, the "Dniester Moldavian" leader said that he would be willing to join a federal Moldova, together with Moldova and Gagauzia. In 1990, the Gagauz, a non–Moslem, Turkic–speaking minority, had proclaimed a separate republic in southern Moldova. Like "Dniester Moldavia," they objected to the idea of merging with Romania.

In October, President Snegur publicly broke with the leadership of the *Popular Front of Moldova* and said that he favored an independent Moldova. "A union with another state is out of question," he said. "At present Moldova promotes a policy pursuing the assertion of our independence internationally." Snegur also supported continued economic ties with the former Soviet republics.

The Moldovan presidential elections had been set for December 8, 1991 and the question of independence versus merging with Romania became the major issue. In addition to President Snegur, there were originally two other candidates, Grigori Eremei, the former first secretary of the *Moldovan Communist Party* and Gheorghe Malarciuc, a writer. The other two candidates withdrew in the middle of November, however. The *Popular Front of Moldova* did not nominate a candidate because the head of the front, Mircea Druc, did not meet the residence requirements. Instead, the front urged voters to boycott the election. The leadership of "Dniester Moldavia" adopted the same position.

"Dniester Moldavia" and the "Republic of Gagauzia" held their own separate elections on December 1. Smirnov was confirmed as president of "Dniester Moldavia" and Stepan Topal was elected president of Gagauzia. Neither area permitted voting in the December 8 republican elections.

President Snegur was running unopposed in the December 8 elections, so the fact that he got 98% of the vote was unsurprising. On the other hand, the vote count indicated that 83% of all registered

voters actually voted in the election, thereby rejecting the *Popular Front of Moldova's* call for a boycott of the election. This gave President Snegur a great deal more leeway in dealing with the front than he had had before.

Unable to resolve its differences with either "Dniester Moldavia" or Gagauzia, the Moldovan Government formally nullified the results of the December 1 elections in the two breakaway republics on December 11. Later, President Snegur offered to establish a free economic zone in "Dniester Moldavia," if it would withdraw it declaration of independence. Neither carrot nor stick worked. The main issue remained the question of Moldova's merging with Romania. Even though President Snegur publicly supported an independent Moldova, the leaders of "Dniester Moldavia" and Gagauzia remained convinced that union with Romania was still on the agenda.

Later in the month, President Snegur broke his long–standing opposition to any form of political agreement of the ex–Soviet republics by going to Alma Ata on December 21 and taking Moldova into the Commonwealth of Independent States. Moldova did not agree to maintain a CIS military command, however, and began to create its own national army. The plan called for it to be a cadre army of about 12,000 persons, with a larger number of citizens serving in an army reserve.

In March 1992, a weekend of clashes that left 23 dead caused President Snegur to issue an ultimatum to "Dniester Moldavia," to lay down their arms or face the use of force against them. Igor Smirnov, leader of "Dniester Moldavia," then declared a state of emergency, closing the enclave to outside contact. According to reports, "Dniester Moldavia" had by this time created its own 10,000 man militia to defend the enclave.

Meanwhile, the unstable political situation was contributing to a deteriorating economic situation. This led on June 1 to the resignations of the Prime Minister, Valeriu Muravsky, and his cabinet. President Snegur then nominated Andre Sangheli, outgoing Agriculture Minister, as the new prime minister.

President Snegur was more concerned about establishing political control throughout all of Moldova than about the economy. Fighting with "Dniester Moldavia" flared up again in June 1992 when President Snegur's troops tried to take control of the city of Bendery. It appeared for a while that Moldova might find itself involved in a confrontation with Russia when elements of Russia's 14th Army, stationed in eastern Moldova, supported the "Dniester Moldavia" forces. It turned out that it was only rogue elements of the 14th Army that were involved, however. Moldova has been quiet for some time now, but that is mainly because President Snegur refrained from further attempts to extend his authority outside the ethnic Romanian areas.

Moldova held its first parliamentary elections since independence on February 27, 1994, and followed that up a week later with a referendum on whether Moldova should remain independent or seek unification with Romania. More than 90% of all voters participating in the referendum supported remaining an independent state within current borders. In the parliamentary elections, most of the parties that did well favored closer relations with Russia and reconciliation with the breakaway region of Transdniestria. The Agrarian–Democratic Party got about 45 percent of the vote, while the pro–Russian Socialist Bloc got 25 percent. Andrei

Sangheli, the prime minister, was the leader of the Agrarian–Democratic Party.

Subsequent discussions between the Moldovan and Russian Governments resulted in an agreement, signed in October 1994, calling for a three–year phased withdrawal of the troops of the 14th Russian Army from the region of the self–declared Trans–Dniester Republic. Although the 14th Russian Army is still in Moldova, President Lucinschi said in January 1998 that he had President Yeltsin's "clear promise" that Russia would withdraw its forces from Transdniestria whenever Moldova wishes. One problem appears to be logistical—how to get the 14th Russian Army's arms and equipment to Russia. Lucinschi indicated, however, that he had obtained the Government of Ukraine's agreement to allow everything to be shipped across its territory. Still, most people believe that the Russian troop pullout will not occur until some sort of final agreement is reached between the Moldovan Government and the leadership of Transdniestria.

There have also been periodic talks between the Moldovan Government and the leadership of Transdnestria. Although the two sides are still at odds, the Transdnestrians did agree to allow the circulation of the leu, Moldova's official currency, along with Transdnestria's own largely worthless coupons. The Moldovan Government, for its part, agreed to recognize Transdnestria as an autonomous republic with its own parliament. Even more important, it was agreed that Transdnestria had the right to opt out should Moldova ever decide to merge with Romania. In addition, the two sides agreed not to use force against each other. The issue that is apparently holding up a final agreement is Moldova's insistence that defense remain the exclusive prerogative of the Moldovan Government. "They can have their own symbols and parliament—an autonomous republic," said Ion Gutsu, a deputy prime minister; "but Moldova must have a single domestic policy and army."

In yet another development, the government reached an agreement with the Gagauz in August 1995. The Gagauz are a second rebellious group which had hitherto refused to recognize the authority of the government and was demanding autonomous republic status for its own area. The agreement granted the Gagauz a broad measure of autonomy in return for agreeing to lay down their arms.

New presidential elections were held on November 17, 1996. President Snegur stood for reelection but was opposed by several candidates. Since no candidate obtained a majority of the votes, there had to be a run–off election between the two highest vote–getters, who were President Snegur and Petru Lucinschi, who at that time held the position of Chairman of the Parliament. Lucinschi won the run–off with approximately 53 percent of the vote.

Lucinschi, a Central Committee Secretary of the Communist Party of the Soviet Union in its final days, now calls himself a social democrat and most people would classify him as a centrist. Though Lucinschi reportedly had the support of the Communist Party of Moldova in the election, it appears that the main reason why Snegur lost is that he had a falling out earlier in the year with his Prime Minister,

**President Petru Lucinschi**

Andrei Sangheli. Snegur had, in fact, accused the government of incompetence and involvement in corruption in April 1996 and urged the Moldovan parliament to dismiss it. Although there may have been other issues involved, the falling out appears to have been the result of a political disagreement between Snegur and Sangheli. Snegur had attempted to dismiss the Defense Minister on corruption charges in March 1996, but Sangheli carried the issue to the Constitutional Court and won. This led to a tacit alliance between Sangheli and Lucinschi and a bitter Presidential campaign, won in the end by Lucinschi.

Lucinschi appointed Ion Ciubuc as his new prime minister in January 1997. Because of the political make up of the legislature, the Ciubuc cabinet was rather heterogeneous, with representatives of several parties and even two communists serving as individuals. Essentially one would classify the cabinet as centrist—supportive of reform but aware that the reforms, although necessary, were hurting many individual Moldovans.

New parliamentary elections took place on March 22, 1998. The political situation in Moldova is still rather fluid, however, so the political parties that competed in these elections were rather different from those that competed in the 1994 elections. Fifteen political parties and electoral blocs—plus some 70 independents—competed in the parliamentary elections. Only four of the contesting parties or blocs won representation in the parliament, however; no independents won seats.

The largest winner was the Party of Moldovan Communists (PCM), which, with approximately 30 percent of the vote, won 40 seats. Although there were communists in the previous parliament and two of them even held portfolios in the previous cabinet, the PCM is a new party to the parliament, for it was still banned at the time of the 1994 elections. The center–right but pro–reform Democratic Convention of Moldova (CDM), which is led by former President Snegur, came in second with approximately 20 percent of the vote and 26 seats. The pro–presidential For a Democratic and Prosperous Moldova (PMPD) bloc, led by Prime Minister Ciubuc, came in third with approximately 18 percent of the vote and 24 seats. The Party of Democratic Forces (PFD) won some 9 percent of the vote and 11 seats. The Agrarian–Democratic Party, which had been the dominant party in the previous parliament (with 56 seats), fell below the minimum 4 percent barrier and so is eliminated from the new parliament.

Since no single party had a majority in the 101–seat parliament, negotiations began in early April for creation of a coalition government. The PCM opened negotiations by announcing its willingness to set up a coalition with the PMPD and the PFD; it rejected cooperation with the CDM. Since such a coalition would have meant the end of reform, the PMPD did not respond to the overture of the PCM but, instead, opened discussions with the PFD and the CDM. These discussions were successful and resulted in an agreement on a coalition government which was announced on April 21. Under the terms of the agreement, each party was to receive government representation proportional to the number of votes each received in the March elections. The agreement also stipulated that the PMPD would have the chairmanship of the parliament, while the Prime Minister would be a member of the CDM. In addition, the three parties agreed to form a joint faction in the parliament and elected former President Mircea Snegur as the joint faction leader. Dumitru Diacov is the coalition's choice for the position of chairman of the parliament. Although it has not yet been announced, it appears that Mircea Snegur would be the logical choice for the position of Prime Minister.

**Nature of the Regime**

The Republic of Moldova has a presi-

# Moldova

dential–parliamentary system, with the executive President recognized as spokesman for the nation and also responsible for setting general policy. The President appoints a Prime Minister who must be confirmed by the parliament. The President also appoints members of the Council of Ministers on recommendation of the Prime Minister. The Prime Minister and members of the Council of Ministers must be approved by the parliament before they can take office and the Prime Minister must retain the support of a majority in the parliament in order to remain in office. The Prime Minister handles day–to–day policy and presides over meetings of the Council of Ministers.

There is also a Supreme Economic Council, created in October 1991, which is headed by the Prime Minister. The presidential decree that created the council gave it the task of defining "the main direction of state economic policy under the conditions of the transition to a market economy." This may be, therefore, a temporary organization.

Moldova has a unicameral parliament of 101 members. Formerly known as the Supreme Soviet, it is now referred to as the Supreme Council or Parliament. There are four political parties/blocs represented in the new Parliament elected in March 1998. The largest is the Party of Moldovan Communists (PCM), which holds 40 seats. The PCM is a new party to the parliament, for it was still banned in 1994. The pro–reform Democratic Convention of Moldova (CDM), an amalgamation of the Christian Democratic Popular Front and the Party of Revival and Conciliation, came in second with 26 seats. The pro–presidential For a Democratic and Prosperous Moldova (PMPD) bloc, headed by Prime Minister Ciubuc, came in third with 24 seats. The Party of Democratic Forces (PFD) won 11 seats.

After the election, the PMPD, CDM, and PFD formed a joint faction in the parliament and a coalition government with representation in the cabinet proportional to the number of votes each party received in the March 1998 elections.

Moldova adopted a new constitution in July 1994. The new constitution made some changes in the administrative divisions of the state, but otherwise mainly codified changes adopted since 1991. On one interesting point, however, the constitution created a Supreme Court, but specified that there should be no judicial review of legislative acts.

## Culture

The Republic of Moldova is primarily an agricultural society, with about two-thirds of the population still living in the countryside. On the other hand, Moldovan villages are large, averaging over a thousand inhabitants, and fairly modern.

All have electricity, for example, and most are supplied with natural gas as well. Because of the ethnic identity of most Moldovans, the culture of Moldova is similar to that found in Romania. Most people think of themselves as members of the Orthodox Church and that has become more important since all restraints on religion were lifted three years ago.

The border with Romania is also now open, so that reinforces the connection.

Most Moldovans are literate, and there is a comprehensive system of primary and secondary schools throughout the republic. Around 70% of the children go to preschool before entering primary school. The most prestigious institute of higher education is the State University at Chisinau (Kishinev), but there are eight other institutions of higher education in other parts of the republic. There are also 51 technical schools scattered throughout the republic. The Moldovan Academy of Sciences was established in 1961. It has 17 research institutes under its jurisdiction.

## Economy

The Moldovan economy is still predominantly agricultural, with approximately two–thirds of the people still employed on the land. Its equable climate and fertile soil, plus the extensive mechanization that has taken place since 1940, mean that agriculture is fairly productive, in spite of the fact that most land is still organized into successor organizations of the old collective or state farms. President Lucinschi said in March 1998 that some 700,000 land titles had been distributed, though the titles were for parcels of land varying in size from one to three hectares (2 1/2 to 7 1/2 acres). Saying that it was "high time to end the useless debates about land privatization," Lucinschi urged the country to accelerate reforms in the villages. His personal choice, he said, would be a model where peasants would work their land in "well–equipped peasant associations."

Winter wheat and corn are the main grain crops grown. Wheat is consumed within the republic, while some of the corn is exported to other republics. Average grain production is about three million tons. Other crops that have traditionally produced surpluses for export include sugar beets, tobacco, and sunflower seeds. Moldova also produces significant quantities of fruits, vegetables, berries, grapes and walnuts, all of which

**An aerial view of Chisinau**

Courtesy: NOVOSTI

have been exported to other republics in the past.

Moldova has a diversified industry, though the most significant branch is food processing. These include sugar refining, wine making (including champagne and brandy), oil pressing, canning and the processing of essential oils. All of these branches have traditionally exported to other parts of the Soviet Union. Flour mills, dairies, meat processing and candy making industries also exist, but these serve the domestic market.

Other light industry includes things such as the processing of pelts for fur coats, footwear, and textiles, particularly knitting and the processing of silk. There is relatively little heavy industry, though the republic does have some machine-building, including tractors, and it also manufactures building supplies, including bricks, tiles, cement, slate, and concrete blocks.

The Department for Privatization submitted a draft privatization program to the Supreme Economic Council in January 1992, but it was rejected as being too narrow in scope. Cabinet members who participated in the discussion favored an alternate program drawn up by government experts. The disagreement appeared to be more political than economic. The parliament created the Department for Privatization as an agency separate from the cabinet, but several cabinet members wanted the cabinet to be in charge of privatization. Parliament, which wanted privatization to start immediately, opposed this.

This quarrel caused privatization to be put on hold for the next year. Another factor was the bad economic situation. By some estimates, real income had dropped by two–thirds between 1990 and 1994. Some privatization finally began in 1994 and some new private companies began to appear. Change was painfully slow, however, until 1994, when the government finally began to implement a voucher program which privatized 940 companies. Today, around 50% of the national economy is in private hands.

Much still remains to be done to make the privatized companies competitive, but GDP growth is now positive, having increased by 1.3 percent in 1997. With low inflation since 1995, a broadly convertible currency and a declining budget deficit, Moldovans can look forward to continued growth over the next several years unless something unforeseen happens.

## The Future

Having endured several years of economic difficulties as they struggled to transform from a command economy to a market economy even as they argued with each other over whether to merge with Romania, Moldovans may now begin to look somewhat more confidently toward the future. It is true that Transdnestria has not yet reconciled itself to being part of Moldova, but that problem now appears likely to be resolved in the not too distant future.

Moldova has also made significant progress on privatization in recent years, and the economy is growing again. Economic growth, 1.3 percent of GDP in 1997, is not yet something to brag about, but economic growth in 1998 should be better. The future is beginning to look more hopeful.

# TRANSCAUCASIAN REPUBLICS (of the former Soviet Union)

Due to their shared histories as well as frequent geographical and cultural similarities, there is necessarily some repetition from one entry to the other.

Showing only capital cities and political boundaries

## The Republic of Armenia

**Area:** 11,500 sq. mi. (29,784 sq. km.), slightly smaller than Maryland.

**Population:** 3 million.

**Capital City:** Yerevan (Pop. 1.2 million, estimated).

**Climate:** Dry and continental.

**Neighboring States:** Georgia (north), Turkey (west), Nakhichevan Region of Azerbaijani (southwest), Azerbaijan (east), a slender border with Iran (southeast).

**Language:** Armenian.

**Ethnic Composition:** Armenian (94%), Azerbaijani and others (6%).

**Principal Religion:** Armenian Orthodox. Until recently, religious worship was officially discouraged.

**Chief Commercial Products:** Livestock, chemicals, textiles, wine, grain, footwear.

**Currency:** Dram (introduced in Nov. 1993).

**Recent Political Status:** The Armenian S.S.R. was established in 1920; from 1922 to 1936 it was joined with Georgia and Azerbaijan into the Trancaucasian S.S.R., but reverted to status as a constituent republic of the former USSR. It declared independence on August 23, 1990.

**Chief of State:** Robert Kocharian, President (elected March 30, 1998).

**National Flag:** Three equal horizontal stripes, red, blue, gold.

### The Land

Modern Armenia, which emerged as an independent state as a result of the collapse of the Union of Soviet Socialist Republics in 1991, is located in a landlocked area south of the Caucasus Mountains. The ancient empire of which it is a remnant included Turkish Armenia, an area of about 57,999 square miles (147,000 sq. km.) across the western border in present–day Azerbaijan.

Today, it consists of 11,503 square miles (29,800 kq. km.). It borders on Turkey to the west, Iran to the south, Georgia to the north and Azerbaijan to the east. Its principal cities are Yerevan, the capital, and Khodjent (formerly Leninabad).

All except about ten percent of Armenia is extremely mountainous. Its "lowlands" are over 3,000 feet high, while the average height above sea level for the entire country is slightly over a mile high; its highest mountains are in the northwestern part of the country. Mt. Aragats, the highest peak, is 13,418 feet high. The northern part of

Armenia consists of a series of ranges and elevated volcanic plateaus, into which deep river valleys have been cut.

In the east, the dominant feature is a high mountain lake surrounded by mountains. Lake Sevan, which is 525 square miles in size, lies at 6,200 feet, while the surrounding mountains soar to 11,800 feet. In the south is the Ararat Plain, only the northern half of which belongs to Armenia. The Ararat Plain is divided by the Aras River, which forms Armenia's southern border.

Armenia's rainfall varies considerably, with over 300 inches in the high mountains and an average of 80 inches on the Ararat Plain. Most of this precipitation falls in the form of heavy rains in the autumn and as snow in the winter.

Armenia's many rivers arise in the mountains in the north and west. Because of the sharp drop in elevation, they tend to be short and turbulent, with many waterfalls and rapids. Armenia accordingly has great hydroelectric power potential, estimated at nearly 22 billion kilowatt–hours a year. Four of these rivers—the Akhuryan, the Razdan (which flows out of Lake Sevan), the Arpa, and the Bargushat—provide water to irrigate the Ar-

# Armenia

menian half of the Ararat Plain before emptying into the Aras River, itself a tributary of the Kura River, which flows into the Caspian Sea.

Since it lies at the northern edge of the subtropical zone, Armenia has long, dry, hot summers with long, mild, sunny autumns. Because of the elevation of most of the land, it also has a winter with average temperatures below freezing, though only the plateau and mountains in the north have really inclement weather.

In spite of its small size, Armenia has an unusually large variety of landscapes. Because of a combination of location and variation in altitudes, it possesses five different vegetation zones: semidesert, steppe, forest, alpine meadows, and high–altitude tundra. The semidesert landscape is found in the south at altitudes below 4,600 feet. This region, unless irrigated, produces only a scanty vegetation of mostly sagebrush and similar drought–resistant plants.

The land between 4,600 and 6,600 feet is mostly steppe, and here, if not watered, mainly drought–resistant grasses grow. The forest zone is found mostly in the southeast at altitudes between 6,200 and 6,600 feet, and in the northeast, at altitudes between 7,200 and 7,900 feet. Oak grows mainly in the southeast, while beech grows in the northeast.

The alpine zone lies above 6,600 feet, where thinning forests give way to mountain meadows. Such meadows are used as summer pastures for goats and sheep. Finally, above the alpine zone is the area of tundra, where little grows other than cushion plants such as moss.

The Ararat Plain produces fruits such as figs, grapes, pomegranates, apricots, peaches and melons. The plateau and the mountain valleys produce cereals and grains, tobacco, vegetables, and orchard crops such as cherries, apples, pears, almonds, and hazelnuts. Higher altitudes produce potatoes, grain and fodder grasses.

The population of Armenia was 3,283,000 as of the 1989 census and is now probably close to 3.5 million. The republic is extremely homogenous, 94 percent of the population being Armenian. There are another 1.5 million Armenians living in the other former republics of the Soviet Union. The remaining six percent of Armenia's population is made up of Azerbaijanis and Russians, with smaller numbers of Ukrainians, Kurds and other groups. Many Azerbaijanis left Armenia and moved to Azerbaijan in the period 1989–91 because of the quarrel between the two republics over the Nagorno–Karabakh, the majority–Armenian enclave in Azerbaijan which wanted to become part of Armenia. Similarly, many Armenians living in Azerbaijan have moved back to Armenia.

## History

Armenians, who refer to themselves as the Hayk, are an Indo–European people who migrated into the area in the 7th century B.C., overrunning and conquering an earlier, high civilization. They subsequently came under the influence of the Medes, Persians and Greeks as they became part of these empires. The first Armenian Empire came into existence during the period of the rise of the Roman Empire. As the Roman Empire became ever more powerful, however, this empire disintegrated and Armenia became a sort of buffer zone between Rome and the Parthian Empire. The people of Armenia converted to Christianity about 300 A.D.; the Armenian Orthodox Church is known for its ancient and rich liturgy. Under communism, the role of the Church was severely limited but there has been a resurgence in recent years, and today the Church is playing an important role, particularly in the cultural sphere.

An independent Armenian state first emerged around 190 B.C., but it was not until the middle of the first century B.C. that a united Armenian state was created under Tigranes I the Great (c.94–c.55 B.C.). The first capital of this state was Artaxata, located on the Aras River not far from modern–day Yerevan. This kingdom lasted for almost 500 years and it reached its pinnacle under Tigranes, who extended his kingdom eastward to include parts of modern–day Iran and westward to encompass Syria. His conquests brought him to the attention of the Roman General Pompey, who defeated him in battle in 66 B.C. Tigranes was forced to relinquish Syria and become an ally of Rome.

**President Robert Kocharian**

For the next 120 years, Armenia remained a buffer state between Rome and Parthia, each manipulating Armenia to achieve its ends. The area was annexed by the Emperor Trajan in 114, but abandoned by his successor, Hadrian. An army of Marcus Aurelius destroyed Artaxata in 163. Caracalla attempted to annex Armenia in 216, but his successor, Macrinus, abandoned the attempt and recognized Tiridates II as King of Armenia. The resurgent Persian Empire then began pressing Armenia from the east. In 238, it conquered Armenia and established it as a vassal state holding it for fifty–some years later before another Roman Emperor, Diocletian, intervened and restored Tiridates III, son of Tiridates II, to the throne.

The reign of Tiridates III is extremely important for Armenian history, for this is when Armenia was converted to Christianity. Tiridates III was himself converted by St. Gregory the Illuminator and he made Christianity the official religion of the realm in 300 A.D. From this time onward, the Armenian patriarchate also became an important symbol of Armenian unity, holding the people together in periods of political instability.

Tiridates was later assassinated by his own court chamberlain in league with local nobles and Armenia split into two parts, with the smaller part gradually being absorbed into the Byzantine Empire. The larger part came under Persian domination in 428 when the Armenian nobility deposed their king and requested a Persian governor. The religion of Persia at this time was Zoroastrianism and the Persian ruler made the mistake of attempting to impose it on the Armenians. An Armenian revolt in 451 caused the Persians to declare that they would not attempt to impose Zoroastrianism by force. A second revolt in 481–484 won Persian recognition of a native Armenian ruler and a Persian promise to honor Armenia's political and religious freedom in return for Armenia's agreement to provide military assistance to Persia when called upon.

The Armenians asserted their religious freedom even further in 554 when an Armenian Church Council got into a quarrel with the rest of the Christian Church over a minor point of dogma, the dyophysite formula enunciated by the Council of Chalcedon in 451. The Armenian Church, by rejecting this formula, isolated itself from the rest of Christianity and turned the Byzantine Empire into an enemy.

Armenia came under attack from the Arabs beginning in 640. Thirteen years later, Armenia came under Arab control as an autonomous region under its own native ruler. This situation continued for the next three hundred years. In the tenth century, however, a resurgent Byzantine Empire invaded from the west, effectively destroying Armenia politically. The final

143

# Armenia

blow came in the 11th century when Armenia was invaded from the east by the Seljuk Turks. The Seljuk Turk conquest was complete by 1071, although a few minor Armenian kingdoms survived for a time in the more remote mountains. In the 12th century, part of northern Armenia was annexed to the Georgian Kingdom. However, Armenia was overrun again in 1236–42 by the Mongols.

Most of Armenia eventually became part of the Ottoman Empire and, after the fall of Constantinople in 1453, the Armenian bishop of Bursa was transferred to Constantinople and appointed leader of the Armenian Church in the Ottoman Empire. The eastern area fell to the Ottoman Empire in 1516, but it soon became a battlefield as Persia and the Ottoman Empire fought for control. Persia gained control of the regions of Yerevan, Karabakh, and Nakhichevan as a result of the peace of 1620. In the mountainous region of Karabakh, however, five Armenian princes managed to assert their independence at the beginning of the 18th century. The Ottoman Empire occupied the area in the 1730s, but were driven out by the Persians.

Amid the swirling events that ultimately resulted in the end of the Ottoman Empire, Armenians claim that 1.5 million of their people were mercilessly slaughtered by the Turks in the late 19th and early 20th centuries. Many fled, and a substantial number were admitted to the U.S.

## Armenia under Russian–Soviet Rule

The Russians began to focus their attention on the area of the Caucasus at the beginning of the 19th century. A war between Russia and Persia beginning in 1809 gave Russia Georgia, northern Azerbaijan and Karabakh. In 1828, Yerevan and Nakhichevan were added. A large part of traditional Armenia still remained under Ottoman control, but the area that was to become modern Armenia had become part of the Russian Empire.

The Russian Government tended to treat Armenians as co–religionists throughout most of the 19th century and being part of the Russian Empire meant that Armenians had greater access to western ideas than before. The 19th century therefore ushered in a cultural renaissance in Armenia.

This changed toward the end of the century, however, when the government of Nicholas II began to get worried about Armenian nationalism and introduced repressive measures to stamp it out. In 1897, hundreds of schools and libraries were closed and Armenian newspapers were banned. And since the Armenian Orthodox Church was closely associated in people's minds with Armenian nationalism, the government moved in 1903 to confiscate all property of the Armenian Church.

Armenian nationalists joined with Georgians and Azerbaijani to form the Transcaucasus Federal Republic in April 1918, but the new state collapsed in just over a month. An independent Armenia was then declared on May 26, 1918. The republic, which lasted until March 1922, had a bumpy independent existence as it attempted to secure as much of the lands occupied by Armenians as it could. It fought short wars with Georgia and Azerbaijan—the latter over the area of Nagorno–Karabakh—and a war in 1920 with Turkey. The loss to Turkey in 1920 led to a change in government and the creation of the Soviet Republic of Armenia in December 1920.

The new government was established as a coalition of communists and nationalists, but the nationalists were soon eliminated and it became a purely communist government. In March 1922, this new government joined with Georgia and Azerbaijan to form the Transcaucasian Soviet Federated Socialist Republic. On December 30, 1922, it became a part of the Union of Soviet Socialist Republics.

The Transcaucasian Soviet Federated Socialist Republic was dissolved in 1936 when a new Soviet constitution was adopted and Armenia at that time became the Armenian Soviet Socialist Republic. Armenia did relatively well as a part of the

**Armenians fleeing Turkish lands in the early 20th century**

144

Soviet Union. Quite a bit of industry grew up around Armenia's chief cities, and individual Armenians held important positions in industry and the professions in major cities throughout the Soviet Union. Yet Armenia was one of the first republics to "explode" after Gorbachëv launched his program of *glasnost.* The most important reason for this was the Nagorno–Karabakh Autonomous Republic, the Armenian enclave in the neighboring republic of Azerbaijan. The situation in Nagorno–Karabakh is treated in greater detail under the Republic of Azerbaijan (See page 120). Suffice to say here that this became a galvanizing issue for the vast majority of Armenians when the Nagorno–Karabakh regional council petitioned in February 1988 to become part of Armenia.

Within weeks, the Armenian political leadership had endorsed the Nagorno–Karabakh position. The Azerbaijani leadership angrily rejected Armenia's claims on Nagorno–Karabakh and began to encourage popular demonstrations in support of its position. The demonstrations got out of control, however, and turned into an anti–Armenian move in the Azerbaijani city of Sumgait. Within weeks, an incipient state of war existed between Armenia and Azerbaijan.

Gorbachëv dismissed the *Communist Party* leaders of both Azerbaijan and Armenia in May 1988, on the grounds that they had not acted quickly enough to control the situation. The new first secretary of the Armenian Communist Party leader was Suren Arutunyan, a Gorbachëv loyalist who had spent the previous several years working in Moscow. He tried his best, but he was constantly caught between Moscow loyalists on the one side and nationalists organized as the Karabakh Committee on the other. In the process, the Armenian Communist Party lost much of its authority.

Armenia was hit by a natural disaster in December 1988, when a major earthquake killed over 25,000 persons and injured thousands more. Other thousands were left homeless. International aid poured in, but Armenians lost further faith in both the Armenian and union leadership when help was slow in coming.

The people applauded in January 1989 when Gorbachëv announced that he had decided to suspend Azerbaijan's control over Nagorno–Karabakh and put the autonomous republic under Moscow's direct control. They suffered when the Azerbaijan Popular Front instituted its road and rail blockade against Armenia, but they refused to give in. They were, therefore, extremely angry when Gorbachëv gave in to the Azerbaijan Popular Front's blackmail and requested the USSR Supreme Soviet to relinquish control back to Azer-

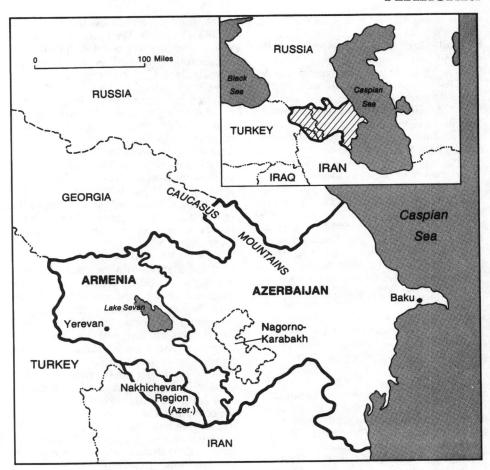

baijan. Armenian delegates refused to participate in that vote.

Armenians now turned conclusively against the Communist Party. By the spring of 1990, there were an increasing number of armed clashes between Armenian nationalists and Soviet troops. In July, Gorbachëv ordered all such vigilante groups to be disbanded, but then the Armenian Supreme Soviet defied Gorbachëv, declaring that his order "contradicts the Armenian people's natural right to self–defense." In August 1990, the Armenian Supreme Soviet elected Levan Ter–Petrossian to the top post in the republic, Chairman of the Supreme Soviet. Ter–Petrossian, a leader of the Karabakh Committee, was Armenia's first post–communist leader. On August 23, 1990, the Armenian Supreme Soviet followed this up by passing a declaration of Armenian independence.

Ter–Petrossian turned out to be a cautious leader in practice. He did not attempt to challenge Moscow, but, again, his quarrel was not really with Moscow. The confrontation with Azerbaijan continued and Armenia continued to suffer from an Azerbaijani blockade of fuel and most other supplies, but it would not cede on the po-

litical question. In the spring of 1991, it boycotted discussions about a new union treaty. Armenia took advantage of the *coup* attempt against Gorbachëv in August 1991 to reiterate its declaration of independence. This was followed by a popular referendum that received overwhelming approval. The Armenian Supreme Soviet also created the office of President to be elected by popular vote. The election took place on October 16 and Ter–Petrossian won 83 percent of the votes. He formally assumed the office in December 1991.

Armenia accepted Russian–Kazakh mediation of the Nagorno–Karabakh dispute with Azerbaijan in September 1991 and agreed to yield its claims over Nagorno–Karabakh at this time. It subsequently recognized the independence of the Republic of Nagorno–Karabakh, however, so its confrontation with Azerbaijan continues.

Armenia agreed to join the Commonwealth of Independent States at the December 1991 founding meeting. Unlike Azerbaijan, it opted to not establish a separate republic army at that time, even though large numbers of Armenian "freedom fighters" were already involved in the fighting in Nagorno–Karabakh. Partly this was because it hoped to win CIS back-

# Armenia

ing for its position on Nagorno–Karabakh; partly it was because the Azerbaijani blockade had been successful and its economy was in terrible shape.

As a result of strains between individual CIS members and a continuing fear of being dominated by Moscow, however, most CIS members began to create national armies in 1992. Armenia created a Ministry of Defense and an Armenian army and began to equip these forces with heavier equipment such as tanks, transferred mainly from Soviet forces.

The war between Azerbaijan and Armenia widened somewhat in the spring of 1992, when forces within Nagorno–Karabakh extended their control over areas formerly occupied by Azerbaijani forces. These same forces then overran Azerbaijani territory lying between Nagorno–Karabakh and Armenia, creating a corridor connecting the enclave with Armenia at the point where the two territories are the closest together. This had a military significance, since Armenia, which had been shifting supplies in by air up to this point, could begin bringing supplies in by truck.

Azerbaijan was going through a great deal of domestic political turmoil at this point, at least partly because of its military defeats. Azerbaijani forces in the enclave of Nakhichevan (cut off from Azerbaijan by a strip of Armenian territory), then began shelling Armenian villages across the border. This led to an Armenian attack on the enclave city of Sadarak, and so the war widened further. Fighting continued intermittently over the summer and into the fall, in spite of a series of truces negotiated with the assistance of international third parties; however, no further significant changes in the military situation occurred. But Azerbaijan maintained its blockade of Armenia, so the economic situation within Armenia deteriorated further.

The situation within Armenia became desperate in January 1993 when the sole gas pipeline leading into the country through Georgia was blown up. A new temporary pipeline was opened in February and some gas is once again flowing from Georgia. But even with almost all Armenian factories closed because of a lack of energy, there was no sign that Armenians were ready to compromise or lessen their support for fellow Armenians in Nagorno–Karabakh. Demonstrations in Yerevan calling for President Ter–Petrossian's resignation and for new parliamentary elections did occur in February 1993, but many of the demonstrators were critical of the President precisely because he had not pursued the war against Azerbaijan firmly enough.

Russia brokered another cease-fire between Armenia and Azerbaijan in March 1994. Under the agreement, Russian troops were to be stationed around the borders of Nagorno–Karabakh and both sides were to withdraw troops, heavy guns and aircraft. The ceasefire lasted approximately six weeks before heavy fighting erupted in April. A new cease-fire eventually set in, however, and things have been quiet since that time. With no solution to the problem of Nagorno–Karabakh in sight, however, Armenia remains cut off from outside energy supplies and its industries continue to operate only at an extremely low level.

Parliamentary elections, carried out in 1995, were won by President Ter–Petrossian's political party, but only after the government had moved to ban one of the opposition political parties. International observers later reported that the elections were unfair.

New presidential elections took place in September 1996, with President Ter–Petrossian a candidate for reelection. The President's chief opponent in the election was Vazgen Manukian, a former Prime Minister. The other candidates were Sergei Badalian, leader of the Communist Party, and Ashot Manucharian, the President's former national security adviser. The two chief issues in the campaign were the continuing stalemate with Azerbaijan over Nagorno–Karabakh and the state of the economy. A cease-fire with Azerbaijan had largely held since 1994 and the economy, which had grown by 7 percent in 1995—albeit from an extremely low level—continued to expand at about the same rate in 1996.

President Ter–Petrossian won with just under 52 percent of the vote, but the results were tainted by widespread charges of voting irregularities during the election. In consequence, his opponents protested the result and thousands of demonstrators gathered near the presidential palace to demand that the President step down. After three days of demonstrations, the government called in the armed forces to break them up. Most of the opposition political leaders were jailed or went underground. All serious opposition was then banned.

Concerned about his growing unpopularity, President Ter–Petrossian dismissed his Prime Minister, Grant Bagratian, in November 1996, supposedly because Bagratian, who had been Prime Minister since February 1993, had become increasingly unpopular because of his close identification with painful economic reforms. He then appointed Armen V. Sarkisyan as his new Prime Minister.

It was certainly true that conditions for most Armenians remained severe, in large part because of the trade embargoes put into effect by both Azerbaijan and Turkey. Most outside observers were also convinced that Armenia could expect no significant longtime economic improvement unless it were able to reach a settlement of the conflict with Azerbaijan over Nagorno–Karabakh.

The Organization for Security and Cooperation in Europe (OSCE), which had been attempting to promote such a settlement, put forth its terms for peace in November 1996. These terms, which became known as the Lisbon principles, essentially called for the restoration of Soviet-era borders, broad autonomy for ethnic Armenians in the disputed region of Nagorno–Karabakh, and international guarantees of such a settlement.

The leaderships of both Armenia and Nagorno–Karabakh rejected the OSCE terms at that time, but President Ter–Petrossian, anxious to cultivate better relations with the United States and Russia, found himself coming under increasing international pressure to accede to the Lisbon principles in succeeding months. Recognizing that these demands from abroad threatened to weaken domestic support from among top military leaders as well as hardliners within his own party, Ter–Petrossian, in March 1997, asked Robert Kocharian, then President of the unrecognized Republic of Nagorno–Karabakh, to become his Prime Minister.

The President and his Prime Minister worked closely together over the next several months, drawing up plans for economic reform. Then President Ter–Petrossian dropped a bombshell in September 1997 when he gave a press conference in which he admitted publicly for the first time that the status quo was untenable. He then went on effectively to endorse the OSCE Lisbon principles, suggesting that Nagorno–Karabakh could retain effective independence, but would technically have to remain part of Azerbaijan. The President had apparently become persuaded that all of his plans for economic reform would fail without peace.

But this was the beginning of the end for Ter–Petrossian. Not only did his opponents call him a traitor, he also came under severe attack from members of his own party and of the government, particularly from his military allies. One of his severest critics was his Prime Minister, Robert Kocharian, who essentially argued that Ter–Petrossian was wrong and that Armenia could rebuild its economy while continuing its support for Nagorno–Karabakh.

President Ter–Petrossian's resignation came on February 3, 1998. Speaking on national television, he said that he was resigning in response to demands by "state bodies well known to you." Although he characterized his resignation as "the defeat of the honorable party of peace in Armenia," he argued that differences over Nagorno–Karabakh were just a pretext that hardline forces were using to make him resign.

In line with the Armenian constitution,

Robert Kocharian then became Prime Minister and Acting President. He also became a candidate for election to a full term as President, in spite of the fact that, as a former President of Nagorno–Karabakh, he could hardly claim to have been a citizen of Armenia for ten years as required by the constitution. In the first round of voting, which took place on March 16, Kocharian came first with 38.82 percent of the vote, followed by former communist leader Karen Demirchian, with 30.62 percent. Vazgen Manukian came third with 12.22 percent and Sergei Badalian came fourth with 11.02 percent. Since no candidate won a majority, a second round of voting took place on March 30. Here Robert Kocharian came in first with 59.7 percent of the vote to Karen Demirchian's 40.3 percent. Eleven days later, he chose Armen Darpinyan, his 33–year old Finance and Economy Minister, as his new Prime Minister. Darpinyan, who also served as first deputy chairman of the Armenian Central Bank from 1994 until May 1997, when he became Finance Minister, is known internationally as an economic reformer. His appointment, plus the convincing victory at the polls, should help Kocharian to consolidate his power both domestically and internationally. However, Kocharian's victory does not bode well for the possibility of a settlement of the war with Azerbaijan.

**Foreign Policy**

Armenia is essentially at war with its eastern neighbor, Azerbaijan, though the 1994 ceasefire is still holding as of the moment. It has fairly good relations with Georgia and Iran, but its relations with Turkey are cold, partly because Armenia refuses to renounce its traditional claim to Armenian Turkey and partly because Turkey tends to favor Azerbaijan in its war with Armenia. There are no diplomatic relations between Armenia and Turkey, and Turkey currently maintains an embargo on Armenian goods.

Armenia has cultivated good relations with Russia and is an active participant in the Commonwealth of Independent States. In 1996, Russia and Armenia signed a series of bilateral agreements that boosted military cooperation. In August 1997, Russia and Armenia signed a treaty "on friendship, cooperation, and mutual assistance" under which Russia, for the first time, committed itself in an accord to defend an ally militarily in the event that the ally is attacked by a foreign country. The treaty also calls for coordination of military–technical policy, mutual development of defense industries, standardization of military hardware, and joint financing of military projects. Since that time, Russia and Armenia have signed another accord which establishes a joint venture for the re–export of Russian gas to Turkey.

Americans tend to be sympathetic to Armenia and this is reflected in the aid program that the U.S. Government instituted in 1993. Under the program, the United States provided $18 million that year to be used to purchase kerosene and heaters to heat classrooms and schools. Japan also contributed to this same program. Since that time, American aid to Armenia has been growing and now amounts to about $100 million a year, making Armenia the second–biggest recipient per person of American foreign aid.

Paradoxically, Armenia also has excellent relations with Iran, which has become Armenia's chief trading partner. The reason, from Armenia's point of view, is not difficult to discover, however. At war with Azerbaijan and with Turkey enforcing an embargo against Armenian products, only Iran and Georgia remain. And Georgia is nearly as badly off as Armenia. Iran, on the other hand, has poor relations with Azerbaijan, partly because it fears Azerbaijani influences on Azeris within Iran, partly because Azerbaijan has welcomed American companies and their billions of dollars of investment.

**The Nature of the Regime**

The Armenian Governmental setup is similar to that of the Russian Federation. An executive President sets policy and makes major appointments, while a prime minister and cabinet handle the imple-

**Looking down the main boulevard in Yerevan**

Courtesy: NOVOSTI

# Armenia

mentation of policy. The Armenian Supreme Soviet has considerable authority, but generally takes its lead from the President. Armenia has a multiparty system, though there have been charges of corruption and vote–fixing with regard to the last two elections. The major political force at the moment is the Armenian Pan–National Movement, successor of the Karabakh Committee (Armenia's version of a Popular Front). The dominating ideology is nationalism, even among opposition parties. The military also appears to have a major influence on political decision–making.

The current government is a coalition of parties called the Hanrapetutyun bloc. The largest opposition party is the National Democratic Union, led by Vazgen Manukian. There is also a Communist Party, led by Sergei Badalian, but it has far less support.

Armenia was admitted to the United Nations at the same time that the other members of the Commonwealth of Independent States were admitted and it is a member of the Council for Security and Cooperation in Europe. It has held membership in the IMF and World Bank since April 1992.

## Culture:

Traditional Armenian culture has deep historic roots that reach back as far as the 5th century when the first written literature began. Two works that date from that period are Moses of Khorem's *History of Armenia* and Erzik Koqhbutsi's *Refutation of the Sects*. The two themes represented by the works, history and religion, continued to be important in subsequent centuries, but they gradually began to be expressed in new forms.

Gregory Nare Katzi, who lived in the 10th century, was Armenia's first great poet. A deeply religious man, his mystical poems and hymns heavily influenced the Armenian Orthodox Church and led to his canonization after his death.

A secular tradition began to emerge in the 16th–18th centuries with the appearance of popular bards (troubadours). Known as *ashugh,* they produced numerous love songs which are now known by the people. The 19th century saw the emergence of both the novel and the short story. Famous Armenian novelists include Hakob Paronian, Ervand Otian and Hakob Maliq–Hakobian, whose pen name is "Raffi." Paronian also wrote plays, as did Gabriel Sundukian.

The communist era had a negative effect on Armenian culture; it rejected nearly every theme associated with traditional literature. Pre–revolutionary novelists and playwrights continued to be read and performed, but modern writers were required to conform to communism's "socialist realism," a requirement which turned them

into party hacks. It is no surprise that the 20th century produced no great Armenian literature, but it did produce its first great composer, Aram Katchaturian, probably because it was hard for Moscow authorities to apply "socialist realism" to classical music.

Communism did leave behind an established society which will help Armenian culture to develop further in the future. There is both a state radio and television broadcasting system with studios in Yerevan. The city is also the site of a State Academic Theater of Opera and Ballet. Several drama theaters also exist, a national dance company, several orchestras and a film studio.

Old folk arts such as dancing, singing and artistic crafts were left undisturbed by communism. Thus, the new non–communist government has a firm basis on which to build. An Armenian Academy of Sciences runs a number of research institutes throughout the country.

## Economy

Armenia today is overwhelmingly an urban and industrial society, with agriculture perhaps accounting for a fifth of the national income. Three fifths of the country's industries are located in and around the city of Yerevan, however, and because so many of them are types of heavy industry which heavily pollute, Yerevan today is one of the most polluted cities of the former Soviet Union. These include factories which produce synthetic rubber, fertilizers, chemicals, nonferrous metals, machines and equipment. It also produces other polluting minerals; all of these have badly polluted large areas of the countryside. The government will probably deal with this problem in the coming years.

It also has light industry—textiles, carpet–weaving, food processing, wine–making, fruit, meat–canning and creameries. Medium industries include electrical equipment, precision instruments and machine tools. It is also a large producer of cement, marble, pumice, volcanic basalt and fireproof clay.

Industry has been in extremely poor condition for a number of years, primarily because of Armenia's political quarrel with Azerbaijan over the Armenian–populated enclave of Nagorno–Karabakh, as can be seen by the fact that GDP fell by 63 percent between 1991 and 1993. Azerbaijan has maintained an almost continuous siege against Armenia since the beginning of the fighting, and it has since been joined by Turkey, which also instituted a blockade against Armenian goods. As a result, Armenian industry has had great difficulty obtaining energy supplies and raw materials. Petroleum and gas formerly came from Azerbaijan and Turkmenistan and they remain short. Armenia has, however, found some alternate

sources of supply and, in addition, has begun using more electricity, of which it now has adequate supplies, ever since it reopened the Medzamor nuclear plant in 1995.

The economic turnaround began in 1994, when GDP grew by 5.4 percent. It then grew by 6.9 percent in 1995 and by 5.8 percent in 1996. Inflation, which has been in four figures in 1993, dropped to 5.7 percent in 1996. This situation was somewhat reversed in 1997 when GDP grew by only 2.7 percent, while inflation had rebounded to 21 percent. What growth was recorded was in trade and services, while industrial output stagnated.

Part of the problem was a budget deficit that was 6.8 percent of GDP in 1997. The Armenian Government, recognizing this fact, is committed to shrinking the size of the deficit in future years. In addition, the World Bank announced in November 1997 that it would provide $200 million in 1997–1998 to finance the budget deficit and infrastructural investment. The IMF has also provided some funds, beginning with a $23.6 million loan in December 1994 and a three–year $148 million loan in February 1996. More recently though, it has twice delayed payments out of concern for such factors as the government's energy pricing policy and the management of privatization.

Armenia launched a program of privatization based on vouchers in 1994 and the program is due to be completed in 1998. The voucher privatization was not very successful, however, because it failed to inject new capital into enterprises or change the way that they were managed. Last year, the government launched a new program which involved a shift toward market capital. That approach is already beginning to pay off. For example, 90 percent of Armentel, the national telecommunications company, has been sold to a Greek consortium. A Canadian company has also agreed to invest $200 million in gold mining, and there are prospects for other large–scale investments in mining. Currently, even the famous Yerevan Cognac Company is up for tender. Still, total foreign investment remains tiny, and interest among private investors is growing only slowly.

Agriculture contributes far less to the economy than industry, but it continues to support employment for almost half the population, together with related processing industries. As elsewhere, it had been organized into state and collective farms, but one of the first decisions of the non–communist government was to begin phasing them out.

As a result, Armenia had begun creating a privatization of agriculture even before it attained independence in 1991. The most valuable resource is probably grapes, from which famous wines, brandies and champagnes are made. Orchard crops are next in importance—peaches, apricots, apples cherries, pears, pomegranates, walnuts, hazelnuts and almonds are abundant. Tobacco is another important cash crop. Extensive mountain pastures support a significant dairy industry, plus many sheep for wool and meat. Pigs and poultry are also raised.

**The Future**

Armenia's future is clouded by its continuing quarrel with the Republic of Azerbaijan. So long as the Nagorno–Karabakh situation remains unsettled, Armenia will find it difficult to do much about its economy. This is unfortunate, since Armenia was among the first of the republics to take advantage of Gorbachëv's restructuring

and begin the privatization of its economy. There is no political crisis, since the overwhelming majority of the people support the policies of the government, but there is an economic crisis which is unlikely to be overcome unless and until a political accommodation is achieved with Azerbaijan.

Presidential candidate Robert Kocharian campaigns in Yerevan

# The Republic of Azerbaijan

*A view of Baku with the Adjarbek Mosque*

Courtesy: NOVOSTI

**Area:** 33,428 sq. mi. (86,579 sq. km.), about the size of Maine.

**Population:** 7.7 million.

**Capital City:** Baku (Pop. 1,782,000).

**Climate:** Generally dry, sub–tropical.

**Neighboring States:** Russia (north), Georgia (northwest), Armenia (west and east where the Nakhichevan Region is separated from the rest of the country), Iran (south).

**Language:** Azerbaijani.

**Ethnic Background:** Azerbaijani (78%), Armenian, mainly within the enclave of Nagorno–Karabakh which lies within its borders (8%), Russian (8%), others (6%).

**Principal Religion:** Islam, principally Shi'a.

**Chief Commercial Products:** Agriculture—grain, cotton, rice, grapes. Industry—oil, concrete, carpets, processed food (fish and caviar), wine, processed meat, cheese.

**Currency:** Manat.

**Recent Political Status:** Azerbaijan S.S.R. was founded in 1920. Part of Transcaucasian Federation (1922–1936), Constituent republic of the USSR (1936–1991).

**Chief of State:** Geidar Aliyev, President (October 1993).

**National Flag:** Three equal horizontal stripes, sky blue, red and green, with a crescent moon and star superimposed in the center of the red.

## The Land

The Republic of Azerbaijan, which was one of the 15 Soviet republics before the collapse of the Union of Soviet Socialist Republics in 1991, is located in an area south of the Caucasus Mountains along the western shores of the Caspian Sea. It covers an area of 33,428 square miles (86,579 sq. km.). Iran lies to the south, Armenia and Georgia to the west, and the Russian Federation to the north. It also includes two autonomous republics, the Nakhichevan Autonomous Republic, occupied mainly by Azeri but separated from the rest of Azerbaijan by the southeastern part of Armenia, and the Nagorno–Karabakh Autonomous Republic, mainly occupied by Armenians.

More than 40 percent of Azerbaijan is lowlands, most of which are in the Kura River valley, which runs in a northwest direction beginning at the Caspian Sea and ending in the mountains of Georgia. The Kura River actually originates in the Small

150

Caucasus Mountains, which stretch along the border between Georgia and Turkey. It flows down through the high valley of central Georgia before crossing the border into Azerbaijan. The Aras River, a southern branch of the Kura, originates in the Aras Mountains of Turkey. It forms the southern boundary between Armenia and Turkey, between the Nakhichevan Autonomous Republic and Turkey and Iran, and between Azerbaijan and the Iranian province of Azerbaijan. It then turns northeast and joins the Kura River. The remaining lowland areas include the Lenkoran Lowland in the southeast, plus a strip of land beginning at the Apsheron Peninsula, which juts out into the Caspian Sea to the north of the mouth of the Kura River, and then running north along the western shores of the Caspian.

To the northeast of the Kura River Valley, the chain of the Great Caucasus Mountains runs southeast, ending just before the Apsheron Peninsula. Here the highest mountains are over 14,000 feet, though most of the territory is covered by foothills running perpendicular to the line of the higher mountain ridge and varying in height from 1,300 to 4,900 feet. Southward across the Kura River Valley, the ground again flows upward, becoming foothills then rising to become the Small Caucasus Mountains, which mark the border between Azerbaijan and Armenia. The Karabakh upland, where the Nagorno–Karabakh Autonomous Republic is situated, is also in this area.

The annual rainfall of the Kura–Aras Lowland varies from 8 to 16 inches and so has the plant life of the steppe and the semi–desert. A well–developed system of dams and canals means that most of the lowland is irrigated, however, and today most of the area is devoted to the cultivation of cotton. The largest of these dams is the Mingechaur, built in 1953 along the Kura River in northwestern Azerbaijan. Mingechaur Dam, which is also a major hydroelectric station, forms a lake that covers an area of 234 square miles and has a storage capacity of 565 trillion cubic feet.

The Kura River Valley has a dry, subtropical climate with hot summers and mild winters. Southeast Azerbaijan, which receives the most rainfall of any part of the republic, has a humid, subtropical climate. Here the annual rainfall is about 50 inches, which falls mainly in the winter. The Nakhichevan Autonomous Republic, with altitudes between 2,300 and 3,300 feet, has a dry, continental climate, with cold winters and dry summers. The Caspian Sea shoreline has a Mediterranean type climate, cool in winter and dry in summer. Forests are found on the upper slopes of the Great Caucasus and Small Caucasus Mountains. The main trees are beech, oak and pine.

## The People

According to the most recent estimates, Azerbaijan's population is approximately 7,450,000. Azeris or Azerbaijani, who make up about 78% of the population of the republic, are a Turkic–speaking people. They migrated into the area in the 11th century as part of the Oguz Seljuk migrations. There are another million Azeris living across the border in the province of Iranian Azerbaijan. Russians, the largest minority, make up about 8% and Armenians about 7.9%. Most Russians reside in the major cities, particularly Baku, the capital and largest city, and Sumgait, an industrial city located 22 miles to the north. Daghestanis make up another 3.4% of the population; other smaller minorities include Iranians, Ukrainians and Kurds.

## History

After the Bolsheviks came to power in Moscow, national groups in Azerbaijan, Armenia and Georgia got together and established the Transcaucasian Federal Republic on April 22, 1918. It collapsed after one month. In Azerbaijan, a National Council of the Tatars, dominated by the *Mussavat (Nationalist) Party*, announced the birth of the Azerbaijanian Democratic Republic on May 28, 1918. This government continued to exist until April 1920, when it was overthrown by the Red Army. The communists established the Azerbaijan Soviet Socialist Republic on April 28, 1920.

This was the beginning of Azerbaijani political history. Prior to that time, the Azerbaijani were an undifferentiated Islamic people, first under Persian then under Russian rule, of the area of the Transcaucasus. Peter the Great was the first Russian ruler to take an interest in the area, when he occupied Baku in 1723. The coastal region actually became Russian in 1813 by the Treaty of Gulistan, under which Persia ceded the lands bordering the western shores of the Caspian Sea from the Lenkoran Lowland northward to Derbent. The interior was annexed by Russia in 1829.

Although Azerbaijan came under communist control in 1920, it remained theoretically independent until March 1922. It was then merged with Armenia and Georgia to form the Transcaucasian Soviet Federated Socialist Republic. The Transcaucasian SFSR became a formal part of the Union of Soviet Socialist Republics in December 1922. Fourteen years later, under the terms of Stalin's 1936 Constitution, the Transcaucasian SFSR was dissolved and the Azerbaijan Soviet Socialist Republic reemerged.

Azerbaijan was a pliant republic under the communists until Gorbachëv's policy of *glasnost* began to challenge the old *status quo*. The situation had been building up over a number of years, however, in

connection with jobs in the modern, industrial sector. Azerbaijanis were traditionally either nomads or farmers, so when the Baku oil industry was developed, most of the jobs went to Armenians or Russians. After the Russian Revolution, literacy campaigns gradually carried education to the countryside where most Azerbaijanis lived.

As more and more Azerbaijanis became educated, they began to be recruited for positions in industry and government. For a long time this was nominal, but the Brezhnev leadership, in particular, encouraged the development of native elites in the republics. This new Azerbaijani leadership founded numerous institutes of higher education and, increasingly, favored a policy of edging out non–Azerbaijanis and replacing them with Azerbaijanis. Thus there was a very distinct bias among the Azerbaijani political leadership to favor Azeri speakers. Armenians were a particular target of this policy.

Many Armenians had taken jobs in the Baku area in the past. When they found themselves edged out of a job, however, they could always return to Armenia. This presented a different problem for the Armenians of the Nagorno–Karabakh Autonomous Republic, however, since this was a relatively poor area without significant industry. The Armenians of Nagorno–Karabakh also felt that the leadership at the republic level ignored needs of the autonomous republic. Thus they formally requested to be transfered to Armenian jurisdiction in February 1988. When the Armenian Republic leadership supported Nagorno–Karabakh's request two weeks later, apparently spontaneous riots broke out in the Azerbaijani city of Sumgait which turned into a slaughter of Armenians. When this was followed by retaliatory moves against Azerbaijani living in Armenia, the result was a dual stream of refugees, Armenians fleeing to Armenia and Azeris fleeing to Azerbaijan.

This first, open manifestation of Azerbaijani nationalism was exacerbated when Gorbachëv dismissed the first secretaries of the Azerbaijani and Armenian Communist Parties in May 1988 for allowing the situation to get out of hand. The Azerbaijani educated classes, up to this time loyal supporters of the party, now began to think of the party as Moscow–dominated. Gorbachëv aggravated the situation even further when he announced in January 1989 that he was suspending Azerbaijan's authority over Nagorno–Karabakh and putting the autonomous republic under direct Muscovite control.

That summer the *Azerbaijan Popular Front* was founded for the specific goal of safeguarding Azeri national interests. And the national interest was defined as meaning the territorial integrity of Azerbaijan. In a challenge to the Communist Party, the

# Azerbaijan

front launched a series of mass demonstrations and labor strikes in August.

In September 1989, the front organized a road and railroad blockade of Armenia. With 85 percent of Armenia's freight entering the country by way of Azerbaijan, this action brought Armenian industry almost to a halt. The success of the blockade also brought the front a political victory over the *Azerbaijan Communist Party*. On September 13, Abdul Vezirov, the first secretary, signed a protocol with the front in which he agreed to call a special session of the Supreme Soviet to pass a law on sovereignty. The law was passed ten days later. Meanwhile the front threatened to maintain its blockade of Armenia until Moscow dissolved its special commission and allowed control over Nagorno–Karabakh to revert back to Azerbaijan. On November 28, the USSR Supreme Soviet voted to end Moscow's direct rule over Nagorno–Karabakh. The rail blockade was eased, but not lifted entirely.

A new 1990 series of killings of Armenians broke out in Baku, the Azerbaijani capital. The government declared a state of emergency to handle the matter. Gorbachëv then sent in Soviet troops to restore order and to forestall a *coup* by the Azerbaijani Popular Front against the Azerbaijan Government. Soviet Defense Minister Yazov later said that the Soviet troops were sent in "to destroy the organizational structure" of the *Azerbaijan Popular Front*. The Azerbaijan Communist Party leadership was changed as well. Ayaz Mutalibov, who had been Prime Minister up to this time, was installed as the new party leader and head of state.

Azeris were extremely angered by Gorbachëv's actions. Elmira Kafarova, chairman of the Azerbaijani Supreme Soviet, referred to the events of January 1990 as "a gross violation of Azerbaijani sovereignty." More than a million people turned out for the funeral of the approximately one hundred Azerbaijanis killed when Soviet troops entered Baku.

There were also rallies when *Communist Party* membership cards were burned, but Gorbachëv kept the troops in Baku and eventually order was restored. Mutalibov survived as party first secretary, though he never dared to lift the state of emergency declared in January 1990.

Mutalibov was abroad on a visit to Iran while an attempted *coup* against Gorbachëv was going on. He never condemned the the attempt, but, after it failed, he resigned as head of the party and issued a decree banning party cells in government and industry. The party later dissolved itself.

Mutalibov announced Azerbaijan's independence on August 30. He then had the Azerbaijan Supreme Soviet modify the constitution by creating a popularly elected, executive Presidency. He was later elected President in an uncontested election.

Mutalibov remained under intense pressure from a growing political opposition, however. In September 1991, he created an 8–member Defense Council and appointed members of the *Social Democratic Party*, the *National Independence Party* and the *Popular Front* to it. By this time, Tamerlan Karayev, leader of the *Azerbaijan Popular Front* had been elected deputy head of the Supreme Soviet.

The front demanded that the Supreme Soviet be replaced by a temporary "National Council" which would prepare for new elections. When Karayev threatened to resign his post as deputy leader in October, Mutalibov agreed to the creation of a National Council and to a second demand that Azerbaijan establish its own army.

On October 18, 1991, the Supreme Soviet passed a law formally reestablishing Azerbaijan's independence. It declared the present government the legitimate successor to the Azerbaijanian Democratic Government, overthrown by the communists in April 1920. The law further declared that "all acts and treaties concluded by the republic since April 1920" were considered invalid.

In early November, Mutalibov closed down the gas line to Armenia, cutting off the delivery of gas. Later in the month, when an Azerbaijani helicopter was downed over Nagorno–Karabakh, Mutalibov announced that he was calling an extraordinary session of the Supreme Soviet and would request them to dissolve the Nagorno–Karabakh government. At the same time, he cut all railway links with Armenia. The Azerbaijani Supreme Soviet endorsed Mutalibov's actions on November 26. By this time, Azerbaijan had its own defense minister and had created a military force of about 25,000. Mutabilov ordered his defense minister to restore order in Nagorno–Karabakh. Something approaching full–scale war existed in the area.

The Azerbaijan National Council met for the first time on November 29. Its first act was to pass a law putting all of Azerbaijan's borders under state control, to be guarded by Azerbaijani border guard troops. The purpose of the legislation was to give Azerbaijan control of its border with Armenia.

Meanwhile, the Armenian political leadership in Nagorno–Karabakh had declared the area to be an independent republic. A referendum, held on December 10, brought overwhelming popular approval.

The war between Azerbaijan and Nagorno–Karabakh continued for the next two months. All of Nagorno–Karabakh's connections with the outside were cut off

**At prayer in the Mashtagin mosque**

and Azerbaijani troops carried out raids into the area from the east. There were reports that the city of Stepanakert had been virtually destroyed, but the Armenian leadership of Nagorno–Karabakh refused to give in. They were also being assisted by elements of the Armenian National Army, which had opened a corridor between Armenia and Nagorno–Karabakh.

When Mutalibov said that he was still seeking a political solution to the problem, the *Azerbaijan Popular Front* demanded his resignation on February 20, 1992, charging that the course of military actions in Nagorno–Karabakh was detrimental to Azerbaijan. As Azerbaijani nationalists continued to press the government to step up the fighting against the Armenians in Nagorno–Karabakh, Mutalibov resigned as President on March 6.

The *Azerbaijan Popular Front* never accepted Mutalibov's conversion to nationalism, and they never forgot that he was installed by Moscow after Soviet armed forces had been used against the front. Under their prodding, an Azerbaijani legislative commission, appointed to investigate the events of January 1990, had concluded that Moscow had deliberately chosen Azerbaijan as a test case to see whether an independence movement could be crushed through the massive use of force. Forcing Mutalibov's resignation was therefore part of their revenge for the events of January 1990. They did not take any personal revenge against him, however. In addition to a grant of immunity against prosecution and a 10–man bodyguard, the legislature provided him with a pension of 10,000 rubles a month and a villa in the countryside.

Following his resignation, the legislature transferred presidential authority to the newly elected Chairman of the legislature, Yagub Mamedov. One of the first acts of the new government was to launch new attacks against Nagorno–Karabakh. Their target was the city of Askeran, located not far from the capital city of Stepanakert. They were driven back by Armenian forces, however.

Ordinary Azeribaijanis reacted by calling for greater efforts to reclaim Nagorno–Karabakh. Mamedov, however, called for diplomatic efforts to get negotiations under way.

In March, the prime minister, Hasan Hasanov, said that "the chance of the conflict erupting into an all–out war and the chance of a political solution are 50-50. This depends on how much world public opinion realizes that the Armenian state terrorist army must immediately leave the occupied territory of Azerbaijan. If it continues its occupation of Nagorno–Karabakh, the chances of a military outcome will greatly increase."

In fact, Azerbaijani attempts to extend their control in Nagorno–Karabakh were

**View of the port area of Baku**

Courtesy: NOVOSTI

unsuccessful. In May, forces of the Nagorno–Karabakh Defense Council managed to capture the Azerbaijani stronghold of Shusha and drive most Azerbaijani forces out of the enclave. Even as the Armenian and Azerbaijani Governments continued discussions aimed at bringing an end to the fighting, the Nagorno–Karabakh Defense Council forces captured a corridor across the Azeri territory separating Nagorno–Karabakh and Armenia, thereby creating a ground connection with Armenia.

Later in May, the war widened when fighting broke out along the border between Armenia and the Azerbaijani enclave of Nakhichevan, separated from the rest of Azerbaijan by a strip of Armenian territory. According to Armenian reports, the fighting began after Armenian villages were shelled from across the border. Armenians retaliated by launching attacks on the Azeri villages of Sadarak and Lachin. Both Turkey and Iran protested the Armenian "aggression" at this point, however, and a sort of quasi–truce settled in along the border.

The next development came on June 7, when the Azerbaijani population went to the polls to elect a new president. There were five candidates, but the easy winner was Abulfaz Elchibey, leader of the *Azerbaijan Popular Front*, who won 60 percent of the vote. Elchibey was 53 years old at the time of his election and a noted historian. He was also one of the founders of the *Azerbaijan Popular Front*. Though the *Popular Front* came into existence as part of a popular response to Nagorno–Karabakh's demand that it be permitted to become part of Armenia, it claimed democratic credentials and was determined to break the

old–line Communist leadership's hold on power. Strongly nationalist, it also opposed cooperation with the other former Soviet republics in the CIS. One of Elchibey's first acts as President was to announce that Azerbaijan would withdraw from the Commonwealth of Independent States and that Azerbaijan would deal with the other republics only on a bilateral basis. Elchibey was particularly incensed that several of the CIS members had negotiated a mutual security pact which included Armenia, though he had been cool to the CIS from its first inception.

Aside from that, however, Elchibey was relatively moderate in his actions after becoming President. This may be partly because he looked to Turkey as a model for his own government and the Turkish Government was urging that course on him. He was committed to an economic reform based on free market principles, but did little in that direction, partly because of his continued preoccupation with Nagorno–Karabakh.

The struggle over Nagorno–Karabakh did not cause the bad economic effects in Azerbaijan that it did in Armenia, but it did appear to preclude Azerbaijani leaders from thinking about anything else.

Unfortunately for Elchibey, however, Armenian forces overran the northern part of the strip separating Nagorno–Karabakh from Armenia in April 1993, capturing the Azerbaijani regional town of Kelbajar and in the process bringing about ten percent of Azerbaijan's territory under Armenian control. The defeat at Kelbajar also produced an estimated 100,000 new refugees for the Azerbaijani Government to cope with. This was a severe setback for President Elchibey, made worse by the

# Azerbaijan

fact that the Azerbaijani forces suffered a series of humiliating defeats when they attempted to regain control of the overrun territories in subsequent fighting.

President Elchibey then found himself challenged by his own forces when he tried to discipline one of the regional commanders, a 35–year old army colonel by the name of Suret Guseinov. Instead, Guseinov rebelled and ordered his troops to march on Baku. As Guseinov's troops approached the capital, Elchibey fled to his home base in the Nakhichevan enclave, leaving a political vacuum in Baku.

The Azerbaijani parliament now elected Geidar Aliyev to the position of Chairman of Parliament and acting head of state, then called on Guseinov to negotiate an end to his uprising. After discussions, the matter was resolved when Aliyev agreed to nominate Guseinov as prime minister, and the parliament confirmed him in this position on July 1.

In a separate move, the Azerbaijani parliament stripped Elchibey of his authority and set a referendum for August 29 so the public could decide whether they wanted him to continue as president. In the resulting referendum, more than 90 percent voted against Elchibey. Geidar Aliyev was then elected president in new elections that took place on October 3.

Desirous of bringing the war to a conclusion, Aliyev reversed his predecessor's policy toward Russia, welcoming Russian mediation in the Nagorno–Karabakh dispute and rejoining the CIS in September 1993. This eventually resulted in the cease-fire signed in 1994. Since that time, there has been only the occasional, isolated skirmish. Peace talks have been continuing in Minsk under the auspices of the OSCE, but the so–called Minsk plan is not acceptable to Armenia. President Ter–Petrossian of Armenia was, in fact, forced out of office in February 1998 after he had indicated his willingness to consider the OSCE plan. President Aliyev is in a similar situation. He has indicated that he would be willing to consider a corridor linking Armenia and Nagorno–Karabakh but he cannot go further without losing domestic support. Meanwhile, Armenia continues to occupy Azerbaijani territory while Azerbaijan has up to 800,000 refugees that it somehow has to take care of. Even so, most Azerbaijani appear to be convinced that time is on their side, and they might even be right. The large sums that have flowed into the country over the past several years in the form of foreign investment mean that a number of large western companies have a growing stake in a peace settlement. If they put pressure on their home countries to support a settlement favorable to Azerbaijan, that could have some effect.

Although President Aliyev appears to be thoroughly in control of what is still viewed as an authoritarian country, he has twice

**President Geidar Aliyev**

had to put down armed rebellions and there have been a number of attempts on his life. Such events are symptoms of a badly divided country where regional loyalties are strong and a significant percentage of the people live below the poverty line.

## Foreign Policy

Azerbaijan's foreign policy since independence has been held hostage to its relations with neighboring Armenia and the war that raged between the two countries over the status of Nagorno–Karabakh, the enclave located in western Azerbaijan which is inhabited by ethnic Armenians. Although a cease-fire has held since 1994, the two countries are still at odds over Nagorno–Karabakh's future. The OSCE has proposed a phased settlement of the conflict, withdrawing Armenian forces from territory occupied in Azerbaijan and negotiating Nagorno–Karabakh's future status, but this is unacceptable to Armenia. That situation became even more complicated in March 1998 when Robert Kocharian, the former President of Nagorno–Karabakh, was elected President of Armenia.

Under the government of President Elchibey, Azerbaijan had very poor relations with Russia, partly because of Elchibey's nationalism and partly because he believed that Russia was siding with Armenia in the dispute. Reversing this policy when he came to power in 1993, Geidar Aliyev took Azerbaijan back into the CIS, then began rebuilding relations with Russia. This has paid off in better relations with Russia, which in 1997 agreed to become one of the three co–chairs of the Minsk peace talks.

Azerbaijan's relations with the United States have never been good, largely because of the influence on U.S. foreign policy of the significant Armenian diaspora in the United States. Under this influence, the U.S. Congress instituted a ban on U.S. assistance to Azerbaijan in 1992, even as Armenia was becoming the second largest recipient of American assistance on a per capita basis. Azerbaijanis naturally interpreted this to mean that the United States had allied itself with Armenia, and this limited the influence of the U.S. Government on Azerbaijan. Accordingly, the United States played no significant role in outside attempts to bring a peaceful resolution to the conflict until 1997 when, at the urging of both Armenia and Azerbaijan, the United States assumed the role of one of the three co–chairs of the Minsk peace talks.

Azerbaijan's relations with its other neighbors are for the most part correct but not cordial. Iran, its southern neighbor, has become Armenia's largest trading partner, undercutting Azerbaijan's attempts to isolate Armenia. Religious differences are one factor, but the fact that there are about 50 million Azeris in northern Iran is another. It probably has the best relations with Turkey, which has closed its borders with Armenia in support of the Azerbaijani position on Nagorno–Karabakh.

### Nature of the Regime

Azerbaijan has completed its transition to a pluralistic political system in principle, but the political situation associated with Nagorno–Karabakh has tended to polarize the society and to make moderate political stances suspect. In one sense, Azerbaijan may have an excess of "democracy." Currently there are over 30 political parties. The three largest political groupings are the *Azerbaijan Popular Front*, the *Social Democratic Party* and the *National Independence Party*. The *National Independence Party*, led by Ikitbar Mahmedov, had been part of the *Azerbaijan Popular Front* until 1992. It split off amid accusations that the *Azerbaijan Popular Front* was abusing its power.

The present legislature was elected during the previous regime and it is a rump body of 50–members consisting of ex–communists and their opponents. It cannot be considered to be representative, but the various political forces are unwilling to hold new parliamentary elections with significant areas of the country, variously estimated currently at close to 20 percent, controlled by Armenian Karabakh forces.

### The Azerbaijan Government

Azerbaijan's government resembles that of the French Fifth Republic. There is a popularly elected President who is considered to be the spokesman for the nation. He is responsible for general policy, but has a Prime Minister who handles day–to–day affairs of government. The President is Commander–in–Chief of the armed forces. He also presides over the State Council and the Defense Council.

The Prime Minister and members of the cabinet are appointed by the President, but must be confirmed by the legislature.

### Nagorno–Karabakh

Nagorno–Karabakh, which declared itself an independent republic in December 1991 after a referendum earlier in the month had received overwhelming approval, was for many years an Armenian enclave located in Azerbaijan with the status of an Autonomous Republic. Around 180,000 Armenians live here and make up approximately 90% of the population of the republic.

They have organized their own 81 seat legislature (with 11 seats reserved for Azeris). The new head of state (whose position is chairman of the legislature) is Arthur Mkrtchyan, a man in his mid–30s who formerly had been a museum director.

Azerbaijan abolished Nagorno–Karabakh's autonomous republic status in November 1991 and has had the republic under siege since that time. It is receiving some support from Armenia, but is otherwise on its own. All CIS troops have been removed from the enclave itself, though Russian soldiers are stationed along the truce line between Nagorno–Karabakh and Azerbaijan.

Nagorno–Karabakh's current problems began in February 1988 when its regional council, feeling itself discriminated against by the Azerbaijani Government, asked that the region become part of the Armenian SSR. The matter quickly became an in-

ter–republic dispute after Armenia endorsed Nagorno–Karabakh's request. Popular demonstrations in Azerbaijan and Armenia soon turned to violence, producing hundreds of thousands of refugees on both sides.

In January 1989, with the situation as bad as ever, Moscow announced that it was suspending both Azerbaijan's control over Nagorno–Karabakh and the local provincial committee and instituting "a special form of administration" for the rebellious autonomous republic, thus putting it under Moscow's direct control.

This led to the creation of the *Azerbaijan Popular Front*, which demanded the return of Nagorno–Karabakh to Azerbaijanian jurisdiction. To back up its demand, the front organized a blockade of railway traffic going into Armenia. Moscow then gave in to the pressure and returned Nagorno–Karabakh to Azerbaijanian control in November 1989.

Russia and Kazakstan attempted to mediate the dispute between Azerbaijan and Armenia in September 1991. This produced a cease-fire agreement between Armenia and Azerbaijan, and Armenia also agreed to give up its claim to the enclave in return for a promise by the Azerbaijan leadership that it would allow free elections in Nagorno–Karabakh and bestow additional autonomy on the enclave. The agreement also called for the disarming of illegal local militias and the resettling of Armenian and Azeri refugees in their homes.

But President Mutalibov of Azerbaijan never implemented the agreement for fear of the nationalist opposition. Mutalibov had little popular support and deliberately appealed to nationalism in an attempt to outflank his nationalist opposition. When an Azerbaijani helicopter was downed in November 1991, President Mutalibov suspended talks with Armenia. He then called an emergency session of the Azerbaijan legislature, which abolished Nagorno-Karabakh's autonomous republic status.

Turkey and Iran next attempted to mediate the dispute and at least six truce agreements were actually signed during this period. None held, however. In 1992, the Conference on Security and Cooperation in Europe (CSCE) offered to sponsor new negotiations. The talks appeared to be near success at one point, and eight nations agreed to provide unarmed observers to monitor a cease-fire, but nothing came of it in the end.

The nature of the conflict then changed in 1993 when forces from Nagorno–Karabakh (with covert assistance by those from Armenia) overran significant parts of Azerbaijan. As Armenian and Karabakh forces continued to advance during the summer and fall, a large part of western Azerbaijan was overrun and occupied. This brought a rebuke from the United Nations

and a demand that Karabakh pull back from its occupied territories. Negotiations now reopened and a number of cease-fires were negotiated but it was not until 1994 that, at last, a cease-fire held. Technically the war continues, though there have been only occasional outbreaks of violence along the cease-fire line since 1994.

The CSCE has continued its mediation efforts and, in 1997, its Minsk Group, co–chaired by the United States, Russia and France, produced its most recent new peace plan. Both Armenia and Azerbaijan accepted the proposal "as a basis for peace," but Nagorno–Karabakh rejected the peace plan because it would have required Karabakh to withdraw all of its forces from Azerbaijani territory before any talks took place on Nagorno–Karabakh's final status.

The leadership of Nagorno–Karabakh has publicly stated that it is willing to trade territory for an assurance that Azerbaijan will not again invade the enclave. But Azerbaijan refuses to negotiate directly with Nagorno–Karabakh because it is unwilling to concede a separate status. President Aliyev did indicate, in July 1997, that Azerbaijan would agree to continued use of the Lachin transit corridor linking Nagorno–Karabakh and Armenia, but he made it clear that he would never accept an independent Nagorno–Karabakh.

The latest twist came in March 1998 when Robert Kocharian, a former President of Nagorno-Karabakh who had been made Prime Minister of Armenia by President Ter–Petrossian, was elected President of Armenia. Kocharian has taken the position that Armenia can never abandon its fellow Armenians in Nagorno–Karabakh.

### Culture

The Azerbaijani are historically a Shiite Moslem people, unlike their Moslem neighbors in Central Asia, who are mostly Sunni. This probably results from the fact that the area of Azerbaijan was for several centuries part of the Persian Empire. It became a part of the Russian Empire at the beginning of the 19th century, however, and the Azerbaijani became merely one of the Moslem peoples of Russia.

There was no sense of national Azerbaijani identity until fairly recently, but there have been a number of famous Azerbaijani thinkers, poets and scientists. Abul Hasan Bakhmanyar, who lived in the 11th century, wrote a number of books on mathematics and philosophy. Abul Hasan Shirvani, a later contemporary, left behind a book on astronomy. Nezami was a later poet and philosopher.

The Azerbaijani have an ancient musical tradition which has survived. Musicians improvise the words to songs as they play a stringed instrument called a *kobuz*. There are also vocal and instrumen-

# Azerbaijan

tal compositions that have been kept alive in a folk tradition.

They also have modern composers with international reputations. Two of these are Uzeir Hajjibekov, author of a number of operas, and Kara Karayev, who writes ballets. The Baku Film Studio also has an international reputation. *Little Vera,* a recent film, tells a depressing story of a young girl growing up as a member of a working–class family in Baku.

Although a large part of the population was still illiterate in 1917, modern Azerbaijan now has 16 institutes of higher education with a student population of over 100,000. The largest of these is the Azerbaijan Institute of Petroleum and Chemistry.

In January 1992, the Azerbaijan National Council passed a law adopting the Latin script for the Azerbaijani language. It acted on the basis of a recommendation from a special commission, appointed two years ago, to look into the question. The commission, made up of a number of linguists, historians, and literary specialists, concluded that the Azerbaijan language's phonetic "peculiarities are best 'superimposed' on the Latin script." Azerbaijan had used the Latin script in the 1920s but, under pressure from Moscow, went over to the Cyrillic script at the end of the thirties.

## Economy

Baku, now the capital and largest city, was the center of the oil industry of Imperial Russia. In 1901, the Baku fields produced over 11 million tons of oil, which was 50% of the world's oil production at the time. The fields lost much of their earlier significance after World War II, but the region still produced three percent of the Soviet Union's oil in 1991. Even then, Baku was still surrounded by oil derricks, though natural gas came to rival petroleum in significance in the last years of the Soviet Union.

Once a beautiful city that spread out along natural terraces running down to a gulf of the Caspian Sea, Baku was, by 1991, a grimy industrial city with terrible pollution problems. The emergence of Azerbaijan as an independent country has given the city new life, however. Today, it is the center of a boom associated with new oil fields that are being opened up on the seabed of the Caspian Sea. Recent drilling by international companies has proven oil reserves of between 15 and 20 billion barrels beneath the Caspian Sea, with the possibility that the basin might hold between 40 and 178 billion barrels. Azerbaijan's share of this treasure trove is estimated to be worth $100 billion over the next 30 years. International companies have already signed contracts with Azerbaijan worth an estimated $30 billion.

Almost all of this wealth is still years off, but the first oil from the Chirag Caspian field began flowing in November 1997.

The Chirag field was developed between 1994 and 1997 by a consortium of western oil companies plus Russia's Lukoil.

There are, however, diplomatic problems to be solved, since the countries bordering on the Caspian have not been able to agree on how to divide up the new wealth. Russia and Iran have contended that the Caspian is a saltwater lake and therefore, according to international law, its various resources can only be exploited on the basis of an agreement signed by all bordering states. Kazakhstan and Azerbaijan argue that the Caspian is a sea and its resources should therefore be divided into national sectors that each country would have the right to exploit as it pleases. Turkmenistan is divided on the issue, having sided first with Kazakhstan and Azerbaijan but then switched its position in late 1996 and is now supporting the Russian–Iranian position. This disagreement has not stopped Azerbaijan from signing agreements with international oil companies for the development of what it considers its national sector, however.

Sumgait, a city located 22 miles north of Baku, is Azerbaijan's second most important industrial center. Major chemical and oil–drilling industries are located here. In fact, Sumgait was the primary manufacturer of oil-drilling equipment in the now defunct Soviet Union. Since 95% of its customers for oil–drilling equipment were located in other parts of the Soviet Union, the area is currently suffering badly. Three other cities with significant industry are Mingechaur, Gyanja (formerly Kirovabad), and Stepanakert. Mingechaur manufactures appliances and instruments and electrical equipment of all kinds, plus textiles, shoes and other consumer goods. Gyanja and Stepanakert manufacture consumer goods, including textiles, and things like knitwear and souvenirs. All have suffered with the loss of customers in other parts of the ex–Soviet Union but certain industries, in particular those manufacturing consumer goods, have begun to recover somewhat.

Most of Azerbaijan's industry was developed to process its petroleum and natural gas supplies. Thus it has refineries producing gasoline, herbicides, industrial oils and kerosene and it also manufactures chemical fertilizers, synthetic rubber and plastics. Although many of these industries suffer from obsolete or outdated technology, they have been given a new life as Azerbaijan begins to rebuild its petroleum production.

Another issue is privatization. Azerbaijan was slow to begin the process of privatization, but it did initiate the privatization of companies with fewer than 50 employees after 1991. Approximately 15,000 such companies were sold between then and 1997, most of them to the man-

agers who had run them under communism.

Finally, in March 1997, Azerbaijan launched a mass privatization program that was supposed to result in the privatization of 70% of all enterprises by the end of 1998. This is a voucher program in which each citizen is issued a coupon book of four vouchers. (War veterans received eight vouchers.) All enterprises that are to be privatized are turned into joint–stock companies and 55% of their shares are then auctioned off for vouchers. The vouchers were distributed between March and August 1997 and voucher auctions have been held regularly since that time. By December 1997, approximately 400 large enterprises had been privatized.

All medium–scale enterprises are to be privatized, but the state intends to hold on to many large–scale enterprises. For example, the state oil company will not be privatized. Other companies that will remain in the state sector include railroads, water facilities, pension funds and the state bank. In addition, companies involved in fuel and energy production, petrochemicals, and telecommunications, plus bakeries and wineries, can only be privatized by presidential decree.

Azerbaijan is also a major producer of electric power and traditionally has exported electricity to neighboring republics. There is a handicraft industry in the South along the border with Iran. Here the Talysh, and Iranian people, live in their mountainous villages and support themselves by weaving rugs and carpets by hand in the traditional way.

Fishing is another industry that makes a major contribution to the gross domestic product, though it has declined in importance in recent years. The Caspian Sea is famous for its sturgeon, and Azerbaijan is a major source of caviar. But the sea is being rapidly polluted and the caviar supplies are quickly diminishing.

Agriculture is less significant than industry insofar as total value is concerned, but it still provides employment to over a third of the population. Cotton is the most valuable crop, followed by tobacco, grapes, vegetables, fruits and nuts. Most of the grapes are used to produce wine. There is also a small silk industry.

The Lenkoren region in southern Azerbaijan produces subtropical crops such as citrus and tea. It also produces rice and tobacco and is a major source for winter and spring vegetables.

The Nakhichevan Autonomous Republic has a semi–desert climate, but irrigation allows it to raise grapes, cotton and grain. It is also famous for its mineral water from local springs, which is bottled and sold as far away as Moscow.

**The Future**

Azerbaijan has not only suffered as a result of its war with Armenia over Nagorno–Karabakh; it has also experienced political instability and a collapsing economy. Although the war is technically not over, a cease-fire has held since 1994. President Aliyev has also brought some political stability to the country. And, lastly, the economy is starting to recover, partly fueled by large foreign investments in the petroleum industry. Azerbaijan still has its problems, but things are looking up.

The fortress at Baku (ca. 1300)

# The Republic of Georgia

**The Vorontsov Bridge across the Kura River, Tbilisi**

Courtesy: NOVOSTI

**Area:** 26,903 sq. mi. (69,700 sq. km; half the size of Wisconsin).

**Population:** 5.5 million (1989 census).

**Capital City:** Tbilisi (Pop. 1,260,000).

**Climate:** Humid, subtropical.

**Neighboring States:** Russia (north), Turkey, Armenia (south), Azerbaijan (southeast).

**Official Language:** Georgian.

**Ethnic Composition:** Georgian (69%), Armenian (9%), Russian (7%), Azerbaijanis (5.1%), others (9.9).

**Principal Religions:** Georgian Orthodox 65%; Russian Orthodox 10%.

**Chief Commercial Products:** hydroelectric power, mining, electrical equipment, metals and alloys, automobiles, electrical manufactures, instruments, Wines, fruits, tea, vegetables, livestock.

**Currency:** Lari (as of October 2, 1995).

**Per Capita Annual Income:** About U.S. $700.

**Recent Political Status:** Soviet Republic (1921), part of Transcaucasian SSR (1922–1936), Republic of the USSR (1936–1991).

**Chief of State:** Eduard Shevardnadze, President (since November 1995).

**National Flag:** Red, with a "field" in the upper left–hand corner made up of two equal horizontal stripes, black, then white.

## The Land

The Republic of Georgia is the independent successor state to the Georgian Sovi-
et Socialist Republic, which was one of the fifteen republics of the Union of Soviet Socialist Republics. The Georgia Supreme Soviet announced the republic's intention to separate from the Soviet Union in November 1990, but it was the August 1991 failed *coup* against Mikhail Gorbachëv that created a situation of *de facto* independence for Georgia. Georgia covers an area of 26,903 square miles (69,700 sq. km.) It includes The Abkhazian and Adjarian Autonomous Republics, plus the South Ossetian Autonomous Region.

Georgia lies at the eastern end of the Black Sea, just to the south of the Great Caucasus Mountains. Eighty–five percent of the country is mountainous, the exception being a small area in the west bordering on the Black Sea known as the Kolkhida Lowland. This is the site of ancient Colchis, where Jason and the Argonauts sought the golden fleece. The Kolkhida Lowland is a delta region formed by the deposits of three rivers that flow through the area, the Inguri, Rioni, and Kodori. It was once mostly swampland, but drainage projects have turned it into a major producer of subtropical crops and winter

158

vegetables. Here winter temperatures average 41°F. and there is a plentiful year–round rainfall.

Behind Kolkhida, the land rises until it reaches two saddle ridges which connect the Great Caucasus and the Little Caucasus Mountains. Beyond that is a high plateau which runs eastward to the border of Azerbaijan. This high plateau, known as the Kartalinian Plain, is the heartland of Georgia. Most of it is covered by a loess type soil. Drier than the western coast, it nevertheless gets sufficient rainfall to sustain agriculture. In addition, the Kura River flows down out of the Little Caucasus in the southwest and then eastward across the plateau, providing plenty of water for irrigation. Open to the warm, moist air from the Black Sea and protected on the north by the wall of the Great Caucasus Mountains, the Kartalinian Plain has winters warm enough that citrus groves thrive. The high mountains to the north and south of this plateau are covered with forests of oak, chestnut, beech, ash, linden, alder, and Caucasian fir. Fruit trees also abound, including apples, pears, and various kinds of nuts. Dairying is practiced on the lower slopes of the mountains and on parts of the plateau. Vineyards are also widely cultivated. Grapes are sold fresh or turned into wine, brandy, or champagne. The eastern part of the country consists of the Alasari River Valley plus a saddleland to the south between that valley and the Kara River Valley. This area receives only between 16 and 28 inches of rainfall and therefore makes use of the water from the Alasari River for irrigation.

## The People

Georgia's population as of the 1989 census was 5.5 million. Georgians make up approximately 69% of the population. The two largest minorities are Armenians (9%) and Russians (7.4%). Azerbaijanis come next (5.1%), followed by Ossetians (3.2%), Abkhazians (2%) and others (4.3%).

Georgia is an ancient center of civilization. Archaeological excavations place the beginning of the bronze age here as early as 3,000 B.D. The ancestors of the Georgian people emerged for the first time in the first millennium B.C. in the annals of the Assyrian Empire. The Georgian language itself is classified as one of the Caucasian languages, meaning that, as far as it known, the Georgians originated here.

Among the Georgian tribes were the Kulkha (Colchians), who once dominated most of the eastern shores of the Black Sea. Their city, Colchis, was known for its fabulous wealth and gave rise to the legend of Medea and the golden fleece. Colchis was later colonized by Greeks and still later incorporated into the Roman Empire.

## History

Georgia converted to Christianity about the year 330. Over the next three centuries it became a battlefield between the Byzantine Empire and Persia. However, in 654 it fell to the Arqab caliphs, who established an emirate in Tbilisi. In reaction to the Arab presence, the various Georgian tribes united around a princely family long prominent in the affairs of Armenia, and this family eventually brought most of Georgia under its sway. King Bagrat III (975–1014) ruled all of Georgia except for the Tbilisi emirate, and that was conquered in the year 1122 by one of his descendants, King David II ("the Builder").

The Georgian Kingdom reached its zenith under Queen Tamara (1184–1213), when it included most of the Caucasus.

The end came in 1220 with the appearance of the Mongols from the east. Eastern Georgia became part of the Mongol Empire, with only the area west of the mountains along the Black Sea maintaining its independence. The decline of the Mongol Empire brought part of the high central plateau back under Georgian control, but the new kingdom was destroyed by a fresh onslaught by Tamerlane, who created a great empire stretching across Central Asia.

The fall of Constantinople to the Ot-

**An artist's concept of the medieval fortress of Queen Tamara in the towering Caucasus Mountains**

# Georgia

toman Turks in 1453 isolated Georgia. In the sixteenth century, it, too, was incorporated into the Turkish Empire. The Turks were in turn driven out by Shah Abba I (1587–1629) ruler of the Persian Empire. In the process, thousands of Georgian Christians were transported to distant parts of the Persian Empire. There was a brief respite after 1658, when the Persians installed the House of Mukhran as viceroys at Tbisili, but this was brought to an end by a fresh Turkish invasion in 1722. The Persians expelled the Turks twenty–two years later. Another kingdom based on Georgia was installed by the Persians and lasted until near the end of the eighteenth century.

In 1783, Erekle, the Georgian king, signed the Treaty of Georgievsk with Catherine the Great, whereby Russia guaranteed Georgia's independence and territorial integrity in return for Erekle's acceptance of Russian authority. When Georgia was invaded by Persia in 1795, however, Russia offered no assistance. Tbilisi was sacked in 1795 and Erekle died three years later. His son, George XII, offered the kingdom to Paul, the Russian Tsar. Paul died before the treaty could be signed, so it was Alexander I who incorporated Georgia into the Russian Empire. In spite of the treaty of 1783, Alexander I then deposed George XII and replaced him with Russian military governors. Erekle's kingdom had included only the areas of Kartalinia and Kakhetia, so other parts of Georgia were incorporated in the Russian Empire between 1810 and 1864. The Black Sea ports of Poti and Batumi were added at the time of the Russo–Turkish War of 1877–78.

Georgia's incorporation into the Russian Empire provoked a number of popular uprisings at various times, but it did have the merit of ensuring the corporate survival of the Georgian nation. Georgia also benefited economically and culturally from its connection with Russia. A railroad connecting Tbilisi with Poti on the Black Sea opened in 1872 and mines, factories and commercial farms were established with Russian and foreign capital. Alexander II's reforms also included the end of serfdom and the spread of education. Alexander III's policy of Russification fostered nationalism among the middle–class intelligentsia, however, and marked the beginning of a national revival.

A number of illegal nationalist groups were founded in the 1890s, the most important of which was the "Third Group," a Marxist group affiliated with the *Russian Social Democratic Party*. In 1898, the Third Group recruited Joseph Dzhugashvili, better known by his later revolutionary name, Joseph Stalin. Five years later, Stalin became a Bolshevik when the *Russian Social Democratic Party* separated into Bol-

shevik and Menshevik factions at its second congress. The Georgian Marxist party, on the other hand, was controlled by Mensheviks.

Georgia saw widespread disturbances and guerrilla fighting during the 1905 Russian uprising, but these were put down by Cossacks in 1906. After the 1917 Revolution, an autonomous Transcaucasian committee was established under the authority of the Provisional Government. After the Bolshevik Revolution in the fall, however, this Transcaucasian committee, which was dominated by Mensheviks, broke with the national government and established the Transcaucasian Federal Republic on April 22, 1918. When this collapsed a month later, the Georgian National Council set up the *Georgian Social Democratic Republic.* The republic was under German protection for a while, but then was occupied by the British. The Georgians refused to cooperate with the British, however, and the latter departed Batumi in July 1920.

Georgia had signed a treaty with the Russians in May 1920, and this allowed the Bolsheviks to dispatch a mission under S. M. Kirov to Tbilisi. Kirov's task was to undermine the Menshevik regime and prepare for a Bolshevik *coup.* It received diplomatic recognition from the Allies in January 1921. One month later, a Red Army under the control of two Georgian Bolshevik leaders, Joseph Stalin and G. K. Ordzhonikidze, entered Georgia. A Soviet regime was installed on February 25.

Georgia was incorporated into the Transcaucasian Soviet Federated Socialist Republic in March 1922. This became a part of the Union of Soviet Socialist Republics on December 30, 1922.

Stalin, who was People's Commissar for Nationalities in the Moscow government, was determined to stamp out nationalist tendencies among his Georgian compatriots and carried out a purge of active nationalists, including even members of the *Georgian Communist Party.*

The Transcaucasian SFSR was formally dissolved in December 1936 when the Union of Soviet Socialist Republics adopted a new constitution and the Georgian Soviet Socialist Republic became one of the constituent republics in its own right. It was at this time that another Georgian Communist, Lavrenti P. Beria, rose to prominence when he was named head of the Soviet secret police, at that time known as the NKVD. Beria remained a top member of the CPSU until after Stalin's death in March 1953. He was then accused of planning a *coup* against the rest of the party leadership and was executed.

Georgia certainly derived some benefits from its participation in the Union of Soviet Socialist Republics. Illiteracy was wiped out, schools of higher education were set up, a Georgian Academy of Sci-

ences was established, and a great deal of industry was built. Yet the price was conformity to Marxist–Leninist ideology and a suppression of traditional Georgian culture.

When Gorbachëv launched his policy of *glasnost* after he took over in 1985, therefore, one of his early supporters was Eduard Schevardnadze, first secretary of the Georgian Communist Party from 1972 to 1985. Schevardnadze, made a full member of the Politburo and Minister of Foreign Affairs, became a strong voice at the center urging on Gorbachëv the necessity for further reforms.

Gorbachëv's reforms were endorsed and exploited as much in Georgia as any part of the Soviet Union. The *Georgia Communist Party* soon found itself outbid by Georgian nationalists, who did not have to worry about loyalty to Moscow. When Gorbachëv decided to permit real elections in 1989, the nationalists were given their chance. A seven party coalition called *Round Table–Free Georgia* managed to win 62% of the seats in the October 1990 republic elections. They took control of the Georgian Supreme Soviet, then elected a longtime nationalist dissident and anti–Communist, Zviad Gamsakhurdia, as Georgia's head of state. At the same time, they changed the name of the country to the Republic of Georgia and announced the beginning of a transition to full independence. Gamsakhurdia, founder of the Georgian Helsinki Group, had been jailed in 1977 by the former Brezhnev regime. He was imprisoned again in 1989, after Soviet special forces fired on peaceful demonstrators outside the parliament building, killing more than 20 persons.

In April 1991, the Supreme Soviet declared Georgia's independence, then changed the constitution to create a popularly elected, executive President. In the elections that took place on May 26, 1991, Gamsakhurdia won 86.5 percent of the vote. Valerian Advadze, who accused Gamsakhurdia of planning to turn Georgia into a personal dictatorship, came in second with 7.6 percent of the vote. Jimmy Mikeladze, head of the Georgia Communist Party, got 1.6 percent. Two other candidates polled less than two percent of the vote. It appeared that democracy had triumphed in Georgia.

Almost immediately after this overwhelming vote of confidence, however, Gamsakhurdia began to take actions that lent credence to the charge that he indeed wanted to create a personal dictatorship. A law signed by Gamsakhurdia made "maligning" the president a crime punishable by six years in prison. Gamsakhurdia also accused reporters of lying and had them thrown out of a news conference. And he began an attempt to remove the political autonomy enjoyed by Moslem

# Georgia

**Centenarian dancers of *Narta'a* go to give a concert**    Courtesy: NOVOSTI

South Ossetians in the north of the country.

When the attempted *coup* against Gorbachëv began in August 1991, Gamsakhurdia promised *coup* leaders that he would cause no trouble in Georgia and then issued an appeal to Georgians to remain calm; this caused a split in the government coalition. Tengiz Sigua, the prime minister, and Gyorghi Khoshtaria, the foreign minister, opposed the *coup* and may have been privately critical of Gamsakhurdia's policy of inaction. As a result, Gamsakhurdia dismissed both of them in the days following collapse of the *coup*. When the two dismissals led to popular demonstrations in the main square of Tbilisi on September 2, Gamsakhurdia ordered the national guard to fire on the demonstrators.

But when Gamsakhurdia ordered Tengiz Ketovani, commander of the national guard, to use force against subsequent demonstrations, the latter refused. Gamsakhurdia then attempted to fire him also, but he refused to recognize the dismissal. In the meantime, the situation in South Ossetia deteriorated after Gamsakhurdia abolished its autonomous status. By September, there had been over a hundred deaths in the area and 50,000 Ossetians had fled over the mountains to North Ossetia, in the Russian Federation.

As daily demonstrations against Gamsakhurdia continued in Tbilisi, members of the government coalition began to go over to the opposition. Gamsakhurdia then had Georgi Chanturia, leader of the opposition *National Democratic Party*, arrested. The charge was that he and Eduard Shevardnadze were plotting a *coup* to overthrow the government.

This brought additional demonstrations, now led by Tengiz Sigua and Tengiz Ketovani, demanding Gamsakhurdia's resignation. On September 22, anti-Gamsakhurdia demonstrators seized control of the government radio and televi-

sion station. They were later joined by members of the Georgia national guard. Following this, more than ten thousand demonstrators marched on government house to demand President Gamsakhurdia's resignation. Meanwhile, Gamsakhurdia supporters harassed the demonstrators from the sidelines. Later, they, in turn, occupied the opposition party offices.

The next three months were punctuated by a series of riots, shootings and demonstrations. Through it all, Gamsakhurdia remained penned up in the parliament building. In late December, then, a major battle broke out. After two weeks, Gamsakhurdia fled the country on January 6, going first to Armenia, then making his way to western Georgia. Here, where he had lived prior to coming to power, he rallied his supporters and attempted, without success, to force his way back to power. He continued to have some support in the country, but not enough to return.

Meanwhile in Tbilisi the victorious opposition set up a Military Council to govern the country. Tengiz Sigua was installed as provisional Prime Minister while Tengiz Ketovani continued as commander of the national guard.

Soon after that, rumors began that Eduard Shevardnadze would return to Georgia and reenter Georgia politics. Schevardnadze refused to either affirm or deny the rumors, but he did congratulate Georgians "on this victory" after Gamsakhurdia fled Tbilisi. In February, however, he agreed to serve as honorary chairman of an opposition umbrella group called the *Democratic Union*. The Military Council then publicly announced that it would welcome Shevardnadze's return. In early March, the Military Council called a meeting of the legislature and relinquished power to that body. The legislature created a governing State Council to run the country until elections could take

place. On March 10, Shevardnadze was elected chairman of the State Council.

New elections were held in October 1992. A new legislature was selected and Shevardnadze was elected to the office of Speaker of the State Council. He ran unopposed. In spite of his new title, however, Shevardnadze had to share power with his Prime Minister, Tengiz Sigua, and his Defense Minister, Tengiz Ketovani, the two men who arranged for his installation as chairman of the State Council in the first place. Meanwhile, Gamsakhurdia continued to have support in certain parts of the country, particularly in north–western Georgia, so unrest continued in the country. Gamsakhurdia's supporters even organized a coup to overthrow Shevardnadze in June 1992, though they only managed to seize the television tower and were easily routed by Georgia national guard troops.

Former President Gamsakhurdia launched a new attempt to come back to power in November 1992. The insurrection was only put down after Russian troops were deployed on the railway running through the area. Gamsakhurdia fled across the border into North Ossetia, where he later committed suicide.

### Georgia's Sesessionist Movements.

Shevardnadze inherited two secessionist movements from his predecessor, one of which he has managed to solve and another which has continued to give him difficulties. The first of these, South Ossetia, was tied in with North Ossetia's wish to separate from Russia. Tengiz Ketovani, defense minister and head of the Georgian National Guard, ordered an attack on Tskhinvali, the capital of South Ossetia in May 1992. Shevardnadze preferred a negotiated settlement, however, and responded favorably when President Yeltsin offered to mediate the dispute. This eventually produced a negotiated ceasefire and a joint Russian-Georgian–Ossetian force to police the peace.

The second, Abkhazia, began originally in 1990 when Abkhazian nationalists demanded greater local autonomy. In August 1992, the Abkhazian legislature voted to reinstate the region's 1925 constitution, in effect asserting its independence. Several Georgian officials were also kidnaped in the Abkhazia area. In August, Shevardnadze sent in a force of 3,000 men armed with tanks and helicopter gunships to take control of the capital city of Sukhumi. There was resistance and approximately 10 Abkhazians were killed in street fighting. More were killed somewhat later. The Abkhazian Government, headed by Vladislav Ardzinba, fled the capital, and Georgia faced the possibility of a long period of guerrilla warfare. When President Yeltsin offered to mediate this dis-

# Georgia

pute, however, Shevardnadze accepted and in September he and Vladislav Ardzinba signed a cease–fire agreement.

The cease–fire did not hold, however. Fighting broke out again in October and the Abkhazians, this time supported by other mountain tribes of the Caucasus plus some Russian Cossacks, managed to gain control over a large part of northwest Abkhazia.

Russia mediated a new cease-fire in the summer of 1993 which required heavy weapons and most of the soldiers to be withdrawn from both sides. The Georgian Government complied, but the Abkhazians did not. After the Georgian troops had been withdrawn from the area, the Abkhazians launched an attack on Sukhumi, the regional capital. Shevardnadze personally flew to Sukhumi to organize the defense, but the situation was hopeless. Sukhumi fell on September 27.

Since it was clear that the Abkhazians were receiving military assistance from Russian units stationed in the area, Shevardnadze had earlier appealed to General Grachev, commander of Russian and CIS forces, to stop the attack. Grachev offered to send three divisions to separate the two sides, but Shevardnadze turned down the offer, fearing that the Russians would turn into an occupation force. On the night before Sukhumi fell, however, Shevardnadze agreed to General Grachev's proposal and also offered to join the Commonwealth of Independent States.

In February 1994, President Yeltsin flew to Tbilisi, accompanied by General Grachev, to sign a treaty, under whose terms Georgia not only joined the CIS but also granted Russia the right to establish military bases within the country; in turn, Russia agreed to train and arm the Georgian army and to provide Georgia with 40 billion rubles ($25 million) in trade credits. After Georgia's entry into the CIS, it was agreed that a CIS peacekeeping force should be stationed along a 13 km. stretch of the Inguri River, which marks the internal border between Abkhazia and the rest of Georgia. Its purpose was to expedite the return of an estimated 200,000 ethnic Georgians who had fled from Abkhazia when fighting broke out in 1992–93. This force, which consists entirely of Russian soldiers, was installed in July 1994. It had no success in facilitating the return of ethnic Georgians to Abkhazia, however.

Later in the year, the United Nations brokered a peace agreement whereby refugees from the fighting in 1993 and early 1994 were to be permitted to return to their homes and talks were to begin on a political settlement. The resulting talks between the Georgian Government and Abkhazia continued until November but broke down when the Abkhazian parliament adopted a constitution declaring the region to be a "sovereign democratic state." In addition, on December 6, Vladislav Ardzinba was inaugurated as president. Reports now began to circulate that both sides had begun stockpiling arms. The situation remained quiet, however, possibly because neither side wanted to be labelled an aggressor by the 134–member UN observer group sent to monitor the peace arrangements.

The next development came on February 10, 1995, when the Abkhazian leadership announced that it was abandoning its demands for complete independence from Georgia because of what had happened when Russia invaded Chechnya. Based on those events, the Abkhazian leadership said, it had concluded that the West would do nothing to help independence–seekers and nothing to stop them from being crushed. Later, the Abkhazian leadership reverted to its pro–independence position after it became clear that Russia would be unable to reassert its control in Chechnya.

In March 1997, Russia backed a resolu-

**Picking citrus fruit on a state farm near Batum, Georgia**　　　Courtesy: NOVOSTI

**Farmers graze flocks high up in the Caucasus mountains**

Courtesy: NOVOSTI

tion at the CIS heads of state summit that extended the geographical area in which the CIS peacekeeping force operated and gave them more extensive powers to protect refugees attempting to return to their homes in Abkhazia. The Abkhazian leadership refused to recognize the legitimacy of the 1997 CIS resolution, however, so almost no refugees managed to return to their homes.

Angered, President Shevardnadze threatened to veto the extension of the mandate of the CIS peacekeeping force when it came up for renewal on July 31, 1997. In addition, the Georgian parliament passed a resolution in May 1997 suggesting that Georgia leave the CIS if the 1997 CIS resolution were not implemented. Alarmed, President Yeltsin invited Shevardnadze and Abkhazian President Vladislav Ardzinba to meet with him in Moscow on August 2 for "one last serious talk." Russia announced, at the same time, that only the CIS could cancel the mandate of the CIS peacekeeping force, so that meant that the force would remain in place at least until the next CIS meeting in October. Shevardnadze accepted Yeltsin's invitation to come to Moscow, as did the Abkhazian leadership. Although Russia

attempted to get the two sides to sign a peace protocol at the Moscow talks, both sides refused, so the meeting was essentially a failure.

The United Nations also became actively involved in the Georgia–Abkhaz dispute once again during the summer of 1997. In July, the UN Secretary–General asked the United States, Germany, France and the U.K. to form a Friends of Georgia group (Russia was invited as an observer) to provide a new venue for talks. This group sponsored a series of meetings between Georgia and Abkhazia which at least got the two sides to promise not to use violence or the threat of violence against each other. Georgia refused to lift its economic sanctions against Abkhazia, however, and Abkhazia refused to allow the repatriation of refugees.

The Friends of Georgia group then invited the two principals to another round of talks in Geneva on November 17–19. At Geneva, the Georgian and Abkhaz delegations agreed to create a coordinating commission with three working groups that would focus on security issues, repatriation, and economic and social issues. These working groups have been meeting on a regular basis since November 1997,

but there has been no breakthrough. In March 1998, Georgia signaled its impatience at the lack of progress by suggesting that it would present a draft plan to the CIS summit in Moscow on March 19–20 calling for a special administrative region in Abkhazia's Gali district to facilitate the return of refugees.

**Shevardnadze Consolidates His Power.**

By the beginning of 1995, Shevardnadze had begun to assert a greater leadership role in the country. It also helped that, with the end of the civil war, Georgia was beginning to turn around again economically. That summer, Shevardnadze and his supporters pushed through a new constitution which established a presidential-parliamentary system. Elections for the presidency and a new parliament were set for November.

In August 1995, as things seemed to moving toward a new era of political stability under a strong and popular president, several persons attempted to assassinate Shevardnadze by throwing bombs at his vehicle. Although the instigators were never definitely identified, the Georgian Government accused Igor Giorgadze,

# Georgia

**Tea leaves are harvested from tea–bush fields**

Courtesy: NOVOSTI

a former Security Minister, of being behind the attempt on Shevardnadze's life. He was never arrested because he managed to get out of the country before he could be taken into custody. He made his way to Moscow and has been there ever since.

After the assassination attempt, Shevardnadze won the presidency with approximately 70 percent of the vote; in addition, the Union of Citizens Party, the political party Shevardnadze had founded, won a dominant position in the new parliament as well. Since that time, Shevardnadze has been the dominant voice in Georgian politics.

Perhaps that explains the new attempt on President Shevardnadze's life that occurred on February 9, 1998, the second attempt on his life within 2 1/2 years. President Shevardnadze was returning to his residence in his limousine, a bullet–proof Mercedes provided by the German Government, when his vehicle was fired on by a several–man hit team armed with high caliber weaponry. In the battle that ensued, two presidential guards and one attacker were killed. Five suspects arrested six days later were identified as supporters of ex–President Gamsakhurdia. The government eventually identified approximately fifteen possible plotters, most of them Gamsakhurdia supporters. But it is still not clear what the motives of the assailants might have been or who they might have been working for. Gamsakhurdia is, of course, dead, so killing Shevardnadze would not have brought their faction back to power. Nevertheless, a group of approximately 20 individuals who identified themselves as Gamsakhurdia supporters abducted four members of the UN observer mission in Zugdidi on February 19 and demanded the release of seven men arrested in connection with the assassination attempt. The UN hostages were released six days later, on February 25, after talks between President Shevardnadze and Nemo Burchuladze, who had

been deputy parliamentary leader under former President Gamsakhurdia. Burchuladze, who has been in exile in Russia since the fall of the Gamsakhurdia regime, was given immunity for the duration of the talks.

## Foreign Policy

Under Gamsakhurdia, Georgia was a maverick nation. It not only refused to join the Commonwealth of Independent States; it also attempted to sever all ties with the other former Soviet republics. Since Gamsakhurdia also began to act in an authoritarian manner domestically, he was soon faced with a civil war, which eventually drove him from power. The United States withheld diplomatic recognition while Gamsakhurdia was president; after Shevardnadze was installed as chairman of the State Council, however, the United States formally recognized Georgia. An embassy was opened in April 1992 and Secretary of State Baker paid an official visit to Tbilisi in May. Relations between the two countries have been good since that time.

Shevardnadze began working for a better working relationship with Russia from the moment he returned to power in Georgia, but it was not until the fall of Sukhumi in September 1993 that he agreed to more formal ties. A new treaty signed in February 1994 gave Georgia membership in the Commonwealth of Independent States and tied her to Russia militarily.

Georgia's continued struggles with its breakaway province of Abkhazia have also played an important role in its relations with Russia. Prior to 1994, Russia was inclined to support Abkhazia's attempts to break away. When Georgia agreed to join the CIS and to allow Russia to establish military bases within the country, however, Russia's position changed and, in early 1996, Russia even agreed, at the urging of the Georgian Government, to impose economic sanctions on

Abkhazia. Since then, Russia has generally supported the Georgian position on Abkhazia.

## Nature of the Regime

Georgia adopted a new constitution in 1995 which established a presidential-parliamentary system. Eduard Shevardnadze was elected the new president with approximately 70% of the vote in elections that took place in November 1995; a new 250–seat legislature was elected at the same time. Shevardnadze is the founder of the center–right *Union of Citizens* Party, which also won a dominant position in the new parliament.

## Culture

Georgia is a land of ancient culture, a surprising amount of which has survived, considering that it was for centuries a battleground between the Persian and Byzantine Empires and, later, the Ottoman Empire. Georgian architecture is particularly interesting because of the role it played in the development of the Byzantine style of architecture.

Georgia has also had a written language since the fifth century A.D., and there are a number of great works which have survived. The earliest of these is an epic masterpiece from the twelfth century by the poet Shota Rustaveli, called *The Knight in the Tiger's Skin*. A cultural renaissance at the end of the nineteenth century produced a number of poets, including Ilia Chavchavadze, Akaki Tsereteli, Vazha Pshavela, novelists such as Alexander Qazbegi, and writers like Mikheil Javakhishvili, Paolo Iashvili, Titsian Tabidze, Giorgi Leonidze and Irakli Abashidze.

Most of these artists were later executed by Stalin when he decided in the 1930s to stamp out Georgian nationalism in his native state. Georgia has also produced important painters (Niko Pirosmanashvili, Irikli Toidze) and composers (Zakaria Paliashvili, Meliton Balanchivadze). Vakhtang Chabukiani was the founder of the Georgian national ballet. There is also a vibrant Georgian theater and film industry. *Resurrection*, a recent surrealistic film about a Stalin–like dictator, was one specifically Georgian contribution to *glasnost*.

Nor should one forget Zviad Gamsakhurdia, the first anti–communist leader of the country, elected in 1990 and forced out as President at the beginning of 1992. Gamsakhurdia, the son of Georgia's best-known modern novelist, was a leading Georgian author in his own right, as well as a translator. Among the authors he translated are Shakespeare and Baudelaire. Tengiz Sigua, currently the provisional Prime Minister, was a professor before he entered politics, while Tengiz Ketovani, is a sculptor.

Georgia has one major university, Tbil-

# Georgia

isi State University, which was founded in 1918. In addition, the Georgia Academy of Sciences, established in 1941, consists of a number of scientific institutions which conduct research throughout the republic. There is also an extensive library system.

## Economy

Georgian industry has four main branches—mineral extraction, machine-building, chemicals and textiles. Extensive coal deposits have been developed along the southern slopes of the Great Caucasus Mountains, particularly at Tkvarcheli and Tkibuli. Georgia also has petroleum and some natural gas. Other minerals include manganese and talc.

The machine–building industry produces railway locomotives, heavy vehicles, several types of planes, and earth moving equipment, but it also produces things like lathes and precision instruments. The chemical industry produces pharmaceuticals, synthetic fibers and mineral fertilizers. The textile industry produces cotton, woolen and silk fabrics and some clothing.

Agriculture contributes importantly to the economy, in spite of the fact that agricultural land is in short supply and much of it is located along mountain slopes. Major crops tend, therefore, to be labor intensive—and with a higher cash value—such as citrus fruits, tea and nuts. Georgia produced 97% of the citrus fruits and 92% of the tea of the now defunct Soviet Union. Georgia was also a major exporter of wines, brandy and champagne to other parts of the Soviet Union, though here Armenia is a major competitor and Azerbaijan produces wines as well. Georgia was

also a significant exporter of dairy products and canned foods. Other major agricultural products include sugar beets, tobacco, perfume oils, poultry, bees and silkworms. With independence and the collapse of the Soviet Union, Georgia's problem now will be how to retain those markets for its traditional agricultural surplus.

This state has great potential for tourism. It already has several resorts and sanatoria located on the Black Sea coast, some of which are famous for their mineral springs. In the interior, there are many monasteries and churches which qualify as architectural monuments.

The Georgian economy suffered terribly in the first years after independence, however. The gross domestic product (GDP) dropped by nearly 73 percent between 1991 and 1994 and inflation soared at 1,500%. Georgia was forced out of the ruble zone in late 1992 and for the next three years they made do with "coupons" issued by the state.

During those years, anecdotal evidence portrayed an economy in deep collapse. In Tbilisi, the subway didn't run most of the time because of a lack of electricity. Buildings also remained unheated for the same reason. A female computer operator, earning the equivalent of $12 a month, commented that "that's a very good salary." Yet she also reported that butter was selling for the equivalent of $5 a pound. An academic at the Institute of Philosophy at the Georgian Academy of Sciences reported that his monthly salary was the equivalent of $3.

When Shevardnadze first took over, his government was tied down by a civil war

so it was not immediately able to launch a program of reform. The economy stabilized in 1995, then grew by 11 percent in 1996. It grew by 11.3 percent in 1997. Inflation was 7.9 percent in 1997, down from 13.8 percent the previous year. The currency, the Lari, has been stabile since its introduction in October 1995. The average monthly wage, although still low, has begun to climb and now stands at about $50 a month.

On the financial front, the banking system has been strengthened. Privatization, launched in 1995, then temporarily halted by a presidential decree in 1966, was re-launched in July 1997 when 266 enterprises were sold. Foreign direct investment, still small, was $105.3 million as of October 1997. Among the firms that foreign investors have bought are a brewery, a bottler, and a producer of sparkling wine.

Georgia will still have a budget deficit of approximately 2 percent of GDP in 1998, though this is down from 4.4 percent of GDP in 1997. The IMF and World Bank, along with the EU and the United States, are helping to finance Georgia's current account deficit. Georgia's foreign debt stood at about $1.485 billion as of October 1997. Although data on imports and exports is unreliable, it appears that Georgia's trade deficit was approximately $600 million in 1997.

It is obvious that Georgia still has a distance to go before it gets on its feet economically, but it is, at least, moving in the right direction.

### The Future

Georgia's greatest problem after independence was its lack of political stability. With the situation in Abkhazia still unsettled, Georgia will find it difficult to attract foreign direct investment and this will retard any significant improvement in the economy. Shevardnadze has brought some political stability to the country, but the recent attempt on his life, the second attempt in two and a half years, puts a question mark on the future. As everybody says, Georgia has great potential as an independent country, provided it can work out its political problems. But no one says how the leadership might go about doing that.

**Traditional cuisine restaurant in Tbilisi**　　Courtesy: NOVOSTI

# CENTRAL ASIAN REPUBLICS (of the former Soviet Union)

Due to their shared histories as well as frequent geographical and cultural similarities, there is necessarily some repetition from one entry to the other.

Showing principal cities and railroads

# The Republic of Kazakstan

**Area:** 1,049,155 sq. mi. (2,717,300 sq. km., almost twice the size of Alaska, second largest state in the former USSR).

**Population:** approximately 16 million as of December 1997.

**Capital City:** Akmola or Aqmola (Pop. 270,000) Akmola was designated the new capital in 1995 and the government formally moved to the new capital in December 1997. Most of the government ministries, as well as most foreign embassies, remain in Almaty, however.

**Climate:** Continental, with very hot summers and extremely cold winters.

**Neighboring States:** Russia (west and north), China (east), Kyrgyzstan, Uzbekistan, Turkmenistan (south).

**Principal Languages:** Kazak and Russian.

**Ethnic Composition:** Kazakh (51%); Russian (32%); German (2%); Ukrainian (5%); Other (10%).

**Principal Religions:** Islam, Christianity (Orthodox). Until recently, religious worship was officially discouraged.

**Chief Commercial Products:** Agriculture—grain, livestock production. Industry—Oil. Kazakhstan was the second–largest oil producer in the former USSR. The republic is also very rich in mineral resources.

**Currency:** Tenge (issued November 1993).

**Annual Per Capita Income:** About U.S. $1,800.

**Recent Political Status:** The Kazak SSR was formally a part of the Russian Soviet Federative Republic (RSFFR) but in December 1936 it was proclaimed a separate constituent republic of the former USSR, remaining in that status until 1991.

**Chief of State:** Nursultan Nazarbayev, President.

**National Flag:** A golden sun rising above mountains superimposed upon a sky-blue background, with the left edge showing a stylized pattern in worked gold.

### The Land

The Republic of Kazakhstan, successor government to the Kazakh Soviet Socialist Republic, declared its independence on December 16, 1991. The Kazakh Soviet Socialist Republic had existed only since December 1936. Its predecessor was the Kirghiz (later renamed Kazakh) Autonomous Soviet Socialist Republic, which had been founded in August 1920 as an autonomous republic of the Russian SFSR.

In spite of its size, Kazakhstan is geographically rather homogeneous. Essentially it is a great tableland, with lowlands, plains and plateaus making up approximately 80 percent of the landscape. Mountainous regions in the east and southeast make up the remaining parts of the land.

Kazakstan is actually a Eurasian land, with its western border beginning at the northern end of the Caspian Sea, just east of the mouth of the Volga River. It then turns slightly west and runs northward just east of the Volga River before bending northeast and skirting the southern edges of the Ural Mountains. East of the Urals, it zig–zags north until it passes the

166

# Kazakhstan

Russian city of Magnitogorsk before turning eastward. After passing just south of the city of Omsk, it turns southeastward and pushes to the top ridge of the Altai Mountains. It then turns at a sharp angle and runs in a southwestern direction along the ridges of the Tarbagatay Range and the Ulu–Tau Mountains until it passes just south of the republic's capital of Almaty. Here it turns westward and runs along the foothills, crossing the Syr–Darya River, until just north of Samarkand. It then crosses the Kyzylkum Desert and passes through the center of the Aral Sea, bending from there southward to reach the center of the Caspian Sea.

The western portion of the republic is dominated by the Caspian Depression. The Mogodzhar Hills, a southern extension of the Ural Mountains, separates the Caspian Depression from the Turan Plain, which stretches west–east just north of the Aral Sea. To the east of the Aral Sea is the Kyzylkum Desert. To the northeast of that, separated by the valley of the Syr–Darya River, is an area called the Hunger Steppe. These areas in the south are all desert and only the presence of the Syr–Darya River makes any agriculture possible. The northern part of Kazakhstan is known as the Kazakh Steppe, however, and here there is sufficient rainfall to support grasses. The northern part of Kazakhstan is an area of farms that concentrate on growing wheat and other cereal crops.

Some irrigation is also possible in this northern area, using water from the Ural River in the west and the Irtysh River in the east. Two smaller rivers, the Ishim and Tobol, also provide water for irrigation. Overall, the republic has over 7,000 streams and rivers, plus about 48,000 small lakes. Kazakhstan also has 1,450 miles of coastline along the Caspian Sea.

The weather is sharply continental, with cold winters and hot summers. Temperatures in the southern part of Kazakhstan are much milder, however, with January temperatures averaging 23–29°F. Average July temperatures are 68° in the north and 84° in the south. The area of the North had rich, black soils; south of that the soils are chestnut-brown, but still fertile. In the extreme South, soils tend to be infertile and alkaline, or sandy desert. Woodlands, found most in the mountains, make up only 3% of the total land surface.

## The People

The population of Kazakhstan has been shrinking since the collapse of the Soviet Union and now stands at just under 16 million, down from 16,538,000 at the time of the 1989 census. The reason for the drop in population has been an out-migration of approximately one million Russians and 600,000 ethnic Germans since 1991. Meanwhile, the number of ethnic Kazakhs has grown by 1.5 million during this period. As a result, ethnic Kazakhs now constitute 51% of the population, making them the majority group in Kazakhstan for the first time since the 1950s. Russians, who were 40% of the population as of the 1989 census, have slipped to 32%. Ethnic Germans, 6% of the population in 1989, are now under 2%. Nearly a hundred nationalities make up the remaining 15%, among them Ukrainians, Tatars, Uzbeks, Belarusians, Uighurs, Dungans and Koreans. The Kazakh people, who are mainly Moslem, speak a Turkic language, but are Mongol in physical appearance.

## History

The first reference to Kazakhs living in Central Asia is found in a Russian source dated 1534. Subsequently, the Russians referred to these people as Kaisak–Kirgiz or simply Kirgiz. Undoubtedly, the reason for this is that the Russian word *Kazaky* means Cossacks and it describes Russian peasants living on the frontier. It appears, in fact, that modern Kazakhs are descendants of the old Kipchak tribes, which were part of the East–Central Asian "Golden Horde."

In the 15th century, there was a Kazakh Empire that controlled the steppe land to the east of the Caspian Sea and north of the Aral Sea stretching as far east as the western approaches of the Altai Mountains. This empire lasted until the beginning of the 18th century, but then was weakened by attacks from a revived Oyrat Empire to the east. The Kazakhs were at this time organized into three principalities, the "Little Horde," "Middle Horde" and Great Horde.

When the Russians began their advance into this area in the 18th century, the Kazakhs decided to accept Russian protection against their enemies to the east. The "Little Horde" accepted Russian protection in 1731, followed by the Middle Horde in 1740 and the Great Horde in 1742.

The Kazakhs began to fear Russian control, however, and this led to a series of uprisings toward the end of the 18th century. As a result, Russia began to suppress the autonomy of the Kazakh Khans. The Khanate of the "Middle Horde" was suppressed in 1822, the "Little Horde" in 1824; and the "Great Horde" in 1848. In 1854, the Russians founded the fortress of Verna, which eventually became the modern capital of Almaty. The area was administratively divided into four areas. In the latter part of the 19th century, there were large–scale settlements of Russian peasants established in the northern part of the territory.

A small Kazakh nationalist movement came into existence at the beginning of the 20th century, and a number of Kazakh deputies were elected to the first and second legislatures. The first Kazakh newspaper began publication in 1910. In 1916, a revolt broke out when the Russian Government ordered the mobilization of all persons between the age of 19 and 43. It was put down harshly.

After the Bolshevik seizure of power in November 1917 in Moscow, Kazakh nationalists demanded full autonomy for Kazakhstan. A Kazakh nationalist government was formed, but was suppressed in 1919–20 when the Red Army occupied the area. The Bolsheviks did sponsor creation of the Kirgiz Autonomous Soviet Socialist Republic in August 1920, however. In 1925, the name was changed to Kazakh, but in 1929, the capital was established at Alma–Ata. Kazakhstan became a Soviet Socialist Republic in December 1936.

The *Kazakh Communist Party* was estab-

**Kazakhstan's former capital of Almaty as seen from Mt. Kok Tyube**  Courtesy: NOVOSTI

167

# Kazakhstan

**The dam in the Maly Almaatinsky Gorge at Medeo**

lished in 1937 and during World War II, Zhumabay Shayakhmetov became its first head. He was replaced in 1954 by P. K. Ponomarenko, a Slav, because of insufficient support for the Moscow–sponsored newly–launched Virgin Lands campaign. Ponomarenko was later replaced by Leonid Brezhnev, who remained first secretary of the *Kazakh Communist Party* until 1956. After he became General Secretary, Brezhnev appointed another Kazakh party hack, Dinmukhamed Kunaev, as first secretary of the *Kazakh Communist Party*. He held that position until December 1986, when he was removed by Gorbachëv and replaced by another Slav, Gennady Kolbin.

When word reached Alma–Ata that Kunaev had been dismissed and was being replaced by an ethnic Russian, violent rioting broke out and several persons were killed. Gorbachëv, recognizing that he had to be more sensitive to nationalist sentiments, later reassigned Kolbin and replaced him with another Kazakh.

When hardliners launched their *coup* against USSR President Gorbachëv on August 19, 1991, President Nursultan Nazarbayev condemned the action and called for Gorbachëv's return. After failure of the *coup*, Nazarbayev severed all ties with the *Kazakh Communist Party*, then banned all political activity in government, the courts and police. The *Kazakh*

*Communist Party* disbanded, then subsequently reconstituted itself as a Socialist Party. The Socialists held their first congress at Alma–Ata in December 1991. They do not have much influence, however.

Nazarbayev strongly supported some form of continued union of the republics and, almost alone among the republic leaders, he did not press for a declaration of independence until it became clear that the old union was dead. This made sense from the point of view of Kazakhstan, for it is a large republic with a relatively small population and its economy is heavily tied to Russia. Most people still live in the countryside and support themselves from the land. The only industry is mineral extraction, most of which has traditionally been shipped to other republics for further processing. In addition, a significant percentage of the population has ethnic ties to Russia or one of the other republics.

The pace of change, fairly rapid just after Kazakhstan declared its independence in 1991, slowed thereafter. Foreign investment is still being encouraged, but there has been some retrenchment on market-oriented economic changes introduced in 1991 and early 1992. In addition, terms like "pluralism" and "moving toward democracy" are not heard much any more. As Kazakhstan's new constitution indi-

cates, the best characterization for Nazarbayev is that he is an "authoritarian modernizer" who is putting economic development before political liberalism.

On the other hand, Nazarbayev, an ex–communist, is in many ways rather pragmatic. He is aware of growing nationalist currents within the country. Though sensitive to those feelings, he is also aware that there are approximately as many Russian speakers in the country as there are Kazakh speakers. Moves in this area have accordingly been moderate. For example, the amount of instruction in the Kazakh language has been increased in the schools, but Russian is still the medium of instruction.

Kazakhstan's new constitution designates Kazakh as the national language, but Russian is described as the language of inter–ethnic communication. The constitution also requires the President to have a good command of the Kazakh language, but does not stipulate that he be an ethnic Kazakh.

One of the strange things of Kazakhstan after 1992 was the almost total lack of any political opposition to Nazarbayev. Nobody challenged him at the executive level and the legislature remained compliant to his wishes. Yet Nazarbayev did not act in a particularly dictatorial manner and appeared to favor the development of at least some political pluralism. The ethnic split in the republic may have been part of the explanation. Nazarbayev was one of the few individuals who managed to win significant support from both Kazakhs and Russians.

All of that changed in late 1994, however. On the one side, ethnic Russians began to agitate for greater recognition within the state, including the designation of Russian as the second official language, and they also began demanding the right to dual Russian–Kazakh nationality. Nazarbayev's efforts to placate them brought a reaction from ethnic Kazakhs. For the first time, voices of criticism were heard in the Kazakh parliament. In early 1995, a majority rejected the president's proposals to give the Russian language equal status with Kazakh. The parliament also rejected a proposed law establishing procedures for the privatization of land.

The Constitutional Court then offered Nazarbayev an unusual opportunity when it declared the March 1994 elections to be illegal on the basis that they offended the "one man, one vote" principle. Nazarbayev immediately disbanded the parliament and accepted the resignation of the government. He then announced that he would rule by decree until a new parliament was elected. Parliamentarians protested, and some threatened to form an alternative assembly. Nazarbayev, however, used the interregnum to push ahead with measures he had favored but which had not had majority support in parliament, such as privatization, enhancement of the status of the Russian language, and streamlining the tax system. New parliamentary elections took place in December 1995. There were multiple candidates for most of the 67 seats, with the result that only 43 candidates won a majority of the votes in the first round of voting. A second election then followed to fill the remaining seats. Although many of the winners had run without a party affiliation, most have since generally supported government policies.

The out–migration of ethnic Russians since 1991 has been of much concern to Nazarbayev. In an attempt to address their concerns, Nazarbayev has made a number of gestures toward the Russian community. In 1994, or example, he extended the time when residents would have to decide whether to opt for Kazakh citizenship. When it became clear that many Russians were hesitant to relinquish their Russian citizenship, Nazarbayev, in 1995, endorsed the concept of dual Russian and Kazakh citizenship. The migration of ethnic Russians to Russia and elsewhere continues, however.

Nazarbayev has also been concerned about the possibility of a separatist movement in the north of the country where most Russian speakers live. Attempting to address that problem, he proposed in 1995 that the capital be moved from Almaty in the extreme southwestern part of the republic to Akmola (or Aqmola), a town of 270,000 located near the center of the country. Akmola has the advantage that it is nearer the main population and industrial centers. Moreover, the northern half of the country contains most of the country's natural resources, including oil, gas, gold, chrome and copper, as well as much of its best farmland.

On the other hand, Akmola was only a provincial town in 1995 and it lacked the facilities to house a government. Over the past several years, therefore, whole new districts were constructed to house the government, the parliament, the foreign embassies and the governmental workers. This also involved constructing new luxury hotels, new residential areas, an additional business center, and an enlarged airport.

The formal move to Akmola took place in December 1997 when President Nazarbayev sent state symbols, including the flag, coat of arms, and the presidential banner, to the new capital. In fact, much of the construction ordered in 1995 has not yet been completed, so most of the government ministries have remained in Almaty, as have most foreign embassies. Those government officials who have been transferred to Akmola have had to be housed in temporary quarters for the most extent. Parliamentary deputies have been assigned to hotel rooms, while government officials have been put up in hostels or even kindergartens. Nevertheless, the task of building a new capital is continuing and the population is growing. If all works out as planned, the population of Akmola will reach a half a million by the year 2000.

President Nazarbayev changed prime ministers in October 1997. Akezhan Kazhegeldin, who had been prime minister since 1994, was in Switzerland for medical treatment when he tendered his

**President Nursultan Nazarbayev of Kazakstan**

resignation. His successor, Nurlan Balgimbayev, was named the same day. Although Kazhegeldin's resignation was allegedly for health reasons, it is possible that he was asked to step down by President Nazarbayev, possibly because of policy disagreements. The same day that President Nazarbayev accepted Kazhegeldin's resignation, he told the parliament that "reforms had been insufficient and in some aspects have not produced the desired results." Nurlan Balgimbayev, the new prime minister, was previously head of the Kazakhstan National Petroleum Company. An engineer by training, he had spent the years from 1986 to 1992 in the former USSR Oil and Gas Industry Ministry in Moscow. He then spent two years in the United States, first at MIT, then at Chevron's headquarters. He was appointed Kazakh gas and oil minster in October 1994, then head of the state oil company that replaced the ministry in March 1997.

## Foreign Policy

After the Presidents of Russia, Ukraine and Belarus agreed to formation of the Commonwealth of Independent States in December 1991, Nazarbayev was active in getting other republics to join and actually hosted the Alma–Ata meeting where the general agreement was signed. Kazakhstan has since been an active participant in the CIS. At the same time, President Nazarbayev has been at the forefront in encouraging cooperation among the Central Asian republics. In September 1991, Nazarbayev joined Boris Yeltsin in a mediation effort between Azerbaijan and Armenia. Unfortunately, the agreement reached was never fully implemented.

In May 1993, President Nazarbayev, who had earlier said that he wanted Kazakhstan to become nuclear–free, asked for security guarantees from the U.S., Russia, and China in return for agreeing to give up Kazakhstan's nuclear weapons. He was asking for the pledge, he said, because some Chinese textbooks showed parts of Kazakhstan as being part of China. There was also other evidence to show that at least some Kazakh officials were having second thoughts about the merits of going nuclear–free. As one of Nazarbayev's advisers pointed out, Kazakhstan would not be receiving the attentions of Secretary of State Baker and high–ranking officials of other countries, if it didn't have nuclear weapons. Nazarbayev paid an official visit to Washington later in May, however, and here he reversed himself once again and agreed to the withdrawal of nuclear weapons from Kazakhstan within seven years. Kazakhstan subsequently signed both the START–1 agreement and the Non–Proliferation Treaty.

Nazarbayev visited the United States again in February 1994. A major purpose

# Kazakhstan

*Sazgen*, the folk music quintet, shown at the Old Instruments Museum in Almaty
Courtesy: NOVOSTI

of this visit, his advisers announced, was to get American help in reducing Kazakhstan's dependence on Russia. Nazarbayev had apparently become uneasy as a result of the rise to prominence in Russia of Vladimir Zhirinovsky, an ethnic Russian from Kazakhstan. Kazakhstan was also at that time under pressure from the Russian Government to regularize Russian control of the Baikonur space launch facility and several military bases. During the visit, President Clinton promised to increase U.S. aid to Kazakhstan from the previous year's $91 million to $311 million in 1994–95. A number of agreements were signed, including one by President Nazarbayev formalizing Kazakhstan's adhesion to the nuclear proliferation treaty. Kazakhstan is also a member of the NATO–sponsored "Partners for Peace" and participated in military maneuvers in Central Asia in 1997.

Nazarbayev has always supported close relations with Russia but these relations were expanded in January 1995 when Kazakhstan and Russia signed an agreement calling for closer economic and military links. This was followed, a few days later, by a second agreement establishing a customs union between Kazakhstan, Russia and Belarus. Nazarbayev has also worked to strengthen ties with the Central Asian republics.

## Nature of the Regime

Kazakhstan adopted a new constitution in 1993 which only slightly modified the presidential–parliamentary system (modeled rather closely on that of Russia) which had been set up after independence. The popularly elected, executive presidency was retained, but there were modifications in the nature of the legislature. The new constitution created a 177-member parliament, with 42 seats to be filled by direct presidential appointees an another 11 by the official trade unions. Elections took place in March 1994. In ear-

ly 1995, however, the Constitutional Court ruled the March 1994 parliamentary elections to be illegal because they violated the principle of "one man, one vote."

In response, President Nazarbayev disbanded the legislature and began to rule by decree. In redrafting the electoral law to bring it into line with the decision of the Constitutional Court, Nazarbayev made all seats elective but reduced the size of the parliament to 67 members. He then set new parliamentary elections for December 1995.

In the ensuing elections, there were multiple candidates in most constituencies, with the result that only 43 seats were filled in the first round of voting, and a second round of voting had to be scheduled to fill the remaining seats. Although many of the winning candidates were elected as independents, most can usually be counted on to support government policies.

Kazakhstan has had three prime ministers since independence. The latest is Nurlan Balgimbaev, appointed prime minister in the fall of 1997 to replace Akezhan Kazhegeldin, who was ousted in October. Balgimbaev has no independent political base, and so serves at President Nazarbayev's pleasure.

## Culture

It is difficult to identify a separate culture for Kazakhstan. Kazakhs are basically a rural people who, until recently, played very little public role. Nearly all are Moslems, but there never has been a major center such as can be found in the Central Asian republics to the south, such as Tashkent, Samarkand, or Bukhara. Thus it affects the lives of the people, but in an easy–going way. There is a specific Kazakh style of clothing or interior decoration but there are no specifically Kazakh foods. Women still tend to wear a long, wide dress with a stand–up collar and bloomers gathered at the ankle, particu-

larly in the countryside. Elderly men wear wide, white shirts, wide trousers and woolen or cotton robes. Young people of both sexes tend to wear European clothes.

Kazakh homes exhibit specific Kazakh designs in stucco work and wall facings, while floors are covered with carpets.

There is a small national literature as well, most of it recent in origin. Abay Ibragim Kunanbayev, a 19th century humanist and poet, is usually considered to be the father of Kazakh written literature. Early twentieth century writers include Aqmet Baytursinuli, an author and newspaper editor, and Jambil Jabayev, a folk poet. The best known of the Kazakh literary figures of the Soviet period is Mukhtar Auezov, a playwright and novelist. His long novel, *Abay*, deals with Kazakh steppe life in the 19th century. It has been translated into English.

The population of the northern part of the republic is mostly Russian or Ukrainian and the culture here doesn't differ significantly from Russian areas across the border. The presence of significant numbers of Koreans and "Volga" Germans does introduce a greater element of cultural diversity, but these are mostly rural peoples who practice mainly a village culture.

Almaty is the largest city and the center for most higher education. The Kazakh S. M. Kirov State University is located here, as is the Abay Teachers College. Almaty also has polytechnical, agricultural and veterinary institutes. Karaganda has a medical institute and a teachers training college. Other institutes of higher learning are also found in regional centers.

There is a Kazakh Academy of Sciences, founded in 1945. This has particularly encouraged scholarship in ethnographic studies of the Kazakh language and the history of Kazakh literature. It also finances industrial and agricultural research.

## Economy

A majority of the residents of the republic support themselves from agriculture or stock raising. The northern part of Kazakhstan is a major grain growing area, with supplemental crops like fruits, vegetables, grapes, sugar beets and potatoes grown. Stock raising is concentrated in the dryer area to the south of the grain belt, in the area of the grassy steppe. Cotton, tobacco, grapes, and mustard are grown in the Syr–Darya and Ili River Valleys.

Kazakhstan had already instituted a number of reforms in agriculture during the Gorbachëv era which began to break down the old system of command control. For example, a 1987 law abolished all restrictions on the number of animals that a farmer could have. This led to an increase of about 2.5 million in the sheep and goat population and about a million additional

170

cattle. Meat sales in the cooperative sector also quadrupled in that time. In addition, 890,000 families received plots of land in 1991 and 46,000 private houses were constructed with state assistance.

In February 1992, Nazarbayev signed a decree on privatizing the property of enterprises in the agro–industrial complex, apparently intending to end the collective and state farm system. At the time, Nazarbayev commented that Kazakhstan did not need loss–making farms. "Private farming works because it is private," he was quoted as saying. There was bitter resistance to this approach at the local level, however, and as a result most agricultural land is still controlled by collective and state farms, now organized as cooperatives. While President Nazarbayev continues to favor a conversion to private farming in principle, few changes are expected in this area of the economy any time soon. Agricultural production has been increasing, however, as evidenced by the fact that Kazakhstan had a grain surplus of about 2.3 million tons in 1997.

Kazakh industry is mainly of the extractive variety. Most industry is located in the northeastern part of the republic, in and around the cities of Karaganda, Zelinograd and Semipalatinsk. It has large deposits of coal and iron ore. It also produces lead, zinc, copper, chromite, nickel, molybdenum, tin, antimony, cadmium, bauxite, gold, silver, phosphates, and oil. In addition to the processing of ferrous and nonferrous metals, it has chemical, machine–building, cement, and textile industries. Light industries associated with agriculture include food processing and leather.

In September 1991, the government approved a program for the "first stage of destatization and privatization" of state property. The program, which included a coupon mechanism, proposed privatization in trade, public catering, construction, motor transport, agriculture, consumer services and small enterprises. Medium and large enterprises were to be converted to joint–stock companies, collective enterprises or partnerships. In a speech to the legislature in January 1993, however, Nazarbayev spoke of mistakes associated with free–market reform in Russia and Kazakhstan and declared that a significant decree of state control and regulation would be necessary in the future. He indicated that major enterprises would be run along commercial principles, but most would remain in state hands. Most small and medium–scale industries have been privatized since that time, but plans to extend privatization into the areas of gas and oil have been stalled. Prime Minister Balgimbaev announced in February 1998 that privatization could not proceed in these areas until the government had selected a "strategic partner."

One colonial leftover that the Kazakhs are rather ambivalent about is the massive space complex at Baikonur Cosmodrone. There is no question but that the space program has given tremendous stimulus to the advancement of hi–tech education, but it has been almost exclusively Russians, not ethnic Kazakhs, that have benefited from the program. Another problem is that the complex continues to be run by Russia. The Government of Kazakhstan, which favors close cooperation with Russia, has made it clear that it does not want the complex closed down, but it would like ethnic Kazakhs to be able to benefit more from its presence.

Kazakhstan is one of the few ex–Soviet republics to have attracted significant interest among foreign investors since independence. The reason for this is that Kazakhstan has some of the largest unexplored oil, gas and mineral deposits on earth. As of June 1997, foreign direct investment had grown to $6 billion while Kazakhstan had commitments from foreign companies to invest more than $60 billion in the coming years.

For example, the Chevron Corporation and the Government of Kazakhstan signed an agreement in April 1993 establishing a 40–year, $20 billion joint venture (Tengizchevroil) to develop the Tengiz and Korolev oilfields on the northeastern coast of the Caspian Sea. By June 1997, Chevron had invested $800 million in Kazakhstan and had committed itself to invest another $500 million over the next three years, with plans to invest $20 billion in the Tengiz oil field over the next 40 years.

The Tengizchevroil joint venture was producing 160,000 barrels of oil a day as of June 1997 and planned to increase this to 700,000 barrels a day by 2003.

## The Future

Kazakhstan is a relatively poor republic without a particularly developed infrastructure. It is heavily dependent on Russia for manufactured goods. It is also divided ethnically, with Russians and other Slavs in the majority in the north and Kazakhs and other Turkic peoples in a majority in the south. Out-migrations of Russians and other Slavs since 1991, combined with high birth rates among Moslems, have made Kazakhs once more the majority ethnic grouping, but that may have actually raised tensions with Russian speakers. This ethnic division therefore remains a problem.

On the positive side, Kazakhstan has an astute political leader in President Nazarbayev who understands the problems of the country. He does not hesitate, for example, to make gestures toward the ethnic Russians, even as he attempts to provide a greater role for Kazakhs. Again, the majority of the people, both Russians and Kazakhs, live on the land and so share some common values. Lastly, Kazakhstan has been the recipient of approximately $6 billion in foreign investment since 1991 and agreements with foreign companies have been signed which will produce much more. Most of this investment will be in the oil and gas industries, however, so may not make much of a difference in the standard of living for ordinary Kazakhs. Nevertheless, foreign investment of this size cannot but have a positive influence on the country in the long run.

**Drying astrakhan pelts of the new–born Persian lambs, used like fur for garments**
Courtesy: NOVOSTI

# The Republic of Kyrgyzstan (Formerly Kirghizia; roughly pronounced *Keer*–zhee–stan).

**President Akayev at dinner with his wife and children**

**Area:** 76,640 sq. mi. (198,500 sq. km., slightly smaller than Nebraska).

**Population:** 4,567,000 (1992 est.).

**Capital City:** Bishtek (formerly Frunze); Pop. 631,000.

**Climate:** Hot, dry valleys; cold, high deserts.

**Neighboring States:** Kazakhstan (north), Uzbekistan (west), Tajikistan (west, southwest), China (southeast).

**Languages:** Kyrgyz, Russian.

**Ethnic Composition:** Kyrgyz (52%), Russian (22%), Uzbek (12%), others (14%).

**Principal Religion:** Islam. About 25% of the people are nominally Orthodox Christian.

**Chief Commercial Products:** Livestock, cotton and cotton oil, vegetables, sugar beets, refined sugar, hides, flour, mining enterprises, metals, textiles.

**Currency:** Som (May 1993).

**Annual Per Capita Income:** About U.S. $1,000.

**Recent Political Status:** Autonomous Republic within the USSR (1926), Constituent Republic of the USSR (1936–1991).

**Chief of State:** Askar Akayev, President.

**National Flag:** Red, in the center a 28–armed golden pinwheel spinning on a rim.

## The Land

The Republic of Kyrgyzstan is the independent successor state to the Kirghiz Soviet Socialist Republic. Situated on a western spur of the Tien Shan Mountains, it is a mountainous country surrounded by more mountains; most of its borders run along mountain crests. Thus it is separated from Tajikistan by the Turkistan and Zaalay Ranges. The Kokshaal–Tau Range, a part of the Tien Shan, forms the border with the People's Republic of China.

The exception is in the southwest, where the border dips down to cross the upper reaches of the Fergana River Valley. Apart from the Fergana Valley, the only lowland areas are the downstream parts of the Chu and Talas River Valleys along the northern border. The capital, Bishtek, is located in the Chu River Valley. These lowland areas make up about 15 percent of the total surface of the republic.

Kyrgyzstan's most unusual geographical feature is Lake Issyk–Kul, a high mountain lake found in the eastern part of the country. Set in a massive hollow much like the Fergana Valley in western Kyrgyzstan, it is surrounded by mountains with a high, alpine plateau to the west. A deep clear lake, it is rich in fish and supports fishing communities around its edges.

## The People

The population of Kyrgyzstan is very mixed, with Kyrgyz speakers constituting only 52% of the population. Russians, the largest minority, are about 22% of the population. Other minorities found in the republic include Uzbeks (12%), Ukrainians

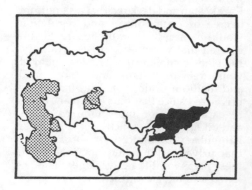

(3%), Tatars (2%), Chinese Moslems, Germans, and Dungans. The Kyrgyz language belongs to the Turkic group of languages.

## History

The Kyrgyz have lived in the Tien Shan Mountains at least since the 16th century and some Soviet ethnographers postulate that they arrived as early as the 12th century. Since they had no written language until recently and continued to live as a nomadic people until modern times, archaeological evidence provides most of what we know of them.

They came under the nominal control of the Kokand Khanate until about 1850, when this area became a major region of Russian colonization. Since the Kyrgyz, as nomads, had no permanent claims on the land, the Russian colonists moved in and took most of the best land, leading to an uprising in 1916, which was put down with great force.

After the Russian Revolution, this area became a part of Soviet Turkistan. In 1921, it then became part of the Turkistan Autonomous SSR of the Russian SFSR. In 1924, it was separated from the Turkistan ASSR and given the status of an autonomous *oblast* (area) of the Russian SFSR. Two years later, it became the Kirgiz Autonomous SSR of the Russian SFSR. It was not until December 1936 that it became a constituent republic of the USSR as the Kirgiz Soviet Socialist Republic.

Much changed during the Soviet years. The nomadic life of the people ended when they were settled on collective and state farms. Some mechanization was also introduced in the countryside, and irrigation projects increased cultivated land in the lowlands. The exploitation of minerals found in the mountains has increased the number of jobs in industry and drawn more of the Kyrgyz people into cities and modern life. Most have preferred to remain in stock raising or farming, however, so the overwhelming majority of people in industry and in the urban areas are non–Kyrgyz.

Gorbachëv's *perestroika* left the republic untouched until 1990, when ethnic riots broke out in the Fergana Valley along the border with Uzbekistan. The riots left 200 people dead and damaged the reputation of Absamat Masaliev, the *Kyrgyz Communist Party* leader. Masaliev tried to repair the damage by calling on the republic's Supreme Soviet to create the office of President, to be elected by that body.

Masaliev's political opposition in the Supreme Soviet organized themselves into a new party, called *Democratic Kyrgyzstan*, and elected Askar Akayev instead. Akayev, who is a physicist by training, worked for twenty years in St. Petersburg before returning to Kyrgyzstan.

In August 1991, there was an organized attempt to depose President Akayev as part of the attempted *coup* against Gorbachëv. The local military commander threatened to send tanks into the street and the local KGB chief attempted to arrest Akayev. The president's loyal troops surrounded the *Communist Party* headquarters and then had the KGB chief arrested. He subsequently banned the *Communist Party* from government offices. When the *coup* failed, the *Kyrgyz Communist Party* dissolved itself. After his own return to power, Gorbachëv asked Akayev to come to Moscow to become his vice president. He turned it down, saying that he wanted to stay in Kyrgyzstan.

As part of the further democratization of the country, the Kyrgyz Supreme Soviet modified the constitution to make the presidency an elective office and called for new elections on October 12. Akayev's position was so strong by that time that no candidate bothered to oppose him. Kyrgyzstan still has a predominantly agrarian economy which is heavily dependent on trade for survival. Thus the break up of the Soviet Union had a particularly devastating impact on the standard of living. One effect has been that Russians, who make up Kyrgyzstan's professional elite have been leaving in large numbers for Russia.

Akayev has pushed democratic reforms and the creation of a market economy, but he has been frustrated by opposition in the legislature. This led him to organize a referendum in February 1994 in which the people were asked whether he should be allowed to finish his term ending in 1996. Ninety–six percent of those voting answered yes. Akayev then dismissed the old 350 member Supreme Soviet, elected during the Soviet era in 1990, and submitted a referendum to the people proposing a new "Assembly of the People of Kyrgyzstan" of 105 members, divided into two chambers. When the electorate responded favorably, Akayev set new elections for February 5, 1995. Over a thousand candidates vied for the 105 seats, about 80% of them running as independents. In the first round of voting, 13 candidates won a majority of ballots cast and claimed their seats, only four of them members of a political party. The results during the second round of voting was similar. This produced a cooperative legislature for Akayev to work with.

Since that time, Akayev has pushed through a whole sheaf of constitutional amendments, many of which significantly increased his powers. He has also pushed through legislation authorizing some forms of privatization, including land. Some 61% of state–owned industrial enterprises had been privatized by May 1997 when President Akayev ended all forms of privatization after he became convinced that state–owned facilities were being sold at unjustifiably low prices. President Akayev has promised that the ban would be temporary, however, and forty of Kyrgyzstan's leading companies are to be put up for sale when the government becomes convinced that they can be sold for something near to what the government feels they are worth.

One of Kyrgyzstan's major problems is that thousands of ethnic Russians have left Kyrgyzstan for Russia over the past several years, leaving many technical jobs unfilled. Hoping to stem the tide, President Akayev has pushed through a law restoring Russian as a national language on a par with Kyrgyz. So far, the migration is continuing, however.

## Foreign Policy

Akayev's reputation as a genuine democrat has caused some problems with his neighbors, all of whose rulers are much more conservative and still attuned to the traditional communist ways of doing things. The partial exception is Kazakhstan, whose President, Nursultan Nazarbayev, although an ex–communist, has gained a reputation for pragmatism.

The U.S. Government showed its own support for Akayev when it opened the first U.S. Embassy in Central Asia in Bishkek on February 1, 1992. In 1993, Kyrgyzstan received the highest amount of U.S aid on per capita basis of any of the ex–Soviet republics. President Akayev made an unofficial seven–day visit to the United States in July 1997. Among those he met with were George Soros, who has invested several million dollars in Kyrgyzstan, UN Secretary–General Kofi Annan, and IMF Deputy Managing Director Alassane Outtara.

Kyrgyzstan was also the first ex-Soviet republic to meet World Bank and IMF requirements for obtaining finance assistance. It has received loans from the World Bank and has negotiated a full standby agreement with the IMF. In 1997, the IMF increased its credits to Kyrgyzstan.

## Nature of the Regime

Kyrgyzstan has a presidential-parliamentary form of government with the president responsible for general policy and a prime minister, responsible to the Supreme Soviet, handling implementation of policy. The president is advised by a State Council, while the prime minister presides over his cabinet.

The republic legally has a multiparty system, though most persons elected to the legislature in the last elections ran as independents. Democratic Kyrgyzstan, the party aligned with the president, is the dominant political force since the Kyrgyz Communist Party dissolved itself in 1991.

# Kyrgyzstan

Kyrgyz family waiting at typical mosaic bus stop which dot the countryside. Man wears a "kalpak" hat

Photo by Hermine Dreyfuss

## Culture

Most Kyrgyz are Moslems, and continue to live a largely traditional life within the context of changes forced on them during the Soviet period. An oral tradition among the people has kept alive epic cycles and lyric poetry. This has saved much that would otherwise have been lost, for the written language has been in three different forms in the twentieth century. The first written language used the Arabic script, but that was abandoned after World War I and the Roman script was introduced. In 1940, Stalin forced all of the Central Asian republics to adopt the Cyrillic alphabet. Now it is likely that they will switch back to the Roman script.

Kyrgyzstan has produced two writers of note in modern times, the playwright and novelist Chingiz Aytmatov and the playwright Kaltay Muhamedjanov. Aytmatov is the author of *Tales of the Mountains and Steppes*, which has been translated into English. It won the Lenin Prize in 1963. The two collaborated on the play *The*

*Ascent of Mt. Fuji*, which has also been translated into English and was performed on stage in Washington, D.C. in 1973. Its theme is the moral compromises that people had to make under Stalin.

Newspapers and magazines are published in both Russian and Kyrgyz and radio and television broadcasts are made in both languages. National broadcasts are also received from Moscow by way of relay lines. The Russian cultural influence is, therefore, very strong. The State University of Kyrgyzstan is located in Bishtek; in December 1991, it opened a business school, support for which came partly from IBM, which donated a roomful of personal computers.

Since its emergence as an independent republic in 1991, Kyrgyzstan has seen a resurgence in interest in the old epic poems and, in particular, a poem of over a million verses called "Manas," parts of which may date back a thousand years. A story of a wise folk hero who unites the Kyrgyz nomads against foreign enemies,

the poem has become the center of a nationalistic upswelling throughout the country, plus something more. "This is our Bible," Jenishbek Sydykov, director of linguistics and literature at the Kyrgyz National Academy of Sciences, said of it. "As a people, we are one with this poem. In our eyes, the hero Manas is just below God—and higher than Lenin ever was to us." The United Nations was impressed enough to declare 1995 the International Year of Manas, commemorating the poem's thousand year anniversary.

## Economy

The Kyrgyz were once mainly nomads who pastured their herds in summer on the alpine–like slopes of the mountains where 30–40 inches of rainfall annually provide lush meadows for grazing. During the Soviet period, they were settled into villages and made part of collective or state farms. Livestock includes sheep, goats, cattle and horses. Mare's milk is the source for *koumiss*, the local fermented drink. Pigs, bees and rabbits are also raised in the mountains. Agriculture, practiced mainly in the lowland areas, is dependent on irrigation, since these areas receive an average of 7 inches of rainfall a year. The main crops include sugar beets, cotton, tobacco, opium poppies and cereal grains. Approximately two–thirds of the population is still engaged in agriculture or stock raising.

The number of people involved in industry has grown greatly in recent years. Extractive industries are important and Kyrgyzstan is a major source of antimony and mercury ores. Lead and zinc are also mined. It also has large coal reserves, which have begun to be exploited. Hydroelectric power provides about half the energy needs of the republic. It also produces petroleum and natural gas. Food processing and light industry have been developed, and the republic also manufactures machinery and instruments.

Kyrgyzstan is still a poor land, however, with a standard of living that is perhaps 65% of the former Soviet average. The reporter Georgie Anne Geyer, who visited the capital, Bishtek, in February 1992 to be present at the opening of the first U.S. Embassy in Central Asia, described it as "horrendously poor." "This isn't the end of the world, but you can see it from here," quip westerners, commenting on its isolation.

Kyrgyzstan has religiously followed the prescriptions of the World Bank and IMF since independence, liberalizing the economy and privatizing shops and some enterprises. The results have been unusually good. They have the lowest inflation among the members of the Commonwealth of Independent States and their currency, the *som*, is the strongest currency in Central Asia.

174

**Kyrgyz woman in traditional head–dress of a married woman making a felt rug ("shirdak")**

Photo by Hermine Dreyfuss

They still have serious problems, however, for many of their larger enterprises are heavily indebted and may never become competitive. Currently, twenty–nine of those enterprises considered to be most in need of help have been put under the wing of the Enterprise Restructuring and Rehabilitation Agency, a state organization set up with the help of the World Bank. At the moment, the money to finance the restructuring is coming from the World Bank. The big question, however, is whether these enterprises can really be rehabilitated or whether they should be shut down.

## The Future

A large part of the Kyrgyz republic budget has been subsidized from Moscow in the past and Kyrgyzstan has had to develop alternate sources of outside assistance to cover the shortfall. In spite of that it has had to make drastic cuts in spending to lower the budget deficit. Whatever economic progress comes is therefore not likely to be fast. The two–thirds of the population that lives on the land is largely self–sufficient, however, so at least they won't starve.

# The Republic of Tajikistan

Grandfather shows his newly–fashioned whistles to his grandson and friend

Courtesy: NOVOSTI

**Area:** 57,250 sq. mi. (143,100 sq. km., slightly smaller than Illinois).

**Population:** 5,680,000 (1992 est.).

**Capital City:** Dushanbe (Pop. 602,000).

**Climate:** Continental, with sharp changes depending upon altitude.

**Neighboring Countries:** China (east), Afghanistan (south), Uzbekistan (west and north), Kyrgyzstan (north).

**Principal Language:** Tajik.

**Ethnic Composition:** Tajik (62%), Uzbek (23%), Russian (7%), other (8%).

**Principal Religion:** Islam. Until recently, religious worship was officially discouraged.

**Chief Commercial Products:** Mining, food processing, textiles, clothing and silk; fruit and livestock. The Ghissar sheep is famous for its meat and Karakul sheep produce wool and glossy, curly lamb pelts. The Republic has tremendous existing and potential hydroelectric resources.

**Currency:** Tajik Ruble.

**Annual Per Capita Income:** About U.S. $600.

**Recent Political Status:** Autonomous Republic within the former USSR (1924) as part of Uzbek S.S.R. Constituent Republic of the former USSR (1929–1991).

**Chief of State:** Imamali Rakhmonov, President.

**National Flag:** Three horizontal stripes; on top a narrow red and on the bottom a narrow green, with a broader white stripe across the center. Superimposed on the white a golden stylized mountain peak topped with a flag and surrounded by a semicircle of stars (a representation of Communism Peak, highest peak in the old USSR).

## The Land

The Republic of Tajikistan is the independent successor state to the Tadzhik Soviet Socialist Republic. It declared its independence in September 1991.

Tajikistan is a small land, which includes the autonomous region of Gorno–Badakhshan. It is located in the extreme southern part of Central Asia.

It is also a mountainous land, with more than half of its territory lying above 10,000 feet. The northern border forms a loop around the western part of the Fergana Valley, running along the top ridges of the Kuramin Range in the north before turning south, crossing the valley, and then tracing its way westward along the foothills of the Zeravshan Range. Here the western and eastern borders almost meet before turning south. The western border continues south, turning somewhat westward, while the eastern border bends sharply eastward and runs along the northern slopes of the Zeravshan Range, continuing until it reaches the China border.

The center of the republic is dominated by the Turkistan Range and the slightly lower Zevavshan and Gissar Ranges. In the east are the Pamirs, which contain the highest peaks found anywhere in Central Asia. In the south, a series of transverse ridges and river valleys slope down to the Pyandzh River in Afghanistan.

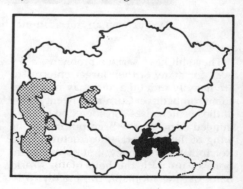

# Tajikistan

Valleys make up about ten percent of the land of the republic. In addition to the western part of the Fergana Valley, there are the smaller Gissar, Vakhsh, Yavansu, Obikiik, Lower Kafirnigan and Pyandzh valleys in the south. There are also a number of small lakes in the eastern part of the country, in the Pamir Mountains. There is a dense river network. These include the stretch of the Syr–Darya that flows through the western part of the Fergana Valley and the upper reaches of the Amu Darya. Most rivers flow northward into Central Asia.

Tajikistan has two climatic zones. The valleys are subtropical, with average July temperatures in the eighties and January temperatures hovering around freezing. Annual rainfall in the valleys is only 6–10 inches, so agriculture depends entirely on irrigation. In the highlands, average January temperatures are 0°F. or below. The mountains get very little precipitation in the summer, but the high ranges get 30– 60 inches in the form of snow in the winter. In the highest ranges, there are also huge glaciers that partially melt in the summer, only to be replenished in the winter. The spring and summer runoff from the mountains provides water for irrigation on the lower slopes and in the valleys.

## The People

Tajiks comprise approximately 62% of the population, estimated in 1992 as 5,680,000. Uzbekis, found mainly in the Northwestern part of the republic, comprise another 23%. Other minorities include Russians (7%), found mainly in urban areas, Ukrainians, Tatars, Germans, Kyrgyz, and Jews.

Tajik belongs to the southwest group of Iranian languages, which set the Tajiks off from the rest of their Central Asian neighbors. It is also spoken in the Hindu Kush area of northeast Afghanistan, where it is called Farsi. Because of the nature of the terrain, Tajiks actually speak a variety of dialects, depending on which part of Tajikistan they live in. The two most important sub–groups are Pamir Tajik, which also includes Bartang, the language spoken in the Gorno–Badakhnabi Autonomous Region, and Yaghnabi, the modern version of the language spoken in the ancient Kingdom of Sogdiana.

## History

The Tajiks are the descendants of Iranian–speaking people who entered Central Asia as early as 2,000 B.C. They were incorporated into the Persian Empire and the subsequent Empire of Alexander the Great. The ancient kingdom of Sogdiana, conquered by the Arabs in the eighth century, was Tajik–speaking. In the tenth century, an invasion of Turkic–speaking peoples overran Central Asia. Many Tajiks were assimilated at this time, with Tajik culture surviving mainly in the mountains.

The Tajiks were later brought under the control of the Emirate of Bukhara. In the eighteenth century, Afghanistan extended its control over the area. The Russian Empire gained control over this area in the 1860s. Bukhara became a Russian protectorate in 1868.

After the Russian Revolution, part of the area occupied by the Tajik people was incorporated into the Turkistan Autonomous Soviet Socialist Republic, established in April 1918. When the Red Army took over Bukhara in 1920, it also claimed most of the territory of modern Tajikistan. The Red Army captured Dushanbe early in 1921. The Basmachi revolt, which began in 1922 and lasted to the summer of 1923, was an attempt to throw off communist control, but it was ultimately unsuccessful. In 1924, the communist authorities decided to divide up Central Asia along ethnic lines. This led to the creation of the Tadzhik Autonomous Soviet Socialist Republic, at the time made part of the Uzbek SSR. In December 1929, the Tadzhik Autonomous SSR was separated from the Uzbek SSR and made a constituent republic in its own right.

Mountainous and isolated and divided into different tribes that had a long history of rivalry, the Tadzhik SSR was run throughout most of the Soviet period by officials sent out by Moscow. Even as late as 1990, Tajiks were a minority in the *Tajik Communist Party*. Gorbachëv's programs of *glasnost* and *perestroika* changed that. By 1988, Tajik officials had recognized the opportunity offered by the Gorbachëv reform program and had begun to implement Tajik solutions to local problems. This led the Tajik Supreme Soviet to assert Tajikistan sovereignty in August 1990.

After the attempted *coup* against Gorbachëv collapsed in August 1991, Kakhar Makhkamov, who had supported the *coup*, resigned as party leader and Chairman of the Supreme Soviet. He was replaced by Kadriddin Aslonov. Upon taking office, Aslonov resigned his membership on the Politburo of the *Tajik Communist Party* and issued a decree banning the *Communist Party of the Soviet Union* on Tajik territory.

This irritated a majority of the members of the Tajik Supreme Soviet, 95 percent of whom were communists. Accusing him of "unconstitutional actions," they ousted him as Chairman of the Supreme Soviet. In his stead, they elected Rakhmon Nabiyev, who had been first secretary of the *Tajik Communist Party* before Makhkamov. At about this time also, the Dushanbe party leader gave permission for a statue of Lenin to be torn down. He, too, was ousted and a state of emergency was declared in Dushanbe. In a related development, a hastily called congress of the *Tajik Communist Party* "dissolved" the party and established a new *Socialist Party* in its stead.

This combined set of developments appeared to political opponents to prove that the communists were determined to retain power. They organized a series of protest rallies in Dushanbe where they demanded that the state of emergency be lifted, the Supreme Soviet be dissolved and new elections called, and that Nabiyev resign as Chairman of the Supreme Soviet.

On September 30, after the rallies had continued for several days, the Supreme Soviet voted to lift the state of emergency in Dushanbe. Two days later, the Supreme Soviet suspended the activities of the officially dissolved *Tajik Communist Party* and its successor, the *Socialist Party* "until the party's participation in the *coup* attempt is estimated." Finally, Nabiyev submitted his resignation as Supreme Soviet Chairman on October 6. Akbarsho Iskandarov took over as acting chairman. The opposition had won every one of their points.

In September, the Supreme Soviet had created a new popularly elected presidency. That election had been set for October 27. The election date was postponed until November 24. As the presidential contest began, there were ten candidates, including Rakhman Nabiyev. Three later withdrew. There were also a number of political parties active, some registered and some not. Registered parties included the *Democratic Party of Tajikistan* and the *Popular Movement Rastokhez (Revival)*. The *Islamic Revival Party* was still in limbo at this point.

The government first banned all religious–oriented parties, then lifted the ban on October 22. At this point, a number of organizations had nominated Akbar Turadzhonzoda, head of the Spiritual Administration of Moslems of Tajikistan, for president. Turadzhonzoda's subsequent statement was therefore significant. "I support a secular parliamentary state with a free economy. Religion should be separated from the state so the sins of society cannot be attributed to Islam, which is what happened to the *Communist Party*." Turadzhonzoda did not stand as a candidate for the presidency.

When the election was finally held on November 24, Rakhman Nabiyev won with 56.9% of the vote. His chief opponent, Davlat Khudonazarov, who had been supported by the united opposition, won 30.7 percent of the vote.

Nabiyev's victory in the elections did not put an end to the struggle, however. In the early spring, the Islamic–led opposition, organized as the *Union of Popular Forces*, launched a campaign demanding multi–party elections and more freedom of religion, though their real purpose was to drive Nabiyev from office. Responding to the threat, the Tajik parliament attempted to strengthen Nabiyev's hand by giving

177

# Tajikistan

him the power to rule by decree. As demonstrations continued, Nabiyev declared a state of emergency. Instead of calming the situation, this brought calls for Nabiyev's resignation. In early May, opposition forces seized control of Dushanbe, the capital, and declared the creation of a revolutionary council. In a compromise, Nabiyev then lifted the state of emergency and agreed to form a "government of national reconciliation." In the new government, eight seats were assigned to an opposition coalition consisting of democrats and moderate Islamics, plus the *Islamic Revival Party*, whose program calls for the creation of an Islamic state.

Nabiyev's compromise calmed the situation briefly, but there was no reconciliation. Not only did the two disparate groupings find it difficult to work with each other; Nabiyev also found himself under attack from ex–communist allies in the northern part of the country who accused him of ceding too much power to the opposition. In addition, the government began to lose control of the country as ex–communists took control of local governments in the north and Islamics took control of local governments in the south and east. Then fighting broke out between regions, eventually resulting in about one thousand deaths.

To restore order, Nabiyev negotiated an agreement with the Commonwealth of Independent States for the dispatch of peace-keeping troops to the country. The opposition reacted by declaring an open rebellion and seizing control of Dushanbe. Nabiyev, taken prisoner by demonstrators as he fled to the Dushanbe airport, was forced at gunpoint to resign as President. The Islamic–democratic coalition then declared itself to be the new government and named Akbarsho Iskandarov as Acting President.

The Islamic–democratic coalition was unable to consolidate its control over the country, however. The northern, and most developed, part of the country was con-

**Spectators watch horses and riders at a popular equestrian event**

Courtesy: NOVOSTI

trolled by ex–communists associated with Nabiyev and they would have nothing to do with the new government. Meanwhile the situation in Dushanbe remained so unstable that the new government was unable to convene a new session of the parliament. This government lasted two months and then resigned on November 12, turning power over to an interim council. Meanwhile the parliament, meeting in the northern town of Khojand, accepted President Nabiyev's voluntary resignation, then elected Imamali Rakhmonov, an ex–communist, as Chairman of the legislature. On December 10, forces loyal to the former president took control of Dushanbe and at this time Rakhmonov was designated Acting President. Islamics fled to their strongholds in the mountains of eastern Tajikistan, pursued by elements of the Tajik army. Other Islamics sought refuge across the border into Afghanistan.

As the civil war continued, the Tajik Government received more assistance from Russia. By the fall of 1993, there were more than 20,000 Russian troops in the country and Russia was providing subsidies amounting to 50% of the budget. Russia's interest was apparently its fear that the Islamic forces, allied with Afghan Islamic militants, would seize control of the government and establish a militant Islamic regime in Tajikistan. The Tajik Government received significant assistance from the Uzbekistani Government as well, partly for the same reason.

The government's control remained fragile, however. A reporter who visited Dushanbe in May 1994 reported that it was calm there during the day but that the streets were deserted at night and, in the distance, one heard a "chorus of automatic rifle shots. With daybreak come reports of assassinations of public figures or of men disappearing from sight."

Russian soldiers have guarded Tajikistan's border with Afghanistan since 1994. Eleven Russian soldiers were killed in skirmishes over the summer before government and oppositional forces reached agreement on a ceasefire in that year. The two sides later held talks in Islamabad which produced a ceasefire between government forces and guerillas based in the eastern mountains. Since that time, the Russian foreign ministry has been supporting a settlement that would reintegrate the rebels into the society. There have been periodic contacts between the rebels and the government since that time, but thus far no agreement is in sight.

In November 1994, the Tajik Government held a combined presidential election and referendum on a new constitution. With the real opposition excluded from participating, the presidential contest was between the acting president, Imamali Rakhmonov, and Abdumalik Abdulajanov, a former prime minister.

Though not democratic by western standards, election observers said that the voting itself was free and fair. Rakhmonov won with about 60% of the vote and the new constitution was approved as well. At this time, Rakhmonov appointed Jamshed Karimov as his Prime Minister and announced that the government would launch a new privatization initiative. This has resulted in some small–scale privatization of firms having fewer than 20 employees, mainly firms providing catering and consumer services, but the economy is still basically state–run.

In the early part of 1996, a split among the forces supporting the government produced a new crisis. Two regional leaders who had been supporters of President

**President Imamali Rakhmonov**

Rakhmonov charged his government with incompetence and corruption and demanded its dismissal. They also demanded that he do something to improve the state of the economy. One of them, Colonel Makhmoud Khudoyberdyev, moved his troops within 10 miles from the capital, though no actual battle took place. Faced with the possibility of another civil war and informed by the Russian Government that it would not intervene again to save his government, Rakhmonov opened negotiations with the rebels. During the discussions, he agreed to dismiss several officials, including his First Deputy Prime Minister, his Chief of Staff and a southern governor. In return, the rebels agreed to return to their barracks.

A few days later, Rakhmonov dismissed his Prime Minister, replacing him with

Yakhyo Azimov, a little–known northerner who up to this time had been a carpet factory manager. It appears that this change was made because of the poor performance of the economy. In a news conference which he called after assuming office, Azimov announced that he favored market reforms and would cooperate with international donor organizations to rebuild the economy.

President Rakhmonov's greater, long-term problem was how to deal with the Islamic–democratic opposition, however. No real political stability could be achieved until he either came to terms with them or found some way to defeat them or deprive them of their popular political support. Many of Rakhmonov's supporters pushed for the second alternative, but this looked increasingly unrealistic to outside observers, in particular the Russians. According to Russian estimates, Rakhmonov's forces controlled, at best, a third of the republic, and the war would already have been lost but for the presence of 25,000 Russian troops.

Under strong pressure from the Russian Government to come to an understanding with the opposition, Rakhmonov travelled to Moscow in December 1996 to meet with Sayed Abdullo Nuri, leader of the Islamic Renaissance Party, largest of the parties in the United Tajik Opposition (UTO). The talks went well and a peace agreement was signed which provided for a general amnesty and called for creation of a Reconciliation Council. When President Rakhmonov got back to Dushanbe, however, he found that he was unable to sell the peace agreement to his political supporters.

Under continuing pressure from the Russian Government, Rakhmonov travelled to Moscow again in March 1997 for new talks with the UTO. Here, Rakhmonov signed an agreement which called for integration of opposition troops into the regular Tajik armed forces. No agreement for a political reconciliation had been reached, however, so another round of talks was scheduled to begin in Tehran on April 9, 1997. No breakthrough occurred at this point, but the two sides did agree to meet again in Moscow in June. It was in Moscow that President Rakhmonov, under pressure from a Russian Government that had grown tired of the war and the continuing death of Russian soldiers, signed a final accord with Sayed Abdullo Nuri on June 27, aimed at ending the years of fighting in the country.

The accord, which has still not been fully implemented, created a power–sharing arrangement and legalized the parties of the United Tajik Opposition (UTO), including the Islamic Renaissance Party, the Democratic Party, the Rastokhez People's Movement, and the Laadi Badakhshan. The accord also created a National Recon-

# Tajikistan

ciliation Commission which was charged with laying the groundwork for elections by the end of 1998, including recommending amendments to election laws. The interim power–sharing arrangement provided that the UTO was to obtain 30% of the ministerial posts in the government. It also specified that members of the UTO were to be allowed to return to Tajikistan accompanied by their own armed guards.

After the accord was signed, the two parties supporting the government—the People's Party and the Political and Economic Renewal Party—merged themselves into the National Unity Movement. Thus the stage was set for Tajik politics to be dominated by two large political groupings, one representing President Rakhmonov and his allies and the other representing the political opposition. To the extent that these two political groupings represent most of the people of Tajikistan, they create the circumstances whereby disagreements may be transferred from the battlefield to the political stage.

Implementation has not gone entirely smoothly, but it appears that one major reason for this was the Tajik Government's desire to assert greater control over subordinate commanders inclined to operate rather too independently of the government. This appears to have been the case with regard to Colonel Mahmud Khudaberiyev, commander of the Tajik army's First Brigade, who was accused of launching a military coup to overthrow the government in August 1997. According to Colonel Khudaberiyev, whose First Brigade was the rapid reaction force of the presidential guard, his unit was attacked by another unit of the presidential guard, led by its commander General Gafar Mirzoyev, and he and his unit only defended themselves. Two other outbreaks of military violence seem to have had similar roots. In each case, military forces loyal to the Tajik Government were able to assert their control. There have been numerous other "incidents," but these seem, in the main, to reflect the current state of instability within the country.

There is still a great deal of distrust between the two sides. Although Sayed Abdullo Nuri, head of the UTO, returned to Dushanbe in September 1997, Ali Akbar Turajonzoda, deputy leader of the UTO, had still not returned to Tajikistan as of February 1998. One explanation for this is that Turajonzoda is demanding the post of Foreign Minister in the government, but this is opposed by President Rakhmonov. In the meanwhile, a group of opposition commanders have announced that they will not permit their units to be integrated into the Tajik army until Turajonzoda returns home.

## Foreign Policy

The leaders of the Tajik Government have had to deliver themselves into the arms of the Russians in order to remain in power, so Tajikistan really isn't capable of an independent foreign policy at the moment. The agreement signed in June 1997 with the United Tajik Opposition holds the promise of an end to the civil war that has ravaged the country over the past several years, but it still hasn't been fully implemented as yet. Perhaps once some form of internal political stability has been created, Tajikistan will be able to begin focusing on relations with countries other than its immediate neighbors. Currently, Tajikistan's best relations are with Russia, which keeps 25,000 troops stationed in the country as a prop to the government, and Uzbekistan, which originally intervened to help President Rakhmonov come to power.

## Nature of the Regime

Tajikistan established a presidential-parliamentary form of government with a popularly elected president and a multiparty system in September 1991, shortly after it emerged as an independent republic. The subsequent struggles between the various factions that emerged led to parts of this system being changed or suppressed, but the new constitution that was approved in a popular referendum in November 1994 largely rebuilt the system put into effect in 1991.

Under this constitution, the key political figure in the system is the popularly elected President, who acts as the spokesman for the nation and establishes general policy. Next in line comes the Prime Minister, who is appointed by the President but must be confirmed in office by the Supreme Soviet, the country's legislature. The Prime Minister and his cabinet are responsible for the day–to–day operation of government.

The Supreme Soviet represents the sovereignty of the nation. It is responsible for all legislation and has final authority over the budget. Most top government officials must also be confirmed in office by the Supreme Soviet.

President Rakhmonov and most of the people allied with him were formerly leaders in the now disbanded Tajik Communist Party. Since June 1997, there has been a power–sharing agreement in effect which brought the United Tajik Opposition into the government with thirty percent of the seats in the cabinet. This is an interim arrangement, for the agreement calls for new, free elections by the end of 1998.

Currently, there exist two political groupings in the country, the National Unity Movement (made up of the People's Party and the Political and Economic Re-

newal Party), representing the old communist elites, and the United Tajik Opposition (which brought together three opposition parties, the Islamic Renaissance Party, the Democratic Party, the Rastokhez People's Movement, and the Laali Badakhshan).

Before the series of *coups* and counter-coups of 1992, Tajikistan appeared to be evolving toward an institutionalized pluralism. Some experts speculated that this was because the Tajik Communist Party had always had its organized political factions, based on differences between regional clans, and this was now coming out in the open. That trend suffered a severe setback in 1992 as first one side, then the other, resorted to force to get its way. Then the coalition of democrats and Islamics that held power briefly in 1992 was overthrown and many of its members fled into hiding, either in the mountains to the east or in Afghanistan.

After that, the new government in Dushanbe went about systematically eliminating the opposition. "It was a real blood bath," said one western diplomat.

Now the country is edging back toward political pluralism again, even if painfully and slowly. But this appears to be the only chance that Tajikistan has for political stability. Because the different parts of the country are so disparate, regional loyalties are extremely important and excluded elements are all too ready to resort to force. The government between 1992 and 1997 was essentially an alliance of the Leninabad and Kulyab areas, but that excluded other important areas such as Garm and Badakhshan. The current power–sharing arrangement provides representation to those parts of the country. The big question now is whether the civil war is now over. The answer to that question will depend on whether the two political groupings that currently share power can accept the democratic principle that only one of them can win the new elections scheduled to be carried out before the end of 1998.

## Culture

Traditional Tajik festivals have always featured songs and dances and there is also a long tradition of theatrical and circus performances. Tajik circuses specialize in tightrope walkers, conjurers, singers and musicians. There is also a vigorous folk literature which is still being collected.

In 1929 the Tajik National Theater was founded. It has nine separate theaters, performing operas, ballet, musical comedy and puppetry. There is also a Tajik film studio which makes both feature films and documentaries. Dushanbe has had its own television center since 1960.

# Tajikistan

Two pre–Soviet Tajik cultural figures are Abdalrauf Fitrat, author of *Last Judgment*, and Sadriddin Ayni, famous for two novels, *Slaves* and *Dokhunda*. His autobiography is titled *Bukhara*. Tajik writers of the Soviet period include the poets Abu ol–Qasem Lahuti and Mirzo Tursunzade. Tursunzade won the Lenin Prize in 1960 for his poem *The Voice of Asia*.

The Tajik State University, located in Dushanbe, is the largest of ten institutes of higher education. There are also 41 technical colleges. A Tajik Academy of Sciences was established in 1951. It now has sixteen institutions and oversees 61 research institutions located in various parts of the republic. The Pamir research station, located in the Pamir Mountains in the eastern part of the country, is a major regional meteorological observatory.

Most Tajiks are Sunni Moslems of the Hanafi school, although there are some Shiite communities among the Mountain Tajiks. Throughout the Soviet era, Islam was a barely tolerated religion and there were few mosques. But Islam is as much a way of life and a culture as it is a belief, so it survived in the villages in spite of official hostility. There has been a clear revival of Islam since about 1989, with many mosques being built, but it does not appear to have a great political significance.

## Economy

Tajikistan is primarily an agricultural economy and its most significant crop is long–staple cotton. Cattle raising (including sheep and goats) is also important, as is the growing of fruits, grain and vegetables. Fruits grown include apricots, pears, apples, plums, quinces, cherries, pomegranates and figs. Grapes and almonds are other major crops.

Tajikistan's light industry mainly involves processing agricultural products, such as cotton and silk processing, fruit canning and wine making. Related industries include knitted goods, shoes, leather working and carpet making. Light industry manufacturing plants tend to be small.

Its larger industry is either ore extraction or non–ferrous metallurgy. Tajikistan is rich in mineral deposits. It mines coal, iron, lead, zinc, antimony, mercury, gold, tin, and tungsten. Its mountains are the source of a number of non–metals, including salt, carbonates, fluorite, arsenic, quartz sand, asbestos and precious and semiprecious stones. Petroleum and natural gas have also been discovered and are beginning to be exploited, though it still imports natural gas from Afghanistan by means of a pipeline constructed in 1974. There are a number of large hydroelectric stations plus a number of thermal electric stations. Tajikistan exports some of its electricity to other republics.

Gold is mined at two sites in the northern part of the republic. Current production is fairly small, only 3.79 tons in 1991. A major new gold combine is currently under construction, however, and gold production is expected to double after it becomes operational.

Tajikistan manufactures a number of engineering or metalworking products, including looms, power transformers, cables, and agricultural and household equipment. There is also a nitrogen fertilizer plant, built in 1967. Most workers in industry are non–Tajiks.

The 1992–1997 civil war left Tajikistan with a badly damaged infrastructure and a continued distrust between factions that makes reconciliation extremely difficult at best. But there are signs of hope. In November 1997, Tajikistan received a pledge of $56.6 million from a United Nations–sponsored international donor conference in Vienna, to be used for demobilizing the army, preparing for multiparty elections, the resettlement of refugees and displaced persons, and generally repairing the country's damaged economy.

## The Future

Independence has not been kind to Tajikistan—political instability, then five years of civil war. Now that may be over. A political accord, reached in June 1997, established a power–sharing arrangement between the government and the political opposition that is supposed to last until new, free elections occur sometime before the end of 1998. There is now a hope—but only a hope—that Tajikistan is finally moving toward a stable political situation.

**Famous woodcarver Sirodzhitdin Nuritdinov in his studio**          Courtesy: NOVOSTI

181

# The Republic of Turkmenistan

**Inside a typical Turkmen home in Ashgabat**

**Area:** 186,400 sq. mi. (488,100. sq. km., as large as California and half of Oregon).

**Population:** 4.5 million.

**Capital City:** Ashgabat (formerly Ashkabad) (Pop. 407,000).

**Climate:** Hot and dry summers, very cold in winter.

**Neighboring Countries:** Kazakhstan (north), Uzbekistan (north and east), Iran, Afghanistan (south).

**Language:** Turkmen.

**Ethnic Composition:** Turkmen (77%), Russian (6.7%), Uzbek (9.2%), Kazakh (2%), others (5.1%).

**Principal Religion:** Islam. Until recently, religious worship was officially discouraged.

**Chief Commercial Products:** Oil, natural gas minerals, cotton, jute, fruits (grapes), vegetables, sheep, goats.

**Currency:** Manat (issued November 1993).

**Per Capita Annual Income:** About U.S. $1,600.

**Recent Political Status:** A republic was formed in 1924, but in 1925 it was incorporated into the former USSR and remained so until 1991.

**National Day:** October 27.

**Chief of State:** Saparmurad Niyazov, President. He is also head of the Government Cabinet of Ministers.

**National Flag:** A solid green background; superimposed against the green on the left, a red–brown fabric pattern consisting of five medallions runs slightly indented from top to bottom; to the right of that in the upper left, a crescent moon with five stars.

## The Land

The Republic of Turkmenistan, independent successor state to the Turkmen Soviet Socialist Republic, declared its independence following the collapse of the attempted *coup* against the USSR's Gorbachëv in August 1991. October 27 has been established as the official independence day.

Although it borders on the Caspian Sea in the west, Turkmenistan is almost entirely a land of deserts and passes. The entire central part of the republic is occupied by the largest of these, the Kara Kum, or Black Sand Desert. Topographically, it is also the southern part of the Turan Plain. Only in the south are there foothills and mountains. The Kopet–Dag forms the border with eastern Iran, while northern–reaching spurs of the Pamir Alay Mountain Ranges form the border with Afghanistan and the south part of the border with Uzbekistan. On the northeast, the Amu Darya River flows along the border with Uzbekistan. It borders on the Caspian Sea in the west.

Three other rivers, the Tedzhen, Murgab and Atrek, flow north out of the southern mountains and provide water for irrigation. In the 1950s, the Kara Kum Canal was constructed from Kerki on the Amu Darya northwestward across the southern part of the Kara Kum to the city of Merv and Ashgabat, the capital. It is the world's largest irrigation and shipping canal. Oases exist along the rivers plus in the foothills of the Kopet–Dag Mountains. The rest of the country is desert.

Turkmenistan has a strongly continental climate, extremely hot in summer (average of 95° F.), and bitterly cold in winter (temperatures as low as −27° F.). Precipitation averages 3 inches a year in the northwestern desert and 12 inches in the southern mountains. Except in oases areas, only desert vegetation grows.

## The People

Turkmen make up 68% of the republic's population. The two largest minorities are Russians (13%) and Uzbeks (9%). In addition, there are smaller numbers of Kazakhs, Tatars, Ukrainians, Armenians,

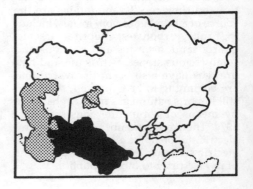

Kara Kalpaks and Azeris. Russians are found mainly in urban areas. About half the people live in urban areas, the rest in rural settlements and villages. Turkmen is, as the name implies, a Turkic language.

## History

The Turkmens were mostly nomads up to the time of the Russian Revolution, though some had settled in oases and taken up agriculture. Divided up into a number of tribes, their main loyalty was to their tribe or clan, with almost no sense of a Turkmen identity. The creation of the Turkmen Soviet Socialist Republic in October 1924 provided a strong impetus toward creation of a Turkmen nation. Turkmens are the most distinctive of the Turkic peoples of Central Asia. Their language is closer to that of the Ottoman Turks and Azerbaijani than it is to the other Turkic peoples of Central Asia. Their origins are disputed, however. They have apparently been Moslems since the tenth century but, because they were desert tribes, the only record of their past is oral. Their main tribes were the Tekes, Ersaris, and Yomut. There were bitter rivalries between the tribes. Thus when the Tekes were fighting a struggle to drive back the Russians in the 1860s and 1870s, the other tribes offered no assistance whatsoever.

In 1869, a Russian military force landed on the eastern shore of the Caspian Sea and founded a settlement at the location of present–day Krasnovodsk. Five years later, the Transcaspian military district was established. This became the Transcaspian *oblast* in 1881. There was fierce resistance to the Russian advance, but it was broken at the battle of Geok–Tepe in 1881. In 1899, the area was incorporated into the Governor Generalship of Turkistan.

Turkmenistan was the scene of intermittent fighting during the Russian civil war that followed the Bolshevik Revolution. Red Army troops conquered Ashgabat in July 1919 and Krasnovoksk in February 1920. The Bolsheviks organized the western part of present–day Turkmenistan as a separate *oblast* of the Turkistan Autonomous SSR. The remaining parts were included in the Bukharan and Khorezmian Soviet Socialist Republics. In 1924, a Turkmen Soviet Socialist Republic was formed, which took in all three Turkmen–inhabited areas. The Turkmen SSR was formally incorporated into the USSR in May 1925.

The life of the Turkmen people changed almost completely during the seventy years of the Soviet period but, through it all, the Turkmen SSR remained one of the most obedient of the constituent republics of the USSR. This began to change somewhat after Gorbachëv became General Secretary in 1985 and launched his program of *glasnost* and *perestroika*. In August 1990, the Turkmen Supreme Soviet passed

**President Saparmurad Niyazov**

a declaration of sovereignty, though there was still no real challenge to Soviet authority. However, Saparmurad Niyazov, first secretary of the *Turkmen Communist Party*, had the Supreme Soviet create the office of president and he was elected to that office in October 1990.

The attempted *coup* against Gorbachëv in August 1991 changed this situation again. Following the collapse of the USSR President Niyazov issued a declaration of Turkmen independence and called for a referendum on the question, which took place on October 26. When the referendum received a 94% favorable vote, President Niyazov declared October 27 Turkmen independence day.

He confiscated all assets held by the *Communist Party of the Soviet Union* within the republic, but he remained first secretary of the *Turkmen Communist Party,* and on November 18–19, the Central Committee of the party held a plenum to consider the future. It called a party congress for December 16 and recommended that the party be renamed the *Turkmen Democratic Party.* This recommendation was implemented by the party congress when it met in December. President Niyazov was elected chairman. According to the program of the *Democratic Party,* it is "oriented towards market reforms, sale of the

state's property and support of all forms of property."

On November 15, Niyazov, who had appointed his prime minister as the chief of a newly formed Turkmen Railroad, decided to take on direct leadership of the government himself. His assumption of the duties of the prime minister was temporary, according to a government spokesman. There was no question of abolishing the office of prime minister. By January 1992, it appeared that the deputy prime minister, Nazar Suyunov, had become the *de facto* head of government.

In April 1993, President Niyazov signed a decree approving a new alphabet of the Turkmen language based on Latin. This change marks the third alphabetic reform for the Turkmen language since the beginning of the century.

Over the past several years, President Niyazov has been increasingly referred to in the press and in public announcements as "Turkmenbashi," or "Leader of the Turkmen." His portrait is ubiquitous, appearing in every parade float, office building and hotel. Every park in the country has a statue of him. The purpose is apparently to increase his popularity among the people by portraying him as a traditional tribal leader and it appears to be working. In a referendum held in January 1994, the people were asked whether they approved extending his term of office until 2002. The final result of the vote was 1,959,408 votes for, 212 against and 17 spoiled ballots. Talking to a western reporter in December 1995, Niyazov admitted that the new cult of personality had gone too far. "I admit it, there are too many portraits, pictures and monuments. I don't find any pleasure in it, but the people demand it because of their mentality."

Elections to the newly created Majlis (legislature) took place in December 1994. Since no oppositional party managed to gain official registration, the candidates were almost all members of the *Democratic Party of Turkmenistan*. All ran unopposed.

President Niyazov had cardiac surgery in Germany on September 1, 1997. The operation was a success and there were no complications. Five weeks later, he chaired his first cabinet meeting since the operation, then later attended a ceremony commemorating the victims of the 1948 earthquake that destroyed Ashgabat. President Niyazov's mother and brothers were among the victims.

## Foreign Policy

Although Turkmenistan has maintained good relations with Russia since emerging as an independent nation in 1991, it has also begun cultivating improved ties with its neighbors to the south. Turkmenistan is a major producer of natural gas. It wishes to export its gas to Europe for hard cur-

# Turkmenistan

rency, but thus far it has had to export its gas to old customers such as Ukraine, Armenia and Georgia, who can't afford to pay in hard currency. Turkmenistan's solution is to build a pipeline through Iran and Turkey and it signed an agreement to do this in August 1994. A new railroad to Iran is also under consideration.

Some of this courting of southern neighbors is mutual. When Turkmenistan celebrated its national day on October 27, 1994, President Niyazov had among his guests Prime Minister Benazir Bhutto of Pakistan, President Ali Akbar Rafsanjani of Iran and President Suleyman Demirel of Turkey. President Niyazov also paid an official visit to Hungary in December 1994.

In what appears to be a slight change in policy, the Turkmen Government signed a agreement with Russia in December 1995 under which Russian troops would take responsibility for protection of Turkmenistan's border with Iran and Afghanistan. Russia and Turkmenistan signed an accord on dual citizenship at the same time. Both agreements were signed during a CIS meeting being hosted by the Turkmenistan Government at Ashgabat.

## Nature of the Regime

Turkmenistan finally got rid of the governmental system inherited from the Soviet era in December 1994. Under the new system, the President acts as both head of state and head of government. He will serve for five years. There is no separate prime minister. The Majlis (legislature) consists of 50 members. It will also be elected for a term of five years.

There is also a constitutional court and a supreme court. The consitution created an additional entity, referred to as the *Khalk Maslakhaty* (People's Supreme Council). The *Khalk Maslakhaty* appears to be some kind of supreme consultative body. Its membership includes the president, the majlis deputies, the chairs of the constitutional, supreme and supreme economic courts, the prosecutor–general, members of government, heads of local government, and representatives from various political parties, public organizations and the clergy. According to a subsequent government announcement, the *Khalk Maslakhaty* adopted a new economic policy for the republic in December 1995 which called for privatization of 15 percent of industry during the following year.

## Culture

Prior to the Russian Revolution, most educated Turkmens were graduates of one of the several seminaries located in Bukhara. Perhaps the most famous of these was Abdulhekim Qulmuhammedoghli, a writer, editor, researcher and cultural organizer, who eventually joined the *Communist Party*. He was killed in 1937 at the time of the great Soviet purge. The level of literacy increased greatly during the Soviet era, but the strait–jacket of socialist realism, instituted by Stalin in 1930, has meant that most work has been written "for the masses." In addition, many Turkmen writers' works were in Russian. This is true also of films, television, radio and theater, which appear in Russian.

Since the fall of communism, there has been a concerted effort to revive traditional Turkmen culture. Mosques have been reopened, various ancient customs and rituals have been revived, and some old taboos are once again observed. Turkmens are Sunni Moslems, but religion, though important, often is less important than tribal loyalties. Turkmenistan is still essentially a tribal culture, dominated by its five major tribes. Tribal ties, officially suppressed under communism, are once again coming to the fore.

Arranged marriages are still the norm in the society, particularly in rural areas. Traditionally, the bride and groom must belong to the same tribe. This causes problems for young people of different tribes who fall in love. Occasionally, a young man will "steal away" the girl he favors, hoping thereby force the parents to agree. This doesn't always work, however. As one Turkmen commented, "it's no joke. Some parents sue the husband in court. Others kill the bride."

## Economy

The Soviet era brought about major changes in the lives of the Turkmen people. Prior to the Russian Revolution, most Turkmens were nomads who constantly moved from place to place in search of forage for their herds. Beginning in the 1930s, great engineering projects were launched to increase the irrigated areas. These irrigated lands were organized into state farms and the Turkmen people were settled on them, their nomadic life at an end.

Cotton became the chief crop grown throughout the area. New engineering projects in the 1950s and 1960s, in particular the Kara Kum Canal, brought additional lands under cultivation and increased Turkmenistan production of cotton even further. Local reports of increasing salinity in the soil or the constant drop in the level of the Aral Sea as a result of the new engineering projects were ignored by the central planners in Moscow.

After 1985, however, Gorbachëv's reforms allowed for greater local autonomy. Beginning about 1987, Turkmenistan began an attempt to restructure its agricultural economy. Moscow was asked to lower its cotton quota somewhat, and some land was removed from cotton production and switched to other crops. Turkmenistan began to grow more grain and feed, and the number of livestock grown also increased. This improved the situation somewhat, but the republic has not yet been able to restructure its economy. This is the likely direction for agriculture in the future, however.

President Niyazov has endorsed the idea of private property, but he has said that he favors transforming money–losing state farms into smaller collective farms and then allowing leasing and creation of rural cooperatives. Some degree of centralization will continue to exist in any case, because all farming depends on irrigation, which must remain centralized.

**A catch of wild carp is hauled from the Kara Kum Canal**          Courtesy: NOVOSTI

**Turkomen carpets for sale in a bazaar outside of Ashgabat**                    Photo by Hermine Dreyfuss

In February 1998, President Niyazov address the Majlis on the subject of agriculture, which he said needed improving. He reported that the country had met only half of the target for grain in 1997, while cotton production was only 41% of the expected total. He did not give any indication of a change in government policy, however. The government sets all purchasing prices for agricultural products.

Turkmenistan is the least industrialized of all the Central Asian republics, with only 14.4% of material production provided by industry. What industry it has is mainly extractive. The petroleum industry began to be developed in the 1930s and Turkmenistan now comes third after Russia and Azerbaijan in the production of oil. Natural gas was also found and exploited and Turkmenistan now has a surplus which it sells to neighboring republics. According to recent estimates, Turkmenistan has the third–largest gas reserves in the world, while its estimated oil reserves in the Caspian Basin are second only to Kazakhstan's. Unlike Kazakhstan and Azerbaijan, however, very little foreign investment has flowed into the country since independence. Meanwhile, President Niyazov has spent what revenues do flow in from gas sales on presidential estates, fountain–filled parkways along the road to his suburban estate, and a vast palace downtown. The highly personalized nature of the government means that foreign investors cannot rely on contracts remaining in force beyond the term of of-

fice of the official that signed them. Corruption in the form of kickbacks is also universal. As a result, Turkmenistan vies with Tajikistan for the honor of being the poorest of the Central Asian republics.

Until 1997, Turkmenistan's only customers for its natural gas were the other ex–Soviet republics. When Turkmenistan began raising natural gas prices toward world prices, several were unable to afford the higher prices and fell behind in their payments. The war between Azerbaijan and Armenia also meant the loss of Armenia as a customer. Armenia, without gas of its own, had been a large customer, but the pipeline from Turkmenistan passes through Azerbaijan, which cut the flow of gas to Armenia.

Last year was a particularly bad year for Turkmenistan as industrial production slumped by 32.7% over 1996. Almost all sectors suffered, but the 44% decrease in natural gas production was particularly important. Essentially, Turkmenistan reduced deliveries of natural gas to several ex–Soviet republics that had not paid for earlier deliveries of natural gas. All of that began to change in 1998 with completion of a pipeline between Turkmenistan's Korpedzhe gas field and the Iranian town of Kord Kuy. Turkmenistan will export 4 billion cubic meters of natural gas to Iran in 1998 and expects to raise this to 12 billion cubic meters in 1999. In addition, Turkmenistan, Iran and Turkey signed an agreement in December 1997 with Royal Dutch/Shell for the construction of a $1.6

billion pipeline to Turkey. If this second pipeline is completed, Turkmenistan will be able to export an additional 30 billion cubic meters of natural gas a year.

Little has changed in the rest of the industrial sector thus far. Some privatization of small enterprises was carried out in 1992, but everything else remained in state hands. In November 1997, however, President Niyazov announced that 50 state–owned enterprises would be auctioned off in March 1998. Half of these companies are in the textile sector, while the remainder are in the energy, industry, construction, and food and fruit sectors. Turkmenistan eventually intends to auction off 350 such companies.

### The Future

As one of the poorer societies of Central Asia and the least developed, Turmenistan's evolution over the past several years has been painful and it has made no progress whatsoever in evolving toward a democracy. Things may begin to improve economically, however, since the completion of a new pipeline to Iran, which has allowed it, for the first time, to export natural gas to a country able to pay in hard currency. If it could now achieve some political progress, it might be able to use its new hard currency earnings to finance the transition in the rest of the economy. That doesn't appear to be likely in the near future, however.

# The Republic of Uzbekistan

**Tashkent, the ancient capital of Uzbekistan shows its modern face**

Courtesy: NOVOSTI

**Area:** 186,400 sq. mi. (447,400 sq. km.; as large as New York, Pennsylvania, Ohio, West Virginia, New Jersey, Maryland and Delaware combined).

**Population:** 23 million.

**Capital City:** Tashkent (Pop. 2,073,000).

**Climate:** Very hot and dry with average annual rainfall of only 8 inches.

**Neighboring Countries:** Kazakhstan (west and north), Kyrgyzstan, Tajikistan (east), Afghanistan (south), Turkmenistan (south and southwest).

**Principal Languages:** Uzbek and Russian.

**Ethnic Composition:** Uzbek (71%), Russian (8%), Tatars (4.2%), Kazakhs (4%), Tadzhiks (3.9%), others (8.9%).

**Principal Religion:** Islam. Until recently, religious worship was officially discouraged.

**Chief Commercial Products:** Cotton, livestock, melons, fruit, vegetables, wheat and rice, all due to vast irrigation. Textiles, food processing and construction materials.

**Currency:** Sum (Issued November 1993).

**Annual Per Capita Income:** About U.S. $1,100.

**Recent Political Status:** The republic was proclaimed in 1924 and became part of the former USSR in 1925, which it remained until 1991.

**Chief of State:** Islam Karimov, President.

**National Flag:** Three equal, horizontal stripes, sky blue, white, green, separated by narrow red stripes. In the upper left against the blue, a crescent moon and to the right of it three rows of stars (3,4,5), aligned on the right.

## The Land

The Republic of Uzbekistan, independent successor of the Uzbek Soviet Socialist Republic, declared its independence on August 26, 1991. Its large area stretches from west of the Aral Sea to the Fergana Valley in the east.

Uzbekistan takes in parts of the Amu Darya River Valley plus the southern half of the Kysyl–Kum Desert. In the east, the republic includes the Fergana River Val-

ley up to the foothills of the Tien Shan Mountain Range, which surrounds the valley on three sides. It is almost exclusively a landscape of deserts and dry steppes, with fertile oases formed by rivers flowing across the dry plains from out of the mountains to the south and southeast.

That part of Uzbekistan which lies west of the Aral Sea is known as the Ust–Urt

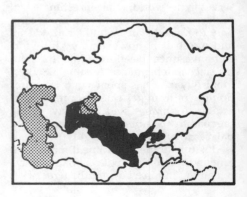

186

Flatland. This area is a dry steppeland, flat and sun–baked and useful only for certain types of grazing. The Aral Sea, which Uzbekistan shares with Kazakhstan, was once the world's fourth–largest body of inland water and supported a large fishing industry. In the last 30–40 years, however, the sea and the land bordering on it have become an ecological disaster area. Since 1960, the Aral Sea has lost 60 percent of its water by volume and the level of the water has dropped nearly 50 feet. Each year, it drops another 9–10 inches.

The problem is that it receives its water from two main rivers, the Amu Darya and the Syr Darya, and those two rivers flow through 600 miles of desert and semi–desert before emptying into the Aral Sea. They form natural oases along their banks, but these cultivated areas were greatly extended in the Soviet era through new irrigation projects. Uzbekistan today has 10.75 million acres of land under irrigation, mainly along the lower reaches of the Amu Darya. There are another 8.25 million acres of irrigated land in Turk-

menistan, the Fergana River Valley of Krygyzstan and Kazakhstan. To stabilize the Aral Sea at its present level, the republics would have to agree to cut water usage sufficiently to allow the annual flow into it to grow from 11 million cubic kilometers to 35 million cubic kilometers per year. To raise it to its 1960 level, the republics would have to agree to cut out all water usage for three decades. Neither alternative is practical, so the Aral Sea will continue to shrink. Its salinity is steadily increasing.

## The People

Uzbekistan is the largest of the Central Asian republics in terms of population. Uzbeks make up about 71% of the population of the country. Russians, who constitute another 8%, are the largest minority, followed by Tatars (4.2%), Kazakhs (4%), and Tajiks (3.9%). Since 1936, Uzbekistan has also included the Kara–Kalpakia Autonomous Republic, located along the southern shores of the Aral Sea in the delta region of the Amu Darya River. Kara–Kalpakia has a population of about

1.2 million, with Kara–Kalpakians, Uzbeks and Kazakhs each constituting a little less than a third of the population. Both Uzbek and Kara–Kalpakian are Turkic languages.

## History

The area where modern–day Uzbekistan is situated was an ancient center of civilization, beginning with ancient states like Bactria and Sogdiana. It was incorporated into the Persian Empire of Darius the Great and the Empire of Alexander the Great. In the eighth century, it was invaded by Arab forces and Islam was introduced for the first time. It became part of the Mongol Empire in the thirteenth century, then of the Empire of Tamerlane.

The Uzbeki people were late–comers to the area, however, arriving probably sometime in the fifteenth century. They are believed to be subordinate tribes of the Kipchak Khanate who called themselves Uzbeks in honor of the greatest Kipchak Khans, Uzbek or *Uzbeg*. Originally settled in the area of the Irtysh River, they began

**A metro station in Tashkent**                                          Courtesy: NOVOSTI

# Uzbekistan

**Registan Square in Samarkand**

to move southeastward in the fifteenth century under their ruler Abu al–Khayr Khan. His grandson, Muhammad Shaybani, conquered Samarkand and most of the Syr–Darya River Valley and the land south of it up to the Amu Darya.

The Shaybani dynasty ruled at Samarkand until 1598, with a collateral branch ruling in Khiva (called Khwarezm until the eighteenth century). Another dynasty, the Janids, ruled a portion of the country until the eighteenth century, when a reinvigorated Persia invaded and conquered Bukhara and Khiva.

The area between the Amu Darya and Syr–Darya was dominated by three khanates by the beginning of the nineteenth century—Bukhara, Khiva and Kokand. More city–states than empires, they exercised very little control over the nomadic tribes of the desert and semi–desert. These tribes subsisted by raids on settlements to the north.

As Russian settlers pushed into the area, raids became more frequent and a problem for the Russian military which was charged with protecting the area. Building first a line of forts along the frontier, they then began retaliatory raids. Finally they began annexing the border areas. Kokand was attacked in 1864–65 and

the emir was forced to cede Chimkent and Tashkent. In 1868, Bukhara was forced to accept the status of Russian vassal. Khiva fell in 1873. Kokand was formally annexed in 1876. The Imperial Russian Government referred to the areas it had annexed as Russian Turkistan. Bukhara and Khiva continued to be semi–independent khanates.

At the time of the Russian Revolution, a Turkistan Committee of the Provisional Government was set up in Tashkent, but it was soon replaced in April 1918 by the Autonomous Soviet Socialist Republic of Turkistan. Lenin extended his direct control over this organization in the fall of 1919. In 1920, the semi–independent Khanates of Khiva and Bokhara were conquered by the Red Army and made into People's Republics. Khiva was transformed into a Soviet Socialist Republic in 1923, Bokhara in 1924.

A fundamental redrawing of Central Asian boundaries along ethnic lines took place in 1924. The republics of Khiva, Turkistan, and Bukhara were abolished and five new republics were created. As a result, the Uzbekistan Soviet Socialist Republic was created in October 1924. It included a large part of the Samarkand region, a large part of the Fergana Valley,

part of the upper reaches of the Syr–Darya River, including Tashkent and the surrounding area, plus the western plains of Bukhara. Between 1924 and 1929, it also included the Tadzhikistan Autonomous SSR, Tadzhikistan became a republic in its own right in 1929.

Uzbekistan received certain parts of Kazakhstan in 1956 and 1963, including part of the Hungry Steppe. Some of that land was returned in 1971.

Soviet rule imposed many changes on Uzbekistan, but perhaps the greatest change was the development of huge state farms that use irrigation to make Uzbekistan one of the principal producers of Central Asian cotton. Most people are, in effect, state employees and they have been mostly docile. Throughout the entire Soviet era, the *Communist Party* monopolized political power, so there was little chance for a political opposition to grow. The *Uzbek Communist Party* did begin making nationalist noises after several years of Gorbachëv's perestroika and in June 1990 the Uzbek Supreme Soviet adopted a resolution of sovereignty.

The leader of the *Uzbek Communist Party*, Islam Karimov, remained silent in August 1991 until it had become clear that the *coup* against Gorbachëv was

# Uzbekistan

failing. He then joined in condemning it and banned communist party cells in the armed forces, police and civil service. He declared Uzbekistan independent on August 31. In mid–September, Karimov called a congress of the *Uzbek Communist Party* and the name of the party was changed to the *People's Democratic Party.* There has, however, been no change in the personnel running the government, though Karimov began allowing some criticism in the Uzbek Supreme Soviet.

Karimov adopted Uzbek nationalist slogans, but he said publicly that Uzbekistan was not ready for democracy or a market economy. Later, he attempted to give himself a democratic aura by having the Uzbek Supreme Soviet provide for a popularly elected presidency and elections were set for December 29, 1991. Other political parties were legalized, but they were not able to operate freely. The Uzbek popular front *Birlik,*, potentially the largest opposition grouping, was not permitted to field a candidate. The *Islamic Renaissance Movement,* which advocated an Islamic state, was banned. Only the *Erk Democratic Party,* which split from *Birlik* in 1990, was permitted to field a candidate. Karimov won 86% percent of the popular vote. His opponent, Mohamed Salikh, got 12.4%. In a separate referendum, 98.2 percent cast their votes in favor of Uzbek independence.

When U.S. Secretary of State James Baker visited Tashkent in January 1992, he met with Abdurahmin Pulatov, co–chairman of *Birlik.* Pulatov urged Baker to recognize Uzbekistan independence, but he admitted that there was no democracy in Uzbekistan. "Politically, we have no freedom at all. The totalitarian regime has been destroyed in Moscow, but in Tashkent it continues to exist."

Very little has changed since January 1992 and current reports out of Uzbekistan indicate that the government still tolerates very little dissent. One reason may be the very volatile nature of the Uzbeki people. In January 1992, for example, riots broke out in Uzbekistan after price increases, and calls were heard for the resignation of President Karimov. The virtual civil war in neighboring Tajikistan between 1993 and 1997 was almost certainly a major factor as well. Karimov was concerned that a similar situation could develop in Uzbekistan. For that reason, the government has not permitted political demonstrations, it has banned religious-oriented political parties, and it has arrested and imprisoned numerous members of the political opposition. The activities of Birlik, the main opposition movement, were suspended in January 1993. Since that time, a number of Birlik leaders have been arrested. Even the registered opposition party, Erk (Freedom), has suffered

tremendous harassment from the government, its newspaper shut and its bank accounts seized.

Parliamentary elections took place in December 1994 under the terms of a new constitution that reduced the number of deputies from 500 to 250. The governing *People's Democratic Party* won 205 seats. Real oppositional political parties were not permitted to participate in the elections, but there was a second party, the *National Progress Party,* which was created by the government to represent business interests. It took 6 seats. Thirty–nine seats went unfilled because no candidate got a

majority of the votes; they were filled later in a second round of voting.

New presidential elections were originally scheduled to take place in 1996, but they were postponed. In March 1995, a referendum was held which asked the people to approve extending the term of the president until the year 2000. The excuse was that this would put the elections for the presidency on the same schedule as that for the legislature.

The relative calm of the past several years was broken in December 1997 when four policemen were killed in the city of Namangan, known as a center of Islamic

At *Uzbekistan Restaurant* in Tashkent, chef Bikhadyr Iskhakov prepares a traditional Uzbek dish—*lagman,* pasta with mutton
Courtesy: NOVOSTI

189

# Uzbekistan

fervency. Although no one claimed responsibility for the killings, the government blamed Islamic militants and launched a massive crackdown. It also enforced a 9 p.m. curfew in Namangan and the neighboring city of Andizhan. Following the crackdown, veiled women organized demonstrations before the presidential palace in Tashkent to protest the arrest and detention of their sons and husbands without charges. As one of the demonstrating women said of her husband, "there are no charges. He has a beard, so they accuse him of being a Wahabi." The government routinely uses the word Wahabi as a catch-all pejorative which it applies to all Islamic devotees.

Abid Khan Nazarov, a religious leader expelled in 1995 as the imam of an important mosque in Tashkent, said of the current situation, "Government policy is becoming tougher and people are losing their tolerance. There is the danger that the situation will provoke the emergence of some terrorist group."

## Nature of the Regime

Uzbekistan has created a presidential–parliamentary system similar to those found in the other ex–Soviet republics. It is different from other republics in one major respect, however. The old ruling *Uzbek Communist Party* merely changed its name but continues to exercise the dominant political role in the republic. It is now the *People's Democratic Party.*

Thus far, the new parliament has been as subservient to the political leadership as its predecessor had been. There is a Prime Minister who presides over the cabinet, but he has no independent political role. Appointed by the president, he must be confirmed by the legislature.

In January 1992, a law on the reorganization of the local authority bodies created a new executive official at the region, district and town level. These *khokim* report to the republic president and to the legislative body over which they also preside. The decree did not specify whether the *khokim* were appointed or elected. They would appear to exercise authority similar to that of a prefect in the French system.

## Culture

Uzbekis are among the most traditional of the Central Asian peoples and national costumes are still often worn. Men wear a robe striped with bright colors and an embroidered skullcap. Women wear bright silk dresses with a shawl over the head. Rugs cover the floors of Uzbeki houses and often folk art decorates the walls. There are also traditional Uzbeki festivals in various times of the year when the people dress up in their finery and there is singing and dancing. Another specialty of the festivals is horse dancing. This is also

**Students at Alisher Navoi University in Samarkand listen to a lecturer**
Courtesy: NOVOSTI

the time for games and tests of strength, dexterity and skill. And of course food plays a role. Some of the distinctive foods include *d'ighman* (meat with pastry in a strong broth), spicy chopped meat wrapped in a thin dough, and *plov* (rice with meat, vegetables, spices and dried apricots).

Religion also plays a great role in the lives of the Uzbeki people, and attendance at the Friday mosque service has been increasing in recent years. Uzbekis are Sunni Moslems of the Hanafi school. Sufism is also practiced by some, and there is a famous Sufi school, the Naqshbandi or *tariqat–al–Khwajagan,* in Bukhara.

The government has taken an ambivalent attitude toward Islam. Moderate leaders have been wooed, but when 400 Moslems tried to hold a congress in Tashkent, the leaders were arrested and non–Uzbekis were expelled from the republic. On the other hand, no effort is made to discourage the practice of Islam, and new mosques are being built every day. New Islamic seminaries have also been opened.

Tashkent is the Islamic center for Central Asia. The "Spiritual Department of Moslems of Central Asia," headed by the Mufti of Tashkent, is located here. It is allowed to receive large sums of money from Saudi Arabia, which has also donated a million *Korans* for distribution in Central Asia. It also publishes a newspaper, *Dawn of Islam,* and a magazine, *Islamic Faith.*

Uzbekistan has produced a number of writers in the twentieth century. Perhaps the best known is Abdullah Qadiri, famous for two historical novels, *Days Gone By* and *Scorpion from the Pulpit,* published in the 1920s. Qadiri was later killed in the Soviet purges of the late 1930s. *Sisters,* the novel of Asqad Mukhtar, has been translated into English. Uzbeks have also made some original contributions in modern graphic arts. Some of the ancient skills such as ornamental wall painting, wood carving and fabric printing have also been kept alive. There is an Uzbek film studio where films in the Uzbeki language are made, and the republic also has its own radio and television facilities. The Navoi Theater of Opera and Ballet in Tashkent is also famous for its productions.

## Economy

Uzbekistan has what is traditionally referred to as a commercial single–crop agricultural economy. What this means is that the republic is heavily dependent on the production of a single agricultural product, cotton, which is mainly exported outside the republic. In fact, Uzbekistan is by far the largest producer of cotton in what was Soviet Central Asia, being responsible for two–thirds of all cotton production.

Almost all agriculture is dependent on irrigation, and practically all irrigated land is now organized into huge state farms whose sole product is cotton. The majority of the people are employees of these huge state farms.

Silkworms are raised in the Fergana Valley, with mulberry trees planted along the streets and irrigation canals. Orchards of apricots, peaches, figs, and pears, and vineyards, used to produce table grapes, raisins and wine, are found in the Fergana Valley, the Zeravshan oasis and the Chirchik and Agren Valleys. Farm wages are low. Uzbekistan has a standard of living that is just half of the old Soviet average. Moreover, the republic has the second highest birth rate of Central Asia, which has resulted in a surplus rural population. The unemployment rate in the republic was over ten percent even before the collapse of the Soviet system.

Uzbekistan has large reserves of natural gas, petroleum and coal. Most local industry use natural gas. Gas is also exported to Russia via a pipeline that runs from Bukhara to the area of the Urals and then on to European Russia. Petroleum is being produced in the Fergana Valley, in the area around Bukhara, and in the area south of the Aral Sea. The Angren coal field produces coal for local use, but coal deposits have not been developed to any great extent.

Plentiful energy supplies are used to support some industry as well. Uzbekistan produces machines and heavy equipment, its specialty being machinery for cotton cultivation and harvesting. Machinery for irrigation projects and road construction are also manufactured, plus some for the textile industry.

Uzbekistan also mines copper, zinc and lead ores, plus tungsten and molybdenum. It also produces fertilizers, cement, cotton textiles, coke and chemicals.

Uzbekistan has been the most reluctant of all the Central Asian republics to reform, but there has been some movement forward in recent months. The first steps were taken in February 1994, when President Karimov decreed a package of economic reforms designed to set up a market economy. Subsidies on basic foodstuffs and public transport were to be phased out and subsidies on utilities were to be reduced. Peasant farmers were also granted private plots of land.

There brought some improvement in the economy. Inflation, running at an annual rate of 1,100% at the end of 1993, dropped to 270% by the end of 1994. Foreign reserves also grew in 1994 and there was a bumper cotton crop. A Mercedes–Benz joint venture began turning out its first trucks as well.

Agricultural production fell below expectations in 1995–97, however, with a grain harvest in 1997 of only 2.86 million tons, two–thirds of the target figure for the year. The government may have been worried that there would not be enough food to feed the entire population, for it introduced "centralized purchasing" in August 1997, under which the government controls sales of flour, sugar, edible oil and butter.

### The Future

Uzbekistan has two problems which appear unsolvable—the shrinking Aral Sea and a standard of living that has been dropping for a number of years. Both of these are related to an overdependence on the production of cotton using irrigation. Greater industrialization is a possibility that could provide more jobs for Uzbekis, but they have been reluctant to leave the land. Even today, a majority of jobs in industry are held by ethnic Russians.

All of this puts a great strain on government and helps explain why the country has not made greater progress toward democracy or a market economy. President Karimov is extremely paternalistic, but he recently began moving Uzbekistan in the direction of change. Progress is likely to be slow, however.

**Women doing gold embroidery—a traditional art form—at factory in Bukhara**

Photo by Hermine Dreyfuss

**EASTERN EUROPE**
The Danube River at Budapest, Hungary.

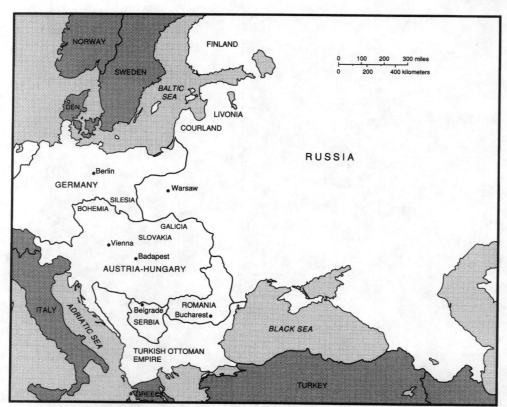

. . . in 1877

. . . in 1914

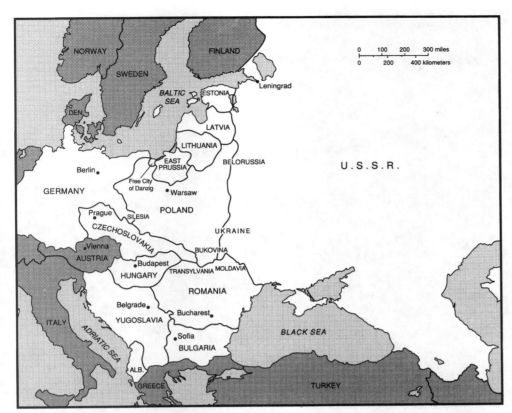

## . . . in 1921

## . . . and today

# The Republic of Albania

**Installation of new traffic lights in Tirana**

Photo by Martha Grenon

**Area:** 28,749 sq. km. = 11,000 sq. mi.
**Population:** 3,350,000 (1991 est.)
**Capital City:** Tirane (or Tirana) (Pop. 210,000; 1990 est.)
**Climate:** Mediterranean, with wet winters and hot, dry summers on the coast. The interior is colder in the winter.
**Neighboring Countries:** Rump Yugoslavia (North and Northeast); Macedonia (East); Greece (South).
**Official Language:** Albanian.
**Other Principal Tongues:** Greek
**Ethnic Background:** Illyrian, an ancient Indo–European group, mixed with Slav, Greek and Turkish ancestry.
**Principal Religions:** Islam (70%); Eastern–rite Orthodox Christianity (20%); Roman Catholic Christianity (10%). Most people refer to themselves now as non–practicing, though interest in religion is growing.
**Chief Commercial Products:** Tobacco, cigarettes, timber, wood, dairy products.
**Currency:** Lek.
**Former Political Status:** Part of the Roman and Byzantine empires; conquered by the Ottoman Turks in the 15th century and under Turkish control until 1912, following which there were six years of conflicts and change associated with the Balkan Wars and World War I. Incorporated into Italy by Mussolini in 1939. Communist state from 1945 to 1991.
**National Day:** November 28, Independence Day.
**Chief of State:** Rexhep Meidani, President.
**Head of Government:** Fatos Nano, Prime Minister.
**National Flag:** Red, with a black, two–headed eagle.

## THE LAND AND THE PEOPLE

Albania is a small, largely mountainous land located along the eastern shores of the Adriatic Sea. In spite of its small size, it has a widely varied climate, the major factor being the mountains. About one– seventh of Albania consists of a series of small plains running north to south down along the coastline. Here the climate is hot and humid in the summer and relatively warm in most winters. Semi–tropical crops such as citrus can be produced, but other crops include figs, wine grapes and olives. Further inland, the plains are at increasing elevations and are correspondingly cooler— the average temperature in July is 63°F. in these regions. Here the chief crop grown is grain. As the elevation rises even further, the green foliage of rolling pastures gives way to sparse evergreens and scattered brush, which in turn is replaced by gray and brown craggy peaks rising steeply to the sky. The air is thin, cold and clear—this is the home of the eagle, where few sounds interrupt the stillness.

In this setting the people continue the isolated life they have experienced for centuries. There are some settlements that have little or no contact with the rest of Albania because of their inaccessibility. The few towns that exist are usually the result of a need for a place to trade agricultural goods. Fishermen ply the cool waters of Lake Shkodër in flat–bottomed boats. Although there is mineral wealth, it

is almost impossible to extract it profitably because of the lack of transportation.

Most of the Albanians of today are remote descendants of the Illyrians, an ancient people of the Indo–European group; at one time, they were to be found throughout most of the Balkan Peninsula, but they were either gradually absorbed or driven out as successive waves of Slavs moved into the area; now they are found only in the western part of the Balkans. Even so, they spill across borders and are found in Serbia, Macedonia, and Greece. There are also colonies of Albanians in Italy, but that is the result of past migrations. In addition, there are about 600,000 persons of Albanian descent living in the United States.

Southern Albania (in Greece, known as North Epirus), has a significant Greek minority, estimated by Albania to be 90,000 and by Greece to be 200,000. Because of the poor economic conditions in Albania, however, most of the men of this area actually live and work in Greece, with only the women and children left behind.

## HISTORY

### Early Albanian Governments

The Kingdom of Illyria came into being in the 3rd century B.C., centered around an ancient city on the site of present–day Shkodër. Conquered by the Romans in 167 B.C., the area remained a part of the Roman Empire for the next five centuries. When the Empire dissolved in the 4th century A.D., Illyria became a part of the Eastern Roman—later Byzantine Empire.

As the Slavs arrived in the Adriatic re-

gion in the 6th and 7th centuries, most of the Illyrians were absorbed; the rest settled along the southern Adriatic coast where Albania is now located. During the centuries which followed, Albania was conquered and reconquered by various eastern and western armies. The most lasting influence was that of the Serbs and the Venetians (Italians).

The Albanians were conquered by the Ottoman Turks in the 15th century and incorporated into their Empire. Although the Albanians had put up stiff resistance to the Ottoman conquest, once they had been absorbed politically, they allowed themselves to be absorbed culturally as well. Albania was the only part of the Balkan Peninsula where the majority of the population converted to Islam.

Albanian nationalism was awakened by the decisions of the major powers at the Congress of Berlin which was held after the Russian–Turkish war of 1877–1878. The great powers awarded to Montenegro (now a part of Yugoslavia) and Greece territories which the Albanians claimed as their own.

They formed the *League of Prizren* to protest the division of lands they felt should not be given to neighboring countries, but this effort was not successful. They also demanded local control within a reformed Turkish Empire rather than independence which would have put them at the mercy of other foreign powers. Both Italy and Austria–Hungary had been showing interest in the area. Although the Turks supported the *League* in its protest against the expansion of neighboring states, the demand for local control was turned down. The Turks suppressed the *League* in 1881, and banned use of the Albanian language in 1886.

The *League* was a means of expressing the first national feelings of the Albanians in their native land, and when it and Albanian liberty were crushed, the national movement was taken up by Albanian communities living in Italy and the United States. Oppression by the Turks continued and there was a series of rebellions from 1909 to 1912 which resulted in Albanian control of almost all of what is now that country.

The remaining Turkish power was eliminated in the First Balkan War of 1912, and on November 28 of that year, a national assembly met at Vlore and proclaimed Albania's independence. Ismail Qemal headed the first provisional government.

### The Birth of a Modern Albania

The Treaty of London ending the First Balkan War (1912) left the question of Albania to a conference of the major powers' ambassadors. They agreed with the demand for independence, but as might have been expected, they redrew the map of the region. Shkodër, demanded by

Montenegro, was left to Albania; Kosovo, inhabited by a large number of Albanians, was given to Serbia, creating a problem that lingers to this day. In the south, the powers gave part of northern Greece to Albania, but with Greek support, the people revolted.

The great powers also provided a hand–picked ruler for Albania—William of Wied, a German Prince. Italian–supported Essad Pasha, successor of Ismail Qemal, was actually the most important man in the country. The years 1912–1914 were turbulent—there were rebellions in the north and south where borders were disputed and general dissatisfaction throughout the country. Prince William fled at the outbreak of World War I.

Four years of utter anarchy followed, with the armies of Serbia, Montenegro (now both part of Yugoslavia), Greece, Italy, France, Austria and Bulgaria occupying parts of Albania. At the end of the war, Albania was occupied by Italy, with Serbia holding the northeastern region and Korcä in the possession of the French.

On December 25, 1918, delegates from all parts of Albania met at Durrës to elect a provisional government and to send a delegation to the Paris Peace Conference to present a demand that Albania's 1913 borders be restored. Greece, Italy and Yugoslavia had made a secret deal to divide

**Albanians under the Turks (1910), and as an independent kingdom (1912).**

# Albania

Albania between them. This was firmly rejected by U.S. President Woodrow Wilson—his action and the determination of the Albanian leaders saved the tiny nation.

In order to understand events that followed World War I, it is necessary to remember that Albania was still a primitive country. Although unique and interesting culturally, it was backward—there was no written Albanian language and no education system. There were only a few miles of road and one bridge. There was no industry in the whole country. Albania was divided into many localities along social, religious and geographic lines and the basic unit of power was the clan. Government control was at best scanty.

A parliamentary and cabinet system of government emerged in 1920. Italy, preoccupied with its own problems, reluctantly recognized Albania's government. The border questions were finally resolved by the major powers in 1926. Two political parties were organized, the *Progressive Party* dominated by Moslem leaders and the *Popular Party* headed by a liberal Greek Orthodox Bishop, Fan S. Noli, who had a U.S. college degree.

Ahmed Bey Zogu, one of the leaders of the *Popular Party* became Albania's premier in 1922 when he stayed to defend the capital against a revolt after the rest of the government had fled. Two years later, he resigned and fled to Yugoslavia when an angry band of demonstrators marched on the capital. Noli, his successor, hoped to introduce a reform program which would literally drag Albania into the 20th century. This could not be done without massive outside aid or internal unity. Noli could muster neither. Zogu returned with the support of Yugoslav troops; the National Assembly proclaimed Albania a republic and elected Zogu president for 7 years.

Ruthless and determined, Zogu had a constituent assembly proclaim Albania a "democratic, parliamentary and hereditary kingdom" in 1928 with himself as King Zog I. He sought financial assistance from Italy; by the mid 1930's this ripened into Italian control of Albania's economy. The fascist Italian dictator, Benito Mussolini, sent an invasion force which swept Albania on April 7, 1939; Victor Emmanuel, figurehead King of Italy also became King of Albania. Italy mounted an invasion of Greece through Albania; it was repulsed by Greek and Yugoslav armies which were able to occupy much of Albania until a German attack in 1941.

## Albania Reborn as a People's Republic

Resistance groups were organized in 1941–42 by communists and non-communists. The *Albanian Communist Party* was founded in 1941 with Yugoslav help; among its leaders was Enver Hoxha, a

**King Zog I**

young man educated in France and Belgium and considered one of the "intellectuals" in the party. The party set up the *National Liberation Movement (LNC)*, which for a time included the clan chief Abbas Kupi and his guerrilla fighters.

Another resistance group, the *National Front (Balli Kombetär)* had an anti–royalist and strongly nationalistic outlook. The two groups came close to joining in 1943, but the *LNC*, on the advice of the Yugoslav communist leader Tito, backed out and soon the two groups were fighting each other. A provisional government headed by Enver Hoxha was formed in October 1944, moving to Tirana as the government of Albania upon withdrawal of the German forces.

Albania was proclaimed a People's Republic in 1946. The absence of political parties and assistance from Yugoslavia's communists enabled Hoxha to assume power with relative ease. After World War II, the Yugoslavs desired to assume the role the Italians had before the war. An economic treaty providing for a customs union, coordination of economic planning, currency equalization and the formation of "joint companies" was entered into in 1946. Yugoslav advisers appeared

**Enver Hoxha**

in greater numbers, and there was even talk of union between the two nations.

The Yugoslavian embrace was apparently too stifling for Hoxha, but there was little he could do about it at the time. In the meantime, the Yugoslavs threw their support to Koci Xoxe, who as Minister of the Interior controlled the police and security forces. What saved Hoxha was the Soviet–Yugoslav split which occurred at this time. Accusing Xoxe of being a supporter of Tito, Hoxha had him and his followers purged at the First Congress of the Albanian Party of Labor in November 1948; Xoxe was later executed.

Hoxha clearly dominated the *Albanian Labor Party (APL)* but he was not without his critics. The next major challenge came in the early 1950's, this time from moderates who objected to dislocations caused by a policy of industrialization and collectivization. After 1953, they also began calling for de–Stalinization as was occurring in Russia. The spokesmen for this point of view were two members of the Politburo, Bedri Spahiu and Tuk Jakova. With Stalin dead and the Soviet leadership moving cautiously toward de–Stalinization, Hoxha could not simply purge these critics.

He actually made a gesture toward the moderate wing of the party in 1954 when he gave up the position of Chairman of the Council of Ministers, though he turned it over to one of his own supporters, Mehmet Shehu. A year later, he managed to get both Spahiu and Jakova expelled from the Politburo.

Yet another challenge came in 1956 at the Third Party Congress, but this came from middle–ranking bureaucrats and military officers; Hoxha crushed it rather easily.

The last contest occurred in 1974–75. It appears not to have been a direct challenge to Hoxha, but rather to some of his policies. Now wielding absolute power, Hoxha purged the dissenters. Between July and December 1974 he removed the entire top level of the military establishment, including the Defense Minister, Beqir Balluku, who was also a member of the Politburo. His dispute with the military was apparently over the extent of party control in such areas as military training and discipline. He followed this ouster with a purge of the nation's top economic and managerial elite when they challenged the role of the party in their areas.

An ailing and tired Hoxha died in early April 1985 at the age of 77. He was succeeded by Ramiz Alia, whom Hoxha had been grooming as successor. Alia, born in 1925, had been a long–time associate of Hoxha, though it was only in 1982 that he became the designated successor.

Although 17 years younger than his mentor, Alia nevertheless belonged to the first generation of Albanian communist leaders. He became a member of the par-

Enver Hoxha makes a point to elderly villagers, while Ramiz Alia (left) listens attentively.

ty in 1943 when it was still only an aspirant to power and became a full Politburo member and a member of the powerful Secretariat in 1961. When he was appointed President of the Presidium of the People's Assembly (titular head of state) in 1982, he retained all of his party posts. Thus, he was already a member of the Secretariat at the time of Hoxha's death and only had to assume the additional duty of First Secretary.

Although no one challenged Alia for the office of First Secretary, it soon became clear that the other members of the Politburo considered him to be not more than a first–among–equals. Since the Politburo was dominated by hard–liners, he was extremely cautious in initiating changes for the first few years. No additions were made to the Politburo, even though that body had three fewer members than in 1982. Alia did make two lesser appointments—the addition of one person to the Secretariat and the replacement of the Chairman of the State Planning Commission.

At the Ninth Congress of the *Albanian Party of Labor* in November 1986, Alia had fulsome praise for Hoxha, to whom, he said, Albania owed boundless gratitude. At the same time, the new Five Year Plan adopted at the congress put much more stress on foreign trade than in the past. Alia indicated that he wanted exports to increase by nearly half over the period.

The new emphasis on trade was accompanied by a slow, and extremely cautious, movement away from the old Hoxha sys-

tem in general. But that movement remained glacieral until March 1990 when Alia, probably responding to the recent extraordinary changes elsewhere in Eastern Europe, launched his own campaign of "democratic" change. Among other things, Alia promised contested elections by secret ballot, including within the *Albanian Labor Party*; limits on terms of office; a decentralization of decision–making authority to district officials and individual enterprises; some price decontrol; and the introduction of economic incentives in industry and agriculture.

Subsequent changes were, in some ways, even more significant. In April, the assembly approved a law lifting criminal penalties for attempts to escape across the frontier and this was followed up in May by a new law explicitly granting citizens the right to travel abroad. The Assembly also lifted the old laws outlawing the practice of religion and declared religious belief to be a matter of individual conscience. Finally, it created the office of Justice Minister, and gave him the task of creating a new system of courts and defense attorneys. None of this represented a basic change in the system, however, for there was no change in the monopoly role of the party.

The May 1990 law granting citizens the right to travel abroad obviously raised expectations among the Albanian populace which were subsequently frustrated by Albanian officialdom. Toward the end of June, some 5,000 Albanians took refuge in a dozen foreign embassies in Tirana and

demanded to be allowed to leave the country. After several days, the Albanian authorities gave in to the demands and the refugees were allowed to leave. Over the next four months, an additional 25,000 persons were issued passports and left the country legally.

In the cities, demonstrations began occurring periodically and some people took to wearing crosses and shouting anti–communist slogans in the streets. Occasionally, violence erupted when officials of the secret police ripped the crosses off people's chests.

Meanwhile the government continued its program of liberalization. Collective farmers were told that they could have private plots and that they would be permitted to sell excess produce in local open–air markets. Cultural controls were also relaxed. At Enver Hoxha University in Tirana, a disco began playing rock music every Saturday night. The prohibition against individuals owning private automobiles was also lifted, though that change had little practical significance since almost no private individual could afford to own an automobile.

These gestures on the part of the party leadership probably only emboldened people to demand more, however. Nearly all of the protests were in the cities and overwhelmingly made up of young people, particularly young men. Then in December, about two thousand students at Enver Hoxha University organized a protest demonstration demanding greater democracy. After three days, the ruling *Party of Labor*, meeting in emergency session, gave in and endorsed "the creation of independent political organizations" and scheduled new elections for February 10. Albanian communists, like their fellow party members in Eastern Europe and the Soviet Union, had been persuaded to give up their monopoly of political power. The next day, the first oppositional political party, the *Democratic Party*, was organized. Approximately 80,000 people attended the rally for the new party.

By January 1991, three additional oppositional parties, the *Republicans*, the *Forum for Human Rights*, and the *Ecological Party*, had come into being. Charging that an election date of February 10 would not give them adequate time to prepare, they demanded that the elections be postponed until a later date. The government gave in and rescheduled them for March 31.

The period January–March was filled with demonstrations, political rallies, additional student strikes, and some violence. Oppositional newspapers also began appearing. At Enver Hoxha University, students decided that Hoxha's name should be stricken from the university's official title and organized a strike which later was turned into a hunger strike. The authorities allowed the strike

# Albania

to continue for twelve days, then surrounded the university with special troops. Demonstrations in support of the students erupted in urban areas across Albania and in two cities, Tirana and the port city of Durres, statues of Hoxha were toppled. The government again backed down and agreed to remove Hoxha's name from Tirana University.

Ramiz Alia, under attack from hardline party members, decided to dismiss Adil Carcani, the hardline Chairman of the Council of Ministers, and assume personal control of the government apparatus by creating a "temporary presidential council." Named head of the new government was Fatos Nano, an economist who had been made Deputy Chairman of the Council of Ministers in January. Alia's actions made clear what up to that time had been only suspected—that the communist *Party of Labor* had split into two factions, orthodox Marxist–Leninists who wanted to stamp out dissent and reformers who supported Ramiz Alia.

Meanwhile, thousands of Albanians again began fleeing the country, first to Greece, and then, at the beginning of March, in commandeered ships to Italy. Many appeared to be fleeing the violence and bloodshed that were accompanying the street demonstrations. The government declared martial law in the port city of Durres in an attempt to stop the exodus, but about twelve thousand Albanians eventually made it out of the country anyway. They were not well–received in Italy, however, and many later returned home.

The March 31 elections were something of an anticlimax. The political opposition won in the cities, but the *Party of Labor*, managing to retain its hold over the countryside, won two–thirds of the seats in the People's Assembly. Ramiz Alia lost his own race in the city of Tirana, but was re-elected Chairman of the Presidium of the People's Assembly on April 30. Fatos Nano was reappointed as Chairman of the Council of Ministers.

But as the *Party of Labor* very quickly learned, electoral majorities do not necessarily create a mandate to rule, particularly if, as in this case, that majority might have been the result of intimidation and fraud. At least, those were the sort of charges hurled by the political opposition against the party, though no evidence was ever produced to substantiate the claim. But no evidence was really necessary. The party's almost total repudiation in the cities meant that it had lost the support of the workers, the very class it claimed to represent, and therefore its political credibility.

As it turned out, the new mandate lasted just over one month. After two weeks of verbal sparring between the government and the political opposition, a group of newly–formed, independent trade unions called for a general strike. With almost total worker support, the strike made clear, as nothing else could, that the party's claim to be the party of the workers was a fraud. During the three–and–a–half weeks that it continued, the general strike brought industrial production to a complete halt and established conclusively that the party had lost control of the cities. On Skanderberg Square in central Tirana, where demonstrators had torn down a huge statue of Enver Hoxha in February, 50,000 demonstrators battled police with rocks, bottles and fire bombs on May 29, leaving the front steps of the Palace of Culture on the Square shattered and fire–blackened.

The political opposition demanded the resignation of the communist government and the formation of an new interim government which would include representatives of the opposition parties. The workers demanded that their wages be doubled and the 48–hour work week be reduced. The party gave in and acceded to all demands in the first week of June. Fatos Nano, in submitting his resignation as Chairman of the Council of Ministers to the legislature, warned of food shortages and the threat of famine. "You have no idea how bad the situation is," he told the legislators.

The new cabinet, which was sworn in on June 12, was headed up by Ylli Bufi, a member of the *Party of Labor* but whose training was as an engineer, not a party apparatchik. His reputation was that of an open–minded reformer. Half of the 24–member cabinet was selected by the communists, while another 12 members came from the opposition. In theory, this government of national unity was supposed to be a government of technicians, with members selected as individuals, without reference to party. In fact, seven of the 12 opposition cabinet seats went to members of the main opposition party, the *Democratic Party*, the other five seats were allotted to the smaller *Republican, Social–Demo-*

*cratic*, and *Agrarian* parties. Sali Berisha, head of the *Democratic Party*, was one of the opposition leaders entering the cabinet. Two other members of his party named to important posts were Gramoz Pashko, who became first deputy premier and minister of the economy, and Genc Ruli, who became minister of finance.

The Tenth National Congress of the *Party of Labor* was scheduled to take place on June 10–12. Prior to the beginning of the congress, President Ramiz Alia submitted his resignation as head of the party, so the keynote address was given by Xhelil Gjoni, the new party secretary. The speech probably shocked some of the delegates with its attacks on Enver Hoxha's collectivization of agriculture and his "brutal pursuit of 'class struggle,' under which intellectuals and churchgoers were persecuted and jailed, some merely for listening to foreign radio broadcasts or reading the Bible." The congress had its surreal moments as well, as when Hoxha's widow, Nexhmije, asserted that, if her husband were still alive, he would be a supporter of democracy and Albanian membership in the European Community. At the conclusion of the congress, the party voted to become the *Socialist Party of Albania*, hoping apparently that a change in name might help to stem a further decline in popular support.

The task of the new government was not an enviable one. Shops were empty and the people were angry. Industrial production was down drastically and exports were down by 50% over the previous year. In the countryside, communists and anti-communists quarreled about whether to break up the collective farms, while peasants held off on planting.

The government tried to solve the land problem first. In July, the legislature passed a law authorizing peasants to obtain small parcels of land from the collective farms. That helped, though communists in the legislature insisted on a clause forbidding peasants to sell any of their newly acquired land. In addition, because the legislation was passed so late in the crop year, a good percentage of the land never did get planted. The fall harvest would be much smaller.

The new government did get some good news, however. The aid already being provided from Italy, the United States and Turkey would continue and be expanded. The European Community offered a trade and co–operation agreement that would allow additional sales of such Albanian products as chromium to the EC and make Albania eligible for technical assistance. In addition, the EC promised Albania 50,000 tons of wheat.

None of this was enough, however. The food situation grew worse over the summer and unemployment continued to grow, reaching over 35% by August. As a

This once isolated nation had built bunker fortifications (which are still in place) along the entire coast.
Courtesy: James V. Elias

result, an estimated 10,000 Albanians commandeered a freighter, the Vlora, and sailed for Italy. Five months earlier, the Italian Government, faced with 24,000 refugees on its hands, had tried to persuade them to return to Albania. About half went willingly.

Most of the rest remained in Italy, unemployable because they were unskilled. This time, the government decided it would use different tactics. When the Vlora arrived, its passengers were taken in hand by riot squads and locked up in a sports stadium. Five days later, most were given $40 in cash, a T–shirt and a pair of jeans, and flown back to Albania. If the treatment was rather brisk and perhaps a little harsh, the Italian Government did counterbalance this with an offer of $85 million in food aid and another $50 million to purchase imported materials to keep the factories running.

The Albanian Government, grateful for the aid, agreed to try to stop future mass departures by placing its ports under military control and instituting joint coastal patrols with Italian warships. Barbed wire was later strung around the port of Durres to keep would–be stowaways out of the port area.

The government announced a privatization program in September which called for 25,000 state businesses to be sold, but this brought protests from the unions that up to 100,000 jobs would be lost as a result. They demanded that the government guarantee unemployed workers 80 per-

cent of their usual salary and this was actually written into law in November. The average worker's salary was less than $30 a month, but, even so, there was a question where the government would get the money to pay the unemployed workers. The budget deficit was already over 20% of GDP, and climbing.

Meanwhile, in the countryside, the people had gotten tired of waiting for the government to make up its mind about the collective farms and they had begun sharing out land and livestock on their own. These "spontaneous privatizations" produced a sort of anarchy in the countryside as looters stripped farm buildings of floors, window frames, roof tiles and even bricks. There were also reports of embittered ex–farm directors dynamiting greenhouses and farm buildings on their way out and farmers burning fields they claimed as their own rather than let a rival family have them.

Ylli Bufi visited the United States in November and thus became the first Albanian prime minister to visit Washington. He had high level conversations with officials at State, Treasury, Commerce and Agriculture, plus meetings with the House Foreign Affairs and Senate Foreign Relations committees.

Shortly after his return, however, the Democratic Party pulled out of the government coalition and it fell. Sali Berisha, head of the Democratic Party, accused the Socialists of hindering economic and political reforms. While the charges were

true—the Socialists were chary of market economy solutions to problems and did force the Democrats to compromise with them—the real reason for the pull–out was that new elections were supposed to take place in May and the Democrats wanted them to take place as early as February. When the People's Assembly refused to agree to move up the elections, the Democrats withdrew from the cabinet. It is also likely that the Democrats wanted to fight the elections from outside the government.

The Democratic Party's withdrawal from the government coalition more or less coincided with new food riots which broke out in December 1991, apparently triggered by a comment by Bufi that food reserves would last only a week.

Bufi submitted his resignation as Chairman of the Council of Ministers at this point and was replaced by Vilson Ahmeti. Ahmeti was to preside over a caretaker government which would prepare for new elections. On December 23, President Alia announced that the elections would be moved up after all and take place on March 22.

The period between December and March was a trying time for Albania. With the population barely surviving on foreign humanitarian assistance, there were once again attempts to flee the country, followed by food riots as thousands of people stormed warehouses and seized what goods they found there. With anarchy spreading, it became unsafe to go out

# Albania

An Albanian street vendor hawks his products.

at night as armed groups of young men roamed the streets attacking people.

During the election campaign, there were also disturbing signs that Albanians were being given an exaggerated idea of what the world could do for them. For example, one journalist quoted "ragged peasants in the countryside" as saying that Albania's *Democratic Party* leaders and U.S. Secretary of State Baker "will be bringing them shoes and food." A common shout at election rallies was "America will save us."

The *Democratic Party* won 62% of the vote in the March 22 elections, giving them an absolute majority in the People's Assembly. Including the votes of the *Republican* and *Social Democratic* parties, the opposition actually got three–quarters of all votes cast. The big losers were the *Socialists* with their 25% percent of the vote, down from 67% a year earlier. Since the *Democrats* had made it clear that they would remove Ramiz Alia as President if they and their allies won a two–thirds majority in the People's Assembly, Alia saved them the trouble and submitted his resignation on April 3. The People's Assembly then elected Sali Berisha, leader of the *Democratic Party*, as the new President of

the Republic. Berisha appointed Aleksander Meksi as Chairman of the Council of Ministers. Meksi said that he would include representatives of the *Republican* and *Social Democratic* parties in his cabinet.

Sali Berisha, a French–trained cardiologist, had very little political experience when he became President. Similarly Aleksander Meksi, his Chairman of the Council of Ministers, graduated from Tirana University with a degree in engineering and most of his subsequent experience was with the Institute for Cultural Monuments and the Institute of Archaeological Excavations as a "restorer and student of monuments of medieval architecture." These two men took control of a country that was, and still is, the poorest in Europe, that was suffering from a breakdown in political and economic life, and with an unemployment rate that approached 50%. The electoral campaign also raised exaggerated hopes among the populace.

The Albanian economy did begin to grow again in 1993, but most people saw no improvement in their own situation. As a result, support for the government began to wane. Under extreme pressure to

turn matters around, President Berisha adopted an authoritarian approach, thereby antagonizing some of the members of his own *Democratic Party*. This led to the expulsion of five MPs, including Gramoz Pashko, a former deputy prime minister, while two other party members resigned. Meanwhile, the *Social Democratic Party*, completely reorganized by Fatos Nano, a young economist who had served as Chairman of the Council of Ministers for a short time in 1991, began gaining in popularity and appeared to have a good opportunity to win new parliamentary elections scheduled for 1996.

Perhaps for that reason, the government brought charges against Fatos Nano for misappropriating state funds in early 1994 and put him on trial. The charges related to the administration of Italian aid money provided during the time that Fatos was Chairman of the Council of Ministers. It was easy to show that the program had been administered incompetently, but the government was unable to provide any evidence that Nanos benefited financially. Nevertheless, the court found him guilty and sentenced to 12 years years in prison. In June 1994, Ramiz Alia, Albania's last Communist leader, was also brought to trial and, found guilty of abuse of power and other charges, was sentenced to nine years in prison. Nine other former top communists were found guilty at the same time and given sentences ranging from three to nine years. Enver Hoxha's widow was also imprisoned. Some of these individuals were undoubtedly guilty of the crimes they were charged with. There is some irony in Alia's conviction, however, since it was he who permitted Albania's first multi–party elections that swept him from power in March 1992.

These various trials had a chilling effect politically. They also led to growing fears that Berisha was becoming just another in a long line of authoritarian Albanian rulers. That latter perception may help explain the severe defeat that Berisha suffered in 1994 over approval of a new constitution. The draft constitution, drawn up by a parliamentary committee with advice from Western experts, lost in parliament when it failed to win the two–thirds majority necessary to pass it, mainly because of opposition by defectors from Berisha's own party. Rather than working for a compromise in parliament, Berisha then decided to submit the draft constitution to the people in a popular referendum. Campaigning throughout the country for its adoption, Berisha turned the referendum into a vote of confidence in himself. The result was that the constitution was rejected by a 54 percent vote.

Ismail Kadare, an Albanian writer, commented afterwards that "Albanians were not against the constitution but against the style of the propaganda. The television propaganda was frentic. It annoyed everybody and recalled the days of Communism."

New parliamentary elections took place on May 26, 1996, but there were such crude irregularities in the run–up to the election, including clubbing of opposition supporters by the police, polling stations packed with Berisha people, plus charges of ballot–stuffing, that independent observers found them rife with fraud. The opposition, which won only a handful of seats, refused to take their seats in parliament, and they maintained their boycott over the next nine months.

Things came to a head in January 1997 when an "investment" scheme that had promised savers interest rates of 50% a month collapsed. This was, it developed, only one of at least nine such pyramid schemes that had been operating in the country and which, collectively, had managed to skim off at least $1 billion in Albanian savings. The government now moved to close down the schemes, but it was too late. There now began six weeks of rioting and unrest that led to the collapse of nearly all authority. The whole southern part of the country passed out of

government control and even parts of the army went over to the opposition.

Berisha tried everything—the threat of force, a promise to partially reimburse what people had lost—but it was to no avail. Finally, Berisha dismissed Aleksander Meksi, Chairman of the Council of Ministers, on March 1, 1997 and, after consultations with the various opposition parties, replaced him with Bashkim Fino, a 35 year old *Socialist* from the southern town of Gjirokaster. Fino headed a caretaker cabinet, made up of representatives of all major political parties, charged with holding new parliamentary elections by June.

These concessions had no immediate effect on the revolt in the south. Although the *Socialists* appeared to be well–poised to benefit from the political unrest, they, in fact, had little or no control over the insurgents in the south. The two, apparently non–negotiable, demands of the rebels appeared to be, first, Berisha's resignation

and, second, reimbursement for money lost in the collapsed pyramid schemes. In early March, Berisha arranged for his re-election as President by the parliament, but that act may turn out to be irrelevant. By March 13, when the new government was sworn in, the country had disintegrated into anarchy and the government had lost control even in Tirana, the capital. All over the country, the people had armed themselves by breaking into or taking over military depots, and a civil war appeared to be eminent. As the government lost control, about 300 prisoners were also released from the Central Jail in Tirana, including Fatos Nano, the leader of the *Socialist Party*, and Ramiz Alia, the last *Communist* ruler of Albania. On March 16, President Berisha granted an amnesty to both men plus 49 others who had been released.

By early April, Fino had begun to assert some authority in most parts of Albania

**Albanian farmers selling their fruits and vegetables along the roadside.**
Courtesy: James V. Elias

# Albania

**Prime Minister Fatos Nano**

and a 6,000 force, assembled under the auspices of the Organization for Security and Cooperation in Europe, had begun to arrive at major ports. The OSCE force was led by Italy, which also provided 2,500 of the troops. The force quickly moved to ensure, first, the distribution of aid, then, the establishment of stability to allow new elections took place at the end of June.

These elections were won by the Socialist Party, which took 47.6 percent to the Democratic Party's 30 percent. Since not all seats were awarded in the first round of voting, a second round took place on July 6. In the final tally, the Socialist Party won 101 seats, while its allies, the Social Democrats and the Democratic Alliance, won an additional 17 seats. That gave the coalition 118 of the 155 seats in the parliament, or more than a two-thirds majority. The Democrats won 27 seats, while their ideological allies won an additional 10 seats. The remaining seats were held by independents.

The Socialists and their allies immediately announced that they would use their two-thirds majority to amend the constitution to create a parliamentary republic. The new parliament convened on July 23, though the Democrats boycotted the session in a protest against plans to change the constitution. Sali Berisha submitted his resignation as President on the same day. The following day, the parliament elected Rexhep Meidani as Berisha's successor. Meidani, a 53-year old physicist,

who had only shortly before become a member of the Socialist Party, immediately accepted the resignation of Bashkim Fino, the caretaker Prime Minister, and appointed Fatos Nano, the Socialist Party leader, in his stead. Skender Gjinushi, a Social Democrat, was elected Speaker of the parliament. Prime Minister Fatos Nano's cabinet was overwhelmingly approved by the parliament on July 29.

The Socialists had announced on July 12 that they intended to change the constitution in order to concentrate executive power in the hands of the Prime Minister. From the beginning, therefore, President Meidani accepted his non-executive role as a symbol of national unity. Fatos Nano, on the other hand, immediately took charge of the country. This took the form of a purge of the judiciary, security forces, and the military of those the Socialists labelled "incompetent political appointees." In fact, these were, in the main, persons who had some connection with the Democratic Party, while they were replaced by persons associated with one of the parties of the government coalition. The Democrats accused the government of appointing its loyalists to all government jobs, and there was undoubtedly a great deal of that. On the other hand, a number of persons appointed to positions in the media were persons of professional ability with no particular ties to the Socialist Party. In addition, most mayors retained their positions, even though many were members of the Democratic Party.

Aside from the personnel changes, however, change has come slowly. Even some of the pyramid schemes have continued to operate. A report issued in February 1998 noted, for example, that the pyramids as a whole continued to generate losses. The 1998 budget, passed on February 3, 1998, sought to reduce the deficit to 8 percent of GDP, from the 11.5 percent it had been in 1997. The government hopes to accomplish this partly by increasing revenues. It has, therefore, raised the Value Added Tax from 12 percent to 20 percent and it hopes to increase customs revenues as well. There is still a great deal of disorder in the country and political polarization is still a fact. Albania is now getting more external assistance, but no one expects major progress soon.

## Foreign Policy

Because of Albania's small size, foreign affairs have always played an extremely important role. Between 1945 and 1948, it was Yugoslavia which played "Big Brother" and attempted to dominate Albania. When Hoxha rebelled, he had no choice but to throw Albania into the arms of the Soviet Union. This marriage lasted as long as Stalin was alive, but Hoxha had no difficulty switching his loyalty to the new Soviet leadership in 1953—at least for

awhile. The country entered the Council for Mutual Economic Assistance (CMEA), the Soviet-dominated economic organization for Eastern Europe in 1949 and the Warsaw Pact in 1955. Almost all foreign trade was with Russia and other members of the CMEA.

Signs of a Soviet-Yugoslavian reconciliation in 1955 gave Hoxha a degree of apprehension. Apparently Hoxha feared that the Soviets might accept his removal as the price for Yugoslavia's renewed friendship. But the situation was saved for Albania by an international crisis—Soviet intervention in Hungary in 1956, which led to a decided cooling in Russian-Yugoslavian relations.

Further, the Soviet leader Khrushchëv continued to push "de-Stalinization" after 1956, which was at cross-purposes with Hoxha's desire to retain absolute, one-man power. He also was disturbed by Russia's proposal in the CMEA for an "international socialist division of labor," for it appeared that Albania's role would be to furnish the CMEA with foodstuffs and raw materials. That would spell the death of Hoxha's cherished industrialization program. When it became evident that China was also becoming disgruntled with the Soviets' leadership, Hoxha decided to sound out the possibilities of becoming a Chinese protégé. Toward the end of 1959, Albanian speeches were already assuming a Chinese slant on political issues. The Chinese were delighted to have at least vocal support in their disputes with the Russians.

The new direction of Albanian policy became clear at a meeting in Bucharest, Romania in mid-1960 when the Albanian delegation backed the Chinese. The next occasion for a confrontation came in November at a Moscow conference of 81 communist parties. In spite of, or perhaps because of, Soviet pressure in the intervening months—including a denial of wheat deliveries at a time when famine threatened Albania—Hoxha attacked Russia's Khrushchëv in language which outdid even the Chinese criticism.

The dispute was plainly brought into the open in late 1961 when Khrushchëv attacked the Albanian party and they, in turn, denounced Khrushchëv. When the Chinese countered with an attack on Yugoslavia, the style of the dispute was set until the later open break between Moscow and Peking in 1963.

Diplomatic relations between Moscow and Tirana were broken in 1961. Albania also refused to participate in the Council for Mutual Economic Assistance (CMEA) or the Warsaw Pact after the break.

Albania accepted Chinese "guidance" in party and state affairs after its break with the Soviet Union in 1961 and between 1960 and 1975 received approximately half a billion dollars in interest-free credits from China. With almost 2,000 Chinese technical experts, Albania was able to set up some thirty new industrial projects, chiefly for the production of energy, irrigation and processing of raw materials. Albania was even exporting modest amounts of oil to Greece, with which it had concluded a trade agreement for the first time since World War II.

When Russia invaded Czechoslovakia in 1968, Albania announced officially its withdrawal from the Warsaw Pact. Apparently concerned about its security, it also launched an effort to improve relations with neighboring countries; for the first time since 1948, Albania began to cultivate better relations with Yugoslavia. This policy began to bear fruit in 1970. Trade between the two countries increased; Yugoslav tourists were permitted to enter Albania and cultural exchanges between the University of Tirana and the University of Pristina (in Kosovo Province) were approved. The two countries raised their diplomatic staffs to embassy level shortly thereafter.

The presence of 1.6 million ethnic Albanians living in Yugoslavia, so often in the past a basis for disagreements between the two countries, for a time helped contribute to a healing as cultural contacts between the ethnic Albanians on both sides of the border increased in frequency. Relations worsened again in 1976, however, as a new wave of unrest and Albanian "unity" activity began in the Kosovo region of Yugoslavia.

A number of violent demonstrations occurred among the students at Pristina University in 1981, accompanied by demands to exclude Kosovo from its program of cultural cooperation with Albania when the program came up for renewal in 1984. In retaliation, the Albanian Government accused Yugoslavia of practicing a policy of "cultural genocide" against ethnic Albanians living within its borders and broke off talks on a new cultural exchange agreement in October 1984. Yugoslavia continued to be Albania's chief trading partner but the level of trade dropped somewhat after 1984 and then stagnated at that lower figure. Economic factors probably played a role in this development, but political factors were clearly dominant. The Serbian Government's subsequent actions against ethnic Albanians in the province of Kosovo, in particular the destruction of that province's autonomy in 1990, only decreased the possibility of improved relations between the two countries.

The situation was further compounded in 1991, when Albania extended diplomatic recognition to the self–proclaimed independent "Republic of Kosovo."

Albania's relations with the People's Republic of China soured in the late 1970's, apparently because of a change that oc-

curred in China's foreign policy at this time. Hoxha disapproved of the warming trend in Chinese–American relations that had begun in the early 1970's, but he was particularly angered when the People's Republic extended an invitation to Marshal Tito to visit China. Albania launched an anti–China campaign in mid–1977 and this led to a break in Chinese–Albanian relations in 1978. China discontinued all economic and military assistance to Albania and withdrew all of its technical experts.

Diplomatic relations were resumed in 1979, but they did not regain their earlier warmth, largely for ideological reasons. This time the reason was the economic reform which Deng Xiaoping launched when he came to power in 1978. Hoxha disapproved of Deng's move and considered him to be a revisionist. Relations began to improve after Hoxha's death in 1985, however. Albania does not have extensive relations with the People's Republic of China, but they now would be considered good.

Albania continued to reject diplomatic relations with either the United States or the Soviet Union so long as Hoxha was alive, but it did come out of its self–imposed isolation to a limited extent in the early 1980's. There was an improvement in relations with Greece, Italy and France, and Albania opened talks with Great Britain and the Federal Republic of Germany in an attempt to resolve bilateral

differences that prevented the establishment of diplomatic relations.

British–Albanian differences were over an Albanian gold reserve placed in London prior to World War II and British demands that Albania pay compensation for sinking a British ship off the Albanian coast in 1946. The sticking point in Albanian–West German relations was Albania's demand for $2 billion in reparations from the Federal Republic for damage done in Albania during World War II.

The Federal Republic was unwilling to concede the principle of reparations, but did suggest the possibility of a loan or credits to finance a major industrial plant in Albania. Some improvement in relations became evident in 1984 when Franz Joseph Strauss, Premier of Bavaria, made a private trip to Albania. In spite of the unofficial nature of the visit, Strauss was received by Manush Myftiu, a Deputy Prime Minister and member of the Politburo. Strauss's presence was also reported in the Albanian press.

This process speeded up somewhat after Enver Hoxha died in April 1985. His successor, Ramiz Alia, though committed to a general continuation of Hoxha's policies, supported a policy of opening up more to the rest of the world. For example, Reiz Malile, the Albanian Foreign Minister, attended the 40th session of the United Nations General Assembly in 1985 and while there, held meetings with the

**Old part of the medieval city of Gjirokastër in southern Albania**

Photo by Martha Grenon

# Albania

foreign ministers of 16 other countries, including Italy, Greece, Turkey and Austria. In addition, Tirana played host to high–level diplomatic delegations from Italy and France as well as trade delegations from West Germany and Japan during 1985–86. An agreement on border demarcation was signed with Greece. In general, diplomatic contacts increased with Western European and Third World countries.

On the other hand, the *Albanian Labor Party* continued to reject party–to–party relations with other communist countries during this period and the only ones represented by an ambassador in Tirana were Romania, North Korea, and the People's Republic of China. Albania did sign a major trade agreement with the German Democratic Republic, however. Under the terms of the agreement, the GDR agreed to provide Albania with industrial technology, including agricultural machinery, in return for Albanian chrome ore.

A further, if still cautious, breakthrough then occurred in September 1987 when Albania reestablished diplomatic relations with Canada. One week later, the Albanian Government followed this up by agreeing to establish diplomatic relations with the Federal Republic of Germany. The near simultaneity of the announcements appears to be coincidence, however, for talks with West Germany had actually been going on for three years.

A further interesting development occurred in January 1988 when Albania and Bulgaria agreed to raise diplomatic relations between the two countries to the ambassadorial level. Albania also agreed to attend a foreign ministers conference on the Balkans hosted by Yugoslavia. The six foreign ministers (of Albania, Yugoslavia, Romania, Bulgaria, Greece and Turkey)

**President Rexhep Meidani**

met in Belgrade in February 1988. Their talks covered a number of issues, including trade, regional economic interests, communications, and creation of a nuclear–free and chemical weapons–free Balkans. Not much of a concrete nature was accomplished, but they did agree to meet again. For Albania, of course, the very fact of its participation represented a breakthrough of sorts. There have been two follow–up meetings of Balkans foreign ministers, the last in Tirana in the spring of 1991.

The wave of political change sweeping across Eastern Europe in the last months of 1989 did not affect Albania directly, but it did change the world in which it operated. Prefacing his remarks with a specific reference to recent international developments, Alia told the Central Committee in April 1990 that "the problem of the reestablishment of diplomatic relations with the United States of America and the Soviet Union is on the agenda." Albania resumed diplomatic relations with the Soviet Union soon afterwards. The first contacts between American and Albanian diplomats occurred in May 1990, but the United States Government was concerned about internal Albanian developments and the discussions continued for some time before they were successfully concluded. Diplomatic relations were officially renewed in March 1991.

After a government of national unity in which half of the cabinet seats were held by members of the political opposition was installed in early June, Albania found additional doors opening to it. It was admitted to the European Bank for Reconstruction and Development in September and the IMF and World Bank in October. Membership in these organizations made Albania eligible for technical assistance and also loans.

Albania's relations with the United States also improved after the change in government in June 1991. The U.S. Government supported Albania's membership applications to international organizations and promised it humanitarian economic assistance. Ylli Bufi, Chairman of the Council of Ministers, traveled to the United States in November, the first Albanian leader to come to Washington. Although the visit was technically private, Bufi did meet with Arnold Kanter, U.S. Undersecretary of State for Political Affairs.

The main purpose of the visit was economic, however. In addition to an agreement which he signed with the Overseas Private Investment Corporation to guarantee American investments in Albania, Bufi met with officials of the Treasury, Commerce, and Agriculture Departments, and with members of the House Foreign Affairs and Senate Foreign Relations committees. He also met with officials of the World Bank.

Since the election of Sali Berisha as President in March 1992, relations with the United States have undergone a major change. Flora Lewis, who visited Albania in the spring of 1993, reported that there's "a constant flow of American military personnel coming and going to give advice and check the situation." With Albanians fearful that the Yugoslav war might spread first to Kosovo and then to Albania, "America is seen as a protector." The United States has, in fact, made no commitments to Albania, though the Clinton Administration, worried about the war spreading to Kosovo, has expressed its disquiet to the Serbian Government. Albania has said that it would resist any attack from across the border, but its weapons, almost entirely Soviet or Chinese–made versions of Soviet weapons from the 1950's and early 1960's, would be almost useless against well–armed Serbian forces. This is probably one reason why President Berisha, visiting NATO headquarters in Brussels in December 1992, said that Albania would like to join the western alliance.

In another change, John Paul II became the first pope to visit Albania since the middle ages when he arrived there in April 1993. Only about ten percent of the population is Roman Catholic, but the Pope got a warm welcome. President Berisha welcomed the Pope and the two speeches made an interesting dialogue about the Balkans. John Paul II, addressing a rally in Tirana, advised:

"Do not let the sense of nation that you feel strongly at this moment degenerate into the kind of intolerant and aggressive nationalism that claims its victims still today and fuels ferocious hatreds in several parts of the world, some not far from here."

President Berisha's speech touched on the same theme. "The Holy Father," he said:

"has come to the Balkans today at a time when not far from us, in Bosnia–Herzegovina, criminal demons are committing massacres and ethnic cleansing, are exterminating an entire people. We can never permit the ethnic cleansing of Albanians from their territory, and we insist that the region's crisis will never be resolved without a solution of the question of Albanians in Kosovo."

Following this, the Albanian Government became even more outspoken in its support for Albanians outside its borders; this caused it to be accused by the Government of Macedonia of interfering in events in that country. There were, in fact, two separate issues involved here. The first is the dream of a "Greater Albania" uniting all 6 million Albanians in a single government. Nationalists espouse this viewpoint, but they represent only a tiny fraction of the population. The second, and more significant, issue was the formerly autonomous Serbian province of Kosovo, where Albanians make up 90 percent of the population. President Berisha's fear was that the Bosnian War could spread to Kosovo, for he was convinced that, if that happened, Albania, and probably Macedonia, could be drawn in as well.

President Berisha's position might be characterized as "the first priority is the prevention of a conflict." Yet he was influenced by Albanian nationalists, who acknowledged that their dream of a Greater Albania depended on a major upheaval in the Balkans. Worried by the war in Bosnia, Berisha increased his government's contacts with more radical ethnic Albanians in Macedonia—those who favored joining Albania—presumably to be ready to act should the war spread. When it became clear that this was undermining the main party of ethnic Albanians who were part of the governmental coalition in Macedonia, however, Berisha reversed the policy in 1995, reducing ties with the radicals and reiterating his support for Macedonia's current borders.

Albanian relations with Greece also changed under Berisha, though here the issue was primarily the fate of ethnic Greeks living in southern Albania. The Greek Government refers to southern Albania as Northern Epirus and claims the right to speak on behalf of ethnic Greeks living in the area. In recent years, the situation was exacerbated by the Orthodox Bishop of the Greek Province of Epirus, who argued that the government ought to be willing to use force to protect the rights of ethnic Greek minorities in Albania. The Greek Government was never willing to go that far, but it did threaten, in 1995, to expel the 150,000 Albanian citizens living and working in Greece. Another factor affecting Albanian–Greek relations was that Greece was Serbia's strongest supporter during the Bosnian War.

After President Berisha began acting in a more and more authoritarian manner in 1995–6, Albania found its relations with both the United States and Western Europe cooling. The United States was particularly critical of irregularities in the parliamentary elections in 1996 and several times called for new elections. By March 1997, Washington had taken the position that Berisha's resignation was essential. When, therefore, Berisha appealed for the European Union and NATO to send peacekeeping troops to restore order after his government had lost control, the word he received was that the first step toward restoring order had to be his own resignation.

After President Berisha resigned and Fatos Nano became Prime Minister in July

1997, the U.S. Government extended an official promise to provide financial support for the reconstruction and democratization of Albania. Other countries have also extended offers of economic assistance, including Germany which pledged $18 million in November 1997. Albania's relations with Greece have also improved in the past year.

## NATURE OF THE REGIME

### The Albanian Government

The "supreme organ of state power" is a 155–member People's Assembly, which is elected for a four year term. In the latest elections, which took place on July 1997, the left won overwhelmingly. In those elections, the Socialist Party won 101 seats, while its two allies, the Social Democrats and the Democratic Alliance, won an additional 17 seats. That gave the coalition 118 seats in the parliament, or more than a two–thirds majority. The Democrats, who had 92 seats in the previous parliament, won 27 seats, while their ideological allies won an additional 10 seats. The remaining seats are held by independents.

Using their two–thirds majority, the Socialists and their allies have changed the nature of the operation of the government in practice, though they have not yet officially changed the constitution to reflect this change. Under the new arrangement that has been in effect since July 1997, the office of the presidency has become a ceremonial position without political authority, while the office of prime minister has become the fulcrum of authority. Since the Socialists announced in July 1997 that they intended to create a parliamentary republic, it is expected that a new constitution will be drawn up in the near future reflecting this new practice.

There is also a Constitutional Court, though it was suspended in February 1998 because, according to the law, three of the court's nine members were supposed to rotate off the court in December 1997, but as the law did not specify which three should step down, all refused to do so. The Court will presumably be reinstated as soon as its membership conforms with current law.

### The Economy

Before Enver Hoxha's death in 1985, Albania always billed itself as the world's first "true socialist economy." One reason for this claim was that 100% of the "means of production" had been nationalized under Hoxha. Until 1990, this extended even to motor vehicles, which could be owned only by the state. Citizens were permitted to own bicycles, however. That proud boast lost all of its glitter long before the defeat of the *Socialist Party of Albania* in the May 1992 elections, but the truth behind

that boast continues to give government ministers headaches as they work to privatize the economy and move Albania toward a market economy.

Albania launched its first Five Year Plan in 1951 with a goal of a rapid development of industry and national self–sufficiency in both industrial and agricultural products. Growth during the first two Five Year Plans was fairly rapid, since Albania was starting from literally nothing. It slowed thereafter, but this can largely be blamed on the halt in Soviet economic aid after the break in relations in 1961. There was fairly rapid growth between 1966 and 1970—reflecting the assistance that the country got from China—but there was a slowdown after 1970 which some blamef on a breakdown in labor discipline in the early 1970s. It may be connected with the fact that Albania achieved full collectivization of agriculture in 1967 and followed this up by a reduction in the size of peasants' private plots. Albanian agriculture regularly achieved only about 50% of its assigned production targets in the late 1960s and early 1970s. This sector also suffered from the loss of Chinese assistance after the Albanian–Chinese diplomatic break in that year. As a result, the government abandoned it long–term goal of self–sufficiency and began to develop foreign trade.

Albania is still the least developed country in Europe, but the regime's policy of industrialization did produce substantial changes in a number of areas. For example, Albania has significant resources of chrome, iron, coal, copper and petroleum, and these have been developed over the past 40 years or so. Albania has the capacity to produce over 800,000 tons a year, which makes it the world's third–largest producer of that vital metal. In the 1970s, Albania constructed an oil refinery with an annual capacity of one million tons and began exporting crude oil and refined petroleum products to Italy, Greece, the Federal Republic of Germany, Switzerland and Romania.

Other exports included electric power, copper, coal, textiles and food industry products. Albania's exports began dropping drastically beginning in 1989, partly as a result of a severe drought that didn't leave the government enough money to import spare parts or raw materials

The severe drought that began in the late 1980s had a devastating effect on agriculture, but the overall economy was having difficulties even before that. Red tape and too much control from Tirana had created a situation of slow growth that the bureaucrats were unable to reverse. Severe shortages developed, particularly of raw materials, modern machinery and consumer goods. Food items such as meat and cheese had to be rationed, though staples such as bread, sugar and milk re-

# Albania

Happier faces for long–isolated Albania: music students in the city of Korce

mained adequate until 1990. Fruits and vegetables were still freely available at that time.

In March 1990, however, Ramiz Alia promised to institute a number of economic reforms aimed at decentralizing decision–making and creating some economic incentives in industry and agriculture. Though developments elsewhere in Eastern Europe were an important influencing factor, the state of the Albanian economy played the more important role in the political developments in 1990–91. A common complaint, both of people demonstrating in the cities and of others who fled the country was the lack of any hope as far as their own futures was concerned. Part of that pessimism was caused by the failure of the communist system itself but not all of it.

The other serious, long–term problem is that of Albania's rate of population growth, which was higher than its rate of economic growth even before three years of drought in 1989–91 exacerbated that situation further. The Albanian Government obviously has its hands full dealing with immediate economic problems, but it will have to address this problem eventually or see its gains in the economic area negated by continued increases in population. According to the latest Albanian Government statistics, however, Albania continues to have the fastest growing population in Europe and over 50 percent of its population is under 30. This creates particular pressure on farmland, since most Albanians are still farmers.

The new democratic government was committed to the privatization of state-owned industry and the creation of a mar-

ket economy, but it wasn't able to make much progress in the area of privatization because of the dire state of the economy by the time it took power. When the previous coalition government removed subsidies on state industry in November 1991, about half of industry closed down or laid off workers and went on short hours. With social discipline breaking down, Albania entered a period of effective anarchy. The new democratic government managed to reverse that trend and to restore order in the cities, though roving bands of robbers still existed in parts of the countryside. Meanwhile, industrial production continued to drop with many plants working at five percent capacity by November 1992.

The situation stabilized after that and the economy began growing again in 1993. For the next couple of years, in fact, Albania had one of the fasting growing economies in Europe, though obviously from a very low baseline. The government launched a major program of privatization in 1994, selling off 1,800 small state–owned enterprises—essentially all state–owned enterprises with fewer than 300 employees and less than $500,000 in assets. Many new small and medium-sized private companies were also started and this resulted in the creation of an estimated 100,000 jobs. At the same time, state industry remained in a state of collapse.

As a plus, the estimated 350,000 Albanians working abroad remit more than $300 million a year, equivalent to 16 percent of GDP. This made it possible for the government to stabilize the value of the Lek and it contributed heavily to the success of privatizations. Albania was still

running a large trade deficit in 1994, however, and its external debt stood at $736 million. Foreign investment, still extremely small, reached $80 million by the end of 1994, and this was mainly in the hotel and tourism industry. Albania thus remained heavily dependent on foreign assistance.

Albania did begin to tap an unusual source of assistance about this time, however. Because of past migrations from this poor land, about 600,000 persons of Albanian descent live in America. They were heavy contributors to the Democratic Party in the run up to the March 1992 elections and, for a while, they began to invest in their old homeland, and some even returned to offer their foreign skills. Most of this consisted of Albanian–Americans providing capital to Albanian relatives to set up or buy businesses, however, and a lot of this was invested in pyramid schemes instead that began to collapse in early 1997.

Albania was also the recipient of increasing amounts of foreign assistance beginning about 1992. The United States was one of the donors, but a number of European countries began providing assistance as well. International assistance greatly increased in 1993, but the government's lack of competent officials meant that it was, in practice, incapable of taking advantage of many of these offers. For example, the International Monetary Fund provided Albania with a credit of $40 million in July 1992 to finance vital imports. A year later, the government had managed to spend only $12 million, even though many factories were idle because of the lack of raw materials.

For a while, the news from the countryside was a little better. First of all, the old collective form of farming basically disappeared as a result of the legislature's 1991 decision to allow peasants to obtain their own parcels of land. Most of the implementation of that decision was carried out by the peasants themselves, however, and they did so in a haphazard manner. Basically, the peasants were unable to agree among themselves about who owned what lands. As a result, only about half the agricultural land was planted in 1991. Most of the quarrels over land ownership were resolved by 1992, and the harvest was much better. Still, perhaps 80 percent of the land was in private hands by the end of 1992, though the distribution of land deeds has been a much slower process. This has had a negative economic effect, for peasants without land deeds are unable to use their land as collateral for borrowing.

The collapse of several pyramid "investment" schemes in January 1997 led to a complete loss of confidence in the government of President Sali Berisha and by early March the government had lost control of almost all of the country. It was estimated that a third of Albania's capital reserves evaporated in the collapse and the resulting anarchy set the country back even further. Since Albania was already receiving one third of its annual budget of $960 million from the European Union, Italy organized a rescue operation which involved moving Italian and other troops into Albania to restore order. This led, in turn, to new parliamentary elections in July 1997 and the ouster of President Berisha and the *Democrats*. Since July 1997, the country has been controlled by the Socialist Party and its allies. Little economic progress has been made thus far, but the country is now somewhat more stable.

## Culture

The two elements that defined traditional Albanian culture were religion—primarily Islam—and the way of life associated with the peasantry of the Balkans. After 1945, the *Albanian Party of Labor* introduced its own double agenda, an economic goal of industrialization and a social goal of creating the "new socialist person." Industrialization increased the urban population and led to increased mechanization of the countryside. In addition, because of its need for trained technicians, the regime set up many new technical schools that eventually produced an educated, urban elite. Albania is still basically a rural and peasant society, however, with 63% of the people living in villages in the countryside where clan or feudal relationships tend to persist.

In 1964, Hoxha launched an ideological and cultural revolution aimed at eliminating religion, the influence of family and sectional loyalties, and prejudices toward women. All churches and mosques were closed and most religious leaders were imprisoned. In addition, a major effort was made to end the traditional Islamic seclusion of women and to bring them into the workplace. Three years later, Albania became the world's first officially atheist country.

The party relaxed some of its controls beginning in 1970, but the cultural revolution resumed again in 1973. Now the targets were young people, the military and the technicians. The party reorganized the education system to make it stricter. Party officials who had advocated a moderate line were purged. Intellectuals were sent to factories and collective farms to do manual labor.

This cultural revolution didn't actually succeed in changing the basic culture of the country, but it did enforce a surface conformity. It is not even clear that closing all of the mosques and churches reduced the number of believers—though it did succeed in driving religion underground.

The prohibition against all public religious rituals left a void, however, and the regime attempted to fill this by creating a new calendar of secular festivals. National holidays such as Albanian Independence Day (November 28) formed the core of the new calendar, but there are also days set aside for honoring the worker and a number of agricultural festivals.

In April 1990, the regime rescinded laws prohibiting the practice of religion. In November, the party voted to return all houses of worship to their respective religious communities. Most churches and mosques had been converted into things like gymnasiums, movie theaters and warehouses or had been allowed to fall into disrepair, however, so implementation has been slow. About 40 churches had been turned over to religious authorities by April 1991. A much more serious problem in rebuilding the church is the shortage of priests, however. There were fewer than 10 Greek Orthodox priests in the country in April 1991 and only 32 Catholic priests. All were elderly and most had spent long years in prison. The head of Albanian Catholics, the Apostolic Administrator of Durres, was a 76–old man who lived in total retirement in a small village in the north of the country.

On March 21, 1991, a symbolic mass was said in Shkodër Cathedral, though the building was not really in a condition to be used. Its two towers had been demolished in 1967, its portal was boarded up, and inside the yellow plaster was peeling everywhere. In another symbolic act, Mother Theresa, an ethnic Albanian born in nearby Macedonia, came to Shkodër in March 1991. She attended the first mass at Shkodër Cathedral and opened a convent nearby. The three nuns in residence opened an orphanage for unwanted Albanian children.

The Islamic community has taken back perhaps 10–15 mosques but they are, like the churches, in a dilapidated condition. One mosque, the Xhamia e Plumbit, an eighteenth century mosque that stands before the gates of Shkodër, had been rehabilitated somewhat and is currently in use. Moslem clerics suffered a treatment similar to Christians and they are also elderly men who have served long terms in prison. In many ways, in fact, they are even more badly off. There are between 10 and 15 Moslem dignitaries in the country and most of them have had no theological training.

## The Future

The left now controls Albania and, although it difficult to argue that they could do a worse job of governing than their predecessors, the *Democrats*, it appears that they have no real idea of Albania's future direction economically. Perhaps it is too early to judge them, however. The country they took over in July 1997 was in both a state of anarchy and a state of economic collapse. Things are still in extremely poor shape, but they have been making an attempt to reestablish some political stability. Still, Albania's future promises to be heavily dependent on foreign assistance for a good number of years.

**A cigarette factory in Durres**

Photo by Martha Grenon

# The Baltic Republics

Due to their shared histories as well as frequent geographical and cultural similarities, there is necessarily some repetition from one entry to the other

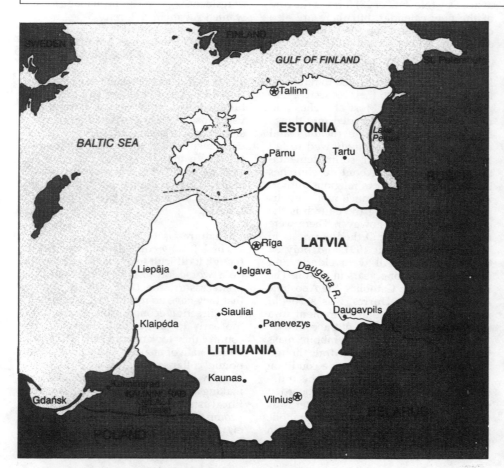

currently make up about 61.5% of the population.

**Other Ethnic Groups:** Russians (30.3%); Ukrainians (3.1%); Belarusians (1.8%); Finns (1.1%).

**Principal Religions:** Lutheranism, Russian Orthodox Christianity.

**Chief Commercial Products:** Ships, mineral fertilizers, paper products, peat, agricultural products, fish.

**Currency:** Kroon.

**Annual Per Capita Income:** About U.S. $1,300.

**Former Political Status:** Conquered by German and Danish Knights in the 13th century, it came under Swedish control in the 17th century. Peter the Great annexed it in 1709 and it remained part of the Russian Empire until 1918. Independent state, 1918-1940. Annexed to the Soviet Union by Stalin in 1940; declared its independence in August 1991.

**Independence Day:** February 24.

**Chief of State:** Lennart Meri, President.

**Head of Government:** Mart Siimann, Prime Minister (February 1997).

**National Flag:** tricolor—blue, black and white.

**Lennart Meri**
**The President of Estonia**

# The Republic of Estonia

**Area:** 18,370 square miles (47,549 sq. km.).
**Population:** 1.6 million.
**Capital City:** Tallinn (506,000).
**Climate:** Temperate with cool summers and cold winters, somewhat tempered by an arm of the gulf stream that reaches into the Baltic.
**Neighboring Countries:** Russia (east); Latvia (south).

**Official Language:** Estonian.
**Other Principal Tongue:** Russian.
**Ethnic Background:** Estonian is linguistically close to Finnish. There is some German influence as a result of being ruled by German Knights from the 13th to 17th centuries, and extensive Russian influence as a result of being part of the Russian Empire 1709–1918. Estonians

# The Republic of Latvia

**Area:** 25,400 square miles (65,786 sq. km.).
**Population:** 2.7 Million.
**Capital City:** Riga (Pop. 915,000).
**Climate:** Temperate with cool summers and cold winters, somewhat tempered by an arm of the gulf stream that reaches into the Baltic.
**Neighboring Countries:** Estonia (north); Russia (east); Belarus (southeast); Lithuania (south).
**Official Language:** Latvian.
**Other Principal Tongues:** Russian.
**Ethnic Background:** Latvian belongs to the Letto–Lithuanian family of Indo-European languages. It is closely related to Lithuanian, but contains words taken over from Swedish, German and Russian, the languages of peoples that controlled the country at various times in the past. Letts currently make up about 52% of the population.
**Other Ethnic Groups:** Russians (33%); Ukrainians, Belarusians, Others (14%).
**Principal Religions:** Lutheran, Russian Orthodox Christianity.
**Chief Commercial Products:** Machinery, electrical equipment, agricultural engineering, paper products, timber, building materials, chemicals, pharmaceuticals, dairy products.
**Currency:** Lats.
**Annual Per Capita Income:** About U.S. $2,500.
**Former Political Status:** The Latvian lands were part of the territory governed by the Teutonic Knights from the 13th to the 16th century. They were subsequently ruled by Poland, then Sweden. Peter the Great annexed Riga in 1710; the remainder of the country fell to Russian rule in the 18th century. With the collapse of the Russian Empire, Latvia declared its independence in 1920. Occupied by Soviet forces in June 1940, it was annexed by Stalin in August 1940; declared its independence May 4, 1990.
**Independence Day:** November 18.
**Chief of State:** Guntis Ulmanis, President.
**Head of Government:** Guntars Krasts (August 1997)
**National Flag:** Three vertical stripes—dark red, white (half as thick), dark red.

**Guntis Ulmanis
The President of Latvia**

# The Republic of Lithuania

**Area:** 25,174 square miles (64,445 sq. km.).
**Population:** 3,690,000.
**Capital City:** Vilnius (Pop. 582,000).
**Climate:** Temperate with cool summers and cold winters, somewhat tempered by an arm of the gulf stream that reaches into the Baltic.
**Neighboring Countries:** Latvia (north); Belarus (southeast); Poland (southwest); Russia (Kaliningrad Enclave) (west).
**Official Language:** Lithuanian.
**Other Principal Tongues:** Polish, Russian.
**Ethnic Background:** Lithuanian belongs to the Letto–Lithuanian family of Indo-European languages. It is closely related to Latvian, but contains heavy influences from the Polish language. Lithuanians, mentioned in Tacitus's *Germania* as excellent farmers, have occupied the southern shores of the Baltic for over two thousand years. A dynastic union with Poland in the 14th century brought a Polanization of the Lithuanian upper classes. Russian influence began in the 18th century when Lithuania became part of the Russian Empire. Lithuanians currently make up 80% of the population.
**Other Ethnic Groups:** Russians (8.6%); Poles (7%); Other (4.3%).
**Principal Religion:** Roman Catholic Christianity.
**Chief Commercial Products:** Agricultural products, timber, paper, ships, textiles, synthetic fibers, leather, cellulose, metal goods, tape recorders, televisions.
**Currency:** Litas.
**Annual Per Capita Income:** About U.S. $1.500.
**Former Political Status:** An independent Principality in the 13th century; A dynastic union with Poland in 1385 led to an increasing closeness between the two countries until they were merged in 1569. Lithuania became part of the Russian Empire in the 18th century and remained so until 1918. Independent state 1918–1940; annexed to the Soviet Union in 1940; declared its independence again in March 1990; took control of its borders on August 26, 1991.
**National Day:** February 16 (Independence Day).
**Chief of State:** Valdas Adamkus, President of the Republic.
**Head of Government:** Gediminas Vagnorius, Prime Minister.
**National Flag:** Three horizontal stripes—yellow, green, red.

**Valdas Adamkus
The President of Lithuania**

Lachemaa National Park, Estonia

## THE LAND AND THE PEOPLE

The three republics of Estonia, Latvia, and Lithuania are located along the eastern shores of the Baltic Sea. Finland lies to the north, separated from Estonia by the Gulf of Finland, while Sweden lies to the west, across the Baltic Sea.

Estonia, the most northern of the three republics, borders on Russia to the east, though the two countries are physically separated along most of the border by a series of lakes that stretch from just north of Pskov to the Baltic Sea. Tallinn, the capital, major port and largest city, lies on the Gulf of Finland, directly across from Helsinki, the capital of Finland. Latvia, to the south of Estonia, shares borders with Belarus and Russia on the east. Its capital, Riga—located on the Gulf of Riga at the mouth of the Daugava [Western Dvina] River—is at the same time its largest city and best port.

Lithuania, the most southern of the three republics, borders on the Kaliningrad enclave of the Russian Republic to the south and the Republic of Belarus on the east. Its shoreline, only 99 kilometers long, is relatively narrow and it has only one good port, the city of Klaipeda. Vilnius and Kaunas, its two major cities, lie considerably inland, Kaunas along the upper reaches of the Nemunas [Niemen] River and Vilnius on the Neris River, a tributary of the Nemunas. Vilnius, the current capital and the ancient capital of the Grand Principality of Lithuania, lies quite close to the current border of Belarus and was actually part of Poland between the first and second world wars.

The entire Baltic coastal area is a plain with occasional higher elevations, particularly as one moves away from the sea, but the highest of these elevations are never more than about 900 feet in height. Nevertheless, they are the reason why a number of small rivers flow through the Baltic Republics and into the Baltic Sea. The shoreline itself consists mostly of low dunes running along the beaches. There are plenty of sandy beaches, but the water tends to be extremely shallow for a good distance into the sea, making swimming difficult. Pine forests, which predominate throughout the Baltic coastal area, often come down almost to the shore.

It is these pines that help to explain amber, the symbol of the Baltic. Fifty million years ago, the Baltic Sea was a vast marshland covered by pine trees. The resin oozed out of the pine trunks and dripped into the silt of the marsh where it eventually hardened, then petrified over succeeding millenia. Today, amber is often found along the shore, washed up by the sea.

Most of the area was originally a combination of marsh and forest and even today farms give the appearance of having been cut out of the forest. Small lakes are very common, with an estimated 3,000 in Lithuania alone. Soils, which are usually gray, tend to be relatively poor, and most farming is dairy farming. One arm of the Gulf Stream reaches into the Baltic, making the climate milder than it would otherwise be. Summers tend to be cool with frequent light rains. Winters are cold and damp.

### Languages

The Estonian language belongs to the Finnish branch of the Ural–Altaic family, though it contains words taken from Swedish, German and Russian. The Estonians, along with the Finns, are the remnants of tribes which once lightly peopled much of the northern two–thirds of what is today European Russia. Although still existing in some places in small pockets in Russia, particularly in the Karelian Peninsula, most were absorbed into the larger Slavic population over the centuries.

The Lithuanian and Latvian languages belong to the Letto–Lithuanian family of Indo–European languages. Lithuanian was heavily influenced by the Polish language, however, while Latvian shows influences from Swedish, German and Russian, the languages of peoples that controlled the country at various times in the past.

## HISTORY

The peoples living along the southern shores of the Baltic have had a relatively long history, and have occupied this same area for over two thousand years. The first historical reference to be found is in Tacitus's *Germania*, where he praises the Lithuanians for their talents in farming. At that time, the Baltic area had some contact with the civilizations to the south because of amber, which occurs along the Baltic coast and became the basis for a trade route which actually came into existence as early as the second millennium B.C. The decline of the Roman Empire turned this area once more into a backwater, however, and nothing more was heard for several centuries.

The next historical reference dates from the seventh century, when Viking raiders swept down out of Scandinavia and launched a series of raids along the coast and up the rivers. These invasions, continuing for the next two hundred years, eventually resulted in some Viking settlements along the rivers and, in 862, the beginning of the Kievan Rus State at Novgorod when Riurik established himself as ruler at Novgorod. Most of the Baltic Sea area was under the control of the Vikings at this time, but their main interest was on expansion of the trade route across Russia down to Constantinople. Accordingly, they only levied an annual tribute on the Baltic peoples and otherwise left them alone.

Remaining on the periphery, the Baltic peoples all remained pagan even as their neighbors to the west and the south embraced Christianity. That led, at the beginning of the thirteenth century, to a Christianizing effort by German missionaries. These first efforts were peaceful, and a bishopric was actually established at Riga in 1201. This peaceful penetration was soon followed by an invasion of crusading knights, the most significant being the Knights of the Sword and the Order of Teutonic Knights. The Teutonic Knights conquered the area of present–day Latvia in 1225. Gradually, the area of Estonia was also brought under the control of the Knights of the Sword, who subsequently turned it over to the Order of Teutonic Knights. The Latvians and Estonians were enserfed and converted to Christianity, but managed to retain many of their customs and their own languages.

Meanwhile the Lithuanians, who up to this time had been organized into separate tribes, formed a federation under the Grand Duke Ringaudas. His successor, Mindaugas, defended the federation against the Russians, Poles and the Teutonic Knights and even converted to Christianity in an attempt to put an end to the outside pressure. He was assassinated, however, and his successor, Vitenis, continued the struggle against the Teutonic Knights. It was Vitenis' brother and successor, Gediminas [1316–1341], who, building on the victories won by his brother, founded the Jogaila [Jagellon] dynasty and laid the basis of the Grand Duchy of Lithuania. During his lifetime, Gediminas extended his conquests southward, fighting both Russians and Tatars until his kingdom extended from the Baltic to the Black Sea. He thus freed the western part of Kievan Rus from the control of the Tatars, including the city of Kiev itself. At this time, a majority of his subjects were either White Russians or Ukrainians, and Russian became the official language of the realm. Although Gediminas was himself still a pagan, most of his subjects were Orthodox Christians.

Gediminas was slain in 1341 while once again attempting to drive back the Teutonic Knights. He was succeeded by his son, Jagellon [Jogaila], who married Hedwige, Queen of Poland. Jagellon, having converted to Roman Catholicism, took over as ruler of Poland and turned over the Grand Duchy of Lithuania to his cousin, Vytautas. Vytautas died without an heir in 1430, however, so the crown reverted back to the Jogaila line. From that time, the Grand Duchy of Lithuania was increasingly tied to Poland until, in 1569, the two kingdoms were merged in the Union of Lublin.

Lithuania continued to have its own

# The Baltic Republics

## Baltic Area – 15th to Early 18th Centuries

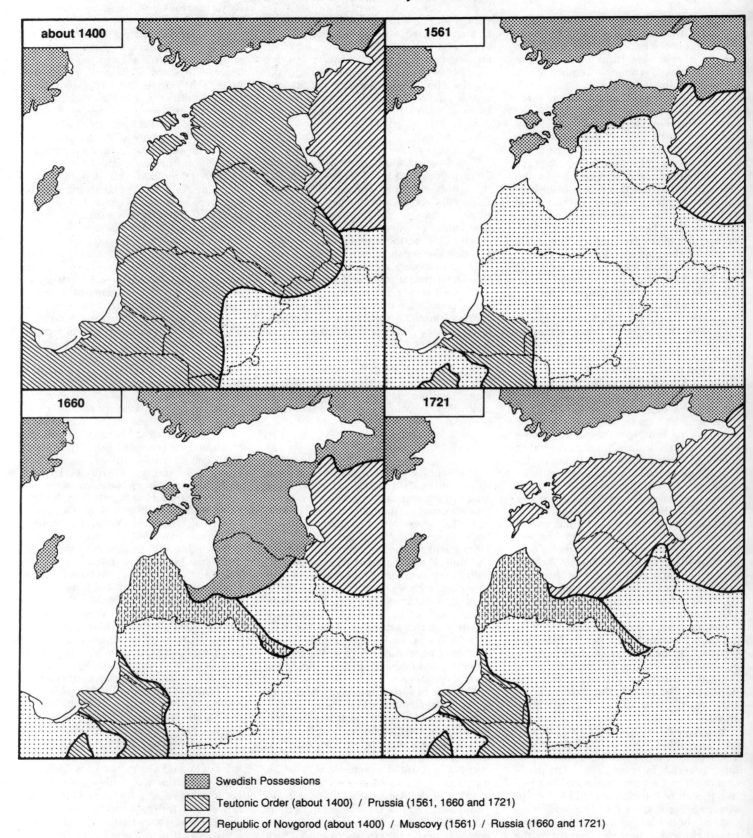

Legend:

- Swedish Possessions
- Teutonic Order (about 1400) / Prussia (1561, 1660 and 1721)
- Republic of Novgorod (about 1400) / Muscovy (1561) / Russia (1660 and 1721)
- Lithuania (about 1400) / Poland-Lithuania (1561, 1660 and 1721)
- Duchy of Courland: Dependency of Poland-Lithuania (1660 and 1721)

Maps labeled: about 1400, 1561, 1660, 1721

**Mindaugas**

laws and army, but the upper classes became increasingly Polanized and most of them became Roman Catholic. Polish replaced Russian as the language of administration in the 16th century.

In the last half of the 18th century, Poland–Lithuania was partitioned among its neighbors, in 1772, 1793 and 1795. As a result, Russia obtained the Ukrainian and White Russian territories plus all of Lithuania proper up to the Nemunas River. Russia obtained the remaining Lithuanian territories in 1815.

The spread of the Protestant Reformation in the 16th century led to the creation of the two secular states of Courland and Livonia and the dissolution of the Teutonic Knights in 1560. The former knights converted to Lutheranism and became a secular nobility. Their Estonian and Latvian serfs were also converted at this same time.

Courland and Livonia also became takeover targets of their neighbors at this time. The Russian Tsar, Ivan IV, wanting to gain control of ports along the Baltic, launched his Livonian War in 1558. He was successful in the beginning but, when the Teutonic Knights collapsed in 1560, Poland stepped in and stole his conquests, annexing Livonia and Courland to Poland–Lithuania. Then, at the beginning of the 17th century, the Swedish King, Gustavus Adolphus, intervened and seized most of Livonia in 1626. The Swedish territory, which included most of modern day Estonia, was given a relatively liberal regime. The privileges of the German nobility—the so–called Baltic Barons—were curtailed somewhat and a university was established at Dorpat. It was also as a result of Swedish rule that the Lutheran Church continued as the established church in Estonia.

Then, at the end of the 17th century, Pe-

ter the Great came to the throne in Russia and launched his Great Northern War against Sweden in 1700. The war lasted until 1721, but Riga fell to Russia in 1710 and Tallinn [Revel] soon afterwards. Russia obtained Livonia and Estonia by the Peace of Nystadt. Courland gradually became a Russian protectorate during the 18th century, and was formally annexed in 1795.

### The Baltics Under Russian Rule

Peter the Great allowed his new Baltic subjects to retain their own laws and the autonomous status which they had enjoyed under the Swedes. There was no attempt to introduce Russian institutions or to encourage the spread of the Orthodox religion to the area. Peter's second wife, Catherine, was actually a Baltic peasant girl whom he took as a mistress during the Baltic campaign and later married. On the other hand, it was basically the German–speaking nobility that benefited from this autonomy; the Letts and Estonians were at this time still mainly serfs. There were some economic benefits to the area, however; in the 18th century, Riga became Russia's second major port after St. Petersburg, a position it would continue to hold in the 19th century.

A major change occurred at the beginning of the 19th century when Alexander I became Tsar. Alexander detested serfdom and as early as 1803 issued a decree

permitting the voluntary emancipation of the serfs. Later in his reign, Alexander abolished serfdom in the Baltic Provinces, in Estonia in 1816, Courland in 1817, and Livonia in 1819. In Lithuania, which was under a separate administration, serfdom continued. It was abolished there in 1861, as part of the general serf emancipation throughout the Russian Empire.

In the Baltic Provinces, the short–term consequences of emancipation were mainly negative. The Baltic serfs were freed without land and, with no alternate means of employment, found themselves working as day laborers for the same large landowners who had been their masters before emancipation. On the other hand, the long–term consequences were both positive and far–reaching. The presence of free labor made Estonia and Latvia logical places to locate manufacturing plants when foreign capital began pouring into Russia after Alexander II launched his great reforms in the 1850s.

Russian rule also had its negative aspects in the 19th century. In Lithuania, in particular, the Russian Government resented the role of the Roman Catholic Church and actively fostered the spread of the Orthodox Church in this area. It did not help that Lithuania participated, along with Poland, in the uprisings of 1830 and 1863. The University of Vilnius was closed down after the 1830 uprising and the Russian language was introduced in all

**On the way to church, Estonia (19th century)**

# The Baltic Republics

215

# The Baltic Republics

schools. After the 1863 uprising, land ownership was limited to adherents of the Orthodox faith.

Perhaps the greatest sustained effort at Russification came during the reign of Alexander III [1881–1894]. Alexander III, a Slavophil and strong adherent of Russian Orthodoxy, extended previous Russification efforts to the areas of Estonia and Latvia and even applied them to the previously exempt German–speaking upper classes.

On the other hand, the industrialization process, begun by Alexander II, was continued by his son, Alexander III, and one result was the creation of both an urban working class and a middle class, including professionals and intellectuals, in the Baltic provinces. All of this provided the basis for the beginning of Estonian and Latvian national movements.

In Lithuania, a similar development occurred, though on the basis of a different class, the peasant landholders who emerged as a result of serf emancipation in 1861. Many of these peasant proprietors sent their sons off to be educated in Russian universities and they came back as doctors, lawyers, teachers and engineers. This led to the creation of the first specifically Lithuanian nationalist movement in the 1890s.

By 1905, illegal nationalist political parties existed in Estonia, Latvia and Lithuania and took an active part in the Revolution of 1905. The Lithuanians were perhaps the best organized, having suffered longer from repression, but similar activities were carried in all three areas. A provisional revolutionary government was established in Riga and two separate congresses met in Vilnius in December 1905. With the collapse of the revolution, widespread arrests were carried out, but government repression only succeeded in forcing the more prominent nationalist leaders to emigrate while the nationalist movements themselves went underground.

The beginning of World War I provided a new opportunity for the nationalists, however. Although the majority of the Baltic peoples loyally supported the war effort in the beginning, the subsequent course of the war brought disaffection here as it did in other parts of the Russian Empire. After March 1917, the Baltic nationalists supported the democratic aspirations of the first Russian Revolution of 1917, but began pressing for their own governments. The *Bolshevik* Revolution of November 1917 further alienated the Baltic peoples for the vast majority favored the creation of democratic states.

The *Bolsheviks* wanted to retain the Baltic provinces but one of the results of the *Bolshevik* seizure of power was disintegration of the Russian army. Unable to stop the German advance, the new Com-

munist government signed the Treaty of Brest–Litovsk with Imperial Germany in March 1918, thereby giving up all claims to the Baltic provinces. The entire Baltic coastal area was at this time occupied by the German army. Now the threat which the Baltic nationalists faced was annexation by Germany. The collapse of the German Empire in November 1918 put an end to that threat but, as the German armies began to pull out, the *Bolsheviks* poured back in, and the Baltic peoples had to fight another round with the *Bolsheviks* in order to establish their independence. The last *Bolshevik* forces finally withdrew from the Baltic area at the beginning of 1920 and the Soviet Government then signed agreements with the governments of the three Baltic States recognizing their independence. The treaty with Estonia was signed on February 20, 1920; that with Lithuania was signed on July 12 and that with Latvia on August 11.

## Creation of the New Baltic Governments

Developments in the Baltic provinces followed a fairly similar pattern after March 1917, though the fact that almost all of Lithuania and the southern half of Latvia were occupied by German troops obviously made for differences. The most important factor between March and November 1917 was the attitude of the Russian Provisional Government. Although not sympathetic to independence movements, it actually authorized establishment of an autonomous Estonian Government in April 1917, which led to elections for an Estonian National Council in July.

A group of middle class parties plus the allied *Labor Party* won 60 percent of the seats. Konstantin Paets, leader of the *Farmers' Union*, was installed as President of the National Council on July 14.

Lettish delegates to the Russian Duma had organized a *Latvian Refugees' Committee* even before the March Revolution. After March 1917, they began urging the Provisional Government to establish an autonomous administrative district for the part of Latvia still under Russian control. Local elections were held in the north, but the fact of German occupation of the south militated against any further developments at this time.

The situation with regard to Lithuania was even worse, for almost the entire country was under occupation. Nevertheless, Lithuanian deputies to the Duma organized a Lithuanian National Council in Petrograd and began to demand political autonomy from the Provisional Government. This was the situation in November 1917.

The *Bolshevik* seizure of power in November 1917 proved to be a turning point, for the national movements rejected Bolshevism and tried to break away from the

new Communist government. The *Bolsheviks*, in turn, rejected the national movements and tried to suppress them.

A Latvian National Council, established after the November Revolution, declared Latvian autonomy on November 16 and called for election of a constituent assembly to form a Latvian government. The Estonian government proclaimed its independence on November 28 and also called for elections to a constituent assembly.

The *Bolsheviks* not only refused to recognize the Latvian National Council; they also abolished the local government bodies set up by the Provisional Government. In Estonia, they arrested President Paets and dispersed the National Council. The *Bolsheviks* did permit elections to a new constituent assembly but, when the parties of the old government won a majority of the seats in the January 1918, the *Bolsheviks* moved to suppress the winners. A civil war now broke out and lasted about a month before German troops moved into Estonia and the *Bolsheviks* were forced to flee. The Lithuanian National Council, split between radicals and moderates, did not take a specific stand against the *Bolsheviks*, but the *Bolsheviks* moved to suppress the Lithuanian National Council anyway.

The *Bolsheviks* soon lost control of the Baltic provinces, however, first, because of advances of the German army, then, through agreement to the Treaty of Brest-Litovsk. Now the nationalists had to contend with the desire of the Germans to annex the Baltic provinces and make them part of the German Empire. Once again, the Baltic nationalist movement found itself suppressed and its leaders imprisoned. This phase ended in November 1918 with the collapse of the Imperial German Government.

The armistice called for the German army to begin evacuating the Baltic provinces, a process that eventually stretched over several months. In the meantime, the nationalist leaders began organizing independent governments. Estonia, which had an operating government once before, began reconstituting itself immediately after the armistice. The Estonian National Council met on November 20, President Paets was released from prison soon afterwards, and the new government began operating on February 24, 1919. Two months later, Paets was replaced by Otto Strandman, a member of the leftist *Workers' Party*. A few months later, Strandman was replaced by Jaan Tonisson, the leader of the *People's Party*, who served until 1920.

Governments had to be created in Latvia and Lithuania, but the nationalist leaders had been active for some time and so were well known. An All–Latvian Council of State met at Riga on November 18, 1918, formed a Provisional Govern-

Newspapers (top to bottom) from Estonia, Latvia, and Lithuania

ment and appointed a president and prime minister. Karlis Ulmanis, leader of the *Peasants' League*, became the first president. He held this office until 1920.

In Lithuania, a Provisional Government was also set up in November. A provisional National Assembly met in Kaunas in January 1919. The first Lithuanian president was elected on April 4. Even as they were organizing their governments, however, the nationalists found themselves again under attack as *Bolshevik* armies reopened the war following the German surrender. By February 1919, Latvia had been completely overrun and most of Lithuania was under occupation by *Bol-*

*shevik* forces. Estonia, which had begun to form its own army, was a little luckier. It had to defend itself, but managed to drive the *Bolsheviks* back to the border.

The situation in Latvia was more complicated. A Latvian army was created and began driving back the *Bolsheviks*, with some assistance from German army units still in the country. Once they had regained control of most of the country, however, the German army supported a *coup d'etat* against the Latvian government, installing a new government controlled by Baltic Germans. The Estonian and Latvian armies first joined to drive out the *Bolsheviks*, then turned on the pup-

pet Baltic German government and overthrew it. The Latvian government was reinstated on July 7. Riga, the Latvian capital, came under attack again by German forces in October, but managed to hold out. Meanwhile, part of Latvia was still held by *Bolshevik* forces, but they were driven out in January 1920. Lenin, finally recognizing that the Baltic provinces had been lost, agreed now to recognize the independence of the Baltic States. International recognition soon followed and all three states were admitted to the League of Nations in 1922.

# The Baltic Republics: Estonia

**Tallinn's harbor with its sign: The Baltic Sea—The Sea of Peace**

Courtesy: NOVOSTI

## ESTONIA SINCE WORLD WAR I

### Independent Estonia, 1919–1939

Estonia had elected a constituent assembly charged with drawing up a constitution for the country in April 1919. The assembly was dominated by the left, so that the constitution that was eventually produced was what might be called "radical liberal" in orientation. Approved by the assembly in June 1920, it went into effect on December 21, 1920. All power was vested in a single–body legislature of 100 members called the *Riigikogu*. This was a parliamentary system. The "commission of the legislature" was essentially a cabinet, while the presiding officer, called the "Senior Statesman" [*Riigivanem*], performed the functions of a premier. There was no separate head of state, however, so the "Senior Statesman" performed all ceremonial functions as well. Another unusual feature of the constitution is that it provided for popular participation in decision–making by means of the referendum and the initiative.

Although early elections had produced leftist majorities, new elections held in 1921 produced a swing to the right with the *Farmers' Union* emerging as the dominant party.

A survey taken in 1922 gives us a good

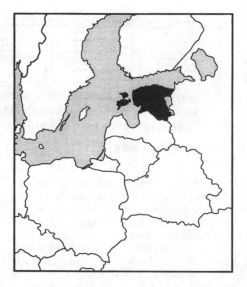

picture of the country. The total population was 1,107,300 with Estonians making up 87.6 percent of the total. Another 8.2 percent of the population spoke Russian, while 1.7 percent spoke German. Estonia was thus the most homogeneous of the Baltic states at this time. It was also religiously homogeneous, with 78.3 percent of the population declaring themselves to be Protestant, with another 19 percent

professing Russian Orthodoxy. And it was rural, with 58.5 percent of the population earning their living from agriculture.

In 1918, two–thirds of the rural population had owned no land whatsoever but, instead, supported themselves by working as day laborers for the large estates which made up 58 percent of the land. Land reform legislation, passed in October 1919, expropriated nearly all of the estates and provided for distribution of the land to the landless rural laborers. An additional 56,000 small holdings were created as a result of the land reform law. This undoubtedly made political sense, since a majority of the estates had been owned by Baltic Germans, but the small holdings turned out to be too small, so that a majority of the new owners were unable to make a go of it without extensive governmental assistance. The eventual answer found by the Estonians was to organize the small holders into cooperative societies, which were able to buy modern machinery which could be used on several farms.

Although the land reform was pushed through by the left, it resulted in additional support for the *Farmers' Union*, a more or less conservative agrarian party. Its support grew from 8 delegates in the constituent assembly to 21 in 1920 and 24 in

218

1929. Between 1919 and 1934, it also produced ten of the twenty premiers.

The *Farmers' Union* was opposed on the left by the *Social Democratic Party*, with the space in between filled in by the *Independent Socialists*, the *Radical Democratic Workers' Party*, the *People's Party*, the *Christian People's Party*, and the *Settlers' Party*.

The *Communist Party* maintained an organization in Estonia until 1924 and its candidates did well in places like Tallinn and Tardu. It was driven completely underground after a communist insurrection in Tallinn in December 1924, though individual communists continued to stand for the legislature using an assumed party name.

The relative strength of the parties can be seen from the number of premiers each produced through 1934. The *Social Democrats* produced one, the *Workers' Party* four, the *People's Party* four and the *Christian People's Party* two.

Because of the number of political parties, governments were invariably coalitions. The most centrist of the parties was the *People's Party*, which participated in seventeen of the twenty coalitions between 1919 and 1933. Over time, there was some merging of the parties. In 1923, the *Independent Socialists* merged with the *Social Democrats* to form the *Socialist Workers' Party*. In 1931, the *Christian People's Party* merged with the *People's Party*; one year later, the *Workers' Party* also merged with the *People's Party*. In 1933, this became the *National Center Party*. In 1932, the *Farmers' Union* joined with the *Settlers' Party* to form the *United Agrarian Party*.

Most of these mergers were the result of the economic crisis that had begun in 1929 and then turned into what the Americans called the "Great Depression." Estonia was heavily dependent on agricultural exports, and the sharp drop in the international price of these products led to great distress in Estonia, particularly in the countryside. People were seeking answers which none of the political parties was competent to provide. The result was a drop in support for all of the established parties and their partial collapse. In 1933, eleven percent of the parliamentary delegates either changed their party or dropped all affiliation whatsoever.

It was at this time that a new political grouping, the *Association of Estonian Freedom Fighters*, began to grow in significance and power. Organized in 1929 as a veterans' organization espousing patriotism, nationalism and anti–communism, by 1932 it was beginning to show increasing tendencies toward anti–parliamentarianism and anti–liberalism. The *Freedom Fighters*, organized into paramilitary organizations, wore grey–green shirts, with black and white arm bands bearing a hand grasping a sword and the dates 1918–1920.

Their most important demand was for the creation of a separate executive power that would be independent of the legislature. Such ideas had already been proposed by the *Peoples' Party*—and defeated in a referendum—in 1926 and again in 1932. The *Freedom Fighters* proposal for constitutional reform was submitted to referendum in October 1933—and passed. This constitutional change created the office of President of the Republic, to be popularly elected for a term of five years. It also vested executive power in the President rather than the legislature. The President could appoint and dismiss governments, declare states of emergency and dissolve the legislature. The revised constitution went into effect on January 24, 1934, and elections were set to fill the new presidency. Among the candidates was General Andreas Larka, president of the *Freedom Fighters*. Another candidate was Konstantin Paets, then serving as premier. The *Freedom Fighters* swept urban local elections at the beginning of 1934 and it appeared that their man would win the presidency as well.

Paets decided to take preemptive action by pulling off his own *coup* before elections could occur. He therefore gave the commander–in–chief of the army special powers to maintain law and order and then banned the *Freedom Fighters* as a "threat to the security of the state." He also banned all political assemblies. The Estonian legislature met, approved Paets' emergency legislation, then was dismissed. Paets next issued a decree postponing presidential elections indefinitely. The legislature met for a short time in September 1934, but it was dissolved when it did not prove to be completely pliant. Paets continued to rule by decree. In February 1935, another decree dissolved the political parties. In their stead, a number of "corporations" representing various interest groups were formed to represent the interests of the people.

In February 1936, Paets began moving to "legitimatize" his authoritarian regime by submitting a referendum to the people asking them to approve calling a new constituent assembly to draft a new constitution. This passed and the new assembly met in February 1937 to ratify a new constitution drafted by the Paets government. This constitution, which went into effect on January 1, 1938, provided for a strong presidency on the order of the one approved in 1933, except that the president was to be elected by a special electoral chamber, not by popular vote. The new parliament also consisted now of two chambers, with the upper chamber partially appointed by the president. The electoral chamber met in April 1938 and confirmed Paets in office.

A small oppositional group was permitted to exist in the lower body of the legislature, but it held only seven out of eighty seats. This was the structure that was still in operation in 1939–40 when Stalin signed his pact with Hitler putting the Baltic States in the Soviet sphere of influence.

Hitler launched his invasion of Poland on September 1 and Soviet troops entered to occupy the eastern third of Poland on September 17. With Poland settled, Stalin moved to cash in his other chips. On September 19, the Estonian Government was informed that the Soviet fleet had extended its defense perimeter to include the Estonian coastline. Six days later, the Soviet Foreign Ministry presented the Estonian Government with a treaty for a military alliance between the two countries, which included the establishment of Soviet bases in Estonia. Left with no alternative, the Estonian Government signed the agreement. On September 28, the first Soviet troops entered Estonia.

Nothing happened for several months, probably because the Soviet Union was tied down in its "Winter War" with Finland. Once that was resolved, the Soviet Union turned its attention back to the Baltic States. Toward the end of May 1940, the Soviet Foreign Ministry accused all three states of violating the 1939 mutual assistance pacts with the Soviet Union. Then all three were pressured into installing popular front governments. These did not last long, however. In July all political parties other than the *Communist Party* were banned and most non–communists were dismissed from office.

This was followed by waves of arrests in all three countries. Then, with only communists, organized as the *Working People's League*, standing for office, new elections were held on July 14. The newly elected legislatures met on July 21. Their only piece of business was to vote on whether to join the Soviet Union, which they did by acclamation. The following month, the USSR Supreme Soviet acceded to their request. They thus became Soviet Socialist Republics.

Nazi Germany's invasion of the Soviet Union beginning on June 22, 1941 reversed this situation somewhat, for German troops overran and occupied the three Baltic Republics later in 1941. They remained under German occupation until 1944. However, with the German retreat, the Baltic Republics once again fell under Soviet control. Guerrilla movements in the three republics continued to oppose Soviet control for some time after the end of the war in 1945, but such efforts were, of course, ineffectual. The movements got no outside assistance, and they were eventually suppressed.

Many changes occurred in the three republics over the next thirty–five years. Soviet policy was to integrate the republics so thoroughly that there would be no

# The Baltic Republics: Estonia

question of their ever leaving the union. To that end, the Soviet Government first carried out policies of nationalization and collectivization. Next it sought to bind the Baltic Republics to the rest of the Soviet Union economically by locating branch factories of Soviet industry in the three republics. Such factories received most or all of their raw materials from other parts of the Soviet Union, and delivered most of their finished products to customers in the other republics. This economic integration was so successful that the three Baltic Republics became more integrated into the Soviet economy than any other republic. Between 1945 and 1959, approximately 250,000 non–Estonians were resettled in the republic, some as employees of the Soviet Government, particularly its security agencies, but most as part of a project to develop Estonia's lignite and brown coal fields. Another wave began arriving in the 1960s when the Soviet Government began developing a branch of its military–industrial complex in the Narva area. As a result, the population in areas such as Narva was eventually 90 percent non–Estonian.

This program of economic integration was accompanied by a program of "Soviet Russification," aimed at transforming the cultures of the three republics. All students received Russian language training in the schools, plus general indoctrination lectures on the nature of Soviet culture. In addition, there was a systematic effort made to settle non–Baltic nationals in the republics. When a new factory was built, most of the workers would be transferred there from elsewhere in the Soviet Union.

The effects of this policy can be seen by examining the figures of the 1989 Soviet census. Ethnic Estonians by this time made up only 61.5 percent of the population of the republic. These overall figures also masked the fact that, in certain industrial regions near the border, Estonians had become a tiny minority. On the positive side, the heavy industrialization carried out since 1945 meant that the standard of living in Estonia was above that of any part of the Soviet Union.

## Estonia Regains its Independence

The Estonian people accommodated themselves to Soviet rule, but they were

never happy with it. When, therefore, Gorbachëv launched his programs of *glasnost* and restructuring after coming to power in 1985, Estonians were among the first to take advantage of them.

In enunciating his policy of *glasnost*, Gorbachëv called on the Soviet peoples to speak out against negative tendencies in the society, and to support his reforms. This became a manifesto which led to the creation of thousands of "unofficial" organizations all over the Soviet Union. Formed originally in support of Gorbachëv's policy of reform, many of them soon began to push their own agendas. For Estonians, Gorbachëv's policies were a welcome breath of fresh air, and they were among the first to throw their enthusiastic support to him. At the same time, and almost from the beginning, the Estonian people used *glasnost* for their own purposes.

The first unofficial Baltic organization was the *Estonian Heritage Society* (*EHS*), founded in December 1987. Ostensibly aimed at preserving the national heritage, the *EHS* very quickly became a vehicle for Estonian nationalism. It stressed Estonian

**The 13th century City Hall, Tallinn**

Courtesy: NOVOSTI

# The Baltic Republics: Estonia

**Celebrating Independence Day, Tallinn**

Courtesy: NOVOSTI

history; it honored Estonian heroes killed while fighting for Estonian independence; and it resurrected the old Estonian blue–black–white flag. Opposed by the government at first, its programs proved to be so popular that the Estonian Government eventually endorsed some of its positions. For example, the Presidium of the Estonian Supreme Soviet legalized the pre–revolutionary flag in June 1988.

An organization destined to play a much larger role than the *EHS* was the *Popular Front of Estonia (PFE)*, first suggested by Edgar Savisaar, a sociologist and planning official, in April 1988. Many communists quickly threw their support to the idea so that the *PFE* quickly won preliminary approval both from the *Estonian Communist Party* Central Committee and the Estonian Government. This gave the *PFE* access to the public media, and it quickly began to build up public support.

This led to a split in the *Estonian Communist Party* for Karl Vaino, Party Secretary since 1978, began to fear the challenge raised by the *PFE* and sought to limit its influence. He was challenged by reformers within the party, however. Moscow sided with the reformers and Vaino was replaced as Party Secretary by Vaino Valjas.

Valjas officially addressed the first congress of the *PFE*, held in October 1988, and expressed his support for the goals of the *PFE*. With some 22 percent of the delegates also belonging to the *Estonian Communist Party*, it appeared that the *PFE* was merely a popular arm of the party. That was misleading, however; although communists

made up a significant percentage of the membership, it was overwhelmingly reform communists who joined the *PFE* and, increasingly, the *PFE* was used to allow reform communists to take control of the *Estonian Communist Party* and the Estonian Government. For example, Savisaar, head of the *PFE*, was appointed deputy chairman of the Estonian Council of Ministers and head of the state planning committee.

Another Estonian unofficial organization was the *Estonian National Independence Party (ENIP)*, established in August 1988. Political parties other than the *Communist Party* were illegal at this time, so the *ENIP* was given a hard time by the government in the beginning. and it was undoubtedly the existence of the *ENIP* that helps explain the significant communist support for the *PFE*. Other unofficial organizations that came into existence in 1988–89 were the *Estonian Green Movement*, the *Estonian Council of Churches* and a *Rural Movement*. In addition, the *Social Democratic Party* was revived in 1989 and a *Christian Democrat* movement came into being.

Meanwhile, there was a further split in the *Estonian Communist Party*. Faced with a choice between nationalism and communism, more and more Estonian communists were opting for nationalism. Valjas tried to control this tendency by specifically catering to it. He reduced the size of the Central Committee, purging mainly non–Estonians, and he carried out a similar purge of the Estonian Supreme Soviet, increasing the number of Estonians to two–thirds of the membership.

Meanwhile, the goals of the *Popular Front of Estonia* were shifting. The original emphasis had been on breaking the control of the "centralized administrative–bureaucratic system" and establishing the right of Estonians to decide their own affairs without outside interference. This had been symbolized by the call for sovereignty. Increasingly, however, the argument was made that these goals could not be achieved without political pluralism and that political pluralism was not possible without a break from the communist system. For people who accepted this argument, independence became the necessary goal.

The elections to the USSR Congress of People's Deputies in March 1989 gave the *PFE* the chance to test its strength, though the results were somewhat obscured by the fact that many *PFE*–endorsed candidates were also members of the *Communist Party*. Nevertheless, *PFE* candidates basically swept the slate, winning 18 out of 21 seats that they contested.

A new test came in February 1990, when republic elections were scheduled. The *Popular Front of Estonia* adopted a platform in October 1989 calling for sovereignty and independence. Thus the *PFE* went on record for the first time as publicly favoring independence.

Meanwhile, the *Communist Party of Estonia* was moving in the same direction. In February 1990, Prime Minister Indrek Toome, a former head of ideology for the *CPE*, founded the *Free Estonia Group* as his vehicle for reelection. He ran on a platform of experience and competence. Arnold Rüütel, President of the Supreme Soviet, also maneuvered to assure his reelection. As presiding officer for the Full Assembly of People's Deputies—a meeting of deputies at the local, republic and union level—he squired through a resolution declaring that Estonia's independence should be restored on the basis of the 1920 Tartu Treaty (with Soviet Russia). Thus Rüütel was also on record as supporting Estonian independence.

Reform communists who had endorsed Estonian independence did well in the February 1990 elections, but it was the candidates endorsed by the *Popular Front of Estonia* who made the best showing, winning a clear majority of the seats. When the new Supreme Soviet met at the end of March, it first passed a resolution declaring that it did "not recognize the legality of state authority of the USSR on the territory of Estonia." The next day, it elected Edgar Savisaar—head of the *Popular Front of Estonia*—as the new Prime Minister. Since he had resigned his membership in the *Communist Party* some months earlier, he became the first non–Communist to be elected head of Estonia's government since 1940.

Savisaar's government now began tak-

# The Baltic Republics: Estonia

**Arnold Rüütel**

ing on many of the trappings of independence. Postage stamps were issued and plans were announced to issue an Estonian currency, the Kroon. The government also launched a campaign aimed at privatizing service industries and state distribution networks. The Estonian Supreme Soviet also passed a law prohibiting the drafting of Estonian youths into the Soviet military.

Then, on May 8, 1990, Estonia became the third of the Baltic republics to declare its independence. Six days later, Gorbachëv issued a decree invalidating the declaration. Vadim Bakatin, Soviet Minister of the Interior, ordered troops into Estonia to enforce Gorbachëv's decree. However, Prime Minister Savisaar telephoned Bakatin and got the order reversed. Bakatin later signed an order guaranteeing the Estonian Government control over law enforcement in Estonia. Bakatin's leniency toward the Baltic republics was probably an important reason why he was later dismissed as Interior Minister and replaced by a hardliner, Boris K. Pugo, one of the plotters of the August 1991 *coup*. Estonia was to remain in a sort of state of suspended animation for another year before its independence would be recognized.

Periodically, Gorbachëv would condemn Baltic demands for independence and he continued to insist that the Baltic States could only obtain their independence by complying with legislation passed by the Supreme Soviet on the question. This was out of the question for the Baltic States, since their legal position

was that they were reasserting an independence which, under international law, had never been lost. Meanwhile, the Communist Party of Estonia, which had voted the previous March to separate from the Communist Party of the Soviet Union, actually carried through its break in September 1990. One more connection was thus severed.

During the fall of 1990, Gorbachëv, surrounding himself with more and more conservative officials, sought to enforce a more hardline position. This lasted until May 1991, when it finally became clear to Gorbachëv that his policy had alienated reform–minded individuals without producing anything positive. Moreover, Gorbachëv now began to realize that he could not achieve a new union treaty without reaching a new accommodation with reformers—which would include accepting a major transfer of power and authority to the individual republics. Boris Yeltsin's election as President of the Russian Republic in May 1991 was another factor. Negotiations for a new union treaty went on during the summer and it was due to be signed on August 17, 1991.

Hardliners opposed to the new union treaty launched their *coup d'etat* against Gorbachëv on August 16. The failure of that *coup* finally broke the logjam on recognition. Estonia and Latvia actually declared their independence while the *coup* was still in progress. After the *coup* failed, most of the world rushed to extend recognition to all three Baltic Republics. The post–*coup* Soviet Government extended its own recognition in September.

Edgar Savisaar remained as Prime Minister of an independent Estonia for approximately 5 months. In January 1992, he came increasingly under attack for the state of the economy and he proposed a state of emergency to strengthen his hand in dealing with the situation. The parliament voted to impose a state of emergency, but criticism of Savisaar continued. He submitted his resignation after the parliament failed to agree on the membership of an anticrisis commission being set up under the state of emergency ruling and the *Coalition Party*, which controlled 5 seats in the cabinet, called for Savisaar's resignation. Tiit Vähi was selected as the new Prime Minister of a government of experts. Individuals entering the cabinet dropped their party membership for the duration of their time in the cabinet. Vahi himself had been Minister of Transport and Communications in the previous cabinet. One of his first acts as Prime Minister was to repeal the state of emergency and to promise to work closely with the parliament. He said that he expected to remain in office only about 6 months. His political agenda included a new constitution and a new law on Estonian citizenship, to be followed by new elections to

the parliament. The Supreme Council approved the new citizenship law on February 26 1992. Automatic citizenship was granted only to those persons—and their descendants—who were Estonian citizens prior to June 16, 1940—the date of Estonia's incorporation into the Soviet Union.

*The 600,000 persons who moved to Estonia after 1940—and their descendants—thus became aliens.* The law turned approximately 38 percent of the population into "resident aliens" and excluded them from the scheduled parliamentary elections. These individuals could become Estonian citizens through a process of naturalization, whose requirements included three years residence in Estonia, ability to speak Estonian, and a loyalty oath. As an exception, persons who had resided in Estonia for more than ten years were not required to take the language test, but still had to qualify for naturalization. The government also decided not to accept applications for citizenship until after legislative elections. All of this became even more important when a new law on the privatization of land stipulated that one had to be a citizen in order to purchase land.

In April 1992, another law restructured the government by replacing the Supreme Council by the *Riigikogu*, a single–chamber assembly consisting of 101 members. The same law created a President of the Republic to replace the Chairman of the Supreme Council.

The new constitution was submitted to a referendum in June 1992. The question of denying citizenship to individuals who had moved to Estonia after 1940 was also included on the ballot. Both measures were approved overwhelmingly. The new

**Prime Minister Mart Siimann**

legislative elections that took place in September were therefore limited almost exclusively to ethnic Estonians.

That helps explain why the right–wing *Fatherland Alliance* became the dominant group in the new legislature. The September elections also included a popular vote to fill the office of President of the Republic. Arnold Rüütel, who had steered Estonia to independence as head of the *Estonian Communist Party*, actually came in first with 43% of the vote. Because he failed to win an absolute majority, however, the new President was elected by the *Riigikogu* when it convened in October. Their choice was Lennart Meri, candidate of the *Fatherland Alliance*, even though he came in a poor second in September with only 29% of the vote.

Meri is a former foreign minister and Ambassador to Finland. His family, which comes from the city of Tallinn, was also among those deported to Siberia in 1941. They were permitted to return to Estonia in 1946.

The new Prime Minister, Mart Laar, headed a coalition government made up of the *Fatherland Alliance*, the *Moderate Bloc*, and the *National Independence Party*. These three groups together controlled 53 out of the 101 seats in the *Riigikogu*.

Even though the new government had a right–wing orientation, it was outflanked on the right by the *Eesti Kodanik*, a rightist–nationalist movement headed by Juri Toomepan, a U.S. citizen and retired U.S. Army colonel, who repeatedly attacked the government for being too lenient toward residents who are not ethnic Estonians. In 1993, Toomepan proposed a new, more–stringent citizenship law to deny permanent residence status to any person who had not entered the country on a residence permit issued by the Estonian Republic "in compliance with the legislation of 1940 replicated in 1992." As passed by the parliament in mid–1993, the legislation gave individuals who arrived before 1990 two years to apply for permanent residency status or Russian citizenship. Failure to comply with the law made one subject to deportation.

The new law brought an immediate reaction from Russia. The government cut off all gas shipments to Estonia, then President Yeltsin threatened to intervene if inter–ethnic relations in Estonia deteriorated. "If the Russian–speaking population expresses the natural desire to protect itself from crude discrimination," he was quoted as saying, "Russia will not be able to remain in the position of an indifferent onlooker."

Alarmed, President Meri announced that he would not sign the new legislation until it was reviewed and approved by international organizations. He then submitted it to the Council of Europe for review. The government subsequently sponsored

new legislation that granted non–citizens the right to vote in local elections.

This defused the situation somewhat, particularly after ethnic Russians and a moderate center coalition that favored accommodation with the Russians managed to win majorities on many urban councils. In the capital city of Tallinn, for example, two Russian groups won 27 out of 64 city council seats, while the nationalists were reduced to a tiny minority.

The nationalists suffered a further loss in the March 1995 parliamentary elections. The *Fatherland Alliance*, utterly routed, barely scraped over the 5% threshold and won a mere 8 seats. Perhaps even more telling, an ethnic–Russian party, called *Estonia Is Our Home*, won 6 seats, only two fewer than the *Fatherland Alliance*.

The principal winners were two allied parties, the *Consolidated Faction*, led by Tiit Vahi, and the *Rural Alliance*, led by Arnold Rüütel, which together won 41 out of 101 parliamentary seats. The other important winner was the *Reform Party*, led by Siim Kallas, which came in second with 19 seats. Although the major issue in the election campaign was economic reform, the winning political parties are on record as favoring a more flexible policy toward non–Estonian ethnic groups and better relations with Russia.

The new Prime Minister, Tiit Vahi, basically continued the policies of the previous government. This was not unexpected. Vahi, after all, had sponsored the original citizenship law which stripped non–Estonian ethnics of automatic citizenship when he was Prime Minister in 1992. And in foreign policy, Vahi, like most Estonian politicians, was a supporter of Estonia's entry into NATO and the European Union. As for the economy, it was Vahi who originally pegged the Estonian *kroon* to the *Deutsche Mark* and modelled Estonia's privatization agency on Germany's *Treuhand*. The one area of disagreement within the coalition was with regard to agriculture. Arnold Rüütel, deputy parliamentary speaker and leader of the *Rural Alliance*, opposed efforts to phase out collectives and end agricultural subsidies. Members of the coalition who wanted to apply liberal principles to agriculture were supported from outside the coalition by Siim Kallas and his *Reform Faction*, whose 1995 platform had stressed liberalizing the economy.

New presidential elections occurred in 1996. President Meri stood for reelection where he was opposed by Rüütel. Neither was able to command the necessary 68 parliamentary votes to become elected, so the matter passed to the jurisdiction of the electoral college. Here Meri prevailed by a vote of 196 to 126.

The most recent political change occurred in February 1997, when Tiit Vahi resigned as Prime Minister. Vahi, who had

been in that office since since April 1995, stepped down after a no–confidence vote which he narrowly won. Vahi had been accused of taking part in shady privatization deals and he apparently felt that the margin of victory was too narrow for him to stay on as Prime Minister. When Vahi stepped down, President Meri named Mart Siimann as his successor. Siimann, previously head of the parliamentary caucus of the *Consolidated Faction*, is a former television and radio manager.

Siimann has since proved himself to be a competent, if uncharismatic, Prime Minister. Since his government is a three party coalition which sometimes differs internally over individual issues, the opposition has sometimes managed to influence government policy in a significant way. The best example of this is the 1998 budget, which was held up for three months while the government and opposition wrangled over spending limits. In particular, the opposition wanted to see teachers' salaries raised and proposed an additional 200 million *kroons* for this purpose. The final budget, adopted in December 1997, called for expenditures of 14.97 billion kroons (approximately $1 billion), including an additional 133 million kroons for a teachers' salary increase.

Estonia also received an international vote of confidence in 1997 when it became the only one of the Baltic States to be invited to join the European Union. The invitation appeared to be well merited, however, since Estonia has been consistently in the vanguard of reforming its economy since 1991. It has also been the recipient of the largest amount of foreign investment of any of the Baltic States and its annual rate of growth has been over 5% since 1994. This is expected to continue. The predicted economic growth rate for 1998 is 5.5%.

The European Union did express some concern about Estonia's treatment of aliens and this may have motivated the government to announce, in December 1997, that it was considering an amendment to the citizenship law which would grant citizenship to all children born in Estonia, if their parents had lived in the country for at least five years. In welcoming the Estonian Government's statement, a spokesman for the European Union referred to the decision as a constructive step toward the integration of non-Estonian citizens.

## Foreign Policy

The U.S. Government, having always refused to recognize the incorporation of the Baltic Governments into the USSR in 1940, was an early and enthusiastic supporter of their efforts to regain their independence. One example of just how far the U.S. Government is willing to go in that regard relates to Aleksander Einseln,

# The Baltic Republics: Estonia

recruited by the Estonian Government to head the newly–created Estonian Defense Forces. Einseln, an Estonian native who had fled with his family to America in 1944, is a former tank commander and Vietnam veteran who retired from the U.S. Army as a colonel. Not wanting to jeopardize either his U.S. citizenship or his army pension, Einseln requested permission from the U.S. Army to accept the assignment. When permission was denied, however, Einseln accepted the assignment anyway; his pension was suspended.

It soon became clear, however, that the U.S. Government's action was being interpreted as being anti–Estonian. To get rid of an embarrassing issue, the U.S. Government, reversing itself, granted Einseln's request and reinstated his pension. To legalize the situation, Senator John McCain introduced a bill allowing retired officers, with the permission of the Secretary of State and the relevant service secretary, to

**Major General Aleksander Einseln, Former Commander, Estonian Defense Forces**

serve in the armed forces of newly democratic countries. Einseln became involved in domestic Estonian politics in December 1995 when he criticized Defense Minister Andrus Oovel in public. As a result, President Meri demanded his resignation as chief of Estonia's army.

Since 1991, Estonia has worked to establish close and friendly relations with Scandinavia, and it has expressed an interest in eventually becoming a member of the European Union. It would also like to get into NATO, though a territorial dispute with Russia makes that unlikely. In 1945, the Soviet Union annexed 2,020 square kilometers of land that the Soviet Government had recognized as being a part of Estonia in the 1920 Treaty of Tartu. Estonia continues to press its claim to the territory, though there is little possibility that the present Russian Government will relinquish its claim. In fact, the Russian Government has begun installing a barbed

**Lecture in Tartu University's physics department**

wire fence along the Russian–Estonian border. The withdrawal of the last Russian troops from Estonia in 1994 removed one bone of contention, but Russo–Estonian relations remain cool because of the continuing dispute over Estonian denial of citizenship rights to most ethnic Russians. This situation has been changing recently, however, since the parties that won the 1995 parliamentary elections favor a better working relationship with Russia. One of the things they have done is to speed up the process of issuing residence permits and noncitizen passports to replace old Soviet passports that many ethnic Russians carry. These passports guarantee that noncitizens who visit their relatives in Russia may return to Estonia.

## NATURE OF THE REGIME

Estonia is a multiparty, parliamentary democracy in transition from the earlier communistic system. Most of the forms of government have recently been changed, with the legislature reassuming the name of *Riigikogu*. In a departure from the past, a new executive President of the Republic has been created, modeled somewhat on the French Fifth Republic. Estonia remains essentially a parliamentary system, however.

### The Estonian Government

Under the new constitution, executive power is shared by the President of the Republic and the Prime Minister. The President, as head of state, is responsible for general domestic policy. He is also considered to be the chief spokesman for the nation internationally.

The constitution originally provided for a popular vote to fill the office of President with the stipulation that, if no candidate won a majority of the vote, then the President would be elected by a vote of the *Riigikogu*. President Lennart Meri was elected by the *Riigikogu* in 1992 after coming in second in the popular vote. Subsequently, the constitution was amended to have the president elected by the *Riigikogu*. Since the amendment stipulated that a candidate needed a two–thirds majority to win, however, it also created an electoral college to take over, should no candidate be able to obtain the required 68 votes. The *Riigikogu*, following this procedure in 1996, deadlocked between Meri and Rüütel. The matter was then referred to the electoral college, which reelected Meri.

The Prime Minister presides over the cabinet and oversees day–to–day operations as head of government. Although appointed by the President, he must be approved by, and maintain the support of, a majority in the *Riigikogu* in order to remain in office. The Prime Minister's cabinet must also be approved by the legislature. The legislature is made up of numerous political parties, none of whom controls a majority of the seats, so the government is a coalition.

In the March 1995 elections, the *Consolidated Faction* and the *Rural Alliance* won 41 out of 101 seats, routing the former ruling *Fatherland Alliance*, a coalition of four parties (*Christian Democratic Union, Unified Party of Republicans, Conservative People's Party,* and *Liberal Democratic Party*), which won only 8 seats. Five other parties are represented in the *Riigikogu*, the *Reform Faction* (19 members), the *Centrist Faction* (16 members), the *Moderates* (6 members), *Estonia Is Our Home* (6 members) and the *Rightists* (5 members).

### Economy

Estonia is an overwhelmingly urban society, with approximately 72 percent of the population living in cities or towns. One of the problems which the current government is facing, however, is that Estonians actually constitute a minority of workers in industrial concerns. Most of the workers are Russians, Belarusians and Ukrainians brought in to staff new factories built during the Soviet era. Until recently, the economic policy of the Estonian Government stressed privatization, a policy likely to affect these factories the most, partly because of the strong antipathy toward such workers.

The *Fatherland Alliance*, main component of the government coalition between September 1992 and March 1995, was obviously hoping that, given bad enough economic circumstances, many Russians and others would choose to leave and go back to their home republics. As Klara Hallik, Minister for National Minorities phrased it, the Estonian Government would be delighted if the Russians in Estonia would leave voluntarily—"in a civilized manner, of course."

This is particularly true with regard to the area of Narva, located in the northeastern part of Estonia. Narva is inhabited almost entirely by Russians, the result of the fact that the Soviet Government decided in the 1960s to build a branch of its industrial–military complex there. Until recently, almost no Russian in the Narva area had bothered to learn Estonian. As one said, "Why should I bother, when everybody here speaks Russian?"

According to Yuri Mishin, a deputy in the Narva city council, about 12,000 Estonian Russians have applied for Russian citizenship under the terms of a new law passed by the Russian parliament making it easier for Russians living abroad to obtain Russian citizenship. Many of these are undoubtedly thinking of emigrating, but almost none have actually done so. The fact that living conditions in Estonia are still better than those in Russia continues to act as a limiting factor.

In spite of the numerous factories built in the 1960s and 1970s to serve as suppliers of the Soviet arms industry, Estonia's largest industry is still that of primary extraction, the production of oil from oil shale. Two other major industries are the manufacturing of mineral fertilizers and shipbuilding. It also has consumer industries such as textiles and medium industry such as electrical and mechanical equipment. Most of the rest of the republic's industry is concerned with the processing of forest products (timber, wood pulp for paper manufacturing, peat) or food processing. Fishing is another major industry.

In 1992, Estonia was the first of the Baltic Republics to establish its own currency, the *kroon*. It subsequently wrung inflation out of the economy by tying the *kroon* to the *Deutsche Mark*. It also began to dismantle the command economy inherited from the Soviet Union, setting up a privatization agency modelled on Germany's Treuhand in 1992. Progress has been fairly rapid since that time. In December 1992, Prime Minister Laar announced that private enterprise had provided 64.3% of all tax income over the preceding eleven months. The privatization process continued in 1993, and by the end of 1994 was 90% complete.

Economic reform had a negative side as well. In December 1992, the Estonian Department of Statistics reported that the volume of production had dropped by 39.5% during the year. This was, however, the result of a near collapse of production in certain areas—building materials, glass works, metal processing and chemical production. During this same time period, production actually increased in areas such as dry goods, concentrated foods, starch, butter and a few other foodstuffs.

Six months later, the situation was visibly improving. By 1994, GDP was growing at an annual rate of 6%, giving Estonia one of the fastest growing economies in Europe. The government also managed to run budget surpluses in both 1993 and 1994—by law the budget must be balanced—while reforming its system of taxation, instituting a flat income tax of 26%. Cutting off subsidies to industry and allowing wages to rise freely, while keeping wages down, stabilized the value of the Estonian *kroon* and gave a great spurt to both foreign investment and exports. As a result, new stores, restaurants and other service enterprises sprouted while foreign investment, particularly from Scandinavia, led to additional jobs in private industry, replacing the ones lost in the crumbling state enterprises. By 1996, foreign direct investment had reached more than 10% of the country's GDP. Not only have exports grown greatly since 1991; this has also been accompanied by a massive redirecting of exports. In 1991, 90% of all ex-

# The Baltic Republics: Estonia

**Marja Bussov**     Photo by Hermine Dreyfuss

ports went into the Soviet economy. By 1995, over 80% of all exports went to the European Union, Sweden and Finland. Estonia's GDP has also been growing between 4% and 6% since 1994.

Recent visitors to the capital, Tallinn, report that it is beginning to look more Nordic than Soviet. Retail shops have all been privatized and the number of foreign companies opening headquarters has ballooned. Foreign investment doubled in the first half of 1994, then doubled again in the last half of the year. Trade grew by 50% in 1994, while the GDP grew by 5%. Unemployment was officially only 2%. On the negative side, wages averaged only $100 a month, while there was an actual drop in the income of farmers and retirees. It is probably this latter statistic that helps explain the results of the March 1995 elections, which turned out the previous government.

Agriculture and the processing of agricultural products still employ about 28 percent of the population. The legislature has passed a law on land privatization, but this has gotten bogged down in the politics of nationalism. Only individuals who can trace Estonian citizenship prior to 1940 may buy land. Most agricultural land remains organized into collective and state farms, but they are no longer supervised by the government. Progress in this area has been slow because of the problem of restitution for land national-ized after 1940, though it is also true that many farmers appear to be satisfied to remain in the collectives.

## Culture

Estonia's culture is very much associated with its historic cities, the most important of which are Tallinn (the capital), Narva and Tartu. Tallinn, historically known as Reval or Revel, was founded by King Waldemar II of Denmark in 1219 on the site of an earlier fortress and it has played an important role in Estonian history ever since. The city became a member of the Hanseatic League in 1284 and a major trading center. Over the centuries, it belonged to the Danes, the Teutonic Knights, the Swedes and, from 1710 onward, Russia. The old city was surrounded by a city wall, about two–thirds of which still stands. Most of the guard towers and some of the gates are also still extant. Medieval buildings include the Dom Castle and the Long Hermann Watchtower.

The oldest of the churches is the Domkirk, which dates from 1232. Other churches of interest are St. Nicholas, built in the fourteenth century, St. Olaf's, built in the thirteenth but with a Gothic spire from the seventeenth century, and the Bremer Chapel of St. Mary, built in the sixteenth century. Most Estonians are Lutherans, but there is also a Russian Orthodox Cathedral, St. Alexander Nevsky's, built in the late nineteenth century. Other cultural treasures include the Town Hall, built in 1371–74, and the Blackheads' Club, which dates from the fourteenth century.

Being the capital, Tallinn also has Estonia's Academy of Sciences, established in 1946, an Art Institute and Conservatoire, founded in 1919, the Vilde Pedagogical Institute, a Polytechnical Institute, the Estonian State Opera House and numerous theaters.

Tartu, known historically as Dorpat, was founded in 1030 by Grand Prince Yaroslav of Kievan Rus. Then called Yuriev, it was built at the site of an earlier Estonian settlement, Tarpatu. Yuriev was conquered by the Teutonic Knights in 1212 and it later became the seat of the Livonian bishops. The Germans gave it the name of Dorpat. Fought over numerous times over the centuries, it passed back under Russian control in 1710 when Peter the Great took it from Sweden. The modern name dates from the first period of Estonian independence following World War I.

Tartu, also a member of the Hanseatic League, was a major trading center; its chief claim to fame is its university, founded in 1632 by King Gustav II of Sweden. Transferred for a time to the city of Parnu during the eighteenth century, it was returned to Tartu in 1802. Today Tartu Uni-versity has seven faculties and 4,000 students. The university library, most of which is housed in the Cathedral of Peter and Paul, contains over two million volumes. The cathedral, in ruins in 1802 when it was reconstructed as a library, is probably the oldest building in Tartu. Most of the other university buildings date from the nineteenth century.

Although the ancient Estonians had an oral literature, very little of that survived the centuries of domination by other cultures. The roots of modern Estonian culture should probably be traced to the formation of the University of Tartu in 1632, for that marked the beginning of a small educated Estonian elite. The first book of Estonian grammar appeared in 1637, followed by an Estonian translation of the Bible in 1739.

Little more happened until the nineteenth century when an attempt was made to revive a folklorist tradition. Many songs, sayings and fairy tales were eventually collected, most strongly reminiscent of Finnish folklorist survivals. Somewhat later, Friedrich Reinhold Kreutzwald used many of these oral works to create an artificial epic which he called *Kalevipoeg* [The Son of Kalev]. It was published by the Estonian Learned Society in 1857–1861.

Kreutzwald's epic marked the beginning of an Estonian national literature, exemplified by the appearance of poets such as Lydia Koidula, Friedrich Kuhlbars and Jacob Tamm, novelists such as Eduard Vilde and Juhan Liiv and Ernst Scrgava, and the playwright August Kitzberg. Estonian writers worked under a great handicap, however, for the Russian Government enforced a censorship down to 1905 that attempted to suppress themes that might encourage Estonian nationalism.

The Revolution of 1905 forced a number of writers to flee abroad, but the constitutional regime established in 1906 led to the abolition of most censorship and the appearance of a vigorous Estonian press. It also marked the birth of a new literary movement called Young Estonia, whose chief representative was the poet Gustav Suits. But Suits, who had fled to Finland in 1905, continued to live abroad until after the Russian Revolution of 1917. Suits eventually became a professor of Estonian Literature at Tartu University. Another figure from this period was Friebert Tuglas, a writer of short stories and novels. Suits and Tuglas, along with a third writer, Ernst Enno, and the poet Marie Under, became the dominant figures in Estonian literature during the period of independence down to 1940. Tuglas, a member of the Social Democratic Party prior to 1917, succeeded Suits as Professor of Estonian Literature at Tartu in 1944, after Estonia had come under Soviet domination. However, Tuglas made no literary contribution after that time except for a travelogue, *The First Trip Abroad*, which appeared in 1945 except for a volume of musings called *Thoughts and Moods*, published in 1960.

A number of Estonian writers made their way abroad during World War II. These included Marie Under, Karl Rumor, Artur Adson, August Mclk, and August Gailit. These and other writers kept Estonian literature alive as an emigre literature even as the Soviet occupation regime was imprisoning figures such as Hugo Raudsepp, Estonia's greatest playwright, and exiling others, such as the poet Heiti Talvik, to Siberia. Most of these figures are too well integrated into their new environments to resettle in Estonia, but their influence on the new generation of emerging Estonian writers is likely to be great.

## The Future

Estonia is a small state with a well–educated population and its long–term prospects are probably rather bright, if its neighbors will leave it alone. With its economy currently developing at a 5% rate, its greatest remaining problem is how to deal with the large Slavic minorities that make up so much of the industrial work force. How Estonia resolves this problem will essentially determine its relations with its neighbors, in particular Russia, and its own domestic tranquillity. The rout of the nationalists in the March 1995 parliamentary elections may make this problem easier to solve.

Foreign language bookstore in Tartu

Photo by Hermine Dreyfuss

# The Baltic Republics: Latvia

**Dressed for a festival on a street in Riga**

Courtesy: NOVOSTI

## LATVIA SINCE WORLD WAR I

Latvia's history as an independent state after World War I bears many similarities to that of Estonia. That is not surprising, since the two countries were alike in many respects. Like Estonia, Latvia created a 100 member single–chamber parliament (called the *Saeima*) based on proportional representation. The Latvian constitution, approved in February 1922, did provide for the election of a President of the Republic to a fixed five–year term, however. The President, who was made commander–in–chief of the military, was also authorized to issue decrees when parliament was not in session, subject to parliamentary confirmation when it reconvened.

The first President of the Republic elected under terms of the new constitution was Janis Cakste. A lawyer and early nationalist leader, he had headed the Latvian delegation to the Paris Peace Talks.

Latvia's population at this time was approximately 1.9 million, with Latvians making up about 75 percent of the population. The largest single minority was Rus-

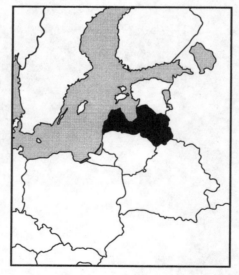

sian, which made up about 7.8 percent of the population. Another 8.1 percent were other Slavs, mainly White Russians and Poles. Other minorities included Jews (5.2 percent), Baltic Germans and Lithuanians.

Like Estonia, Latvia had an agrarian–based economy, with 66.2 percent of the population supporting themselves through agriculture. One difference is that Latvia had significantly more industry, particularly in and around the city of Riga. The majority of the population was Protestant (57.2 percent), but there were significant Russian Orthodox (13 percent) and Roman Catholic (22.6 percent) populations.

Latvia also began its existence with a land reform which expropriated the old landed estates and provided for their distribution to landless peasants. As a result of the reform, 22.2 percent of the land was held by small holders who had obtained their land at this time. In general, Latvia had better luck with its land reform than Estonia and food production, particularly of beef and dairy cattle, continued to grow through the 1920's and 1930's.

With the same kind of legislative system and similar type of population, it is not surprising that Latvia's political parties were similar to those in Estonia. There was, for example, a *Peasants' League* on the

# The Baltic Republics: Latvia

right with the *Social Democratic Party* on the left, with the *Democratic Party*, the *Radical Democratic Party* and the *People's Party* filing up the middle. In 1922, these three centrist parties merged to form the *Democratic Center*. Thereafter it was to be found in every coalition, for neither the left nor the right was able to obtain a majority on its own.

Latvia's use of proportional representation also made it more difficult to form stable governments, since it increased the number of political groups vying for seats. In the 1931 elections, for example, 27 different political groupings won representation in the legislature. Twelve of the groups managed to elect only a single member, however. At the other end, only two groups had more than ten members. To be sure, this proliferation of political parties was partly a reaction to the bad economic conditions since 1929—characterized by a drop in exports, especially agricultural products, and a rise in unemployment—which had led to a loss of confidence in the older political parties.

## Latvia's Move Toward Authoritarianism

The bad economic situation also led to a growth of anti–parliamentarianism in Latvia, mainly led by right–wing, nationalist forces. The resurgence of a nationalist movement can be traced back as far as 1926, but the first proposals for a change in the nature of the regime came after the major economic crisis began in 1929. It was at this time that the *Nationalist Association*, then a small and relatively insignificant right–wing party, proposed giving additional political powers to the President of the Republic. A number of fascist or semi–fascist groupings also emerged at this time, and began pushing anti–communist, anti–socialist, anti–Jewish and anti–foreign policies. The Latvian Government proscribed most of these, but the mainline political parties began to take a more nationalist and anti–foreign stance as well.

In August 1933, Karlis Ulmanis, leader of the *Peasants' League* and one of the founders of modern Latvia—he served as first provisional president from 1918 to 1920—proposed a number of constitutional changes to strengthen the executive. He could not get sufficient support from among the other members of the legislature, however, so his constitutional proposals were tabled at this time. Then, on March 16, 1934, Ulmanis was made Premier. Four days earlier, President Paets had asserted authoritarian control in Estonia. Although there is no evidence of any direct connection, the program which Ulmanis implemented as Premier was strikingly similar to the Paets program in Estonia.

Claiming that he had discovered a communist plot to overthrow the government,

Ulmanis declared a state of emergency, suspended the parliament, banned party political activities, and proscribed the *Thunder Cross Association*, a fascist organization. Two months later, Ulmanis organized a separate government committee to take on certain of the functions of the parliament, that is, to handle matters which would normally require legislation. President Kviesis gave his approval to this new arrangement in June.

Most Latvians quietly accepted this new authoritarian regime, apparently convinced by Ulmanis' argument that he needed the additional powers to defend Latvian democracy. Two years later, when President Kviesis' term came to an end, he stepped down and was succeeded by Ulmanis. Since Ulmanis continued to hold the office of Premier, the effect was to merge the two offices from this point onward.

## Latvia under Soviet Rule, 1939–1991

The authoritarian direction of the Latvian Government after 1934 weakened it internationally, especially insofar as the Western democracies was concerned. When the leaders of Nazi Germany and the Soviet Union got together to negotiate a "non–aggression" pact in August 1939, therefore, their stipulation that Latvia fell within the Soviet sphere of influence caused less of a reaction than it might otherwise have done.

Hitler launched his invasion of Poland on September 1 and Soviet troops entered to occupy the eastern third of Poland on September 17. With Poland settled, Stalin moved to bring the remaining areas of the Soviet "sphere of influence" under his control. Latvia was forced to sign a mutual assistance pact with the Soviet Union on October 5.

Nothing happened for several months, probably because the Soviet Union was tied down in its "Winter War" with Finland. Once that was resolved, the Soviet Union turned its attention back to the Baltic. Toward the end of May 1940, the Soviet Foreign Ministry accused the Latvian Government of violating the 1939 mutual assistance pact signed with the Soviet Union. Almost immediately thereafter, the Latvian Government was forced to resign and a popular front government was installed in its place.

But Latvia's popular front government had a remarkably short life. In July, all political parties other than the *Communist Party* were banned and most non–communists were dismissed from office. This was followed by a wave of arrests. Then, with only communists standing for office, new elections were held on July 14. The newly elected legislature met on July 21. Its only piece of business was to vote on a resolution asking to join the Soviet Union. The resolution was passed by acclamation.

The following month, the USSR Supreme Soviet acceded to the Latvian request. Latvia thus became a Soviet Socialist Republic.

During the period from August 1940 to June 1941, the new communist government nationalized the land, then launched a program of "land reform" whereby larger estates were turned into state farms while smaller parcels were distributed to landless laborers. Nazi Germany's invasion of the Soviet Union beginning on June 22, 1941 reversed this situation somewhat, for German troops overran and occupied Latvia later in 1941. Latvia remained under German occupation until 1944. With the German retreat, however, Latvia once again fell under Soviet control. A guerrilla movement arose to oppose Soviet control after the end of the war in 1945, but such efforts were, of course, ineffectual. Latvia got no outside assistance, and the opposition was eventually suppressed.

Many changes occurred in Latvia over the next thirty–five years. Soviet policy was to integrate the Baltic Republics so thoroughly that there would be no question of their ever leaving the union. To that end, the reestablished Latvian communist government reinstated its 1941 nationalization decree, then followed this up by carrying through a general collectivization of agriculture. Meanwhile, the Soviet Government sought to bind Latvia and the other two Baltic Republics to the rest of the Soviet Union economically by locating branch factories of Soviet industry in the three republics. The first factories in the 1950s emphasized primary extraction, but a much larger range of factories was built there in the 1960s and 1970s. Such factories received most or all of their raw materials from other parts of the Soviet Union, and delivered most of their finished products to customers in the other republics. This economic integration was so successful that Latvia and the other two Baltic Republics became more integrated into the Soviet economy than any other area of the Soviet Union.

This program of economic integration was accompanied by a program of "Soviet Russification," aimed at transforming the cultures of the Baltic Republics. All students received Russian language training in the schools, plus general indoctrination lectures on the nature of Soviet culture. In addition, there was a systematic effort made to settle non–Baltic nationals in the republics. When a new factory was built, most of the workers would be transferred there from elsewhere in the Soviet Union.

The effects of this policy can be seen by examining the figures of the 1989 Soviet census. Ethnic Latvians made up only 52 percent of the population of the republic. Latvians had nearly become a minority in

# The Baltic Republics: Latvia

their own country. These overall figures also masked the fact that, in certain industrial regions near the border, Latvians had become a tiny minority. In many urban areas, it was more common to hear Russian spoken than it was to hear Latvian. Russians also tended to monopolize many types of jobs, particularly in management and in parts of government. Everywhere, the Russian way of doing things became the acceptable way. On the positive side, the heavy industrialization carried out after 1945 meant that the standard of living in Latvia was above that of any other part of the Soviet Union.

## Latvia Regains Its Independence

The Latvian people accommodated themselves to Soviet rule, but they could not forget their brief period of independence between the wars. When Gorbachëv launched his programs of *glasnost* and restructuring after coming to power in 1985, Latvians were therefore among the first to take advantage of them. In enunciating his policy of *glasnost*, Gorbachëv called on the Soviet peoples to speak out against negative tendencies in the society, and to support his reforms. This became a manifesto which led to the creation of thousands of "unofficial" organizations all over the Soviet Union. Formed originally in support of Gorbachëv's policy of reform, many of them soon began to push their own agendas.

Latvians were among the early supporters of Gorbachëv's policy of *glasnost* and restructuring, and Latvian unofficial organizations also sprang up, taking advantage of the new atmosphere. One of the first such organizations was *Renaissance and Renewal*, a religious rights organization. The *Popular Front of Latvia* (*PFL*), organized in October 1988, incorporated many of these earlier unofficial organizations into its overall structure. The leader of the *PFL* was Dainis Ivans, a journalist. Within a year its membership had grown to 250,000, about 85 percent of whom were Latvians. This provided an important contrast with the *Latvian Communist Party*, which had a membership of 184,000, only 39.7 percent of whom were Latvians.

The ethnic issue was a greater one in Latvia than in either of the other two Baltic republics, because of the much larger percentages of non–Latvians in the republic. Conservatives were particularly disturbed by what the front represented and managed to get the *PFL* decertified in January 1989.

This did not stop the front from continuing to operate, however. In the March 1989 elections to the USSR Congress of People's Deputies, front–supported candidates won three–fourth of the seats.

Like Estonia, Latvia had a political party specifically committed to independence, the *Latvian National Independence Movement* (*LNIM*). Labeled an extremist organization, it nevertheless exercised influence on the *PFL*. Under the prodding of the *LNIM*, the *Popular Front of Latvia* went on record in June 1989 as favoring "Latvia's independent statehood."

Russians and other non–Latvians had become very concerned about Latvian nationalism, and there were rising fears of ethnic strife. The *Popular Front of Latvia* sought to alleviate these anxieties by advocating equal rights for all persons living in Latvia, regardless of nationality or other affiliation. The front specifically supported the right of other nationalities either to receive instruction in their own language in the public schools or to set up their own schools. It also advocated political pluralism. This defused a lot of the opposition and helped to win additional support for independence from among the non–Latvian sections of the population.

The *Latvian Communist Party*, with more Russians than Latvians among its membership, proved to be the most conservative of the Baltic communist parties, but even it came under pressure from its Latvian members to take a more nationalistic stance. In September 1989, Janis Vagris, the First Secretary, endorsed the concept of a sovereign Latvia, including republican economic autonomy.

The overlap between the *Latvian Communist Party* and the *Popular Front of Latvia* can be seen in the list of delegates to the second congress of the *PFL*, held in October 1989. Twenty–four percent of the delegates were members of the *Latvian Communist Party*, while 45 out 100 of the members of the steering committee were *LCP* members. They obviously represented members of the reform wing of the party, however, for the Congress not only endorsed Latvian independence and creation of a multiparty political system, but called upon the Latvian Supreme Soviet to declare illegal Latvia's 1940 incorporation into the Soviet Union.

New elections to the Latvian Supreme Soviet were scheduled to take place in March 1990. Hoping to co–opt the nationalism issue, the communist members of the old Supreme Soviet adopted a declaration, on February 15, endorsing an independent Latvia. That statement proved to be too weak for the new delegates elected in March. On May 4, the new Supreme Soviet proclaimed Latvian independence, though with a transition period before implementation. Although the declaration got 138 positive votes, 57 deputies refused to participate in the vote, claiming that the declaration was unconstitutional. Most of the delegates abstaining had been elected

**Latvian folk dancer**

Courtesy: NOVOSTI

by the large non–Latvian element within the population. Nothing happened for ten days, probably because the Soviet Government was preoccupied by its economic war against Lithuania. On May 14, however, Gorbachëv issued a decree invalidating Latvia's declaration of independence. The Soviet military also became involved in the issue when it began dropping leaflets on Riga, accusing the Latvian Government of counter revolution. The next day, several hundred Soviet army soldiers, accompanied by cadets from an officers' training school in Riga, joined a protest march against Latvian independence.

By June, however, the Soviet Government had begun ignoring the situation in Latvia, even as it began easing off on its pressure on Lithuania and Estonia. The negative international reaction to the Soviet moves in the Baltic was clearly a factor in this change of policy. Thereafter, Moscow virtually ignored what was happening in Latvia until January 1991, when hardliners launched another intervention. Once again there was an international protest, however, and Moscow eased off.

By May 1991, Gorbachëv apparently decided that his conservative policies of the past several months had been a failure and threatened the new union treaty which he wanted to get negotiated and signed over the summer. He began a rapprochement with Boris Yeltsin, which led to nine of the republics agreeing to sign a new union treaty on August 17. This became the signal for conservative hardliners to organize a *coup* with the aim of overthrowing Gorbachëv and reasserting centralized control.

The *coup* failed but, even as it was going on, the Latvian Government declared its independence. The post–*coup* Soviet Government temporized for two weeks but it soon found the number of states granting recognition to Latvia and the other Baltic Republics to be irresistible. In early September, it, too, recognized the independence of the Baltic Republics. Latvia was admitted to the United Nations in October 1991.

A major preoccupation of the Latvian Government since that time has been the continuing presence of ex–Soviet troops in the Republic, plus the problem of an extremely large non–Latvian population. These troops were originally under the jurisdiction of the Commonwealth of Independent States, but the Russian Government assumed responsibility for Russian troops stationed in the ex–Soviet Republics in the summer of 1992 after establishing its own Ministry of Defense. Subsequent negotiations between the Latvian and Russian Governments elicited a Russian promise to have all troops out of Latvia by the summer of 1993; however, President Yeltsin rescinded this agreement in September 1992 after the Latvian Government stripped non–Latvians of citizenship.

The Latvian Government took this action because it was under pressure from Latvian nationalists within its ranks concerned with the extremely large non–Latvian element in the population. It should be remembered that the government at this time had been elected in March 1990 and that its leaders were essentially the leaders of the *Popular Front of Latvia*. Most of the *Popular Front's* leadership were originally reform communists who eventually broke with the party. One of the problems of the *Latvian Communist Party*, in fact, was that it was dominated by Russians and only about 40 percent of its membership was Latvian. Although most of the support for the *Popular Front of Latvia* came from ethnic Latvians, the government pursued moderate policies toward minorities and attempted to win them over to support of the government. It was fairly successful until 1992.

A new citizenship law was discussed in the legislature, but the legislature was badly divided over the issue. It was then decided to handle the matter administratively. Under new government regulations issued at this time, automatic citizenship could be claimed only by persons who were Latvian citizens—or their direct descendants—prior to Latvia's incorporation into the Soviet Union in 1940. This rendered about 48 percent of the population of the Republic "stateless." These regulations were subsequently incorporated into a new electoral law passed in October 1992. Under the terms of this new law, non–Latvians needed to establish a fluency in the Lettish language and permanent residence in the republic for at least 16 years in order to qualify for naturalization.

In December 1992, the government announced the first partial results of a citizen registration that it had begun carrying out. About 67% of the inhabitants of the republic had been registered by that time. Of those registered, 1,339,530 were classified as Latvian citizens, while an additional 452,378 persons were classified as non–citizens. However, the government also announced that 405,124 of these non–citizens—or 89.5%—had expressed a desire to become citizens.

Perhaps partly in response to that expressed sentiment, the government subsequently reduced the minimum permanent residence requirement to five years. According to figures published in 1995, 40% of non–ethnic Lett speakers have passed Lettish–language and history tests and qualified as citizens. That still leaves nearly one–third of Latvia's adult population voteless, but the problem now appears well on its way to being resolved.

The October 1992 electoral law also gave the government the right to pass laws "within the limits of the laws and resolutions adopted by the Latvian parliament." After that time, the government essentially ruled by decree. A significant part of retail trade had already been privatized by that time in the cities, but the government used its new powers to complete the process throughout the republic. Many shops were subsequently either sold at auction, leased to individual entrepreneurs, or turned into retail outlets of individual manufacturing plants.

Since the government did not process citizenship applications during this period, almost all residents who are not ethnic Latvians were excluded from the elections which took place in June 1993. Those elections were won by the *Farmers' Union* and *Latvian Way*, which together took 48 of the 100 seats in the new *Sejm*. The previous legislature had created the new office of President, and Guntis Ulmanis, grandnephew of Karlis Ulmanis, leader of pre–1940 Latvia, was elected to that post. Ulmanis is a member of the *Farmers' Union Party*. The presidency is largely a titular position, however.

The new parliamentary elections which took place in the fall of 1995 produced a heavily fragmented assembly with nine political parties or blocs. More ominously, the *People's Movement for Latvia*, led by Joahims Zigerists, a German citizen who also heads the German national political organizations of conservatives, came in second with 15% of the vote. *Latvian Way*, the ruling party in the previous government, came in third with 14.65% of the vote. Since the other political parties wanted nothing to do with the *People's Movement for Latvia*, it took nearly three months to form a new government. After two designated candidates failed to form a majority coalition, President Ulmanis asked Andris Skele, a Latvian businessman who was not even in the legislature, to attempt to form a government. He put together a six party coalition which was finally confirmed in office on December 21, 1995. Skele announced that his new government "should raise the spirit of private enterprise, ensure the stability of the local currency, improve the investment climate, and create conditions which will realize the people's potential." Although Skele headed what was technically a non–party government, he won the support of 73 out of 100 deputies at the time of his confirmation vote. That support was always soft, however, and he resigned as Prime Minister in January 1997 when his honesty was impugned after he nominated a controversial businessman, Vassily Melnik, as the new Finance Minister. President Ulmanis then consulted with all of the Saeima factions about a successor. When the parties were unable to agree on a replacement, President Ulmanis renominated Skele as Prime Minister

# The Baltic Republics: Latvia

**Enjoying their work: Chimney–sweeps, Riga**

and he was confirmed as Prime Minister on February 13.

Seven political parties pledged their support to this new government, so it should have been stronger than the previous one. That turned out not to be the case. Skele and the parties had a falling out shortly afterwards and he was forced to resign again on July 28, 1997, after the parties withdrew their support. His replacement as Prime Minister was Guntars Krasts, the Economics Minister in the previous government. Unlike Skele, Krasts is a politician, a member of the Fatherland and Freedom Party. The change in Prime Ministers did not produce significant changes in government policy, however. Although Krasts promised to increase the pace of reforms and bring in a balanced budget for 1998, he otherwise continued the policies of the previous government. Perhaps that is not surprising, considering that he was supported by six of the parties that had previously supported Skele, his predecessor. For that same reason, it is perhaps not surprising that Krasts has also begun quarreling with individual political parties in his coalition, in particular deputies from Latvia's Way and the Democratic Party, who recently voted with the opposition on several issues. There is, as yet, no indication that his coalition is about to collapse, however.

## Foreign Policy

Since 1991, two ideas have tended to guide Latvia's foreign policy—building Baltic solidarity and reorientation of the economy toward the west. But while pursuing these policies, the Latvian Government has had to also spend a great deal of its time on its relations with Russia. In theory, Latvia would like to have good relations with Russia and sees the necessity of a continuing, if diminished, economic relationship as well. The large number of ethnic Russians in the country, plus the continuing presence of Russian troops, have been major concerns for the government. The problem of ethnic Russians remains unresolved, but Latvia did negotiate an agreement with Russia in May 1994 that resulted in the withdrawal of all Russian troops from the country by August 31, except for military technicians manning an anti–missile radar station at Skrunda.

## NATURE OF THE REGIME

Latvia is a multiparty, parliamentary democracy. After regaining its independence in 1991, the government revived the 1922 constitution but retained those articles of the constitution of the Soviet Republic of Latvia which were not in contradition to the 1922 constitution. The 1922 constitution was then fully reinstituted as of July 6, 1993.

### The Latvian Government

The President of the Republic is the ceremonial head of state. Guntis Ulmanis, when elected to this position in June 1993, was little known in political circles. His main distinction was that he was the grandnephew of Karlis Ulmanis, leader of Latvia before 1940. During his first three years in office, however, he won the reputation of a man of fairness and balance in domestic affairs who also had the ability to defend Latvian interests in dealing with the Russian Government. As a result, he was reelected by the legislature on the first ballot in June 1996, obtaining 53 out of 100 votes. This contrasted sharply with the situation in 1993, when several votes were taken before he received the necessary majority.

Executive power is exercised by the Prime Minister and his cabinet, who jointly govern on the basis of majority support in the legislature. Because of the extreme-

ly fragmented nature of the current *Saeima*, with its 100 members currently divided among seven political parties or blocs plus 13 independents, there has been a non–party government since the 1995 elections. Prime Minister Andris Skele submitted his resignation in January 1997, but was renamed as Prime Minister by President Ulmanis after consultations with all the *Saeima* factions. He was reconfirmed as Prime Minister on February 13, 1997.

The highest legislative body in Latvia is the single–chamber *Saeima*. Recreated by an electoral law passed in March 1992 and then modified in October 1992, delegates to the *Saeima* serve three years and are elected on a proportional basis. For this purpose, the country has been divided into five constituencies and party representation is on the basis of the percentage of votes won in each constituency. The *Saeima* itself has 100 members; however, the number of deputies per constituency is based on the number of voters per constituency.

### The Economy

Latvia is the most industrialized of the Baltic republics. Its major industries include machinery, metalworking, electrical equipment, light industry, agricultural equipment, chemicals, and pharmaceuticals. Forestry products and extractive industry are also important, including things like timber, paper, peat, limestone, dolomite and clay. Riga, a major center for industry, manufactures consumer goods like radios and other electrical appliances, cars and trucks, and agricultural equipment. Light industry, including food processing and woodworking, is also important. In the past, about 80 percent of Latvia's exports went to other parts of the Soviet Union but now the figures are almost entirely reversed with most exports now going to the countries of the European Union.

In agriculture, most of the old collective and state farms have been turned into cooperatives but there are still very few private farms. Partly, this has been because relatively few peasants favor a return to private agriculture, but there has also been no political majority in the *Sejm* that supported passage of the necessary legislation. Although the new Prime Minister publicly supports privatization, it is not clear that his government will be any more successful than previous ones. Meanwhile, a March 1996 report from Latvia characterized collective farms as "dying," leaving behind pockets of "hard–drinking, bitter people who have abandoned their fields."

Agriculture no longer has the significance in the economy that it formerly had, but Latvia still has an important dairy industry. Dairy products, one of Latvia's important exports, have been redirected to the West since 1991, though this has been somewhat hindered by a world–wide surplus in dairy products.

After 1991, the government used its decree–issuing authority to carry through a general denationalization of domestic retail trade, but the privatization process as applied to other parts of the economy slowed after the government announced in November 1992 that it would not sell any more state–owned facilities for Latvian rubles. There has been relatively little foreign private investment in Latvia so far, but the government has worked at establishing ties with the Scandinavian countries and this is beginning to pay off. The first private bank in Latvia was established by the Parex Finance Company with collaboration of the Swedish company Kungsorden AB Foretags. The bank has a capitalization of 100 million rubles.

The economy suffered a setback in the summer of 1995 when about one–third of the country's 67 commercial banks collapsed, but it has since recovered and is now as robust as any in the area of the former Soviet Union. Inflation and unemployment are both low and the economy is steadily growing.

## Culture

Latvian culture was historically the culture of the peasantry, the upper classes being mainly German. The same was also true of the cities, for that was where the German and Jewish merchants and tradesmen lived. Thus a great deal of Latvia's historical culture is not Latvian at all, though as Latvians became educated and entered the middle class in the nineteenth century, they tended to adopt elements of that earlier culture. Modern Latvian culture is no longer a peasant culture and it is, in fact, mainly an urban culture.

Approximately a third of the population lives in the city of Riga, Latvia's capital, its chief port, and its largest industrial center. In the twelfth century, German merchants of the Hanseatic League began trading with Latvian tribes living along the Daugava [Western Dvina] River. In 1201, Bishop Albert of Bremen, who had been given the title of Bishop of Livonia by the Pope and dispatched to the area accompanied by the Teutonic Knights, built a fortress along the right bank of the river. Bishop Albert also founded his own militant Order of the Brethren of the Sword and he used it to spread Christianity among the Latvians. A town grew up around the fortress and the town, Riga, quickly became a major center for trade. It became a member of the Hanseatic League in 1282. But Bishop Albert's religious order controlled the city until the Reformation. Riga became an independent merchant city–state in 1561, but it was soon taken over by the Polish king. It passed back and forth between Poland and Sweden until 1710, when Peter the Great captured it and it became part of the Russian Empire.

Riga remained mainly a city of foreigners until the late nineteenth century, when it gradually became a Latvian city. Today it is not only the political and cultural center of the republic, but the industrial center as well. Riga University, founded in 1861, is the main university of the country, though there are a number of colleges and technical schools as well. The Latvian Academy of Sciences and its 14 affiliated research institutes is also located here. The city has an Opera and Ballet Theater, numerous other theaters for plays, and four concert halls. It is therefore the center for higher Latvian culture.

The city itself is full of historic buildings, including guild halls, medieval warehouses and private residences, dating back as far as the fourteenth century. One of the oldest buildings is the Riga Castle itself, headquarters of the Livonian Order in Riga, which dates from 1330. There are also many churches, a few of which date from this same period, though most of them were at least partially rebuilt in subsequent centuries. The oldest of these is the Domkirk, a brick church consecrated in 1211. For centuries the seat of the archbishop of Livonia and Prussia, it has been rebuilt or remodeled many times and shows evidence of many architectural styles, stretching from the Romanesque to the Baroque. The Reformation reached Riga in the middle of the sixteenth century and the Domkirk became a Lutheran Church at that time. Today it is a museum. The city also has many operating churches representing many denominations—Roman Catholic, Russian Orthodox, Baptist, and, of course, Lutheran. There is also one remaining synagogue.

Latvia has a strong folklorist tradition, but because most Latvians lived historically in the countryside, most of the early collections of Latvian folk tales were made by Germans resident in the cities and most of these were translated into German before being published. A written literature by Lettish writers first appeared in the nineteenth century as the number of educated Latvians began to grow. The man usually given credit for laying the foundations stones for a Lettish literature was Juris Neikens, a nineteenth century author of numerous short stories. A contemporary, Juris Alumans, was the first Latvian poet, but he helped to start a school of poetry, represented by Krisjanis Barons, Fricis Brivzemnieks, and Atis Kronvalds. Another nineteenth century figure, Adolfs Alunans, is considered to be the father of Latvian drama. The novel was given Latvian form by two brothers, Reinis and Matiss Kaudzites, who jointly wrote The Times of Land–Surveyors, published in 1879.

Two novelists of the early twentieth century were Augusts Deglavs, author of Riga, a three volume work published between 1912 and 1921, and Jekabs Jansevskis, author of The Native Land, a six volume work published in 1924–25. Realism is represented by the dramas and short stories of Rudolfs Blaumanis and the poems of Vilis Pludonis. Romanticism is represented by the dramas of Janis Rainis, whose greatest work, written in 1905, is a epic tragedy dealing with early Latvian history entitled Fire and Night. Rainis was also a social reformer who spent several years in tsarist prisons before 1905. He participated in the 1905 revolution and subsequently had to escape to Switzerland, where he lived until 1920. Fire and Night became the basis for an opera written in 1921 by the composer Janis Medins.

Literary figures of the period of Latvian independence include the novelist Janis Akuraters, the poets Karlis Skalbe and Edvards Virza, the short story writer Janis Ezerins, and the novelist Janis Jaunsudrabins. Jaunsudrabins is unusual in that he also made a reputation for himself as a painter.

A novelist of the Soviet period is Jonas Miesnieks, whose historical novel, The Judge of the Livonian District, was published in 1948. Most other better writers of this period belong, however to that group of individuals who managed to make their way abroad. These include the playwright Martins Ziverts, the essayist and novelist Zenta Maurina, and the novelists Anslavs Eglitis, Girts Salnais, and Antons Rupainis.

## The Future

Latvia basically has two problems for which it has found no solution—an extremely fragmented electorate that has often meant that there was no majority for any specific action and an extremely large non–Latvian population which threatens the political stability. The two problems are, of course, interrelated, for part of the political fragmentation has resulted from disagreements over how to treat the non–Latvian population. Both problems may, therefore, be diminishing as more and more non–Latvians qualify for citizenship.

Another factor contributing to political fragmentation is the dissatisfaction of pensioners whose buying power has diminished during the transition to a market economy. Because of their large numbers, they remain a significant, negative political force. On the plus side, Latvia's well–educated work force and fairly disciplined populace have helped make the transition to a market economy more successful than in any of the other ex–Soviet republics, with the exception of Estonia.

# The Baltic Republics: Lithuania

**Wedding Day, Vilnius**

## LITHUANIA SINCE WORLD WAR I

### Independent Lithuania, 1919–1939

Elections to the Lithuanian Constituent Assembly took place in April 1920. A provisional constitution was adopted two months later, though the permanent constitution did not go into effect until August 1, 1922.

This constitution created a parliamentary system with a single–body legislature, called the *Seimas*. It also created a ceremonial President of the Republic, elected for a five–year term. Aleksandras Stulginskis became the first president under the new constitution.

Lithuania was overwhelmingly rural at this time with 79 percent of the population earning their living from agriculture. It was also relatively backward; according to the 1923 census, approximately a third of the population was illiterate. There was no individual agriculture among the peasants, since their holdings were organized into communes similar to the *mirs* of Rus-

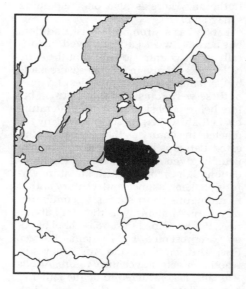

sia and farmed in common. The large estates were mainly in the hands of either Poles or Russians, though the Poles were

mainly descendants of individuals of Lithuanian extraction who had been Polanized in the 16th to 18th centuries, when the Polish monarchy and Polish culture dominated the united Poland–Lithuania.

A 1922 land reform program expropriated the land of Russian estate owners and limited the size of other estates to 375 acres. These lands were subsequently redistributed to peasant small holders. The land reform also provided for the break up of the peasant communes and the distribution of the land to the peasants to create private farms. Turning the peasants into individual farmers brought increased prosperity to the countryside. However, the plots of land given out after the breakup of the large estates were so small that the peasant small holders thus created had great difficulty making a go of it on their own. In the 1930's, many either sold or abandoned their land, and then sought employment in the cities or emigrated.

Lithuania was the most densely populated of the three Baltic States. With a population of 2,035,121 in 1923, it also had the largest population of the three. Its population was rather mixed ethnically, with approximately 80 percent speaking Lithuanian.

Jews were the single largest minority [7.6 percent], followed by Poles [3.2 percent], Russians [2.5 percent] and Germans [1.4 percent]. There were also a few White Russians and Latvians. Religiously, Lithuania was rather homogeneous, with 85.7 percent professing Roman Catholicism. The remainder were either Jewish or Protestant.

The party system that developed in Lithuania bore some similarity to the pattern already seen in Estonia and Latvia, except that the dominant right–wing party was the *Christian Democratic Party*. The *Christian Democrats*, allied with the *Lithuanian Peasants League* and the *Workers' Federation*, was a broad–based party with its main base among the peasants of the countryside, but with an urban wing of industrial workers who rejected Marxism. Its broad base made it the majority party in the period up to 1926.

The *Social Democratic Party* was the principal left–wing party, though Lithuania, with its smaller urban population, proved to have a less congenial climate for Marxism than either Estonia or Latvia. The *Social Democrats* were also unable to make any inroads into the countryside because of the existence of a leftist liberal party, called the *Peasant Populists* [literally, Party of Rural People], which espoused a sort of agrarian populism similar to the *Socialist Revolutionaries* of Russia. The other political party, the *National Party*, had played a role in formation of the republic—Antanas Smetona, leader of the *Nationalists*, served as the president of the country in 1919–20—but remained insignificant during the 1920's down to 1926.

## Lithuania's Border Disputes

Lithuania's chief problem in the period of the 1920's was in securing acceptable international borders. Although there were a number of border disputes, its most significant problem by far was with regard to the city of Vilnius, the historic capital of Lithuania. The problem was that a number of the leaders associated with the new Polish State, including Joseph Pilsudski—sometimes called the father of modern Poland—had strong ties to the Vilnius area. Pilsudski, descendant of a Polonized Lithuanian noble family, had been born in Vilnius. These Polish leaders wanted to recreate the old Polish–Lithuanian union. When the Lithuanian leadership opted for a separate, independent Lithuania, Pilsudski, in particular, decided that the Vilnius area ought to be part of Poland. His real aim, of course, was to recreate the old Polish–Lithuanian Empire.

But here it is necessary to provide a little background in order to understand just what happened and why. The original Lithuanian proclamation of independence had been made in the city of Vilnius, but the newly–proclaimed Lithuanian Government was forced to abandon that city in January 1919 as *Bolshevik* forces approached the city. They fled to Kaunas, which became the provisional capital. The *Bolsheviks* were forced out in April 1919 by Polish forces, who then occupied the city. In the summer of 1920, the *Bolsheviks* launched a counter–offensive, driving the Poles back.

Now Soviet Russia and Lithuania signed a peace treaty on July 12, under which the *Bolsheviks* recognized Lithuanian independence. Three days later, they offered to restore Vilnius to Lithuania, if Lithuania would ally itself with Soviet Russia against Poland. Basically, this required Lithuania to allow Soviet troops to pass through Lithuania during their invasion of Poland. In the process, they took and occupied Vilnius. The Soviet invasion force continued westward toward Warsaw and was only stopped by a major battle at the Vistula River in August. As the Soviet forces retreated, they turned Vilnius over to the Lithuanian Government, which took possession of the city on August 26, proclaiming it once again the national capital.

Meanwhile, the Polish armed forces pressed further and further eastward, hoping to fulfill Pilsudski's dream of restoring the ancient borders of Poland–Lithuania. Since the Polish Government was desirous of Allied support against Soviet Russia, it gave in to Allied pressure to end its border dispute with Lithuania. On October 7, therefore, Poland signed the treaty of Suwalki granting Lithuania the city of Vilnius and the surrounding district.

By this time, however, the Polish invasion force, defeated by a Soviet force, was beginning its retreat westward. Two days later, a Polish force under General Lucjan Zeligowski broke away from the main Polish force and advanced into Lithuania, apparently acting under secret instructions from Pilsudski. Vilnius was quickly occupied and then General Zeligowski moved further into Lithuania, apparently intending to conquer the entire country. Lithuanian forces counter–attacked, however, and General Zeligowski was forced to withdraw to Vilnius.

The Polish Government disavowed Zeligowski, but that was only for international consumption. Zeligowski, acting on orders from Pilsudski, now proceeded to create a Central Lithuanian Republic, supposedly independent of both Poland and Lithuania. There were a number of attempts to solve the matter diplomatically,

but all failed. Then General Zeligowski arranged for "elections" to take place in January 1922, which were won by pro–Polish candidates. The puppet legislature then voted for union with Poland. The Polish *Sejm* now proceeded to annex the Vilnius area. The Allied ambassadors, tired of the whole thing, accepted the annexation, thereby recognizing the existing line as the final frontier. Lithuania, refusing to accept the annexation, broke diplomatic relations with Poland. These were not resumed until 1938. In the case of Vilnius, therefore, Lithuania never did achieve an acceptable international frontier.

The second boundary question was with regard to Memel, located on the Lithuanian coast a short distance from the mouth of the Nemunas, Lithuania's largest river. Memel had been part of Prussia since the 18th century, but was taken from Germany by the Treaty of Versailles. The Allies had intended that Memel go to a reconstituted Poland–Lithuania. Although Lithuania's decision to seek its separate independence ended that possibility, the Allies, refusing to recognize Lithuanian independence because of its border dispute with Poland over Vilnius, could not bring themselves to turn Memel over to Lithuania. Instead, Memel was placed under French military administration and the matter was put on hold.

Memel itself was a town of only about twenty thousand, most of whose citizens were German nationals. Lithuania's interest in the city was that it needed a seaport, and Memel was the only good seaport along the entire Lithuanian coast. Its interest in Vilnius was much greater, however, so it did nothing until it had become clear that the international community had recognized Poland's annexation of Vilnius. With nothing further to lose, the Lithuanian Government decided to seize Memel by force. On January 7, 1923, days after the French had begun their own occupation of the German Ruhr, Lithuania sent troops accompanied by a large number of Lithuanian "volunteers" to invade and occupy Memel. The Lithuanians lost twenty men, while two Frenchmen and a German policeman were killed on the other side. With the French tied down in Germany and the German and Soviet Governments supporting Lithuania, the Allies decided that nothing could be done and agreed, in February 1923, to formally transfer Memel to Lithuanian sovereignty.

Thus in the Memel dispute, Lithuania got both the desired seaport and international recognition of that fact. The government immediately gave the Lithuanian name of Klaipeda to the city and the region, and established it as an autonomous province with its own government. Klaipeda, with all of Lithuania as its hinterland, flourished in subsequent years, though it continued to have a significant

# The Baltic Republics: Lithuania

German population, and that would become a diplomatic issue between Germany and Lithuania after Hitler came to power.

## Lithuania's Move Away From Democracy

The May 1926 elections resulted in a political transformation when the *Christian Democrats*, who had dominated every government up to this time, were defeated. A new coalition government under the premiership of Mykolas Slezevicius now took power, composed of the *Social Democrats* and the *Peasant Populists*. One month later, in June 1926, the coalition's candidate, Dr. Kazys Grinius, a prominent leader of the *Peasant Populists*, was installed as President.

Among the changes introduced by the new government was a change in the attitude toward the Soviet Union, symbolized by a non–aggression pact which the two countries signed in September 1926.

The *Christian Democrats* and the *Nationalists* had opposed an agreement with the Soviet Union from the beginning, and they now began planning a counter–stroke. On the night of December 16, with the support of the army, they carried out their *coup d'etat* against the government. Entering the parliament building accompanied by a group of officers, they seized control, then dismissed the cabinet, adjourned the session of parliament, and deposed the President of the Republic. Antanas Smetona, leader of the *Nationalists* and first President in 1919–20, was appointed President of the Republic.

The *coup* having succeeded, the left decided to cooperate to save what they could of Lithuanian democracy. Grinius submitted his resignation as President, and Slezevicius resigned as Premier. The parliament then met and elected Antanas Smetona as President of the Republic. The *coup* had been legalized. One of Smetona's first acts as President was to name Augustinas Voldemaras, a prominent *Nationalist*, as the new Premier. Voldemaras formed a cabinet composed of *Christian Democrats*, *Nationalists* and members of parties of the center.

The *Social Democrats* and *Peasant Populists* continued to control a majority in the legislature, however, and when, after a period of cooperation, they challenged the government in April 1927, the government dissolved the legislature. Smetona ruled for approximately a year by decree, then proclaimed a new constitution in May 1928 which formalized the new structure. From that time onward, Smetona and his Premier, Augustinas Voldemaras, ruled the country by decree. Lithuania was thus the first of the Baltic countries to abandon democracy and replace it with a form of authoritarianism.

## The Lithuanian Authoritarian Regime

Lithuania differed from its two Baltic neighbors in that its authoritarian regime involved two figures, Smetona and Voldemaras, in the beginning and because some political organizations continued to operate. The *Nationalist Party* was the most significant of the political groups at this time, though a semi–fascist group, *Iron Wolf*, was created by Voldemaras at this time. Voldemaras was forced out in September 1929, however, after he came under clerical criticism and became the target of a failed assassination attempt by three Lithuanian students. He was succeeded as premier by J. Tubelis, President Smetona's brother–in–law. Tubelis remained premier until 1939.

In 1934, spurred on by worsening economic conditions, a number of military officers attempted a *coup* to restore Voldemaras to power. When the *coup* failed, Voldemaras was arrested and sentenced to several years in prison. Released in 1938, he left the country and settled in southern France.

There were also a number of peasant revolts in 1934 which were put down by force. Believing that the revolts were the result of political agitation, Smetona banned all political parties other than the *Nationalists*. The government permitted the election of a new legislature in 1935, but this was largely meaningless, since the government nominated all electoral candidates. A new constitution was also approved in 1936. In essence, it legalized the authoritarian Presidency which had existed since 1926. In one innovation, Smetona

**Ornamental cats**

Courtesy: NOVOSTI

was henceforth to be addressed as *Tautos Vados*, or "Leader of the People."

## Lithuania Under Soviet Rule, 1939–1991

Although the Lithuanian people had failed in some respects with regard to domestic policies, their greatest mistake was internationally. Perhaps nothing they could have done would have made any difference, but it is nevertheless true that they were at odds with almost all of their neighbors and had no international friends. Thus when Nazi Germany and the Soviet Union got together to negotiate their "non–aggression" pact in August 1939, Lithuania was among their victims. Dividing eastern Europe into spheres of influence, the original agreement assigned Estonia and Latvia to the Soviet Union; Lithuania to Germany. A September 23, 1939 protocol assigned Lithuania to the Soviet Union, while Nazi Germany got an extra piece of Poland.

Hitler launched his invasion of Poland on September 1 and Soviet troops entered to occupy the eastern third of Poland on September 17. With Poland settled, Stalin moved to cash in his other chips. During the month of October all three Baltic States were forced to sign mutual assistance pacts with the Soviet Union. As an aside, Lithuania was the only one to get anything out of the agreements. The Soviet Union transferred the city of Vilnius and surrounding area, which it had just taken from Poland, to Lithuania.

Nothing happened for several months, probably because the Soviet Union was tied down in its "Winter War" with Finland. Once that was resolved, the Soviet Union turned its attention back to the Baltic States. Toward the end of May 1940, the Soviet Foreign Ministry accused Lithuania of violating the 1939 mutual assistance pact. Then, on June 14, Soviet Foreign Minister Molotov demanded the arrest of the Lithuanian interior and security ministers and the creation of a new Lithuanian Government capable of supporting the 1939 treaty. In addition, Molotov demanded that Soviet troops be authorized to enter the country and to occupy "the most important centers."

Lithuania had no choice but to give in to the Soviet request. After the Red Army had entered the country, Molotov demanded the right to name a new premier. A popular front government was now established. The *Social Democrats* and *Peasant Populists* were given ministerial seats, but all the important ministries were controlled by the *Communists*.

But the popular front government had a remarkably short life. In July, all political parties other than the *Communist Party* were banned and most non–communists were dismissed from office. This was followed by a wave of arrests. Then, with only communists, organized as the *Work-*

The old part of Vilnius, the Lithuanian capital whose "sister" city is Madison, Wisconsin
Courtesy: NOVOSTI

*ing People's League*, standing for office, new elections were held on July 14. The newly elected legislature met on July 21. Its only piece of business was to vote on whether to join the Soviet Union, which it did by acclamation. The following month, the USSR Supreme Soviet acceded to this request. Lithuania thus became a Soviet Socialist Republic.

The new communist government immediately began to implement general Soviet policies. A government decree nationalized all of the land. Larger estates were taken over directly and turned into state farms, but there was also a promise of

land to landless laborers. Smaller farmers were permitted to retain up to 75 acres, though technically they did not own it any longer. Nationalist elements now began to organize opposition to the new policies. In retaliation, the communists began rounding up oppositional elements and deporting them to Siberia.

Nazi Germany's invasion of the Soviet Union beginning on June 22, 1941 reversed this situation, for German troops overran and occupied Lithuania later in 1941. It remained under German occupation until 1944. With the German retreat, however, Lithuania once again fell under

# The Baltic Republics: Lithuania

Soviet control. A anti–communist resistance movement once again arose, often consisting of individuals who had been active in guerrilla actions against the Germans. By the summer of 1945, this movement had approximately 50,000 members and was operating throughout Lithuania. Units tended to operate in rural parts of the country, with their encampments in the middle of a forest. Guerrilla units would move out to attack centers of communist control while, back at the encampment, others worked to organize popular resistance. The reconstituted Lithuanian Communist Government countered the resistance movement by creating its own "People's Defenders," though the main struggle against the guerrillas was carried out by the NKVD. This war between the Lithuanian resistance and the NKVD went on until 1947. Such efforts were, of course, ineffectual. Lithuania got no outside assistance, and the resistance movement was eventually suppressed.

Many changes occurred in Lithuania over the next thirty–five years. Soviet policy was to integrate the Baltic Republics so thoroughly into the Soviet system that there would be no question of their ever leaving the union. To that end, the Soviet Government first carried out policies of nationalization and collectivization. Next it sought to bind the Republics to the rest of the Soviet Union economically by locating branch factories of Soviet industry there. Such factories received most or all of their raw materials from other parts of the Soviet Union, and delivered most of their finished products to customers in the other republics. This economic integration was so successful that the three Baltic Republics became more integrated into the Soviet economy than any other republic.

This program of economic integration was accompanied by a program of "Soviet Russification," aimed at transforming the cultures of the three republics. All students received Russian language training in the schools, plus general indoctrination lectures on the nature of Soviet culture. In addition, there was a systematic effort made to settle non–Baltic nationals in the republics. When a new factory was built, most of the workers would be transferred there from elsewhere in the Soviet Union.

It was Estonia and Latvia that became the chief victims of this policy, however. According to the figures of the 1989 Soviet census, Lithuania is still 80 percent ethnic Lithuanian. By comparison, ethnic Estonians by this time made up only 61.5 percent of the population of the republic, while in Latvia the figure was only 52 percent. On the positive side, the heavy industrialization carried out since 1945 meant that the standard of living in the three Baltic Republics was above that of any part of the Soviet Union.

## Lithuania Moves Toward Independence

The Lithuanian people accommodated themselves to Soviet rule, but they were never happy with it. Thus when Gorbachëv launched his programs of *glasnost* and restructuring after coming to power in 1985, Lithuanians were among the first to take advantage of them. In enunciating his policy of *glasnost*, Gorbachëv called on the Soviet peoples to speak out against negative tendencies in the society, and to support his reforms. This became a manifesto which led to the creation of thousands of "unofficial" organizations all over the Soviet Union. Formed originally in support of Gorbachëv's policy of reform, many of them soon began to push their own agendas. For the Baltic peoples, Gorbachëv's policies were a welcome breath of fresh air, and they were among the first to throw their enthusiastic support to him. At the same time, and almost from the beginning, the Baltic peoples used *glasnost* for their own purposes.

The Lithuanian people were a little slower to get organized than the Estonians and Latvians but, once organized, they proved to be even more determined to split with Moscow than either Estonia or Latvia. *Sajudis*, the Lithuanian Popular Front, traces its origins to a commission established by the Lithuanian Academy of Sciences on May 23, 1988 to propose changes to the Lithuanian constitution to accommodate Gorbachëv's policies of *glasnost*, *perestroika*, and democratization. The commission brought together party and non–party intellectuals and professionals who, in turn, decided that the times demanded something more. On June 3, they created an "initiative group" which subsequently took the name of *Sajudis*. Over the summer, *Sajudis* organized mass meetings and demonstrations on issues such as the 1939 Molotov–Ribbentrop Pact, the status of the Lithuanian language and the possibility of some form of economic autonomy. From the beginning, the animating spirit behind *Sajudis* was a non–party intellectual, a musicologist by the name of Vytautas Landsbergis.

*Sajudis* held its founding congress in October. Here a resolution was passed calling on the republic government to issue an assertion of Lithuanian sovereignty. Algirdas Brazauskas, who had just been appointed First Secretary of the *Lithuanian Communist Party*, was one of the invited speakers at the congress. He supported the measure initially, but was then forced to reverse himself on orders from Moscow. The *Lithuanian Communist Party* lost a great deal of its credibility as a result, as can be seen by looking at the results of the March 1989 elections to the USSR Congress of People's Deputies. *Sajudis* candidates won 36 out of 42 seats to the Congress and might have won

**Vytautas Landsbergis**

even more had they not deliberately refrained from challenging certain top communists, including First Secretary Brazauskas, who was liked personally, in spite of his having toed Moscow's line on the sovereignty issue. In fact, there was a tremendous overlap in the electoral positions of *Sajudis* and the *Lithuanian Communist Party*, for the latter advocated economic autonomy, pluralism of opinions, democracy and *glasnost*.

The *Lithuanian Communist Party* came under tremendous pressure after it had lost to *Sajudis* in the spring elections. In an attempt to create nationalist credentials, the party began discussing a split with the *Communist Party of the Soviet Union* in mid–1989. Another indication of the way opinion within the party was evolving came on August 22, 1989 when a commission of the Lithuanian Supreme Soviet, at that time still controlled by communists, voted to condemn the 1940 Soviet annexation of Lithuania and to declare it invalid. The party's formal split with Moscow came in December, at the *Lithuanian Communist Party* Congress. The *Lithuanian Communist Party* became the first republic party to split with the *CPSU*.

Even so, the *Lithuanian Communist Party* still found itself following along in *Sajudis's* wake. On August 23, 1989, the governing council of *Sajudis* voted unanimously that Lithuania should "take the peaceful course to becoming an independent democratic republic once again." In December 1989, Brazauskas, going further than he had ever gone before, could only bring himself to advocate a "sovereign Lithuanian state in a new union of free republics."

And even that position caused a split in the *Lithuanian Communist Party*, when a faction claiming to represent one–fourth of the membership broke away and reaffirmed its ties with Moscow.

# The Baltic Republics: Lithuania

It was against this background that elections were held to elect a new Lithuanian Supreme Soviet. The elections took place on February 24, 1990 with run–off elections on March 10. The *Sajudis* slate, which included reform communists as well as representatives of the newly legalized *Christian Democrat*, *Social Democrat* and *Green* parties, won an overwhelming majority.

When the newly installed parliament met to elect its Chairman of the Presidium, it chose Vytautas Landsbergis, head of *Sajudis* and a non–communist. Lithuania had its first non–communist government since 1940. On March 11, the Lithuanian Supreme Soviet adopted a declaration of Lithuanian independence.

The Soviet Union not only did not recognize Lithuanian independence; it also organized a partial economic boycott against the republic. Orders went out to all state enterprises in the republic to obey only orders from Moscow. There was also public discussion about presenting Lithuania with a bill for Soviet capital investments over the years—estimated at 21 billion rubles—payable in hard currency. There were also Soviet military maneuvers held in March 1990 in and around the city of Vilnius, though Gorbachëv claimed at the same time that force would not be used except to prevent bloodshed.

The Lithuanian response to the Soviet demand for indemnities was to raise counterclaims for goods and services extracted from the republic, environmental damage and for the tens of thousands of Lithuanians killed by Soviet officials over the years. The rhetoric escalated still further in April when Gorbachëv threatened to sharply reduce the flow of gas and oil to Lithuania if it did not immediately retract its declaration of independence. The

Lithuanian Government offered to discuss the question of the effective date of independence but not the question of independence itself. Oil shipments to Lithuania's sole refinery were then cut off and cuts were made in the delivery of other raw materials.

Meanwhile, Lithuania got some support of sorts when the Estonian and Latvian Governments joined Lithuania in issuing their own declarations of independence, though the declarations were not to take force immediately. In addition, the United States Government threatened to withhold most–favored–nation trading status from the Soviet Union if it blockaded Lithuania. As a result, after some further threats, the Soviet Union lifted its partial embargo on Lithuania. Things remained quiet for several months, but there was a new move against Lithuania by Moscow hardliners in January 1991. Gorbachëv claimed no advance knowledge when USSR Ministry of Interior troops seized a television tower in Vilnius, but he did not repudiate the action.

The issue of Baltic independence was one of the issues that precipitated the *coup* against Gorbachëv in August 1991. The failure of that *coup* led most of the world to extend recognition to the Baltic States and led the post–*coup* Soviet Government to extend its own recognition in September 1991. Lithuania was admitted to the United Nations in October 1991.

The newly–independent Lithuanian Government concentrated mainly on domestic problems at first, although it also pressed for the removal of Soviet troops from Lithuania as soon as possible. That presented a particular problem so long as the troops remained under the aegis of the Commonwealth of Independent States, but the Russian Government set up its

own Ministry of Defense in the summer of 1992 and subsequently negotiated an agreement with Lithuania for the removal of the troops as soon as possible.

There were approximately 20,500 troops in Lithuania at this time. Some small token force withdrawals began in September, and Russia promised that all would be out by sometime in 1993. President Yeltsin suspended the troop withdrawals in October, however, asserting a "profound concern" over the treatment of ethnic Russians in the Baltic Republics. Since Lithuania, unlike the Estonians and Latvians, had extended citizenship to all persons who were resident prior to mid–1990, it is not certain why Lithuania was included in the decree. Apparently, the Russian Government wanted guarantees concerning the pensions and status of retired Russian military personnel living in Lithuania. In any case, new negotiations with Russia led to the evacuation of the last Russian troops from Lithuania in the summer of 1993.

Lithuania has also had some problems with minorities within the country, mainly Poles and Russians. District governments in and around Vilnius where Poles were in a majority were suspended, apparently because the Poles elected communists to office. In spite of nationalist demands to the contrary, however, the Government eventually ended up extending citizenship rights to its minorities.

A new constitution was adopted in 1992 and new parliamentary elections were subsequently held in October, with a run–off election in November. In a surprise, the electorate gave *Sajudis*, the party of President Landsbergis, only about 22 percent of the vote. The winner was the *Democratic Labor Party*, the successor party to the *Lithuanian Communist Party*, led by Algirdas Brazauskas, which got over 40 percent of the vote and a majority of the seats in the *Seimas*. This result was reaffirmed in the subsequent Presidential elections which were won by Brazauskas, who then took office on February 25, 1993. In one sense, therefore, one could say that the communists returned to power in Lithuania in 1992.

That would be a misreading of the election results, however. In fact, Brazauskas was a nationalist, first and foremost, and it was he who was responsible for the *Lithuanian Communist Party*'s split with Moscow in 1990, and its subsequent support for Lithuanian independence. Moreover, when Brazauskas founded the *Democratic Labor Party* after independence, many communists became politically inactive, with the result that only about 5% of its membership in 1992 were formerly members of the *Lithuanian Communist Party*.

In actuality, it was not politics but economics that was responsible for the victory of Brazauskas and the *Democratic Labor Party*. By 1992, the Lithuanian economy

**Weaving wicker baskets**                    Courtesy: NOVOSTI

# The Baltic Republics: Lithuania

was in relatively poor shape, with salaries frozen and many people being paid up to three months late. Moreover, Lithuania had been forced to cut its imports of oil and gas beginning in July 1992, after Russia began charging world prices payable in hard currency for exports to areas outside the ruble zone. By October, therefore, Lithuania did not have sufficient fuel to heat most buildings. As one commentator explained the vote, "the simple people know only that before it was warm, and now it is cold."

After his victory, President Brazauskas spelled out his essential program: "we support the idea that there can be no sharp turns, that we cannot do anything at any price. We have already done that. We have frozen salaries and removed subsidies. Can you imagine how a person receiving a small salary can survive, with world prices coming down upon their heads? A government has to reply to the people's cries."

The victory of the *Democratic Labor Party* and Brazauskas' election as President did not, therefore, bring about a change in direction, though it did involve a change in style. In an attempt to cushion the transition to private enterprise, for example, the government made a point of working out its policies in close consultation with factory managers. This slowed the process somewhat, but it did not reverse it. Lithuania's macroeconomic policies, in fact, continued to have the support of the IMF.

One political change occurred in February 1996, when the Lithuanian legislature voted 94 to 24 to oust Prime Minister Adolfas Slezevicius after it was learned that he had withdrawn his personal savings from Lithuania's largest bank two days before it shut down. President Brazauskas then nominated Mindaugas Laurynas as the new prime minister. Because Slezevicius was removed for essentially personal reasons, this change had no significant effect on policy, though it did sully the reputation of the *Democratic Labor Party*.

New parliamentary elections in October 1996 brought a reversal once again as the governing *Democratic Labor Party* won only 10 out of 70 contested seats. This result was confirmed in a second round of voting on November 10. The big winner was Vytautas Landsbergis, who had used his four years out of power to reshape the center and right of the political spectrum by founding a new political party, the *Homeland Union*. It took 70 seats in the 141–seat *Seimas* during the two rounds of voting, falling just one seat short of a majority. A coalition with the *Lithuanian Christian Democratic Party* resulted, which came in second in terms of seats won in the voting. Landsbergis decided to take the position of Chairman of the *Seimas*, while Gediminas Vagnorius was elected Prime Minister. Since Brazauskas' term as

President runs through February 1998, this marked the beginning of a period of shared government for Lithuania.

Although economic issues played an important part in the campaign, with the *Homeland Union* portraying itself as a force for modernization which could facilitate Lithuania's entry into the European mainstream, charges of mismanagement and corruption stemming from the events of February 1996 hurt the ruling party as well. On the other hand, the Homeland Union's unfulfilled promises of tax cuts and increased spending on social programs may have played a role in the Presidential elections which took place in December 1997.

There were three candidates in those elections. No candidate won a majority of the vote, but Vytautas Landsbergis, candidate of the government coalition, was eliminated from further contention when he came in third after winning only 15.85% of the vote. The "winner" of the first round of voting was Arturas Paulauskas, with 45.35% of the vote. Paulauskas, the son of a KBG colonel, had the support of most of the old communist establishment, as well as the endorsement of the sitting president, Algirdas Brazauskas. The man who came in second was Valdas Adamkus, with 27.89% of the vote. The surprise came in the runoff election that took place on January 4, 1998, for the narrow winner was Valdas Adamkus.

Even more surprising, Valdas Adamkus, now 71, is an emigre who spent most of the period since World War II in the United States, in later years as an official of the U.S. Environmental Protection Agency. Because of that background, he had to fight a lawsuit to get on the ballot, and an important issue in the election was his emigre past. In the end, the Lithuanian people, forced to choose because an outsider and a member of the old communist establishment, opted for the outsider— presumably in the hope that Mr. Adamkus will be able to lead Lithuania westward. Since the job of a Lithuanian President is to represent the country abroad, they may have made an excellent choice. In any case, he speaks excellent English and German and knows American ways. The Lithuanian President doesn't have much power domestically, so Adamkus will have to build a working relationship with the parties of the government coalition if he is to have much influence there. He has made a beginning, since he was endorsed by the Prime Minister, Gediminas Vagnorius, before the election. Still, unless he is able to create a local power base for himself, he is likely to be frustrated if he pushes for major changes domestically.

## Foreign Policy

Lithuanian foreign policy under Vytautas Landsbergis tended to be confronta-

tional toward Russia, partly because of the continuing presence of Russian troops after Lithuania reestablished its independence in 1991, partly because Landsbergis was not interested in better relations with Russia. With the change in administrations and election of President Brazauskas, therefore, there has been a significant change in foreign policy. During the campaign, Brazauskas had pledged himself to work for a closer working relationship with Russia, particularly in the economic area, and he has, in general, succeeded. He also managed to negotiate an agreement with Russia whereby it agreed to remove the last of its troops by September 1993. Lithuania was thus the first of the Baltic republics to be totally free of Russian troops. Even Brazauskas managed to annoy Russia, however, when he announced in January 1994, in a television address, that the Lithuanian Government had submitted a formal request for membership in NATO. Moscow's reaction was swift and negative, with a spokesman for President Yeltsin warning that any moves to expand NATO could "trigger military–political destabilization in the region." In fact, there is little possibility that NATO will extend an offer of membership to Lithuania, as Brazauskas must have known. Therefore, this request should be seen as the Lithuanian Government's attempt to burnish up its pro–western credentials.

## NATURE OF THE REGIME

Lithuania completed its transition from the earlier communistic system in October 1992 when the Lithuanian people approved a new constitution in a national referendum and is now a multiparty, parliamentary democracy. Under the terms of a new constitution, transition titles adopted after Lithuania became independent in September 1991 have been replaced by permanent titles, some of which reflect titles current during the earlier Lithuanian Republic. For example, the legislature, known as the Supreme Soviet when Lithuania was a Soviet Republic, became the Supreme Council after September 1991. Under the new constitution, it reverted to its previous name, the *Seimas*. The head of state, formerly known as the Chairman of the Presidium of the Supreme Council, is now the President of the Republic. The head of government, formerly referred to as the Chairman of the Council of Ministers, is the Prime Minister.

### The Lithuanian Government

The President of the Republic is the highest official of the state. Popularly elected for a term of five years, he is expected to represent the country internationally and to provide general political leadership domestically. He appoints and

# The Baltic Republics: Lithuania

dismisses state officials as provided by the constitution and other laws. He may issue decrees under certain circumstances, and only he may declare a state of national emergency. Laws passed by the *Seimas* may either be approved and published or returned with remarks for reconsideration.

The current President of the Republic is Algirdas Brazauskas, leader of the *Democratic Labor Party*, who was elected to that office on February 14, 1993. Brazauskas was originally named Chairman of the Presidium and Acting President by the *Seimas* in November 1992, following the victory of the *Democratic Labor Party (DLP)* in the Fall elections. The *DLP* is the renamed *Lithuanian Communist Party*, though it has been transformed by Brazauskas into a "left of center," democratic party.

The official next in importance to the President is the Chairman of the *Seimas,* a position held since November 1996 by Vytautas Landsbergis, leader of the *Homeland Union.* Landsbergis, Chairman of the Presidium from 1990 to 1993, was one of the founders of *Sajudis*, the Lithuanian Popular Front, and a leader in Lithuania's struggle for independence.

The Prime Minister comes next in terms of importance. As the constitutionally-designated head of government, he and his cabinet are responsible for the day-to-day operations of government. The Prime Minister is also responsible for implementation of laws and resolutions of the *Seimas*, decrees issued by the President of the Republic, plus the maintenance of diplomatic relations with foreign countries and international organizations.

Appointed by the President, the Prime Minister must be confirmed by the *Seimas*, and must retain the support of a majority of that body to remain in office. Thus, among his other functions, the Prime Minister is expected to maintain a close working relationship with the *Seimas*. Ministers are appointed and dismissed by the President of the Republic upon the recommendation of the Prime Minister. The current cabinet is a coalition made up of the *Homeland Union* and the *Lithuanian Christian Democratic Party*, which together control a majority of the seats in the *Seimas*.

The *Seimas* is a single body legislature with a total of 141 members elected for a period of four years. Under Lithuania's voting system, 71 of the seats are filled by direct vote; the remaining 70 seats are awarded on a proportional basis, each political party being assigned seats on the basis of its share of the popular vote. The *Seimas* has the power to amend the constitution, enact laws, control the activities of the government, approve the budget, appoint and dismiss chairs of the state institutions, and settle other issues pertaining to state power.

## Culture

Lithuanian culture was essentially a rural, peasant culture until the end of the nineteenth century. After that, it developed an urban culture, based on the rising professional and middle classes, though the population of most Lithuanian cities remained largely non–Lithuanian until fairly late in this century. Vilnius, the current capital and largest city, continues to have a large Polish population. It was, in fact, part of Poland until 1939, and only became Lithuanian shortly before Lithuania itself was incorporated into the Soviet Union. In one sense, then, Kaunas, the second city and the capital of Lithuania in the inter–war period, is more Lithuanian than Vilnius.

Vilnius does have Gediminas Castle, the fortress–residence of the Grand Dukes of Lithuania, the Gothic Church of St. Anne that dates from the fourteenth century, the University building in the oldest part of the city, and the "Medininku vartai," all that is left of the nine gates in the former wall that surrounded the city when it was the capital of the Grand Duchy. There are also some houses that date from the fifteenth–seventeenth centuries. But the city became Polanized after the Union with Poland in 1569. Vilnius University, the republic's greatest center of learning, was originally founded in 1579, but it was closed by the Russian Government in 1832. When it reopened in 1919, Vilnius was part of Poland, so it was located in Kaunas until after World War II. Today, of course, Vilnius is home to the Lithuanian State Opera and Ballet Company and to numerous theaters for the presentation of plays, as well as the republic's main philharmonic orchestra.

Kaunas also has its own philharmonic and numerous theaters, though it lacks an opera and ballet company. It also has numerous churches and museums. There are five institutes of higher education in the city, including a medical college. Another is Kaunas' Polytechnical Institute, founded in 1951 after the university was shifted to Vilnius. There are also a number of scientific research institutes.

## Lithuanian Literature

Although the Lithuanian people had a strong oral folklorist tradition, a written literature was rather late in developing. In fact, the first book published in the Lithuanian language was a religious text, *Simple Words of the Catechism*, published in 1547. The religious controversy associated with the reformation led to the translation of the *Bible* into Lithuanian in 1590 but, as a result of the triumph of Catholicism in Poland–Lithuania, it was never published but remained in manuscript form in the library of Koenigsberg University. The Jesuits, who were primarily responsible for the triumph of Catholicism, did produce several things in Lithuanian, including a catechism, a collection of sermons, and a dictionary, the latter published in 1629.

The first example of secular literature in the Lithuanian language, a translation of ten of Aesop's fables, appeared in 1706. The first Lithuanian author, the poet Kristijonas Donelaitis, lived in the eighteenth century, though his epic poem, *The Sea-*

**Founded in 1570—Vilnius University Library with over 4 million volumes**

Courtesy: NOVOSTI

241

# The Baltic Republics: Lithuania

sons, circulated only in manuscript form during his lifetime and was not published until 1818. Donelaitis was a Protestant pastor in the town of Tolminkiemis and parts of his poem appear to be paraphrases of his sermons. Yet the poem also presents a realistic portrayal of the life of the peasants, at that time still struggling serfs. The German poet Goethe, who was familiar with the poem, compared Donelaitis to Homer.

A second poet, Antanas Baranauskas, who lived and wrote in the nineteenth century, had a background similar to that of Donelaitis in that he also followed a religious avocation, and in later life became the Catholic bishop in Seinai. Baranauskas actually wrote his poems during his youth, however, before being ordained as a priest. His most important poem, written during summer vacations at home in 1858–59, was *The Forest of Anykščiai*. Baranauskas projects a mystic oneness with nature that is almost pagan in its orientation:

"Forest and peasant knew no discord,
Grew up together, aged in accord.
To the Lithuanian, caveman of yore,
The forest gave a strong wooden door;
And since he never would hew the
  wood,
Till aged it fell, the dry trees still
  stood."

Lithuania became a part of the Russian Empire at the end of the eighteenth century, along with parts of eastern Poland. At that time, there was no separate Lithuanian nationalism, but Lithuanians supported Polish attempts—in 1831 and again in 1863—to throw off the Russian yoke. As a result, the Russian Government attempted to stamp out Polish–Lithuanian nationalism by Russifying the people and the culture. The University of Vilnius was closed after the 1831 uprising; then the Latin alphabet was replaced by the Cyrillic alphabet after the 1863 uprising. These efforts to stamp out the local culture were unavailing, however.

Instead, Lithuanian political and cultural leaders arranged to have Lithuanian-language books and newspapers published in East Prussia, then smuggled them across the border. The first Lithuanian–language newspaper, *The Dawn* began publishing in Tilset in 1883. In addition, increasing numbers of Lithuanians entered universities either in Russia or abroad and subsequently added their literary output to the stream. Jonas Maironis–Mačiulis studied at Kiev and St. Petersburg and later became a professor and a priest. His collection, *The Voices of Spring*, published in 1895, glorified the Lithuanian countryside. He also wrote ballads and satires and even a drama in verse, *The Death of Kestutis*, which, however, was not published until 1921. Another dramatist, Vilius Storasta, who wrote under the name of Vyduanas, produced *The Shadows of Ancestors* in 1908, *The Eternal Flame* in 1912, and *Bells of the Sea* in 1914. A fourth play, *The World on Fire* was produced in 1928.

Vincas Krėvė, another playwright, produced his first dramas before World War I, but his most important plays appeared in independent Lithuania. Important plays include *Skirgaila* (1922), *On the Roads of Destiny* (1926), *The Death of Mindaugas* (1930), and *The Son–in–Law* (1939). Krėvė served for a short time as Minister of Foreign Affairs in the new Soviet–dominated government in 1940, then went into hiding before fleeing abroad. In 1947, he became a member of the faculty of the University of Pennsylvania and remained there until his death in 1954.

The second major figure of the period of Lithuanian independence was Vincas Mykolaitis, who wrote under the *nom de plume* of Putinas. Extremely versatile, Putinas, who was also an ordained priest, produced poetry, novels, and plays. His two best novels are probably the autobiographical trilogy, *In the Shadow of Altars* and *The Crisis*, both written in the 1930's. Putinas, who died in 1967, continued to write after the Soviet occupation of the country in 1940, but these works, favorable to the new regime, are lesser works.

There is also a body of works done by Lithuanians in emigration. Antanas Vaičiulaitis taught at several American universities after World War II, then joined the Voice of America. His books include three volumes of short stories, legends and myths. Jurgis Gliauda, who also made his way to America after World War II, is the author of *House Upon the Sand* (1951), *Ora pro nobis* (1952), and *The Sonata of Icarus*. Other writers in emigration include Nėlė Mazalaitė, Alfonsas Šešplaukis, Henrikas Radauskas, and Stepas Zobarskas.

## Economy

Lithuania is the least industrialized of the Baltic Republics, with only about 40 percent of the work force involved in industry. Even so, industry contributes more to the overall economy than agriculture.

Most of Lithuania's industry is located in or near its major cities. Kaunas, Lithuania's second largest city, has metal and woodworking industries as well as light and food industries. Kleipeda, Lithuania's third largest city and its major seaport, is home to a large deep–sea fishing fleet, and it has one of the largest shipyards in the Baltic. The main local industry is fish processing. The town also has a pulp and paper mill, a woodworking factory, textile mills, plus a large plant that manufactures radios and telephones. In addition, it is a traditional center for the working of amber. Vilnius, Lithuania's largest city and its capital, is a center for computer manufacturing, machine tools, electric meters, drills, farm machinery, building materials and food processing. There is also a small amount of industry located in smaller towns.

A large part of Lithuania's agricultural land is still organized into collective and state farms, even though the previous government supported the privatization of agriculture. That government did manage to create some private farms, though a major problem was that individual peasants had to be persuaded to accept the responsibility of private farming. The process has slowed down somewhat under the new government. President Brazauskas said in December 1992 that it was "a mistake to get rid of the remaining collective farms . . . by giving their property to individuals." Brazauskas said that farmers who "wished and were able to keep their private farms should be provided with all the necessary facilities for it" but that those still on collective farms should be allowed to choose their own form of privatization.

Forestry products are another source of income for persons residing in the countryside. With approximately 25 percent of the land covered by trees, Lithuania produces both timber and pulp wood. There are also considerable deposits of peat plus materials used in construction such as limestone, chalk, dolomites, clays and gravel, whose exploitation provides additional jobs in the countryside.

In the past, about 55 percent of Lithuania's exports went to other parts of the Soviet Union. Negotiations with Russian and some of the other republics have extended those arrangements, but the *Sajudis* government was committed to reorienting its trade more toward the west. President Brazauskas has said that he would like to improve economic relations with the ex–Soviet republics, but the collapse of inter–regional trade in 1991-92 has made that difficult.

Approximately one–third of the republic's industrial workers work in engineering or metal–working factories created during the Soviet period. These factories, which were built to serve customers located mainly in the other republics, have been particularly hard pressed recently. Overall, the Lithuanian economy has suffered fairly steep declines over the past two–three years, but these declines have been similar to developments elsewhere in the former Soviet Union and less than in some republics. One of Lithuania's major problems has been obtaining energy supplies from Russia.

In June 1993, Lithuania began issuing its own permanent currency, the *litas*, to replace the *talon*, an interim coupon is-

**Mass is celebrated in Kaunas**

Courtesy: NOVOSTI

sued after independence. When this did not bring inflation under control, it introduced legislation in February 1994 to establish a currency board system, modelled after the system successfully tried beginning in June 1992 in Estonia. The essence of the system is that the currency board issues only as much currency as is backed by the country's reserves of gold and foreign exchange.

What that meant in practice is that the Lithuanian central bank had to curtail credits to state–owned industries and fail-

ing enterprises and stop issuing paper money to cover government budget deficits. As the system began working, inflation dropped drastically and prices, wages, and pensions stabilized. This permitted the government to begin on a program of general privatization, which was largely implemented by the end of 1996.

**The Future**

Lithuania's larger agricultural population probably gives it a cushion that the other two Baltic states lack. Its greater eth-

nic unity and the strong unifying role of the Roman Catholic Church are other pluses. It has also shown that it can have a peaceful change of government. On the negative side, it is the poorest of the Baltic republics, so its reserves are that much less. During the most recent parliamentary elections, in October–November 1996, the winning political party campaigned on making Lithuania part of the European mainstream.

# The Republic of Bulgaria

An expensive purchase in Sofia: costume jeweley

**Area:** 42,729 sq. mi. (111,852 sq. km.).

**Population:** 8.3 million (1997 est.).

**Capital City:** Sofia (Pop. 1.2 million; 1991 est.)

**Climate:** Mediterranean in the South, cooler in the North.

**Neighboring Countries:** Romania (North); Turkey, Greece (South); Serbia, SFRY (formerly Yugoslavia), Macedonia (West).

**Official Language:** Bulgarian.

**Other Principal Tongue:** Turkish.

**Ethnic Background:** Slav, Turkish.

**Principal Religions:** Bulgarian Orthodox, Islam.

**Chief Commercial Products:** Machinery and equipment, agricultural and forest products, fuels, minerals, metals, rose oil, wine.

**Currency:** Leva.

**Annual Per Capita Income:** Unknown, but average monthly wages, which had dropped to under $25 in February 1997 after an economic collapse, had risen to almost $108 by December 1997.

**Former Political Status:** Part of Ottoman Empire, 1393–1878; Autonomous Principality, 1878–1908; Independent, 1908–1944; Communist State, part of Soviet Empire, 1945–1990.

**National Day:** Undetermined.

**Chief of State:** Petar Stoyanov, President.

**Head of Government:** Ivan Kostov, Prime Minister (May 1997).

**National Flag:** Three horizontal stripes, white, green, red.

## THE LAND AND THE PEOPLE

The Republic of Bulgaria is a relatively small, square–shaped country bordering on the Black Sea to the east and bounded by the Danube River to the north. The Black Sea coast has not only beautiful sandy beaches which are now being developed, but it is also the site of the major industrial center of Varna. Stretching from west to east is the Balkan Range (Stara Planina) separating the fertile Danubian Plain in the north from the Thracian Plain in the south.

In the exact center of the country there is the Kazanlik "Valley of Roses" where fragrance and beauty combine with commercial value in the production of rose oil. The southwest is dominated by the rugged Rila Mountains—which include Mount Musala, the highest peak in the Balkans—and by the snow–capped Pirin Mountains. South of Plovdiv, Bulgaria's second largest city built on a cliff overlooking the Maritsa River, lie the Rhodope Mountains, where hundreds of mineral springs can be found.

In the 7th century an Asiatic people called the Bulgars crossed the Danube River and settled in the area which is known today as the Republic of Bulgaria. Within two centuries after their conquest of the region, the Bulgars had become completely absorbed into the native Slav population, adopting their language and culture. The Bulgarians were converted to Orthodox Christianity during the 9th century by Cyril and Methodius, two missionaries, who devised a Slav alphabet in order to translate the Bible and religious writings into the language of the people. The conversion of the Bulgarians thus brought them their first literary language and early contact with the Byzantine Empire.

## HISTORY

The rise of Bulgarian power began when they challenged the Byzantine Empire, which had become a powerful Greek super–state of the medieval period that grew with and through the eastern Orthodox Church. On two occasions, the Bulgarians were able to seize and control substantial lands in what are now Bulgaria, Greece, Turkey, Russia, Yugoslavia and Romania. The swirling tides of battles during this period are complicated, involving both the eastern Orthodox Church and the Roman Church. The expanding Ottoman Turks conquered Bulgaria in 1393 and remained in control until 1878. The inhabitants of the Ottoman Empire were organized into administrative units on the basis of their faith, with a religious leader as head of each unit. The Orthodox Church was thus used by the Turks to administer the Bulgarians.

# Bulgaria

## The Birth of Modern Bulgaria

The liberation of Bulgaria from Turkish control was the product of a war between Russia and Turkey which ended in Turkish defeat. The Russians had envisioned a single, large Bulgarian state and this was stipulated in the resulting Treaty of San Stefano. The Austrians and British objected, however, and Russia was forced to permit a rewriting of the treaty at the Congress of Berlin. The result, signed in 1878, was that the southern portion of Bulgaria was returned to Turkey while the remaining area was divided into two parts, separated by the Balkan Mountains. The northern part became Bulgaria and was established as a self–governing territory with the right to select its own Prince. The portion south of the mountains became the autonomous Turkish territory of East Rumelia. The division did not last, however; in 1885, the East Rumelians voted to merge with the rest of Bulgaria. The nation as a whole remained a self–governing autonomous principality until it declared its complete independence from the Ottoman Empire in 1908.

There were three main problems that Bulgaria inherited from the period following Ottoman rule. The first concerned territory—the Great Bulgaria envisioned in the Treaty of San Stefano had included much of the territory the Bulgarians had lived in at the time of their greatness in the 10th century. The Treaty of Berlin had reduced those territories by nearly two–thirds. The Union of East Rumelia and Bulgaria in 1885 partially cured the situation, but still left Bulgaria with claims to additional territory. It was this question that led to Bulgarian participation in the two Balkan Wars of 1912–13, to an alliance with Germany and Austria in World War I and to an alliance with Germany in World War II.

The second problem was the status of neighboring Macedonia. In the nineteenth century, it was still part of the Ottoman Empire. A majority of its inhabitants were Slavs but had no developed national identity. Most outsiders assumed that they must be either Serbians or Bulgarians and the Bulgarian and Serbian Governments took this same position, each claiming the Macedonians as separated brethren. To complicate the situation more, Greece also claimed the area, arguing that Macedonia was historically Greek. As a result of this Greek–Serbian–Bulgarian rivalry, each state waged a constant battle to increase its influence through a variety of means, including political propaganda, school subsidies, Orthodox Church authority and, worst of all, terrorism.

The third problem was the nature of Bulgaria's relationship with Russia. On one hand, there had been a great deal of popular affection for Russia as the liberator of Bulgaria from Turkish rule. On the other hand, this affection had been mingled with a fear that the price of Russian friendship may be Bulgarian servitude.

This was the only nation in the Balkans to join the Central Powers (Germany Austria) in World War I; this not only resulted in defeat in 1918, but a loss of even more territory. The terms of the treaty settling the war and the boundaries of the southern Balkans were denounced by Bulgaria as harsh during the interwar period.

From 1919 to 1939, Bulgarian history was troubled. There were political plots from left and right–wing groups, assassinations, mass murders and constant acts of individual terrorism. One of the most important groups in the country, especially in the years between 1923 and 1934 was the *Internal Macedonian Revolutionary Or-*

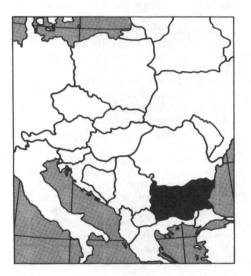

*ganization (IMRO).* This was a terrorist group fighting for Macedonian self–government and undermining any political leaders who pursued policies inconsistent with this goal.

The early post–World War I period years were dominated by Alexander Stambuliski, a colorful, strong–willed leader of the *Agrarian Party*. During the period he was premier, which lasted until 1923, reforms in the tax structure, legal system and land ownership were carried out. The land reforms were not as drastic as they were elsewhere in the Balkans since Bulgaria was basically a peasant society with few large landholdings.

While Stambuliski was in office, the *Communist Party of Bulgaria* was the second–largest party in the country. After a right–wing military regime came to power in 1923, the party was banned, and its leaders, such as Georgi Dimitrov, had to go into exile.

After ten years of *IMRO* terrorism and government inefficiency, a military *coup* was engineered in 1934. Colonel Kimon Georgiev, the leader of the *Zveno* group—an organization of reform–minded intellectuals and politicians—became premier. In less that a year he was out of office; his powers went to King Boris, who ruled Bulgaria as a royal dictator from 1935 until his death in 1943.

Bulgaria joined the Axis in 1941, but refused to declare war on the Soviet Union when that nation was invaded by Germany. During 1941, as a by–product of a German attack on Yugoslavia, Bulgaria occupied the Yugoslav portion of Macedonia, part of Serbia and also took over Western Thrace, a part of Greece.

245

# Bulgaria

Boris was succeeded in 1943 by his six–year–old son, Simeon. A three–man regency exercised state power. Under the administration of Premier Ivan Bagrianov, a less pro–Axis policy was soon adopted. Thousands of political prisoners were released and persecution of Jews decreased.

Bulgaria announced in 1944 that it was ready to seek a separate peace with the Allies. However, the Soviet Union declared war on Bulgaria within a few days and the Soviet army entered the country.

## Bulgaria Becomes a People's Republic

Technically, the government was overthrown at this time by a native resistance group calling itself the *Fatherland Front*. This was a "popular front" grouping which had come into existence during World War II with the assistance and under the sponsorship of the Communist International (Comintern). An undoubted factor in this sponsorship was that Georgi Dimitrov, the Bulgarian communist who had fled the country in 1923, was now Secretary General of the Comintern.

The communist role in the *Fatherland Front* was very strong, but it was a genuine "popular front," encompassing the Agrarian Union, one wing of the Social Democrats, and Zveno. In fact, the premier of the new government was Colonel Kimon Georgiev, a member of Zveno. The communists were a minority in the cabinet, but they controlled the key ministries of Justice and Interior. This gave them control over both the police and the courts, and they used this to institute a systematic purge of opposition figures.

Since all the parties of the *Fatherland Front* were pro–Russian and united in their hatred of the "German collabora-tors" who had frozen them out of power in the past, there was strong support among the other parties for these actions. Those executed included the three regents, former premiers Bagrianov and Bozhilov, twenty–six former cabinet ministers and sixty–eight deputies from the wartime Assemblies. In addition, special "People's Courts" were set up throughout the country and thousands of additional individuals were sentenced to death and executed.

Having eliminated the "German collaborators," however, the communists next turned to their partners in the *Fatherland Front*. Under the terms of the Yalta Declaration of February 1945, free elections were to be held throughout eastern Europe. The communists, determined to establish their own political dominance, demanded a common *Fatherland Front* list of candidates with a prearranged ratio giving them half the seats in the new Assembly. *Zveno,* more a military faction than a political party, accepted these terms. The *Agrarian Union* and the *Social Democrats* did not. The communists thereupon produced their own Agrarian collaborator, Alexander Obhov, and, by packing the congress of the *Agrarian Union*, managed to get him elected head of the party. Similar tactics were used against the *Social Democrats.* The elections, which took place in November 1945, produced an 86% majority for the *Fatherland Front*.

Georgi Dimitrov, who had been elected President of the Central Committee of the *Bulgarian Communist Party* at a Party Congress in March 1945, returned to Sofia in the midst of the election campaign. Although clearly the preeminent leader of the party that dominated the government, he did not enter the government at this time. One reason may have been that the American and British governments challenged the validity of the November elections and demanded that the true leaders of the *Agrarian Front* and *Social Democrats* be brought back into the government. This became the subject of the Moscow Conference of December 1945, but American and British pressure was of no effect.

By the summer of 1946, in fact, the communists felt strong enough to campaign against *Zveno,* the remaining independent element in the *Fatherland Front*. An attack was launched in the communist press against the founder of *Zveno,* General Velchev, who held the position of Minister of War. Velchev eventually was forced to resign from the cabinet. Colonel Georgiev remained on as premier until the autumn when he, too, was forced out.

Bulgaria was still technically a monarchy up to this point; however, a plebiscite, held in September 1946, resulted in a vote in favor of a republic. A month later, new elections were held for a Grand National Assembly which was charged with preparing a new constitution.

The *Fatherland Front* won those elections and Georgi Dimitrov took the office of premier in the new government. Some legal opposition continued for awhile, however, since the independent factions of the *Agrarian Union* and the *Social Democrats* had both run candidates in the elections and had managed to get a few of their candidates elected. For awhile, they were permitted to make speeches in the Assembly, but this was soon replaced by a campaign of intimidation. Things came to a head in June 1947 when Nikola Petkov, leader of the independent faction of the *Agrarian Union,* was arrested on the floor of the Assembly—even though his parliamentary immunity should have protected him. Charged with preparing for a *coup d'etat*, he was found guilty and sentenced to death.

Somewhat later, Georgi Dimitrov addressed a specific warning to the few Social Democrats remaining in the Assembly. "As you remember," Dimitrov informed them, "from this rostrum I many times warned your political allies from Nikola Petkov's group. They did not listen to me. They took no notice of all my warnings. They broke their heads, and their leader is now under the ground. You should now think it over, lest you share their fate . . ."

The following July, Kosta Lulchev, head of the *Social Democrats,* was arrested, along with six of the nine remaining deputies from that party, and was subsequently sentenced to fifteen years imprisonment.

The Dimitrov government presented Bulgaria with a new constitution in December 1947. As might have been expect-

**Plaza 9th of September, Sofia**                    Photo: Miller B. Spangler

Entertainers at Mt. Vitosha, south of Sofia

Photo: Miller B. Spangler

ed, it was modeled closely after the 1936 "Stalin Constitution" of the U.S.S.R. Bulgaria now became a "people's republic" while its government became almost a carbon copy of the Soviet model, except that the legislature consisted of one house only, since Bulgaria had no need for a separate house representing different nationalities such as existed in Russia and Yugoslavia. Like the Soviet Union, theoretical sovereignty rested with the legislature, but the actual decision–making was carried out by a Presidium and a separate Council of Ministers. Reflecting the fulcrum of power, Georgi Dimitrov took the position of President of the Council of Ministers for himself.

### Internecine Struggles

Having eliminated the opposition, the communists turned against each other. The charge was "nationalist deviation" and the ostensive cause was Tito's break with the Soviet Union. It tended to turn into a struggle between communists who had served an apprenticeship in the Soviet Union and those who had remained behind. It appears to have been largely directed from Moscow, for Stalin apparently became convinced that he couldn't trust any of the "native" communists.

The most significant of that group was Traicho Kostov, who had risen to the position of Vice–President of the Council of Ministers in charge of economic affairs and who was widely considered to be Dimitrov's probable successor. The list of charges eventually filed against him was rather extensive, but the most serious charge was that he had kept secret information on Bulgarian economic matters from Soviet representatives, not realizing, as *Rabotnichesko Delo*, the communist party newspaper phrased it, that "secrets and commercialism do not exist in our dealings with the Soviet Union." Kostov was sentenced to death and executed in late 1949. Several of his associates, including the Finance Minister, the Foreign Trade Minister, the Director of the National Bank and the Commercial Attaché in Moscow, were sentenced to long terms in prison. Other leading native communists were tried, sentenced and eliminated. In addition, a purge of the party ranks resulted in about 20% of the membership being expelled from the party.

In the midst of the purge, Georgi Dimitrov died while on a trip to the Soviet Union. His immediate successor was Vasil Kolarov, but he died six months later in 1950, and was in turn replaced by Vulko Chervenkov. The latter was Dimitrov's brother–in–law and had spent many years in the Soviet Union. Known as an arch–Stalinist, he was almost certainly responsible for the severity of the purge of the "native" communists. By using the weapon of "nationalist deviation," he eliminated all possible rivals and consolidated his own power position.

The purges had one final result. At the Kostov trial, an attempt was made to portray the defendant as an American agent who had been encouraged in his actions by U.S. Minister Donald Heath. This was followed by the arrest of five Bulgarians employed by the U.S. Mission and a subsequent "spy trial" of other alleged U.S. agents. Finally, the U.S. had enough, and in early 1950 it broke off diplomatic relations with the Bulgarians.

Chervenkov was the most ruthless of Bulgaria's post–war rulers, but he did not get to enjoy his power for very long. Stalin's death in 1953 was the first change, for now his old patron was dead. Khrushchev's rise to power threatened Chervenkov's position, for Khrushchëv was determined to heal the breach with Tito of Yugoslavia, and Chervenkov had distinguished himself as an enemy of Tito. In 1954 he gave up the position of General Secretary of the Central Committee—the leading Party position—although he managed to retain the leading state position, that of premier. Chervenkov actually managed to hold on to most of his power for another two years, but he was never able to overcome his Stalinist past. And when Khrushchëv launched his attack against Stalin in 1956, Chervenkov found himself accused of Stalin's chief crime—promoting a "cult of personality"—and was again forced to accept a demotion, this time to Deputy Chairman of the Council of Ministers.

### The Beginning of the Zhivkov Era

The man who got Chervenkov's party position in 1954—changed at this time

# Bulgaria

**Cleaning the streets of Sofia** AP/Wide World Photo

from General Secretary to First Secretary—was Todor Zhivkov. His first membership in the Bulgarian Communist Party dates back to 1932 and he had been one of the organizers of the partisan underground in the Sofia area during World War II; he commanded the partisan regiments in and around Sofia at the time of the 1944 *Fatherland Front* seizure of power. Lacking close ties to the "Moscow" communists, who had returned to Bulgaria to take charge of the party, Zhivkov spent the next four years in various subordinate positions. His breakthrough came in 1948 when he became First Secretary of the Sofia City Committee, and simultaneously, a member of the party Central Committee. From this time, his rise was more rapid. He became an alternate member of the Politburo in 1950 and a member of the Secretariat. A year later, he was admitted to full Politburo membership. Thus, when Chervenkov came under attack in 1954 as a Stalinist, Zhivkov was able to move into the position of First Secretary of the Central Committee, a position he held until November 1989.

Zhivkov's rapid rise after 1948 would indicate that he got his start as Chervenkov's protégé, and his actions after 1954 would bear that out. It was not until Chervenkov had been further demoted in 1956 that Zhivkov made his own bid for greater power: in 1957 he increased his control by removing some of his opponents, but it was not until 1962 that he consolidated his position by taking the additional title of Chairman of the Council of Ministers (Premier). At the same time, he severed his last connection with Cher-

venkov and had him dismissed from the government. The break apparently was over foreign policy—Zhivkov favored closer relations with Yugoslavia and, in general, wanted to bring Bulgarian foreign policy closer into alignment with Soviet foreign policy under Khrushchëv. After Chervenkov's dismissal, Zhivkov publicly endorsed Soviet policies in the Cuban missile crisis of 1961, made moves toward establishment of better relations with Yugoslavia and totally supported the Soviet Union in its disputes with China.

One of the problems Zhivkov also had to face was the trend toward a more relaxed and liberal leadership which had started prior to the time he became Premier. Detention camps had been closed, and limits were placed on the secret police. Writers and scholars were given more freedom to express their views—in some cases this new freedom was used to criticize the government. But Zhivkov's position was not secure enough to tolerate such criticism. He had eliminated his rivals from the top level of the party, but was still faced with the opposition of lesser members who had been supporters of Chervenkov.

Other problems were created by popular discontent with a shortage of food, consumer goods and housing. Economic reform was needed to stifle criticism, but it would have met with opposition from the "dogmatists" and those who profited from the present set-up. Zhivkov's only alternative was to end the brief period of liberalization and to reimpose restrictions. Even though this was a step backwards, it was not a return to the repressive atmosphere of the Stalinist days. Meanwhile,

Zhivkov tried to shore up his own position by tying himself closely to his Soviet benefactor, Khrushchëv. When Khrushchëv lost power in November 1964, Zhivkov's position became precarious and his gestures of loyalty toward the new Soviet leadership could not disguise the loss of support which he experienced at this time.

A few months later the inner turmoil of Bulgaria was underlined by the most unusual event in its postwar history. In April 1965 a plot to overthrow the government was discovered in Sofia. The *coup* had been planned for the April 14 meeting of the Politburo, at which time the plotters intended to arrest leading party members and to occupy important areas to prevent Soviet military action within Bulgaria.

The plot was discovered by Soviet military spies and the *coup* was quickly prevented. It was not until mid–May, however, that the Bulgarians received their first official explanation of the plot. It was declared to be an unimportant event caused by a small group of pro–Chinese plotters. This was not the case—the conspirators were not insignificant people but were former World War II freedom fighters, Bulgarian communists, high– ranking army officers and top–level party members. It is probable that they wanted to remove Zhivkov in the hope that a new leadership would bring a new course of independence for Bulgaria in its relations with the Soviet Union.

After the attempt failed, one member of the Central Committee of the party committed suicide, others were tried secretly and there was the usual purge of anyone with questionable loyalty. There was a renewed pledge of allegiance to the Soviet Union.

Perhaps shaken by the events of 1965, Zhivkov initiated a series of reforms, particularly in the area of the economy. These were designed to allow some decentralization of decision–making, but they were so strenuously opposed by the entrenched bureaucracy and conservatives they were phased out in mid–1968. Although he had initiated them, Zhivkov's support was never more than half–hearted, so it did not reflect adversely on him when they were discontinued.

Zhivkov continued as Chairman of the Council of Ministers until 1971 when a new constitution created the position of President of the State Council. When Zhivkov gave up his previous position, it went to Stanko Todorov and Zhivkov was named *President of the State Council*. This relieved Zhivkov of many day–to–day duties connected with running the government, but still gave him a government post as titular head of state. Todorov was subsequently replaced as Chairman of the Council of Ministers by Grisha Filipov, who continued to hold that position until 1986.

By this time, Zhivkov was 75 and the Bulgarian Politburo had gotten old along with the Secretary General. The example of Gorbachëv's significant personnel changes since coming to power a year earlier began to create strong pressure on Zhivkov to step down and allow a new generation of leadership to take over. As a result, a significant reshuffle occurred among Bulgaria's senior government and party leaders, though Zhivkov managed to retain his own hold on power.

Grisha Filipov retired as Chairman of the Council of Ministers and was replaced by Georgi Atanasov. One Politburo member and one candidate member were retired and four younger men—all combining strong party credentials with technical backgrounds—were added. This was accompanied by a streamlining of the government, including the elimination of six ministries.

Atanasov, the new Chairman of the Council of Ministers, was still in his forties and the government which he then headed was both distinctly younger and better–educated than the previous regime.

The Party Congress which took place in April 1986 was a low–keyed affair with no significant additional changes. Zhivkov was reelected to another five–year term. There were no changes made in either the Politburo or Secretariat, though there was a fairly significant turnover in membership on the Central Committee. About 80 out of 250 members were retired and replaced by younger individuals from the city and regional party organizations.

The Congress also created a new "Economic Council," with the delegated authority to make decisions which would have the force of actions decreed by the Council of Ministers. This Economic Council apparently took the place of the six recently abolished ministries. It was thus a part of the streamlining of government that Zhivkov began emphasizing in January 1986.

In January 1988, the *Bulgarian Communist Party* held a special party conference whose purpose, according to advance reports, was to discuss the progress of *perestroika* in Bulgaria. What was outlined was a relatively cautious approach to reform modeled closely on developments in the Soviet Union. Enterprises were to operate under a form of self–management with the right to set prices, salaries and production goals, but all of this would be within general guidelines set in Sofia. There was also a suggestion that terms of office of higher party officials might be limited, though implementation was not to begin until the next party congress in 1991.

A new political shake–up of sorts occurred in July 1988 when Zhivkov ousted three men from the Politburo who had been strong supporters of reform. It appears that Zhivkov might also have been concerned about his own political survival, however, for one of those removed, Chudomir Alexandrov, a young technocrat in the mold of Gorbachëv, had been tipped by many as the next leader of the party. In any case, the result, according to Stephen Ashley, head of Bulgarian research at Radio Free Europe, was "to reduce the Politburo to a tight clique of former partisans and Zhivkov's long–standing proteges."

In spite of Zhivkov's purge, pressure for change continued to build within the country. Domestically, Bulgarian industrialization had brought into existence a significant and growing "middle" class—of technicians, engineers, teachers, doctors, and other better educated individuals— who wanted a larger role in decision-making and resented the interference of political operatives in their areas of expertise. Internationally, the Bulgarians had always looked to the Soviet Union for leadership and so were inevitably affected by the wave of changes occurring there. Actually, Zhivkov's own first reaction was to go along with Moscow's reforms and for a while *glasnost* and *perestroika* became the new watchwords in Bulgaria. Local newspapers were suddenly filled with unprecedented debates and "independent associations" were authorized by law.

But when a human–rights group was formed to monitor human rights abuses, Zhivkov considered this to be too great a challenge. Moving to isolate the group, he expelled those who happened also to be members of the *Bulgarian Communist Party*. Another leading communist, Svetlin Rusev, lost his seat on the Central Committee when he organized and independent environmental committee to protest pollution in the city of Ruse.

Perhaps the greatest challenge came in November 1988 when a group of 100 leading intellectuals formed the "Club for the Support of *Perestroika* and *Glasnost*." Once again, Zhivkov reacted by arresting the leaders and expelling them from the party. In effect, Zhivkov had rejected *glasnost* and *perestroika* and opted for repression and the status quo. While pleasing some people, such actions alienated intellectuals and set the stage for Zhivkov's own eventual departure.

That came in November 1989 in a palace coup organized by Zhivkov's Foreign and Defense Ministers, in a sort of counterpoint to the revolutionary ferment then sweeping across Eastern Europe. Petar Mladenov, the man who engineered the coup, had been Zhivkov's Foreign Minister for the previous 19 years. Over the years, he had kept his mouth shut and was awarded by promotions that eventually put him in the Politburo. After Gorbachëv launched his policy of *perestroika*, however, Mladenov became attracted to the new ideas, and in particular as they applied in the international arena.

Increasingly, however, he found his efforts frustrated by actions Zhivkov was taking for domestic reasons. Thus, in May 1989, only four months after Mladenov had signed a new international human rights accord in Vienna, Zhivkov launched a new campaign encouraging the emigration of ethnic Turks. Then when Mladenov organized a 35–nation environmental conference in Sofia in October and invited an independent Bulgarian group, *Eco–Glasnost*, to participate, Zhivkov had his secret police rough up *Eco–Glasnost* members in a Sofia park. Mladenov was embarrassed and his attempt to polish up Bulgaria's image was largely negated.

Mladenov first submitted his resignation and, when it was not accepted, he decided that Zhivkov had to go. Cautiously, he began sounding out other Politburo members. This brought a promise of support from Dobri Dzhurov, the Defense Minister. Dzhurov, a World War II partisan colleague of Zhivkov and longtime Politburo member, had been revolted for years by Zhivkov's behavior and incessant efforts to advance the career of his son, Vladimir. His support was particularly important because he could guarantee the loyalty of the army. Mladenov also got promises of support from Georgi Atanasov, the Chairman of the Council of Ministers, and Andrei Lukanov, the Minister for Foreign Economic Relations.

Meanwhile, a wave of change was beginning to sweep across Eastern Europe and this strengthened Mladenov's case even further. Even Zhivkov realized by this time that some concessions were nec-

# Bulgaria

essary. In a statement published in the party newspaper on October 29, Zhivkov conceded the failure of earlier Bulgarian reform efforts and promised to introduce changes along Soviet lines. He had very little credibility left by that time, however.

The pivotal Politburo meeting took place on November 9. Mladenov made a motion calling for Zhivkov's resignation and proposing himself as General Secretary. He won on a vote of five to four. The next day, Gorbachëv put his stamp of approval on the change by sending Mladenov a highly complimentary, congratulatory message.

One of Mladenov's first actions as General Secretary was to reinstate 11 former party members who had been purged because of their membership in a dissident organization called the *Independent Discussion Club for the Support of Glasnost and Perestroika.* He followed this up with a statement pledging support for greater diversity and promising that, in the future, street rallies by anti–Government groups would be allowed. That same week, *Eco–Glasnost* was granted official recognition, making it a legal organization.

Mladenov next called a meeting of the Central Committee for November 16. Here, Zhivkov and three of his supporters were removed from the Politburo, while a fourth was dropped as a Central Committee secretary. Half a dozen other men were also dismissed, including two non–voting members of the Politburo. In addition, the Central Committee recommended that Mladenov take over Zhivkov's other post as head of state.

The next day, the National Assembly met to implement the recommendation of the Central Committee. At the same time, it also repealed a law making it a crime to say anything likely "to create dissatisfaction with the government and its undertakings" and declared an amnesty for persons convicted under the old legislation. Speaking afterwards, Mladenov told the legislature that he favored political and economic restructuring and that the National Assembly "should play a democratic alternative to the administrative command system that reigned before." Later, he told journalists "personally, I am for free elections." Another interesting aspect of the proceedings was that a number of the members of the Assembly rose to give anti–Zhivkov speeches. All of this was broadcast to the nation via live television.

Mladenov clearly wanted controlled change but news of the events happening elsewhere in Eastern Europe reverberated through Bulgaria and popular demands began to mount. Mladenov visited Moscow at the beginning of December. Asked there by journalists what his reaction was to the decisions of the Czechoslovak and East German *Communist Parties* to give up

their constitutional monopoly of power, he first suggested that he would leave that up to the Bulgarian people to decide, then that, though he couldn't predict how the issue would be resolved, "I foresee changes in the Constitution."

Back in Bulgaria, popular demonstrations, which had begun occurring on an almost daily basis, grew larger in size and their demands became more far–reaching. A new, umbrella organization, the *Union for Democratic Reform,* was also formed to coordinate the actions of the opposition. Responding to these pressures, Mladenov called another meeting of the Central Committee on December 8. Six more members of the Politburo were ousted, plus 27 members of the Central Committee.

This second purge in a month only seemed to whet the appetite of the opposition. Two days later, 50,000 of them gathered for another pro–democracy rally in the middle of Sofia. All of this was fully covered by the controlled press and state television. The next day, Mladenov went on television to promise that the Communist Party's monopoly on power would be abolished and that there would be free elections in the spring. "We need to adopt the principle of a multiparty system," he said.

Mladenov's promises did not placate the opposition. On December 14, when the National Assembly took up a bill to scrap Article I of the Constitution, which guaranteed the party's leading role, 20,000 demonstrators surrounded the legislature and began shouting for an immediate end to the party's monopoly on power. When Stanko Todorov, the assembly's chairman, told them that Article I had already been suspended but could not be repealed for a month because of another constitutional provision, he was met by cries of "we do

**A newly privatized music shop**

not believe you," "resign," and "Berlin, Prague, Sofia." The next day, the Assembly unanimously passed a declaration affirming that Article I would be stricken from the constitution at its next session in January. Mladenov also announced that round–table discussions with opposition leaders would begin the following week.

In a new development, thousands of ethnics organized a mass rally against government persecution at the end of December. That same day, the Party Central Committee met and voted to reverse Zhivkov's policy of assimilation, calling it "a grave political error." Under the new policy, ethnic Turks could take back their old names and speak Turkish in public. This policy was subsequently adopted by the government. For the first time, this led to a demonstration of another sort, as thousands of anti–Turkish Bulgarian nationalists gathered outside the National Assembly chanting "Bulgaria for the Bulgarians" and demanding that the government's action be rescinded. In a curious reversal of past developments, the communists and the democratic opposition now came together to reaffirm the new policy.

When the National Assembly met on January 15, 1990 and voted to delete Article I from the constitution, the action came as a sort of anticlimax. Roundtable discussions between the communists and the opposition, a coalition of 13 new parties, movements and groups collectively referred to as the *Union of Democratic Forces,* began in January. At the beginning of February, Mladenov offered to form a coalition government with the opposition. When this offer was refused, Georgi Atanasov was replaced as Chairman of the Council of Ministers by Andrei Lukanov.

At a hastily called party congress, the party voted to change its name and to become the *Bulgarian Socialist Party.* This was accompanied by a general restructuring of the party. The old power position of General Secretary was abolished, replaced by a Chairman. In another change, the congress also endorsed the creation of an executive presidency.

These changes were voted into law by the National Assembly at the beginning of April. Mladenov was then elected President. Alexander Lilov then became the new Chairman of the *Bulgarian Socialist Party.*

Multiparty elections took place in June and they were won by the *Bulgarian Socialist Party* with almost 53% of the vote. The *UDF* got only about a third of the seats in the Assembly, with the rest going to a third party, the *Movement for Rights and Freedoms,* which represents the one million or so Turkish–speakers, plus independents. Although the socialists won in the overall vote, their main support came from the countryside. The *UDF* actually won in the urban areas. For this reason,

# Bulgaria

the *UDF* thought of themselves as having won the election, and they refused to co-operate with the socialists.

Before the socialists could get their new government installed, President Petar Mladenov came under attack for remarks he had made in December 1989 about ordering tanks to be used against the Bulgarian people. Mladenov resigned on July 6. After almost a month of stalemate, Zhelyu Zhelev, who had led the democratic opposition in the June elections, was named President by the Bulgarian Assembly. Zhelev, who had spent 17 years under house arrest under the former regime, was a compromise candidate backed by all the parties.

Meanwhile the socialists, divided between conservatives and reformers, were having difficulty getting a government organized. They first offered to form a coalition government with the *UDF*. When the opposition refused, it took the socialists three months to get their new government chosen and approved. Andrei Lukanov was reappointed Chairman of the Council of Ministers in September but his tenure turned out to be short. By November, thousands of Bulgarians were demanding his resignation. Lukanov won a vote of confidence in the Assembly, but the demonstrations continued. One issue was an unpopular austerity plan put into effect by the government and widespread shortages of food, gasoline and consumer goods, but a greater issue was a lack of confidence in a government led by an ex–communist. Lukanov finally stepped down on November 29, 1990 after the Confederation of Independent Trade Unions began a general strike aimed at forcing him out of office. His successor, Dimitar Popov, was chosen on December 7.

Popov, a non–politician who had been head of Sofia's municipal court before becoming Chairman of the Council of Ministers, was apparently selected to stand above the parties and lead a coalition government that could be supported by all factions.

Although originally considered to be a caretaker government, Popov submitted a far–reaching program in January 1991 that began moving Bulgaria toward a free market. Price controls were loosened, interest rates were increased, a new land ownership law was passed and proposals were submitted to reform the banking and tax laws and begin the privatization of state–owned enterprises. Prices rose ten-fold, interest rates soared to about 50% and unemployment began edging up. On the positive side, shop windows and market stands began filling up and food became plentiful, though things like medicines, fertilizers, toilet paper, sugar, petroleum products and pesticides remained scarce. Polls indicated that Bulgarians had become more optimistic, ap-

Enjoying a soft drink in a park along the Danube

parently convinced that their present sacrifices would pay dividends later.

New parliamentary elections were set for October 1991. In the lead up to the elections, the *Union of Democratic Forces* broke down into four factions and numerous new political parties came into being. The number of seats in the National Assembly was reduced from 400 to 240, so each candidate had to campaign in a larger constituency. A form of proportional voting was utilized, but an attempt was made to keep out fringe parties by establishing a threshold of 4% before a party would become eligible for a seat.

When the election was over, only three parties had crossed that threshold, the *UDF* with 34.36% of the vote, the *Bulgarian Socialist Party*, with 33.14% and the *Movement for Rights and Freedoms* with 7.54%. This gave the *UDF* 111 seats, the *BSP* 106 seats, and the *MDR* 23 seats. President Zhelev designated Filip Dimitrov, head of the *UDF*, to form a cabinet on November 5. Since it lacked a parliamentary majority, Dimitrov offered to form a coalition with the *MDR*. The *MDR*, an ethnic Turkish party that represents Bulgaria's Moslem population, refused to enter the cabinet but agreed to support the government in the National Assembly. In the end, the 14–member cabinet contained a number of "technicians" chosen for their expertise and belonging to no party.

Only 8 of the 14 were members of the parliament. For example, Yordan Sokolov, a Sofia lawyer with no political affiliation, was appointed Minister of the Interior.

In his beginning policy statement, Prime Minister Dimitrov set forth long and short–term goals. His long–term goal would be to replace the previous system; his short–term goal would be to stabilize the country's economy and curb inflation. His specific policies included amending

the Foreign Investment Act passed by the previous government, privatization, the reform of banking, tax reform, and amending the Land Act.

President Zhelev also managed to win a popular mandate for himself when he ran in popular elections for the presidency in January 1992, though he won only a plurality in the first round of voting and had to participate in a second round run–off. In that race, the *Socialists* supported Velko Vulkanov, while a third candidate was George Ganchev, a former fencing champion who had lived for a number of years in the United States. Zhelev got 45 percent of the vote, Vulkanov 30 percent, and Ganchev 17 percent. In the run–off, Zhelev got just under 53 percent while Vulkanov polled 47 percent.

This was the last significant victory for the *Union of Democratic Forces*, however. Although Prime Minister Dimitrov managed to make an important start on most of his short–term goals, the economic pain they engendered produced a split in the *Union of Democratic Forces*, which in turn led to the fall of his ministry later in the year.

After a period of political instability in which two previous nominees for the office failed to win a vote of confidence in the National Assembly, Lyuben Berov was installed as the new prime minister in December 1992. At the time, Berov's selection represented a widening of the governing coalition for he was nominated by the *Movement for Rights and Freedoms*, the party of the nation's one million ethnic Turks. Although he belonged to no party, Berov had previously served as an economic adviser to President Zhelev. The man named as his deputy prime minister, Yevgeny Matinchev, was, however, a member of the *Movement for Rights and Freedoms*. At this time, the government was supported

251

# Bulgaria

**The Kliment Ohridski University, Sofia.**

by the *Union of Democratic Forces*, which held 110 out of 240 seats, plus The *Movement for Rights and Freedoms*, with 24 seats. Previously, the *MRF* had refused to enter the cabinet even as it supported the government in the Assembly.

This arrangement did not last very long, however. As the *Union of Democratic Forces* continued to splinter, it appeared that the Berov government would fall. In a switch, the *Bulgarian Socialist Party*, which held 106 seats, joined with the *Movement for Rights and Freedoms* in support of the government, and it survived.

Berov remained in power through most of 1994, but stepped down and was replaced by a caretaker prime minister, Reneta Indzhova, in the lead–up to the December elections. These new parliamentary elections gave the *Bulgarian Socialist Party* an absolute majority. Their victory had been expected—the collapse of the *Union of Democratic Forces* assured that—though the margin of victory was a little more than anticipated.

Zhan Videnov, the 35 year old leader of the *Socialists*, became the new prime minister. Although Videnov was protrayed at the time as a reformer who supported the creation of a market economy and who wanted to see Bulgaria integrated into the

rest of Europe, he was actually a product of the old communist system. Groomed from an early age for leadership, he studied at Moscow's elite Institute of International Relations, then later worked in the youth organization of the *Bulgarian Communist Party*. During the campaign, the *Socialists* promised to continue restructuring the economy, though, they said, with less pain. Yet the party was badly divided over the issue. Moreover, the party had been returned to power through the votes of the pensioners and the poorer classes who opposed further change.

At the time that Videnov assumed power, Bulgaria was already in poor economic shape as a result of the years of drift. It is true that the economy had grown slightly in 1994, but inflation was already running at 122%. Moreover, there had been almost no privatization other than retail businesses, and the large, badly–run state companies required large subsidies in order to continue to exist. Yet people were optimistic, for they thought they had elected a man who could take charge and set things right.

This, however, was not so. It is not clear whether Videnov really thought in terms of reform but, if so, he was persuaded otherwise by the old guard in the party. Some

privatization did occur, to be sure, but it consisted mainly of turning over control of companies to leading ex–communists, who simply stripped them of their assets. The government also began discouraging foreign investment.

In the spring of 1995, the government even tried to turn back the clock by reintroducing collective farming. The only reason the plan did not go into effect was because President Zhelev insisted on referring it to the constitutional court. The court overruled the government, saying that the plan would have violated private property rights. After that, the government began marking time, apparently unsure what it wanted to do. Meanwhile, inflation was growing, the country's hard currency reserves were plummeting, and Western companies began pulling out of the country.

Polls now indicated that the majority of Bulgarians wanted the government to begin moving forward again on reform, but the old guard of the ruling *Socialists* became more outspoken in their opposition to any reform whatsoever. By the middle of 1996, Bulgaria was essentially bankrupt, unable to repay more that $1 billion in debts. Two prominant banks closed, 64 state–run businesses faced bankruptcy,

Bulgaria

**President Petar Stoyanov**

while a further 72 businesses were placed under strict financial supervision.

The government now agreed to a reform plan drawn up by the IMF which would have made $465 million available to meet foreign debts. By the fall of 1996, however, the arrangement with the IMF had collapsed after the government had refused to implement any real economic reforms.

This is the background to the presidential elections that took place in November. The first sign that the people were determined to bring about change came in the national primary organized by the *Union of Democratic Forces* to nominate a presidential candidate to oppose Ivan Marazov, the candidate of the *Bulgarian Socialist Party*. President Zhelyu Zhelev was challenged by Petar Stoyanov, then a little-known lawyer, and defeated, apparently because he was viewed as one of the "ins." Another, disturbing sign of the times was the assassination of Andrei Lukhanov on October 2. Although a member of parliament for the *Socialist Party*, he had been loud in his criticism of the policies of Prime Minister Videnov. His murderer has never been identified, but many believe he was killed for political reasons.

Stoyanov accused the *Socialists* of isolating Bulgaria from the rest of Europe and he argued that Bulgaria had to implement sweeping reforms such as had been so successful in Central Europe. He also said that he wanted to bring Bulgaria into the European Union and NATO. On November 3, 1996, Stoyanov was elected president with 60% of the vote.

Although the office of president is largely a ceremonial position in Bulgaria, Stoyanov's landslide victory was seen as a vote of non-confidence in the ruling *So-*

*cialists*. As a result, Videnov resigned as Prime Minister in December. At first, it appeared that the party would give him a renewed vote of confidence and he would remain in power. But public demonstrations calling for new parliamentary elections caused the *Socialists* to nominate Nikolai Dobrev as the new Prime Minister. The public demonstrations continued, however, and the political opposition also began boycotting the parliament.

Stoyanov was sworn in as president on January 22. The *Socialists* had agreed to new elections "in principle" by that time. Thus Stoyanov's call for new elections after the swearing-in ceremony was part of a negotiation which subsequently produced an agreement for a care-taker government under Stefan Sofiyansky and new parliamentary elections on April 19, 1997.

In those elections, victory went to the *Union of Democratic Forces*, which won 52.2% of the vote and 137 out of 240 seats in the legislature. The *Socialist Party* came in second with 22% of the vote, which gave them 58 seats. The remainder of the vote was divided among the *Movement for Rights and Freedoms*, an ethnic Turkish party, with 7.6% (19 seats), the *Euroleft Party*, which includes many *Socialist* dissidents, with 5.6% (14 seats), and the populist *Bulgarian Business Bloc*, with 4.9% (12 seats). Ivan Kostov, leader of the *Union of Democratic Forces*, was installed as the new Prime Minister in May.

Although the economic policies of the care-taker government of Stefan Sofiyansky had reversed the downward plunge in the economy by shutting down most of the largest money-losing state enterprises and raising energy prices to world levels, Prime Minister Kostov's government decided that additional measures would be needed to restore confidence in the econ-

omy. He therefore persuaded the Bulgarian parliament to pass a law creating a currency board within the Bulgarian National Bank in June. The law, which went into effect as of July 1, was specifically designed to prevent the National Bank from fueling inflation. The value of the Bulgarian lev was set at a ratio of 1,000 lev to one German Mark. The law also specified that the domestic currency had to be 100 percent backed by the Bulgarian National Bank's foreign reserves. In other words, the only way that the domestic money supply can be increased is by converting foreign currency inflows into domestic currency. In addition, the National Bank is forbidden to finance government budget deficits.

The concept of creating currency boards to regulate the currency is controversial among economists, but in Bulgaria's case it has had an extremely positive influence thus far. This has been recognized by Ann McGuirk, the IMF's chief representative in Bulgaria, who was quoted as saying in February 1997 that Bulgarian economic performance was "very positive" and "better than expected." That same day, Olivier Descamps, regional director of the European Bank for Reconstruction and Development, said that Bulgaria's credibility with foreign investors and bankers was "the best it has been in the past five years."

The improvement has indeed been impressive. For example, the foreign currency reserve tripled during the first hundred days of the operation of the currency board, growing to 3.8 billion German Marks. Foreign investment has also soared. In 1996, U.S. companies invested $66 million in Bulgaria; that figure soared to $410 million for the first nine months of 1997. And inflation, which reached 243

**Frigid in the valleys, hikers find the sun warm enough to run bare-chested across the snow-covered Rhodope Mountains in southern Bulgaria.** AP/Wide World Photo

253

# Bulgaria

*Bar America* in Roussé, Bulgaria's fourth largest city

percent in February 1997 alone, was 2.1 percent in January 1998. Moreover, average monthly wages have also recovered somewhat, going from $25 in February 1997 to $108 in December 1997.

The government's new economic policies have not created miracles, however. Although the economy has stabilized greatly since introduction of the currency board, GDP nevertheless declined by 7.4 percent in 1997. Moreover, although banks are flush with liquidity, they are using their funds to purchase government bonds rather than lending to enterprises. Yet another problem is that the prices of Bulgarian exports will tend to rise and the price of imports to fall if Bulgaria continues to operate under a fixed exchange rate regime and domestic inflation continues at its current rate. Thus Bulgarian goods may become less competitive at home and abroad. But these worries are only theoretical at the moment and they may produce their own remedies if the economy begins growing again.

## Foreign Policy

Bulgarians have always admired the Russian people and looked to Russia for assistance and leadership. Even after the Bulgarian Government banned a domestic communist party in 1923, it continued to maintain good diplomatic relations with the Soviet Union. When Bulgaria became a communist state after 1945, therefore, it was not surprising that the first principle of Bulgarian foreign policy be-

came loyalty to the Soviet Union. This would probably have happened regardless, because Georgi Dimitrov, the new Bulgarian leader, had been a loyal servant of Stalin since the 1920s.

After 1948, Bulgaria's traditional rivalry with Yugoslavia reinforced this orientation. Following Tito's quarrel with Stalin, Bulgaria replaced Yugoslavia as the principal country through which Soviet influence was projected in the area of the southern Balkans.

This relationship with the Soviet Union was reflected not only in Bulgaria's relations with its neighbors, but in its relations with the United States as well. As the Cold War began, Bulgaria joined the Soviet Union in making extravagant attacks on the United States. As a result, relations broken by the U.S. in 1950 were not renewed until 1959. Formal, but cool, relations continued until the 1970's, when Bulgaria became interested in exports to the United States.

The government agreed to end jamming of Voice of America radio broadcasts and also signed a consular convention which accorded greater protection for Americans in Bulgaria. Deputy Premier Ivan Popov then paid a visit to the United States in 1974 and it appeared that U.S.–Bulgarian relations would continue to improve. Then the Soviet Union renounced its trade agreement with the United States in 1975 over the issue of Jewish emigration, and the Bulgarians followed suit, abandoning their efforts to expand trade. Thereafter,

American–Bulgarian relations simply mirrored the state of American–Soviet relations. For example, when the Soviets announced a boycott of the 1984 Olympic contests in Los Angeles, Bulgaria was the very first country to indicate that it would not participate either.

The country had no diplomatic relations whatsoever with Greece until 1964. Relations then remained cool for another ten years, becoming cordial only after 1974. They were particularly good during the years of the left–wing Papandreou government.

Relations with Yugoslavia followed the pattern of Soviet–Yugoslav affairs. There has been one additional complication, however—the traditional rivalry over Macedonia. The Bulgarian Government has never recognized Macedonian as a separate nationality and on occasion it did feel called upon to speak out on behalf of "Bulgarians" living in the Yugoslav republic of Macedonia. The death of Tito in 1980 brought no change, for better or worse. The collapse of Yugoslavia in 1991 when Croatia and Slovenia seceded, coupled with the subsequent decision of the Republic of Macedonia to seek recognition as an independent country, has changed that situation. Bulgaria was one of four states that extended diplomatic recognition to the Republic of Macedonia in 1991. The Bulgarian Government still does not recognize that there is such a thing as a Macedonian "nationality," but it has recognized the existence of a Macedonian "state."

Romania is the one nation with which Bulgaria has maintained consistently friendly relations over the years. Of course, Romania was the only one of Bulgaria's neighbors that was also a member of the communist bloc. The two nations have continued to cooperate since 1989, however. At first, one factor may have been that ex–communists continued to play important political roles in both societies and both were at first denied economic assistance by the EC and the United States. Today, the important factor is that the two nations are involved in a number of joint economic projects dealing with hydroelectric works on the Danube River.

There was an evolution toward greater independence in Bulgaria's relations with the Soviet Union in the 1980s, particularly after the death of Brezhnev in November 1982. The first signs came in 1984–85 when the Soviet Union instituted a political–economic boycott of Western Europe after arms negotiation talks had failed to resolve the issue of intermediate range ballistic missiles in Europe. The Bulgarian Government, interested in obtaining new technology from Western Europe to reverse several years of declining growth rates, was unwilling to go along at first. After some pressure from the Soviet Government, it went along with a political freeze, but did everything it could to maintain its economic ties to Western Europe.

Gorbachëv's rise to power was welcomed in Bulgaria and his foreign policy of cooperation with the West found particular support. Bulgaria's Zhivkov instituted his own political opening to the West in June 1987, when he paid an official visit to the Federal Republic of Germany. Bulgaria, he told his hosts, wanted to expand its economic relations with West Germany and the European Community.

Even then, West Germany was Bulgaria's largest trading partner outside of the CMEA. Since that time, Germany has been unified, the CMEA and the Soviet Union have collapsed, and Bulgaria has lost most of its markets in eastern Europe and the former Soviet Union. Bulgaria has been granted associate membership in the European Union and it is looking to Germany and the EU as major trading partners in the future. At the same time, Bulgaria is working to create closer economic relations with the successor states to the old Soviet Union, in particular Russia and Ukraine.

## The Nature of the Regime

The Bulgarian Government is of a presidential–parliamentary type. A popularly elected president presides over the executive branch, assisted by a prime minister who is nominated by the president and confirmed by the 240 member National Assembly. The president, who is considered to be the spokesman for the nation, is responsible for general policy. He is also commander–in–chief of the armed forces. The prime minister presides over the cabinet and oversees day–to–day affairs of government. He thus is responsible for implementation of policy.

## The Economy

Bulgaria was still predominantly an agricultural society at the end of World War II. Using the Stalinist model, the government started the first of its Five Year Plans in 1949. The emphasis has always been on the industrial sector, and this has resulted in a transformation of the Bulgarian economy. Today, over three–quarters of the gross national product is attributable to either industry or construction.

In spite of this significant shift, agriculture continues to play an important role in the Bulgarian economy. Although the population has become predominantly urban, nearly one–fourth of the people are still employed in agriculture–related jobs.

Bulgaria placed a heavier emphasis on the development of agriculture than did the other Eastern European countries. Collectivization, begun in 1948, was car-

ried out more quickly than elsewhere. By 1950, 43% of the land had been collectivized; by 1960 this figure reached 100%. This is even more surprising when one considers that Bulgaria is a mountainous country and much of the land is not suitable for intensive cultivation. Extensive wineries have been established in the hills, however, and produce good wines which are reasonably priced by western standards.

Originally some 3,200 collective farms were set up, roughly corresponding to the number of villages in the country. These were then merged into 930 economic units beginning in 1960. A further consolidation began in 1969 when Bulgaria launched what it termed Agro–industrial complexes *(AICS)*. The *AICs* became the model for subsequent Soviet experiments of this same nature. There were 281 such *AICs* in the country and they had their own factories for the processing of the harvests.

After the victory of parties committed to creation of a market economy in the October 1991 elections, the government launched a new economic program which

included liquidation of the *AICs*. In a two–step process, peasants were granted immediate ownership of the private plots they cultivated under communism, while the remainder of the land was made available for their use on a temporary basis. A complicated land reform law has resulted in over 1.7 million conflicting claims, however, so thus far less than ten percent of the remaining land has been privatized. As a result, the average size of the private plots is less than 3 acres. Meanwhile, since the remaining land has been transferred on a temporary basis only, it cannot be used for collateral or be sold.

The situation in industry is in many ways worse than that of agriculture. Almost all of Bulgaria's industry was created after World War II and it consists mainly of large monopoly units which have always operated on the basis of orders from Sofia. Many were created specifically to produce goods for export to the Soviet Union or other members of the Council for Mutual Economic Assistance (CMEA). In 1989, over 80 percent of Bulgaria's foreign trade was carried on with other member

**Picking roses near Karlovo—which starts before dawn. Some 2,000 rose petals are needed to produce a single gram of attar, an essential oil in making perfume.**

# Bulgaria

**From exciting skiing in the Rhodope Mountains ...**

states of the CMEA. Most of those markets have since evaporated with the collapse of communism in Eastern Europe and the disintegration of the CMEA. The disarray in the Soviet economy has been particularly painful for Bulgaria, since over 50 percent of Bulgaria's foreign trade was with that country alone. The situation has become even worse since January 1, 1991, when all CMEA trade began to be expressed in dollars. The Soviet Union, short of hard currency, canceled 70 percent of its Bulgarian orders. One example of how these events effected the Bulgarian economy can be seen by looking at the individual case of Balkancar, a manufacturer of

electric fork lift trucks. In 1990, the company manufactured 50,000 trucks, almost all of which were exported to the Soviet Union. In 1991, it produced 29,000 trucks, and 20,000 in 1992. The company is exploring new markets in Argentina and the United States, but it is also attempting to win back its markets in the former Soviet Union by creating dealer networks in the CIS. Bankancar's recent history is typical of Bulgarian enterprises that depended on the Soviet market.

Meanwhile, although previous Bulgarian governments said that they were committed to creating a market economy in the country, they basically managed to do

so only in the area of retail trade. As of the end of 1994, only 34 enterprises classified as either medium and large had been privatized.

Under plans drawn up by the previous government, profitable state enterprises were to be turned into joint stock companies, with stock then sold to the public. Unprofitable state enterprises were to be broken up and absorbed as part of other groups. The *Bulgarian Socialist Party*, which won the December 1994 elections, partially implemented these plans, but they so were marred by wide–scale corruption that most privatized enterprises ended up in the hands of the old communist elite. When the new owners proceeded to strip the privatized exterprises of their remaining assets, a near collapse of the economy resulted, causing such a revulsion against the *Socialists* that they were effectively driven from power in early 1997.

The caretaker government of Stefan Sofiyansky, which was installed in February 1997, reversed the policies of the previous government and put an end to the downward plunge of the economy. In particular, he closed down most of the major state–owned money–losing enterprises and cut out all energy subsidies, thus forcing prices up to world market levels. That restored some of the confidence in the Bulgarian lev and caused inflation to drop drastically, from 243 percent in February to 12 percent in March.

The new government of Ivan Kostov, installed in May 1997, built on this beginning. Most importantly, he got the Bulgarian parliament to pass a law creating a currency board within the Bulgarian National Bank which made it impossible for the National Bank to continue to fuel inflation. In particular, the value of the lev was fixed at the ratio of 1,000 lev to one German Mark. Further, the National Bank was required to maintain 100 percent foreign reserves backing for all currency in circulation. The effect of these measures has been to restore confidence in the domestic currency and to reduce inflation to negligible amounts.

These moves have restored international confidence in the Bulgarian economy and this, in turn, has led to increased foreign investment. For example, U.S. investment went from $66 million for all of 1996 to $410 million for the first nine months of 1997. The international financial institutions have also resumed lending to Bulgaria. The IMF provided a $320 million loan in 1997, while the World Bank provided $100 million and the European Union $250 million.

The government has also begun a policy of privatization aimed at completing Bulgaria's transition to a market economy. Many banks have already been privatized with international bankers playing a leading role. Several large privatization deals have also been signed with foreign investors.

It should be emphasized that, although the new government has stabilized the economy, the country remains in deep recession. Again, average monthly wage rates grew from their nadir of $25 a month in February 1997 to approximately $108 a month in December 1997. Yet average Bulgarians recall that their average monthly wage in December 1995 was $127, and they would like to see it reach that figure again fairly soon.

## Culture

Bulgaria was still mainly a peasant society when the communists came to power in 1945 and began to transform it. They got rid of the private farms and herded the peasants into either collective or state farms. Some of the traditional peasant culture died as a result, but much of it survived and is starting to reemerge. The *Bulgarian Communist Party* had greater success in the cities, though not in the way it had hoped. The workers who came to the cities to work in the new industry did abandon most of their traditional peasant ways, but the party's attempts to create communist intellectuals through its emphasis on education actually produced the new elite that overthrew the communists in 1990–91.

Religion is being accorded a greater role, and the government has become officially neutral. Anti–Turkish legislation has been withdrawn and the Turkish–speaking minority may now use Turkish in public. They have also been permitted to take back their old Turkish names. There are about a million ethnic Turks in the country, about 800,000 of whom are Muslim.

The Bulgarian Orthodox Church, which was accorded a special position even under the old regime, has begun to speak out and take a more active role. Its membership is estimated at three million. There are about 60,000 Roman Catholics in the country, plus an extremely small number of Protestants, divided up into Pentecostals, Congregationalists, Seventh–Day Adventists, Methodists and Baptists. There are also several other identifiable minority groups—about 250,000 Macedonians with smaller numbers of Gypsies, Armenians and Albanians.

## The Future

The economic situation in Bulgaria is beginning to look brighter as the government of Prime Minister Ivan Kostov, installed in power in May 1997, implements policies designed to restore confidence in the government and the economy. The currency has been stabilized, privatization is proceeding apace, and international investors and lending agencies are once again looking at Bulgaria with favor. Although personal incomes have recovered somewhat from their nadir in February 1997, the country is still in recession. It may be several years before ordinary Bulgarians really begin feeling good about themselves again.

**. . . to the sandy beaches and warm waters of the Black Sea.**

# The Czech Republic

From the heights above Prague's Vltava River, the Czech capital's medieval heritage comes into full splendor

Photo by Jon Markham Morrow

**Area:** 78,742 sq. km. = 30,441 sq. mi.
**Population:** 10.4 million.
**Capital City:** Prague (Pop. 1,206,098).
**Climate:** Continental, with lower temperatures in the higher elevations of the north.
**Neighboring Countries:** The Federal Republic of Germany (West); Poland (North); Slovak Republic (East); Austria (South).
**Official Language:** Czech.
**Other Principal Tongues:** Slovak, German.
**Ethnic Background:** Slav.
**Principal Religions:** Roman Catholic (39%), Protestant (4.6%), Orthodox (3%), Atheist (37%), Other (16.2%) .
**Chief Commercial Products:** Machinery and equipment, coal, aromatic oils, energy ores, metals, consumer goods.
**Currency:** Czech Koruna (crown).
**Annual Per Capita Income:** About U.S. $3,000.
**Former Status:** Part of the Austro–Hungarian Empire until 1918 (ruled from Vienna); Part of Czechoslovakian Republic, 1918–1938; Part of Nazi Germany, 1939–45 (incorporated into the Third Reich as Bohemia and Moravia); Part of Communist–influenced Czechoslovakian Republic, 1945–48; Communist State, 1948–89; Part of democratic Czech and Slovak Federal Republic, 1990–1992.
**National Day:** The Czech Republic has two national days, May 8 (Liberation Day) and October 28 Foundation of the Czechoslovak Republic in 1918).
**Chief of State:** Vaclav Havel, President of the Republic.
**Head of Government:** Josef Tosovsky, Prime Minister (Interim caretaker until June 1998 elections).
**National Flag:** White and red horizontal stripes with a blue triangle extending from the staff to the center of the flag.

## THE LAND AND THE PEOPLE

The Czech Republic is the modern successor state to that ancient region known as Bohemia and Moravia. Most of the countryside consists of rolling hills except for the Sudeten Mountains in the north, where individual peaks rise to over 5,000 feet. Although most of the land is suitable for cultivation, there are extensive forest areas, the largest being the Bohemian Forest, located in the west along the border with the Federal Republic of Germany.

The Czech Republic is today almost exclusively inhabited by ethnic Czechs, except for a tiny remnant of German–speakers in the western part of the country, left over after the mass expulsions that followed World War II. In addition, the dissolution of the Czech and Slovak Federal Republic in January 1993 left approximately 300,000 Slovaks living in the Czech Republic. Most of these are individuals from rural parts of Slovakia who came west seeking employment. They are mainly to be found in industrial areas in the eastern part of the Czech Republic. With employment opportunities scarce in Slovakia and with many married to local Czech girls, they are likely to be a permanent part of the population.

## HISTORY

### Ancient Kingdoms

In the early centuries of the Christian era, a sub–group of the Slavs, subsequently to be known as the West Slavs settled in the area to the south of the Carpathian and Sudeten Mountains and along the Vltava and Danube Rivers. According to the

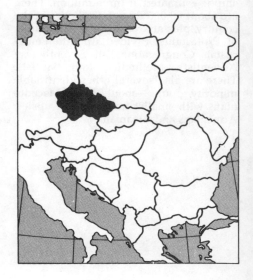

# Czech Republic

Frankish chronicle of Fredegar, they were organized into a unified state at the beginning of the 7th century by a Frankish trader named Samo. This first state collapsed at Samo's death in 658, however, and the West Slavs reverted back to their tribal form of government. It was not until the ninth century that the West Slavs were again brought together under a single government with the establishment of the Moravian Empire.

It was also at about this time that Christianity was introduced into the area. The first missionaries were Roman Catholic monks and they came mainly from Germany. The language which they used for church services was Latin. Somewhat later, the Moravian king, learning of missionary efforts among the South Slavs, requested missionaries from Constantinople. Two young monks, Cyril and Methodius, came to Moravia and, following Eastern Orthodox practices, began teaching the Slavs in their own language. In the process, they developed a script, later known as Cyrillic, to write the Slavic language. Cyrillic eventually became the basis for the written languages of the eastern and southern Slavs, though for historical reasons not of the Czechs. The reason is that, although the two brothers had great success in converting the people, they were ultimately unable to supplant the western missionaries backed by Rome. After Methodius's death in 885, the Latin form of Catholicism became predominant and the area came under the sway of Rome. As a result, written Czech uses Roman rather than Cyrillic characters.

At the end of the 9th century, the Moravian Empire came under attack from groups of Magyar peoples moving into the area from the east. According to Czech historians, the Magyars "drove a wedge" between the western and southern Slavs, and also separated the Czechs from the Slovaks. In the process, the Moravian Empire disintegrated. By the beginning of the 10th century, the center of Czech development moved westward into what is called Bohemia, while the Slovak lands began a thousand-year period under the Hungarian crown.

The old Moravian Empire was replaced by the Kingdom of Bohemia, ruled by the Princes of the Premyslid Dynasty, who became powerful in the tenth century. One of the members of this family was the legendary "Good King Wenceslas" (also known as St. Wenceslas). He was murdered by his brother, who took the throne as Boreslav I. Boreslav I brought much of the former Moravian Empire under his rule but later, under the continued harassment of the Magyars, he agreed to bring the Kingdom of Bohemia into the Holy Roman Empire. Although the Holy Roman Emperor recognized the right of the

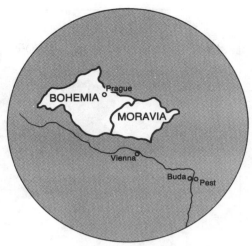

**Moravia and Bohemia ca. 1360**

Bohemian nobles to elect their own ruler who would be the highest authority in Bohemia, there was a substantial German migration into Bohemia and Moravia after this and German influence grew steadily.

Nevertheless, a new line of Czech rulers that came to power in the mid-fourteenth century began to reverse this trend somewhat, even managing to assert a growing influence over neighboring states. The "golden age" of Czech history occurred under Charles IV, the King of Bohemia who also became the Holy Roman Emperor. For a generation, Prague became the capital of the Holy Roman Empire. Deter-

mined to make his capital worthy of its imperial status, Charles IV supported the construction of new palaces and churches. He was also responsible for founding Prague's great Charles University and for the still-standing, famous Charles Bridge across the Vltava River.

The fourteenth century also saw the beginnings of a movement for church reform in Bohemia. Though couched in religious language, the movement was primarily a reaction against the extensive landholdings of the Roman Church and the dominant role of Germans in religious and political matters. This was also the period of the Great Schism, when two separate popes, one in Rome and one in Avignon, each claimed to be the one true pope. John Hus, the young preacher who led the reform movement, criticized the papacy and accused the clergy of being corrupt. Echoing ideas expressed earlier by John Wycliffe in England, he also maintained that the Bible is the sole authority for Christians, not the teachings of the Church. The Council of Constance, called to heal the breach in the church and end the Great Schism, rejected Wycliffe's and Hus's teachings and ordered Hus to appear before them to answer charges of heresy. Hus, receiving a promise of safe conduct from Sigismund, the Holy Roman Emperor, traveled to Constance to defend his positions. Upon his arrival, the Council, refusing to meet with him, condemned him to death. Sigismund then withdrew his safe conduct and Hus was burned at the stake in 1415.

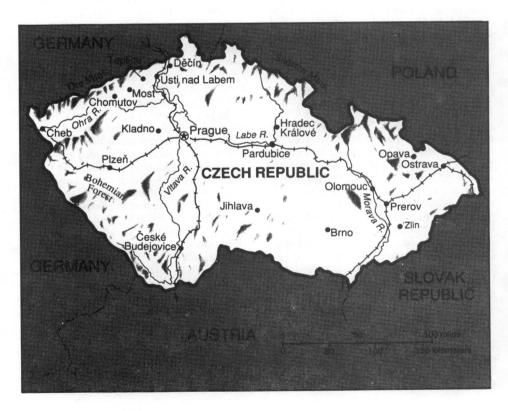

259

# Czech Republic

Hus became a martyr even to those Czechs who had not been his followers—a national hero who died at the hands of the Germans. Thus when Sigismund attempted to succeed to the Bohemian throne after the death of the Czech king in 1419, he set off the Hussite Wars, which were to last from 1420 to 1436. Although the wars were fought in the name of religion, they had great political and social overtones as well and, in that sense, were an expression of Czech nationalism. The conflict was complicated by the fact that the Hussites were sometimes divided among themselves and in 1434 even waged war against each other. Ultimately, however, the Hussites prevailed, and the Church signed a separate agreement with them, allowing them to retain Hussite rituals in return for their acknowledging the pope as head of the church.

## Part of the Multi–National Hapsburg Empire

This agreement failed to endure, however, partly because the more radical Hussites were repressed and partly because the Czech Catholic nobility resisted the treaty terms during the following decades. In 1462, the Pope declared the agreement invalid and requested King Mathias of Hungary to send in troops to enforce his decision. With the support of Czech Catholics, Bohemia was then incorporated into the Hungarian Kingdom. Hungarian rule continued until 1526 when the last Hungarian king was killed at the battle of Mohacs and the crown passed to Ferdinand of Hapsburg. Since Bohemia was included among the possessions of the Hungarian crown, Ferdinand was "elected" King of Bohemia as well. In 1547, the right of the Czech nobles to elect their king was abolished and the Crown of St. Wenceslas became the hereditary property of the House of Hapsburg.

Conflict between the predominantly Protestant Czechs and their Roman Catholic kings continued during the next decades. Although the Protestants were able to obtain promises from their Hapsburg rulers allowing freedom of worship, they continued to fear persecution. The situation was further exacerbated when Calvinism began to spread into Bohemia.

Conflict erupted in May 1618 after two Protestant churches were closed. Angry Protestant leaders then stormed Prague Castle and, in an act since known as the "Defenestration of Prague," tossed the two royal governors out of a castle window. According to tradition, they landed on a dung–heap and were unhurt.

The Czech nobility then met and deposed the Hapsburg ruler and, reclaiming their ancient electoral rights, named Frederick, Elector of the Palatinate, as King of Bohemia. Frederick was both a Calvinist and the head of the Protestant Union of

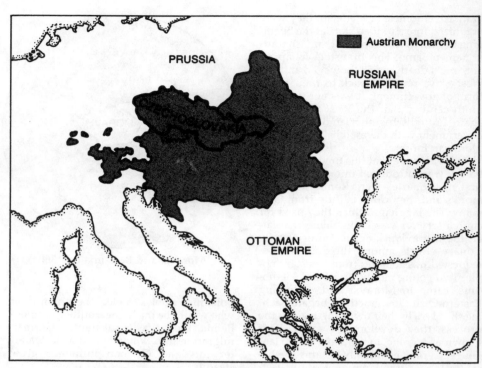

**The Austrian monarchy ca. 1793 (showing pre–1993 Czechoslovakia)**

German Princes. This was, therefore, a direct challenge to Hapsburg power and marked the beginning of the *Thirty Years' War*. Frederick is known to history as the "winter king," for he retained the Bohemian crown only briefly, being defeated in 1620 by a Hapsburg army at the battle of White Mountain.

After the Hapsburgs reclaimed the Bohemian Crown, they decided to put an end to all dissent within the kingdom. The leaders of the revolution were executed and other suspected opponents had their property confiscated. More than 30,000 families, including members of the Czech nobility, fled from the terror that gripped Bohemia at this time. The Czechs thus lost an important part of their national leadership. In addition, Roman Catholicism was imposed and German was accorded equal status with Czech. Publications were censored and books were burned. The Hapsburgs first reasserted their hereditary claims to the Bohemian Crown, then went further and abolished the Bohemian Government entirely. The Bohemian lands were governed by a separate administration located in Vienna until 1749.

The Thirty Years' War ended with the Peace of Westphalia in 1648. During the century that followed, there was a large–scale migration of German peasants into traditionally Czech lands, and this was accompanied by a gradual process of Germanization in education, in culture and in urban life.

In 1749, Maria Theresa abolished the separate Bohemian administration and merged Bohemia and Austria into a single

state. Although it thus lost the last shadow of a separate political existence, the tariff union that followed shortly afterwards, between Bohemia, Moravia and Austria, benefited Bohemia economically, as it quickly became the most industrially–developed part of the Empire.

Joseph II (1765–90), who succeeded Maria Theresa, introduced a series of other changes and reforms, whose chief result was to increase the number of German government officials and to create a secret police. On the other hand, Joseph II's policy of religious toleration led to a decrease in the influence of the Catholic Church. This period also marked the beginning of a period of Czech cultural revival.

The French Revolution and the Napoleonic era that followed it had a major effect on the power of the Hapsburgs, but Bohemia remained largely unaffected. The period of relative tranquility that set in after the fall of Napoleon was misleading, however. As the industrial revolution spread to Bohemia in the first half of the nineteenth century, it brought a prosperity that encouraged the growth of a new Czech nationalism. Thus while the Hapsburg rulers devoted their energies to maintaining themselves and other royalty in power throughout Europe, their position was being undermined at home.

When rioting erupted in Paris in February 1848 and then spread to Berlin and Vienna, Prague also exploded in turmoil. On March 11, an assembly in Prague demanded freedom of the press, equality of languages, a legislature to represent the

# Czech Republic

Czech people, and the abolition of serfdom. In June, the first Pan–Slav Congress assembled in Prague. It was dominated by Francis Palacky, a Bohemian historian who believed that Czechs could find freedom and remain within the empire at the same time.

While the Congress was meeting, riots broke out against the commander of the Austrian forces in Prague. He suppressed the revolutionary movement, and set up a military dictatorship. Moderate Czechs continued to press for a new constitution, but to no avail. Order was now restored throughout the empire under a centralized, absolutist regime.

The creation of the "dual" monarchy in 1867 provided for a national legislature for the Austrian part of the Austro–Hungarian Empire, and gave Czechs representation at Vienna for the first time. Between 1867 and World War I, Czech nationalists used this new forum to demand self–government within the Austro–Hungarian Empire. The goal of independence was not actively pursued until the fortunes of the war presented the opportunity to sever the centuries–old domination of Austria. Attainment of this goal was helped by an extensive propaganda campaign carried on by Czech people living in Paris and in the United States.

### Birth of an Independent Czecho–Slovak State

The first direct contribution to independence was made by the thousands of Czech—and Slovak—soldiers who refused to fight with the armies of the Central Powers during World War I, choosing instead to surrender to the Russians. These prisoners of war formed a special force, the Czecho–Slovak Legion, which then fought on the side of the Russians against Germany and Austria.

When the Russian *Bolsheviks* (communists) signed the Treaty of Brest–Litovsk, taking Russia out of the war with Germany, the western allies suggested the transfer of the legions to the western front by way of Siberia and Japan. They became briefly involved in the Russian Civil War, after the Bolsheviks attempted to disarm them. Seizing control of the Trans–Siberian Railroad, they made their way eastward through Siberia to Japan.

Although Bohemia remained under Austrian control during World War I, a Czech National Council started to function in early 1916. Located in Paris and composed of such leading personalities as Thomas G. Masaryk, Eduard Benes, and Milan Stefanik, it maintained contact with a resistance organization, the "Mafia," back in Bohemia.

The Council's goal, which was close to being achieved by mid–1918, was to win support for the creation of an independent Czechoslovak state. Masaryk was instrumental in gaining American support for this cause. His wife was Charlotte Garrigue, an American, and this gave him connections he would have otherwise not have had. Two documents signed in America would be of historic importance in laying the basis for the future Czechoslovak state. The Pittsburgh Agreement, signed on June 30, 1918, expressed Slovak support for the union of Czech and Slovak lands in return for the promise that Slovakia would have considerable independence within the new state. The Philadelphia Agreement, signed in October by Masaryk and the leader of American Ruthenians, promised autonomy for Ruthenia, the ethnic Ukrainian part of prewar Czechoslovakia (now a part of the Ukraine).

A National Committee representing three parties, the *National Democrats, Agrarians* and *National Socialists*, was set up in Prague in July 1918. This Committee, headed by Karel Kramar, proclaimed the Independent Czechoslovak State on October 28, 1918. Two days later, the Slovak *National Council* voted to be part of the proclaimed state. The *Central National Council of the Ruthenians* opted to become part of Czechoslovakia on May 8, 1919.

### The First Czechoslovak Republic 1918–1939

The frontiers of the Czechoslovakian state were drawn during 1918–1919, partly as a result of military action and partly by the decisions of the post–war peace conference between the major powers. The borders between the Czechs and Poles, and between the Slovaks and Hungarians, were contested. The final settlements resulted in confusing and potentially troublesome borders. A large number of Hungarians were included in Slovak territory and a number of Slovaks resided in Hungary.

The resulting Czechoslovakian state included minorities of Poles and Hungarians as well as about three million Germans, living mainly in northern and western Bohemia. Denied the status of one of the "state" peoples, the Germans tended to become culturally identified with Germany during the period that followed World War I. They participated fully in Czechoslovak politics, however, and were represented by several political parties.

The Czechs, who dominated the national government, had their problems with other ethnic groups as well. Slovaks, in particular, not only felt excluded from the political process but were concerned about their cultural integrity as well. Throughout the interwar period there were a number of differences that divided the Czechs and the Slovaks. The conflicts centered on the form and concept of the Czechoslovakian nation. The Czechs were more advanced industrially than the Slovaks and, being in the majority, Czech civil servants dominated the government. The Slovaks insisted that the term "Czechoslovak nation" was no more than a cover–up for Czech–dominated centralization of government.

However, the problem was even more complex—Slovak political leaders who favored a decentralized government joined with Czechs in urging a single Czechoslo-

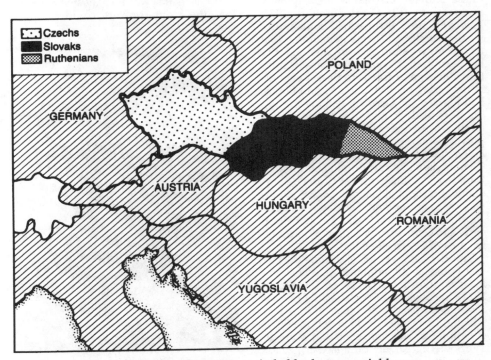

**Czechoslovakia, 1918–1938, encircled by hungry neighbors**

# Czech Republic

vak nation. Slovaks opposed to this even asserted that they had the right to secede from Czechoslovakia.

Ruthenia presented another problem. Czechs were willing to concede that they were a separate people, but they refused to grant them the self–government that they thought they had been promised. The problem was its strategic location. Backward and inhabited by poverty–stricken peasants, Ruthenia nevertheless enabled the nation to have a border with Romania, an important ally.

In spite of these problems, the Czechoslovak Republic was an economically developed country with a democratic pattern of government. Political parties represented a wide range of outlooks. The Communist Party was legal throughout the years of the republic and claimed a substantial following. Although the government was a coalition of parties, the Agrarian Party was continuously a part of the government after 1922.

Stability was also provided by the top political leadership. Masaryk, Czechoslovakia's first president, was reelected in 1927 and 1934. When he died in 1935, he was succeeded by Eduard Benes, who had been Foreign Minister since 1918.

Benes' policy as foreign minister had been directed toward encouraging strict observance of the Treaty of Versailles. He formed alliances with Romania and Yugoslavia. Later, he turned first to France and then to the Soviet Union among the major powers.

Domestically, government relations with ethnic Germans deteriorated badly during the last several years before 1938. These Sudeten Germans had originally pressed for political autonomy. By 1938, however, most of them had come under Nazi influence and were demanding that territories where they were in a majority be permitted to join Germany. Hitler threw his open support to these demands in the spring of 1938. England and France had rejected the German demand in May, but were ready to give in to Hitler by September. Mussolini now proposed a four–power conference to resolve the matter. Hitler and Mussolini, plus Prime Minister Chamberlain of Great Britain and Premier Daladier of France, met at Munich, Germany, at the end of September. Czechoslovakia was not invited. Seeking a solution short of war, France and Great Britain agreed to German annexation of the Sudeten area of Czechoslovakia.

This decision was made despite the fact that France had guaranteed Czechoslovakia's borders by a treaty of alliance in 1924. The Soviet Union also had a mutual assistance pact with Czechoslovakia which it had signed in 1935, but the Soviet Union was not represented at Munich. The Soviet agreement promised armed assistance if France also fulfilled its commit-

**President Thomas G. Masaryk**

ment. As a result of the Munich Pact, Germany occupied some 10,000 square miles of territory inhabited by three and one–half million people, one–quarter of whom were Czechs.

President Benes accepted the pact under duress, partly because he was pressed by both France and Great Britain to do so. Czechoslovakia was thus dismembered so that the major powers could gain, in

**President Eduard Benes**

Prime Minister Chamberlain's words, "peace in our time." The four great powers guaranteed the territorial integrity of the remaining parts of Czechoslovakia, but no one did anything when Hitler announced the annexation of Bohemia and Moravia on March 15, 1939, and sent in German troops to occupy the area. Slovakia became a nominally independent state, while Ruthenia was ceded to Hungary.

### Czechoslovakia: "Divided and Reconstructed, 1939–1948"

During World War ll, many of Czechoslovakia's leaders left the country. Eduard Benes, who had resigned on October 5, 1938, became the head of the Provisional Government organized in London in 1940. Klement Gottwald and other important Czech communists sought support in Moscow. Negotiations between Benes, Gottwald, and Joseph Stalin in Moscow in March 1945 resulted in a decision to create a "national front" government, consisting of Benes' government–in–exile plus Gottwald and his communists. Benes arrived in Kosice in March 1945 and there established his new government.

This first post–war government was drawn exclusively from parties belonging to the *National Front*, consisting of four Czech and two Slovak parties. Their programmatic statement, known as the Kosice program, stipulated that Czechoslovakia's future foreign policy would have an "all–Slav" foundation and would be based on an alliance with the Soviet Union. This declaration was even more meaningful because of the territorial closeness of the Soviet Union after Ruthenia was made a part of the Soviet Ukraine.

For the next three years, Czechoslovakia was governed by the *National Front*, and functioned as a democratic nation. During this period, the Soviet Union was willing to tolerate parliamentary politics so long as the communists held the upper hand on matters of importance. Although they seized total power in February 1948, they could have done this at any time from 1945 onward, since they were the strongest party of post–war Czechoslovakia. As it was, they dominated the *National Front* through their occupancy of Deputy Premiership, plus the Ministries of Information, Interior, Agriculture and Education.

The communists received by far the largest number of votes in free elections held in 1946. By the winter of 1947–48, however, there were signs that their popular support was dropping sharply. It appeared that the communists were headed for defeat in elections set for May 1948.

The circumstances leading up to the communist *coup* began with the dismissal of eight police officers in Prague and their replacement by communists. When the

Minister of Interior refused to reinstate the non–communist officers, twelve non–communist ministers resigned in the hope that this would force new elections in which the communists would be defeated.

Instead of submitting to elections, the communists threatened to use force—a threat strengthened by the arrival of Soviet Deputy Foreign Minister Valerian Zorin in Prague. Communist "action committees" took control of newspapers and occupied the headquarters of non–communist parties. Faced with this show of strength and organization, coupled with the fear of a possible civil war, President Benes accepted a new government formed by Klement Gottwald. When Benes resigned in June 1948, Gottwald succeeded to the presidency and Antonin Zapotocky became premier.

Jan Masaryk, son of Thomas G. Masaryk, had been Foreign Minister under Benes. At the time of the *coup*, he was reported to have committed suicide by leaping from a high window of a government building to a stone courtyard below. In 1989, after the fall of the communist regime, it was officially confirmed that he was pushed.

## Czechoslovakia Becomes a People's Republic

After the 1948 coup, Czechoslovakia was a faithful ally of the Soviet Union, imitating the Stalinist pattern of rule at home and supporting Soviet policies abroad. As in other East European communist countries, a series of purges occurred between 1949 and 1954, aimed at cleansing the party of individuals who might have a greater loyalty to nationalism than to communism. Both Vladimir Clementis, Foreign Minister, and Rudolf Slansky, Secretary General of the Czechoslovak Communist Party, were among eleven victims hanged in 1952 after having been found guilty of "Titoism" and "nationalist deviation."

The death of Joseph Stalin in the Soviet Union in 1953, followed by Gottwald's a few days later, brought no visible change to the government. This was because the domestic scene was stable—economic growth and an increase in the standard of living made for a relatively placid population. In the party, because no single individual was able to assume all of Gottwald's authority, there began a period of collective rule. Antonin Zapotocky, who had been Premier since 1948, succeeded to the Presidency—the dominant political position within the Czechoslovak system—while Antonin Novotny became party leader. Reflecting a change also carried out in the Soviet Union at this time, Novotny's title was downgraded to First Secretary.

The denunciation of Stalin by Soviet leader Nikita Khrushchev in 1956, plus the neighboring Hungarian revolution of the same year, failed to bring any substantial changes. The communist leadership of Czechoslovakia, rendered more monolithic by purges, remained Stalinist even after his death.

President Zapotocky died in 1957 and was succeeded by Antonin Novotny who, however, retained his position as First Secretary of the *Czechoslovak Communist Party*. Novotny's succession to the Presidency thus marked the beginning of his political ascendancy and, since Novotny was no reformer, a further period of Stalinist rule in Czechoslovakia.

Novotny distinguished himself by opposing nearly every proposal for political innovation and resisting any move toward de–Stalinization within Czechoslovakia. Almost alone among the members of the Communist bloc, Czechoslovakia continued to have political prisoners left over from the Stalinist purges of the early 1950s.

One symbol of the Novotny era became a huge statue of Stalin, erected in 1955 on an embankment overlooking the Vltava River in Prague. The statue survived Khrushchev's 1956 de–Stalinization campaign and even the 1961 decision of the 21st Party Congress to remove Stalin's body from the mausoleum on Red Square. It was finally taken down in October 1962.

Perhaps Novotny's proudest achievement was the new constitution which he pushed through in 1960. According to its terms, Czechoslovakia had become the second country—after the USSR—to make the transition to "Socialist Republic." Since the name was identical to that of the individual Soviet republics, it has even been suggested that Novotny had in mind the incorporation of Czechoslovakia into the USSR.

Novotny's troubles began after 1960. Domestically, there was a growing intellectual ferment that was pressing for greater cultural freedom while, in the economic field, industry began to show the strains of the Stalinist command model. By 1962, the situation had reached crisis proportions. The government was forced to abandon its third five year plan and to rely on make–shift annual plans for the next three years. Internationally, there was Khrushchev's continuing de–Stalinization campaign.

The events in the USSR reinforced the more liberal, reform elements in the Czech party. Rudolf Barak, Minister of the Interior and a member of this faction, was an obvious challenger to Novotny's leadership. Even the influence of events in Moscow was not sufficient to boost Barak to power as long as he lacked firmer support within the party, however. In early 1962 Barak was removed from all positions, arrested, and sentenced to fifteen years in jail for embezzlement and "conspicuous consumption," which probably meant that he had been living too luxuriously.

The removal of Barak did not end Novotny's troubles. At a party congress in Prague in 1962, the Central Committee decided to conduct an inquiry into the purges of 1949–1954. The result was a declaration that Clementis and Slansky had been wrongfully convicted.

As pressure increased on Novotny, he dismissed the top officials in Slovakia. These included Karol Bacilek, First Secretary of the *Slovak Communist Party*, and Viliam Siroky, Slovak Premier. Both men had aroused Slovak hatred because of their support for Prague's policies of centralization. Siroky was replaced by Josef Lenart, a more popular Slovak, and Bacilek was succeeded by Alexander Dubček (pronounced *Doob*–chek). These changes quieted the situation and allowed Novotny to be elected to another term as President of the Republic in 1964.

Long before Novotny's term of office expired, however, he fell from power. Numerous popular complaints in 1962–63 had caused Novotny to promise economic reforms, but this remained largely a promise. It eventually became clear that political reform would have to precede economic reform. The reason was that the party disagreed over two major issues, how fast economic reforms should be implemented and how much autonomy ought to be granted to Slovakia.

Both surfaced in late 1967 when Dubček accused Novotny of undermining the program of economic reform and of refusing to meet Slovak demands for more self–government. At the same time, there were protests from the Czechoslovak Writers' Union and demonstrations by students in Prague. This series of events, taken together, would probably have led to Novotny's dismissal, had Soviet party chief Brezhnev not thrown his support to Novotny during a visit to Prague.

As it turned out, however, Brezhnev's gesture of support only postponed the date of Novotny's fall. The internecine fighting between Novotny's and Dubček's supporters continued to sharpen. Two months later, the Central Committee separated the functions of the presidency from those of the First Secretary of the *Communist Party*. On January 5, 1968, Alexander Dubček took over Novotny's functions as First Party Secretary of the *Czechoslovak Communist Party*. A clumsy attempt at a military coup, apparently an attempt to save Novotny, was discovered and the participants were removed from office by Dubček. One army general committed suicide while a second fled the country, eventually making his way to the U.S.

# Czech Republic

## "Socialism With a Human Face": An Experiment and its Consequences

The change in party leadership generated even greater hope that wider political, economic and social changes would follow. When Novotny finally resigned from the presidency in March 1968, it was clear that Czechoslovakia was proceeding in a new direction. A popular national military hero who had been decorated by both Tsarist and Soviet Russia, General Ludvik Svoboda (pronounced Sfo–boh–dah) was chosen president. Oldrich Cernik (pronounced Chur–nik) became Premier, and formed a cabinet which supported Dubček.

The party's program for the future was adopted in April under the title of "The Czechoslovak Road to Socialism," also known as the "Action Program." The program endorsed important changes such as an end to most censorship, restrictions on the powers of the secret police, and guarantees for the expression of minority viewpoints. In light of what subsequently happened, it is also important to stress that the Action Program was concerned only with domestic matters, with nothing to suggest any change in Czechoslovakia's policies either toward the Soviet Union or the Warsaw Pact. Dubček also repeatedly declared that the Communist Party had the leading role in the government and that his administration was committed to a continuation of socialism. In Dubček's words, the purpose of the reform movement was to create "socialism with a human face."

These developments raised great anxiety among some of the leaders of neighboring communist countries, however. The great fear was that, once liberalization was set in motion, it would inevitably get out of control. Moscow also began to express its worries. In May 1968, Czechoslovak visitors were advised to beware of counter–revolutionary attacks on the leading role of the party. When, two months later, more than seventy writers released a document entitled "Two Thousand Words" calling for "pressure from below" for further liberalization and democratic reform, the Soviet press cited this as proof that counter–revolutionary forces existed in Czechoslovakia. In addition, the Soviet Union added some psychological pressure by delaying the departure of Soviet forces that were in Czechoslovakia for Warsaw Pact maneuvers.

At the beginning of July, neighboring communist nations suggested a joint meeting to address their concerns. The Czechoslovak Government countered with a suggestion of bilateral talks. Rebuffed, Czechoslovakia's communist neighbors held their own meeting in Warsaw in mid–1968. This conference produced a document known as the "Warsaw Letter" which warned that Czechoslovakia could maintain its independence only as a "so-cialist" (i.e., communist) country. The letter added that reactionary forces were diverting Czechoslovakia from socialism and asked that immediate action be taken to reinstitute censorship of the press and radio and to clamp down on anti–socialist political movements.

Prague, which responded by a letter of its own, argued that the party was in complete control but that it could not take the suggested actions for its authority was based on being responsive to the will of the people, who desired more freedom of expression. This exchange of letters thus did nothing either to settle the situation and may have inflamed it further. In fact, Prague's reply brought a Soviet request for a special meeting with the Czechoslovak leadership.

In the end, two meetings were held, the first in late July and the second in early August. At the second meeting, all the other Warsaw Pact nations were in attendance, with the exception of Romania. Pressed to modify their program, the Czechoslovak leadership stood firm, though they did agree to a joint statement which made reference to the need to strengthen the forces of socialism against imperialist aggression.

## Invasion And Its Aftermath

On the night of August 20–21, military units of the Soviet Union, Hungary, the German Democratic Republic, Poland and Bulgaria invaded Czechoslovakia. Within a few hours they had overrun the country and occupied the leading cities.

TASS, the official Soviet news agency, announced that the occupation had been in response to a request for assistance against "counter–revolutionary" forces. None of the Czechoslovak leadership had made any such request, however. In fact, the entire Czechoslovak leadership—Dubček, Cernik and Josef Smrkovsky, President of the National Assembly—had been placed under arrest at the time of the invasion.

The Soviets did attempt to find Czech collaborators who would confirm the Soviet explanation of the invasion but without success. Instead, the Czech Foreign Ministry publicly denounced the military move as a violation of the Warsaw Pact, and President Svoboda flatly refused to participate in the formation of a Soviet–dominated government.

The deadlock was broken when Svoboda agreed to go to Moscow for direct talks with the Soviet leaders, provided Dubček and the other leaders traveled to Moscow with him and participated in the talks. At the meeting, it was agreed that the Dubček administration would be allowed to remain in office, though it was made clear that Czechoslovak leaders would have to change their political outlook. In October, a treaty was signed which legal-ized the stationing of Soviet troops within Czechoslovakia for an unlimited time. The Czechoslovak party congress, which had met during the first week of the invasion was also declared invalid and the strongly liberal Central Committee selected at that time was repudiated. Finally, the Executive Committee of the Presidium was created to counteract liberals in the Presidium itself.

## Retreat from Reform

One element of the reform movement survived, however. At midnight on December 31, 1968, Czechoslovakia became a federal state. With the creation of separate Czech and Slovak Republics, the Slovaks had finally achieved their goal of a separate, autonomous state. Basically, the Soviet leadership had decided to try and co–opt the nationalistic, but more conservative Slovaks.

Dubček's position soon became impossible. On the one hand, he refused to abandon his commitment to reform; at the same time, he tried to placate conservatives by criticizing anti–Soviet attitudes, denouncing student demonstrations and reimposing censorship. None of this saved him, however.

In April 1969, Dubček was demoted from First Party Secretary to Chairman of the Federal Assembly. Gustáv Husák, the new First Party Secretary, was a Slovak who earlier had been a supporter of reform. After the invasion, however, he had switched positions, arguing that the first priority for Czechoslovadia was to live in harmony with the Soviet Union. During the remainder of 1969, most of the rest of the pre–invasion reform leadership was either demoted, forced to resign or dismissed. Dubček, removed as Chairman of the Federal Assembly in the fall of 1969, was sent to Ankara as ambassador to Turkey. Eight months later he was expelled from the communist party.

With pro–Moscow conservatives now in control of the party, the Central Committee repealed the resolution condemning the Warsaw Pact Invasion. Czechoslovakia was back in line. In May 1970 a new treaty of friendship was signed with the Soviet Union.

In early 1970 Cernik was dismissed as Premier and was replaced by Lubomir Strougal. The general assumption at the time was that Srougal, then known as a conservative, had been installed as a counter–weight to Husák and a possible rival for power.

An extensive purge of the party was carried out between 1970 and 1975 which resulted in the dismissal of about 450,000 members—nearly one–third of the total. In general, it was the more liberal members who were purged. It was also during this time—in 1972—that Husák's party title was changed from First Secretary to

**Curious youngsters mill around a Soviet tank and armored personnel carrier in downtown Prague on the morning of August 21, 1968.**

AP/Wide World Photo

General Secretary, thereby mirroring the change Brezhnev had pushed through in the Soviet Union in 1966.

Having consolidated his power, Husák announced in 1976 that he was ready to begin a policy of reconciliation. Purged members were invited to apply for readmission to the party. There was one major stipulation, however: they had to formally repudiate the policies and leaders of the Prague Spring. In spite of this precondition, some ex–members were accepted back into the party and it began to grow again.

The government was reorganized at both the federal and national levels in early 1971. Chief among the changes was that the Federal Cabinet was given the right to veto decisions of the Czech and Slovak national cabinets. In mid–1975, Husák replaced an ailing Svoboda as President of the Republic, retaining his position as head of the party. The Czechoslovak power structure thus reverted to the pattern that had existed prior to Dubček's replacement of Novotny as First Secretary of the Czechoslovak Communist Party in early 1968. Husák continued to occupy both positions for 12 years, becoming a symbol and instrument of Soviet domination of Czechoslovakia (even though he once was thrown into jail for "bourgeois nationalism").

In early 1977 a group of Czech intellec-tuals released a document called "Charter 77", which charged the government with a long list of human rights violations, including the exclusion of young people from institutes of higher education on the basis of their parents' political views. The document also accused the government of systematically violating the right of public expression guaranteed in the Czechoslovak constitution. A number of western newspapers picked up the story, however, and news of the document soon filtered back into Czechoslovakia. The reaction of the Czechoslovak Government was predictable. Charter signatories were investigated by the secret police, and several were sent to prison. The government never managed to suppress the *Charter 77* movement, however, and its attempts to do so only further tarnished its international reputation. This latter charge was quickly confirmed when the domestic press refused to publish the "Charter 77" declaration.

## The Beginning of the End of Communism

The way in which the Czechoslovak leadership had been installed probably guaranteed the policies carried out after 1969. Precisely for this reason, however, political changes in the Soviet Union after 1985 had an unsettling effect in Czechoslovakia.

After Gorbachëv launched his campaigns for *glasnost*, *perestroika* and democracy in the Soviet Union, a more or less public debate began to occur within the Czechoslovak leadership as individual members of the Presidium publicly argued whether loyalty to the USSR required them to support a similar program in Czechoslovakia. It soon became clear that the top leadership was sharply divided over the issue. The hardliners, whose spokesman was Vasil Bilak, argued that events in the Soviet Union had no relevance for Czechoslovakia. On the other hand, Premier Strougal, who emerged now as spokesman for the moderates, argued the case for Prague's own restructuring.

President Husák remained publicly neutral until just before a visit of Gorbachëv to Czechoslovakia in April 1987, then endorsed a general program of reform. But Husák was a reluctant reformer; no changes were to be implemented until the next five–year plan, scheduled to begin on January 1, 1991.

During his visit, Gorbachëv used his public speeches to set forth the rationale for reform. While he did not insist that the Czechoslovak leadership implement a similar program, he also, significantly, had no praise for them. It was, in fact, becoming clear that Husák, at 74, was no longer able to provide any clear leader-

# Czech Republic

ship and that the issue of reform was becoming a vehicle to determine the succession.

The issue was resolved in December 1987 when Husák voluntarily retired as General Secretary while remaining on as President. His successor, Milos Jakes [pronounced *Ya*–kesh], a member of the ruling Presidium since 1981, was a compromise choice, a man not associated with either of the two factions within the Presidium. Jakes, although a member of the party secretariat for over 20 years, had never developed a strong political profile.

In fact, his record was a rather ambivalent one. Originally appointed to head the Party Control and Auditing Commission by Dubček, he transferred his loyalty to the new leadership installed after the Soviet invasion and subsequently presided over the post–1968 purge of the party that resulted in the expulsion of most liberals and moderates. Many of these same people, who constituted an important part of the country's cultural and technological elite, were also fired from their state jobs and forced either to take menial jobs or emigrate. Given this background, Jakes had a problem establishing credibility in his new job.

Jakes' own public statements after becoming General Secretary were rather unconciliatory. On at least one occasion, he characterized the Prague Spring as an attempt "to destroy the socialist system." At the same time, his speeches included references to the need for a "fundamental restructuring of all spheres of public life."

Jakes' promotion to General Secretary did not put an end to the Bilak–Strougal struggle and may even have intensified it, since they were now trying to influence a man of untried qualities. Strougal's

**General Secretary Milos Jakes**

speeches in favor of Gorbachëv–style reform apparently became embarrassing to the party, however, for he was forced out as Premier in October 1988.

Ladislav Adamec, who succeeded Strougal was, like Jakes, a man of the middle. During a trip to Moscow in February 1989, he spoke of the need for political as well as economic reforms. At the same time, Adamec remained willing to carry out the will of the conservative majority on the Presidium.

All of this began to change in the late summer of 1989. As the changes sweeping across Eastern Europe reached the German Democratic Republic, the West German Embassy in Prague became a refuge center for East Germans attempting to get to West Germany. This proved to be embarrassing to the Czechoslovak Government and it began putting pressure on the GDR Government to do something about it. Eventually the GDR Government caved in and arranged for trains to carry the refugees to West Germany. As the GDR was forced to give in more to the demands of its people, disaffected Czechs began to organize their own demonstrations demanding greater rights.

The culmination came on the evening of November 17, when a crowd of about 3,000 young people gathered at the entrance of Wenceslas Square (Vaclavske Namesti) and began a chant calling for free elections.

They were met by a line of riot police plus an anti–terrorist squad called the Red Berets who attacked them and bludgeoned them to the ground. The attack, personally ordered by Jakes, was a fatal error. It ignited the emotions of the Czech people, who responded with ten days of singing, chanting and non–stop organizing. This was Prague's so–called "velvet revolution," and at its end the communists had been elbowed from power. On November 24, with 300,000 people in the streets, Jakes called a meeting of the Central Committee and submitted resignations for himself and the rest of the Presidium.

Jakes was replaced as party leader by Karel Urbanek, who issued an unequivocal condemnation of the violence of November 17. But it was Ladislav Adamec, the Premier, who now stepped into the power vacuum and began discussions with the opposition, since November 19 organized as the *Civic Forum*. He continued to play that role for perhaps two weeks. During that time, the party agreed to give up its monopoly of power and to form a coalition government with the opposition. But Adamec wanted to keep a majority of the seats in the hands of the communists. When *Civic Forum* rejected his proposed cabinet on December 3, Adamec resigned and was replaced by Marian Calfa. The new cabinet, installed

on December 10, contained a majority of non–communists. Jiri Dienstbier, a founder–member of "*Charter 77*", became Foreign Minister while Vaclav Klaus, an economist committed to creation of a market economy, became Finance Minister.

As an added benefit, Gustáv Husák now submitted his resignation as President. Vaclav Havel, longtime dissident, founder of *Charter 77*, and prominent playwright, was elected President by acclamation on December 29. Alexander Dubček, reform communist leader of the 1968 Prague Spring, was elected leader of the national assembly.

With the new leaders all in place, the country settled in for a period of consolidation that included some dismantling of the old system. In the political and social arenas, the secret police were dissolved, and required courses in Marxism–Leninism were abolished in the universities. In the area of religion, *Pacem in Terris* was dissolved and the government dropped its system of licensing priests and ministers. Fewer changes were made in the economic sphere, though one reason for this is that everybody seemed to be waiting for new elections scheduled for June 6 in order to have a popular mandate.

One issue, the rivalry between Czechs and Slovaks, resurfaced with virulence, however. Upon Slovak insistence, the name of the country was changed to the Czech and Slovak Federal Republic.

The first democratic elections since 1946 finally took place in June 1990 and resulted in a victory for *Civic Forum* and its Slovak partner, *Public Against Violence*. An astonishing 96% of voters participated in the election. After the election, Vaclav Havel was reelected President and Marian Calfa was reappointed Premier.

After the June elections, there was a struggle of sorts between free marketers and advocates for a "third way" between communism and capitalism within the leadership of the *Civic Forum*. The spokesman for the free marketers was the Finance Minister, Vaclav Klaus, while Foreign Minister Jiri Dienstbier was a major spokesman for the opposing viewpoint, which also included most of the 1968 communists. President Havel tried to stay above the fray. Klaus won the first round in October 1990 when he was elected chairman of *Civic Forum*. In February 1991, however, the two factions decided to divide into two separate organizations, though they would continue to be associated on a coordinating committee of *Civic Forum* chaired by President Havel.

## Separation of the Republics

One other issue that demanded attention after the June 1990 elections was that of Slovak separatism. Slovaks had always been concerned about maintaining a separate identity, but now individual Slovak

**President Havel shares a light moment with his private secretary**

leaders began demanding creation of a separate, independent Slovak state. In effect, their argument was that Slovakia could not maintain its separate identity as part of a federation shared with the Czechs.

In December 1990, the Federal Assembly tried to defuse the situation by passing new legislation spelling out in greater detail the separate powers of the Czech and Slovak regional governments. The legislation also gave President Havel special powers to deal with the threat of Slovak separatism.

Although a majority of both Slovak and Czech deputies voiced support for the legislation, Slovak nationalists remained unappeased. When President Havel visited Bratislava in March 1991, he was greeted by thousands of Slovaks shouting abuse. The situation became even worse after Vladimir Meciar, the Slovak Premier, took up the Slovak nationalist cause—at least partly because he feared the effect of Prague's privatization policies on Slovak industry. Meciar had gotten too far out in front of the political forces, however, and he was dismissed as Premier in April 1991. Yet the issue remained alive. The new Premier, Jan Carnogursky, head of Slovakia's *Christian Democratic Movement*, tried to straddle the issue by supporting continuation of the federation for the time being while favoring an independent Slovakia in principle.

As Slovak nationalism continued to dominate Czechoslovak politics in 1991 and 1992, President Havel was forced to spend more and more of his time on this issue. Acting as a mediator between the Czechs and Slovaks, he brought the two sides together for discussions and, at one point, called for a referendum on the issue. Public polls showed that a small majority of Slovaks supported a continuation of the federation, however, so the Slovak nationalists eventually rejected that suggestion. Havel also proposed some changes in the nature of the federal government, and these were presented to the Federal Assembly in December 1991 in the form of three draft laws.

The first of the draft laws would have replaced one of the houses of the bicameral Federal Assembly with a Federal Council composed of representatives of the Czech and Slovak legislatures. A second draft law would have given the president special powers to issue decrees, should the Federal Assembly be dissolved. The third draft law would have allowed the president to call a plebiscite if he had the concurrence of the federal government.

The three draft laws were not enacted, but they may have acted as a catalyst. An *ad hoc* commission of the Czech and Slovak National Councils (i.e., legislatures) announced on February 9, 1992, that its members had drawn up a draft agreement

on a future common state which would be submitted to their respective legislatures. The draft agreement listed foreign policy, defense, monetary, credit, interest and currency policies and budgetary regulations as falling within the powers of the federation. Czechs and Slovaks would be equally represented in the federal bodies. The agreement also specified that either republic could withdraw from the common state "only on the basis of the will of the majority of its citizens expressed in a referendum."

What appeared as a breakthrough fell to pieces when the Presidium of the Slovak National Council rejected the draft agreement on February 12. Another partial reversal occurred two weeks later when the Slovak National Council passed a resolution asking the Presidium to reconsider. Slovak National Council deputies were requested to submit their views on the draft to the Presidium, which was instructed to compile a comprehensive report on the comments. The resolution further recommended that the Presidium meet with the Presidium of the Czech National Council "to jointly assess . . . the possibility of concluding the treaty."

When these maneuvers failed to produce an agreement, it was decided to hold new federal elections on June 5–6 to resolve the general issue. Slovakia decided to hold its own elections to the National Council on the same days. The *Christian*

# Czech Republic

*Democratic Movement*, the party of Slovak Premier Jan Carnogursky, now split into two factions. The faction that had been pushing for an independent Slovakia formed a new party, the *Slovak Christian Democratic Movement*, and announced that they would run a separate slate of candidates in the June elections. With the radicals gone, the *Christian Democratic Movement* reaffirmed its support for a common state.

In the June 1992 elections, the vote split along national and ideological lines. In the Czech Republic, Vaclav Klaus and his *Civic Democratic Party* won a convincing victory on a program of anti–communism and reform. In the Slovak Republic, Vladimir Meciar and his *Movement for a Democratic Slovakia*, won an equally convincing victory with their blend of statism, socialism and nationalism.

When Klaus and Meciar met after the election to discuss the formation of a new federal government, the latter made it clear that he would not accept a federal state that could dictate policy to Slovakia. Among his demands were that the Slovak Republic be permitted to establish its own army, its own currency–issuing central bank and that it have the independent right to borrow. None of these positions was acceptable to Klaus and the talks collapsed after six and a half hours.

Because a new federal government had to be formed, Klaus suggested giving a new, temporary federal government the power to act until a referendum could be held to ask citizens whether they wanted to live in a federal state. After further talks, Czech and Slovak negotiators agreed to establish a weak interim federal government whose task would be to facilitate bringing the union to a close. The actual constitutional questions relating to the separation would be resolved in the legislatures of the two republics.

When Vaclav Havel, still trying to save the federal state, agreed to stand for re-election to the federal presidency, Slovak nationalists blocked his reelection.

Havel could have stayed on in a caretaker capacity until October, since the dominant Czech party, the *Civic Democratic Party*, had vowed to block any other candidate for the presidency. Havel was unwilling to remain under those circumstances, however, and submitted his resignation instead. Most people saw that as a further step in the dissolution of the federal government. As Havel said, had he stayed, he would have been committed by the constitution to defending a common state that no longer had much purpose.

Further negotiations now produced an agreement, signed on August 26, calling for a split into two independent states by January 1. On October 1, the federal parliament rejected a bill legalizing the end of the federation, then voted itself out of existence on November 25.

Having agreed to a peaceful separation into two independent nations, the Czechs and Slovaks nevertheless recognized that their economies would be tightly bound to each other for some time and that it would be wise to retain certain elements of the former union if they could. These would include a common currency and a customs union which would allow for the free movement of goods. In addition, Czechs and Slovaks would not be required to show passports to pass from one country to another.

## THE INDEPENDENT CZECH REPUBLIC

The Czech National Council adopted a new constitution for an independent Czech Republic in December 1992. It essentially created a presidential–parliamentary system such as had existed in the former Czechoslovakia. The Czech Republic had formerly had only a unicameral legislature, the 200–member Czech National Council. This was renamed and became the Chamber of Deputies. An 81–member upper house, called the Senate, was then added to create a bicameral legislature.

On January 26, the Chamber of Deputies elected Vaclav Havel President of the Czech Republic. His inaugural speech of February 2, given from a balcony of Hradcany Castle, was rather somber in tone, in

Wenceslaus Square, central Prague

**Shoppers look with skeptical amusement at relaxing skateboarders**

Photo by Jon Markham Morrow

contrast to his first inaugural speech. "The revolutionary times are over," he said. "This is the time of every day, common and hard work. To cultivate our best traditions today is infinitely harder than in times of great historical change and the euphoria that came with it."

On the same day, and almost as a counterpoint to his speech, the Czech and Slovak parliaments announced that the agreement on a common currency for the two republics had been terminated and each republic would now be issuing its own currency. Thus the agreement to retain a common currency collapsed after just over a month; the customs union has, however, managed to survive. Trade between the two republics did fall considerably following separation, but it has since recovered. In any case, the emphasis of Czech trade policy since 1993 has been to redirect its exports to Western Europe. Any loss of exports to Slovakia has been more than compensated for by its growing trade with the European Union. By 1994, in fact, one–third of all Czech exports were going to Germany.

The implementation of the Czech Republic's program of economic reform was widely considered to be the best in Eastern Europe and it was widely predicted that Prime Minister Klaus and the government coalition would win easy reelection in the 1996 elections. They did, in fact, win a renewed mandate, but the party that

benefitted most from new elections was the opposition *Czech Social Democratic Party (CSSD)*, which increased its representation from 16 to 61 seats. Essentially, the *CSSD* won on a campaign that endorsed Klaus's pro–market policy while strongly criticizing both the concept and progress of economic reform. The second party that did well in the 1996 elections was the *Communist Party of Bohemia and Moravia (KSCM)*, which won 22 seats, making it the third largest party in the Chamber of Deputies after Prime Minister Klaus's *Civic Democratic Party (ODS)*.

The three parties of the government coalition together won 99 seats, a drop of 14 seats from their 1992 showing. They thus fell one seat short of a majority and, in order to pick up the necessary support to form a new government, they had to make an arrangement with the *CSSD*. Essentially, the *CSSD* agreed to support the government from outside the coalition in return for *CSSD* control of major positions in the Chamber of Deputies, including the chairmanship.

Prime Minister Klaus also had some problems with the other two parties in the coalition over allocation of cabinet seats. Klaus's *ODS* had held a majority in the cabinet of the previous government. Since the constitution specifies that the Prime Minister may act whenever he has the support of a majority of his cabinet, Klaus sometimes took actions opposed by the

other two parties. Although the 68 seats won by the *ODS* meant that it controlled two–thirds of the coalition's seats in the Chamber of Deputies, Klaus agreed to assign half of the cabinet posts to the two smaller coalition parties. Thus the two minority parties controlled four cabinet posts each, while the ODS held eight.

Although Prime Minister Klaus's government coalition took 52 of 81 Senate seats in the November 1996 elections and thus retained control of the upper house, this was not sufficient to counterbalance the government coalition's loss of its majority in the house. Difficult decisions which had been put off because they were too controversial now had to be abandoned entirely and the government began to drift. It became increasingly evident that this had become a *de facto* caretaker government that lacked the power to put its policies into effect. Yet, as it became clear that there were still a lot of inefficiencies in industry and that the government had not developed adequate regulatory mechanisms for the capital markets, the economy began to stumble, business confidence lessened, the trade deficit worsened, and the currency had to be devalued.

Klaus had one final triumph during the summer of 1997 when the Czech Republic received invitations from both the European Union and NATO to apply for membership. But this was soon followed by

269

# Czech Republic

quarreling among the coalition partners that led to the resignation of the Interior Minister, followed in October by the Foreign Minister. Next, Josef Lux, Deputy Prime Minister and leader of the People's Party (KDU–CSL), demanded a new government program and a new vote of confidence by the parliament. President Havel, who up to this time had played the role of the ceremonial head of state, now entered the fray with an attack on the government. Referring to Lux's demand, Havel commented that he doubted whether a new government program "would solve anything because the coalition lacks the energy and the will to act, merely living from one day to the next."

These attacks hurt, particularly since it was becoming increasingly evident that they were true, but what finally brought down the government was a corruption scandal that broke in October over allegations that a political donor gave more than $200,000 to Prime Minister Klaus's party in return for the inside track in a privatization deal. Klaus denied any knowledge of the alleged deal, but the charges brought a split in his party. Meanwhile, the smaller Civic Democratic Alliance (CDA) began to fall apart as well. Klaus formally resigned on November 30 after President Klaus had demanded his resignation and the People's Party and the CDA had pulled out of the government coalition.

Approximately two weeks later, President Havel appointed Josef Tosovsky, the governor of the Czech National Bank, as the new Prime Minister. Tosovsky has since put together a cabinet of technicians chosen without regard to their party affiliation, and new elections were set for June 19 and 20. It is understood that Tosovsky is a caretaker Prime Minister who will not attempt to initiate new policies. Tosovsky did oversee new Presidential elections on January 20. Although President Havel had a malignant tumor and half of the right lung removed in December 1996 after he had been diagnosed with lung cancer, he nevertheless stood for reelection. The voting during the first ballot was by the lower house and the Senate each voting separately. President Havel had two opponents, Stanislav Fischer, a man of the far left whose chief support came from the Communist Party of Bohemia and Moravia, and Miroslav Sladek, the candidate of the rightist Republican Party. In spite of the fact that neither of these men was a viable candidate, Havel failed to win the required majority in both houses. A second ballot then followed in which the two houses voted together. Here President Havel won reelection by a single vote.

Meanwhile, the three parties associated with the previous government coalition have continued to split with major dissident factions developing in Klaus's ODS and the ODA.

The winner in all this is the Social Democratic Party (CSSD), led by Milos Zeman, which currently appears to be set to win the June parliamentary elections. This means that the next Prime Minister will probably be Milos Zeman. The CSSD is a leftist political party which supports the general concept of a market economy but wants to make it more responsive to the needs of ordinary Czechs. Thus the Czech Republic appears ready to take the path already taken by Lithuania, Poland, and Hungary and pull back for a while from the whole process of reform.

## Foreign Policy

While Czechoslovakia was controlled by the *Communist Party*, it had no independent foreign policy. Or, as the Czechoslovak Ambassador to the United States told this writer some years ago, "the foreign policy of Czechoslovakia is the foreign policy of the Soviet Union."

That all changed in December 1989. After that time, the Czechoslovak Government established relations with Israel and the Vatican, President Havel gave orders for the curtailment of worldwide arms exports, and the country carried out successful negotiations with the Soviet Union to get Soviet troops withdrawn from Czechoslovakia. The last of the troops left in June 1991.

In other signs of change, both Alexander Dubček and Vaclav Havel made trips to the United States and Havel gave a major address before a combined session of Congress. Czechoslovakia was also among those nations urging the Soviet Union to drop its insistence that a united Germany either be neutral or hold simultaneous membership in both military alliances. Czechoslovakia wanted a united Germany to be part of NATO.

The demise of both the Warsaw Pact and the Council for Mutual Economic Assistance had some effect on Czechoslovakia's international relations, though Czechoslovakia's participation in both memberships had become increasingly nominal. Czechoslovakia was among those nations insisting that all CMEA accounts be settled in dollar or other convertible currencies as of 1991.

The demise of the Soviet Union in 1991 changed that relationship even further as Czechoslovakia extended diplomatic recognition to the successor republics and opened separate relations with them. Czechoslovakia sought good relations with the newly independent Republic of Ukraine, but the Czechoslovak leadership was more attuned to the new Russian political leadership in Moscow. Its relations with the remaining successor republics have been more nominal.

Czechoslovakia was admitted to Associate Membership in the European Community (now the European Union) in December 1991, along with Hungary and Poland, and the Czech and Slovak Republics have retained that status since independence. The Czech Republic wants to become a full member of the European Union as soon as possible and it has already begun aligning its foreign policy to that of the EU. In the case of the break–up of Yugoslavia, for example, the Czechs extended diplomatic recognition to the successor republics only after the EU had done so.

German Chancellor Helmut Kohl visited Prague in January 1997 and the highlight of the visit was a declaration of Czech–German Reconciliation, signed by Chancellor Kohl and Prime MInister Klaus, which acknowledged wrongs committed by both sides before and after World War II. In the document, Germany expressed sorrow for all the victims of Nazi violence during the period of German occupation. The Czech Government, on its part, expressed regret for the forcible expulsion of an estimated three million Sudeten Germans in 1945–46.

American–Czech relations remain good and the Czech Government would welcome greater American investment in the Czech industry, partly to offset the strong investment drive from Germany but partly also because they would like to see a greater American economic presence. Over the past several years, the Czech Republic has received, after Hungary, the largest amount of foreign investment in Eastern Europe.

The Czech Republic's relations with Slovakia were a little uneven at first. They have since improved, and both sides are committed to good relations.

## Nature of the Government

Under a new constitution adopted in December 1992, the Czech Republic adopted the presidential–parliamentary system of the old Czechoslovak Republic. The parliament consists of a newly created 81–member senate plus the 200 member lower house, called the Chamber of Deputies. In lieu of elections, the Czech members of the Czechoslovak federal parliament filled the Senate seats until November 1996, when new elections were held.

Under the constitution, the President of the Czech Republic is the titular head of state. The functions of the President are largely ceremonial, though the office bestows a moral authority that derives partly from the expectation that the President will remain above politics. Vaclav Havel, formerly the President of Czechoslovakia, was elected President of the Czech Republic on January 26, 1993.

The Prime Minister presides over the Czech Government and is the key political figure in the system. Appointed by the

President, he must establish that he has the support of a majority of the Chamber of Deputies in order to remain in power. The President appoints members of the cabinet upon the advice of the Prime Minister. Their names are then submitted to the Chamber of Deputies for its approval.

## The Economy

Czechoslovakia was already an industrialized nation when the communists took over in 1948. The coalition government installed in office in 1945 had nationalized about 60% of all industry and instituted a land reform aimed at breaking up all large land holdings. Major steps had also been taken toward institutionalizing socialism and state planning. With half their work done for them, the communists only had to complete the nationalization of industry and adapt state planning to the command model developed by the Soviet Union in the 1930's. This was accompanied by a gradual collectivization of agriculture.

Czechoslovakia's first Five Year Plan was launched on January 1, 1949, and it, and the following two subsequent Five Year Plans, placed a major stress on the creation of heavy industry—again a slavish following of the Soviet model. The relative neglect of consumer industries and agriculture produced a lop-sided economy which began to resemble more and more an industrialized copy of the Soviet economy. Food items such as meat became scarce, a severe housing shortage developed in the cities, and the quality of consumer goods declined as well. These developments obviously had an effect on morale and, as the third Five Year Plan progressed, even heavy industry began to fall short of its targets. In 1962, with the economy in a severe recession, the third Five Year Plan was simply abandoned.

A number of Czech economists associated with the Institute of Economics of the Czechoslovak Academy of Sciences had been critical of Stalinist concepts of command planning for a number of years. One of the most prominent and outspoken of these proposed a plan for reordering the economy which became known as the "New Economic Model." The Czech economist had been influenced by a Soviet counterpart, Yevsei Liberman, and his plan, like the Liberman Plan, called for limiting the role of the central planners. Individual enterprises were to be managed on the basis of profitability; worker salaries were to be based in part on individual skills; and there was to be a major stress on upgrading technology.

President Novotny initially opposed the plan but, as the economy continued to flounder, he gave a grudging approval for initiation of the plan at the beginning of 1967, though he did specify that it leave the Party's central policy–making authority intact. But it was a start in name only; as a result of continued opposition by conservatives involved in central planning, it failed to have any significant effect.

A similar effort in the Soviet Union resulted in a victory for the conservatives there. In Czechoslovakia, the reformers decided to challenge the conservative leadership and were instrumental in securing the resignation of Novotny as head of the party. Dubček, his successor, fully supported the reform measures and the economist who initially wrote the plan became deputy prime minister.

Even as the reformers began implementing their "New Economic Model," however, the Soviets were drawing up their own plans to invade Czechoslovakia. Afterwards, economic reform was condemned by the Husák regime as a "romantic notion." The central planners again assumed control of the economy.

Czechoslovakia's problems remained, however, and the new Husák regime had to face them. An injection of Soviet aid plus a vigorous investment effort got the economy back on a positive course, though just barely. Then in 1975, the regime introduced its own economic reform, based on ideas developed in East Germany in the 1960's. Essentially a bureaucratic solution, a new "middle level" of managers between the central planners and the individual managers was created—a sort of regional level of managers whose function was to coordinate the working of the plan within their sub–areas.

There might have been some decentralization in this cautious reform, but it was insufficient to have a noticeable effect on the economy. As a result, the Husák regime continued to tinker with the central planning mechanism, but always in a cautious manner. The frame of reference within which Czech central planners work is perhaps best illustrated by the title of a 1980 proposal "Set of Measures for Improvement of The System of Planned Management in the National Economy After 1980." This concept, put into action in

Prague: wedding couple receives gifts following ceremony

Photo by Jon Markham Morrow

# Czech Republic

1981, developed what might be called the concept of the conglomerate.

Twenty to 40 enterprises were to be organized under a single management which was then to be given a certain amount of independence from the central state planning bureaucracy. A similar system was introduced in the German Democratic Republic in the 1970s, but there the companies were referred to as *kombinate*.

The 1981 reform did not prevent a slowing of the economy, however, nor was it able to reverse an increasing shortage of certain types of consumer goods, particularly pork and beef. The government raised the prices of meat, milk and bread by as much as 150% in February 1982, but when shortages persisted, new price rises were instituted the following year. Official statistics reported a 3 percent average growth rate during most of the 1980's, but industry continued to be plagued by outdated technology, declining productivity and low–level products. Proposals for economic reform were never really put into effect or, if they were, had no effect.

**Dismantling the Command Economy**

The revolution of 1989 put a new set of leaders in power and, although there was some floundering about in the first year, the government then began to take the necessary steps to create a market economy. In February 1991, the Federal assembly passed a broad privatization law which committed the government to denationalize all industry. Companies nationalized after 1948 were to be returned to their original owners or their descendants, while remaining companies were to be privatized through a complex system of government–issued coupons or sold to foreign investors. The key individual responsible for the government's plans was Vaclav Klaus, then Finance Minister.

As the political debate between Czechs and Slovaks over the future of the common state grew in intensity in 1991, however, and Klaus's plans for economic reform were thrust partially aside. In November 1991, the Czech Government announced that it had made significant progress in its small–scale privatization program, having sold 12,333 out of 20,786 business units included in the program. Less progress had been made in large–scale privatization, but the government had held seven auctions, approved five direct sales, and prepared two public tenders.

The government began privatization of large–scale industry through its coupon program in March 1992. Czech citizens were offered books of vouchers for 1,000 crowns (approximately $35), which could then be used to bid for shares. Facilitating the process, approximately 400 investment funds were set up to manage the shareholdings. Though by law they are not permitted to hold more than 20 percent of the shares of any one company, they eventually ended up holding 70 percent of the shares on behalf of individual investors. In June 1993, with over a thousand Czech and Slovak companies privatized, the government sponsored creation of the Prague Stock Exchange to provide a market for the shares.

As of January 1, 1993, 988 Czech companies had been privatized and there were six million stockholders. A second round of voucher privatization in the latter part of 1994 transferred assets worth an additional $5.8 billion. All told, approximately 80% of all Czechs participated in the two sets of voucher privatizations. In addition, more than 100,000 properties worth an estimated $4 billion were returned to their former owners. The process of privatization is now essentially complete.

Some economists are worried that the voucher system of privatization has produced a system whereby ownership is separated from oversight and the effect of this is that companies will not be under strong pressure to restructure in order to become more competitive. Since ownership is widely dispersed and the investment funds are primarily portfolio managers, there is some basis for the worry. On the other hand, companies that do not perform adequately will clearly find it difficult or impossible to raise new capital, and that ought to provide incentives to become more competitive. Perhaps a greater worry is that the biggest investment funds are run by the biggest Czech banks. That presents a potential for a conflict of interest.

There has also been a large flow of foreign capital into the Czech Republic and this has resulted in a significant international presence. Perhaps the most famous company to invest in the Czech economy was Volkswagen, which agreed to invest $5.5 billion to obtain a 70 percent interest in the Skoda automobile plant, located in Mlada Boleslav, about 30 miles outside of Prague. Other companies included Nestlè, which took a 43% stake in the chocolate maker Cokoladovny Modrany, and Philip Morris, which obtained a 65% interest in Tabak, the cigarette maker.

The government has also launched a program to transform the country's agriculture. In earlier, federal legislation, collective farms had been legally transformed into cooperatives and employees were given the right to ask for their own land. After they had taken legal title to their land, however, almost all owners arranged to lease back the land to the cooperatives. Only 1,120 of those who applied for land took more than 25 acres. Most wanted only a couple of acres to work for themselves. This was disturbing from the government's point of view, for the large agricultural subsidies alloted to the cooperatives to make them competitive act as a drain on the national budget. The federal government sought to deal with this problem by passing a "transformation" law which reduced government oversight over the cooperatives and made the elective bodies of the cooperatives responsible for management and decision–making. The government hoped that, given the responsibility, the cooperatives would transform themselves and, to encourage them in this direction, the government cut agricultural subsidies by one–quarter in December 1991.

While the process of transformation has been slow, it appears to be working. In June 1996, this author visited one such cooperative, AGRO Jesenice a.s., located a few miles outside of Prague. This particular cooperative had 2500 hectares of land and 210 employees. That was down from 3200 hectares in 1990, when they also had 720 members, 550 of them actually employed in the cooperative. Thus they now have 38% of the employees they had before to farm 78% of the land they farmed before. This particular cooperative was mainly a dairy farm, but it has been diversifying into other areas and now raises and freezes strawberries, opened a processing plant for processing vegetables and fruit, and now manufactures a yoghurt product with added fruit. It has also created an affiliate to handle sales.

The cooperative now has approximately 700 shareholders, only 30 of which are employed by the cooperative. It made a profit in 1995–96 but paid no dividend, having plowed all of its profits back into the cooperative. Most stockolders apparently agree with the policy, partly because they would have to pay taxes on any paid out dividends.

**The Czech Arms Industry**

Two months after the November 1989 revolution, Foreign Minister Jiri Dienstbier announced that Prague would "simply end its trade in arms" without regard to economic consequences. That turned out to be impossible, though the government did manage to cut the output of weapons plants to 25% of 1988 levels by 1993. Political idealism no longer appears to be a controlling factor, however. In 1993, the Czech parliament began considering a bill to license firms selling arms and Vladimir Dlouhy, the Czech Minister of Industry and Trade, called the old arms–export laws naive. In another sign, the heavy–engineering firm of Skoda Pilsen announced that it would form an arms–manufacturing consortium with several other Czech companies. Skoda–Pilsen did stress, however, that its intention was to participate in large Western defense programs, and that it had already established contact with French and German firms. It was not, it added, interested in arms sales to the Middle East or the developing world. Skoda also pointed out that it had already converted a large percentage of its productive capacity from military to civilian production.

## Culture

Prague, the center of Czech culture, is an achingly beautiful city full of carefully preserved ancient churches with gold–tipped spires, plus baroque, romanesque and art nouveau buildings untouched by the bombs of World War II. On the hill above the Vltava River stands Hradcany Castle, residence of the President. St. Vitus Cathedral, Prague's great Gothic cathedral, is part of that same complex and its spires stand out against the sky. Down the hill from Hradcany and St. Vitus, the 14th century Charles IV bridge—now a pedestrian walkway closed to traf-fic—leads across to the old city center. Here, in the old residence quarter of the city, one finds Wenceslas Square (Vaclavske Namesti) and Old Town (Stare Mesto) Square, with its Jan Hus Memorial.

One must give the old communist government credit; they did put a great deal of money and effort into fixing up the older buildings of Prague in their last years in power. It seemed at the time that scaffolding surrounded half of the city's architectural, historical and religious structures, but visitors to Prague have the benefit of that effort today. Incidentally, soon after it took over, the new Czechoslovakian Government abolished all visa requirements for Americans planning to stay less than 30 days. It is also now possible to rent a room in a private home or apartment and the arriving visitor is likely to receive many such offers. That is particularly important, since hotel space is still extremely limited.

The Czechs have contributed substantially to the world of music and literature. One needs only to recall such persons as Anton Dvorak, composer of the New World Symphony, Vilm Blodek, famous for his comic operas, such figures as Smetana, Janácek and, a contemporary artist, Jaroslav Seifert, who was awarded the Nobel Prize for Literature in 1984. Mr. Seifert was one of the founders of Charter 77, the civil rights group organized to monitor the government's implementation of the Helsinki Accords, and his poetry was not generally available inside the country until after 1989. Mr. Seifert's poetry is not really political, however. A typical example is his "Spring in the Fisherman's Net," which follows:

"In the fisherman's cork–fringed net
is spring. Young bulbs abound
on the trees and smile at us
when we look round.

In the fisherman's cork–fringed net
spaced out in three
are the stars; we are acquainted,
one always remembers me
and lights up the pathway home
in the dark at journeys end.
Not so many have the luck
to find in the stars their true girl friend.

In the fisherman's cork–fringed net
the wind is caught. Its laughter is the
laugh all women know
when they talk about men together.

In the fisherman's cork–fringed net
the claws are caught of tender fear. The
same fear that men know
when they talk about women
together."

(Tr, by ORBIS; used with permission)

## The Future

The Czech Republic has completed the transformation from communism to capitalism and it has done so with less pain than any other country in eastern Europe. Unemployment is low and 80% of its trade is with Western Europe or other industrial economies. Inflation is also under control. There are continuing problems, some of them economic, but the chief problem is the political scandal that led to the collapse of Prime Minister Klaus's government in November 1997. The Czech Republic currently has a caretaker Prime Minister with parliamentary elections scheduled for June 19 and 20. Current polls indicate that the left will win.

**Peace and quiet reign in the Krkonoše mountains**        AP/Wide World Photo

# The Republic of Hungary

**View from Buda across the Danube to Pest, with Parliament building on the right.**

Courtesy: Jon Markham Morrow

**Area:** 35,919 sq. mi. (93,030 sq. km.).
**Population:** 10,375,000.
**Capital City:** Budapest (Pop. 2,113,645).
**Climate:** Continental, with long, dry summers and severe winters.
**Neighboring Countries:** Slovakia (North); Ukraine (East); Romania (Southeast); Serbia, Croatia (South); Slovenia, Austria (West).
**Official Language:** Hungarian (Magyar), a Finno–Ugrian language related to Finnish.
**Other Principal Tongues:** Languages of small minorities, German, Serbo–Croat, Slovak, Romanian.
**Ethnic Background:** Magyar (92.4%) Gypsy (3.3%); German (2.5%), Jewish (0.7%) other (1.1%).
**Principal Religions:** Roman Catholic and Protestant Christianity.
**Chief Commercial Products:** Machinery and equipment, agricultural and forest products, fuels, minerals, metals, consumer goods.
**Currency:** Forint.
**Annual Per Capita Income:** About U.S. $3,500
**Former Political Status:** Independent, 1918–1945; Communist State, part of Soviet Bloc, 1945–1990.

**National Day:** April 4, Liberation Day.
**Chief of State:** Arpad Goncz, President.
**Head of Government:** Viktor Orban, Chairman, Council of Ministers (July 1998).
**National Flag:** Horizontal stripes of red, white and green.

## THE LAND AND THE PEOPLE

The Republic of Hungary, second smallest country in Eastern Europe, lies in the Middle Danube Basin. Two great rivers, the Danube and the Tisza, cross the rolling plains which cover most of the country. The Danube—one of Hungary's few natural frontiers—provides part of the border between Hungary and Slovakia, then turns sharply southward, passes through Budapest, and divides Hungary. Contrary to legend, just like most rivers, its waters are not blue, but are usually brown because of the presence of silt from upstream areas.

To the east of the river lies the great fertile plain, a vast rangeland used for cattle grazing. The northeast section along the Slovak border is covered with forested mountains, abundant with wildlife. Here one can find limestone caverns and Europe's largest stalactite caves. Most im-

portantly, the northeast contains Hungary's famous wine–producing centers, Eger and Tokaj. West of the Danube, plains turn into hills where the easternmost part of the Alps reach into western Hungary.

Although there are several theories concerning the origins of the Hungarian people, it is generally agreed that they are a Finno–Ugrian people, that is, they speak a language related to Finnish. In early historic times, they were first found inhabiting a part of the Russian Plain west of the Ural Mountains. Apparently suffering attacks from even more aggressive neighbors, several Hungarian tribes migrated westward, crossed the Carpathian Mountains and settled the broad plain that speads out from the Danube River east and south of the present–day city of Budapest.

## HISTORY

### Origins of the Hungarian State
Initially led by Arpad, for whom the first dynasty of Hungary was named, the Hungarians did not immediately settle down in central Europe. They terrorized most of the surrounding people until the

274

# Hungary

tenth century when they were defeated by the German Emperor Otto I. Although there was earlier Christian missionary work among the Hungarians, Stephen I of the Arpad Dynasty "converted" the whole nation on Christmas Day, 1000 A.D. when he accepted a cross and crown sent by Pope Sylvester II. After his death, he was proclaimed a Saint by the Church in 1083.

At a later time in the history of Hungary, the Crown of St. Stephen became the symbol of highest authority. It represented the "unity" of all lands claimed by Hungary, including those not inhabited solely by Hungarians. During the 10th century, Slovakia was conquered; by 1003 Transylvania was under the Crown and a century later, Croatia, Slavonia and Dalmatia were united with Hungary. By the late 14th century, the Kingdom of Hungary contained extensive areas inhabited by Saxons (Germans), Slavs, Vlachs (Romanians of Wallachia, and Szecklers (Transylvanian Magyars living in the Carpathian Mountains).

During the Middle Ages, Hungary was not isolated from the rest of Europe. At the end of the 12th century a dynastic connection with France was established when King Bela III married the daughter of the French king; the marriage settlement showed that Hungary's national treasury equalled that of France. Hungary's early constitutional development resembled England's; the Hungarian king was forced to sign a document called the Golden Bull in 1222 which guaranteed the rights of the nobility, similar to the English *Magna Charta*.

A Mongol invasion in 1241 devastated Hungary and resulted in the loss of one-half of the population. However, the Mongols remained only for a year, so their occupation did not influence Hungary as it did Russia.

The Arpad Dynasty ended in 1301 and for two centuries Hungary was ruled by foreign nobility. In the 15th century one of Hungary's greatest kings, Mathias Corvi-

nus, ascended the throne. An enlightened Renaissance monarch, he reformed the country's administrative and judicial systems, reorganized the army, founded universities and preserved Hungary's position as an important European power.

## A Part of the Multi–National Hapsburg Empire

Hungary's defeat by the Ottoman Turks in 1526 was a turning point in the nation's history. After a period of civil war, Hungary was partitioned between the Turks and the Hapsburgs; the central part was controlled by the Turks, the western part was controlled by the Hapsburgs. A third region consisting of Transylvania and sixteen neighboring counties was declared to be a self–governing principality. This area became the center of Hungarian culture during the next two centuries and gave

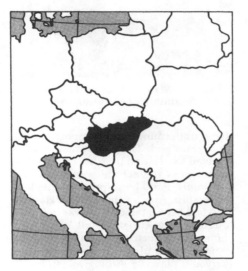

Hungary such heroes as Stephen Bocskay and Gabor Bethlen. Transylvania was a model of religious tolerance among the states of Europe. Its princes, backed by armies, spread the principle throughout the rest of Hungary, forcing its adoption as the law of the land.

The country was the easternmost one to participate in the Protestant Reformation—the great spiritual movement of the 16th century. By the end of that century, 90% of the Hungarians were Protestant, but this figure was reduced later by the Counter–Reformation in the 17th century. However, the Protestant population of Hungary and Transylvania is now still the most significant of that group in Eastern Europe.

By the Peace of Karlowitz in 1699, most of Hungary, Transylvania and Croatia passed from Turkish to Austrian hands. This led to the suppression of protestantism, which had been tolerated by the Turks as a protection against the influence of the Roman Catholic Hapsburgs, and also to a weakening of the traditional Magyar aristocracy and the end of an elected monarchy in Hungary.

Francis Rakoczy led a rebellion in 1703 against Hapsburg domination. Although it was suppressed, it was a foretaste of the nationalist movement which shook the Empire a century later. During the 18th century, Hungary was tied to Austria by the *Pragmatic Sanction,* although it had its own *Diet* (assembly) composed of a Table of Magnates and a Table of Deputies.

The political climate of Hungary in the 1830's and 1840's was infected with the spirit of nationalism and reform. Radicals, such as Louis Kossuth, advocated independence from Austria; other more mod-

Hungary c. 1350

# Hungary

erate leaders wanted Hungarian self–government within the Empire. A program known as the March Laws was adopted in 1848 which made Hungary practically independent, connected with Austria only through a unified monarchy.

This didn't last long—the various non–Magyar people, who numbered half of the population, soon realized that Hungary's independence simply meant that the Magyars could mistreat the minorities within the borders—independence for Hungary meant "Magyarization" for the rest of the people.

Louis Kossuth declared Hungary's complete independence in 1849, but within a few months, the revolution was suppressed by Austria with the aid of Russian troops. A highly centralized system of government was adopted. Many Magyars came to realize that a change in Hungary's status could only come within the limits of Austrian imperial government. The events that followed were largely the result of efforts of a moderate leader, Francis Deak, who constructed a plan of government which was the basis for the *Compromise of 1867*. This created the Dual Monarchy—Austria and Hungary were separated, each had its own constitution and parliament, but there were common ministries set up for finance, foreign affairs and war. The *Compromise* was important because it provided the basis for relations between Austria and Hungary until 1918.

It was natural that Hungary sided with the Central Powers (Germany–Austria) in World War I. Although some leaders favored negotiation of differences which led to the war, they agreed to refrain from quarreling over domestic issues in the so–called "Truce of God" (1914) after Hungary had entered the war. By 1916, opposition to the war had increased; the truce was broken and extremists began a propaganda campaign against the war. Two years later, one of these leaders, Michael Karolyi, became head of the government in a war–weary defeated country. This government proclaimed Hungary a republic in 1918 which lasted only five months; the immediate cause of its downfall was an ultimatum from the allies, demanding that Hungary surrender part of its territory. Unable to accept the demand, Karolyi resigned and the next day, March 21, 1919, the communists were in power.

The communist leadership of Hungary consisted of soldiers who learned of Marxism while prisoners of war in Russia. They had no political experience nor had any of them held any important post in the Hungarian labor movement of the prewar period. Upon their return, they formed the *Communist Party* of Hungary in November 1918 and spread propaganda of peace and prosperity among the mass of unemployed workers and sol-

**Budapest: March 22, 1919. The pouring rain does not deter the celebration of Hungary's communist revolutionaries.**

diers, undermining the support that the moderates had. The government had attempted for the first time in February 1919 to suppress the activities of the young *Communist Party* by imprisoning its local leadership. Among these was Bela Kun, who had been a prisoner of war in Russia, fought in the Russian Civil War on the communist side, then organized the Hungarian section of the *Russian Communist Party* and played a leading role in founding the *Hungarian Communist Party*.

While in prison, the communists and some prominent members of the *Social Democratic Party*, the strongest political group in the country, decided to merge the two. This gave the communists the political strength with which to come to power without a violent revolution and without a popular following. Actually, their success was also because of nationalist sentiment—the ultimatum of the allies to the Karolyi government put it in an impossible position and gave the communists a national issue to use against the government.

Bela Kun became head of the *Hungarian Soviet Republic*. The government nationalized all banks and all enterprises which had more than 20 workers. All titles and ranks of the nobility were abolished. Private property was also ended, but the land from the great estates was not given to the peasants. The failure to carry out land reform had been one of the biggest mistakes of the ruling class and of the Karolyi government, and it eventually

was one of the principal causes of the downfall of Bela Kun.

The young Soviet Republic collapsed because of Kun's inability to deal either with internal problems or with the threat of advancing Romanian troops. He resigned in 1919 and fled the country; the Romanian army occupied Budapest until November, when its western allies persuaded it to withdraw.

A number of pre–war politicians who had been loyal to the old regime had set up an opposition government during the time Kun held power. They raised a small army which, under the command of Admiral Nicholas Horthy, moved into the capital in late 1919, set up an anti–Bolshevik government and asked to be recognized by the allies. However, the response was a demand for a provisional government that would hold elections.

A coalition provisional government including the *Smallholder Party*, the *National Democratic Party* and the *Social Democrat Party* was formed; it announced elections to be held in January 1920. During the months before the elections, bands of terrorists roamed the country, attacking Jews, Social Democrats, members of trade unions and anyone they suspected had communist sympathies, or opposed the return of the conservatives to power.

The first post–war parliament was not representative of the country because of the terrorism which had prevailed during the campaign. The *Social Democrats* decided to boycott the elections because of the

# Hungary

attacks on them. The new parliament, as it first order of business, took up the question of whether Hungary was still a monarchy; King Charles had renounced all power in 1918, but had not abdicated. The parliament's decision was that Hungary would continue to be a kingdom, but without a king—a Regent would be elected to act as head of state. From March 1920 to October 1944, Admiral Nicholas Horthy was Regent of Hungary. The question of Charles' claim to the throne ended in 1922 when he died.

The *Treaty of Trianon,* signed on June 4, 1920, legalized the loss of territory which had been taking place since 1918. By its terms, a weakened Hungary had to submit to immense losses of territory. Slovakia and Ruthenia went to the recently–created Czechoslovakia; Croatia and

**Admiral Horthy**

Slavonia went to Yugoslavia; most of the Voivodina also went to that country. Transylvania and part of the Banat went to Romania. Hungary thus emerged from World War I losing almost three–fourths of its prewar territory and about two–thirds of its population. Since boundary lines could not follow ethnic divisions, a large Hungarian population was left in each of the lost areas.

Arguments during and after the Paris Peace Conference, which ended World War I, about which nation was "rightful" claimant to a piece of territory were not only unresolved, but were also largely very irrelevant. As in all wars, the victor took the spoils. After 1920, Hungarians used the word "dismembered" to describe Trianon Hungary. This was intended to produce the image of a broken state which for a thousand years had been held together under the legal and patriotic symbol of the Crown of St. Stephen.

The interwar period was one that appeared to be peaceful. A Conservative government led by Stephen Bethlen, a Protestant aristocrat from Transylvania, held power from 1921 to 1931. Desiring a return to the "good old days," but without the Hapsburgs, he ignored the need for land reform and had no understanding of the worker's and peasants' problems. Hungary was internationally isolated by the "Little Entente" consisting of Czechoslovakia, Romania and Yugoslavia, which wished to retain Hungarian lands gained by the Treaty of Trianon.

The world–wide economic depression of the 1930's and Hungary's continuing desire to regain lost lands led the nation down a disastrous path to alliance with Nazi Germany in World War II. Government leadership changed five times between 1931 and 1939, but the conservatives remained in control. Anti–Jewish measures were enacted which affected even the political leadership. The last of the five premiers, the patriotic statesman Count Paul Teleki, committed suicide as a dramatic protest against the invasion of Yugoslavia by Germans crossing Hungarian soil.

Diplomatic activity preceding World War II resulted in Hungary's regaining southern Slovakia and Ruthenia; northern Transylvania was recovered in 1940. Hungary signed the *Tripartite Pact* of the Axis powers in November 1940 and in spite of a treaty of friendship between Yugoslavia and Hungary, German troops crossed Hungary to invade Yugoslavia. The next question was whether Hungary should join in the war on Russia launched by the Germans. On the pretext that Russian planes had bombed Kosice, Premier Laslo Bardossy, siding with the military, published a declaration of war against Russia in mid–1941 without the consent of the Parliament. It is probable that the Russian aircraft were really German planes on which Russian markings had been painted.

Parliamentary institutions and political parties functioned until late in the war; there was no German occupation until March 1944 when this was prompted by the advance of the Red Army. A pro–German government dissolved political parties and increased the persecution of Jews to a level not previously experienced in Hungary.

The Regent, Admiral Horthy, and his advisers came to the conclusion in the fall of 1944 that the Axis powers could not win the war. Seeking a separate armistice, Hungary sent a diplomatic team to Moscow and, on October 15, 1944, announced that an armistice with Russia had been requested. Horthy's proclamation was poorly timed—the Germans had time to take control of the capital, seize him and force him to retract his proclamation; he was then forced to abdicate.

General Bela Miklos, the Hungarian Commander–in–Chief, joined with the Russian army when it crossed Hungary's borders. With Russian support, Committees of National Liberation were set up in the Russian–held areas, and a Provisional Government was formed in Debrecen. When Russian forces besieged Budapest, the pro–German puppet government fled, and in January 1945 the Provisional Government concluded an armistice in Moscow. The government of Hungary was based on a coalition of political parties which included three major ones: the *Hungarian Independence Front,* the *Social Democratic Party,* the *Communist Party,* and two smaller ones, the *Smallholder's Party* and the *National Peasant Party.*

According to the terms of the armistice, Hungary was directed to return to its 1938 frontiers; this provision was contained in the Peace Treaty of February 10, 1947. The agreement also provided for an Allied Control Commission with Soviet Marshal K. E. Voroshilov as its chairman.

## Hungary Becomes a People's Republic

By a decree of March 1945, the Provisional Government started an extensive land reform program which was accomplished under the direction of Imre Nagy, the communist Minister of Agriculture. In probably what were the freest popular elections Hungarians had ever experienced, held in late 1945, the *Smallholders Party* received 57% of the vote. The *Communist Party* and the *Social Democratic Party* each received 17%. Zoltan Tildy, the leader of the *Smallholders* became Prime Minister and later President of the Hungarian Republic after the National Assembly proclaimed Hungary a republic in early 1946. Ferenc Nagy succeeded Tildy in the office of Prime Minister. Although the *Smallholders Party* had won a majority of the vote in the election, the government consisted of a coalition; Imre Nagy became Minister of the Interior.

It is inaccurate to describe the process by which the communists came to dominate the Hungarian government as a "seizure" of power. In reality, this was achieved quite slowly and cautiously over a three–year period. The leadership of the *Smallholders Party* was picked off individually in a variety of ways. Bela Kovacs, secretary of the party, was arrested by the Russians on charges of conspiracy. Ferenc Nagy was blackmailed into resigning by a threat of physical harm to his son. Losses of leadership and continued attacks on members weakened the *Smallholders Party* to the point it could not provide any real opposition to the communists.

The *Communist Party* and the *Social Democratic Party* merged in mid–1948 to form the *Hungarian Workers' Party.* Tildy was replaced by a communist sympathizer in that year, and communists dominated the cabinet. The final move was made

# Hungary

in February 1949 with the establishment of the *Hungarian Independent People's Front,* a combination of all parties and mass organizations. It presented a singlelist of candidates which received 96.5% of the vote in May 1949. The newly elected National Assembly proclaimed Hungary a *People's Republic* and adopted a constitution reflecting Hungary's official position as a member of the Soviet bloc.

## The Stalinist Period

The years from 1949 to 1953 have been called the "Stalinist period" in Hungary and other East European nations. Political control of the party, and through the party, over Hungary, was wielded by Mathias Rakosi, a dedicated communist since 1918. He had been a prisoner of war in Russia during World War I, returned to Hungary in 1918 and helped Bela Kun form the *Hungarian Communist Party,* held office in the Hungarian Soviet Republic, left Hungary when the republic collapsed and worked for the *Communist International (Comintern)* for a number of years.

Rakosi tried to reorganize the outlawed *Communist Party* in 1924, but was arrested and spent most of the next 15 years in prison until 1940. He was then traded to the Soviet Union for some Hungarian flags that the Russian army had captured in 1849. He returned to his homeland in 1944 and became Secretary General of the *Communist Party,* Deputy Prime Minister until 1952 and Prime Minister from 1952 until 1953.

Under his supervision, a reorganized secret police conducted a purge of the party, attacked rich landowners, undermined the churches and kept a close watch over social life in general. The most dramatic event of this period was the trial of Laszlo Rajk, a "home communist" and one-time Minister of the Interior and Foreign Affairs. He was accused on falsified evidence of conspiring with Yugoslavia's Tito and was executed in 1949. This was followed by a purge of the party membership which eliminated from it all those suspected of having nationalist or anti-Rakosi sentiments. In the process, several thousand party members were also imprisoned.

By 1949 the new regime had introduced the Stalin model of economic planning with its emphasis on central decision-making and heavy industry. All industry employing more than ten workers had been nationalized and a program for the collectivization of agriculture had been initiated.

Lacking most raw materials, Hungary had never placed any great stress on heavy industry, but had concentrated on the development of agriculture based on the processing of its products and the manufacture of consumer goods. The new emphasis on heavy industry of the first

Five-Year Plan accordingly produced spectacular growth totals in the beginning. Heavy industrial production increased fivefold and the engineering industry showed a sevenfold increase in productivity over 1938.

By 1953, however, serious shortages had begun to appear in both raw materials and fuel supplies, and a serious disproportion had begun to appear between heavy and light industry. Agriculture was beginning to stagnate under the combination of the policy of collectivization accompanied by a decline in investment. Wages and salaries had risen less rapidly than consumer prices, with the result that there was a 20% decline in the general standard of living between 1948 and 1953.

## The New Course and Revolution

There had been some muted criticism of these developments even before March 1953, but Stalin's death at the time brought these out into the open. The lead was taken by Imre Nagy, who challenged Rakosi's handling of the economy, accusing him of forcing the tempo of industrialization all out of proportion to the country's resources. Rakosi was forced to step down as Chairman of the Council of Ministers—though he retained his position as head of the *Hungarian Workers' Party*—and Nagy was named in his place.

In his first speech to the Parliament in 1953, Nagy presented a program which later became known as the "New Course." It included an emphasis on consumer goods instead of heavy industry, abolition of collective farms when such was desired by a majority of the workers, and the release of many political prisoners. Among those released was Janos Kadar.

Continued disputes over these new policies, particularly in agriculture, coupled with a failure to gain support of important party members, led to Nagy's resignation in 1955. He was replaced by Andras Hegedus and Hungary returned to the old policies of heavy industrialization and collectivization. After the unkept promises of the New Course and a disappointing return to earlier policies, protests from writers and scholars began to be heard in the autumn of 1955. The following summer, the *Petofi Circle,* named after a revolutionary poet killed in 1849, was formed, providing a forum for debate among those who were critical of government.

In an effort to appease the critics, the Soviet Union brought increased pressure on the Hungarian party to dismiss Rakosi. He resigned in mid-1956 and was replaced by Erno Gero. This did not quiet the discord. A number of party leaders who had been executed in the purges of 1949 were reburied with honor; the funerals turned into a mass demonstration against the government. A few weeks lat-

er, the students of Szeged University in the city of that name organized a non-communist youth organization.

By late 1956 news of the Szeged students and of the anti-government activities in neighboring Poland reached Budapest. This prompted students and writers to draw up a resolution and to hold a public demonstration expressing sympathy for the Polish cause. Their plan was to march to a statue of General Joseph Bem, a Polish soldier who had fought with the Hungarians against the Austrians and Russians in 1848–49. The resolution demanded the evacuation of Soviet troops from Hungary, the return of Nagy as Prime Minister, free elections and freedom of speech and press. This was not so much in opposition to communism as it was in favor of the development of some form of socialist democracy.

Although planned only as a demonstration, the October 23 events turned swiftly into a mass revolution. This was due to poor judgment of officials and the emotions generated by the mass activity. The Minister of the Interior responded to news of the planned demonstration by banning it, and then agreeing not to interfere. The demonstrators, joined by members of the communist youth movement, marched reading the immensely patriotic poem "Arise, Magyars" and the resolution. By evening a huge crowd had gathered in front of Parliament calling for Nagy, who addressed them briefly and asked them to disperse.

Later in the evening, two specific events triggered an uprising; an untactful and accusing speech by First Secretary Erno Gero which denounced the demonstrators, and the refusal of the radio station director to broadcast the resolution. Fighting which first broke out between the demonstrators and the secret police, quickly spread into the working class districts. A gigantic statue of Stalin in the center of Budapest was toppled; because only the boots remained, the site is now popularly called "Boot Square."

During the night, Soviet tanks appeared and fighting erupted between Soviet troops and revolutionaries who were by then supported by parts of the Hungarian army. The fighting spread even further into the countryside, where Workers' Councils and Revolutionary Councils were organized to replace the local communist administrations.

On October 24, Nagy replaced Hegedus as Chairman of the Council of Ministers and the next day Janos Kadar replaced Erno Gero as First Secretary of the *Hungarian Workers' Party.* Anastas Mikoyen was in Budapest at the time as a representative of the Soviet Politburo. He accepted political changes and negotiated an agreement with Nagy and Kadar for the withdrawal of the Soviet army from Hungary.

**Soviet tanks guard the street intersection leading to the Danube Bridge in Budapest on November 5, 1956.**     AP/Wide World Photo

Mikoyan's agreement was obviously based on the premise that Nagy and Kadar, as communists, were committed to the maintenance of communist control in Hungary. However, Nagy, in announcing the Soviet troop withdrawal agreement, also promised to abolish the secret police and to bring representatives of non–communist parties into the government.

Reports reached Budapest on November 1 that Soviet troops had stopped their withdrawal and, reinforced now by additional Soviet tanks of the latest design, were heading back toward Budapest. Nagy responded by announcing Hungary's withdrawal from the Warsaw Pact (the military organization of Eastern Europe presided over by the Soviets), committing Hungary to a policy of neutrality and appealing for help from the United Nations.

Soviet troops attacked Budapest on November 4, 1956. At the same time, Kadar, now in eastern Hungary, having left Budapest on the evening of November 1–2, proclaimed the establishment of a "revolutionary government of peasants and workers" to replace the "fascist" Nagy government. Although there was a great deal of resistance by the Hungarian people, a basically unarmed people were no match for Soviet tanks, and the revolution was ruthlessly suppressed. Janos Kadar, First Secretary of the Communist Party, was back in power with the backing of Soviet troops.

## Politics Since 1956

Kadar was in a difficult position after 1956 because he lacked party support and general popular support. Within the party, he was opposed by those who favored internal reform, who accused him of selling out the revolution. The Stalinists in the party wanted to return to the style of the Rakosi era.

Large segments of the population, including students, writers and workers who had played such a large role in the revolution, viewed Kadar as a Soviet puppet. He was in power only because he had the support of the man who had suppressed the revolution, Nikita Khrushchëv, leader of the Soviet Union.

During the two years after the uprising, Kadar repressed various social groups and political parties which opposed his government. Hundreds of people associated with the revolution were imprisoned.

In 1959–1960 there were signs that the government was willing to allow a relaxation of its tight control. Partial amnesty was declared and several hundred political prisoners were released. After 1961, Kadar adopted policies intended to win popular support. The "People's Courts" that had convicted the revolutionaries were abolished and in 1962 Rakosi and Gero were expelled from the party, demonstrating Kadar's desire to break completely with the Stalinist policies of the past. Although he became Prime Minister in addition to First Secretary of the party, there was no return to the so–called "per-

sonality cult" of which Stalin had been accused after his death.

Kadar reported to a party congress in 1962 that collectivization had been completed the previous year, with 90% of the farmland in cooperative and state farms. Most industrial products were from socialist enterprises. In foreign policy, he expressed complete support for the Soviet policy of peaceful coexistence, for its actions in the Cuban missile crisis and its position in the disputes with China.

The congress, in turn, adopted Kadar's "one nation" policy, which declared in effect that the government was willing to cooperate with anyone who was not actively opposed to the communist party. In this respect, it was willing, he said, to recruit competent, non–party members for government service. Further liberalization was evident by 1963, when a general amnesty was declared, freeing additional political prisoners numbered in the thousands. Travel restrictions were lowered and tourism increased.

Kadar's popularity greatly increased as a result of these changes and that was a considerable help when Nikita Khrushchëv fell from power in November 1964. Although now "on his own," Kadar managed to hold on to power, though he did have to relinquish the office of Chairman of the Council of Ministers in mid–1965. Julius Kallai got that position, while Kadar remained First Secretary of the party.

Kallai was Chairman of the Council of

# Hungary

Ministers until 1967. He was replaced by Jeno Fock, who held the position until 1975. Fock's resignation came shortly after the Eleventh Congress of the *Hungarian Socialist Workers Party,* where he took personal responsibility for his government's failure in its "Leninist duty" to adequately supervise the functioning of the national economy. His resignation "for reasons of health" almost certainly reflected the Soviet leadership's dissatisfaction with the relatively freewheeling style of economic management in Hungary under the "New Mechanism." His successor as Chairman of the Council of Ministers was Gyorgy Lazar, who held the position until 1987.

The Eleventh Congress of the *HSWP* tightened party regulations by introducing a ban on "propagating dissent," almost certainly a gesture meant to appease their Soviet comrades. In another gesture, this time aimed at Hungarian workers, the congress also endorsed the reduction of the work week to 44 hours by 1980.

Although he held no state office after 1965, Kadar continued to be the key leader in the political system. As such, he tended to run a rather collegial Politburo, though he did not hesitate to dismiss those members who got too far out of line. In general, he tended to prefer technocrats rather than political types. This may have been because he recognized that they were needed to carry out his economic reforms, but he could not have been blind to the fact that they were also less likely to be rivals for power.

Kadar, in fact, always tried to limit the personal power of his associates. In 1978, for example, he dismissed his deputy, Bela Biscku, because the latter had ambitiously extended his personal control over the party apparatus, the military and the security forces. It was the purge of Biscku which opened the way for Karoly Nemeth, who became Kadar's deputy for the party apparatus at this time. Nemeth, although not particularly liked either within the party or by the Hungarian public, was officially designated as Kadar's deputy at the 13th Congress of the Hungarian

Workers' Party in March 1985. Nemeth was considered by many to be a likely Kadar successor. In June 1987, however, he was promoted to the largely ceremonial post of President of the Presidential Council instead.

It was also at this time that Karoly Grosz replaced the ailing Gyorgy Lazar as Chairman of the Council of Ministers. Grosz, former party boss in Budapest, had often been mentioned as a potential Kadar successor, but he was only one of three potential candidates at this time. The other two were Janos Berecz, former editor of the party newspaper, *Nepszabadag,* and Laszlo Marothy. Berecz, party chief ideologist, was promoted to the Politburo in June 1987. Marothy, Deputy Chairman of the Council of Ministers, had been a member of the Politburo since 1976. Although Berecz often took conservative positions on issues, he appealed to many party intellectuals because of the quality of his arguments. Marothy was supported by those who were attracted by his reputation for moderation and pragmatism.

The matter came to a head in May 1988 at a special Hungarian Socialist Workers' Party Conference. It had become clear in the months leading up to the conference that Kadar intended to retire and so, for the first time, there was something of a campaign for the office of party leader. Grosz, who had previously had a reputation as a hard–liner, put himself forward as an aggressive and energetic pragmatist who supported further reform. He also adopted an open style reminiscent of that of Gorbachëv.

It was Grosz who was selected by the party conference to succeed Kadar as General Secretary. As it turned out, however, this was not just a succession but, rather, something approaching a revolution in the party. In addition to the appointment of Grosz, eight of the 13 members of the Politburo were dropped, along with 40 percent of the Central Committee. Kadar was among those dropped from the Politburo, though he was given the honorary title of party president. Marothy was also dropped, though Berecz kept his seat.

Six persons were added to the Politburo, including two well–known advocates of radical reform, Rezso Nyers and Imre Poszgay. Both had previously been Politburo members, but had been dropped because of their political positions.

Nyers, a member of the Economic Institute of the Hungarian Academy of Sciences and a former Minister of Finance, was one of the principal authors of the 1968 reform. Several years ago, he wrote an article for the Budapest daily (*Magyar Hirlap*) in which he advocated a larger political role for the Hungarian parliament. In 1985, when the party established multiple candidacies and moved to give a larg-

**Peasant girls in native costume in the courtyard of Parliament.**

Courtesy: Jon Markham Morrow

280

er role to parliament, it was implementing most of what Nyers had advocated in his article. Imre Pozsgay, Chairman of the Patriotic Peoples' Front since 1982, attempted to give this umbrella organization new life and more influence. He had also argued that the party ought "to withdraw from its present relationship with the state and society—and to establish a new relationship." In addition, he was on record as supporting the creation of autonomous interest groups, including, under certain circumstances, independent trade unions.

Grosz, speaking to the party conference following his election as General Secretary, promised that he would seek "to expand democratic procedures within the party to match some of the 'practical advantages' of western multiparty systems." Later, in an televised address to the Hungarian people, he admitted past mistakes on behalf of the party and promised a new approach "in public life, in production, in human sectors and other fields."

Gorbachëv was quick to put his stamp of approval on the new General Secretary, calling him "a principled communist and authoritative leader" and wishing him "big successes . . . in tackling the task of improving and renovating his socialist society on Hungarian soil."

Grosz continued as Chairman of the Council of Ministers until November 1988, when he turned the office over to Miklos Nemeth. Nemeth, a 40–year–old economist, had been added to the Politburo in May 1988. Known as a strong advocate of change, he was described by Janos Lukacs, another Politburo member, as a "young, dynamic workhorse."

His biography indicates that, after graduating from Karl Marx University in Budapest, he studied at Harvard University. He began working for the party's economic department in 1981. In 1987, he became a member of the Central Committee and, simultaneously, party secretary for economic policy. Mark Palmer, American Ambassador to Hungary in 1988, characterized Nemeth as an affable man who would be easy for the West to work with. "He has," Ambassador Palmer went on to say,

"very rich experience in the area of economic reform. He clearly has the strong backing of Grosz and a great deal of experience in the West. We believe he is committed to reform and will push ahead."

Nemeth's appointment was, in fact, further evidence that the reformers were in more or less complete charge, though they still retained their alliance with the moderate Grosz. And having placed their supporters in all of the key positions, they turned their attention to the subject of institutional reform.

There was some question about where all of this was leading and the situation became even more muddled in December 1988, when Imre Pozsgay spoke out publicly in favor of a multi–party system. One week later, Karoly Grosz rejected Pozsgay's suggestion, but that actually marked the beginning of a struggle within the party over the issue. The matter was largely resolved in February 1989, when the party announced further details of proposed constitutional changes. A multi–party system was to be formally established and additional political parties were to be permitted to operate freely. The draft also provided for the creation of a new executive Presidency. Among other things, the President would be commander–in–chief of the armed forces. Free elections were also scheduled for 1990.

Although the program had not formally gone into effect, independent political groups immediately began to form. In March 1989 the first of those, the *Democratic Forum*, had its first convention in Budapest. In addition, the *Smallholders Party* and the *Hungarian Socialist Party*—both of which had been part of the first government coalition (along with the *Communist Party*) in 1945—were revived and began to operate as independent groups.

However, the *HSWP's* commitment to multi–party elections was too much for conservatives still within the party and they opposed it. To resolve the issue, Grosz proposed at a plenum of the Central Committee in April 1989 that the Politburo "lay down its powers and hold a new secret ballot on its composition." In the subsequent voting, four remaining conservatives were removed from the Poliburo, including Janos Berecz. Two persons, Mihaly Jasso and Pal Vastag, were added. The size of the Politburo was thus reduced from 11 to 9. In a separate move, Janos Kadar was dropped from the Central Committee and his title of honorary president was abolished. He died soon afterwards.

Two months later, the party went through yet another leadership shake–up. In June, the Politburo and the office of General Secretary were both abolished. They were replaced by a four–member Presidium, with Rezso Nyers as President. Karoly Grosz was made a member of the Presidium but lost most of his power.

The winds of change continued to blow strongly in 1989. In October, the party dropped its old name and became the *Hungarian Socialist Party*. Somewhat later, a group of party stalwarts resurrected the old party. As other parties had begun to operate, it became clear that it had little chance of winning in the upcoming free elections, but it still hoped to install its man as president while the *HSWP* controlled the legislature. That hope was dashed in November when opposition

parties forced a referendum to postpone election of the president until after free elections; the referendum favored this move.

In March 1990, in the first free elections since 1945, the Hungarian people repudiated both the communist–reformist *Hungarian Socialist Party* and the communist *Hungarian United Workers Party*. No single party received a majority but it was the centrist *Democratic Forum* that came in first with approximately 42% of the vote and therefore won the right to organize the new government. A coalition was formed with two smaller parties, the *Independent Smallholders* and the *Christian Democrats* with Jozsef Antall, leader of Democratic Forum, as Chairman of the Council of Ministers. Together the three parties controlled more than 60% of the seats in the new Parliament. The main opposition party was the left–liberal *Alliance of Free Democrats*, with the *Hungarian Socialist Party* reduced to a tiny remnant on the left.

Jozsef Antall remained Chairman of the Council of Ministers for the next three and a half years, until his death on December 12, 1993. During that time, he came to dominate Hungarian politics almost completely, giving the country a political stability that distinguished Hungary from most of its eastern European neighbors.

In the beginning, the greatest problems faced by the new government were related to the state of the economy and its early focus was on establishing policies that would move Hungary more rapidly toward a market economy. This task appeared easier in Hungary for the communists had already moved the country the furthest along this path of all the Eastern European nations. Nevertheless, state-owned enterprises still constituted 90 percent of the productive sector of the economy.

First of all, the government drew up a long list of laws and regulations aimed at fostering private initiative, encouraging direct foreign investment, and developing private capital markets. It also committed itself to reducing the state sector to less than 50 percent by 1995.

All over eastern Europe, there were heated discussions about how best to privatize a former communist–controlled economy. In Hungary, the government opted for a company by company privatization, based on finding western companies who would either take over the company entirely or come in as a partner, providing capital and technical expertise. Under this plan, foreign investment increased rapidly and a good number of companies were able to find foreign partners or purchasers. Small and medium-sized companies were privatized locally, some to groups of employees.

In general, the process has been relatively slow and is not yet completed.

# Hungary

**President and Mrs. Arpad Goncz**

Many of the companies have also found it difficult to compete, so salaries are low and unemployment has grown significantly.

As a result, the government came under criticism by those who argued that it was moving too slowly and by others who feared that it was dissipating the nation's wealth. Some of this showed up in the local elections in October 1990, when the parties of the government coalition lost badly. In Budapest, the two major opposition parties won over 50 percent of the vote. In most places, independents won, however, possibly indicating a distaste for the political partisanship that had come to dominate debate.

None of this threatened the coalition's majority in parliament, however. In fact, the government coalition had regained much of its popularity in the country by the beginning of 1992 and Antall, though still not overly popular, was conceded to be the most effective leader in eastern Europe.

Nevertheless, Antall found himself faced with a serious problem within his own party later in 1992 when the party's ideologue, Istvan Csurka, published a tract attacking Jews, journalists and international financiers and blaming them for the country's ills.

Csurka's espousal of right–wing nationalism threatened to split the party and Antall moved to limit the damage. Csurka then tried to seize control of the party in early 1993. After that attempt failed, he

and three of his followers were expelled from the *Democratic Forum* and he went on to form his own party. Although a few members of the *Democratic Forum* defected to the new party, the great fear was that he would split the vote in the next elections.

When Antall died on December 12,

**The Crown of St. Stephen returned**

1993, of non–Hodgkins lymphoma, he was succeeded by Peter Boross, up to that time the Interior Minister. His was essentially a caretaker ministry, since elections were scheduled to take place less than five months later.

The *Democratic Forum* did badly in the May 8 elections, garnering only about 12 percent of the vote. This was not a judgment against Boross, however, for even before Antall's death, the *Democratic Forum* had been expected to do badly. Istvan Csurka, who had tried to move the party to the right, did badly also with his own party, winning only 1.3 percent of the vote. The big winners were the *Socialists*, who led with 32.7 percent of the vote. Their possible alliance partner, the *Free Democrats* got 19.8 percent of the vote.

In the second round run–off vote on May 29, however, the *Socialists* got more than 54 percent of the vote nationwide, which gave them an absolute majority of 209 seats in the 386–member legislature. The *Alliance of Free Democrats* finished second with 70 seats. The *Democratic Forum* was a distant third with 37 seats.

Although the *Socialists* were capable of forming a government on their own, Gyula Horn, the *Socialist* leader, offered to form a coalition government with the *Alliance of Free Democrats*. Horn gave as his reason that the party favored "broad national cooperation." In fact, political analysts were saying that Hungary could be in for a period of political and economic instability if the *Socialists* tried to form a government on their own. Gabor Kuncze, the *Alliance of Free Democrats* leader, was at first hesitant, apparently fearful that, because the *Socialists* had an absolute majority, they would ignore their junior coalition partner. He eventually agreed, however, so the new government controlled over two–thirds of the seats in parliament.

It turned out, however, that serious differences of opinion existed within the leadership of the *Socialist Party*, with the result that almost nothing happened for the next six months. The major point of disagreement was over economic policy. In January 1995, Prime Minister Horn dismissed his privatization commissioner, Ferenc Bartha, after a disagreement over the sale of a Hungarian hotel chain to an American investor. Left–wing members of the government wanted to use the revenues from the profitable hotel chain to help support the cash–strapped social security fund. This led, in turn, to the resignation of the finance minister in protest.

Horn now came under pressure from his junior coalition partner plus members of the more moderate wing of his party, both of whom urged him to make a firm commitment to more rapid reform. The result came in March, when the Hungarian Government announced an economic

# Hungary

reform package aimed at cutting government spending by $170 billion forints ($1.4 billion) and reducing the budget deficit by a third. The package was assembled by Lajos Bokros, the new finance minister, and Gyorgy Suranyi, the new head of the central bank. Prime Minister Horn agreed to the cuts, apparently moved by the fact that the budget deficit in 1994 had soared to $3.9 billion and was projected to grow even worse. The essential problem was that welfare and social services, with its thousands of excess public sector jobs, was eating up the equivalent of 27 percent of Hungary's GDP. Under the government's plan, spending on welfare services, which included automatic child care benefits, two years of maternity benefits, and free higher education, would be cut in all of these areas.

The program caused some pain and led to the resignations of two ministers. Trade unions, unhappy about the cuts in benefits, attempted to change the government's mind by threatening a series of strikes. But it produced the results intended. By 1996, the economy had begun to recover and it has only picked up speed since that time. Hungary's GDP grew by some 4 percent in 1997 and foreign investment, which was $346 million for the first 11 months of 1997, doubled over the preceding year. The United States is the largest investor in Hungary, followed by the Netherlands, France and Germany. Total foreign investment as of February 1998 was estimated at $3 billion.

Hungary got a double vote of international confidence in 1997 when it received invitations to join NATO and the European Union. The Hungarians have already approved membership in NATO in a popular referendum. Membership in the European Union will probably occur some time after the year 2000.

New parliamentary elections are scheduled to take place in May 1998. With the opposition in disarray, the Socialists are expected to do well, though they may well lose their majority in the parliament. However, it appears that the Alliance of Free Democrats is willing to continue as a coalition partner after the elections.

## Foreign Policy

The first non–communist government since 1945 brought a change in Hungary's foreign policy, but not all that much. The biggest change is that its relations with Russia are now the relations of equals. They remain cordial, but businesslike.

Under the communists, alignment with the Soviet Union was a basic component of foreign policy. For example, Hungary followed the lead of the USSR in breaking relations with Israel in 1967 and it joined the Soviet boycott of the 1984 Los Angeles Summer Olympics. It also tended to sup-

port the Soviets in quarrels with the People's Republic of China.

On the other hand, Hungary always maintained a more independent position vis–à–vis the Soviet Union than either Bulgaria or Czechoslovakia. Hungarians were frank about their desire for better relations with the West. Although they participated fully in the CMEA, and the Soviet Union remained their single largest trading partner, they also pushed to increase their trade with the west and were the first to call for reform of the CMEA.

Trade between Hungary and the Federal Republic of Germany grew greatly, exceeding 5.2 billion Deutsche Marks (about $2.3 billion) by 1985. This was roughly 30% of all Hungarian trade with the west, making the Federal Republic Hungary's second largest trading partner after the Soviet Union. There was also extensive cooperation between the two countries designed to facilitate the transfer of technology. Approximately 350 cooperative agreements were signed between West German and Hungarian firms before 1989.

Austrian entrepreneurs have also been active investors recently. According to the Hungarian Government, approximately 1880 joint ventures were established between foreign investors and local partners in the first eighteen months of the new democratic regime. More than 60% percent of the investors were either Austrian or German. US–Hungarian relations have been relatively good since 1973, when the two countries signed an agreement settling claims for damages to American property during World War ll. The U.S. government also returned the St. Stephen's Crown, in American custody since World War ll, to Hungary in 1978. It also granted Hungary "most–favored nation" trade status at about the same time.

Relations, already very good even under the reform communist leadership, have become even warmer since 1989. Arpad Goncz, the new Hungarian President, paid an unofficial visit to the United States in September 1990, followed by an official visit by Prime Minister Jozsef Antall in October. During the visit, President Bush publicly called on the IMF to lend up to $5 billion to the new democracies of Eastern Europe, including Hungary. The United States has, in general, been a strong supporter of multilateral economic assistance to Hungary.

One problem that Hungary has with its neighbors is over minorities. Significant Magyar–speaking populations are to be found in Romania, the Czech and Slovak Republics and Yugoslavia. Romania, with between 1.7 and 2 million ethnic Hungarians, has the most, but there are also at least 600,000 in Slovakia, mainly in the area of the southern plain. There are fewer in rump Yugoslavia, and they are mainly to be found in Serbia, in the area of the

formerly autonomous province of Vojvodina. The "Yugo" Magyars became a particular problem for Hungary after Serbia's destruction of the government of the autonomous province of the Vojvodina in 1989 put these Magyars directly under Belgrade. With the withdrawal of Croatia and Slovenia from the collapsing Yugoslavia in 1991–92, these Magyars became hostages to Hungary's actions as Serbia accused Hungary of assisting the Croatians. On a number of occasions, Yugoslav People's Army troops or military aircraft carried out incursions across the border into Hungary. Partly because of this concern, Hungary supported sending in UN peacekeeping troops, taking the position that the UN ought to be given a greater role in protecting human and minority rights. In his address to the Security Council in January 1992, Geza Jeszenszky, the Hungarian Foreign Minister, argued that:

"protecting human and minority rights is more than a legal and humanitarian issue: It is an integral part of international security. Therefore, a firm assertion of these rights by the UN Security Council is indispensable."

Hungary had a running controversy

**On a Budapest square, a German tourist wonders whether or not he should be photographed with a cardboard likeness of President Bush**

Photo by Jon Markham Morrow

283

# Hungary

with Romania concerning Romanian treatment of ethnic Magyars during the latter years of the Ceausescu regime, but the matter became more low–key after the fall of Ceaucescu. Under Ceaucescu, Hungarians feared that the Romanians were attempting to "denationalize" the Hungarians of Transylvania and that feeling continued to some extent under Iliescu. However, the Hungarian Democratic Federation of Romania, the party that represents ethnic Hungarians in Romania became part of the government coalition in 1997, so that fear no longer exists. In 1997, Hungary and Romania signed an agreement recognizing each other's borders and providing for opening of a Hungarian consulate in Cluj. Prime Minister Horn also paid a two day visit to Romania in November 1997.

Relations with Slovakia have deteriorated since Vladimir Meciar was elected prime minister. Meciar, a former communist who has discovered the power of nationalism in building popular support, has supported legislation requiring the use of Slovak even in areas where Hungarians are in a majority, and in 1997 he suggested that ethnic Hungarians should migrate to Hungary if they were not willing to become good Slovaks. Adding to the bad relations between the two countries is the quarrel over Hungary's abandonment of a 1977 agreement to jointly construct a series of dams and hydroelectric power stations on the Danube river at Gabcikovo–Nagymaros. The Slovaks obtained a decision from the International Court of Justice in 1997 that Hungary had broken international law in abandoning the 1977 agreement.

After coming to power in May 1990, the new non–communist government established diplomatic relations with Israel and the Vatican and also negotiated an agreement with the Soviet Union calling for the removal of all Soviet troops by July 1991. Hungary was also instrumental in the demise of the Warsaw Pact. When the Hungarian Government announced that it intended to leave the Warsaw Pact, Moscow, apparently fearing that other members would join the exodus, proposed that the military aspects of the organization be terminated as of April 1, 1991. The Warsaw Pact plus the CMEA, Hungary's other formal tie to Moscow, were formally dissolved on July 1, 1991.

Hungary was admitted to membership in the 23–nation Council of Europe in November 1990, the first East European nation to seek and receive admittance. Hungary became an associate member of the European Community in December 1991, along with Poland and Czechoslovakia. In 1997, the since renamed European Union extended an invitation for Hungary to become a full member. EU membership will

**Costumed fiddler celebrates two significant events of 1989—President Bush's official visit and the opening of Budapest's McDonald's restaurant (note U.S. and McDonald's flags below)**
Photo by Jon Markham Morrow

probably come some time after the year 2000. Hungary was also invited to become a member of NATO in 1997 and this was approved by popular referendum in November.

## The Nature of the Regime

Hungary is a multiparty democracy in transition to a free market economy. A new constitution was adopted in 1990 which created a parliamentary form of government with a ceremonial President of the Republic as chief of state. The President is elected by the National Assembly for a term of four years. The National Assembly is the new fulcrum of power, with the Chairman of the Council of Ministers as the country's political leader.

## The Hungarian Government

The President of the Republic is Arpad Goncz, a well–known writer and dissi-

dent. He was jailed for six years after the Hungarian Revolution of 1956. A founding member of the *Alliance for Free Democrats*, he became the head of the National Writers Association in 1989, then was elected President of the National Assembly (interim President) in May 1990. He was elected President of the Republic on August 3, 1990.

The Chairman of the Council of Ministers is the head of government and the individual responsible for government policy. He is nominated by the President and confirmed by the National Assembly. He can be removed if he loses a vote of confidence in the National Assembly.

The National Assembly is a single chamber parliament with a total of 386 seats. Its members are elected for a four year term in an election that is part proportional, part constituency.

# Hungary

## The Economy

The economy which the Antall Government inherited when it took power in May 1990 was one which had been moving away from an orthodox communist command economy for a good number of years, though it still retained and retains many aspects of that original pattern. The deviation began in the 1960's under the leadership of Janos Kadar. For the first six years after he became First Secretary of the communist *Hungarian Workers' Party* after the Soviet intervention to put down the Hungarian Revolution, Kadar enforced the old policies of heavy industrialization and collectivization which the regime had tried to get away from after the death of Stalin in 1953. The results were predictably unsatisfactory.

In 1963, with the economy in extreme stress and performing badly, Kadar came across a reform proposal by a Professor Liberman at the University of Kiev. Intrigued, Kadar decided to try out some of Professor Liberman's ideas. To encourage individual enterprise, the Hungarian government granted a one–year tax exemption to new artisan–type enterprises and guaranteed them access to supplies of raw materials. The result was an immediate increase in the number of working artisans in the villages, a welcome reversal of the long–time trend of migration to the cities. The reform also led to increased service facilities in the cities as tailors and repair-

men and mechanics set themselves up in their own shops.

In 1966, a more extensive economic reform began to be discussed. This program, which eventually became known as the "New Economic Mechanism," went into effect in 1968. The New Economic Mechanism postulated the continuation of central planning but proposed a change in the nature of that planning. Instead of concentrating on a minute, day–to–day control over the economy, central planning experts would concentrate on long–range goals.

Day–to–day management of the economy was delegated to the managers of individual enterprises, who were enjoined to go forward with the plan based on market demand. Although industry would remain state–owned, the state's control would be exercised indirectly, by general credit and interest policies and, in the case of individual enterprises, by means of loans provided to finance technological innovations. Wages were to be established by individual factories, though within guidelines set out by the central planners. Most important of all, the government gradually relinquished its control over prices. Before the reform began, there were over one million administered prices; by mid–1970, the figure had dropped to just over one thousand.

The New Economic Mechanism differed from Czech economic proposals of

**Hon. Gyula Horn**

the same time period in envisioning a continued positive role for the central planners. It was also not accompanied by a parallel discussion of possible political reforms. It therefore managed to survive the

**The Hilton Hotel's mirrored facade reflects the Gothic spires of Matthias Church in Old Budapest, site of the coronation of Charles II as King of Hungary in 1916.**

Courtesy: Jon Markham Morrow

285

# Hungary

**Harvesting corn on a collective farm**

Soviet invasion of Czechoslovakia. Kadar's condemnation of the Czech experiments and his participation in the invasion of Czechoslovakia were additional significant factors.

The plan had beneficial effects throughout the economy, but this was particularly true with regard to agriculture. The end of artificially low prices for agricultural products and the accompanying increase in average earnings in the countryside increased incentives and led to greatly increased production. The change was spectacular. In the mid–1960's, Hungary was a net importer of agricultural products. By the end of the 1960's, it had become a net exporter. In 1990, approximately 30 percent of exports were agricultural products.

The Hungarian Government instituted some further economic changes in 1984 which amounted to a strengthening of the New Economic Mechanism. As of January 1, 1985, approximately three–quarters of all enterprises became eligible for a new type of management system which gave them almost complete autonomy. In addition, a new set of financial rules was issued whereby efficient companies were permitted to pay higher wages and were actually encouraged to get rid of unnecessary employees.

The plan called for state subsidies to be eliminated and those inefficient enterpris-es which couldn't make it on their own were to be allowed to go bankrupt. Only one major company was permitted to go bankrupt at this time, however, and all of its viable parts, along with employees, were taken over by other companies.

Following the change in political leadership in May 1988, a further change in the economic program was adopted by the party in July. Essentially, this extended and intensified the reform program of the government, continuing an austerity program begun in 1987. Submitted by Miklos Nemeth, the new Chairman of the Council of Ministers, its object was to create "a genuine commodity, monetary, capital and labor market." A long–range plan, it contemplated several years of austerity and at least 2–3 years of little or growth before a turn–round would occur.

The most important change had to do with Hungary's small private sector. This sector, which constituted only 4–5% of the overall economy in 1988, was to be encouraged to grow until it became approximately 30%. Hungary also joined the International Monetary Fund, the Bank for International Settlements, and the International Bank for Recovery and Development (The World Bank) while the communists were still in control. That same government also established a realistic exchange rate for the Forint, its national currency.

Reorientation toward world markets was undertaken. In the 1970's, it began negotiating with western companies for the opening of manufacturing facilities in Hungary. The most famous of the products is probably Levi jeans, which Hungary exports throughout Eastern Europe and the Soviet Union. In the 1980's, a number of other western companies began operating in Hungary. Among those was McDonald's, which opened its first store in downtown Budapest in 1987. Although fast food restaurants are still pretty much a foreign concept in Eastern Europe, the Hungarian government began opening its own fast food outlets in 1984 under the English name of "City Grill." They proved to be so popular that a state catering firm signed a contract with McDonald's to franchise the real thing.

On the negative side, Hungarian borrowings to finance the importation of Western technology had raised its hard-currency debt to approximately $8 billion by 1981. When the Polish economy collapsed, Western bankers began to worry about Hungary's debt as well. The government, arguing that it had a relatively well–managed, market–oriented economy, managed to retain its access to Western credit. For example, between 1982 and 1984, it received a $596 million medium–term credit from the International Monetary Fund, negotiated a $200 million loan from a West German bank and was awarded a mandate for a $250 million six–year loan.

Nevertheless, the regime also instituted austerity measures designed to produce a positive balance of trade with Western nations. Between 1981 and 1984 the government managed to reduce its hard currency debt by about $1 billion. Then the government began easing off its austerity program and this, combined with a drop in the prices of its major exports caused its hard currency debt to begin growing again. Hungary's export situation worsened in 1986 with the country actually running a deficit in its convertible currency

trade, instead of an expected surplus. This led the government to opt for a new austerity program at the beginning of 1987.

Hungary's adverse trade balance worried foreign bankers and it came under international financial pressure again. The Federal Republic of Germany then came to Hungary's rescue with a credit of a billion marks ($526 million). Additional borrowing after that time raised Hungary's hard currency debt to $17.3 billion. This was potentially a very serious situation for Hungary. In 1989, debt servicing consumed 38.5 percent of Hungary's hard–currency earnings, though the ratio dropped after that time.

Hungary's economic situation improved in the early 1990s and for several years Hungary was the largest recipient of foreign investment in eastern Europe. It suffered a setback in 1994 but an austerity package adopted in January 1995 brought a gradual change for the better. Hungary has now had steady growth and declining inflation for several years and foreign investment is up again. The Hungarian stock market fell after the Asian crisis hit in the summer of 1997, but it has since recovered its lost ground.

Major investors have included American firms such as General Motors, General Electric, Ford, and Ameritech, German

Tourists enjoy ice cream on a street in Budapest.                          AP/Wide World Photo

# Hungary

companies such as Deutsche Telekom, Japanese companies such as Suzuki, and Austrian firms like Julius Meinl and Kleiner Bauder. General Motors invested $193 million in a joint venture project with Hungary's Raba Factory to produce 200,000 engines and assemble an estimated 15,000 Opel Astra automobiles a year. The first Opel Astra rolled off the assembly line in March 1992. Suzuki, a Japanese automobile company, began manufacturing Suzuki Swifts at its plant in the town of Esztergom in the fall of 1992. Ford has paid $80 million for a plant to produce electronic components for cars. General Electric purchased Tungsram, Hungary's lighting manufacturer, in 1989. Other American companies investing in Hungary include the Digital Equipment Corporation, Schwinn Bicycle Company, Cartier, Apple Computer, and US West.

In addition, the Swiss have entered into joint ventures in pharmaceuticals and food, and Ikea, the Swedish–based furniture group, has opened its first store in Budapest. Austrian and German firms have also been large investors, with more than 60% of all joint ventures in 1990 being sponsored by nationals of these two countries.

Hungary is also a major recipient of loans from the new European Bank for Reconstruction and Development, formally established in April 1991 with an initial capitalization of 12.4 billion.

Its greatest problem is that of privatization of industry, of course. Foreign investment, particularly joint ventures, has made a contribution, but it became a political issue as opposition political parties asserted that the government had sold the country's patrimony to outsiders. The potency of the argument is revealed by a 1994 poll of Hungarian workers which indicated that only 4 percent of workers were strongly in favor of foreign investment while 40 percent were opposed. Much of this is perception, since foreign investments currently constitute less than 10 percent of the gross domestic product. In addition, the number of Hungarian–owned small firms continues to grow rapidly even as the state sector contracts. A senior official of the European Bank for Reconstruction and Development has argued, in fact, that the private sector already accounted for over 50 percent of the gross domestic product by 1994. That may be so, but the state–owned sector at that time included most of the country's energy, chemical and pharmaceutical industries and nearly all banks.

The previous government was committed to reducing state ownership down to 21 percent, though even it had identified enterprises that it intended to keep under state ownership. It even set up a new state holding agency, the State Property Company, to operate these firms. It did intend,

**Hungarian children at the library**

however, that the State Property Company would issue stock to be sold to the public. The Hungarian Socialist Party, which has been in power since May 1994, has continued Hungary's development of a market economy, but it did slow down the process of transition for a while in an effort to offer greater protection against layoffs to workers. When this approach began to have negative economic effects, however, it reversed course in early 1995. Since that time, it has pursued a policy aimed at turning Hungary into a fully developed market economy.

Hungarian agriculture remains an important part of its economy and significant changes have taken place in this sector as well. Collective farms had already been given considerable autonomy under the communists and numerous small businesses had also grown up in conjunction with them. All of the collectivized farms have now been privatized, though legal conflicts about the ownership of land has slowed the issuance of deeds in some cases.

## Natural Resources

Hungary is relatively short of natural resources, which means that it is heavily dependent on imports. In the past, the Soviet Union has provided it with approximately 90% of its oil, iron ore and timber needs, plus a high proportion of other raw materials. The CMEA's conversion to dollar prices as of January 1, 1991, plus domestic economic problems the Soviet Union is experiencing, have disrupted CMEA trading patterns and left their future in doubt. Soviet oil exports to Eastern Europe dropped somewhat in 1990–91, but this has become less important since Eastern European countries now have to pay in dollars in any case.

Hungary's main domestic fuel source is a low–quality brown coal. Unfortunately, the country's reserves are not extensive, and coal production has started to decline.

For this reason, the Government several years ago made a commitment to the development of nuclear energy and it currently has three plants in operation, two of which were completed in 1987. Twenty–five percent of Hungary's electricity comes from nuclear energy. The old communist government had committed itself to build four additional reactors by the year 2000—raising the amount of the nation's electricity generated by nuclear plants to 40% but that probably won't occur.

The Soviet nuclear accident at Chernobyl is one factor, but not necessarily the most important one. The Hungarian plants are of a different design than that which exploded at Chernobyl—they make use of pressurized water in their design to slow down the neutrons in the fuel instead of graphite as at Chernobyl. In addition, as Joszef Bognar, director of the World Economics Institute insisted, the Hungarian government has "taken many more security steps than in the Soviet Union and incorporated many Western design elements."

## Culture

Because the Magyar language is not related to any of Europe's major languages, Hungarian culture is rather distinct from that of its neighbors. There tends to be a strong international culture also, since most educated Hungarians are fluent in at least one foreign language. Hungarian plays have to be translated before they can go abroad, but one such play, *Cats Play*, was extremely popular when it was produced in the United States in the 1970's.

Hungarians are also noted for their films, many of which would be classified as new wave or art films. Only about 20 Hungarian films are made in a year, however, so Hungarian theaters show many foreign films. One particularly successful Hungarian producer in recent years, made the films *Colonel Redl* and *Hanussen*, both

# Hungary

of which have been released in the United States. Incidently, both deal with the cultural area of the old Austro–Hungarian Empire and were released with a German soundtrack.

The old communist Hungarian Government was strongly supportive of cultural activities and in the 1980's spent an estimated $27 million to renovate the State Opera House in Budapest. Cultural activities were heavily subsidized, with the average ticket to a full opera or first–class concert costing about $2. The government also sponsored numerous "folk festivals" throughout the country. That did not change significantly under the new regime.

## Religion

Church–state relations were quite bad for many years but they began to improve after Cardinal Mindszenty, who had been residing in the American Embassy since 1956, agreed to go into exile; he died in Vienna in 1975. His successor, Laszlo Lekai, was named a cardinal in 1976. Janos Kadar summed up his position on religion at a press conference in Paris in 1978:

"We have ever considered it most important that honest religious citizens, doing a fair day's work building our country, should not be faced with irreconcilable problems of conscience by the confrontation of state and church. As the result of protracted, patient work settling the relationship between the state and the churches, a religious citizen can now, at the same time, be committed to social progress and socialism, and be a faithful son of his church" . . .

Cardinal Lekai died in the summer of 1986. Negotiations for appointment of his successor and new bishops dragged on for some time before the government finally gave its approval to the appointment of Laszlo Cardinal Paskai. The Hungarian Government had insisted that the Church take action against one of its priests, Father Gyorgy Bulanyi, who was preaching the incompatibility of Christianity and service in the Hungarian military. The Church, which had its own problems with Father Bulanyi, was nevertheless unwilling to repudiate him completely.

Church–State relations improved dramatically after Grosz became General Secretary. It was under Grosz, for example, that the government rehabilitated Joszef Cardinal Mindszenty and extended an invitation for the Pope to visit Hungary. One of the first acts of the new non–communist government, installed in office in May 1990, was to reopen diplomatic relations with the Vatican. It followed this up by dismantling all government controls over religion. The *Christian Democrats* were, of course, part of the last government coalition.

Hungary also has about 80,000 Jews, a tiny remnant of the estimated 600,000 Jews who lived in Hungary prior to World War II. Under the communists, Jews kept a low profile, though the government permitted them to run a school and the only rabbinical seminary in eastern Europe. Since the fall of communism, however, the local Jewish population has opened two Jewish schools, Jewish publications, cultural associations, and youth groups are expanding, and work is currently underway to renovate Budapest's 4,000–seat synagogue. As Peter Maass of the *Washington Post* reported, "it all amounts to the revival of what was one of Europe's largest and most prolific Jewish communities."

## The Future

Hungary has had steady growth and declining inflation for the last several years. Unemployment, which is over 10 percent, is rather high, but not higher than the average for unemployment in the European Union, which Hungary was invited to join in 1997.

The political situation is stable, though there is some possibility that might change as a result of the May 1998 parliamentary elections. The Hungarian Socialist Party, in power since 1994, appears poised to do well in those elections, though it might lose its electoral majority. If so, the Alliance of Free Democrats appears ready to join them in a new coalition government.

Hungary has excellent relations with all of its neighbors with the exception of Slovakia, and in 1997 it received an invitation to become one of three new members of NATO. All in all, the future is beginning to look pretty good.

**Father and son on the way to market.**                                    Courtesy: Jon Markham Morrow

289

# The Republic of Poland

A glimpse of the interior of the Royal Castle, Warsaw

Courtesy: Embassy of Poland

**Area:** 120,727 sq. mi. (312,683 sq. km.).

**Population:** 38.2 million.

**Capital City:** Warsaw (Pop. 1,659,400).

**Climate:** Temperate in the West; continental with colder winters in the East.

**Neighboring Countries:** Ukraine, Belarus (East); Lithuania (Northeast); Russia—Kaliningrad Enclave (North); Czech Republic, Slovakia (South); Germany (West).

**Official Language:** Polish.

**Other Principal Tongues:** Belarusian, Ukrainian, Russian, German.

**Ethnic Background:** Polish (98.7%) other (2.3%).

**Principal Religions:** Roman Catholic (95%; 75% practicing), Uniate, Greek Orthodox, Protestant and other (5%).

**Chief Commercial Products:** Machinery and equipment, fuels, raw materials, partially manufactured goods, light industrial goods, agricultural and food products.

**Currency:** Zloty.

**Annual Per Capita Income:** About U.S. $3,000.

**Former Political Status:** Independent kingdom from the 10th century; joined with Lithuania in the 14th century, decline in power in the 17th century leading to partitions of Poland by Russia, Prussia and Austria at the end of the 18th century; independent from 1918 until German conquest in 1939; "People's Republic" within the Soviet sphere 1947–1989.

**National Day:** May 3 (marking the day in 1791 when Poland adopted the first democratic constitution in Europe).

**Chief of State:** Aleksander Kwasniewski, President (Kvash–*nyef*–skee).

**Head of Government:** Jerzy Buzek, Prime Minister (appointed October 1997).

**Type of Government:** Multiparty democracy.

**National Flag:** Red and white horizontal bars.

## THE LAND AND THE PEOPLE

Poland, formerly the largest communist–governed country of east–central Europe, is shaped in an uneven circle as a result of the boundary changes that occurred after World War II. The land is mostly a flat plain that rises to mountainous heights only along the southern border, where the Sudeten and Carpathian ranges are found. These mountains seldom exceed 2,000 feet in elevation within Poland.

The soil is not very rich, and for this reason, agricultural yields are rather modest except in relatively small areas of black soil and wind–driven topsoil found in the center and south of the country.

Poland is bordered on the north by the waters of the Baltic Sea. The province of Olsztyn has a number of scenic lakes which form about ten per cent of the land area. Almost 26% of the total land is covered by forests. The longest river is the Vistula (*Wisla*) which stretches for 664 miles northward to the Baltic Sea, exiting in the Gulf of Danzig (*Gdansk* in Polish).

The climate reflects the middle position of Poland between Western Europe, with its moist oceanic climate and Eastern Europe with a dry, continental climate. There is slow change between the seasons because of the distinctive features of early spring and early winter. The summers are warm and permit the cultivation of fairly

good crops except during the years when there is not enough rain. The winters can be bitterly cold.

Although Poland prior to World War II had significant Ukrainian, White Russian, Jewish and German minorities, because of events associated with that war, Poland is ethnically and religiously now quite unified—almost every citizen is both an ethnic Pole and a Roman Catholic.

## HISTORY

### The Early Polish Kingdoms

In 1966 Poland officially celebrated its millennium—a thousand years of existence as a state. This date, observed with much pomp by the communist government, is actually the thousandth anniversary of the introduction of Christianity into the area; Roman Catholicism was established in 966.

The Piast ruling dynasty, named after its semi–legendary founder Piast, established itself in control of a number of Slav tribes living in the area between the rivers

**Shifting borders: c. 1150 . . .**

**and c. 1350**

Vistula and Oder. The most important of these were the *Polanie*, which means "inhabitants of the plains"—they gave their name to the nation and the country. In Polish, Poland is *Polska*. Prince Mieszko I (Mee–*ehs*–ko) adopted Roman Catholicism and was joined by those he ruled.

The adoption of Christianity and the submission to the protection of the Virgin Mary, officially called "Queen of the Polish Crown," had a political purpose. One thousand years ago it was an insurance policy against continued pressure of German rulers who justified their incursions into Polish lands as a movement to convert the pagans. The fact that Christianity was adopted in its western form has been of great and lasting influence. With Roman Catholicism came the introduction of the Latin, or Roman alphabet, to which were added letters designed to render some specific Slavic sounds. This was in contrast to the Cyrillic alphabet, developed from the Greek alphabet, adopted by the Russians and other eastern and southern sub–branches of the Slav family.

Because of the split between the Roman Catholic and the Eastern Orthodox churches, the Poles developed the notion that they were an outpost and frontier of Catholicism and western culture. The

Russians, professing what they regarded as orthodox ("correct") religion, viewed the Poles as "intruding Roman heretics." The mixture of political claims and conflicting spiritual values caused a lasting hostility between the two leading Slav nations.

The consequences of this split did not

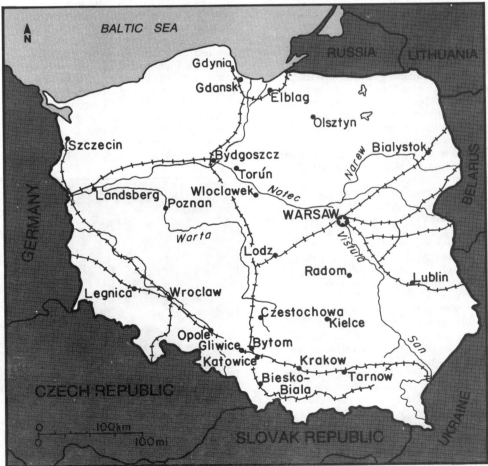

# Poland

fully appear for several centuries. During this time the Polish state, later combined with the much larger Grand Duchy of Lithuania, was one of the most important European realms. What later became known as Russia slowly dragged itself out of isolation, backwardness and a long period of Tartar rule which all but severed its contacts with Europe.

The early history of Poland was marked by attempts to create a solid national state with an independent existence against eastward pressures by the Germans and contests for territory and power with "Russian" princes. There was also competition with the early Bohemian (Czech) rulers whose claims to certain areas overlapped with those held by the Polish rulers.

Early successes by the Piast rulers included the brief occupation of Kiev (now the capital of the Ukraine) and an extension of control toward the Black Sea by Boleslaw the Brave. Important trade routes were also brought under Polish control. These successes were soon followed by a disintegration caused primarily by the so-called *appanage* system of inheritance by which the territory of a ruling prince was subdivided among all his sons, causing endless clashes among brothers and cousins for the position of leadership. The development was similar to what prevailed in the early "Russian" state of Kiev. The competition forced the contenders to rely for support on combinations of fighting men and also of the higher clergy. Support in the battle was paid for with land grants and with political power given to the landed gentry (*szlachta*). This became the basis for the development of the political power of the gentry which hampered the growth of a strong, centralized monarchy. It also led later to a concept of liberty almost bordering on anarchy, thus making orderly government almost impossible.

The most famous—or infamous—example of this development in later centuries was the concept of the *liberum veto*, where a *single* member of the national assembly could block legislation and force the assembly to be dissolved by speaking the words *nie pozwalam*—"I do not allow." In practice, these obstructive votes of minor gentry could be controlled or purchased by powerful magnates, or even by agents of foreign powers meddling in Poland's affairs. Although praised as a "democratic system, the constitutional freedoms and privileges actually were extended almost exclusively to the gentry, which was about 10% of the population. The cities enjoyed some rights, but the peasants were reduced to serfdom. This oppressive system continued with little change during the existence of the Polish–Lithuanian "commonwealth."

The unity of the state was restored in the 14th century under Casimir (Kazimierz) the Great; substantial reforms were introduced. The cities, which had lain neglected were developed, often settled by German artisans and Jewish traders. Culture advanced—the University of Krakow, a distinguished seat of learning and *alma mater* of the astronomer Copernicus, was established in 1364.

In spite of Casimir's wisdom and great contributions to government, law and culture, his rule was characterized by a further retreat of Polish control in the West and Southwest. The province of Silesia was ceded to semi–Germanized Czech rulers; the order of the Teutonic Knights, a Germanic religious group, was allowed to extend its control over areas adjacent to the Baltic Sea. Polish expansion was eastward, bringing closer a future clash with the Russian state once Tartar domination ceased there. For awhile, however, it seemed that the Polish state was safely launched on a course of greatness with its power embracing territory from the Baltic to the Black Sea.

## The Jagiellonians

Casimir the Great was the last of the Piast dynasty—he had no male heir. The throne passed to his nephew, Louis of Anjou, who was also the King of Hungary, and then to the latter's daughter, Jadwiga. A new era in the history of Poland opened when Jadwiga married the Duke of neighboring pagan Lithuania, Jagiello. He adopted Christianity and became king of Poland in 1386, founding a dynasty that lasted until 1572. During this period, in theory, the kings were elected, thus earning Poland the name "royal republic."

One of the reasons for the union of Poland and Lithuania was joint defense against the pressure of the Teutonic Knights along the Baltic Sea. Although the Knights were soundly defeated in 1410 at Tannenberg (Grunwald) and were forced to accept the authority of the Polish kings, they were never fully dislodged from their positions. With the advent of the Reformation in the sixteenth century, the Knights discontinued their role as a pseudo–religious organization and eventually became the nucleus of the kingdom of Prussia, thus establishing a standing menace to Poland's access to the sea. The Reformation also resulted in the adoption of Protestantism by some distinguished Polish families, but the bulk of the people remained stalwart Roman Catholics. Their faith was bolstered by the vigorous activity of the Jesuits during the counter–reformation.

## Decline and Fall

The previously loose organization of Poland–Lithuania was changed in 1569 into a more centralized state. However, soon thereafter, with the end of the Jagiellonians, the process of decline began, Until a final collapse at the end of the 18th century, there was a succession of elected kings, most of whom were foreign.

One of these monarchs, Sigismund III of the Swedish royal house of Vasa, involved Poland in the troubles that raged in Russia following the death of Ivan the Terrible; Polish troops occupied Moscow in 1610 and used false pretenders to the Russian throne to advance Polish policy. These attempts to profit from Russia's weakness were unsuccessful, but they created lasting resentment and distrust.

The rest of the 17th century was one of much misery for Poland. The Cossacks of the Ukraine, whose territory was mostly under Polish control, staged a bloody uprising in 1648, devastating much of the country. The Swedes "deluged" and almost destroyed Poland in 1655—tradition

Shrine to the Virgin Mary, Czestochowa

# Poland

places the reason for the rescue of the country to the miraculous intervention of the Virgin Mary. The invaders were stopped near a shrine to the Virgin Mary at Czestochowa. Soon, Poland was forced to give the eastern part of the Ukraine to Russia in 1667.

The decline of Poland was briefly interrupted by the brilliant performance of Polish forces under the native king, Jan Sobieski, which contributed greatly to the defeat of the Ottoman Turks at the gates of Vienna, Austria in 1683. This victory bolstered the self–image of the Poles as a strong Christian power, but in reality the weakening of Turkey opened the door to the strengthening of neighboring Russia and Austria. They began to plan the partition and destruction of the declining commonwealth.

Throughout much of the 18th century, Russian and other foreign troops occasionally occupied the territory of Poland; foreign ambassadors frequently dictated who was to sit on the throne. The last king of Poland was Stanislaw August Poniatowski, a former favorite of Catherine the Great, Empress of Russia. He was a man of great culture and charm, but possessed only limited talents for governing a country which was in a state of disintegration. Partitions of Poland were carried out in 1772, 1793 and 1795 by neighboring Russia, Prussia and Austria; they diminished and finally ended the independent exis-

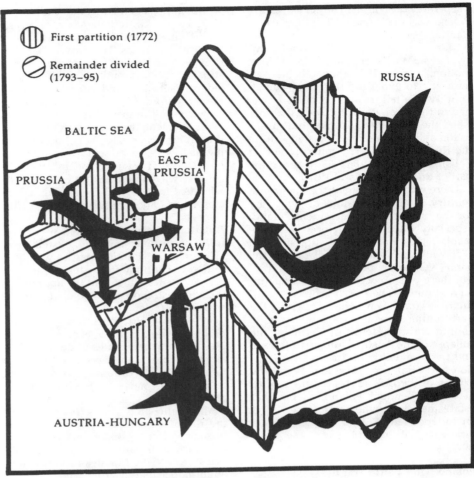

**POLAND: A land devoured**

tence of the once–glorious commonwealth.

Before the final partition, there were tardy expressions of patriotism in Poland. The youthful leader of one movement, Casimir Pulaski, eventually came to the United States and died while fighting the English in the War of Independence. Another Pole, Tadeusz Kosciuszko (Kos–chewsh–ko) led an unsuccessful uprising in Poland after fighting in the U.S. Revolutionary War. There was a last–ditch effort to reform the political structure which resulted in a proposed constitution, referred to with reverence even today as the May 3 Constitution (1791), though it was never actually put into effect.

### "Not Yet Lost"

After the collapse of the old commonwealth, the struggle for the revival of Poland was carried on mainly through efforts to interest foreign powers in sponsoring restoration of an independent Poland. Poles also flocked to various armies involved in fighting or preparing to fight one or another of the partitioners. Many were attracted by the high–sounding and seemingly universal slogans of the French

Revolution; a Polish legion was created by Napoleon in the Italian province of Lombardy. Their official song began with the words "Poland is not yet lost as long as we live." It became the national anthem in later years and still is today. Actually, although glad to see Poles join his armies, Napoleon had little concern for the cause of Polish independence. He revived a symbolic "Polish" state in 1807—the Duchy of Warsaw—which collapsed with the defeat of Napoleon's troops in the historic battles of 1812.

At the Congress of Vienna, Alexander I, the Russian Emperor, demanded that the historic Polish lands be brought together in a Kingdom of Poland. One of Alexander's advisers was a Pole by the name of Adam Czartoryski and he had suggested the idea to the Russian Tsar. Neither Austria nor Prussia was eager to give up their claims to Polish territories obtained as a result of the partitions, but they eventually agreed to Alexander's demands. The Kingdom of Poland thus came into existence in 1815 as a separate possession of the Russian Emperor; Alexander took the title of King of Poland and not only granted the Poles a constitution, but also set up

293

# Poland

a separate Polish army. The actual ruler of Poland was the Russian Grand Duke Constantine, regent.

Many Poles were dissatisfied with this arrangement which implied Russian domination, and in 1830 they rebelled, attempting to expel the Russians. The attempt was a failure and Nicholas I, who had in the meanwhile become Tsar, punished the Poles by abolishing the constitution and making Poland a state within the Russian Empire. In spite of another Polish uprising in 1862–63, it remained part of Russia until World War I.

There were, throughout the nineteenth century, many expressions of sympathy for the cause of an independent Poland, especially whenever there occurred spectacular, but unsuccessful, uprisings in 1830 and 1863. Russia had earned the name "gendarme (policeman) of Europe." But there was no occasion for outside intervention in "The Polish Problem" until the first World War, which involved the partitioning powers in a fatal struggle ending with the defeat of Germany, the collapse of the Austro–Hungarian Empire and the weakening of Russia by revolution and civil war. President Woodrow Wilson of the U.S. advocated the rebirth of an independent Poland, saying that "statesmen everywhere are agreed" that an independent Poland would become necessary with the collapse of the partitioners.

### Poland After World War I

The "new" Poland was officially reborn on November 11, 1918, and it enjoyed an independent existence for a little more than twenty years. The Treaty of Versailles which ended the war granted Poland access to the Baltic Sea through a narrow corridor which separated East Prussia from the main body of Germany, The area around the port city of Danzig (Gdansk) was organized as a Free City with a League of Nations high commissioner, Polish control over its foreign relations and internal self–government by a largely German– speaking population. The demand for its return to Germany would later be used to "justify" the Nazi invasion of Poland.

The reborn Polish state consisted of provinces which had been governed and neglected by foreign rulers for over a century. There was much wartime destruction and hunger, alleviated to some extent by a U.S. relief program. Politically, the nation was divided into a number of parties competing for power. An important outlet for the pressure of a rapidly growing population was formerly provided by emigration, especially to the U.S. This was virtually stopped after World War I, thus making the economic situation even more difficult.

One of the first prime ministers, the world–famous pianist Ignacy Paderewski (Pad–er–*ev*–ski), left the country after a few months, disgusted with the constant political squabbles. The provisional chief of state, Marshal Jozef Pilsudski, a former socialist who had fought for awhile on the side of Germany and Austria in World War I, temporarily retired from politics. However, he returned to power in May 1926, to rescue the country from disaster due, in his opinion, to the political bickering that was ever present. From that time until the end again came in 1939, the country was governed first by Pilsudski, who died in 1935, and then by his associates, especially a group known as "the colonels."

Parliamentary government was never fully abolished, but the system was "streamlined." Political parties were permitted to continue in existence, but only the candidates which had the approval of the administration could be elected to the parliament *(Sejm)*.

In addition to continuing economic problems, the country was beset by activities of ethnic minorities of doubtful loyalty to Poland. Many Germans turned out to be Nazis. The Ukrainians had a strong revolutionary movement, with some terrorist groups.

Many alienated young people joined the illegal *Communist Party;* filling the prisons with these disaffected youngsters only turned the jails into "prison universities" where the inmates received thorough indoctrination from fellow–prisoners who had sometimes been deliberately planted by the party. The fear of communism and the bitter relations with Soviet Russia against which a war was waged in 1920 in another attempt to profit from Soviet weakness, forced Poland to maintain a large, but poorly equipped army; this force proved unable to resist the massive attack launched by Hitler in September 1939.

Aware of their dangerous location between Germany and Russia, the Poles tried to maneuver between the two powerful neighbors. Although they signed a non–aggression agreement with Hitler in January 1934, they refused to enter into a closer, anti–Soviet association with the Nazis. In the end, the Poles aroused the suspicions of Germans and Russians alike. They also alienated western public opinion by participating in the division of Czechoslovakia with Germany that followed the Munich Conference in 1938.

### Poland During World War II

Undeterred by a guarantee given to Poland by the government of Great Britain, Hitler made a series of brash demands on Poland which were rejected as "impossible" by the Polish foreign minister. A week before the Germans launched their attack on Poland, Hitler scored a diplomatic success by reaching an agreement with the Soviet Union. The secret portions of the pact provided for a new partition of Poland, with the Soviet Union receiving the eastern part of the country with its

Signing the German–Russian Pact (August 23, 1939) which divided Poland between them. L. to r.: Germany's Ribbentrop with Stalin, Molotov

heavily non–Polish population. Soviet troops marched into Polish territory on September 17, after the last members of the government had left the national territory to seek refuge in neighboring Romania.

The heroic, but futile Polish resistance to the German armies came to an end in mid–September 1939. Soviet troops marched into the eastern part of the country and stopped along an agreed–upon line, called the Ribbentrop–Molotov Line after the names of the German and Soviet foreign ministers. Between September 1939 and June 1941 when the short–lived "friendship" between Hitler and Stalin came to an end, the partitioning powers energetically tried to wipe out all traces of an independent Poland. A large part of the German share of the land was directly incorporated into Germany; the remainder was formed into a "General Government" under a Nazi governor, Hans Frank.

A systematic policy of exterminating Poland's political and intellectual leaders reflected a Nazi plan to make the Poles a source of manual labor, working for the benefit of the "master race." The Jews were first herded into enclosed ghettos and later subjected to the "final solution"—death in gas chambers that operated around the clock. The eastern portions of Poland that were held by the Russians until they were overrun by Hitler in 1941 were declared to be parts of the Soviet Union. Massive transfers of people occurred in these regions.

Symbolically, an independent Poland continued to exist in the form of a government in exile, located first in France and later in England. Many thousands of Poland's fighting men managed to make their way west and formed military detachments pledged to fight side–by–side with the western Allies. Polish airmen distinguished themselves during the massive German air assault on England.

The position of the Poles was complicated by the fact that while the West was fighting Hitler's forces, the Poles were in conflict also with the Russians, who had joined in the partition of their land. On the surface the situation changed when Hitler launched an attack on Russia in mid–1941. Through British mediation, an agreement was signed restoring relations between the USSR and Poland. This made possible the formation of Polish fighting units from among the prisoners taken by the Russians in 1939 and from the many Polish citizens who had sought refuge in Russia. Because of the serious rifts between the Polish forces and the Soviet leadership, the troops under the command of General Wladyslaw Anders, left the territory of the Soviet Union. They fought gallantly in North African and Italy, especially at Monte Cassino, under British command.

As the war fortunes of the Soviet Union

**Warsaw in ruins, 1944**                    AP/Wide World Photo

began to improve, the Russians showed increasing dissatisfaction with the insistence of the Poles in exile on regaining the prewar frontiers of Poland in the East. When the Germans announced in 1943 the discovery in the Katyn Forest of a mass grave of Polish officers apparently slaughtered by the Russians, a new break between the Russians and the "London" Poles occurred. Pressured by his military staff, the Polish prime minister in exile, General Wladyslaw Sikorski, asked for an impartial inquiry by the International Red Cross. This was used by the Russians as a pretext to break diplomatic relations with the Poles in exile. A *Union of Polish Patriots* emerged as spokesman for the Poles in the Soviet Union; a Polish "army" was formed as an auxiliary of the Soviet troops.

These front organizations became the nucleus of a government set up when the Soviet Red Army in its westward drive reached what the Russians were willing to consider Polish territory. In August 1944, when it looked as if the Germans were withdrawing from Warsaw, the underground loyal to the London leadership staged an uprising, in the hope of obtaining control of the city before it was captured by the Russians. At the last moment, Hitler issued orders for his troops to make a stand, and the uprising was brutally crushed. The city was almost completely destroyed by the Nazis and many thousands perished in the ruins. Russian troops, although they were at one point very close to the suffering city, but across the Vistula, for political reasons, showed little desire to come to the assistance of the Poles.

This attitude, although possibly justified in part by the fact that Soviet forces

had run out of steam after a successful westward push in the summer, added another lasting element of bitterness and resentment to the relations between the two nations. Stalin was determined that no group of Poles not under his control would make a political comeback. At one point, sixteen leaders of the pro–London underground were lured into the open supposedly for the purpose of negotiation with the Soviets, but they were unceremoniously arrested and sentenced to jail.

After the Yalta Agreement of February 1945, the government–in–exile located in London was eventually "de–recognized" by the U.S. and the British; a lame compromise was worked out in the spring of 1945 which led to the creation of a government of "national unity," built around the Russian–sponsored group, with the addition of a few non–communist leaders, the most prominent of whom was the peasant leader Stanislaw Mikolajczyk (Mee–koh–*lie*–chik).

Stalin's vague promises of "free and unfettered elections" offered little protection to non–communist groups which tried to resume their political activities after the war. The fiction of "national unity" came to an end once the illusion of postwar accord between East and West was ended by the opening of the "Cold War." Mikolajczyk had to flee the country in 1947.

### From "People's Democracy" to "People's Republic"

Postwar Poland was and still is, in many respects, an almost entirely new country. It is about 185 miles farther to the west than it had been in 1939. At the expense of Germany, it gained a 325–mile-long coast on the Baltic Sea—a large coast-line when compared to the narrow corri-

# Poland

Map legend:
- Annexed to Russia, 1939
- Annexed from Germany, 1945
- ---·--- 1939 Boundary
- ——— 1945 to present
- ------- Curzon line

0 60 120 mi
0 60 120 km

Jan 85

been active in the pro–Soviet underground during the years of German occupation and who presided over the absorption of the territories "recovered" from Germany, was removed from office and eventually imprisoned. He was never tried and was later able to reemerge as a leader in 1956. Communist control over all aspects of social life and Soviet direction of Polish internal affairs were substantially strengthened in the late 1940's.

Pressure was brought against political parties that had kept their prewar names and occasionally some of the pre–1945 non–communist leaders were induced to merge either with the communists or with the communist–front groups. Thus, the *Polish Socialist Party (PPS)* was forced to merge with the communists, who had been using the name *Polish Workers Party,* to form the *Polish United Workers Party.*

In spite of all of the changes of the wartime and early postwar period, the communists could not compete for the support of the workers against the traditional *Polish Socialist Party,* which had to be merged out of existence largely with the help of one of its younger leaders, Jozef Cyrankiewicz (Tsee–*ran*–kay–vich). He was rewarded with the job of Premier; some years later, he was appointed Chairman of the Council of State (1970–1972). The *Peasant Party,* which had retained a large following under its prewar leadership, was forced to combine with a communist–front group to form the *United Peasant Party.* Independent social organizations were also herded together into "united" groups controlled by the communists.

The high point of Soviet meddling in Polish affairs was reached when Konstantin Rokossowski, a Soviet army marshal, was made commander–in–chief of Poland's armed forces, minister of defense and a deputy premier in the government. Important positions in the army were given to Russian officers, not all of whom could claim, as did Rokossowski, to be of Polish descent. Economic transformation was reflected in stepped-up industrialization plans, and an almost complete elimination of private enterprise in industry and commerce. There was an attempt to shift land ownership from individual peasant holdings to a form of collectivized farms. However, in comparison with other countries of the area, the results of collectivization remained rather limited. Poland is to this day agriculturally the least collectivized of the communist–governed states.

In the years following 1947, increasing pressure was brought to bear on the Catholic Church, directed principally at educational efforts. Church schools were secularized, Church lands were confiscated and restrictions were placed on religious activities. This pressure reached its peak

dor of the interwar period. What had been East Prussia prior to the war was divided between Poland and the Soviet Union, eliminating what many Poles viewed as a "dagger pointed at the heart of Poland."

The frontier line with Germany was substantially shortened. The "recovered" lands taken from the Germans are economically more valuable than those surrendered to the USSR. Another basic change was in the composition of the population. Instead of having over 30% of its people ethnically non–Polish, the country is now inhabited by 38 million people, of whom only a little more than 2.3% are ethnic minorities. The Ukrainians and Byelorussians that had lived in Poland were taken into the Soviet Union; the bulk of the more than three million Jewish population was exterminated by the Germans and most who managed to survive chose to leave the country. Most Germans were expelled or moved westward. Thus, Poland is more Polish and, incidentally, more Roman Catholic than it has been for many centuries.

Until mid–1947, during the period of "national unity," the official claim was

that the system established in Poland was to be different from both the capitalist model of the west and the communist one of the Soviet Union. This claim could not survive the beginning of the Cold War with its divisive effect. While the United States proclaimed a policy of "containment" of communism, the founding of the Communist Information Bureau (*Cominform*) at a conference held in western Poland in 1947, symbolized the beginning of a new era. Under the circumstances, Poland was compelled by Moscow to reject an offer of Marshall Plan aid extended by the U.S. Soon thereafter, the rift between Stalin and the Yugoslav communists made the Russians exert still more pressure to hold the line in the governments of other eastern European states. In one country after another, communist leaders identified with the "national" road to socialism were removed from office, jailed and sometimes executed.

For a variety of reasons, events in Poland did not lead to such extreme measures against leaders accused of "nationalist deviationism," but there were drastic changes. Wladislaw Gomulka, who had

in 1953 when Cardinal Wyszynski (Vee-*shin*–skee) was placed under house arrest in a monastery and forbidden to carry out his functions as primate of Poland. However, the confiscation of Church lands and the general persecution probably had an effect opposite to that intended. The fact that the Church was no longer a landowner probably increased its hold over the rural population and the general persecution mainly served to increase its hold over the masses, which remains remarkably strong.

The Catholic educational system was topped by the Catholic University of Lublin and the Theological Academy in Warsaw. The communists looked upon the Church as a rival organization which competed for the allegiance of the people, and no efforts were spared to make the position of the Church difficult. At the same time, the regime had great respect for the traditional power of the Church in Poland and it was this which protected the Church from an all–out frontal assault. This also produced some anomalies as when, for example, the communist leadership publicized the endorsement of Cardinal Wyszynski in the 1956 elections, even though they had kept him under house arrest since 1953.

### The Polish Struggle of October 1956

Following the death of Josef Stalin in 1953, the Polish government launched a "New Course" which involved some relaxation of the old Stalinist norms. Workers were little affected, but there was a cut in taxes for the peasantry and a slowdown in the process of collectivization. Intellectuals found they could be a little more critical in their comments about Polish life.

Then an event occurred that had widespread repercussions. Jozef Swiatlo, a high official of the Polish secret police, fled westward soon after Stalin's death. In 1954, Radio Free Europe in Munich began a series of broadcasts of Swiatlo's memoirs. His well–documented disclosures of the terroristic activities of the *UB*, the political police organization, became widely known in Poland and led to the abolition of the Ministry of Public Security. This was followed later by the arrest of some leading secret police officials.

Several economic reforms were also introduced, especially in the field of labor discipline. Critical voices began to be heard, first among writers and students and then among the rank and file membership of the party. In the field of communist political theory, "revisionist" views came to the fore, accompanied by a tendency to question some of the most basic tenets of Marxism–Leninism. Students and recent graduates began to organize discussion clubs in which pointed questions embarrassing to the government were raised in lengthy debates.

Poland was thus in a state of political turmoil when Khrushchev made his famous "secret" speech denouncing the evil deeds of Stalin at the 20th Congress of the party in the Soviet Union in 1956. As luck would have it, Boleslaw Bierut, First Secretary of the Polish Communist Party, died in Moscow two weeks after Khrushchev's speech. He was succeeded by Edward Ochab, a shrewd politician who recognized the need for reform. It was Ochab who freed Gomulka, at that time under house arrest in a villa on the outskirts of Warsaw, and facilitated his reentry into the party; this occurred in August.

A wave of strikes by industrial workers broke out in June 1956, topped by clashes in Poznan between workers and troops. The regime at first tried to blame the outbreaks on "capitalist provocation," but soon came to the conclusion that the entire structure of communist rule might tumble unless there was a dramatic change of direction in government.

The logical choice to accomplish this was Gomulka, who because of his insistence on a "Polish road to socialism" became a symbol of independence from the Soviet Union. He was thought likely to satisfy the "revisionist" elements within the party, but also the masses of workers and ordinary citizens. Amid preparations to put Gomulka in the position of First Secretary of the party in mid–October 1956, an impressive delegation of top Soviet leaders suddenly appeared in Warsaw and there were rumors of Soviet troops on the march toward the Polish capital. However, Khrushchev and his comrades, reassured about continued Polish–Soviet ties and possibly impressed by the resolute stand of factory workers who had obtained arms and were converging on the airport, departed.

The Soviet delegation flew back to Moscow, grudgingly, accepting changes in the Polish communist leadership, which included the elimination of Marshal Rokossowsky, a visible symbol of Soviet interference in the internal affairs of a neighboring and friendly country. In this way, a tragic clash such as occurred about the same time in the Hungarian capital of Budapest was avoided. Because of the role he played in the unseasonal "spring in October," Gomulka was thought by many to

**First Secretary Wladyslaw Gomulka (left) chats with President Aleksander Zawardski**
AP/Wide World Photo

# Poland

be a "liberal" who favored popular control of government. Actually he was rather an austere, conservative communist with a political sense for what could be done in Poland and with the Polish people; this sense failed him in later years, however. As the "thaw" of 1956 passed into history, many of the more visionary hopes of the intellectuals were disappointed.

However, the Polish regime continued to differ from those in neighboring communist–ruled countries. There was a reversal of the trend toward collectivization of agriculture. Prior to 1956, progress toward this goal had at all times been slower in Poland, and when Gomulka returned to power, there was a massive abandonment of even the token collectivization that had occurred.

Agricultural Circles were about the only form of cooperative organization in the farmlands. Their main function was the joint purchase and use of farm machinery. This was a far cry from the practice of totally controlling agricultural production through a system of collective farms. Gomulka apparently decided that the Polish peasant had to be left to discover for himself the blessings of socialism rather than be forced into it.

In other branches of the national economy, especially in industry, Gomulka saw less room for non–communist management. Workers Councils, organized during the 1956 upheaval, were later discouraged, and industry once again ran in a centralized manner. There were, however, some attempts to make central planning of the economy less rigid. For a number of reasons, Polish industry continued to suffer from serious shortcomings; various emergency measures occasionally resulted in unemployment and a halt in the movement of people from the overcrowded countryside to the cities.

In commerce, a degree of private enterprise was permitted, although it was overburdened by state controls and taxation. Individual craftsmen were also permitted to work alone or in small groups.

In the cultural sphere, there was a tremendous outburst of creative activity after 1956 as the rigid rules of "socialist realism" were relaxed and it became possible to experiment with new and non conformist forms of artistic expression. Access to the Western press and literature was relatively free and travel permits to areas outside the communist bloc were issued more generously than elsewhere in Eastern Europe.

In political life, an effort was also made to create a real function for the parliament (Sejm). The habit of debating proposed legislation in committee and attempts to critically evaluate the efficiency of government changed the legislature from a rubber stamp completely controlled by the leadership to a reasonably authentic voice of some parts of public opinion. Polls and other studies of public attitudes also came into use. Polish sociologists point with pride to the fact that, under their influence, a revised interest in the social sciences spread to other nations of Eastern Europe and to the Soviet Union. The relatively tolerant Khrushchëv was dismissed from office in 1964 and his successors began a retightening of control. These Soviet events were mirrored in Poland, where the "spring" of 1956 was followed by a new freeze. Although the people continued in various ways to have "little freedoms," a sense of disappointment and distrust characterized the attitude of intellectuals, who had high hopes of basic changes under Gomulka.

Dissatisfaction with the regime came into the open in early 1968 when students and intellectuals clashed with the police. The reasons for the conflict was the suppression of a theatrical performance of a work by Poland's greatest poet, Adam Mickiewicz (Mits–kay–witch). The work, Dziady (Forefathers), contained anti–Russian themes which were lustily applauded by audiences. There also was dissatisfaction with the official attitude of the government, which (following the lead of the Soviet Union) came out in support of the Arabs in their conflict with Israel. This policy enabled one of the groups within the leadership, the so–called Partisans led by the ambitious General Mieczyslaw Moczar (Mo–char) to open an attack on "Zionist" elements supposed to be in the government and the party.

These charges appealed to a deeply-rooted anti–Semitism of the Poles; Gomulka, although himself married to a Jewess, decided to go along with what turned out to be a massive purge of Jews within the government, universities and cultural organizations. Many had to leave the country practically overnight because they could not make a living in Poland.

They had to renounce their Polish citizenship and leave most of their belongings. Thus, the once–flourishing Jewish community of Poland, reduced by Hitler's destruction and postwar emigration from over 3 million to less than 30,000, has by now almost ceased to exist.

Gomulka's political maneuvering and his obedience to the Soviet Union demonstrated in his support for the invasion of Czechoslovakia in 1968 saved him temporarily from political defeat. He was reelected leader of the Party in 1968 in spite of pressure from Moczar and his Partisans, with the support of Edward Gierek, boss since 1957 of the Party organization in the important mining and industrial province of Upper Silesia. But Gomulka (aptly described as a "spent force" by one observer) could no longer control the conflicting trends within the party leadership. Differences were not only over the direction of leadership, but reflected a generation gap between old timers such as Gomulka and younger, better educated, technically–minded elements demanding a share of power.

The final downfall of Gomulka was triggered by an apparently spontaneous outbreak of protests by workers expressing dissatisfaction over increased food prices on the eve of the Christmas holidays of 1970. A coalition of competing factions within the Party leadership agreed to dismiss Gomulka and elected Edward Gierek as First Secretary. Some of the ex–leader's closest colleagues also lost their positions.

Under the leadership of the initially popular ex–miner Edward Gierek, Poland embarked on an ambitious plan of rapid industrialization and economic growth, financed by heavy borrowing of capital from the Soviet Union as well as from a number of Western governments, international financial institutions and private banks.

Until about the mid–seventies the results seemed impressive; there was a substantial rise of the gross national product

**Edward Gierek**

and a striking improvement in the standard of living. However, this economic "miracle" came to an end, in part, because of a dramatic change for the worse in the international economy, but also because of widespread graft and mismanagement within the government.

To service the foreign debt, Poland had to resort to increased export of food, thus cutting into the supply of food for consumption at home. While workers' wages had increased, less and less was available for purchase. An attempt in 1976 to raise prices on basic food articles led to the outbreak of strikes as well as looting and at-

Poland

Swientojanska Street in Krakow—the city's Archbishop became Pope John Paul II

tacks on communist party headquarters in many localities. The decision of the government to *cancel* price increases a bare 24 hours after they had been announced, undermined the prestige of the ruling party. Legal measures taken against workers who had incited strikes led to the creation of an organization for the defense of arrested and dismissed workers known by the initials *KOR*. Another organization came into being in 1977 called *Movement of Defense of Human and Civil Rights (ROPCIO)*.

The new Gierek leadership also expressed a desire to "improve communication with the working masses" and sought a further normalization of relations with the Roman Catholic Church. Several anti-Church measures were dropped, permission was given to construct churches in the new industrial towns and the Church's debts to the state were cancelled.

The election of a Polish Pope in 1978 was another factor in this development.

The election of Karol Wojtyla (*Voi*–chla), Archbishop of Krakow—who took the name of John Paul II—brought an outburst of national pride which extended even to many members of the Communist Party. Gierek sent a handsome message of congratulations to Rome and negotiations began immediately for a papal visit to Poland. It occurred in June 1979 and included a nationally–televised meeting between the Pope and Edward Gierek and other leaders of Party and state.

Gierek was more successful in his relations with the Catholic Church than he was in his second goal of improving communication with the masses. He promised that workers would be consulted and that intellectuals would be heard. He also declared that the Party could not possibly regulate *everything*. The political thaw did not last long.

By 1973 censorship had been fully restored and it soon became clear that the Party, instead of reducing its intervention

in national life, was in practice carrying through a further centralization in the name of reform.

Moreover, while claiming to be the "leading political force in society in constructing socialism," the Party was granting its own members special pay and privileges that set them off from, and aroused the hate of, the masses. Isolated and filled with bureaucrats, the Party became more and more a hollow stem willing to "stonewall" just about anything.

### Strikers and Dissidents

Dissatisfaction with the communist system had been simmering in Poland for a number of years. It brought about the emergence of various dissident groups on the political and intellectual level, ranging from barely legal to illegal organizations; some of these groups claimed belief in the basic tenets of communism, but advocated reform of the system and removal of those who mismanaged it, while others,

299

# Poland

on the extreme right, advocated abandonment or overthrow of the system.

Illegal publications, study circles and "flying universities," often holding classes in church buildings, proliferated over the years. However, the decisive change came when the small intellectual groups identified themselves with the plight of the workers who had resorted to strikes to protest oppressive conditions in the factories and the undercutting of their living standards by a hike in the prices of food.

Opposition in Poland derived substantial support from the outspoken position of the Catholic Church under the leadership of Cardinal Wyszynski (d. 1981). The election of a Polish prelate to be Pope was also a source of moral support. Nevertheless, it was the spectacular collapse of the economy after a decade of what looked like successful development that set off Poland's latest crisis in 1980–81. One could hardly imagine the dramatic and potentially catastrophic pressures for reform without the spectacular collapse of the economy after several years of what looked like successful development.

The government, facing a rapidly deteriorating economic situation and a crushing debt to foreign lenders (estimated at some $28 billion) tried to appease the workers as well as the political dissidents by a number of half–measures and promises of improvements which could not always be kept. Matters came to a head when thousands of workers in the Gdansk (Danzig) shipyard went on strike and occupied the premises of the enterprise.

## "Confrontation," Confusion and Clumsiness

Under the leadership of Lech Walesa (Vah–*len*–sa), an unemployed electrician who emerged from nowhere to a position of prominence, the workers refused to vacate the factory and insisted that the government send a negotiator to deal with the *Twenty–one Demands* posted by the workers' strike committee.

The main point of the demands was permission to establish independent trade unions *in competition with the party–controlled official trade union organization.* When this demand was accepted by the government, a new institution was born: *Solidarity,* which claimed a membership of ten million workers. An extension of the protest movement to the countryside resulted in the creation of a rural branch of *Solidarity.* Whether intended or not, there was underway a confrontation between the Polish workers in association with the Church and, ultimately, the Soviet Union.

What followed was a drastic shake–up of the Party–State leadership. Gierek and his close associates were ousted and the relatively unknown Stanislaw Kania became leader of the Party. The post of

December 1980: Lech Walesa with supporters

Chairman of the Council of Ministers was taken over by the man who already held the post of Defense Minister, a career military officer, General Wojciech Jaruzelski (*Voy*–check Ya–roo–*zel*–skee). For awhile, negotiations involving the communist government, the independent *Solidarity* movement and the Catholic Church raised the hope that Poland might enter a new phase of its history under a rather unusual triangular arrangement between the formal, but discredited communist authorities (with the Soviets lurking in the shadows), the independent trade union movement and the Church (now led by Cardinal Wyszynski's successor, Cardinal Glemp). However, a worker movement independent of the Polish United Workers' Party was, by its very existence, a challenge to the communist claim to be the party of the workers, and it soon became clear that an independent *Solidarity* was unacceptable not only to significant elements in the *PUWP* but to the Soviet leadership.

The true picture became clear in October 1981 when Kania resigned as Party Secretary and was replaced by General Jaruzelski, who, significantly, was not only Chairman of the Council of Ministers (prime minister) but also Defense Minister and therefore head of the Polish armed forces.

During previous periods of unrest, the armed forces had not been used to restore order. On December 31, 1981, however, General Jaruzelski declared martial law throughout the country and ordered the armed forces to begin a roundup of trade

union activists and intellectual dissidents. Thousands were rounded up, including Lech Walesa and most of the other *Solidarity* leaders. A curfew was enforced throughout the country and telephone communications between cities were restricted.

The Polish government also sought to discredit *Solidarity* by attempting to show that the trade union was not merely seeking an improvement in the economic situation as it claimed, but that it was interested in sharing political power with the communists, or taking it away from them. Secret tapes made by the government at a national conference of *Solidarity* in the city of Radom had Lech Walesa and others stating that the time had come for "confrontation" with the government rather than "compromise." The tapes were probably altered. In late 1982 *Solidarity*—and the discredited old official trade unions—were banned and new official trade unions replaced them. According to the government, the new official unions currently have a membership of about 7 million, of which 60% are former members of *Solidarity.* If correct, that figure would represent slightly less than half of the total labor force.

*Solidarity* may have been banned, but it was by no means dead. Lech Walesa, after being held in custody for several months, was eventually released without any charges being filed against him. His receipt of the Nobel Prize for Peace also strengthened his hand. As a result, he was permitted to continue to speak out publicly, though his actions were closely mon-

300

itored by the government and he was continuously under the threat of harassment or worse. An amnesty of mid–1984 resulted in the release of the last 652 *Solidarity* detainees. A few were rearrested after meeting with Walesa. They were subsequently released, but remained subject to government harassment when they attempted to speak out publicly.

While there were those within the leadership of the *PUWP* who opposed the independent *Solidarity* movement, the decisive factor that led the Polish government to declare martial law and ban the movement was the strong pressure being exerted at this time by the Soviets.

Yet another concern of the Soviet leadership under Brezhnev was the still–important position of the Roman Catholic Church in Polish life, and that concern appears to have increased after John Paul II, the former Karol Wojtyla, Archbishop of Krakow, was elected Pope in 1978. It is for this reason that scholars are inclined to accept a connection between the Soviet KGB and a subsequent attempt on John Paul II's life while he was officiating at a ceremony in St. Peter's Square in Rome. The connection is indirect because the man who actually fired the shot was a Turkish national who, the Italian government charged, was an agent of the Bulgarian secret police. The Soviet connection derives from the fact that the Bulgarian secret police would almost certainly not have been operating in such an important matter without the knowledge of the Soviet KGB.

The most important connection between the attempted assassination of the Pope and the government of Poland is that John Paul II is a Pole; there is absolutely no evidence that it knew anything whatsoever about the plan to kill the pontiff. At least up to 1985, the Polish Government was under pressure from the Soviets to reduce the influence of the Church. The government was divided on the issue, with moderates arguing the value of cooperation with the Church and "hard–liners" arguing the danger of such an accommodation. While the internal struggle was still going on, three members of the Polish security police, acting under orders of their superior officer, a colonel, brutally murdered Father Jerzy Popieluszko, a priest. He had become a target because he was an ardent and public supporter of *Solidarity*. Eleven days after he had been reported missing, his body was found, weighted, at the bottom of a reservoir. An autopsy showed that he had been beaten to death before being thrown into the water.

This forced General Jaruzelski's hand. Disassociating himself and his regime completely from the killing, he ordered that the four implicated individuals be put on public trial and that it be televised nationwide. All four were convicted and

**General Wojciech Jaruzelski**

received long prison sentences. In addition, their superior in the Ministry of the Interior was fired. Jaruzelski himself took the further step of assuming direct responsibility for the police and the internal security forces, replacing two members of the Party secretariat who had formerly been in charge of those activities.

In spite of Jaruzelski's actions, State–Church relations reached a new low,

**His Holiness Pope John Paul II**

charged with emotion arising out of the revelations during the trial of the dirty war waged by the security police against the Church. Responding to these emotions, Cardinal Glemp began to take a more militant line, and Jaruzelski answered in kind. In a 1985 press interview, speaking about differences with the Church, the general was quoted as saying somewhat defensively:

*"In Poland the church has a vast, favorable opportunity to carry out its priestly mission. Regrettably, certain priests abuse this freedom to stage unlawful acts. We talk about it openly."*

Church–state relations began to improve again in 1986. They climaxed in January 1987, when General Jaruzelski paid a state visit to Italy and was received by Pope John Paul II. The 70–minute private talk was described by a Vatican spokesman as "earnest, clear and profound." Symbolically, Jaruzelski's daughter, Monika, who accompanied him, was given a rosary and took another home to her mother. Equally symbolically, Jaruzelski invited the Pope to visit Poland and the visit took place in June 1987. According to press reports at the time, Jaruzelski also promised to grant the Church full legal status—a move that would allow the Church's youth organization and its various professional bodies to operate publicly—but nothing was done to put this into effect before the June arrival of the Pope.

When the pontiff arrived, the fireworks began. *Solidarity* banners appeared widely everywhere he went. Crowds ultimately numbering into the millions attended the many masses he said, cheering him with wild enthusiasm. At each mass or appearance he praised *Solidarity* with warm enthusiasm to show his disapproval of the government. Jaruzelski tried to talk him into silence midway during the visit, but to no avail. He kissed the tomb of Father Popieluszko, reviving all of the old emotions surrounding his death. Upon his departure, the General appeared at the airport to say relatively harsh words to the highly respected Pope. Jaruzelski, usually "unflappable," had visibly been disturbed and was shaking with undisguised anger. The damage had been done.

Although Jaruzelski had not gotten what he wanted from the Pope's visit, he was evidently impressed by the response of the Polish people to the Pope. From this, he concluded that some accommodation with the Church was necessary if he wanted to reconcile the Polish people to continued communist rule. As a result, the government began permitting the Church to enlarge its area of activities and to become, in the words of one Pole associated with the movement, "the most interesting

# Poland

independent intellectual and social center in Poland."

As in East Germany, the Church became a refuge for dissident artists. In September 1987, Wroclaw's large Gothic "Church of the Holy Cross" arranged an exhibit of the works of 151 artists from all over Poland under the title "National Biennial of Young Artists." The Government permitted the exhibit, even though many of the 423 works of art on display had secular themes and, according to Polish law, could not legally be exhibited inside a church.

The Church was also permitted to expand its educational role. Church schools teaching secular subjects were established throughout the country and the Catholic University in Lublin added faculties in law, economics, psychology and sociology. In addition, the Church established publishing facilities where it began printing its own textbooks. Many of the activities originally sponsored by *Solidarity* were thus given new life under the patronage of the Church.

But Jaruzelski did not want the Church to be the sole intellectual alternative, and he accordingly moved to grant more freedom generally. This led the government to give approval to *Res Publica*, a privately owned magazine, to begin publishing in July 1987. Although allowed only 25,000 copies, it was important as the first of Poland's many underground magazines to achieve legal status. An even more important move came in January 1988 when the government stopped jamming the broadcasts of Voice of America, Radio Free Europe and the Polish language broadcasts of the BBC.

Although Jaruzelski made the final decision himself, it was reportedly on the advice of Mieczyslaw Rakowski, then Deputy Chairman of the Council of Ministers and an ex–journalist. Rakowski had been editor of *Politika*, Poland's most important journal of politics, before joining the government.

All of this provided background for Jaruzelski's greatest gamble—his attempt to implement an economic reform that had much in common with what Gorbachёv was trying to do in the Soviet Union at this same time. In an attempt to obtain public backing, Jaruzelski submitted the plan to a public referendum in November 1987. Although the three–year program contained elements such as increased private enterprise and a decentralization that was supposed to cut the number of government jobs by a quarter, it also included a cut in subsidies that would have brought an immediate, significant increase in prices. Whether for that reason or because they simply did not trust the communists, voters rejected the reform.

Stung by its defeat, the government decided to begin implementing the reform anyway, although more slowly than originally planned. The first price rises went into effect at the beginning of 1988 with food, rent, and fuel increasing by an average of 45 percent.

It was the official party unions that protested first, and this led to a strike among transport workers in the city of Bydgoscz. The government granted a 60 percent pay increase to the transport workers but, in the meantime, the strike began spreading to other parts of Poland. Among those joining the strike were the workers at the Lenin Shipyard in Gdansk.

The strike now became explicitly political, for this was the birthplace of *Solidarity* and Lech Welesa once again emerged as a local leader. Occupying the Lenin Shipyard and refusing to leave, the Gdansk workers demanded that, in addition to a pay increase, *Solidarity* activists dismissed in 1981 should be reinstated in their jobs. The government agreed to a wage increase but refused to bargain over the political issue. When the government held firm, it soon became clear that this was not to be a replay of 1980–81. There was no national ground–swell of support for the Gdansk workers, and after eight days they were forced to end their strike.

The government thus won a victory of sorts, but not one of much value. For its economic reform to have any chance of success, it had to have the active support of the workers, and this it did not have. In fact, a public opinion poll taken in early 1988 indicated that only 7% of those polled believed that the economic reform had any chance of success.

That is not surprising. After all, the political leadership had been pursuing a program of economic reform since 1980, all without tangible results. This bred a sense of pessimism exemplified by the comment of one Polish journalist in July 1988 that Poland had already been through reform, "and it did not work."

Inflation, already bad, grew worse as the summer progressed and there were increasing shortages of all kinds of consumer goods. In August, a new wave of strikes swept across Poland, spreading for the first time to the Silesian coal fields. Because coal exports were one of Poland's major sources of hard–currency earnings, the government had always gone out of its way to keep the miners happy. But even the miners had seen their standard of living drop in the preceding months, and they were now demanding action.

In a final irony, it was the official trade unions, not the outlawed *Solidarity*, that declared a lack of confidence in the government and demanded that it resign. The government stepped down in September and General Jaruzelski appointed Mieczyslaw Rakowski (*Myek*–cis–lav Ra-*Kov*–skee) as the new Chairman of the Council of Ministers (Premier).

Rakowski, determined to break the political–economic deadlock, introduced a new phrase into the communist lexicon—the "constructive opposition"—and offered four cabinet seats to *Solidarity* supporters. He also called for roundtable negotiations with the opposition. But what he offered the opposition was the chance to participate in the economic reform; there were to be no political reforms. *Solidarity* was not to be legalized and, in fact, *Solidarity* supporters were urged to repudiate their leadership, since "it is impossible to compromise with Walesa." Under the circumstances, no one in the opposition was willing to join the government, and the proposed roundtable negotiations never got started.

Rakowski was left with the alternative of either dealing with Walesa or of somehow discrediting him. The party decided to assign that task to Alfred Miodowicz (*Meeo*–doe–vitz), leader of the official trade unions and a member of the party Politburo. Miodowicz challenged Walesa to a television debate, which took place in November. With 70% of the nation watching, it was Walesa who came across as the statesmanlike leader. This point was conceded even in the USSR. *Komsomolskaya Pravda*, reporting on the debate, said that some of Walesa's "recent speeches have been distinguished by a certain political balance and reasonableness. It would also be possible to agree with a number of his assertions made directly during the debate." The party next tried to co–opt Walesa personally by offering to make him a deputy premier, but Walesa held out for formal negotiations and "laws, rights, positions offered by law, not by privilege."

By December, it had become clear that all of Rakowski's efforts to push through economic reform while ignoring *Solidarity* had been a failure, as were the party's efforts to discredit Walesa. Yet conservatives in the top leadership of the party continued to oppose any compromise with the opposition.

To clear the way, General Jaruzelski called a Central Committee meeting just before Christmas. Six hard–liners were removed from the Politburo and eight persons were added. This was followed by a second two–day meeting of the Central Committee in January 1989, which ended with a communique supporting the legalization of *Solidarity*.

Even at the January meeting, conservatives attacked the leadership decision to deal with Walesa, but Jaruzelski pushed through the decision against their opposition. Among those who opposed the decision was Alfred Miodowicz.

## Roundtable Discussions Begin with Solidarity

Roundtable negotiations between the government and *Solidarity* opened on Feb-

# Poland

**A church courtyard's fence displays a banned *Solidarity* sign**

ruary 6. Once the two sides began talking, they quickly carried their discussions beyond the question of the legalization of *Solidarity* and began to put together an historic compromise. As Tadeusz Mazowiecki, a leading *Solidarity* negotiator, commented, "both the communists and we crossed the Rubicon. It's really surprising how far things went."

In addition to the legalization of *Solidarity*, the April agreement called for creation of a Senate as a second legislative body, all of whose members were to be chosen by popular election. That election took place in June. New elections to the *Sejm*, the old legislative body, also took place at the same time. In the latter case, however, the communists and their allies were guaranteed 65% of the seats, with the remaining 35% to be freely contested.

To provide executive authority and to act as a counter–weight to a more powerful legislature, the post of President was also created. The President was to be chosen by the newly elected legislature.

Most of those in leading positions in the

*Solidarity* movement decided to stand for either the *Sejm* or the Senate. Walesa declined, saying that he did not want to compromise his credentials as a trade unionist. He did, however, create a Citizens' Committee of approximately 100 opposition figures which took over management of the campaign for the opposition, and he actively campaigned for *Solidarity* candidates.

In the June elections, the *Polish United Workers' Party* suffered a crushing defeat. *Solidarity* took 99 out of 100 seats in the Senate, plus all of the open seats in the *Sejm*. In addition, most of the top communist leadership, running unopposed for *Sejm* seats, were rejected because they failed to get 50% of the valid votes. These seats, reserved for communists, were filled in a second round of voting only because *Solidarity* instructed its supporters to support the new candidates.

The newly elected legislature managed to agree to install Jaruzelski as President but the failure of the communists at the polls meant that they were in practice un-

able to form a government. Their allies, the *United Peasants' Party* and the *Democratic Party*, refused to support the *PUWP* candidate for Chairman of the Council of Ministers and opened discussions with *Solidarity*. This led Lech Walesa to propose a *Solidarity*–led coalition government which would include representatives of the *PUWP*. Now came a second decisive Soviet intervention. After Mieczyslaw Rakowski, the new head of the *Polish United Workers' Party*, announced his opposition to such a coalition, he got a 40 minute telephone call from Gorbachëv, the essence of which was that Gorbachëv expected the Polish party to accept a *Solidarity*–led coalition government. Tadeusz Mazowiecki, Lech Walesa's hand–picked candidate, was installed as Chairman of the Council of Ministers at the end of August.

## Poland's First Post–War Non–Communist Government

In December 1989, the legislature made several changes in the constitution. The adjective "People's" was dropped from the official name of the country, making it is once again the Republic of Poland. All references to Socialism and the leading role of the *People's United Workers' Party* were also deleted from the document.

On January 1, 1990, the government instituted its plan to bring about Poland's transition to a free–market economy. In general, prices were freed, subsidies to industry were canceled, the currency was essentially set free to float, and the draft budget showed a surplus. The plan produced hardships throughout the society, but it also began the process of transforming the economy. Unemployment rose as inefficient state industries lost their subsidies and had to begin laying off employees in order to cut their costs, but individual Poles began establishing thousands of small businesses and small amounts of foreign investment began to pour into the country. For the year, foreign investment was estimated at $100 million.

As the year progressed, however, a split became evident in the *Solidarity* ranks. In particular, Walesa began publicly attacking specific policies of the Mazowiecki government. His first target was the program of economic reform which, he argued, was being implemented in a way which made it harder on the Polish people than it needed to be. That was a minor criticism, however. His main objection was that the government was not moving fast enough in clearing communists out of key positions. Poland was, by this time, the only country in Eastern Europe other than Albania which still had a communist as head of state. Communists also held 45% of the seats in the *Sejm*, though the results of the June 1990 elections suggested they would not be able to retain most of those seats in a genuinely free election.

# Poland

**Native costumes in Gdansk**

When Walesa first raised the issue of his becoming President, many of his supporters in *Solidarity* tried to persuade him not to run. Walesa backed down at first, then changed his mind and declared his candidacy for the Presidency on September 17. Two days later, astute General Jaruzelski, sensing the direction of political winds in Poland, elected to a six year term as President in July 1989, agreed to step down because of his "concern to prevent undesirable public sentiment" and to "promote democracy."

The Polish Parliament then modified the office of the Presidency, setting a 5–year term of office and specifying that the President was to be elected by popular vote. The election was set for November 25. Prime Minister Mazowiecki then announced that he would stand for the Presidency himself.

It was never clear why Walesa and Mazowiecki had their falling out. Perhaps Mazowiecki feared that Walesa as President would repudiate his economic program. Or perhaps it was related to the fact that Mazowiecki was a university gradu-

ate and had a reputation as a learned theorist, while Walesa had only a trade–school education and a background as a shipyard electrician. Adam Michnik, editor of the *Solidarity*–founded newspaper *Gazeta Wyborcka*, added another reason when he accused Walesa of having dictatorial tendencies. Whatever the reasons, Mazowiecki's candidacy represented the end of *Solidarity* as the unifying umbrella organization of the non-communist forces.

Walesa, though still the head of *Solidarity*, did not attempt to use that organization in his presidential campaign. His supporters were organized as the *Center Alliance*. Mazowiecki's political organization was known by the acronym *ROAD*. Later in the campaign, a third candidate emerged as a contender based on his promise to bring western business know-how to Poland. This was Stanislaw Tyminski, a Pole who had emigrated to Canada and whose qualification was that he was a successful businessman.

Tyminski, the only one to attack the government's economic reform program,

edged Mazowiecki out for second place, taking 23% of the vote to Mazowiecki's 16%. Walesa came in first with about 40% of the vote, but since he did not get a majority, there had to be a second round of voting on December 9. This time, Walesa got an overwhelming 75% of the vote and was sworn in as President on December 21, 1990. Mazowiecki had submitted his resignation as Prime Minister after his defeat in the first round of voting. Walesa asked him to continue to serve until new parliamentary elections. He refused but remained on in a caretaker capacity. Walesa offered the position to several people, including Leszek Balcerowicz, Finance Minister in the Mazowiecki government. Balcerowicz declined, saying he wanted to stay on as Finance Minister, so Walesa eventually offered the position to Jan Krzysztof Bielecki.

Before becoming Prime Minister, Bielecki was leader of a small free enterprise political party in the parliament, the *Liberal–Democratic Congress*, and head of a consulting company. From Gdansk, he had also been involved in the *Solidarity* underground. The *Liberal–Democratic Congress* is strongly committed to the development of private enterprise in Poland, and Walesa's selection of Bielecki was seen as his way of underscoring his commitment to Poland's program of economic reform.

Walesa was also anxious that new elections to the *Sejm* take place as soon as possible in order to remove the influence of the communist deputies still sitting there. Under the compact negotiated with the communists in 1989, however, new elections were not required until 1993. In March, Walesa urged the legislature to ignore the 1989 deal with the communists. "I am convinced that Poland today needs instant elections," Walesa told the legislature. "One has to put an end to growing disillusion and mistrust of political institutions, including Parliament." Parliament did schedule a debate on Walesa's appeal, but it ultimately decided to postpone new elections until October 1991.

Before the elections occurred, however, the *Sejm* passed a new electoral law that instituted an extreme form of proportional representation in an apparent attempt to protect as many seats as possible held by the communists and their allies. President Walesa vetoed the legislation on the basis that it would produce a too fragmented legislature, but the communists and their allies, with control of 65% of the seats, passed it over his veto.

The election results were more or less what Walesa predicted. Twenty–nine parties won seats in the *Sejm*, with the largest of the parties winning only 12.2% of the vote. The *Democratic Left Alliance*—the renamed communists—came in second with 12.1% of the vote, while their ally, the communist *Peasant Party,* got 8.9%. Creating a coalition government that could count on a stabile majority in the *Sejm* was no easy task and it was not accomplished until the end of December. Walesa even offered to lead a government of national unity himself, but there was no significant support for that idea.

Eventually, however, Jan Olszewski managed to put together a coalition of seven parties and his government was approved by the *Sejm.* Over the next three months, the new government worked on a new economic program that, if enacted, would have negated most of the gains of the preceding two years. Olszewski wanted to put off privatization and increase subsidies to state–owned companies so they wouldn't have to lay off more employees. He would have also increased spending on social welfare. With the Polish budget deficit already running more than 5% of GDP, that would have forced the government to print more money and destroyed the value of the currency. Olswzewski continued to push the policy even after his Finance Minister resigned over the issue, and it was not until after the *Sejm* had voted down his economic program and the IMF threatened to cancel future lending that he abandoned this approach. In late March, he went back to the budget worked out by the previous government and already approved by the IMF.

That opened the possibility of broader support in the *Sejm* and led to discussions in early April between the government coalition and three additional parties about enlarging the coalition. Significantly, two of the parties, the *Democratic Union* and the *Liberal Democratic Congress,* were the parties of the two previous non–communist Prime Ministers, Tadeusz Mazowiecki and Jan Krzysztof Bielecki. A programmic document was actually agreed on by the two groups on April 11, but the talks subsequently collapsed.

Mr. Mazowiecki later remarked that "conditions are not right to form a big coalition and reshuffle the government." It is likely that Mazowiecki and Bielecki were unable to get the guarantees they wanted that Olszewski would not revert to his earlier economic program.

Olszewski's government lasted for another two months. In that time, he lost his finance minister over the issue of the size of the deficit, then his defense minister over that individual's charges that President Walesa was planning a coup against the government. Finally, on June 5, Parliament voted to oust Olszewski himself. President Walesa then proposed Waldemar Pawlak, 33–year old leader of the *Peasant Party* as Prime Minister. Pawlak was never able to put together a majority coalition, however, and he submitted his resignation to parliament on July 2.

Meanwhile a coalition of seven parties with ties to *Solidarity* proposed Hanna Suchocka as Prime Minister. Suchocka, a 46–year old law professor and member of the *Democratic Union,* one of the parties strongly supportive of economic reform, was confirmed as Prime Minister on July 11, 1992. Early on, Prime Minister Suchocka made it clear that Poland would continue its austerity regime and the budget deficit would be kept under 5% of GNP, the figure set by the IMF which Poland had to meet if it wanted IMF aid. She twice had to take a firm stand against strikes whose demands would have increased social spending. In February 1993, she even had to defy the *Sejm* when it adopted social spending bills that would have raised the budget deficit. But she faced them all down, even the *Sejm,* which finally agreed to pass the government's proposed budget.

Making her task somewhat easier, economic reports revealed that Poland's economic decline has stopped and that industrial production had been growing since April 1992. Unemployment, on the other hand, was still at 13.8% and predicted to grow further in the short term.

Prime Minister Suchocka still lost an important bill in the *Sejm* on occasion but, when she did, she just came back and continued fighting. An example is the government's privatization bill, which the *Sejm* rejected on March 18, 1993. The bill would have authorized the privatization of 600 state companies through the mechanism of 20 different investment funds. Prime Minister Suchocka refused to accept the legislature's rejection and on April 30 finally got the bill through the *Sejm.*

Prime Minister Suchocka suffered another defeat on May 28, 1993 when she lost a vote of confidence by a single ballot. At issue was Suchocka's refusal to grant pay raises to striking health workers and teachers and increases in pensions. Suchocka's position was that there was no money in the treasury to pay for the raises. President Walesa then announced that he would dissolve parliament. New elections were scheduled to take place on September 19. In the meanwhile, Suchocka remained on as prime minister but in a caretaker status.

The elections took place under a new electoral law which sought to reduce the number of political parties in the *Sejm.* While retaining the principle of proportional representation, the law specified that individual parties would need 5 percent of the vote to enter parliament; coalitions would need 8 percent. It was expected that the new law would reduce the number of parties represented in parliament from 29 to under six.

Since there are six parties or coalitions (plus six seats representing the German

minority) in the current *Sejm,* the law did what it was supposed to do. Because the center and right parties, which controlled about half the seats in the previous *Sejm,* were unable to get together to form larger alliances, however, they were largely eliminated from the current *Sejm.* On the other hand, the *Democratic Left Alliance* took 171 out of 460 seats to become the largest party in the legislature by bringing together the remnants of the Polish communists plus the communist era trade unions. The *Polish Peasant Party,* an ally of the communists before 1989, came in second with 131 seats. Together, these two remnants of the communist era won just under two–thirds of the seats. The remaining four parties in the *Sejm* are the *Union of Labor* (41 seats), the *Democratic Union* (74 seats), the *Confederation for an Independent Poland* (21 seats), and the *Non–Party Reform Bloc* (16 seats).

Since the election, there has been considerable speculation about why the election turned out as it did. One factor is that there was clearly a backlash against the pain of reform. As one commentator put it, "forty years of communism had ingrained expectations of social security that the new parties failed to provide." A major theme of the left during the campaign was that the post–communist governments had used all the state's resources to support capitalism and ignored the needs of workers, peasants, and pensioners.

Another factor was the matter of social policy, particularly the role of the Catholic Church. Post–communist governments

*Solidarity* **Chairman Lech Walesa addresses Congress, November 1990.**

# Poland

had instituted religious classes in school, negotiated a Concordat with the Vatican and, after considerable arm-twisting by the Catholic hierarchy, passed a rigorous abortion law that largely reflected the Church's position on the issue. Moreover, the rightist parties continued to stress social issues during the campaign, even attacking Hanna Suchoka's *Democratic Union* for not doing enough in this area. A Warsaw businessman, a natural supporter, one would have thought, of the reform parties, explained why he intended to vote for the *Democratic Left Alliance*:

"The last four years [the government hasn't] worried about the economy. They worried about whether the eagle [on the national emblem] should have a crown, about abortion, but not about the economy."

In the event, the *Christian National Union*, which had 49 seats in the previous *Sejm*, didn't even make it into the present parliament. Considering that 75 percent of all Poles are practicing Roman Catholics, it is surprising that not a single political party with a specific religious orientation made it into the parliament. It appears clear that there was a backlash against what was viewed as excessive involvement in politics on the part of the Roman Catholic Church since the fall of communism.

There is another side to the election which should not be overlooked, however. Both the *Democratic Left Alliance* and the *Polish Peasant Party* made it clear during the campaign that they essentially supported both privatization and the creation of a market economy. What they promised was modestly increased social spending and "the just allocation of sacrifice." There was no question of a return to communism.

Although the *Democratic Left Alliance* is the largest party in the *Sejm*, it was Waldemar Pawlak (pronounced vahl–DEH-mar PAHV–lak), leader of the *Polish Peasant Party*, who became Poland's new prime minister. Pawlak, 34, son of a farming family, had been prime minister for 33 days in 1992 but resigned when he was unable to create a majority coalition. Although he chose not to stand for the office of prime minister, Aleksander Kwasniewski (pronounced kvash–*nyef*–skee), leader of the *Democratic Left Alliance*, was a figure of equal importance even at this time.

After the new government took office, it became clear that Pawlak was the more leftist of the two leaders. While Pawlak argued on behalf of more social spending, it was Kwasniewski who stressed the necessity of maintaining a tight monetary policy and continuing market reforms. Relations between the two leaders became cooler and cooler as Pawlak made clear

**Young Poles waiting to begin a march to the Black Madonna**

his party's reluctance to pursue further economic reform and its opposition to closer ties with western Europe. Pawlak also stalled the mass privatization program that had been drawn up by the previous government.

However, it was a quarrel between Prime Minister Pawlak and President Walesa that led to his being forced to step down as prime minister in February 1995. The basis of the quarrel was a disagreement over nominees to fill the posts of foreign and defense minister. Since Pawlak refused to accept Walesa's nominees and vice–versa, both posts had remained vacant for several months. Walesa finally threatened to dissolve the parliament unless there was a change of government. Walesa also accused the government of corruption and of reversing market reforms.

The *Democratic Left Alliance* then withdrew its support from Pawlak because of its own disagreement with him over the pace of economic reform. Pawlak's replacement was Jozef Oleksy, a member of the *Democratic Left Alliance*, who up to this time had been speaker of the parliament. Mr. Oleksy's government was sworn in on March 3. One of his first acts was to accept President Walesa's nominees as foreign and defense ministers. Mr. Oleksy also pledged his government to restart the process of market reform.

The next several months were dominated by the presidential elections scheduled to take place in the fall. Throughout the summer, Walesa, running for reelection, trailed badly in all of the polls. In the first round of voting on November 5, however, Walesa made a remarkable comeback, coming in second with 33% of the vote. His main opponent, Aleksander Kwasniewski, did only marginally better with 34%. Since neither candidate received more than 50%, a runoff election was set for November. Many commentators expected Walesa to win the runoff, but it was Kwasniewski who won with 52% of the vote. Thus the Poles joined the Lithua-

nians and Hungarians in returning the successor party of the communists to power. Not that Kwasniewski can any longer be considered to be a communist or that ideology necessarily played any significant role in his victory. Kwasniewski made it clear throughout the campaign that he supported both privatization and a market economy and favored Polish membership in NATO. But he also stressed that the reforms instituted after the fall of communism have been unnecessarily harsh on the poor, the elderly and the peasants. Not surprisingly, he won an estimated 59.5% of the votes of the unemployed, while also winning the support of peasants and women. On the other hand, he also carried the more prosperous, western part of the country while doing relatively badly in the poorer southeast. Thus the reasons for his victory are complex and hinge at least partly on Walesa's unpopularity after five years in office. Inevitably, Walesa was associated with the pain of the past five years, even though the powers of the presidency are actually quite limited.

After his election, Kwasniewski resigned his membership in the *Democratic Left Alliance*, saying he wanted to "treat all my political and social partners on equal terms" and so would stand above party. He, incidently, speaks good English. He is also rather cosmopolitan, having, in earlier years, worked abroad in Sweden and spent some time in London. In 1976, as a 22–year old student, he also spent three months travelling about the United States, eventually visiting 33 states in all.

Kwasniewski assumed the office of President on December 22, 1995 and almost immediately faced his first crisis—accusations that Prime Minister Jozef Oleksy had spied for the Russians for over a decade. Oleksy handed in his resignation on January 24 after Poland's military prosecutor announced that he was opening an investigation into the charges, though he continued to maintain his innocence. The *Democratic Left Alliance* then showed its continued confidence in Oleksy by naming him party leader. The ruling coalition next proposed the deputy speaker of Parliament, Wlodzimierz Cimoszewicz, as the new prime minister and he was confirmed in office a few days later. Cimoszewicz served as prime minister from then until October 1997, when he was forced to resign after the left had lost its majority in the September 1997 parliamentary elections.

Although Cimoszewicz was a faithful implementer of President Kwasniewski's policies, Poland made some important progress during his term of office. In particular, the economic policies of the left were as market oriented as those of their predecessors in power, so Poland continued to grow during these years even as the government implemented a program of privatization that put 64 percent of all industry in private hands by 1997. Direct foreign capital investment also grew greatly during these years. And in the foreign policy area, Poland was invited to join both NATO and the European Union during this period. Finally, in the political area, the government managed to get a new constitution approved in May 1997.

What, then, produced the stunning reversal that the center–right victory represented? It was clearly a complex of factors at work. On the one side, the government had disappointed some of its supporters of four years earlier because of its adherence to the concept of a market economy. On the other side, there were also many Poles who continued to be suspicious of the left because of its communist past. But the primary reason was that the center–right, which had been badly splintered four years previously, had now been welded into a solid alliance under the leadership of Solidarity leader Marian Krzaklewski. There was, in fact, no deep shift in the voting patterns of the electorate, which actually voted along fairly predictable lines. The difference was that, this time, those votes went to single winning candidates, rather than being distributed among numerous losing candidates, as had been the case in 1993.

Four years earlier, the Democratic Left Alliance, successor to the old communist Polish United Workers' Party, and its ally, the Polish Peasant Party which, as the United Peasants' Party, had been part of the government under communism, reduced to abject minority status the anti–communist coalition that had toppled the Polish communist regime. Now the Solidarity Election Action, an alliance of political parties with roots in the old Solidarity political movement, took 201 of the 460 seats in the Sejm, while the Freedom Union Party, which also includes a nucleus of former Solidarity activists, won 60 seats of the vote. Most of the credit for this resurgence has to go to Marian Krzaklewski, who took over as head of Solidarity in 1990 and then rebuilt the old Solidarity coalition which led to the 1997 victory.

The left was not routed entirely, however. Although they had lost their majority, the Democratic Left Alliance still won a respectable 164 seats, while the Polish Peasant Party took 27 seats. So President Kwasniewski retained significant political clout, based on the fact that he had enough votes in the Sejm to sustain a veto of unacceptable legislation.

Perhaps for this reason, Marian Krzaklewski opted not to become Prime Minister but nominated Jerzy Buzek for this position instead. Krzaklewski, a strong Catholic and anti–communist, had let it be known that he could never work with

President Kwasniewski. On the other hand, it is no secret that Krzaklewski intends to challenge Kwasniewski for the Presidency when the latter comes up for reelection and he may have decided that being Prime Minister might reduce his chances for victory.

As for Jerzy Buzek, he is a chemical engineering professor from the southern industrial region of Silesia who was also chair of the first Solidarity congress in Gdansk in 1981 and later an anti–communist underground activist. Before being nominated as Prime Minister, he was Solidarity's chief policy adviser and had overseen the drafting of its election program. Thus while he is almost entirely unknown outside of Poland, he is no mere puppet of Krzaklewski.

The cohabitation between a president of the left and a government of the center–right did not go very well at first. For example, shortly after he took over as prime minister, Buzek ended a seven year tradition under which presidential representatives attended cabinet meetings. Next, the government passed legislation that would have kept sex education out of the public schools, and overwhelmingly ratified a concordat with the Papacy that had been negotiated by the previous *Solidarity* government in 1993. President

Kwasniewski signed the concordat, but he vetoed the anti–sex education bill and his veto was sustained in the Sejm. In January 1998, Prime Minister Buzek agreed to creation of a new "cabinet council" whose membership consisted of himself, the members of the cabinet, and the president. Thus, although he continued to insist that presidential representatives did not have the right to attend regular meetings of the cabinet, he did agree to periodic meetings with the president for the purpose of greater coordination of policies. At least at the moment, therefore, the cohabitation appears to be working relatively well.

### Foreign Policy

Poland had a communist government from the end of World War II until 1989, then a government dominated by *Solidarity* until 1993. The *Democratic Left Alliance*, which brought together the remnants of the Polish communists plus the communist–era trade unions, won the 1993 legislative elections in alliance with the *Polish Peasant Party*, an ally of the communists before 1989 and this new political alignment was reaffirmed when Aleksander Kwasniewski, leader of the *Democratic Left Alliance*, was elected President in November 1995. Yet, Poland's foreign policy showed considerable continuity after *Soli-*

**President and Mrs. Aleksander Kwasniewski**

# Poland

The Wawel Cathedral of Krakow, Poland. Pope John Paul II was once Archbishop here.

*darity* replaced the communists in 1989, and no great changes occurred after the victory of the *Democratic Left Alliance* in 1993. It should not, therefore, be surprising that there has been an essential continuity in foreign policy since the victory of the leader of the *Democratic Left Alliance* in the 1995 presidential race. In fact, President Kwasniewski made it clear even before the election that he strongly supported Poland's future membership in both the European Union and NATO. Moreover, he resigned his membership in the party immediately after the election, saying that he wanted to be president of all the Polish people.

President Kwasniewski made a four–day official visit to Italy in April 1997. Here he was assured of the Italian Government's support for Poland's entry into NATO and the EU. While there, President Kwasniewski promised that the Polish legislature would soon ratify a Concordat signed with the Vatican in 1993. As it turned out, the Concordat was ratified, but not until after a newly resurgent Solidarity Election Action, an alliance of political parties with roots in the old Solidarity political movement, won the September 1997 parliamentary elections. President Kwasniewski signed the Concordat in January 1998.

Poland's relations with Russia, always satisfactory under President Walesa, have actually cooled somewhat under President Kwasniewski. The charge that Prime Minister Jozef Oleksy had been, in effect, a spy for Russia after 1989, a charge which led to his forced resignation in January 1996, was one factor. Another was President Kwasniewski's support for the proposed enlargement of NATO. The fact that Poland actually received and accepted an invitation to join NATO in late 1997 did not help either. On the other hand, Poland and Russia share too much culture and history and geography for factors like these to affect relations for very long.

The Polish Government has made it clear that it desires good relations with all of its neighbors to the east, but that its own commitment is to become part of Europe. Its economic orientation is also primarily to the West, particularly now that it is a candidate for membership in the European Union. It should also be added that this western orientation has been actually reinforced by the slowness of economic reform in neighbors such as Belarus and, to a lesser extent, Ukraine, Lithuania and the Slovak Republic.

Poland has signed new economic agreements with several of its eastern neighbors, including Russia, Ukraine and Belarus, but trade relations have tended to decline in spite of that. Poland's relations with Lithuania have also been negatively affected by Lithuania's treatment of its Polish minority in the Vilnius area.

### Nature of the Regime

After nine years of effort, the Sejm was finally able to agree to new constitution and it was approved by the Polish people in a referendum in May 1997. Prior to that time, the Polish Government had continued to operate under the constitution of 1952, as amended.

Two controversial issues which had caused considerable controversy since 1989, the question of the power of the presidency and the role of the church, have now been resolved in the new document. The new constitution also clearly spells out the relations between the parliament, the president, and the government, eliminating previous ambiguities. It also provides for an independent judicial review of laws. As for the church, the preamble invokes God as the "source of truth, justice, goodness and beauty," while the body of the constitution provides guarantees for religious instruction in public schools and grants the church autonomy from the state. Although some right–wing politicians attacked the document after it came out, Poland's Catholic Primate, Jozef Cardinal Glemp, said that "many people accept this compromise constitution, regarding it as historically important."

## The Polish Government

The new constitution does not change the structure of government in any basic way. Poland remains a presidential–parliamentary system where the president has significant powers in certain areas, but the government itself is run by the prime minister, who, in turn, is responsible to the *Sejm*. The president is commander–in–chief of the military, and also has general responsibility for foreign and defense policy and the police. He appoints the prime minister and the various members of the council of ministers. He also has the right to dissolve parliament in certain circumstances; an example would be if a submitted budget were not approved within three months.

The prime minister is nominated by the president, but must have the confidence of a majority in the *Sejm*. He is the political leader of the country and is in charge of the government. He has overlapping responsibilities with the president in the area of foreign affairs and the military.

The legislature consists of two bodies, an upper house called the *Senate*, which was created in 1989, and a lower house, called the *Sejm*. The term of office is four years. Of the two houses, the *Sejm* is more powerful. The *Senate* has the right to review legislation and propose amendments, but the *Sejm* decides the final version of any legislation.

The *Senate* has 100 members, all elected by their regional constituents. The *Sejm* has 460 deputies, 391 of whom run in 52 electoral districts and are elected under a complex system of proportional representation. The remaining 69 run on a countrywide list. Under a 1993 law, individual parties need 5 percent of the vote to enter the Sejm while a bloc needs 8 percent. As an exception, the German minority is exempt from the 5 percent rule.

In the September 1997 elections, two blocs and three parties entered the Sejm. The center–right Solidarity Election Action bloc was the winner in the elections, taking 201 seats and winning 33.8 percent of the popular vote. It is actually an alliance of approximately three dozen parties which have in common some connection to the old Solidarity movement. It is allied with the Freedom Union, which also has roots in the old Solidarity movement. The Freedom Union won 60 seats and 13.37 percent of the popular vote. Together, therefore, the Solidarity Election Action bloc and the Freedom Union control a majority of the seats in the Sejm.

The Democratic Left Alliance, which had been the dominant party in the previous parliament, won 164 seats and 27.1 percent of the popular vote. Its ally, the Polish Peasant Party, won 27 seats and 7.31 percent of the popular vote. The right–wing Movement for Reconstruction of Poland, the remaining party to enter the Sejm, won 6 seats and 5.6 percent of the popular vote. The German minority won two seats, down from 6 seats in the previous parliament.

## The Economy

The pattern of economic development in Poland since World War II has been similar in many respects to that in other countries of the area under Soviet domination. Limited natural resources and the resistance of the population to measures of forced savings resulting in fewer consumer goods have slowed the drive to change from a predominantly agricultural economy to one based on industry.

Centralized industrial and economic planning was adopted when the communist regime came to power. Although there were attempts between 1980 and 1989 to reduce the rigidity of central planning, they failed because of the lack of a political alternative and because of the opposition of the entrenched bureaucracy. As a result, Poland continued to suffer from a severe housing shortage, high inflation and the shortage of many consumer goods.

Economic reforms introduced in January 1982 were supposed to be a mixture of Hungarian decentralization and Yugoslavian self–management with the Central Planning Commission limited to forecasting, rather than directing the economy. Because of the shortage of raw materials,

**Wilanow Palace in Warsaw, the summer residence of Polish kings**

Courtesy: Embassy of Poland

# Poland

**Folk dancing in the countryside**                    Courtesy: Embassy of Poland

however, government planners began allocating them to enterprises, and in that way. Because of the shortage of raw materials, the government planners began allocating them to enterprises, and in that way retained their centralized control. The economy did begin to grow again in late 1982 and Poland began to run trade surpluses with the West, though only as a result of a drastic decline in imports, causing serious shortages throughout the economy and leading to a lower standard of living for the Polish people. And even that effort began to falter after 1986.

In March 1987, the government launched what it called "the second stage of the economic reform," aimed at modernizing the economy. The reform, a furtherance of the 1982 efforts, called for introduction of economic accountability and was accompanied by extensive price increases on food, fuel, transportation and postal services. Prices for gasoline, natural gas and electricity rose by 25% and coal by 50%. After complaints from the official trade unions, food price increases were held to 9.6%. The purpose of the increases, to reduce the level of subsidies found throughout the economy, was thus frustrated. This put the government in a bind. It needed the support of the official trade unions in implementing the second stage of economic reform but they publicly opposed the elimination of food and other subsidies.

The government attempted to win public backing for its economic reform by submitting the issue to a referendum in November 1987. Although it offered certain political concessions, it lost that referen-

dum. Refusing to accept defeat, it began implementing the reform in January 1988 and this included a 45 percent increase in the price of most basic goods.

At first, there was sullen acceptance of the increases but, in April 1988, one of the official unions launched a strike among transport workers in the city of Bydgoscsz. Strikes spread quickly to Kracow and Gdansk, but there was, significantly, no national groundswell of support. The government was eventually able to bring an end to the strikes by promising to raise wages.

The country was in deep economic difficulties. By its own estimates the economy would not reach the point where it was in 1978 until the year 2000. A major problem was with agriculture. Although about 85% of all land was privately owned, government policy had always discriminated against the private peasants in an effort to persuade them to join collective farms. There was some modification of this policy under the new reform, but the government did not have large funds it could pour into agriculture, even if it wanted to. The Catholic Church had talks with the government on a plan to funnel money in from abroad to assist the private landowners, but this evaporated as Church–state tensions grew.

The installation of a new non–communist government in 1989 led to a major change in economic policy and a firm commitment to institute a market economy, but that transition, launched as of January 1, 1990, will take time. Some estimates have been overly pessimistic, however. For example, the government esti-

mated that it would take three years for the country to be self–sufficient in agriculture, but this was achieved by the spring of 1991.

Poland's economic reform program became an issue in the presidential elections, but not a significant one. Still, a lot of Poles had mixed feelings about the reform by the fall of 1990. Clearly, there were some successes. Poland's currency, the *zloty*, had been stabilized, bringing an end to the currency black market, and all over Warsaw, thousands of stalls had been set up at which individuals sold a variety of products from farm produce to cassette tapes. In general, store shelves were again full and people no longer had to stand in line or pay bribes to obtain certain products. The other side is that official statistics, which admittedly covered only the state–owned sector, showed that production had plunged by 25%. Strict wage controls had also cut the purchasing power of ordinary Poles. On balance, however, Poles continued to support the reform program, because they expected to benefit eventually, even if there was some current pain.

Some Poles criticized the reform because it was going so slow. Ten months after it was initiated, not a single large state–owned company had been privatized. Parliament debated such issues as the rights of employees in private companies and whether shares ought to be made available at a discount to employees. Many Poles were also concerned about foreigners coming in and buying everything up.

In September, the government announced that it would issue shares in seven state–owned companies and make them available to the public for purchase. It took the government four months to prepare the shares. By that time, the government had reduced the number of companies being sold to five. And when the shares were offered in January 1991, the deadline for purchase had to be extended because there weren't enough takers. Another approach to privatization being discussed would be to issue script or coupons to all Polish citizens, who could use them to purchase shares in companies that were being privatized. There are more than 8,000 companies, however. The process is obviously going to take quite a bit of time.

Poland got some international assistance in March 1991, when western nations agreed to forgive 50 percent of the $33 billion that Poland has borrowed from foreign governments. The United States was even more generous, forgiving 70 percent of the $3.8 billion debt held by it. Poland also reached an agreement with the IMF in April 1991 which made it eligible for $2.48 billion in loans over the next three years.

# Poland

And in a turn–about from the situation just 18 months earlier, when Poles faced long lines for food, Poland, in April 1991, offered to sell the Soviet Union 1.5 million tons of grain, 300 tons of sugar, 2 million tons of potatoes, 10,000 tons of meat, plus an unspecified amount of vegetable oil.

The news was not all good, however. By late summer, it has become apparent that the budget deficit was running at a much higher rate than the target negotiated with the IMF. As a result, the IMF suspended Poland's borrowing authority until new targets were agreed to and met. This was even more serious than the loss of the IMF loan, however, for the governments of the "Paris Club" which had agreed to forgive 50% of loans owed them by Poland had stipulated that the offer only held if Poland fulfilled the stabilization program negotiated with the IMF, scheduled to run through March 1994.

The legislative elections of October 1991 played an important role in all this, for economic reform was probably the most important issue in the elections. As it turned out, no party did well in the elections, but the *Liberal Democratic Congress*, the party of Prime Minister Bielecki, won only 7.2% of the vote, dooming his chances of staying on as Prime Minister. The *Democratic Union*, the party of Tadeusz Mazowiecki, his predecessor as Prime Minister, made the best showing with 12.2% of the vote, but his challenge of Lech Walesa for the presidency argued against their being able to work together in the future. Thus the mantle fell to Jan Olszewski, who had criticized the reforms for causing too much unnecessary pain. He wanted to reflate the economy and do something for growing unemployment. He also spoke of putting off privatization of major state companies even further into the future. He was nevertheless confirmed as Prime Minister at the end of December.

Prime Minister Olszewski, a lawyer rather than an economist, reflected "political realities" as he saw them rather than any particular economic viewpoint. When he set about to supplement his plans, however, he found that he did not have the freedom that he thought he had. His Finance Minister, Karol Lutkowski, soon resigned, citing "major differences of opinion" on socio–economic strategy. Next, the *Sejm* rejected a resolution on the government's socio–economic guidelines for 1992. Finally, the IMF made it clear that future loans would depend on the government's adherence to its agreement with the IMF.

Olszewski finally realized that he had misunderstood the "political realities" and announced on March 23 that the government would "stick to the 1992 draft budget already approved by the IMF. A programmatic statement was actually approved on April 11 and it appeared that the government would soon consist of a 10–party "grand coalition." The talks subsequently failed, however. Olszewski himself lost a vote of confidence in the *Sejm* in early June. After five weeks, Hanna Suchocka was confirmed as Prime Minister. Supported by a seven—later nine—party coalition, Prime Minister Suchocka proved to be a strong proponent of reform. She also showed her ability by facing down strikers and persuading the *Sejm* to accept her budget. In April, she got a major privatization bill through the *Sejm*.

Suchocka lost a vote of confidence in the *Sejm* in June 1993, however, and new elections were set for September. The economy was an important issue in the election campaign, though not the only one. When the left, consisting of the *Democratic Left Alliance* and the *Polish Peasant Party*, won an almost two–thirds majority in the new *Sejm*, however, most people took that to mean that people were growing tired of the pain of reform. The new coalition did promise to increase social spending, but in practice they continued the policies of previous governments, even managing to bring in a 1994 budget with a lower deficit than the previous year. They also made clear that they supported both privatization and the full development of a market economy. Thus Poland continued on its previous course.

Currently, non–agricultural employment accounts for about 73% of the national work force. A significant percentage of industrial establishments remain in state hands, but the great growth in the number of private enterprises means that their significance in the overall economy is decreasing. A study published in April 1994 found that government or state–owned enterprises accounted for only 40% of employed labor. A second study published in February 1996 indicates that the private section is now responsible for 60% of national output. According to Poland's privatization office, more than 2 million private companies have been established since 1989. The lack of local capital and the difficulty of getting credit have meant that the majority of private enterprises are in the areas of wholesale and retail trade, services and handicrafts, however.

The most popular form of privatization has been through "liquidation," which means essentially that the companies have been sold or leased to their employees. At least 900 larger companies have been privatized in this manner. Another method of privatization has been to transform state–owned companies into joint stock companies, then sell their shares through negotiations with investors or through a public offering. As of October 1994, 124 large–scale enterprises had been sold in this manner. That same year, the state drew up its Mass Privatization Program, involving the privatization of 444 of the remaining large state–owned enterprises. Under this plan, 15 National Investment Funds (NIFs) were set up in December 1994 as joint stock companies. The 444 enterprises were then turned into joint stock companies, with their shares distributed to the 15 NIFs. The NIFs possess all the rights of owners, including the right to sell off companies or assets.

There are also companies that the government does not expect to be able to privatize, essentially those which are either too big to close, too sick to sell, or the industries are located in single–factory towns. Included in this category would be Poland's coal mines, currently all state–run and Poland's most significant industry. Although they are run at a loss, they meet most of Poland's energy needs and provide an additional 20 million tons each year for export. Coal production was 131 million tons in 1993, down 3.4 percent from the preceding year. It dropped a further 0.8 percent in 1994. Reformers have since argued that at least 60 coal mines need to be closed to further economic growth and cut the budget deficit. Poland's giant steel mills also fall into the category of ailing industries, though the manufacture of products based on steel actually grew somewhat in 1994.

The government's ability to reduce the deficit in the 1994 budget to 3.9 percent of GDP triggered the second phase of a 50 percent reduction in Poland's $33 billion debt to western governments in the Paris Club. It also led to an agreement between Poland and London Club banks which reduced its $13 billion debt to western private banks by 45 percent. These agreements have meant that Poland has become a more attractive place for foreign investment, as evidenced by the fact that foreign investment doubled in 1995 to $2.5 billion. Another factor is that the government moved to make the zloty a hard currency in 1995. That also contributed to a drop in inflation to about 21 percent. Foreign investment has continued to grow since that time and reached $6.6 billion in 1997, the highest yearly amount for any Eastern European country since the fall of communism. The United States is the single largest investor in Poland, with approximately $4 billion. Germany comes next with $2.1 billion.

The current economic picture is heartening. The economy has been growing now for six years and in 1997 reached a real rate of 7 percent, up from 6.1 percent in 1996. The 1998 budget, approved by the *Sejm* in January 1998, anticipates a budget deficit of 1.5 percent, inflation of 9.5 percent and GDP growth of 5.6 percent.

## Culture

Since Poland regained its independence in 1918, successive governments have al-

# Poland

**Heroes of the Warsaw Ghetto Memorial**

ways accorded respect, sometimes positive and at other times grudging, to cultural endeavors. This tradition may have its roots in the fact that, in the 19th century when there was no independent Poland, culture, particularly literary works, provided an important bond of national unity in spite of the partition of the country among several empires. The communists, eager to win the support of intellectuals, provided lavish government subsidies for various cultural programs.

Rigid insistence on "socialist realism" was never as strong in Poland as it was in the Soviet Union, even during the dictatorship of Stalin; this permitted greater intellectual experimentation than elsewhere in the Soviet orbit. In the post–Stalin period, a cry for greater freedom and a more humane form of socialism originated in Polish literary circles—among writers who considered themselves to be loyal communists but who insisted they had the right to describe things as they were, sordid and often heartbreaking. This was in stark contrast to the cheerful distortions of fact by Party propaganda.

The *Poem for Adults* by the communist writer Adam Wazyk, published in 1955, heralded the beginning of the "thaw" in cultural as well as in political relations in Poland. This wave of writing was denounced as "revisionist" by the Party and eventually suppressed, as were the publications and free discussion groups created by students. No literary works of great value appeared in later years under the communists.

On the other hand, the politically less controversial fields of graphic arts and music continued to flourish. At least one composer of the younger generation, Krzysztof Penderecki, achieved international fame with his "Passion According to St. Luke."

Under the Communist regime, official statistics stressed the numerical growth of cultural institutions; Poland boasted ten philharmonic orchestras, nine symphony orchestras and three musical ensembles associated with the state–run radio network. The theater also continued to enjoy official support, though the quality of plays tended to be poor, with a few significant exceptions such as the plays of Slawomir Mrozek, now better known in the West than in Poland.

Polish education is based on a system of 8 years of compulsory primary schooling, followed by secondary general and technical schools, which about 75 per cent of the elementary school graduates attend. Access to universities and specialized institutes of higher learning is controlled by entrance examinations. According to official figures, the number of students in universities and similar schools rose from 14.4 per 10,000 population in 1937–1938 to 85.9 in 1966–67. As in the Soviet Union and other communist–governed nations, there was particular stress on the exact sciences and less on humanistic subjects which apparently are considered less "relevant" to the efforts of the regime. About half of the students are children of white collar workers; only 17.7% are the sons and daughters of peasants.

One development arising out of the declaration of martial law in December 1981 was the growth of an underground culture. Many cultural workers refused to collaborate with the regime and turned to underground publishing. Novels and short–story collections were published unofficially during this period and then hawked from door to door. Some became underground best–sellers. Art shows were held in apartment houses and churches. There were even underground cabarets. Some mediums, such as film, do not lend themselves to such a culture, however, and they suffered.

With the installation of Poland's first non–communist government in 1989, all of this began to change. The old proscriptions and prohibitions were removed and artists became free to write and publish what they liked, at least insofar as the government was concerned. Commercial considerations have now become important, however, and not everybody likes the new literature catering to popular tastes that has begun to appear. Almost no one wants to go back to the old system of state control, however.

## Religion

Religion has always played an important role in Polish life, usually as a unifying force, since over 90% of all Poles classify themselves as Roman Catholics. Under communism, the church actually prospered and Poland was one of the few countries in the world where the number of persons becoming priests and nuns actually increased. Today Poland has 24,678 priests, up from 20,234 in 1980. That gives a ratio of one priest for every 1,280 church members, compared to one priest for every 1,650 church members in the United States. In addition, nearly 1,000 church and other religious buildings have been constructed in Poland since 1985.

Undoubtedly the fact that Pope John Paul II is Polish plays a role in this. His photograph is to be seen almost everywhere, over shop doors, on placards hanging from rearview mirrors in automobiles, and on keychains. There was a close identity between *Solidarity* and the Catholic Church during the period of the 1980's, so it was not surprising that almost one of the first things the new Mazowiecki government did was to reinstate religious instruction in the schools.

The church has found that its positions are not shared by the people in every case, however. The most important one of these is the matter of abortion, long legal in Poland under communism. In the fall of 1990, the church launched a campaign to ban all abortions, and this severely divided the country. In spite of Pope John Paul II's personal intervention, polls continued to show that a majority of Poles favored continuation of abortion, at least under specific circumstances.

The Polish legislature began debate on the issue of abortion in May 1991. Before it was a bill which would have barred abortion in all cases and set a jail term for anyone who performed an abortion or had one. That was too strong for Parliament, and it refused to take any action on the issue. When Pope John Paul II visited Poland again in June 1991, therefore, he

brought up the issue again. Because of this continued church pressure, the Polish Congress of Physicians adopted a new medical code in May 1992 which effectively prohibited physicians from performing abortions. This was written into law in January 1993 when the Sejm passed a bill setting restrictions on abortion.

The new constitution, approved in May 1997, would have legalized abortion again, but an appeal to the Polish Constitutional Court in the summer of 1997 produced a ruling that the constitution's invoking of God as the "source of truth, justice, goodness and beauty" meant that abortions were illegal. This viewpoint was subsequently endorsed by the new center–right government that was installed after the September 1997 elections.

Other potential church–state controversies are over anti–pornography censorship, divorce, contraception and homosexuality, all areas where the church's position is considerably more conservative and restrictive than what exists today in Poland. On the other hand, since approximately 95 percent of all Poles are Ro-

man Catholic, even if only about 75 percent are practicing Catholics, all of this is essentially a quarrel "within the family." In that sense, it is a societal quarrel, rather than a state–church quarrel.

**The Future**

New elections in September 1997 brought back into power a group of center–right parties whose connection is a common tie to the old Solidarity movement. Since President Kwasniewski is a man of the left, this could lead to a stalemate if the new government tried to ram through its policies against the president's wishes, since the government does not have a large enough majority to pass legislation over the president's veto. That is only potential, however. The fact is the two sides are not that far apart on most issues. In addition, Poland has shown significant economic growth now for six years and that has created a more optimistic outlook on the part of most of the Polish people. What they want is continued progress. That makes compromise a more likely scenario.

**Christmas carolling party consists of many traditional characters such as King Herod, the devil, death, and an angel**
Courtesy: Embassy of Poland

# The Republic of Romania

After work in Bucharest—time for a slow beer and catching up on the day's gossip

**Area:** 91,700 sq. mi. (237,500 sq. km.).

**Population:** 22,400,000.

**Capital City** Bucharest (Pop. 2,014,359).

**Climate:** Continental, with moderate rainfall.

**Neighboring Countries:** Moldova, Ukraine (Northeast); Bulgaria (South; Serbia, SFRY (West); Hungary (Northwest).

**Official Language:** Romanian.

**Other Principal Tongues:** Hungarian, German.

**Ethnic Background:** Ancestry rooted in Dacian and Roman heritage, with some Slav intermixture.

**Principal Religion:** Romanian Orthodox Christianity.

**Chief Commercial Products:** Machinery and equipment, petroleum, minerals and metals, manufactured goods, agricultural products and foodstuffs.

**Currency:** Lei.

**Annual Per Capita Income:** About U.S. $1,300.

**Former Political Status:** Independent states in the east and south from the 13th century; Turkish control from the 15th and 16th centuries in the south and east; increasing Russian influence in the 19th century; independent in 1878 after Russian–Turkish conflict. The western sector was under the Hungarian Crown in the Middle Ages, under independent princes in the 16th century, and under Hapsburg control and later part of Hungary until 1918, when it became a part of Romania. Communist state, part of Soviet bloc, 1945–1990.

**National Day:** December 1 (Date in 1918 when Transylvania became part of Romania).

**Chief of State:** Emil Constantinescu, President (elected November 1996).

**Head of Government:** Radu Vasile, Prime Minister (appointed April 1998).

**Type of Government:** Multiparty democracy.

**National Flag:** Vertical stripes of blue, yellow and red.

## THE LAND AND THE PEOPLE

The dominant feature of Romania's geography is the system of mountains which separate Moldavia and Wallachia from Transylvania in the West. This system has been most commonly described as a giant reverse "S" composed of the Eastern Carpathians and the Southern Carpathians, the latter of which are also called the Transylvanian Alps. They extend westward as far as the magnificent cliffs of the Iron Gate, located on the banks of the Danube River, where it flows through the Alps. This mountain range continues through Bulgaria, where the bottom of the "S" forms the massive Balkan Range. About one–fourth of Romania is covered by forests which are an important source of timber and timber products.

The Danube flows eastward for more than 200 miles from the Iron Gates, forming the border between Romania and Bulgaria. One hundred miles from the Black Sea the river turns north and eventually east again, flowing through Romania to the Black Sea. The area between the river and the sea in this region is known as Dobruja and has been the object of many disputes in the past. Romania's only seaport, Constanta, lies on the Black Sea.

Recently canals have been completed through Dobruja and Bulgaria making transit along the Danube to the Black Sea shorter by more than 100 miles.

The other geographical feature is a plain which begins in the southwest, just south of the Iron Gate, and broadens as one travels eastward. By the time one gets to Bucharest, the "valley"—for it is actually the northern side of the Danube River Valley—has widened to about 80 miles. East of Bucharest, it widens out into a broad plain which becomes the delta of the Danube River. This plain is the chief grain–growing region of Romania. Although mountains dominate the center and north of the country, much of this area actually consists of mountain valleys or plateaus, and so is also productive for purposes of agriculture.

Although most of the population is ethnic Romanian, minorities do make up approximately 12 per cent of the population. The two historic provinces of Moldavia and Wallachia are overwhelmingly ethnic Romanian, but Transylvania has significant Hungarian and German minorities. Latest estimates put the number of Hungarians at 1.7 million, or nearly 8% of the population; the number of ethnic Germans is about 350,000, or about 1.6%. Other minorities includes Jews, Armenians,

# Romania

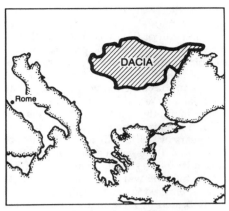

**Dacia c. 110 A.D.**

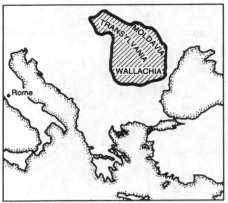

**Wallachia, Moldavia, Transylvania, c. 1555**

Gypsies, Serbs, Turks, Bulgarians and Greeks.

## HISTORY

### Origins of the Romanian State

The Romanians trace their earliest history back to an unknown time when their ancestors, the Dacians, formed a state in Transylvania. Conquered by the Roman Emperor Trajan in 106 A.D., Dacia became a province of Rome, remaining under its rule until the Emperor Aurelian withdraw Roman forces in 271. Although the Latin heritage of the present–day Romanians is reflected in their name and in the character of their language, they are not completely distinct from their Slavic neighbors—this is because the Dacians were subjected to Slavic influence during the centuries that followed the Roman withdrawal.

Not much is known about the life of the Slavic Dacians until the 13th century. Possibly they found safety from the invasions of the barbarians from Central Asia by moving high into the Carpathian Mountains, living in pastoral isolation.

There are three major areas which constitute Romania today—Wallachia, Moldavia and Transylvania. The first two became independent states in the 13th century. Transylvania, which had been inhabited by the ancient Dacians, was under the Hungarian Crown during the middle ages, under independent princes during the time the surrounding area was part of the Turkish Ottoman Empire in the 16th and 17th centuries, under the Hapsburgs after 1699 and under Hungarian (Magyar) control after 1867. It finally became part of Romania after World War I.

The Turkish Ottoman Empire gained control of Wallachia and later Moldavia in the 15th and 16th centuries. They were not incorporated into the Empire, but were allowed a measure of independence in choosing their princes, called *Hospodars*.

At the beginning of the 18th century, the Turkish rulers started to select puppet Greek princes. Until the 19th century, Wallachia and Moldavia were nominally under Ottoman rule, which was not always rigid and was often shared with other powers. In addition to Turkish control of their internal affairs, the Romanians were also subjected to the cultural influence of the French, economic domination by the Greeks and political intervention of the Russians.

Russian interest in the two principalities was recognized by the Treaty of Adrianople signed in 1829 in which the Turkish sultan agreed that rulers elected by the two states could not be removed without Russian consent. It further provided that Russia could occupy the area for a period of time. During this occupation, from 1829 to 1834, the principalities were governed by a Russian commander, Count Paul Kisselev, who helped prepare the "Organic Statutes" which became the basic law of Moldavia and Wallachia.

According to the statutes, the two principalities would be separate, each with its own assembly of wealthy land owners who would in turn elect a prince. This system of separation was soon undermined by the forces of nationalism and revolution. The European revolutions of 1848 spread into Romania—in Wallachia revolutionaries forced the ruler to abdicate and set up a provisional government, which proclaimed as its goal the unification of all Romanians into a single state. This goal was not accomplished for another 13 years because Russia suppressed the revolution.

Russian occupation of Moldavia and Wallachia in 1853 was one of the causes of

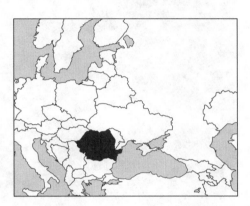

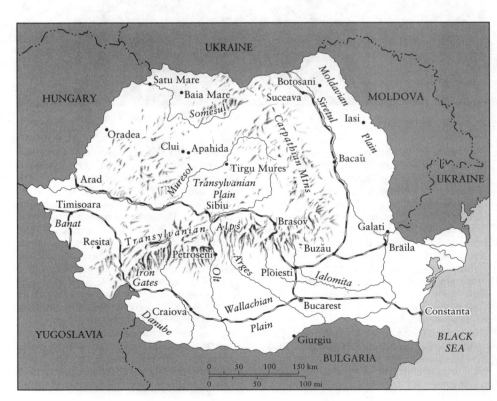

315

# Romania

**A Draculian setting: Bran Castle in Transylvania**

the Crimean War involving Russia and Turkey which followed in 1854–1856. Under the terms of the Treaty of Paris which ended the conflict, Moldavia and Wallachia were placed under the joint protection of the so–called great powers—France, England and Austria. The great powers decided after the Paris Peace Conference that each of the Romanian principalities was to have a separate assembly and prince. On matters of common concern, the parliaments could meet together.

The effect of this decision was overcome in 1859 when both principalities chose Alexander Cuza to be their prince. Two years later, he proclaimed the unified Romanian state, with Bucharest as the capital. He made efforts toward land reform, freeing the peasants from their feudal ob-

ligations. But the peasants were not given enough land to live on, and they remained indebted to the landlords. Cuza was ousted in a military *coup* staged in 1866 by both conservatives and liberals, who favored installation of a member of European royalty as ruler in Romania.

Charles of Hohenzollern–Sigmaringen (Germany) was selected prince, and he ruled until 1881 using that title. From 1881 to 1914, he ruled as King Carol I of Romania. A new constitution was adopted shortly after he arrived, and two political parties alternated in power during his reign—the *Liberal Party* represented the middle class and the *Conservative Party* represented the landowners. The large peasant class had no voice in government.

After another round of Russian–Turkish

conflict, the Treaty of Berlin in 1878 recognized Romania's independence. Under the direction of the major powers, Romania was forced to cede the province of Bessarabia to Russia, receiving in turn the region of Northern Dobruja from Turkey.

Romania avoided involvement in the First Balkan War (1912) but battled against Bulgaria in the Second Balkan War of 1913. It remained neutral during the first two years of World War I. The promise of Bukovina, Transylvania and other Hungarian lands was enough bait to bring Romania into the war on the allied side. Its troops entered Transylvania, but were badly beaten by a German counterattack, which resulted in the fall of Bucharest on December 6, 1916. In early 1918 Romania sued for peace, but as the tide turned against Germany, it reentered the war. Romania was thus on the winning side at the peace conference, and in a particularly good position to press territorial demands because its troops had occupied Transylvania and Bessarabia.

## Romania After World War I

With Romanian troops on the scene, the councils of Bessarabia and Transylvania voted to unite with Romania. In the peace settlement, Romania was awarded Bukovina (formerly part of Austria), as well as Transylvania and part of the Banat from Hungary. It kept Southern Dobruja which had been seized from Bulgaria in the Second Balkan War.

The areas of Transylvania and Bessarabia were the greatest problems. The first had a large Szeckler population related to the Magyars of Hungary. The Hungarians rejected Romania's claim to the area on the ground that the Daco–Romans had been exterminated or removed from Transylvania by the end of the 3rd century. It was argued that the Romanians made no attempt to re–enter the region until the 13th century while Hungarian settlements dated from the 9th century, therefore Transylvania should belong to Hungary.

The region of Bessarabia had been the subject of disputes involving Russia and the Ottoman Turks in the past. Russia had acquired this territory in 1812 from the Ottoman Empire; Moldavia took southern Bessarabia in 1856 and Russia took it back in 1878. The annexation of Bessarabia by Romania after World War I was recognized by the western allies in 1920.

Untroubled by losses of territory as were many of its neighbors, Romania had the opportunity to deal with its fundamental problem: the need for greater land reform. But its governments during the interwar period were inefficient and corrupt. There were land reforms that resulted in the taking of large tracts and distributing them to the peasants, which temporarily appeased them. But it did not provide a real solution to the poverty of the peasants, who then constituted almost 80% of the population.

An important consequence of the land reform was that it reduced the class of wealthy landowners and thereby weakened their representatives from the *Conservative Party*. The *National Liberal Party* came to power in 1922, and except for a brief period from 1926–1927, remained in power. Despite great opposition from Transylvania, a new constitution was adopted which made Romania a centralized state. The government embarked on a program of industrialization for which the peasants had to bear the burden.

The *National Peasants' Party*, organized in opposition to the *Liberal Party*, came to power in 1928 as a result of what was probably the most free election of the interwar period. The government of Iuliu Maniu which had promised to help the peasants did not improve their condition. Instead, it concentrated on attracting foreign investment to boost the industrialization program.

Ferdinand, who had succeeded his father to the throne in 1914, reigned until 1927; his son, Carol II did not take the throne immediately because of a scandal involving an attractive woman, Madame Lupescu, with whom he preferred to live in Paris. The youthful Michael, Carol's son, was nominal ruler from 1927 to 1930 with Nicholas, Carol's brother, as regent. Carol returned to Bucharest in 1930 and persuaded parliament to revoke the law excluding him from the throne.

From 1930 to 1940, King Carol actively promoted the disintegration of the traditional political parties by playing off party leaders against each other and, in the process, strengthening his own power. By 1938 Romania was a royal dictatorship. During the late 1920's a group was organized called *The League of the Archangel Michael*, which, in accordance with its Biblical name, was supposed to do battle with the Devil.

In Romania, the Devil turned out to be anyone who opposed the League, which was fascist and anti–Jewish in outlook. Its name was later changed to the *Iron Guard*. After his return, King Carol subsidized the group and it became the largest fascist party in the Balkans.

In elections of 1937, the *National Peasants' Party* received the largest vote, but the King refused to ask its leader, Maniu, to form a government. Instead, the leader of the fascist *National Christian Party* was named premier. The dismissal of the premier in 1938 marked the beginning of Carol's dictatorship; a new constitution was drafted, the *Iron Guard* was outlawed and political parties were replaced by the *Front of National Rebirth*—Romania's fascist party.

The country had supported the League of Nations and a system of regional treaties to preserve the balance of power in the Balkans after World War I. However, from 1936 onward, closer ties were established with Hitler's Germany. Despite this, in the first year of the war Romania lost the territories acquired after the First World War. Russia got Bessarabia back, as well as Northern Bukovina; Hungary got Northern Transylvania and Bulgaria took back Southern Dobruja.

## An Ally of Nazi Germany

Carol II abdicated and fled Romania in September 1940. General Ion Antonescu, backed by the *Iron Guard*, formed a government and on November 23, 1940, Romania joined the Axis powers. The cooperation between General Antonescu and the *Iron Guard* didn't last long—with Hitler's blessing, he suppressed an attempted revolt by the *Guard* in January 1941. Hitler's concern over stability in Romania was greater than his support for the "like–minded" terrorists whose activities disrupted the country.

From early 1941 until mid 1944 the country was governed by Antonescu's military dictatorship, with the backing of German troops. Romania participated in military operations against the Soviet Union after Germany invaded that country, and it made heavy contributions to the Axis war effort. Although there was only a very weak anti–Nazi movement in Romania, it was the first Axis satellite to defect at the close of the war. On August 23, 1944, King Michael (Carol's son), backed by the *National Peasants' Party*, the *Liberal Party*, the *Socialist Party* and the *Communist Party*, ousted the Antonescu government. Romania then declared war on Germany. Negotiations which had started in Cairo were ended in September in Moscow with the signing of an armistice.

## The Romanian People's Republic is Born

Prior to World War II, the *Romanian Communist Party* had been weak and unpopular. It had been outlawed by the government in 1924; further, its pro–Russian attitude and advocacy of self–determination for Bessarabia and Transylvania were contrary to the prevailing spirit. A communist–sponsored railroad strike in 1933 was quickly suppressed by the government and was followed by the arrest of dozens of party members.

During the 1930's and 1940's there were two groups of Romanian communists— the "home" communists who were behind bars in Romania and the "Muscovites" who had fled to the Soviet Union to avoid being jailed and persecuted. In the early postwar period, the power struggle between the two groups became the most significant feature in domestic politics. The "Muscovite" communists—Ana Pauker ("Red Ana"), Vasile Luca, Teohari

Georgescu and Emil Bodnaras—returned to Romania in 1944.

In October the communists joined with the *Social Democratic Party*, the *Union of Patriots* and the *Ploughmen's Front* to form the *National Democratic Front*. The first objective of this union of parties was to launch an attack on the leadership of the *National Peasants' Party* which controlled important posts in the government, headed by General Constantin Sanatescu. He was replaced by Nicolae Radescu.

Early in 1945 the communists started a campaign to publicize a program which they hoped would bring them to power— agrarian reform, a new government and the return of that part of Transylvania transferred to Hungary during World War II to Romanian administration. There was a communist–supported demonstration in early 1945 in which several people were killed. A few days later, Andrei Vyshinsky of the Soviet Foreign Ministry demanded the resignation of the Radescu government. He further specified that a *National Democratic Front* government, led by Petru Groza should be put in power. Radescu could offer no resistance, since Romanian troops had been ordered out of Bucharest.

The new government included noncommunists as well as communists, but the important Ministry of the Interior was given to Teohari Georgescu, one of the "Muscovite" communists. Northern Transylvania was returned and a land reform program was started. General Ion Antonescu was executed in mid–1945.

The Soviet Union recognized the new government headed by Groza. The United States and Britain, however, did not. It was decided that a special commission should advise King Michael, titular head of state, to include representatives of the *National Peasants' Party* and the *Liberal Party* in the government. The new "broadened" government should then call for elections.

The enlarged government took office in early 1946 and was recognized by the western powers the following month. Elections, in which women could vote for the first time, were not held until November 1946. In the months before the elections, the communists pressured some of the other parties into running a common list of "Government" candidates; the result was a victory at the polls for this bloc.

A peace treaty was signed on February 10, 1947, formally returning Transylvania to Romania; the other frontiers were to follow the line of January 1, 1941, which meant that Bessarabia and Northern Bukovina remained part of the Soviet Union and Southern Dobruja stayed with Bulgaria.

The communists eliminated opposition from other political parties outside the *National Democratic Front* in 1947. Ion Mihalache, Iuliu Maniu and other leaders of the

# Romania

The abdicated King Michael with his bride, Princess Anne of Bourbon–Parma, at their June 1948 wedding in Athens

*National Peasants' Party* were arrested and sentenced to life imprisonment on charges of conspiring with U.S. intelligence officers. The *National Peasants' Party* was outlawed, and government officials from the *Liberal Party* who had agreed to a common list of candidates in the elections were dismissed in late 1947. The left–wing *Social Democrats* who had also joined in the common list of candidates were absorbed into the *Communist Party,* which was given the name *United Workers Party.* (The name was changed back to *Communist Party of Romania* in 1965).

Having eliminated and neutralized all opposition, they removed the last remnant of the old system by forcing King Michael to abdicate at the end of 1947. The monarchy had been retained for more than two years after communist–approved Groza became premier.

A new constitution was adopted in 1948 and the Romanian People's Republic was officially born. The story of internal politics in the following years is concerned with a struggle for power between the "home" communists and the "Muscovite" communists. Initially the government was controlled by the "Muskovite" group—Ana Pauker was Foreign Minister, Vasile Luca was Minister of Finance and General Emil Bodnaras was Minister of War.

A "home" communist, Gheorghe Gheorghe–Dej, had helped organize the rail-road strike in 1933 and was arrested and sentenced to twelve years in prison. He escaped in August 1944 and in October 1945 became Secretary General of the *Communist Party,* which meant that he was titular head of the party while Ana Pauker and her associates were in control of the government. During the postwar years he consolidated his power and gained support from within party ranks to the extent that he was able in 1952 to remove Pauker, Luca and Georgescu from their party and government posts.

The subsequent official Romanian explanation of this purge is an example of rewritten history. The move was described as the beginning of Romania's independence from foreign domination. The fact is that there was no real change in Romanian foreign policy or in Romania's relations with Russia until the late 1950's–early 1960's. Also of significance was the execution in 1954 of Lucretiu Patrascanu, a moderate national communist who had been removed from office in 1948. This event took place two years after the supposed beginning of Romania's new national course.

A more probable explanation of the 1952 purge was that the victory of the "home" communists was the result of an internal power struggle in which Gheorghe–Dej had the support of General Bodnaras and probably Moscow. The reason for dismissal of Pauker and her fol-lowers was their supposed responsibility for economic failures.

In addition to his party post, Gheorghe–Dej assumed the post of Chairman of the Council of Ministers in 1952. Holding the highest party and government offices, he had become the real ruler of Romania. The death of Stalin in 1953 would bring upheavals in the communist world and Gheorghe–Dej would adapt to these changes, but he would continue to exercise the primary power in Romania until his death in 1965.

Following the death of Stalin, the Soviet leadership adopted the principle of collective leadership. Gheorghe–Dej obediently resigned his party post, retaining for himself the position of Chairman of the Council of Ministers. Gheorghe Apostal, the trade union chief, became First Secretary of the Communist Party. Gheorghe–Dej soon realized that the party post was more important than the government position, however, so he took it back in October 1955, giving up his government position instead. Chivu Stoica became the new Chairman of the Council of Ministers. Two further changes occurred in 1961. Gheorghe–Dej decided that it would be convenient for him to have a government post, so he added the title of President of the Council of State (ceremonial head of state). He also decided that Stoica was becoming too ambitious, so he replaced him as Chairman of the Council of Ministers with Ion Gheorghe Maurer.

## The Ceausescu Era Beginning

This was the situation when in 1965 Gheorghe–Dej died unexpectedly at the age of 63. There was no designated successor so his offices were divided among his subordinates. Nicolae Ceausescu (Cha–*shes*–koo) was Gheorghe–Dej's deputy in the party secretariat and he managed to obtain the top party post. (The title of the office, formerly First Secretary, now became Secretary General.) Maurer remained on as Chairman of the Council of Ministers while Chivu Stoica got the title of President of the Council of State.

Ceausescu, the new Secretary General, had joined the Romanian Communist Party in the 1930's through its youth organization. A protégé of GheorgheDej, he became a full member of the party Politburo in 1955, at the age of 37. Over the next ten years, he occupied himself as a member of the Central Committee Secretariat. His special area of responsibility was party organizations and cadres, a position which allowed him to exercise extensive control over party appointments. In 1965, however, he was only one of three individuals who exercised power in a collective leadership.

It was under these circumstances that the Ninth Congress of the Romanian Communist Party met in July 1965. The

# Romania

congress approved a new constitution—the one in force until the revolution of 1989—and a new set of party laws. The adoption of a new constitution was largely symbolic. It did not change the general system in any important respect, though it did announce that Romania was no longer a "People's Republic" and that it would be known as the "Socialist People's Republic of Romania." It also made explicit that it was the *Romanian Communist Party* that exercised all leadership within the state.

The constitution increased guarantees of civil liberties and a general emphasis on national independence. At the same time, it abolished the Szeckler autonomous region, which had originally been set up in Transylvania to give the Hungarian–speaking minority a modicum of self–government.

The most formidible opponent of the new Secretary General was probably Alexandru Draghici, Minister of the Interior, who controlled the secret police. Ceausescu invoked one of his new party laws which provided that government and party functions could not be combined in one man. When the party Congress elected Draghici to the Secretariat, he had to give up his post as Minister of the Interior.

Following this move, Ceausescu had a national party conference in late 1967 reverse the policy of the separation of party and government offices. Instead, plans were made for reorganization of the government on all levels based on the principle of combining state and party offices; this was supposed to avoid duplication of functions between party and state. This principle was immediately carried out at the highest level—Ceausescu was elected by the National Assembly to succeed Chivu Stoica as President of the Council of State; he was on his way toward establishing his preeminent authority within the country.

Over the next several years Ceausescu also became Chairman of the National Defense Council, Supreme Commander of the Armed Forces and chairman, or honorary chairman, of any number of party and state commissions and committees. The culmination of all this came in mid–1974 when the constitution was amended to create the position of President of the Republic—the position was, of course, filled by Ceausescu.

This accumulation of offices was accompanied by the development of a full–blown "cult of personality" around Ceausescu. In speeches and in the press, he began to be referred to as the "hero of heroes" and the years of his rule as "the years of light." In later years, he was given credit for everything that happened in the country. In fact, he often intervened to resolve petty matters at the local level.

**President Nicolae Ceausescu**

More ominously, he also placed his family in important positions of power in the government and party. Three of his brothers held senior posts in the government, one on the Council of Ministers, while his wife, Elena, was First Deputy Chairman of the Council of Ministers, member of the Permanent Bureau of the Political Executive Committee (Romania's equivalent of a Politburo), and Chairman of the National Council for Science and Technology. Finally, his son, Nicu, was First Secretary of the Union of Communist Youth and a candidate member of the Political Executive Committee. Nicu's wife was also a member of the Central Committee.

### Ceaucescu's Fall
All of this was swept away at the end of 1989 in a violent uprising that ended in Ceausescu's death by firing–squad on December 25. Ceausescu, who was proud of his independence from Moscow, had rejected Gorbachëv's policy of reform and

made every effort to isolate his countrymen from events going on elsewhere in Eastern Europe. In November 1989, he had reaffirmed his policies at a Party Congress and had been reelected head of the party for a further five–year term. It was probably this act of reaffirmation that was responsible for his downfall, for those same policies had been responsible for a significant decline in the standard of living of Romanians over the previous nine years.

The revolt, which actually began as an ethnic dispute in the city of Timisoara, in the western part of Romania, spread to Bucharest, the capital, when Ceausescu called a mass meeting for December 21 to denounce the events in Timisoara. Instead, the people began shouting "freedom" and "democracy" and Ceausescu stalked off. That afternoon, the streets were full of people demonstrating against Ceausescu. That evening, Ceausescu ordered the secret police to begin firing on the people. A similar order to the army brought a refusal from General Milea, the Defense Minister. General Milea was executed the next morning, but the army now joined the revolution. Ceausescu and his wife fled the capital, but they were captured, brought back to Bucharest, tried, and summarily executed.

The *Securitate*, Ceausescu's secret police, fought on for a few days more but the army gradually managed to restore order. In the meantime, a group calling itself the *National Salvation Front* emerged as the new political leadership in the country.

### The New Government
The *Front*, at first made up almost exclusively of former establishment figures who had fallen out with Ceausescu, was enlarged within a few days to take in various non–communist elements. It then began referring to itself as the *Council of National Salvation*. In the third week of January, the Council announced that multi–party elections would take place in May

**TV picture shows the Ceausescus upon their capture**

# Romania

**A group of young folk dancers from the provinces**

and that it intended to run its own candidates. This brought a condemnation from the leaders of the three largest opposition parties. After a series of negotiations, the *Council* agreed to make room for representatives of other parties. On February 1, the Council brought the representatives of 29 other political parties into the government coalition. By this time, it had grown to approximately 180 members. It also underwent a name change at this time and became the *Provisional Council for National Unity.* A new ten member Executive Committee, headed by Acting President Ion Iliescu, also came into existence at this time.

Meanwhile, the original *National Salvation Front* reorganized itself as a political party, announced that it, not the Council, would field candidates in the upcoming May 20 elections. As its candidate for President, it nominated Ion Iliescu. Most of the leadership of the *Front* had been members of the old *Romanian Communist Party* and the local branches of the *National Salvation Front* set up at the time of the revolution were largely made up of ex–officials. Thus, while the old *Communist Party* structure had collapsed, a large percentage of its membership transferred their loyalties to the *National Salvation Front.*

Eventually, some 80 political parties came into existence, though only three of them had any significant political support in the country. Two of these, both parties that were outlawed when the communists took over, are the *Liberals* and the *Peasant Party.* The third, the *Hungarian Democratic Union,* represents the interests of ethnic Hungarians. Although the opposition attacked the *National Salvation Front* because of its high component of ex–communists, there was, in fact, little to differentiate between them as far as programs were concerned. All said that they were committed to the creation of a multiparty democracy and a market economy.

In the May elections, Ion Iliescu was elected President with approximately 83 percent of the vote while the *National Salvation Front* took 66 percent of the seats in the National Assembly. Election observers announced that there had been some ir-

regularities in the voting but that, overall, the election was free.

For approximately six months, the policies of the new government remained unclear as factions within the Front debated whether Romania would move toward a free market or attempt to develop some sort of mixed economy with the government continuing to play an important role. Petre Roman, the new Chairman of the Council of Ministers, called for a transformation to a market economy within two years. Others talked about a gradual transition that would safeguard jobs and wages. The *Peasants Party* and the *National Liberal Party* the two main opposition parties, had argued for a rapid transition to a market economy and privatization of land and industry. Their showing in the May 1990 elections strengthened the hand of those who argued for a mixed economy.

Still some progress was made. Over the summer, legislation was passed encouraging the creation of small businesses and authorizing the government to turn state enterprises into privately owned companies. Other legislation authorized the government to sell apartment houses built after 1948. These laws were permissive in nature, however, and longtime bureaucrats found it easy to frustrate their intent.

A larger issue is that the democratic credentials of the government came into question after the government encouraged miners to attack a group of anti–government demonstrators on University Square in Bucharest in June. Six individuals were killed in the resulting violence and the headquarters of some of the opposition political parties were ransacked. Anti–government rallies continued over the summer. As a result, the Romanian government found itself boycotted by potential donor countries, in spite of its desperate need for economic assistance.

In October, Petre Roman submitted another package of land, banking and tax proposals to the Assembly which he said were intended to speed Romania's transition to a market economy. Among the proposals was that prices of nonessential goods and services would be freed, though the government would continue to subsidize the price of energy, fuel and rent for another year and control the price of basic foods and services. Although Romanians were talking about these proposals as radical and likely to contribute further to the spiral of inflation that had hit the country, they were actually yet another example of gradualism which would leave the underlying problems unsolved.

The government did take one set of actions of a positive nature. It redistributed almost a third of the country's arable land to private farmers, and the result was an unusually good grain harvest and an increase in meat and fresh products in the unregulated farmers'areas. The government got some more good news in Janaury 1991, when it was finally admitted to the economic aid program set up a year earlier to provide economic assistance to the emerging democracies of eastern Europe. Separate discussions with the International Monetary Fund resulted in an agreement in April 1991, under which Romania became eligible for up to $1 billion in financial support. In return, Romania agreed to phase out subsidies on basic food products. This led to major increases in the prices of bread, eggs and meat.

The government began converting the National Bank into a western–style central bank in December 1990. The bank was to give up all of its retail operations and confine itself to issuing currency and controlling monetary policy. The Foreign Trade Bank, which formerly performed certain central bank functions, gave up its monopoly over foreign exchange. Private banks were also authorized at this same time. Eight private banks came into existence within the next six months, the first being the Banka Comerciale Ion Tiriac SA,

founded by a Romanian expatriate, the ex–tennis player Ion Tiriac.

In January 1991, the government learned that it had finally been admitted to the economic aid program set up a year earlier to provide economic assistance to the emerging democracies of eastern Europe. Separate discussions with the International Monetary Fund resulted in an agreement in April 1991, under which Romania became eligible for up to $1 billion in financial support. In return, Romania agreed to phase out subsidies on basic food products. This led to major increases in the prices of bread, eggs and meat. In a separate move, the World Bank approved a $175 million loan to Romania in June 1991. The loan was to be used for technical assistance and for financing imports of critically needed spare parts.

Although Roman's economic reforms had the support of international economists, their implementation was causing a drop in the standard of living of most Romanians as inflation outpaced wage increases. The matter became political in September 1991 when 52,000 coal miners in western Romania went on strike over pay and prices. Several thousand of the miners made their way to Bucharest, where they demanded the resignation of Petre Roman. The demonstrations soon turned violent and before they were over three persons had been killed and hundreds had been wounded. President Iliescu, whose relations with his prime minister hadn't been very good for some time, fired Mr. Roman and promised the miners that he would form a new "government of national openness."

Roman afterwards charged that Iliescu and his allies had called in the miners and that it was all a communist plot to remove him and reverse his economic reform. There is no evidence of that. It appears, rather, that President Iliescu took advantage of the miners' protest to get rid of Mr. Roman. It does not appear to have been a policy matter either, for the man Iliescu named as Roman's replacement, Theodor Stolojan, had been at one point Minister of Finance in Roman's government and later was his Minister for Privatization. A strong believer in reform, he pledged his new government to a continuation of Roman's economic policies. His cabinet, a government of national unity, included seven technicians not associated with any political party, four ministers, plus the Prime Minister, from the *National Salvation Front*, three from the *National Liberal Party*, and one from the *Agrarian Democratic Party*.

In fact, economic reform continued and perhaps even speeded up a little under Stolojan. But he was no more successful than Roman in perking up the economy, and dissatisfaction inevitably grew. This surfaced in February 1992, when local elections were held throughout Romania.

The *National Salvation Front*, with its strong organizational structure, held on to a majority of mayorships, but lost in Bucharest and in many smaller cities. Because the second largest total was won by independent candidates, however, this did not yet represent a turning to opposition political parties.

According to the constitution, new elections for the presidency and the national legislature were scheduled to take place in the summer of 1992. These would obviously be a larger test for the government, and at one point President Iliescu may even have considered not standing for re-election. The problem was that, although Iliescu was a founding member of the *National Salvation Front*, he could not be certain of its support. The reason for this is that Iliescu resigned his membership in the party upon becoming president, turning the party reins over to his first Prime Minister, Petre Roman. The two had a political falling out in September 1991 when Iliescu dismissed Roman as Prime Minister, however. Now no one knew whether Roman's political control was sufficient to deny Iliescu the nomination or not.

In the lead up to the September elections, the *National Salvation Front* did, in fact, split over whether to support Iliescu. The pro–Iliescu faction became the *Democratic National Salvation Front*, while Mr. Roman's wing organized itself as the *Front For National Salvation*. This latter group fielded no presidential candidate, but it did run a separate slate of candidates for seats in the parliament.

There were a total of six candidates for the office of President in 1992. Iliescu came in first with 48% of the votes in the first round of voting, followed by Emil Constantinescu, candidate of the *Democratic Convention Alliance*, with 33%. Gheorghe Funar, an ultra–nationalist candidate came in third with 10%. Because Iliescu had not obtained a majority of the votes, a runoff election between Iliescu and Constantinescu took place on October 11. Iliescu won, taking 61.4% of the votes.

The results of the parliamentary elections were far less decisive. The *Democratic National Salvation Front* became the largest of the parties, but controlled only 28% of the seats. Later, it changed its name and became the *Party of Social Democracy*. The *Democratic Convention Alliance* (which is actually a coalition of political parties) won approximately 20% of the seats, followed by the *Front For National Salvation* with about 10%. Five other parties also won representation.

With no party or coalition controlling a majority of the seats, it took five weeks to put together a majority willing to support a new Prime Minister. The selection finally fell on Nicolae Vacaroiu, a 49–year old economist who had been head of a tax department in the Economics Ministry of the

# Romania

previous government. Vacaroiu, a technocrat without close political ties, loyally carried out President Iliescu's policy of slow reform.

The government did remove price controls and introduce a value–added tax in 1993, but privatization remained only a promise. "The government is slow on privatization," explained Dan Pascariu, Chairman of the Romanian Bank of Commerce, in November 1993, "because it represents the big industries. The government still thinks of restructuring as a political concept rather than an economic or business one."

Little changed over the next two years, but the campaign for mayor of Bucharest, which took place in the summer of 1995 became a sort of referendum on Iliescu and the *Party of Social Democracy*. Ilie Nastase, an internationally famous tennis player, was recruited by the *Party of Social Democracy* to return to Bucharest and run for mayor; his opponent was Victor Ciorbea, a lawyer and trade union leader, who ran with the support of the *Democratic Convention Alliance*. Major campaign issues were the slow transition to a market economy and the corruption that pervaded all levels of the society. Ciorbea's easy win over Nastase provided the first evidence that Iliescu could perhaps be defeated the next time around. Then, in June 1996, the opposition's sweep of municipal elections added to the momentum.

When Emil Constantinescu was renominated as the candidate of the *Democratic Convention Alliance*, the 1996 presidential elections became a referendum on Iliescu's rule and a rerun of the 1992 campaign. Only, this time, the result was different.

Iliescu actuallly came in first in the first round of voting. But his 32% was a 16% drop from what he had gotten in the first round of voting four years earlier, while Constantinescu's 28% put him only 4 percentage points behind. Petre Roman came in third with 21% of the vote. Parliamentary elections, which took place at the same time, were more decisive. Here the victor was Constantinescu's *Democratic Convention Alliance*, with the *Party of Social Democracy* suffering severe losses. The parliamentary verdict was reaffirmed two weeks later in the second round of presidential voting, when Constantinescu won 54.43% of the vote to Iliescu's 45.57%.

President Constantinescu is a geologist by training who was elected rector of Bucharest University in 1990. He spent a year as a visiting fellow at Duke University in 1991–92, then returned to run for the presidency in 1992. His loss that year, albeit with 39% of the vote, convinced him that he would have to become a better speaker and campaigner. Over the next four years, he travelled about the country and around the world, in the process becoming a polished speaker. He was the clear winner in

**President Emil Constantinescu**

four nationally televised debates that occurred during the campaign.

However, his campaign document, "Contract with Romania," raised expectations that his administration has found difficult to meet. His promises, which included lowering taxes and providing generous housing loans, have been particularly difficult to fulfill. But another equally difficult promise was that he would end the corruption that pervades all aspects of Romanian life.

The man who was given the job of putting President Constantinescu's political ideas into effect is Victor Ciorbea, the man he appointed prime minister in November 1996. This has not been an easy task and it may be that Ciorbea was ultimately not up to the task. Certainly the IMF was frequently critical, not of the proposed reforms themselves, but of the slowness with which they were implemented. The problem was that each of the reforms hurt groups of individuals who then appealed to supporters in the individual political parties to try to get changes made which would be less painful to their constituents.

An example was a reform announced by Prime Minister Ciorbea in August 1997 which he himself described as the "test of fire" for reforms. Responding to IMF criticism of the slow pace of liquidation or privatization of money–losing enterprises owned by the state, Ciorbea announced

that the government would close down 17 enterprises, including three refineries which had originally been built for export markets which never materialized. The decision was a good and necessary one—but it meant that 30,000 people would lose their jobs. Similar actions with regard to money–losing coal mines produced layoffs for 32,000 miners. These various reforms did produce the desired result, however. Between 1996 and the end of 1997, the private sector grew from 52 percent of GDP to 62 percent.

In spite of these gains, the government, which is a coalition made up of three parties which are actually coalitions themselves, began publicly quarrelling over the future direction of policy. The largest of these political groups is the Democratic Convention of Romania—President Constantinescu's party, to which Ciorbea also belonged. The second of the groupings is the Social Democratic Union, led by Petre Roman. The third grouping is the Hungarian Democratic Federation of Romania (UDMR).

The first crisis came in December 1997 when the UDMR threatened to pull out of the government because of an "anti–Hungarian campaign that has been on going as of late." This was resolved after talks with the other two coalition partners. In January 1998, however, the second partner, the Social Democratic Union, threatened to pull out of the coalition after the Transportation Minister, Traian Basescu, a member of the Social Democratic Union, was dismissed. The quarrel escalated from there and soon the Social Democratic Union was demanding the resignation of Prime Minister Ciorbea. As a result, Ciorbea stepped down as prime minister in April 1998. His successor was Radu Vasile. One could blame this particular government crisis entirely on the Social Democratic Union, but that would be misleading. Prime Minister Ciorbea eventually had to step down because he was unable to control his cabinet and his relations with the other coalition members. Ultimately, he was forced out because he lost the support of even his own political grouping. The change in prime ministers is not expected to lead to major changes in policy.

**Foreign Policy**

Romania first obtained the ability to develop its own independent foreign policy in 1958, when Soviet troops were withdrawn from the country, but the issue over which it split with the Soviet Union, its desire to industrialize, first became an issue in 1961–62. It was at this time that the Soviet Union proposed the creation of a supranational planning group within the Council for Mutual Economic Assistance (CMEA) to decide which country should produce how much of what. The

**Residential/commercial district near central Bucharest.**

Soviets wanted an international division of labor which would allow some countries to emphasize industrial production while others (notably Romania and Bulgaria) were intended to be a source of raw materials and agricultural products. The Soviet–Chinese dispute gave Romania the chance to defy Moscow. The first sign of opposition came in March 1963 when Romania refused to support the creation of the CMEA group.

In April 1964, the Romanian Central Committee issued a statement which has been described as a "Declaration of Independence" in economic as well as in political matters. In the economic area, they asserted the right to develop their own natural resources. In political affairs they rejected the idea that any communist party was superior to another, claiming the right of each party to develop its own policies. Their attitude toward the Warsaw Pact military alliance has been similar to their attitude on CMEA. Soviet attempts in 1966 to strengthen the Warsaw Pact Organization by creating a permanent East European political authority and by increasing the integration of the various military units from each country were successfully resisted by the Romanians. And when the Soviet Union intervened in Czechoslovakia in 1968, Ceausescu criticized the Soviet actions and coupled it with a statement that Romania would re-

sist any Soviet incursion into Romanian territory. Romania maintained this critical attitude toward the Soviet Union from that time onward. It always refused to permit Warsaw Pact maneuvers on Romanian soil and refused even to attend the annual meeting of Warsaw Pact nations in 1971. Relations improved somewhat in the middle of the 1970's but Ceausescu publicly aired his differences with the Soviet Union in November 1979, following the Warsaw Pact meeting in Moscow, over Soviet Middle Eastern policy and Soviet demands that the East European members of the Warsaw Pact increase their military expenditures.

In early 1980, Romania publicly, if indirectly, criticized the Soviet invasion of Afghanistan when Ceausescu attacked countries that "gravely threaten the cause of people's independence." The Romanian position became even clearer in January 1981 when it abstained on a United Nations vote demanding the withdrawal of foreign troops from Afghanistan. All of the Soviet Union's Eastern European client states voted against the resolution.

Ceausescu also took an independent position with regard to Soviet SS–20 missiles and Theater Nuclear Force negotiations. In December 1983, after the Soviets withdrew from the TNF talks in Geneva, Ceausescu issued a public call for both the Soviet Union and the United States to stop de-

ploying nuclear missiles and to resume arms control negotiations. Another example of Romania's independence was the Soviet decision to boycott the 1984 Summer Olympics. Every other Soviet "ally" joined in the move, but Romania sent its athletes to Los Angeles—and brought back 32 medals, including 20 golds, to place third in the total number of medals won.

Romania's relations with the Soviet Union became more complex after the Soviet Communist Party's 27th Congress in early 1986. Ceausescu forthrightly condemned Gorbachëv's programs for economic reform, but, at the same time, Romania's economic ties to the Soviet Union actually increased. Gorbachëv finally paid a visit to Romania in May 1987. The Soviet press gave the visit a rather low–key treatment, but the Romanian press was far more enthusiastic. Several economic agreements were signed, but it was clear that political differences remained.

Under Ceausescu, relations with other countries were basically determined by the relations of those countries with the Soviet Union. Thus the primary thrust of Romanian foreign policy in those years was to establish close relations with those countries opposed to an expansion of Soviet power. A second, related interest was Romania's desire to expand its trade with the West. Neither of these principles involved a turning away from communism.

# Romania

Domestically, Romania remained among the most orthodox of communist nations.

During those years, it maintained its closest relations with the People's Republic of China. The reasons for this are clear. In addition to a common ideology, the two nations strongly opposed Soviet domination of the communist world. Romania consistently supported the Chinese arguments in the Sino–Soviet quarrels. In addition, there was a regular exchange of high–level diplomatic missions between the two countries and an extensive promotion of cultural contacts and trade.

Relations with Western Europe and the United States developed on another basis during those years, with trade perhaps being the most important factor. Romania never made the mistake of thinking it could ignore its geopolitical position entirely, or that it could depend on any country other than itself in case of extreme Soviet displeasure. It was nevertheless the first East European nation to establish diplomatic relations with the Federal Republic of Germany and until about 1985 it went out of its way to encourage better relations with the United States. The breakthrough may be said to date from 1967 when Richard Nixon, visiting various European capitals, stopped in Bucharest and was personally received by Ceausescu. Two years later, then President Nixon decided to pay a state visit to Romania as part of a round–the–world trip. He thus became the first American President to pay a state visit to a communist country. Nixon suggested the visit to "needle our Moscow friends" but he evidently wanted to show his appreciation for the way he had been treated in 1967. The visit took on a symbolic importance beyond that, however.

First of all, a Romanian Communist Party conference, to which the Soviet leadership had been invited, had to be rescheduled in order to make the visit possible. However, Brezhnev and Kosygin, originally scheduled to attend the conference, cancelled out of the rescheduled conference. Secondly, as reported by a New York newspaper, Nixon received "a warm reception from hundreds of thousands of flag–waving Romanians in the largest and most genuinely friendly welcome of his global tour." It also was during this visit that President Nixon asked Ceausescu to act as a channel of communication to the Chinese. The subsequent breakthrough in U.S.–Chinese relations therefore owed something to the Ceausescu connection.

The Nixon visit to Romania was followed up by a Ceausescu visit to the United States the following year. This visit, which lasted two weeks, had an obvious political component, but its major emphasis was economic. Ceausescu met with a number of American businessmen, signed a contract for a $10 million aluminum sheet–rolling mill and signed an agreement for an exchange of researchers and university teaching staff. Ceausescu had been to the United States twice since that time, in 1973 and again in 1978. On the American side, President Ford stopped in Bucharest in mid–1975 and at that time the U.S. accorded Romania the "most favored nation" trade status. The United States also sponsored Romanian applications for membership in international organizations such as the International Bank for Reconstruction and Development (World Bank) and the International Monetary Fund (IMF).

Beginning in the 1980's, the United States became increasingly critical of Romanian internal developments. This was accompanied by occasional threats to withdraw "most favored nation" status unless the Romanian Government made certain internal changes. One instance was a tax on Jewish emigration which Romania had instituted. Under the Reagan Administration, it focused increasingly on Romanian treatment of Christian evangelicals.

The matter came to a head in June 1987 when the U.S. Senate voted to suspend Romania's "most favored nation" status for six months to indicate that it disapproved of Romania's human rights record. To put an end to such recriminations, the Romanian Government responded by voluntarily renouncing all such trade concessions.

Romania's actions did not put an end to U.S. criticism of Romania's human rights record, however. In the last two years of Ceausescu's rule, the U.S. Government several times criticized his program to transform the countryside by razing villages and replacing them with high–rise "agro–industrial" complexes. The basis for the criticism was that the program, although billed as an economic measure, was being implemented almost exclusively in areas where there were Hungarian and German ethnic minorities and a major goal of the program appeared to be to destroy these centers of non–Romanian culture so that their inhabitants could be assimilated into the majority Romanian culture.

Romania's foreign policy changed after the overthrow of Ceausescu in December 1989 and the creation of a new government committed to democracy and a market economy, but less than one might have thought. The new leadership has attempted to establish a friendly relationship with all nations and thus far it has largely succeeded. Even the Soviet Union welcomed the overthrow of Ceausescu and followed this up with friendly gentures such as opening the border between Moldova and Romania for a day so relatives could visit back and forth.

The repudiation of communism following failure fo the August 1991 *coup* against Gorbachév, followed by the subsequent collapse of the Soviet Union, obviously changed that relationship as Romania quickly moved to establish diplomatic relations with the successor republics, but the changes have been more in form than in substance. In any case, with the notable exception of the newly independent Republic of Moldova, Romania's main interest in the successor republics was economic as it struggled to hold on to export markets.

Romania's relations with Moldova are complicated. This area, except for that part east of the Dniester River, had been part of Romania prior to 1940 and a majority of the people living there speak Romanian. The government supports the reincorporation of Moldova, though on a purely voluntary basis. This is an emotional issue in Moldova but, so far, the government has favored an independent Moldova.

The United States welcomed the overthrow of the Ceausescu regime and our early attitude toward the new government was extremely favorable. Among other things, Secretary of State Baker arranged a short visit to Bucharest in the spring of 1990. But the United States was also critical of some of the actions of the new government, and decided after the death of six demonstrators in June 1990 that all assistance to Romania would be put on hold. The United States went along with inclusion of Romania in the aid consortium for eastern Europe, but it was not until Petre Roman visited Washington in April 1991 that one could speak of a noticeable thawing of relations. Relations warmed further in 1992 as the administration began to give the Romanian Government good marks for such things as allowing greater press freedom, holding democratic elections, and bringing the intelligence services under legislative control.

This trend culminated in the granting of "most favored nation" trading status to Romania in October 1993. With the Romanian economy in such poor shape, this new status hasn't yet benefitted Romania much, though it may encourage needed foreign investments now that Romania has a new government committed to privatization and further development of a market economy.

Even under the previous government, Romania had applied for membership in NATO and had joined NATO's Partnership for Peace. The new government supports these goals, and has also expressed its desire to join the European Union. NATO membership appears to be a possibility but the consensus in the European Union is that Romania won't be ready for membership until it has completely remade its economy.

## Nature of the Regime

The Revolution of 1989 overthrew the old Communist regime and installed a

324

revolutionary regime whose stated goals were the creation of a multiparty democracy and a market economy. Free elections occurred in May 1990. The new Government gave itself 18 months to draw up a new constitution and it accomplished that when the new constitution was approved in a popular referendum on December 8, 1991. The new constitution did lack specific guarantees of rights for minorities that ethnic Hungarians had demanded, but this was rectified in September 1996 when Romania signed a new treaty with Hungary which included a section wherein each side promised to treat its minorities according to high "European standards." A 1992 electoral law set up a 147–member Senate and a 310–member lower house. Two sets of presidential and parliamentary elections have since taken place in an orderly fashion and most observers now concede that Romania has completed the transition to a multi–party democracy. No single party or coalition commands a majority in the Grand National Assembly.

## The Government

The president, who is popularly elected, exercises overall executive power. He is expected to set general policy and act as spokesman for the nation. In addition, he has specific responsibilities in the areas of foreign affairs and defense. He nominates the prime minister, who must be confirmed by the Grand National Assembly. The prime minister, in turn, chooses his cabinet, who must also be confirmed by the Assembly. The prime minister articulates specific policies, maintains liaison with the legislature, and oversees the day–to–day operations of government. The current cabinet is a coalition consisting of the *Democratic Convention Alliance*— the party of President Constantinescu— and the *Social Democratic Union*, led by Petre Roman.

## The Economy

At the end of World War II, Romania was still an overwhelmingly agricultural economy with over three–quarters of the workforce employed in farming. Bucharest, center of what industry there was, was large and relatively modern; but there were only three other cities in the country with populations of over 100,000 persons. The political elites who had dominated the government during the interwar period had been committed to a policy of industrialization but, except for the petroleum industry, they were not notably successful.

Immediately following World War II, a land reform act set an upper limit of 123 acres (50 hectares) on all individuals. This act also provided for the expropriation of all real property of individuals held to be fascist collaborators. The collectivization of agriculture was begun in 1949. It was in theory voluntary, but peasants who refused to join a collective found themselves required to deliver a set amount of produce to the state at an artificially low price.

Collectivization was completed in 1962, although there was a subsequent further amalgamation of collective farms that brought together single villages into new multi–village cooperatives. Under the Communist regime, the state purchased, processed, and distributed most agricultural products. It did, however, run town and city markets where individuals and also state and collective farms could market some of their produce. Agricultural output increased considerably during the period 1970–1977 but largely stagnated after that. This was particularly true in the area of animal production. From 1979 onward, Romanians had trouble finding beef and pork in the markets. Perhaps the largest reason for this was the government's decision to place a greater emphasis on the export of agricultural products as part of its program to pay off the foreign debt.

There were some problems with the overall level of production as well, however, for cattle herds were a million below planned levels by 1980 and President Ceausescu publicly complained that exports had to be reduced "year after year" in order to maintain domestic levels of consumption.

One problem appears to have been organizational—state and collective farms fairly efficiently produce grain and fodder crops but perform badly in the production of meat, milk, eggs, fruits and vegetables. Thus, although all but 9.4% if the land was controlled by the state, it was this privately–held land (nearly all located in mountainous areas deemed unsuitable for extensive cultivation) plus the private plots of individual collective farmers which provided over half the country's production of potatoes, fruit, meat, milk and eggs. In fact, these two sectors produced an estimated one–third of Romania's total agricultural production during this period.

Although under communism nearly all capital flowed into state and collective farms and the machine–tractor stations serving them (plus other state units such as experimental stations) their use of capital was actually very inefficient. Between 1962 and the early 1980's, output per unit of fixed capital on state and collective farms was filled by about one–half.

In spite of its shortcomings, however, collectivization, with its emphasis on mechanization, did bring about major changes in the countryside. The old, traditional farming methods were largely supplanted and productivity accordingly increased, so that only 32% of the workforce was still engaged in agriculture by the 1980's. Most of these excess agricultural workers were drawn into the industrial workforce. Starting from a relatively low base in 1948, Romania began an industrialization program using the Stalinist command model which resulted in one of the fastest growth rates in the world. The driving force behind the Stalinist command model was the very high investment level—up to 35% of gross national product—which was determined by the state. This will result in a very rapid growth rate if one is dealing with a situation in which

**The seaside resort of Eforia**

325

# Romania

The Trade Union Cultural Home in Slatina, southern Romania

there is a surplus of labor and adequate raw materials—as was the situation in Romania in the 1950's and 1960's. On the other hand, a high investment level means that there is less left over for consumption, and living standards will necessarily remain low. This has also been the case insofar as postwar Romania has been concerned.

Under communism, Romania's industrialization program also concentrated on the creation of heavy industry rather than consumer goods. The major industries built or expanded during this period include oil refineries, chemical plants and various sorts of metal–working and machine–building enterprises. In later years, a major area of emphasis was electric power generation.

Two huge hydroelectric stations, the Iron Gate II project with Yugoslavia and the Trunu–Magurrele project with Bulgaria, were constructed during the 1980's. Its first nuclear power plant was completed in the second half of the 1980's. These new sources of energy were designed to allow for a continued growth in industry in general and the metallurgical industry in particular. Two other projects pursued by the government in the 1980's were an expansion of the Galati steel complex and construction of a new steel complex at Calarasi.

In the last several years under Ceausescu, however, Romania had largely exhausted the possibilities of the Stalinist demand model and had reached the point where both labor and raw materials were scarce—and in fact many of the raw materials had to be imported. Instead of moving toward decentralized decision–making and placing greater emphasis on quality as opposed to quantity, however, Ceausescu stubbornly clung to the command model.

The situation was also exacerbated by Ceausescu's determination to pay back the foreign debt of approximately $13 billion which he had run up during his industrialization spree in the 1970's. To accomplish that, Ceausescu instituted a harsh austerity program and cut Romania's hard currency imports by more than two–thirds. Romania also began to reorient its trade toward the CMEA countries, in particular with the Soviet Union. Between 1980 and 1989, the proportion of Romania's trade with other members of the CMEA grew from a third to just over a half. The government was also able to pay off its hard currency debt by the beginning of 1989 but only by dropping Romania's standard of living to the lowest in Europe. During Ceausescu's last years, food was rationed, cities were unlighted at night, and gas and electricity were available only on a limited basis.

The first sign that the Romanian people were losing their patience came in November 1987 when riots broke out among workers in the city of Brasov. The riots, triggered by a new government decree announcing additional penalties for workers who failed to fulfill production quotas, were met by tanks, police dogs and tear gas. For several days, Brasov was off–limits to all foreigners.

The government did not, in the end, have any great difficulty putting down the riots, but the blows to Ceausescu's credibility and to the regime's legitimacy were more severe. Once again, workers had risen up in protest against a so–called workers' state. One indication of this loss of credibility was that, for the first time in memory, a number of prominent Romanians dared to criticize the regime publicly. One such was Silviu Brucan, former Ambassador to the United States and the United Nations, who urged the govern-

ment to recognize the legitimacy of the workers' grievances. Several government ministers also dared to defend themselves against charges that they were responsible for the widespread shortages.

In spite of these signs of growing domestic opposition, Ceausescu held to his policy of austerity and used the funds thus accumulated to pay off Romania's foreign debt. As a result, Romania announced in April 1989 that it had paid off the last of its foreign loans and was debt–free.

The big question then was Romania's future economic policy. Its 1989 current–account surplus was expected to be around $3.5 billion, and Ceausescu could have eased off on his austerity program and allowed some increase in imports. Instead, he used the funds to finance such grandiose schemes such as his creation of a grand avenue and Presidential Palace, which he had been building in the middle of Bucharest over the previous five years. Ceausescu also continued the grand program, launched in 1988, of transforming the countryside by razing half of Romania's villages by the year 2000 and moving the inhabitants into new high–rise buildings in "Agro–industrial" centers.

The answer of the Romanian people came in December 1989, when they rose up and brought the entire regime down. Romania has now had a non–Communist government committed to multiparty democracy and a market economy since the beginning of 1990. But the individuals making up the new government were badly divided among themselves as to the proper path to follow and they had been in power for about a year before taking any action to begin transforming the economy. They also took certain decisions during that first year that temporarily eased the lot of the Romanian people, but which had negative longer–term consequences.

One of those decisions was to use part of Romania's foreign currency reserves, then about $1.8 billion, to import food for domestic consumption. The government continued the policy in 1991 but, by that time, it had used up most of its foreign currency reserves and so turned to financing consumption through an enlarged budget deficit. In effect, then, Romania was living beyond its means after 1989 and couldn't afford to do it any longer.

International aid has helped to close the gap, but the standard of living has declined further since 1992.

Economic statistics also look awful. For example, industrial production decreased by over 40% after 1989 and then remained at that lower level. Part of this drop can probably be blamed on the disruptions of the revolution itself, but there are larger causes as well. Domestically, shortages of energy and raw materials play an important role. Internationally, Romania lost a significant part of its market for exports when the Soviet Union collapsed. It also lost a major source of raw material imports.

The Romanian working class has been unhappy about the economic situation for several years, but they were also extremely fearful about change. Freeing prices had produced a virulent inflation that had eroded wages, while talk of privatization of state firms raised the spector of future unemployment. Surprisingly, polls indicate that a majority of the Romanian people continue to favor both privatization and the development of a market economy.

The news from the countryside is also rather negative. The break–up of the collective and state farms has given land to the peasants, but without any farm machinery to work the land. After the revolution, most of the tractors had wagons attached to them and they are now being used in urban areas as a substitute for trucks. The result is that it is common to see peasants using milk cows for plowing. On a more optimistic note, more oxen are also beginning to appear. Romanian agriculture is likely to remain at this primitive level for a number of years. Not only has Romanian industry not yet begun manufacturing small tractors suitable for individual agriculture, even if it did, few farmers could currently afford them.

How soon before Romania turns the corner? It is difficult to say. It will depend partly on the amount of international assistance Romania qualifies for and partly on the economic policies of the Romanian Government. The economy is now stabilized but, because of the severe deterioration in the infrastructure that occurred during the last several Ceaucescu years, a great deal of money is going to have to go into rebuilding before one can begin to talk about new growth.

The voucher privatization program launched by the government in October 1995 has been criticized as being designed more to convince the World Bank that Romania is serious about reform than to promote real privatization. Under the program, citizens exchanged vouchers valued at $325 for shares in 3,905 companies to be privatized. The state retained 40% of the shares, however, thus retaining effective control. Very little information was made available on the companies, thus reducing the ability of the public to choose intelligently. Since very few companies were considered to be profitable, very few citizens bothered to turn in their vouchers.

The change in government after the 1996 elections altered the situation somewhat. President Constantinescu is committed to recreating a market economy, but he realizes that this will require a period of austerity that the people of Romania can ill afford. There has thus been

some progress since 1996, but not a rapid transformation.

Victor Ciorbea, who was appointed prime minister in November 1996, implemented policies that resulted in the private sector growing from 52 percent of GDP to 62 percent, but he ultimately became so disliked that he was forced to resign in March 1998. Petre Roman, leader of the Social Democratic Union, who was ultimately responsible for Ciorbea's resignation, ostensibly opposed Ciorbea because the latter was not moving fast enough on reforms, but its more likely that he was forced out because Roman felt that he was not being consulted enough. His successor, Radu Vasile, will have to show a great deal of tact to hold the three-party coalition together.

## Culture

The Romanians take great pride in their Latin origin, although over the centuries they have also been subject to Hungarian, Slav and Turkish cultural influence. Romania has a large Hungarian minority located primarily in the Tisa Plain and in Transylvania. The Szecklers, though they speak a Magyar dialect, are distinguishable from the Hungarians on historic grounds. They have been in Transylvania since the Middle Ages when they were frontier guards for the Magyar settlements. The Hungarian Magyars recognized them as a free people of noble birth and as one of the privileged nations of Transylvania, along with the Saxons (Germans) and the Magyars.

The Romanian Orthodox Church has the largest following, but Roman Catholicism and Calvinism are strong among the Hungarian population. The old communist constitution guaranteed freedom of religion with qualifications—for instance, the organization of "religious cults" was regulated by law. Schools other than sem-

inaries could not be operated by the Church; the Church budget was under state control and the Church officials had to be acceptable to the state. The Iliescu government took a "hands–off" attitude toward religion, neither supporting nor interfering. The new government of President Constantinescu has tended to take a more specifically pro–religion stance, though so far it has been primarily symbolic. For instance, icons of the Romanian Orthodox Church line President Constantinescu's office shelves and he makes a point of having an Orthodox priest say a prayer at political meetings. It should be added that the *Christian Democratic Peasants Party* is one of the parties making up the ruling *Democratic Convention Alliance*.

There has been considerable movement from rural to urban areas since World War II, but Bucharest is still by far the largest city, containing more than 1/5 of the city dwellers of Romania. It is modern and a center of cultural expression. In the countryside, the folk music, art and colorful costumes prevail.

Free primary education is compulsory for eight years, and there are universities in Bucharest and in four other major cities.

## The Future

The results of the November 1996 presidential and parliamentary elections have put Romania in the hands of a political leadership committed to speeding up the process of privatization across the economy and completing the transition to a market economy. That is the promise. However, converting an inefficient industrial base that has been constructed largely on Stalinist command lines is a task so large, and one which will require so much capital, that one should not expect noticable improvements soon. Romania's economic progress will be slow and painful.

One of Ceaucescu's extravagant legacies is the gigantic House of the Republic, a billion-dollar "white elephant" in central Bucharest which stands empty and unfinished.
Photo: Miller B. Spangler

# The Slovak Republic

**A Slovak peasant woman shows off her daughters after church on a Sunday morning**

AP/Wide World Photo

**Area:** 49,000 sq. km. = 18,819 sq. mi.
**Population:** 5.3 million.
**Capital City:** Bratislava (Pop. 429,743)
**Climate:** Continental, with lower temperatures in the higher elevations of the north.
**Neighboring Countries:** The Czech Republic (West); Poland (North); Republic of Ukraine (East); Hungary (South); Austria (West).
**Official Language:** Slovak.
**Other Principal Tongues:** Magyar, Czech, German.
**Ethnic Background:** Slav.
**Principal Religions:** Roman Catholic (60.3%), Protestant (8.4%), Orthodox (4.1%), Atheist (9.7%), Other (17.5%).
**Chief Commercial Products:** Machinery and equipment, energy ores, metals, consumer goods, arms.
**Currency:** Slovak Koruna (crown).
**Former Status:** Part of the Hungarian Kingdom of the Austro–Hungarian Empire until 1918; Part of Czechoslovakian Republic 1918–1938; Protectorate of Nazi Germany, 1939–45; Part of Communist–influenced Czechoslovakian Republic, 1945–48; Part of Communist Czechoslovakia, 1948–89; Part of Czech

and Slovak Federal Republic, 1990–1992.
**National Day:** May 9 (Liberation Day).
**Chief of State:** The office of the President of the Republic has been vacant since March 2, 1998, when Michal Kovac's term of office came to an end, because there is no three–fifths majority in the parliament to elect a successor. Some of the President's powers have devolved on Prime Minister Meciar.
**Head of Government:** Vladimir Meciar, Prime Minister.
**National Flag:** Three equal horizontal stripes—white, blue, red—with a shield on the left showing a two–armed white cross on a red field with a blue base.

Most of the Slovak Republic is covered by mountains or hills, but it does possess a single large plain, located to the south and east of Bratislava, the capital. It is also here that the Danube River forms the border for some distance between Slovakia and Hungary. Just north and east of Bratislava, a western spur of the Carpathian Mountains begins. The Carpathian Mountains proper then stretch east, northeastward, widening until they cover the

entire country from north to south. The highest mountains are found in the center–north, along the border with Poland. It is here that the steep, rugged peaks of the High Tatras tower over deep valleys dotted with numerous lakes. Gerlachovsky, the tallest peak, is 8,620 feet high.

It, and the surrounding high terrain, form the Tatra National Park. A popular

# Slovak Republic

place for vacationing since the 19th century, it is full of spas and holiday resorts. The Carpathian Mountains diminish in height as one moves further eastward, but they actually run for a couple hundred miles beyond the Slovakian border, traversing Western Ukraine.

As its name implies, Slovakia is essentially a land of the Slovaks. But there are three minorities making up several percent of the population which have the status of "nationalities." These include Hungarians, mainly in the southeast, Poles in the northeast and Ukrainians in the east. The Hungarians, who number about 560,000, are the largest minority. Slovakia also has a fairly large number of Gypsies whose numbers don't show up in official statistics because they are not recognized as a separate nationality. Under the communists, the government attempted to assimilate them, providing them with apartments and jobs, though discrimination continued. Since 1989, while many have felt free to resume their traditional wandering existence, open antipathy to them has also increased.

## HISTORY

In the fifth century, the Slovaks, then one of a group of west Slavic tribes, settled into the area of modern Slovakia, moving there from further east. Other tribes settled further west. Together, these various Slavic tribes settled the area to the south of the Carpathian and Sudeten Mountains and along the Vltava and Danube Rivers. Except for a legendary, short-lived kingdom created by a French trader in the seventh century, these western Slavic peoples continued to be governed by a tribal structure until the ninth century, when the Moravian Empire was established. The seat of this Moravian Empire was in the western part of modern Slovakia, in the modern Slovak city of Nitra. It was also here that the first Christian church among western Slavs was built in the year 850. It is likely that the rulers of this first unified state were Slovak tribal leaders, for it was the Slovak lands that were first unified, with the remaining western Slavic lands being added later.

Although the Moravian Empire lasted less than a century, it was important because the western Slavs were converted to Christianity during this time. The first Christian missionaries came from Rome, but Prince Rostislav, who ruled 850–870, requested the Byzantine Emperor to send a bishop to "enlighten and instruct his people in the true faith and in their own tongue." Methodius and Cyril, the two Greek Orthodox monks sent by the emperor, introduced a Slavonic liturgy and the first written script for the Slavs, later known as Cyrillic. Because later rulers of the Moravian Empire favored the priests

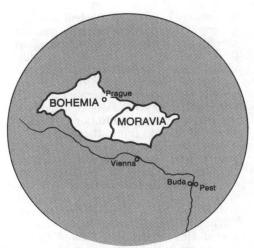

**Moravia and Bohemia ca. 1360**

from western Europe, Cyrillic was later replaced by Roman letters, but a written Slavic literature dates from this time.

The Moravian Empire began to disintegrate toward the end of the ninth century. First weakened from within by revolts by ambitious Czech nobles desirous of creating their own independent kingdom of Bohemia, the Moravian Empire came under attack from the south and east when Magyar peoples swept into the area, overrunning the Hungarian Plain and gradually extending their control northward to the Carpathian Mountains. Although the Slovak rulers fought a rear-guard action against the Magyars for some time, all the Slovak lands were brought under Magyar control by about the year 1000, the date traditionally used to mark the beginning of Christianity in Hungary and the founding of the Kingdom of St. Stephen.

For nearly a thousand years—until 1918—the Slovaks remained under the Hungarian crown. For most of this period, the Slovaks remained simply one of the peoples of the Hungarian Kingdom. Since both Magyars and Slovaks were Roman Catholics and Latin, not Hungarian, was the language used at court and in the churches, Slovaks could have no complaints in these areas. On the other hand, although a few Slovaks managed to rise to high position, most were peasants living on land controlled by members of the Hungarian nobility. And when serfdom spread into central Europe in the later middle ages, the majority of them became serfs.

When the last Hungarian King was killed at the battle of Mohacs in 1526 Hungary became a possession of the Hapsburgs, whose main seat was at Vienna. If anything, this was a positive development as far as Slovaks were concerned, for the Hapsburgs, being German–speaking, had no reason to unduly favor the Hungarians. And when most of Hungary was overrun by the Turks in the sixteenth and seventeenth centuries, it was the Slovak lands that remained unoccupied, in effect becoming the main part of the kingdom. For the next 150 years, the seat of the Hungarian government was Pressburg, better known today by its Slavic name, Bratislava, the present–day capital of Slovakia.

The Revolutions of 1848 ended serfdom in central Europe, but they also unleashed a virulent Hungarian nationalism that led the government to institute a policy of *Magyarization* after 1867. As a result, the government prohibited the use of the Slovak language in public, decreed that all school education was to be only in Hungarian and, in general, did everything it could to suppress a separate Slovak identity.

Yet the Revolutions of 1848 affected the Slovaks as well. It was in 1848, during the

329

# Slovak Republic

revolutions, that an assembly of Slovaks first drew up a demand for political, social and cultural equality. And even as the Hungarian Government attempted to suppress Slovak nationalism, individual Slovak intellectuals worked to counteract the official policy. These included two poets, Jan Holly and Jan Kollar, and Ludovit Stur, a writer and a political leader. Nevertheless, Slovak culture remained largely suppressed down to the collapse of the Austro–Hungarian Empire in 1918.

In spite of this, a Slovak identity did begin to develop, mainly among Slovaks in emigration—in Paris and, particularly, in the United States. During World War I, these Slovaks threw their support behind Thomas Masaryk's vision of an independent Czechoslovak state. The Pittsburgh Agreement, signed on June 30, 1918, expressed Slovak support for the union of Czech and Slovak lands in return for Masaryk's promise that Slovakia would have considerable independence within the new state. The independent Czecho–Slovak Republic was proclaimed in Prague on October 28, 1918. Two days later, the Slovak National Council, meeting in Turciansky Svaty Martin, a town in eastern Slovakia, voted to be part of the proclaimed state.

## The Independent Czecho–Slovak Republic

Slovakia remained a part of the independent Czecho–Slovak Republic until 1939, but that period of co–habitation was not entirely happy. The problem was that the constitution, adopted in 1920, stressed absolute majority rule and emphasized the sovereignty of the state *vis–à–vis* individual citizens. In addition, since Czechs and Slovaks were considered to be one people, there were no separate rights for Slovaks, nor was Slovak recognized as a separate language. In addition, the lesser educated Slovaks found themselves at a disadvantage in applying for jobs in the government. Thus there were less than 200 Slovaks among the 8,000–odd civil servants of the central government. In Slovakia, the public services were staffed mainly by Czechs. Even in the schools, half of all teachers were Czechs. Although almost all industry was located in the Czech part of the country, no effort was made to develop Slovakia and even some of the few factories that predated 1918 were allowed to go under. Many Slovaks believed that the Czechs were treating them as a colony. They particularly resented the presence of so many Czechs in important positions throughout Slovakia.

Individual Slovaks who spoke out on this issue often found themselves the subject of official judicial inquiry and action, charged with violating the 1923 law for the protection of the government, which prohibited "agitating . . . against the state because of its . . . constitutional unitary structure." Thus individuals who advocated federalism—as many Slovak nationalists did—were considered to be guilty of subversion. One of the more prominent cases occurred in 1928, when Professor Vojtech Tuka was arrested and sentenced to 15 years in prison for an assertion in a newspaper article that the original Slovak agreement to join the Czecho–Slovak Republic had required a referendum after ten years. In another such incident, the Slovak People's Party newspaper was closed down in 1933 and the editor arrested, after 100,000 Slovaks had demonstrated for autonomy in Nitra.

A Slovak provincial administration was actually created in 1927, but this did not satisfy Slovak leaders, who continued to press for full autonomy. The most important of these was Monsignor Andrej Hlinka, leader of the Slovak People's Party, largest of Slovakia's parties. Other parties that agitated for Slovak autonomy included the Catholic People's Party and the Slovak National Party. In addition, Slovak members of Social Democrats and Agrarians were often supporters of autonomy.

In 1935, Masaryk died and Dr. Eduard Benes became a candidate for the presidency. During his campaign, Benes sought electoral support from members of the Slovak People's Party by promising autonomy for Slovakia. When Dr. Milan Hodza, a Slovak, became Czecho–Slovak Premier at this time, many Slovaks became convinced that the central government was finally ready to take their interests into consideration. After his inauguration, however, Benes supported the Slovak Government that had existed since

**A mountain village in Slovakia in the late 1900's**

1927, and made no attempt to accord it any greater autonomy.

When a Sudeten German crisis erupted in 1938, therefore, this actually constituted a second crisis, for Slovaks were also beginning to organize their own demonstrations on behalf of autonomy—at the beginning of June, the Slovak People's Party introduced a bill for Slovak autonomy. A few days later, a mass meeting in Bratislava drew perhaps 120,000 persons. When Monsignor Hlinka died in August, the situation deteriorated further, for Monsignor Jozef Tiso, his successor as head of the Slovak People's Party, was an even more outspoken advocate of Slovak autonomy.

Meanwhile, the Sudeten German crisis was coming to a head. As pressure from Nazi Germany grew, Premier Hodza resigned on September 22 and President Benes took charge of the government. He created an all-party coalition with one seat reserved for the Slovak People's Party. Matus Cernak, the man chosen to represent the party, gave President Benes an ultimatum in October—unless Slovak autonomy was granted within 24 hours, he would resign and all Slovak delegates would leave the parliament. Cernak actually resigned the next day but, in an anticlimax of sorts, President Benes submitted his own resignation on October 5. General Jan Syrovy, whom Benes had appointed premier only days earlier, then became the acting president.

The next day, representatives from all of the Slovak political parties and Slovak branches of national political parties—with the exception of the Communists and Social Democrats—met in the town of Zilina. After considerable discussion, they voted to merge their several parties to form the Slovak National Unity Party and then drew up a manifesto which announced the formation of an autonomous Slovakian government.

Acting President Syrovy accepted the Zilina manifesto and appointed Monsignor Tiso as premier of Slovakia. The autonomy of Slovakia was legalized by constitutional amendment, passed by the Prague parliament on November 19. Elections to a Slovak parliament were held on December 18. The Slovak National Unity Party—whose dominant wing was the old Slovak People's Party—ran a single unity ticket and won 97.5 percent of the vote. The remainder of the ballots were cast for small German and Hungarian ethnic parties. The Social Democrats and Communists were unrepresented because the government had deliberately delayed publication of election procedures until it was too late for these two national parties to nominate candidates. Slovakia thus had essentially a one-party government and this situation continued throughout its existence.

Even after achieving its goal of autonomy, however, Slovak relations with Prague remained poor. This may have been because the Czechs were stressing the necessity of Czecho-Slovak unity to guarantee the continued independence of the state, plus Czech anger at the Slovaks for continued contacts with the Carpatho-Germans and for extensive conferences with officials from Hitler's Germany. In any case, Emil Hacha, who had been elected Czecho-Slovak president on November 19, 1938, was extremely upset by these contacts, which he claimed were treasonous. On March 9, he dismissed Monsignor Tiso as premier and declared a state of emergency in Slovakia. Several ministers were arrested, but Hacha did agree to allow the deputy premier, Karol Sidor, to reconstitute the Slovak government.

## "Independent" Slovakia, 1939–45

It was at this point that Hitler made his move. On March 12, a Nazi delegation arrived in Bratislava with a message from Hitler urging Premier Sidor to declare Slovakian independence. Sidor refused, but shortly thereafter Monsignor Tiso and Ferdinand Durcansky, a second Slovak nationalist, flew to Berlin to meet with Hitler. Here they were informed that Germany would recognize and support a declaration of Slovak independence. Hitler warned them, however, that he "would leave the destiny of Slovakia to the mercy of events," if they decided to remain with Prague.

There had already been reports that Hungary, which had already obtained parts of southern Slovakia in November, wanted to annex the rest of Slovakia. Now Ribbentrop, the German Foreign Minister, informed Tiso and Durcansky that Hungarian troops had begun to mass along the Slovak border. Monsignor Tiso returned to Bratislava on March 14 and immediately addressed the Slovak parliament. Following his report, the parliament unanimously adopted a declaration of Slovakian independence.

Meanwhile, President Hacha, who had requested an interview with Hitler, was invited to come to Berlin on that same day. In fact, the declaration of Slovak independence had already been adopted by the time he arrived in Berlin. Hacha met with Hitler late that evening. After a long harangue, Hitler demanded that Hacha sign an agreement accepting a German protectorate over the remaining parts of the country. Hacha collapsed during the interview, but managed to recover enough to sign the Czech capitulation. German troops entered the new Bohemia and Moravia Protectorate on March 15.

The Independent Slovakian Republic has often been referred to as a "puppet state" and it is true that the political realities of the time meant that the Slovak government had to, in general, align its policies with those of Hitler's Germany. It is also true that the Tiso government passed anti-Jewish legislation which, among other things, required Jewish entrepreneurs to sell off 51 percent of their shares to Slovak partners, set a limit of four percent on the percentage of Jews in public services and the professions, and encouraged Jewish emigration to Palestine.

These laws did not satisfy Hitler, however, and in July 1940 he forced the Slovak Government to agree to transfer Slovak Jews to a "resettlement" area in German-held Poland. The deportations continued until July 1942. Monsignor Tiso ordered them stopped after being informed by the Papal Nuncio that Jews were being murdered in the Lublin area. This new policy remained in force over the next two years. When, however, Security Minister Hassik ordered the disbanding of the labor camps and the repeal of anti-Jewish laws, the Germans assumed direct control of all matters concerning Jews in Slovakia.

The Germans deported approximately 9,000 Jews over the next year. With only pro forma cooperation from the Slovak Government, however, an estimated 26,650 Jews managed to escape the Nazi net and were still in Slovakia in 1945 at the end of the war.

Meanwhile, a sort of Slovak government-in-exile came into being in December 1943 in London when a number of Slovak liberals and leftists, including communists, organized a Slovak National Committee and, under the terms of a "Christmas Agreement" signed at the same time, committed themselves to "take over, at an expedient time, all political, legislative, military, and governmental executive power in Slovakia." The Slovak National Committee found some support for its plans in Slovakia, particularly among Protestants and some elements of the army and police. They also established some contact with partisan units in the mountains of eastern Slovakia. In August 1944, these communist-led partisans launched the so-called Slovak Revolt. Its hand forced, the Slovak National Committee endorsed the revolt on August 29, constituting itself a provisional government. The insurgents took over large parts of central Slovakia for a few days, but the bulk of the Slovak population withheld its support. Meanwhile, President Tiso, fearing the success of the revolt, requested the help of the German army. The revolt collapsed within a few days, but German troops remained, not leaving until forced out in 1945. Their presence, of course, destroyed any pretense that Slovakia was an independent country.

## Reintegration into Czechoslovakia

The vanguard of the Soviet army entered Slovakia on October 18, 1944. Slowed by a subsequent German counteroffensive, it took until April 4, 1945, to

# Slovak Republic

**North central Slovakia.**

Photo: Miller B. Spangler

clear the rest of Slovakia of German forces. Meanwhile, President Benes, having reorganized his government–in–exile into a "National Front" government after consulting Stalin in Moscow, arrived in Kosice in eastern Slovakia in March 1945 and set up his government. Here the government announced its "Kosice Program," which spelled out its plans for reconstituting the Czechoslovak state. Under its terms, "the members of the so–called Slovak Governments since March 14, 1939, as well as members of the so–called Slovak Parliament" were to be arrested and charged with high treason. The program also called for the suppression of the "Slovak People's Party, and those parties which joined the latter in 1938."

Most of the members of the Slovak Government fled to Bavaria at the end of the war. Taken into custody by the U.S. Army, they were extradited at the request of the Czechoslovak Government and taken to Bratislava. A National Tribunal appointed to try them sat for nearly a year before rendering its verdict in April 1947. Monsignor Tiso was sentenced to death by hanging, while other members of his government received prison terms.

Labor camps were also set up in Slovakia and thousands of persons deemed to "threaten the reconstruction of the state, security, the peace, public order . . . as well as those persons who profess an ideology inimical to the state" were confined into these camps without benefit of trial.

## The Continuing Problem of Slovak "Particularism"

From the point of view of the Czechoslovak Government, the punishments meted out were because the individuals were fascists, not nationalists, though Benes and the others were well aware that Slovak "particularism" was a continuing problem that was not likely to be ended by the imprisonment or even execution of a few leaders. To defuse this issue, therefore, the central government promised that Slovakia would be granted an autonomous status, with a parliament and a cabinet. Adopting this same approach, the communists, at this time the strongest group in the National Front government, organized a separate Slovak Communist Party. The communists did very badly in the 1946 elections in Slovakia, however, and thereafter began to place greater stress on Czechoslovak centralization.

After the communist seizure of power in Prague in early 1948, the new constitution issued three months later created a highly centralized state with nearly all power centered in the Czech capital. Yet it technically fulfilled the earlier promise of an autonomous status for Slovakia by creating a Slovak National Council with limited legislative powers relating to cultural matters, education, public health, local boundaries, encouragement of agriculture and local trade.

Two months later, however, the presidium of the Czechoslovak Communist Party negated this theoretical grant of autonomy to Slovakia by calling for a united communist party. Responding to this directive from Prague, the Slovak Communist Party voted to merge itself into the Czechoslovak Communist Party. From this time, the communist party organization in Slovakia was merely a branch of the Czechoslovak Communist Party,

though it was allowed to keep its separate central committee and regional organization.

The significance of this change became clear in April 1950, when the national government decided to move against religious communities throughout the country. Without informing the Slovak communist leaders, Prague dispatched policemen to dissolve religious orders in Bratislava and deport their members. When Slovak communist leaders protested, they were immediately suspended from their governmental duties. A month later, charges of "deviationism" and "bourgeois nationalism" were brought against them at the Ninth Congress of the Slovak branch of the Communist Party and a general purge followed. Among those dismissed from office at this time were Gustáv Husák, the Slovak Premier, Karol Schmidke, Chairman of the Slovak National Council and Ladislav Novomesky, Commissioner of Public Education.

Nine months later, Husák, Schmidke and Novomesky, plus Vladimir Clementis, a Slovak who had risen to the rank of Minister of Foreign Affairs in the central government, and several lesser known Slovak Communists, were arrested and charged with "nationalist–deviationist tendencies" as part of a general purge of "Titoist" Communists in Eastern Europe. Clementis, one of the 14 defendants in the so–called Slansky trial, held in Prague, was found guilty of bourgeois nationalism and executed in 1952. The others remained in prison for another two years before being given a formal trial in 1954. All were found guilty. Husák was sentenced to life imprisonment, while the others got lesser sentences. After the trial, there was a widespread purge of Slovak intellectuals from party and government jobs.

Following this purge of leading Slovak Communists, leadership in Slovakia was exercised by Viliam Siroky, a Slovak of Magyar origin who headed the Slovak branch of the Communist Party, and Karel Bacilek, a Czech who had migrated to Slovakia at the end of World War I, who replaced Husák as Premier. Thus there were no ethnic Slovaks in leadership roles in Slovakia.

Although the Slovak Communists had never enjoyed any real popularity among the Slovak people, they were willing to make some concessions to the nationalist aspirations of the Slovak population. Their successors were viewed by ordinary Slovaks as outsiders and agents of Prague and were detested for that reason.

With the general alienation of the Slovak population, it is not surprising that the 1956 Hungarian Revolution led to an outbreak of demonstrations in a number of Slovak cities. In response, a frightened

Prague Government dispatched six divisions of troops to western and central Slovakia to quell the unrest, while Soviet troops were moved in to secure eastern Slovakia. Four years later, the new constitution of the Czechoslovak Socialist Republic abolished the last legal remnants of Slovak autonomy.

Yet the issue of Slovak autonomy would not die. Two years later, a party congress in Prague voted to conduct an inquiry into the purges of 1949–1954. This reopened the Slovak issue for Vladimir Clementis was among those found to have been wrongfully convicted. The inquiry's decision on Clementis then led Slovak writers and scholars to begin agitating for the rehabilitation of those Slovak communists who had been thrown into prison for "bourgeois nationalism." Though this produced no immediate results, one "bourgeois–nationalist" figure, Gustáv Husák, was released from prison in 1960, ostensibly as part of a general amnesty to mark the fifteenth anniversary of socialist Czechoslovakia.

But he and the other victims of the Stalinist trials had to wait another two years for political rehabilitation. When the twelfth party congress met in December 1962, one of the resolutions adopted voided the earlier convictions and made amends by stipulating that those still alive would be readmitted to the party and given better jobs, while relatives of those executed would receive financial compensation.

Karol Bacilek, the immensely unpopular First Secretary of the Slovak branch of the Communist Party, and Viliam Siroky, Slovak Premier, were also removed at this time. Both men had aroused Slovak hatred by a consistent policy of cooperating with the Prague government's policies of centralization. Siroky was replaced by Josef Lenart, while Bacilek was succeeded by Alexander Dubček (pronounced Doob–chek). Czech–Slovak relations now improved and Novotny, basking in his new role as a reformer, got himself unanimously elected for another seven–year term as President of the Republic in 1964. The apparent political calm was misleading, however. It soon became clear that there were a number of differing opinions within the party over the progress of reform as well as a number of other issues, including Czech–Slovak relations.

Alexander Dubček emerged as the leader of the anti–Novotny forces in late 1967. At a meeting of the party Central Committee, he accused Novotny of undermining the program of economic reform and of refusing to meet Slovak demands for more self–government. Though he had raised the Slovak issue, Dubček placed greater emphasis on the issue of economic reform. It was clear that he did not want to be labeled a Slovak particularist. His position was helped by the fact that the Czechoslovak Writers' Union joined in the attack against Novotny at this same time; in addition students launched a series of demonstrations in Prague.

The reformers were not immediately successful, however. In fact, the unrest in Prague led to a visit by Soviet party chief Brezhnev as a gesture of support for Novotny. But the visit was not enough to save the falling president. When the Central Committee convened again two months later, it was decided that the functions of the presidency should be separated from those of the First Secretary of the Communist Party. On January 5, 1968, Alexander Dubček became the first Slovak to assume the top post in the Communist Party of Czechoslovakia.

An unsuccessful attempt at a *coup* showed that not even the army could help Novotny. The plot was discovered and the participants were removed from office by Dubček. One army general committed suicide while a second fled the country, eventually making his way to the U.S.

**Defeat for Reform**

The overall purpose of the entire reform movement was to create what Dubček called "socialism with a human face." Dubček was, in fact, always careful to portray himself as a Czechoslovak leader, though his general plans for political decentralization would have also led to greater Slovak autonomy. Yet the plans of the reformers were not to be. On the night of August 20–21, military units of the Soviet Union, Hungary, German Democratic Republic, Poland and Bulgaria entered Czechoslovakia, and within a few hours occupied the major cities. In the process, the entire Czechoslovak leadership—Dubček, Cernik, and Josef Smrkovsky, President of the National Assembly—was placed under arrest. The Czech Foreign Ministry denounced the invasion as a violation of the Warsaw Pact and President Svoboda flatly refused to participate in the formation of a Soviet–dominated government. The deadlock was broken when he agreed to go to Moscow for direct talks with the Soviet leaders.

At Svoboda's insistence, Dubček and the other leaders accompanied him to Moscow and participated in the talks. After much discussion, it was announced that there would be no change in the political leadership, though it was clear that they would not be permitted to continue their reform political program. This became even clearer in October when the two countries signed an open–ended treaty providing for the stationing of Soviet troops within Czechoslovakia.

**Compensation for Slovakia**

Yet one reform which was of great significance to Slovakia managed to survive the Soviet crushing of the Prague Spring. Since Prague was considered to be the focal point for reform communism, the Soviet leadership dropped its support for a highly centralized Czechoslovak state under Czech leadership and began to favor those conservative Slovak communists who had earlier been removed for nationalistic tendencies. To win their support, it was decided to finally grant Slovakia its autonomy by turning Czechoslovakia into a federal state. This reform, put into effect at midnight on December 31, 1968, abolished the old unitary structure and created in its stead a new federal republic consisting of the two separate Czech and Slovak Socialist Republics. During 1969 there was a gradual replacement of the pre–invasion reform leadership through demotion, resignation or dismissal.

Dubček, caught in the middle of all of this, tried to hang on by playing the centralist role. While assuring the liberals that there had been no surrender to the Soviet Union and that reform was still possible, he reassured the conservatives that there was no danger in reform. At the same time, he attempted to convince the Soviet Union that he would not be the source of additional political strife. Dubček found it difficult to be in favor of so many conflicting political views at the same time. In April, he was replaced as party secretary by Gustáv Husák.

Husák was a rather complex individual himself. Although in many ways a political moderate, he was willing to preside over the end of reform for two reasons; first, because he was inclined toward Slovak nationalism and liked the new federal structure; secondly, because he believed that it was paramount for Czechoslovakia to live in harmony with the Soviet Union. Dubček was expelled from the communist party in June 1970. This victory for the party's "hardliners" left Husák surrounded at the center by conservatives who also wanted to recentralize power in Prague. In early 1971, the Federal Cabinet was given the right to veto decisions of the Czech and Slovak cabinets. Slovak autonomy was once again being eroded.

Husák's own political position was not impaired by this new move toward centralization and, in all likelihood, he went along with the trend because he was, in fact, in charge of the entire country. In May 1975, he further increased his authority by replacing the ailing Svoboda as President of the Republic while remaining head of the party. Husák continued to occupy both positions for the next 12 years. Thus, in a final irony, the man who had once been thrown into prison for "bourgeois nationalism" became both the symbol and instrument of Prague's domination of Slovakia.

Husák became more and more conservative in his later years, so Gorbachëv's

# Slovak Republic

emergence as a reformer after his election as CPSU General Secretary in March 1985 presented him with a problem. After temporizing for some time, Husák announced his retirement as leader of the Czechoslovak Communist Party in December 1987, though he retained his position as President of the Republic. His successor was Milos Jakes (pronounced Ya–kesh). A Czech, Jakes kept his position as party leader for two years, until forced out in November 1989 as a result of Prague's so–called "velvet revolution."

Jakes was replaced by Karel Urbanek, but it was the Premier, Ladislav Adamec, who opened discussions with the opposition. The party now agreed to give up its monopoly of power and to form a coalition government with the opposition. But Adamec wanted to keep a majority of the seats in the hands of the communists. When Civic Forum rejected his proposed cabinet on December 3, Adamec resigned and was replaced by Marian Calfa. The new cabinet, installed on December 10, contained a majority of non–communists.

Gustáv Husák now submitted his resignation as President, thus opening the question as to who his successor should be. Alexander Dubček, leader of the Prague Spring in 1968, and Vaclav Havel, longtime dissident, founder of Charter 77, and prominent playwright, were both mentioned, but the job eventually went to

Havel. On December 29, he was elected President by acclamation, while Alexander Dubček was given the compensatory prize of becoming leader of the national assembly.

## Renewed Separatism

In the run–up to the June 1990 elections, the issue of democracy versus communism dominated political discussions, but the rivalry between Czechs and Slovaks began to emerge as an issue as well. Upon Slovak insistence, the name of the country was changed to the Czech and Slovak Federal Republic. And as new political parties were organized to contest the elections, separate parties emerged in the two parts of the country. While the Czech reform group was organized as the Civic Forum, the Slovak partner took the name of Public Against Violence.

Slovaks were from the beginning concerned about their separate identity, but the issue that led Slovak nationalists to begin demanding the creation of a separate, independent Slovak state was the question of economic reform. Many of the Slovak leaders feared that the swift implementation of a market system as advocated by Czech leaders such as Vaclav Klaus, the new Czechoslovak Minister of Finance, would have a disastrous affect on the Slovak economy.

The Federal Assembly attempted to

**Vaclav Havel**

defuse the situation in December 1990 by passing new legislation outlining the powers of the Czech and Slovak regional governments. The legislation also gave President Havel special powers to deal with the threat of Slovak separatism.

Although most Slovak deputies afterwards expressed their satisfaction with the legislation, the situation continued to

**Slovak hot–dog stand at the Hungarian border.**

Photo: Miller B. Spangler

simmer and President Havel was rushed by thousands of Slovaks shouting abuse when he visited Bratislava in March 1991. Part of the problem was that the Slovak Premier, Vladimir Meciar, had taken up the Slovak nationalist cause. Things improved somewhat after Meciar was replaced in April 1991 by Jan Carnogursky, head of Slovakia's *Christian Democratic Movement*. Carnogursky's position was somewhat ambiguous, however; although he supported continuation of the federation for the time being, he also said that he favored an independent Slovakia in principle.

Slovak nationalism continued to be the dominant factor in Czechoslovak politics throughout the rest of 1991 and into 1992. President Havel spent more and more of his time on this issue as he tried to act as a mediator between the Czechs and Slovaks, bringing the two sides together for discussions and, at one point, calling for a referendum on the issue. Public polls showed that a small majority of Slovaks supported a continuation of the federation, however, so the Slovak political leadership eventually rejected that suggestion. Havel also proposed some changes in the nature of the federal government, and these were presented to the Federal Assembly by the Czechoslovak Government in December 1991 in the form of three draft laws.

The three draft laws were not passed, but they may have acted as a catalyst. An ad hoc commission of the Czech and Slovak National Councils (i.e., legislatures) announced on February 9, 1992, that its members had drawn up a draft agreement on a future common state which would be submitted to their respective legislatures. The draft agreement listed foreign policy, defense, monetary, credit, interest and currency policies and budgetary regulations as falling within the powers of the federation. Czechs and Slovaks would be equally represented in the federal bodies. The agreement also specified that either republic could withdraw from the common state "only on the basis of the will of the majority of its citizens expressed in a referendum."

When the Presidium of the Slovak National Council met on February 12 to consider the draft, however, it was turned down. Two weeks later, the Slovak National Council adopted a resolution requesting Slovak National Council deputies to submit their views on the draft to the Presidium and instructed the Presidium to compile a comprehensive report on the comments that the deputies submitted. The resolution further recommended that the Presidium meet with the Presidium of the Czech National Council "to jointly assess . . . the possibility of concluding the treaty."

When these maneuvers failed to pro-duce an agreement, it was decided to hold new federal elections on June 5–6 to resolve the general issue. Slovakia decided to hold its own elections to the National Council on the same days. The *Christian Democratic Movement*, the party of Slovak Premier Jan Carnogursky, now split into two factions. The more radical faction that had been pushing for an independent Slovakia formed a new party, the *Slovak Christian Democratic Movement*, and announced that they would run a separate slate of candidates in the June elections. With the radicals gone, the *Christian Democratic Movement* reaffirmed its support for a common state.

In the June 1992 elections, the vote split along national and ideological lines. Essentially, the Czechs cast their votes for reform and anti–communist candidates, while the Slovaks supported nationalists and leftists. In the Slovak Republic, Vladimir Meciar and his *Movement for a Democratic Slovakia* won with their blend of statism, socialism and nationalism. In the Czech Republic, Vaclav Klaus and his *Civic Democratic Party* won an equally convincing victory on a program of anti–communism and reform.

When Meciar and Klaus met after the election to discuss the formation of a new federal government, Meciar made it clear that he would not accept a federal state that could dictate policy to Slovakia. He demanded that the Slovak Republic be authorized to establish its own army, its own currency–issuing central bank and that it be permitted the independent right to borrow. He also indicated that he intended to reverse some of the recent national policies as they applied to Slovakia, including restoring subsidies to state industry, increasing social benefits, and slowing privatization. None of these positions were acceptable to the free market. Klaus and the talks collapsed after six and a half hours.

Because a new federal government had to be formed, Klaus suggested giving a new, temporary federal government the power to act until a referendum could be held to ask citizens whether they wanted to live in a federal state. After further talks, Czech and Slovak negotiators agreed to establish a weak interim federal government whose task would be to facilitate bringing the union to a close. The actual constitutional questions relating to the separation would be resolved in the legislatures of the two republics. Further negotiations now produced an agreement, signed on August 26, calling for a split into two independent states by January 1.

The process suffered a setback on October 1, when the federal parliament rejected a bill legalizing the end of the federation. After further negotiations, however, the federal parliament voted itself out of existence on November 25.

By that time, the two national legislatures had begun acting like the federation had already disappeared; this was particularly true in the case in Slovakia. Meciar had said in June that he wanted to slow down privatization and he began submitting bills to the Slovak legislature to accomplish that purpose. The Slovak government called for the renegotiation of several privatization agreements and stopped the privatization of a number of companies. As a result, only 5.3% of Slovak industry had been privatized by the end of 1992 as compared to 25.2% for the Czech Republic. On January 1, 1993, The Czech and Slovak Federal Republic disappeared and in its place there emerged an independent Slovak Republic and an independent Czech Republic. The separation was peaceful, but all of the celebrations were in Bratislava, the capital of Slovakia. There was no ceremony to mark the occasion in Prague. In the speech he gave to mark the occasion, Prime Minister Meciar attempted a note of conciliation. "Two states have been established," he said. "Living together in one state is over. Living together in two states continues."

### Slovakia Since Independence

After achieving independence for Slovakia, Prime Minister Meciar reiterated the positions he enunciated in 1992. In his New Year's Day address, he rejected both free market economics and a ban on former communists in top government positions. He also surrounded himself with reform communists who had been active in the Prague Spring. Meciar's commitment to democracy and pluralism was also not very firm. For example, the government

**Prime Minister Vladimir Meciar**

# Slovak Republic

tightened its control on the press and on television after independence, dismissing individuals suspected of oppositionist tendencies. It also began to restrict the language rights of its Hungarian minority. In October 1993, for example, the government began taking down Hungarian–language signs in border areas and formally announced that Hungarian names for Slovak towns could not be used in Hungarian–language broadcasts.

Meciar's greatest changes were in the area of economics, however. In the first months after independence, privatization came to an end for all but the smallest firms. At the same time, the government increased credits to state industry, thereby enlarging the budget deficit and contributing to the collapse of the common currency arrangement with the Czech Republic. There was a drop of almost 50% in exports to the Czech Republic, and an even greater drop in imports from the Czech Republic. There were also reports that significant deposits had been switched from Slovak to Czech banks.

Meciar undoubtedly expected that his halting of privatization and increasing of credits to state industry would have a positive effect on employment and the overall economy. In fact, they had the opposite effect. As the economic situation worsened and unemployment grew to an estimated 14.4%, Meciar's party split in February 1994. Among those withdrawing from the party were Meciar's foreign minister, Jozef Moravcik, and the deputy prime minister, Roman Kovac. That left the *Movement for a Democratic Slovakia* without a parliamentary majority. Meciar was finally ousted on March 11 when he lost a parliamentary vote of confidence. He was replaced by Jozef Moravcik, who had led the rebellion against him in February. Although a former member of the *Movement for a Democratic Slovakia*, Moravcik promised to revive the reform process.

New elections were scheduled to take place on September 30, so Moravcik didn't have much time to make a record for himself. Nevertheless, he managed to accomplish a number of important things during the next six months, including a controlled state budget, falling inflation, improving GDP growth and rising foreign reserves. He shepherded legislation through parliament extending protection for Hungarian language rights, In a related area, he opened negotiations with Hungary for a treaty to settle border questions and the treatment of each other's minorities and, in connection with that, invited Gyula Horn, the Hungarian prime minister, to Bratislava for an official visit. Having restored Slovakia to international respectability, he was rewarded by a $263 million loan from the IMF and promises of additional loans from the European Union and other industrialized countries.

None of that seemed to matter very much when the people went to cast their ballots on September 30 and October 1, however. The essential problem appears to have been that Moravcik's supporters were a disparate group of *Movement for a Democratic Slovakia* rebels, conservative *Christian Democrats*, and the *Democratic Left Party* (i.e., the successor to the old communist party) that had very little in common other than their opposition to Meciar. Moreover, Meciar's *Movement for a Democratic Slovakia* is still the best organized and financed of all the political parties. Nor did it hurt that his supporters in parliament, in attacking the new government by every means at their disposal, were viewed as heroes by most of those negatively affected by the reforms—in

**Former President Michal Kovac**

particular Slovakia's 15% unemployed, the peasantry and the retired.

While no party won an outright majority, Meciar's *Movement for a Democratic Slovakia* came in first with 35% of the vote, winning 61 of the 150 parliamentary seats. Yet he found it extremely difficult to create a working majority coalition. Although Moravcik had submitted his resignation as prime minister after the results of the election became known, he actually remained on in the capacity of caretaker for another six weeks. Finally, Meciar announced on November 3 that he had negotiated a "voting pact" with the right–wing *Slovak National Party* and the left–wing *Association of Slovak Workers* which would allow him to form a government. Although not then a formal alliance, this voting majority pushed legislation through the parliament sacking the attor-

ney general, dismissing the board of the National Property Fund (thus suspending privatization), blocking the sale of all state–owned companies approved by the previous government, and bringing radio, television, and the state intelligence service under the control of Meciar's party.

This trend continued, and intensified, after that time. In 1995, Meciar launched a series of public attacks on President Kovac, and these continued in 1996 and 1997. Meciar also called, on several occasions, for President Kovac to step down. When this did not work, he attempted to get the parliament to dismiss President Kovac. These moves failed because Meciar lacked the two–thirds majority in the legislature necessary to force out the President.

One of the more bizarre aspects of this struggle between Prime Minister Meciar and President Kovac occurred in August 1995 and involved the President's son, Michal Kovac, Jr. Although all the facts haven't been established, what is known is that Michal Kovac, Jr. was mysteriously abducted in Bratislava and carried across the border into Austria, where he was later arrested on a German warrant. Most observers believe that the Slovak security service was responsible for the abduction, though no one has been able to provide any evidence that Prime Minister Meciar was directly involved. On the other hand, Ivan Lexa, the head of the security service, had been rejected for the post of privatization minister by President Kovac in 1993 and may have arranged the kidnapping because he held a grudge against President Kovac. President Kovac did later say, in an interview, that accusations and attacks against him had begun in 1993, though he never publicly charged that there was a political motive behind the abduction. One other thing that ties Meciar to the kidnapping is that he granted pardons to all persons involved after he took over as Acting President in March 1998.

Meciar has always used appeals to Slovak nationalism to consolidate his support. In 1995, this led him to push through a new language law aimed at restricting the rights of minorities, and particularly the Hungarian minority, to make use of their national language. This law made it illegal for radio or television broadcasts, advertising and official government information to be in anything other than the Slovak language. In August 1997, Meciar carried his antipathy to Hungarian-speakers even further when he officially suggested to Gyula Horn, the Hungarian Prime Minister, that ethnic Hungarian-speakers be repatriated to Hungary or, as he put it at a party rally in Bratislava, "those people who do not want to be Slovak citizens [should] go to Hungary and live there." Subsequently, the Slovak National Party and the Slovak Workers' Party, the two junior parties in the ruling coalition, endorsed Meciar's proposal, characterizing it as a "possible and constructive solution."

During the later part of 1997, people began looking toward the presidential elections which had to come in the early part of 1998, as President Kovac's term of office ended on March 2. It was evident that Prime Minister Meciar wanted to be elected President, but lacked the three–fifths majority in the parliament necessary to win. Thus when the first round of voting took place on January 23, the only persons nominated were two candidates from the opposition plus an independent. None came close to winning the required three–fifths majority as Meciar had announced prior to the vote that none of the candidates were acceptable to his Movement for a Democratic Slovakia.

When President Kovac's term came to an end on March 2, the office became vacant, with some of the powers of the President devolving on Prime Minister Meciar. New parliamentary elections are currently scheduled to take place on September 25 and 26, 1998. The current expectation is that the office of the President will remain vacant until after new parliamentary elections. If Meciar and his coalition partners win those elections, then he will presumably arrange his own election as President.

## Foreign Policy

Slovakia's most important foreign relations are naturally those with the Czech Republic. Having agreed to a peaceful separation into two independent nations, the Czechs and Slovaks nevertheless recognized that their economies would be tightly bound to each other for some time and that it would be wise to retain certain elements of the former union if they could. These would include a common currency and a customs union which would allow for the free movement of goods. In addition, Czechs and Slovaks would not be required to show passports to pass from one country to another.

Although the common currency collapsed after less than two months, the customs union has survived. Trade between the two new republics fell off considerably following separation. It has since stabilized, but it has had a negative effect on both economies.

Slovak relations with the Czech Republic tended to be testy during the earlier prime ministership of Meciar. At one point, for example, Meciar threatened to cut off the oil that flows to the Czech Republic through Slovakia. Relations improved under Moravcik, but they have reverted to their earlier coolness since Meciar returned to power in 1994. At one point in 1997, in fact, Slovakia had withdrawn its Ambassador from Prague and

was demanding an apology from President Havel for some, admittedly impolitic, comments that President Havel had made about Prime Minister Meciar. It has not helped that the Czech Republic has been invited to join both the European Union and NATO, while Slovakia has been rejected by both organizations.

Slovakia's relations with its other neighbors, which improved under Moravcik, have also returned to their previous state. Relations with Hungary are particularly bad for a number of reasons. There is a continuing disagreement over a new dam on the Danube River which Slovakia built after Hungary had backed out of an earlier joint agreement, though this will probably be settled shortly. The more important issue is Meciar's attitude toward ethnic Hungarians. The essential problem is that Meciar is a Slovak chauvinist who appears to believe that allowing Slovakia's 560,000 ethnic Hungarians to use Magyar in areas where they are a significant percentage of the population would

somehow diminish the Slovak language. His continuing actions to limit such use militates against good relations with Hungary. As Geza Jeszenszky, Hungary's Foreign Minister, commented, "it is not possible to maintain good relations with neighbors who oppress minorities."

The one area where relations have improved since Meciar returned to power are with Slovakia's eastern neighbors, Russia, Belarus, and Ukraine. One factor has been the tendency among Slovak nationalists to stress pan–slavic cooperation; more importantly, however, Slovakia has encouraged a rebuilding of trade ties eastward. There has also been the ideological factor. For example, the ex–communist Slovak Association of Workers is a strong advocate of better relations with the east. Meciar, himself, appears to be of two minds in this regard. He declares himself to be a supporter of eventual membership in both the European Union and NATO and he expressed great public disappointment when Slovakia was passed over for

**Industrial plant in central Slovakia**

# Slovak Republic

membership in the EU and NATO in 1997. At the same time, Meciar also stresses Slovakia's "special relationship" with Russia and a dozen treaties were signed during Russian Prime Minister Viktor Chernomyrdin's official visit to Bratislava in February 1995.

## Nature of the Regime

Slovakia's constitution, adopted by the Slovak National Council in July 1992 formally designates the country as the Slovak Republic. The constitution also created a 150 seat assembly as the nation's legislature and bestowed on the assembly the right to elect the head of state, to be known as the President of the Republic.

The independent Slovak Republic came into being on January 1, 1993. It is in principle a parliamentary democracy, with the leading political role that of the prime minister. Eighteen parties competed for votes in the 1994 parliamentary elections, but most of them are weak and uncompetitive. The *Movement for a Democratic Slovakia*, with its mixture of populism and nationalism and its ties to the reform communist movement of the late 1960s, is the richest and best organized of the parties. It controls 61 seats in the parliament. The other two members of the current "voting pact" coalition are the *Slovak National Party*, an ultra–nationalist party on the right, and the *Association of Slovak Workers*, on the far left. Together they control 83 of the parliament's 150 seats.

The most recent President of the Republic was Michal Kovac, nominated by Prime Minister Meciar after his first choice, Roman Kovac, his deputy prime minister, was not able to win the three–fifths majority necessary to be elected. Michal Kovac, elected on the first ballot, was expelled from the communist party in 1970 as a supporter of Dubček. He was Slovakia's Finance Minister from the end of 1989 to the beginning of 1992, then served as the last chairman of Czechoslovakia's federal parliament.

## Economy

Privatization was instituted as a national policy after the fall of communism, but the actual implementation was always in the hands of the Slovak Government. Much of Slovakia's industry was built during the communist era. It is large–scale and has had difficulty competing during the transition to a market economy. There is, for example, an extremely large arms industry. Fears about the fate of its heavily subsidized plants helped fuel the Slovak separatist movement that resulted in the break–up of Czechoslovakia at the beginning of 1993.

Privatization was always a much more controversial policy in Slovakia than in the Czech Republic, and Meciar brought it to a halt after Slovakia achieved its in-dependence. Yet stopping privatization had, if anything, a negative effect on the economy. Under Meciar, GDP declined while unemployment climbed to 14.4 percent and inflation soared to 22%. This led to Meciar's ouster as prime minister in March 1994. His successor, Jozef Moravcik, took office committed to economic reform. Over the next six months, he reduced the budget deficit by slashing various subsidies, and he instituted a major program of voucher–privatization. As a result, inflation fell by several percentage points, GDP turned positive, and foreign reserves rose. It is currently estimated that 55% of production now comes from the private sector.

Since Meciar returned to office in November 1994, however, he has reversed a number of Moravcik's policies and promises to end others. In particular, he threatens to destabilize the budget again by reinstituting subsidies and raising governmental salaries and pensions. If Meciar implements the promised policies, the economy is likely to begin sinking again. Privatization in the area of agriculture got much further because the Federal Government strenuously pursued a program to transform the country's agriculture, and most of this had been fully implemented prior to Slovakia's independence. Federal legislation legally transformed collective farms into cooperatives and stipulated that employees had the right to ask for their own land. Most Slovak peasants opted to remain a part of the cooperative structure, however, with only a tiny minority requesting their own land. Even those few who asked for their own acres mostly wanted only a couple of acres to work for themselves. Meciar recently promised to increase agricultural subsidies.

## The Slovak Arms Industry

In the decade from 1978 to 1988, Czechoslovakia was the world's eighth largest weapons exporter and the global leader in per capita terms. More than 100 plants produced various types of weaponry ranging from Skorpion machine pistols to L–39 jet trainers, exported to Czechoslovakia's Warsaw Pact partners and Third World countries. Most of these plants were located in central Slovakia, which became the center of Czechoslovakia's heavy arms industry. By 1989, military production represented nearly 60 percent of total industrial production in Slovakia and provided employment for more than 100,000 persons.

"These plants were put up in green meadows," says Josef Fucik, head of the department for conversion of military production in the federal Ministry of Economics in Prague. "It was a quick fix in the '50s to give modern jobs to Slovakia. Now the bill has come due." The town of Martin, 230 km north of Bratislava, was the site of a tank plant that employed 11,000; nearby Dubnica built armored personnel carriers, while Povazska Bystrica, down the road, produced jet engines.

Two months after the November 1989 revolution, Foreign Minister Jiri Dienstbier announced that Prague would "simply end its trade in arms" without regard to economic consequences. That turned out to be impossible. With so many jobs dependent on arms production, the bulk of them in a depressed region of Slovakia, the government had to modify its plans. Still, it remained pledged to cut the output of weapons plants to 25% of 1988 levels by 1993. Slovak politicians strenuously opposed the cuts, and this became a major issue in the push for Slovak independence. They did everything they could to frustrate the policy in the interim period and then reversed the policy entirely after January 1993.

While the Slovak Government has halted all efforts to convert arms factories to civilian production, it has not found it all that easy to carry out its stated policy of keeping its arms industry intact. There is, for example, no domestic demand for tanks, since Slovakia must actually destroy some of the tanks it currently has under the terms of the Conventional Forces in Europe agreement. In addition, in the past, three–quarters of all arms exports went to former Warsaw Pact allies. Those sales have disappeared as these countries cut their military budgets, partly for the same reason. The Soviet Union, once Czechoslovakia's largest customer, cancelled almost all purchase orders in 1991 when it would have been required to pay for such purchases in hard currency. The subsequent collapse of the Soviet Union had a psychological effect in Czechoslovakia, but it had already ceased to be a major arms purchaser prior to its collapse.

There have been some sales to Third World countries, but Slovakia is at a disadvantage here because it produces mainly heavy battlefield weapons, not the small arms and specialized explosives most in demand in the developing world. Worse, all of Slovakia's major weapons systems are produced on license from Russia, which in many cases is competing in the same markets with more advanced weapons systems.

Some of these sales have been controversial and sometimes even opposed by western countries. One example, dating from before Slovak independence, was Czechoslovakia's agreement to sell up to 300 T–72 tanks to Syria in a deal worth $200 million. The USA and Israel condemned the projected sale and it eventually fell through after an unsuccessful attempt had been made to deliver the tanks. As it turns out, since Syria owes Czechoslovakia the equivalent of $1 billion for previous arms shipments and this new sale would have been on the basis of long–term government credit, the net effect would have been negative in any case.

Efforts made before independence to convert parts of Slovak heavy industry to peaceful purposes were also not very successful. An example is the Zdeno Velky Steel Mill, located in the city of Kosice in eastern Slovakia. Built in the 1950's to supply Czechoslovak weapons plants and industry throughout the Soviet bloc, Zdeno Velky invested millions of dollars in up–to–date equipment from the west after 1989 in order to make itself internationally competitive. Its extensive efforts to find new markets for its steel paid off initially, but its very success proved its undoing. In 1992, the European Community imposed strict trade limits on steel imports from eastern Europe, including Czechoslovakia. Zdeno Velky has since managed to sell steel to China, India and Thailand, but sometimes it was required to sell it at a loss in order to get the sale.

A somewhat more successful story of conversion relates to the ZTS Martin ("Turcanske Strojarne" factory, located in the city of Martin), a tank manufacturer, which negotiated an agreement with the German firm Hanomag to manufacture earthmoving equipment. The company also began working under license from the Italian manufacturer Lombardini to produce tractor engines and other machinery. In this instance, military production has been reduced to one–quarter of overall manufactures.

## Culture

There has always been a separate Slovak culture. Slovaks, part of the Hungarian Kingdom from the 11th century, were a peasant people heavily influenced by Hungarian culture. Slovakia is particularly known for its unique and lively folk music and dances, performed in brightly–colored traditional dress. Slovakia has changed greatly in recent years, however, and many parts of the country are now urbanized and industrialized.

Slovaks tend to be somewhat defensive about the level of their culture, but the truth is that the works of individual Slovak artists and craftsmen compare favorably with that of other Europeans. On the other hand, because many Slovaks live in small towns or in the countryside itself, Slovak art often has more of a peasant

quality about it. There is also not as large an audience for art, so artists tend to be more marginalized.

## Religion

The old communist regime was extremely hostile to religion and it went out of its way to make its practice difficult. The Catholic Church, to which most Slovaks belong, was particularly restricted by the regime, probably because it is part of an international organization. Since the 1989 revolution, the Catholic Church has revealed that it maintained an underground church in Slovakia during those years. This involved such things as secretly providing theological training in private apartments and homes and ordaining hundreds of individuals as priests who then continued to work in their regular jobs while performing their priestly functions in secret.

As this underground church has emerged, people were surprised to learn of the double lives some of these individuals had been living. As an example, five faculty members at the communist–run Kosice University were actually Jesuit priests, including the Dean of the School of Civil Engineering. It also turns out that a large percentage of the priests in the country belong to religious orders like the Dominicans, Jesuits and Salesians, all of which were banned by the communists. There were even some married men ordained as priests, plus some women who became deacons. The Church is now attempting to sort all of these anomalies out.

## The Future

Slovakia's initial years of independence have not been promising and the future doesn't appear any brighter. Its greatest problem appears to be its long–term lack of self–esteem that persuades many of its politicians that Slovaks cannot compete equally with others and that they must therefore have a separate political existence in order to reach their full potential. For that, Meciar was willing to give up large subsidies that were coming into Slovakia from the federal government. That lack of self–esteem also takes the form of xenophobia aimed at all ethnic non–Slovaks in the country and at nearly all neighbors outside the country. All people, to be sure, exhibit something of this attitude at times, and there are many Slovaks who do not have this problem. But there are still enough that men like Meciar will always find a political following to lend power to their voices. His party's victory in the 1994 parliamentary elections is proof of that. Slovaks have opted for several more years in the wilderness.

**A Slovak peasant tills her plot**                    AP/Wide World Photo

# The Former Yugoslavia

Due to their shared histories as well as frequent geographical and cultural similarities, there is necessarily some repetition from one entry to the other.

**President Slodoban Milosevic of Serbia, left, shakes hands with President Franjo Tudjman of Croatia as President Alija Izetbegovic of Bosnia–Herzegovina, right, looks on following the signing of the Balkan treaty at the Elysee Palace in Paris, December 14, 1995. Behind them applauding, from left, are Spanish Premier Felipe Gonzalez (hidden), President Clinton, French President Jacques Chirac and German Chancellor Helmut Kohl.** AP/Wide World Photo

On April 27, 1992, after four of the six republics which had been integral parts of *The Socialist Federal Republic of Yugoslavia* had declared their independence, the remaining two, Serbia and Montenegro—the largest and the smallest in the former union—proclaimed themselves the successor nation as the "new" *Federal Republic of Yugoslavia*. This rump state has not been accorded diplomatic recognition by any nation and it is, in fact, little more than an extension of the Republic of Serbia.

The basic facts listed immediately below relate only to the new Serbia/Montenegro "marriage" followed by a general history of that area of the Balkans and of the now disintegrated *republic* born on November 26, 1945.

**Area:** 39,408 square miles (102,261 sq. km.).

**Population:** 10,406,742 (April 1991 census).

**Capital City:** Belgrade (Pop. 1.3 million, metropolitan area, projected).

**Climate:** Continental, with marked contrasts between summer and winter, with lowest temperatures in the high elevations. The summers are hot.

**Neighboring Countries:** Hungary (north); Romania, Bulgaria (east); Macedonia (south); Albania, Bosnia–Herzegovina, Croatia (west).

**Official Language:** Serbian.

**Other Principal Tongues:** Albanian, Hungarian, and Romanian.

**Ethnic Background:** Slav, with Albanian ancestry in the southwest, Hungarian in the Vojvodina. About 60% of the population are Serbs.

**Principal Religions:** Serbian Orthodox Christianity, Islam.

**Chief Commercial Products:** Chemicals, farm equipment, paper, glass, textiles, sugar, flour, wheat, corn, tobacco, fruits and vegetables, lead, zinc, copper, silver, gold, chromium, coal, and consumer goods.

**Currency:** New Dinar (since Jan. 1994, at par with the German mark).

**Annual Per Capita Income:** Undetermined.

**Former Colonial Status:** Yugoslavia did not exist as a state prior to World War I;

it was created around the core of old Serbia by adding the Kingdom of Montenegro and territories taken from the Austro–Hungarian Empire.

**National Day:** April 27 (1992), the date on which Serbia and Montenegro declared themselves the successor nation as the "new" Yugoslavia.

**Chief of State:** Slobodan Milosevic, President.

**National Flag:** Horizontal stripes of blue, white and red, with a five–pointed red star in the center, outlined in gold.

## The Land

With the collapse of the Yugoslavian Federal Government in 1991 following the withdrawal of four of the six re-

# Yugoslavia

publics, Yugoslavia has shrunk to a rump of its former self and now consists of the two republics of Serbia and Montenegro. Serbia has two "autonomous" regions, the Voivodina (Vojvodina) and Kosovo–Metohija, the latter of which now seeks its own independence or affiliation with Albania.

The Voivodina is that part of Serbia north of the Danube River. It is a rich, flat plain, divided by tributaries of the Danube flowing across it from the north. The Voivodina borders on Hungary to the north, Croatia to the west, and Romania on the east. It was granted an autonomous status because a majority of the population is ethnically Hungarian.

Kosovo–Metohija, the second "autono-mous" region, is located in the southwestern part of Serbia. About 90 percent of this area is ethnically Albanian. This is a mountainous region, with the highest ones, the Albanian Alps (in Serbian the *Mokra Mountains*), located in the northeastern part of the province. A second mountain, the Sar, arises in the southwest. There is a plateau region in the center, with lower mountains rising again to the east. Northern Serbia is mostly the lowland area of the Danube River Valley. As one travels south away from the river valley, however, the land becomes rolling hills, then mountain ridges cut by river valleys open to the north. Mountains also predominate along the western border with Montenegro, in the south along the border with Macedonia, and in the east along the border with Bulgaria.

Montenegro means "Black Mountain" and that describes most of this mountainous land. The Dinarian Alps extend into the republic from the north. In the south, the Albanian Alps run west–east along the border with Albania. Montenegro also has a fairly long coastline on the Adriatic Sea. Skhoder Lake, also located here, forms part of the border with Albania. The northern half of the lake belongs to Montenegro.

## The People

The rump Yugoslavia of 1992 consists almost entirely of Serbs and the linguistically and culturally closely related Montenegrins, except for the two autonomous

341

# Yugoslavia

regions of Serbia, where Hungarians predominate in the Voivodina and Albanians in Kosovo–Metohija. In 1990–91, the Serbian Government destroyed the autonomous status of both these regions, so today the governments in these areas are appointed by Belgrade. The people of the Voivodina have quietly accepted the situation, but the Albanians of Kosovo held a referendum on independence and declared their own republic in 1991. The area is still occupied by Serbian troops and the situation is far from stable.

## History

The Slavic–speaking peoples of the Balkan Peninsula are classified as South Slavs and they are one of three branches of the Slavic peoples, the other two being the East Slavs (Russians, Ukrainians, Belarusians) and the West Slavs (Poles, Czechs, Slovaks). The Slavic language is, in turn, a branch of the Indo–European family of languages. When the Slavic peoples first appeared in history, they were found mostly in the area of the Pripet Swamps in what are now the republics of Belarus and Ukraine.

The South Slavs began migrating into the area of the Balkans sometime in the sixth century. At first, the Slavs were dominated by two Turkic peoples also present in what became the Balkans, the Avars and Bulgars. When the Avar and Bulgar khanates crumbled in the first quarter of the seventh century, however, the Byzantine Emperor signed an alliance with two of the stronger Slavic tribes, the Serbs and Croats. Supported by this alliance, the Slavic peoples either pushed the Turkic peoples out of the Balkans or submerged them in their greater numbers. By the end of the seventh century, Slavic language and culture was dominant throughout most of the northern Balkans, except for the east where the Vlach (ancestors of modern Romanians) were in a majority and in mountainous areas of the west where the native Illyrian people (ancestors of the modern Albanians) managed to keep their culture alive.

The Serbs and Croats eventually gave their names to the areas of the Balkans they now occupy, while a third tribe, the Slovenes, who had actually been the first of the Slavic tribes to enter the Balkans, settled further west. In 748, the Slovenes were incorporated into the Carolingian Empire and converted to Roman Catholicism. They remained a part of western culture from that time onward. The Croats were also incorporated into the Carolingian Empire for a short time at the beginning of the ninth century and converted to Roman Catholicism. It was not until the end of the eleventh century that they came under the control of the Kingdom of Hungary, however.

The first Serb state rose about the middle of the ninth century when a number of south Serbian tribes united to oppose expansion from the Bulgar state to the southeast. Vlastimir, the ruler of this state, sought the support of the Byzantine Emperor against the Bulgars; in the process, he submitted himself to the over–lordship of the Byzantine Emperor. One effect of this is that Serbia became open to Byzantine cultural influences, the most important of which was Orthodox Christianity. In addition, the two missionaries from Thessalonica, Cyril and Methodius, had created a script for the Slavic language based on Greek letters. The Cyrillic alphabet was adopted by Serbia along with Orthodox Christianity, and in the process a great cultural divide was created in the Balkans that ran down through the middle of the Slavic settlements. Henceforth, Serbs (along with Bulgarians, Montenegrins and Macedonians) were on one side of that divide and the Croats and Slovenes on the other.

In spite of Byzantine assistance, Vlastimir's kingdom eventually fell under Bulgarian control. As a result, the Serb church became a part of the Bulgarian Orthodox Church. The area of Serbia next came under the control of a Macedonian kingdom created at the beginning of the eleventh century. Then the Byzantine Empire overthrew the Macedonian kingdom in 1018 and tried to extend its control over the area of the eastern Balkans. This led to short–lived kingdoms arising in Herzegovina and Montenegro to challenge the Byzantine control. Toward the end of the eleventh century, yet another kingdom rose in the area of Novi Bazar, only to be supplanted by a revived Bulgarian kingdom after the capture of Constantinople by soldiers of the fourth crusade in 1204.

A new Serbian kingdom rose in the area of Skopje ("j" is almost always pronounced "y") beginning in 1282, called the Nemanjid Empire after the name of the dynasty. The founder of this dynasty was Stefan Nemanja. This kingdom reached its height under its ninth ruler, Stefan Dusan, who ruled from 1331 to 1355. Although this kingdom eventually extended its control over a large part of the northern Balkans, its greatest significance was probably cultural. The Nemanjids were committed to the Orthodox Church and it was during this time that the Serbs managed to separate from the Bulgarian Orthodox Church and establish an autonomous *Serbian* Orthodox Church. The seat of the church was later moved to Pec; In 1375, it was raised to a patriarchate.

Equally important, the Nemanjids managed to create a Serbian "high culture" based on religious cohesion. They fought the influence of Roman Catholicism and worked to suppress Bogomilism, a religious heresy centered in Bosnia. They were also responsible for construction of many churches and monasteries, which have come to signify the essence of medieval Serbian Orthodoxy. Among the most renowned of these churches are the Milesevo (c. 1235), Pec (1250), Moraca (1252), Sopocani (c. 1260), and the Decani (1327). Many of these churches are decorated by frescoes, the most important being those of the Rasko school.

In addition, this period produced a number of literary works, including a biography of Stefan Nemanja. A close partnership between church and state produced a courtly culture which was at the same time a religious culture. This continued to define the best of what it meant to be a Serbian long after the kingdom itself was no more. This kingdom came to an end in the fourteenth century, when Turkish armies defeated the Serbs in the Battle of Kosovo which took place on June 15, 1389. The leader of the Serbian forces was Prince Lazar. The Turkish Sultan, Murad I, was actually killed early in the day by a Serbian assassin, Milosh Obilic, who made his way into the Turkish camp pretending to be a deserter. He stabbed the sultan with a poisoned dagger.

Murad's son managed to rally his forces and defeat the Serbians. Prince Lazar, taken prisoner during the battle, was beheaded. For seventy years, Serbs were required to pay an annual tribute and to serve in the Turkish armies, but were allowed domestic autonomy. Then, in 1459, the sultan placed all of Serbia under Turkish rule. All lands became the property of the sultan and all Serbs became bond slaves of the land. The patriarchate of Pec was also suppressed for a time, but was restored in 1557. Henceforth, Serbian culture lived on only within the Serbian Orthodox Church.

Turkish rule continued for another five centuries before the Serbs raised the banner of revolt. Under the leadership of Karageorge (Black George), the Serbs revolted against the rule of the Turks in 1804. The revolt was suppressed in 1813, but a more successful revolt broke out two years later under the leadership of Milosh Obrenovic. In 1817, Serbia won the right to have its own national assembly. Milosh became Prince of Serbia and promptly had his great rival, Karageorge, murdered. This was a beginning of a feud between the Obrenovic and Karageorgevic families which continued into the twentieth century, frequently disrupting the political life of the country.

After the Russo–Turkish War of 1828–29, Serbia was given the status of an autonomous principality, technically still under Turkish suzerainty but effectively a Russian protectorate.

In 1876, Serbia became the cause of another war between Russia and Turkey when it declared war on Turkey. When it

# Yugoslavia

## WESTERN BALKANS 1560–1680

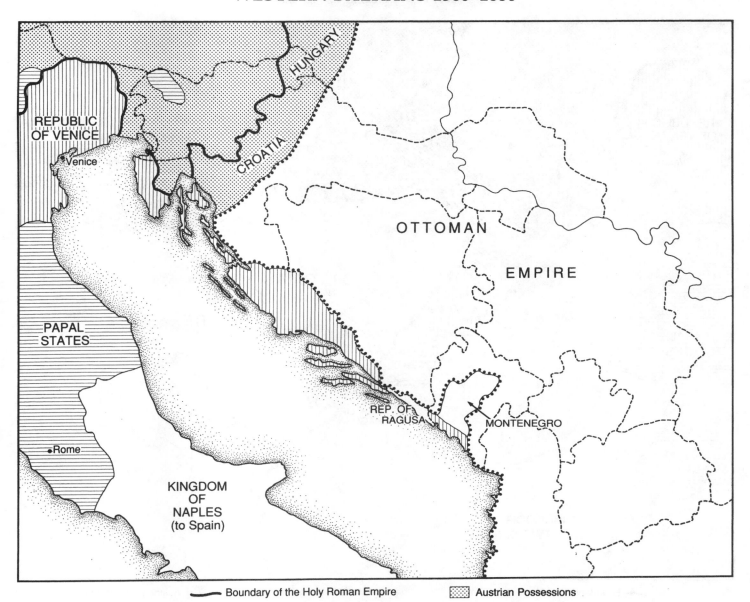

—— Boundary of the Holy Roman Empire     ▦ Austrian Possessions

OTTOMAN (Turkish) EMPIRE at its greatest extent.
MONTENEGRO, an area of virtually inaccessible mountains, never conquered by the Turks.
REPUBLIC OF VENICE, ruled by an elite of wealthy merchant families. Dominated the Adriatic Sea from bases in Dalmatia.
REPUBLIC OF RAGUSA (Dubrovnik), a small city–state which flourished as an important cultural center, developing distinctive
   local styles of architecture and sculpture, and establishing Croatian as a modern literary language.

*These boundaries were essentially stable for over a century as the Austrian Hapsburgs resisted further Turkish advances into Central Europe.*
KINGDOM OF NAPLES, ruled by the Spanish Hapsburgs as a separate kingdom.
PAPAL STATES—In these territories the Pope was the secular ruler. Other Church territories were ruled by bishops or abbots who
   were princes of the Holy Roman Empire.
AUSTRIAN POSSESSIONS—A collection of separate kingdoms, duchies and counties, ruled by the Austrian branch of the House
   of Hapsburg.
HOLY ROMAN EMPIRE—During this period all emperors were from the Austrian Hapsburgs.

### 1680–1740

The Ottoman Empire attempted to expand into Central Europe, but the Turkish army was held at the gates of Vienna in 1683, and
   then forced back, liberating the entire central basin of the Danube River; the new Austro–Turkish border stabilized in 1739.
AUSTRIAN MILITARY FRONTIER—Refugee Serbian communities were settled along the border in Croatia and Slavonia (not to
   be confused with the present republic of SLOVENIA) by the Austrian government. A military constitution to defend the Slavonian borderland was granted in 1702 and later extended to Croatia and Transylvania.
KINGDOM OF THE TWO SICILIES—After changing hands several times, the Kingdom of Naples and the Kingdom of Sicily
   were combined in 1735 under a junior branch of the House of Bourbon.

343

# Yugoslavia

## WESTERN BALKANS 1740–1797

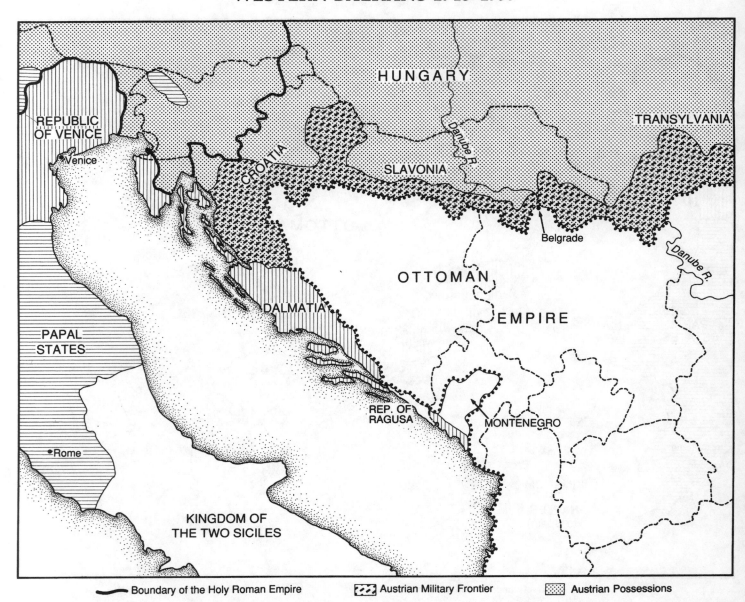

Boundary of the Holy Roman Empire ▰▰▰ Austrian Military Frontier ░░░ Austrian Possessions

The Ottoman Empire was no longer a threat, and Austria was occupied in central Europe with the rise of Prussia and the partition of Poland. Boundaries were basically stable during this period.

---

**1797–1815**

During the Napoleonic wars political boundaries and country names changed frequently.

The Venetian territories were carved up in 1797, the largest part going temporarily to Austria.

The Holy Roman Empire became extinct in 1806.

In 1809 France briefly annexed all of the eastern Adriatic coast as well as Ragusa and nearly all of present–day Slovenia.

By 1809 all territories ruled by the Roman Catholic Church had been acquired by secular states.

Meanwhile, Montenegro won a small expansion of its boundaries.

## WESTERN BALKANS 1815–1860

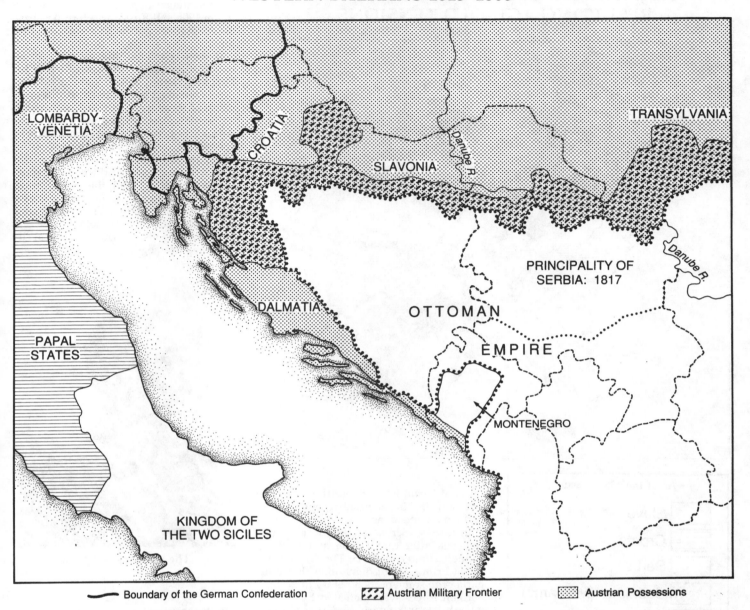

— Boundary of the German Confederation    ▨ Austrian Military Frontier    ▨ Austrian Possessions

In the post–Napoleonic settlements, Austria (re)gained all of the Venetian territories plus Ragusa as well as those Church territories within its borders. The Military Frontier was maintained, becoming a separate crownland in 1849 with special privileges for the Serbian settlers.

GERMAN CONFEDERATION—Created to replace the Holy Roman Empire with the same eastern and southern boundaries.

The Pope was restored as ruler of central Italy, but all other former Church territories remained secularized.

SERBIA—The Serbs had been fighting for their independence since 1804, achieving in 1817 recognition as an autonomous principality under Ottoman overlordship.

These boundaries were essentially stable during this period.

See the text and map of this area (c. 1350) on page 259. Also, note the map on page 331 for later pre–World War I boundaries.

# Yugoslavia

## THE ETHNIC/RELIGIOUS MIXTURE WITH RESULTING AGE–OLD TENSIONS

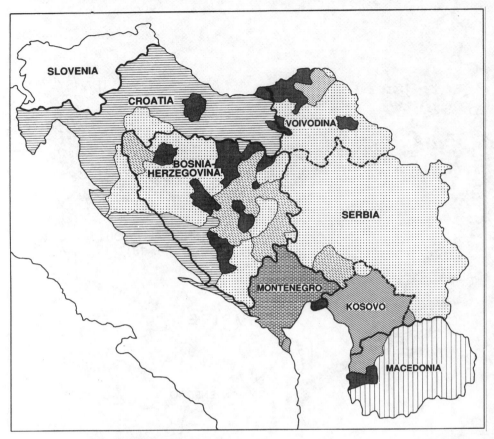

**As of the 1980 census**

- Slovenes
- Croats
- Serbs
- Bosnians (Moslems)
- Montenegrins
- Macedonians
- Hungarians
- Albanians
- Ethnic mixture

annexed them. Serbia, supported by Russia, threatened to go to war against Austria in 1908, but Russia was forced to back down in 1909 and Serbia was left in a lurch.

It then began putting together an alliance of Balkan countries that led to the First and Second Balkan Wars in 1912–13. Serbia obtained additional territories as a result of these wars, but Austria frustrated Serbia's attempts to gain access to the Adriatic Sea coast, among other things by sponsoring creation of an independent Albania. In 1914, Serbia played an important role in the origins of World War I by sponsoring the Black Hand, the Serbian revolutionary group which carried out the assassination of Archduke Franz Ferdinand, heir to the Austrian throne, while he was paying a state visit to Sarajevo, capital city of Bosnia–Herzegovina.

**The last King of Serbia, Peter I**

### Montenegro

Montenegro experienced centuries of independence while the surrounding areas seethed under Turkish control. The almost impassable mountains allowed the Montenegrins to resist repeated Turkish attempts to conquer the area; although they and later the Venetians did occupy parts, it was never completely controlled. Its independence was recognized by the Congress of Berlin in 1878. During the years before World War I, the Montenegrins, like some of their neighbors, were advocates of South Slav nationalism, lending military support to the cause in 1878 against the Turks and during the Balkan Wars of 1912–13.

### World War I

A Bosnian student assassinated Archduke Franz Ferdinand, heir to the Haps-

gress of Berlin in 1878, but the resulting Treaty of Berlin included recognition of Serbian independence.

In 1885–86, Serbia fought a war against Bulgaria after that nation and Eastern Rumelia united in 1885. The war began when Prince Milan demanded that Bulgaria cede some of its territory to Serbia. Serbian forces were defeated by Prince Alexander of Bulgaria and it was only Austria's threat to enter the war on Serbia's side that produced an armistice. Serbia then recognized the union of Bulgaria and Eastern Rumelia.

In 1903, a palace revolution led by forces loyal to the Karageorgevic family led to the murder of the Obrenovic family and the Karageorgevic dynasty to the throne. In a change of foreign policy, the Karageorgevic king set out in earnest to create a Greater Serbia by bringing as much of the Balkans as he could under his control. This brought Serbia into conflict with the Austrian Empire, since Serbia also laid claim to Austrian lands occupied by South Slavs. Relations worsened after Austria formally annexed Bosnia–Herzegovina in 1908. Austria had obtained these lands in 1878 as part of the Treaty of Berlin, but had not formally

became clear that Serbia would not be able to stand against the Turks, Russia intervened in 1877. Russia defeated the Turks and forced Turkey to recognize the independence of Serbia (and Romania) in the Treaty of San Stefano. The Treaty was revised by the great powers at the Con-

# Yugoslavia

**The last King of Montenegro, Nicholas I**

burg throne, in Sarajevo on June 28, 1914. He belonged to the "Black Hand," which was formed in Serbia in 1911 with a goal of the union of all Serbs.

Austria responded to the murder with an ultimatum to Serbia, demanding in part that Austrian officials be permitted to participate in the investigation of the crime. When the Serbian government accepted only part of the terms of the ultimatum, Austria–Hungary declared war on Serbia. Because of a multitude of cross–alliances, France and Russia came into the war on the side of Serbia, while Germany entered as an ally of Austria–Hungary. England entered when Germany violated Belgian neutrality and World War I began. Bulgaria and Turkey later entered on the side of Germany and Austria–Hungary, while Romania entered as an ally of France, England and Russia. Thus almost all of the Balkans became involved in the war.

Austrian armies reached Belgrade by December 1914, but were repelled by a counter–attack. Bulgaria's entry in 1915 helped shift the equation against Serbia. The Serbian army retreated to the Adriatic coast and then to the island of Corfu. In 1918, Allied forces made their way into the Balkan Peninsula. The Serbian army joined with the Allies in defeating Bulgaria, then liberated Serbia.

## A New Nation is Born

During the war, discussions were held on creating a separate state for South Slavs who had been part of the Austro–Hungarian Empire. Serb leaders hesitated at first because their long–time vision was of a single Greater Serbian Kingdom which would include all areas inhabited by Serbs. The remaining South Slavic leaders had in mind a different vision. They wanted a decentralized South

Slavic state organized along federal lines, which would allow a large amount of autonomy to the individual ethnic groups. Representatives of the two points of view signed the Corfu Pact in 1917 in which they agreed to create a South Slav state under the Karageorgevic dynasty after the war.

Although basically South Slav, what became Yugoslavia consisted literally of what was left over after France, Great Britain and the U.S. redrew a new map of eastern Europe after World War I. On December 4, 1918, the Kingdom of the Serbs, Croats and Slovenes was proclaimed in Belgrade with Prince Alexander of Serbia as Regent. Serbia (including Macedonia and Kosovo), which had been independent before the war, formed the core of this new kingdom. The Kingdom of Montenegro, also independent before the war, was added when the King of Montenegro resigned his throne in favor of the new South Slavic State. To this was added territories from the former Austro–Hungarian Empire—Croatia, the Voivodina, Bosnia–Herzegovina, and Slovenia—plus

strategic points taken from Bulgaria along the Serbian–Bulgarian border.

## Politics of the Interwar Period

The question of the political structure of this new kingdom was supposed to be decided by the Constituent Assembly which was elected in 1920. The parties represented in the Constituent Assembly included the *Democratic Party*, the *Radical Party*, the *Croatian Peasant Party*, the *Agrarian Party*, the *Slovene People's Party*, the *Moslem Party*, and the *Communist Party*. Of these, the *Radical Party* was the largest. Led by Nikola Pashich, they were in power almost continuously until 1926. The *Croatian Peasant Party* was the most important in Croatia and its leader, Stepjan Radick, was the most prominent Croatian political figure until his death in 1928.

In 1921, the Constituent Assembly adopted a constitution which created a centralized government. The necessary votes came from the Serbian parties and smaller ones which had "sold" their votes in return for promises of special favors. The *Croatian Peasant Party* boycotted the

**The combatants at the start of World War I, 1914**

347

# Yugoslavia

Assembly because of its opposition to the centralized system outlined by the constitution.

The period 1921–1928 was one of conflict between the Serbs and Croats over the question of centralism vs. federalism. The Serbs prevailed by using increasingly harsh tactics, including the arrest of the Croat opposition leader and dissolving his party. Outraged, the Croatian deputies withdrew from the body, swearing not to return until they had been granted a federal system in which Croatia would no longer be controlled from Belgrade. The demands of the Croats were unacceptable to the Serbian leaders, and also King Alexander. Taking advantage of a decade of disagreement between the Serbs and Croats, the king abolished the constitution and proclaimed a royal dictatorship, later changing the name of the country to the Kingdom of Yugoslavia. The change in name did not alter the fact that Serbs, Croats and Slovenes lived and fought with each other within the boundaries of the kingdom. Alexander's mistake was in thinking he could create a Yugoslav nationalism by decree. He was assassinated in 1934 by a Macedonian terrorist.

From 1934 to 1941 a three–man regency ruled the country with Prince Paul as First Regent. Internal affairs were left to the Premier, who governed with the support of a specially organized party, the *Yugoslav Radical Union*. Parties in opposition formed an alliance and demanded a new constitution which would set up a government capable of dealing with the discontented Croats. When the extent of the Serb–Croat split was revealed in 1938 elections, the government sought talks with the Croatian leadership. The result was an agreement which created an internally self–governing Croatia.

In international relations during the interwar period, Yugoslavia was most concerned about the protection of its borders against the ambitions of neighboring states and against the Great Powers who wanted to use the conflicts among the Balkan states to extend their own influence. Both the "Little Entente" and the "Balkan Entente" were supposed to serve these purposes. In 1920–21 Yugoslavia formed an alliance with Romania and Czechoslovakia, the "Little Entente," which was directed primarily against Hungarian ambitions to revise the Treaty of Trianon. The "Little Entente" was backed by France through treaties with Czechoslovakia (1924), Romania (1926) and Yugoslavia (1927).

After a series of conferences between 1930–1933, Greece, Turkey, Romania and Yugoslavia signed the Balkan Pact (February 1934) guaranteeing the territorial status quo against aggression by any Balkan state. In practice, this meant that the Pact was directed against Bulgaria. Several

**Assassination: King Alexander of Yugoslavia at Marseilles, France, October 1934**

months later, the signatories adopted the Statutes of the Balkan Entente which set up a Permanent Council, provided for regular meetings and for extensive economic and political cooperation. Both alliance systems disintegrated by the end of the 1930's. The rise of Germany and Italy, the inability of the League of Nations to deal with acts of aggression, and the appeasement policy of Britain and France made Yugoslavia search for new means of

**Prince Paul of Yugoslavia**

ensuring her security. Accordingly, it signed a pact of friendship with Bulgaria (1937) and a non–aggression and arbitration pact with Italy in the same year, which moved Yugoslavia closer to the Axis powers.

During the late 1930s, Prince Paul repeatedly appealed to the British for arms and economic assistance in order to ward off an increasingly militant Germany, but his requests fell on deaf ears.

When in September 1940 Germany, Italy and Japan signed the Tripartite Pact which bound their nations into a military alliance, it caused great alarm in Yugoslavia, especially when Germany became insistent that it, too, become a signatory to that Pact. Prince Paul resisted and stalled for time; he wanted to transfer a whole and sovereign nation to his nephew, King Peter, then only seventeen and soon to be of age. The British, notwithstanding the fact that they had ignored Paul's pleas for assistance, were totally opposed to any such action by Yugoslavia which would strengthen the hand of the Axis powers.

Prince Paul, feeling the noose tightening around his multi–ethnic nation, instructed his ministers to draw up three conditions for signing the Pact which he felt certain Germany's Hitler would never accept. The three important clauses were: (1) that the sovereignty and territorial integrity of Yugoslavia would be respected, (2) that no military assistance would be requested of Yugoslavia and also no passage or transportation of troops through the country in the event of war, and (3) acknowledgement of Yugoslavia's interest in a free outlet to the Aegean Sea through Salonika, Greece.

Surprising the Yugoslav government, Hitler readily agreed to its terms (with no thought of respecting them), and the Pact was reluctantly signed, but Hitler purposely omitted the second clause denying German troops access to Yugoslavia's transportation system.

The apparent alliance with the Axis powers infuriated many Yugoslavs, particularly the independent–minded Serbs, and embittered the British with whom Prince Paul had always been so close. According to recently unearthed documents, Great Britain was directly instrumental, through bribery, in staging a *coup d'état* in March 1941 which overthrew Prince Paul's government. The new regime made the young King Peter a temporary puppet and sent a discouraged, demoralized Prince Paul into poverty–stricken exile wrapped in the undeserved mantle of a Nazi sympathizer when, in truth, he hated militaristic Germany.

## World War II

The decision of the government to sign the Tripartite Pact and, thus, apparently join the Axis side in 1941 was bitterly opposed by certain Yugoslav officials and army officers. Following the military coup, the army announced a policy of neutrality, continuing Prince Paul's policy. The Nazis saw through this by now transparent plan and attacked Yugoslavia ten days later, after which Yugoslavia was divided.

Croatia was enlarged and placed in the hands of a fascist dictator, Ante Pavelich. Slovenia was divided between Germany and Italy, Macedonia was occupied by Bulgaria, parts of Bosnia and Dalmatia went to Italy, a small piece in the north was given to Hungary, and German administration was imposed on Serbia. A puppet government was established in Belgrade.

From 1941 to 1944 Yugoslavia was ravaged not only by struggles against the Nazi occupation, but also by civil war between the *Chetnik* and *Partisan* resistance forces. The Chetniks were bands of officers and men drawn from the remnants of the Royal Yugoslav Army; they were loosely organized and generally undisciplined, pro–Serbian and anti–communist. The Partisans, led by Tito and the *Yugoslav Communist Party*, tried to form an organization with a broader, national following.

The *Communist Party* had been one of the largest in the Constituent Assembly elected in 1920. Its goal was the establishment of a Yugoslav Soviet Republic. In 1921, however, the government banned the party after the murder of the Minister of the Interior, although there was no evidence linking the party to the assassina-

tion. The party remained illegal throughout the interwar period, which meant that its members were forced to operate underground. One of its early members was Josip Broz, whose revolutionary *nom de guerre* was Tito. The son of a Croatian peasant who had been inducted into the Austrian army, he was taken prisoner of war by a Russian detachment at the age of 23. He escaped from prison in Russia and joined the Bolsheviks, fighting with them in the Russian civil war. After he returned to Yugoslavia, he became the secretary of the Zagreb branch of the *Communist Party of Yugoslavia*. When the party was declared illegal, Broz was arrested and sentenced to five years at hard labor.

By 1937 he was the Secretary General of the *Yugoslav Communist Party*, which he reorganized and purged in accordance with the latest dictates from Moscow. After the country was occupied by the Germans, he used his control of the party organization to create guerrilla units called "Partisans" for use against the Germans.

At first, Partisans and Chetniks attempted to fight side–by–side, but it soon became evident that while they were both fighting to free Yugoslavia from Axis control, their image of the future of the country was totally different. The Chetniks were fighting for the return of the monarch and Serb–dominated government. The Partisans were fighting for a federally–organized, socialist republic. There also was a disagreement on general military strategy—the Partisans wanted all–out resistance while the Chetniks, afraid of German reprisals, wanted to wait for the arrival of the Allies.

Eventually the Chetniks and Partisans were fighting each other as hard as they

fought the common enemy. In order to combat the Partisans and to prevent the Germans from killing Serbs, the Chetniks began to collaborate with the enemy. Evidence of collaboration resulted in a loss of Allied support for them. The British sent a military mission to aid the Partisans several months before there was a similar move by the Soviets. The contribution of the Partisans to the war effort and the leadership of Tito were thus formally recognized by the Western Powers.

Under Tito's direction, the *Anti–Fascist Council for National Liberation of Yugoslavia (AVNOJ)* was formed in 1942 to function as a government in liberated territories. A year later at Jajce in Bosnia, the *AVNOJ* elected a provisional government which made Tito Marshal of Yugoslavia and Premier. The AVNOJ thus replaced the nominal authority of the government–in–exile, located in London, and forbade King Peter, successor to Prince Paul, to return.

The British prevailed on the king to appoint as premier of the exiled government a man who could negotiate with the Partisans, and Dr. Ivan Shubashich, who had been governor of Croatia until 1941, was selected.

In October 1944 Russian and Partisan forces liberated Belgrade. It is significant that by the time Russian forces arrived in Belgrade the Partisans were in firm control of large parts of Yugoslavia. After the liberation of Belgrade, Tito and Shubashich signed an agreement providing for a Regency Council to act in the king's name, free elections within three months of liberation and a legislature consisting of the *AVNOJ* until an assembly could be convened. This arrangement was approved by the "Big Three"—the U.S., the

**Marshal Josip Broz-Tito, leader of the *Partisans* in World War II**

# Yugoslavia

U.S.S.R. and Great Britain—at the Yalta Conference in 1945, and the king was thus forced to accept it also. Three Regents were chosen in March 1945—a Serb, a Croat and a Slovene, none of whom were communists but all of whom had Tito's approval.

Tito then formed a new government in which he was Premier and Shubashich was Foreign Minister; the cabinet included representatives from each of the six areas of Yugoslavia and of the government–in–exile. Before the elections for a Constituent Assembly took place, Shubashich resigned, protesting the government's refusal to allow "collaborators" to vote—this term was loosely applied to anyone who opposed the government. The elections were boycotted by the opposition parties, the *Serbian Radical Party, Agrarian Party, Democratic Party* and *Croat Peasant Party* in protest against the atmosphere of intimidation created by what had become a very active secret police. As a result, the people could vote only for the *Communist People's Front* list of candidates.

## Yugoslavia Becomes a Federal People's Republic

The Constituent Assembly which was elected declared Yugoslavia to be a Federal People's Republic; when a new constitution was adopted in early 1946, the Assembly changed its name to the People's Assembly. This body consisted of two houses, a Chamber of Nationalities and a Federal Chamber. The Chamber of Nationalities had 30 representatives from each of the six federal republics, plus 15 from the autonomous province of Kosovo and 20 from the autonomous region of the Voivodina. In theory, therefore, it served a function somewhat similar to that of the U.S. Senate. The Federal Chamber was the "popular body", with one representative for every 50,000 inhabitants.

The People's Assembly was not designed as a deliberative body, however. It met only twice a year, on April and October 15th, then only to rubber–stamp decisions of the government. More power resided with the Presidium of the People's Assembly, since the Presidium appointed and dismissed cabinet ministers and had law–making authority when the Assembly was not in session. As with all communist regimes, however, real power rested with the Communist Party.

Although the government remained in theory a "People's Front," the policies which it instituted during this period were based on Soviet models. Larger estates were expropriated and a beginning was made on the establishment of collective farms. In 1947, the government launched its first Five–Year Plan. In industry, emphasis was placed on electrification, chemicals and metallurgy. Foreign trade was oriented toward the eastern bloc nations.

## The Soviet–Yugoslav Dispute of 1948

Yugoslavia had been considered such a loyal satellite that the new Communist Information Bureau, or *Cominform*, set up in September 1947, had established its headquarters in Belgrade. But now a quarrel began over the issue of joint Yugoslav–Soviet companies. Two joint companies were actually set up, for air transport and for river shipping, but the way they were operated appeared so disadvantageous to the Yugoslavs that they refused to allow any further joint companies to be formed. This led to a bitter quarrel between Tito and Stalin and resulted in the curtailment of Russian aid and a reduction of trade between Yugoslavia and the rest of the eastern bloc nations.

The dispute marked the first time a ruling communist party defied the authority of Moscow and still remained in power. The disagreement arose over the question of the power relations between the two countries. Tito's challenge to Moscow was possible because his political survival did not depend on Stalin's support. Unlike the communist leaders of other East European countries, Tito had not come to power by the might of the Soviet army, but because of his personal following in the Partisan movement which had the leading role in liberating Yugoslavia at the end of the war.

After the war, the Yugoslav communists thought of themselves as Moscow's most faithful followers. Tito's desire to follow the correct line was evident in the enthusiasm with which he modeled Yugoslavia's economy and constitution on those of the Soviet Union. It was probably in recognition of Tito's importance that Stalin set up the *Cominform* headquarters in Belgrade.

In light of this background, the real issue in the dispute was not Yugoslav departure from the official Moscow communist line, but the refusal to be controlled by Moscow in matters which affected the interests of Yugoslavia. The question was one of how two communist parties and their leaders should conduct their relations with each other when each was also responsible for the interests of his own state.

Stalin's opposition to any communist power that was not under his personal control was shown by his attitude toward the plans for a Balkan federation authorized by Tito and supported by the Bulgarian communist, Dmitrov. The Bulgarians even agreed that after federation, Yugoslavia should annex the part of Macedonia that lies within Bulgaria. By 1947 the plans included the possibility of also bringing Albania, Romania and Greece into some kind of union and there were hints of a Balkan–Danubian Federation involving Hungary.

Sensing an increase in Tito's power if there were federation, Stalin abruptly reversed his early support for the plan. When the Bulgarian leadership expressed hope for a customs union as a step towards federation, *Pravda*, the Moscow official newspaper, responded with an article stating that the Balkan states did not need any kind of customs union or federation.

At a meeting in the Kremlin in 1948, Yugoslavian and Bulgarian representatives were scolded by Stalin and Soviet Foreign Minister Vyacheslav Molotov. The Bulgarian communists were criticized for planning a customs union with Romania and the Yugoslavs were denounced for helping Greek communists and for sending troops into Albania without Moscow's approval.

There were other issues involved in the break between the two nations. The Yugoslavs were critical of the Soviet failure to send aid to the Partisans during the war and Stalin's instructions to play down the role of the *Communist Party* in the resistance movement. They recalled that Stalin had opposed setting up the AVNOJ as the supreme authority in 1943. Further charges included the failure of the Soviet Union to press Yugoslavia's claim to Trieste against Italy at the close of the war because Stalin did not want to antagonize the Allies by bringing up the claim.

The Soviets accused the Yugoslavs of directing propaganda against the Soviet Union and of having an "unduly large" peasant membership in their communist party; there were also accusations charging that the party was being run "undemocratically." The treatment of Soviet military advisors and civilian experts as foreigners was also a target.

The Yugoslavs requested that the dispute be settled by two–party discussions. Instead, the Soviets called a meeting of the *Cominform* and issued a statement in mid–1948 which indicated that the member parties backed the Soviet position. The *Yugoslav Communist Party* was expelled from the *Cominform*, Tito was denounced by Stalin and his name became a symbol of hatred among communist leaders who courted Moscow's favor. Despite economic and diplomatic isolation, Yugoslavia survived and set a precedent for other challenges to Soviet authority which followed after Stalin's death.

Relations with the U.S. warmed, but didn't boil over. U.S. President Harry S. Truman is reliably rumored to have privately commented that although Tito was a "son–of–a–bitch, at least he's *our* son–of–a–bitch."

## Politics Since 1950

After 1949, Yugoslavia began to search for new trading partners, for a new for-

**The Savica waterfall, source of the Sava River.**            Photo by Prof. Janko Ravnik

eign policy which would demonstrate its independence, and for a new statement of principles which would explain the changes introduced in the Yugoslav system *after* the break with Moscow.

In domestic politics, the two themes which were developed were decentralization and economic democracy. The first step came in 1950 with the creation of "workers' councils" in all state–owned economic enterprises. At the same time, the former economic ministries which had directed the economy were abolished and replaced by national coordinating councils made up of representatives from each of the republics. Thus, the central directive role of the state was reduced while, at the same time, the participatory role of the workers was enhanced at the local level.

In 1953, the constitution was modified to incorporate the concept of workers'

self–management. Beginning in 1952, producers' councils had been created at the local and republic levels. In 1953, a national Council of Producers was created as a second national legislative body to replace the Chamber of Nationalities. The Chamber of Nationalities was not abolished, however, but was partially amalgamated into the Federal Chamber. What was different about the national Council of Producers as well as the local and republic producers' councils was that representation was on the basis of occupation and that persons voted where they worked. It was, in effect, an attempt to give political expression to the term "economic democracy."

On the other hand, decentralization was considered to apply primarily to economic decision–making. In the political arena, other constitutional changes made at this

time had as their purpose to create a more obvious central political authority. To this end, the old executive structure of a "Presidium of the National Assembly" and a Council of Ministers were abolished and replaced by a "President of the Republic" with true executive powers, assisted by a Federal Executive Council. Needless to say, Marshal Tito became the new President.

The Communist Party also changed its name at this time and became the "League of Communists of Yugoslavia." But the League of Communists was not willing to give up its monopoly of political power. When Milovan Djilas, a Vice–Premier and President of the National Assembly, late in 1953 began a series of articles in the communist newspaper *Borba,* in which he argued, among other things, that:

> "No class or political movement can claim the exclusive right to represent society as a whole or to proclaim their ideas as objective truth . . . ,"

he was expelled from the Politburo and Central Committee and forced to resign his government offices. Later he would be imprisoned, but that would be for more critical things he would write, in particular, such things as his study of the new Communist elite, which he entitled *The New Class.*

A new constitution was adopted in 1963 which extended the concept of worker's self–management to that of "social self–management." In a move toward greater economic democracy, more authority was given to local communes, to the governments of the republics and to the organs of self–management in the economy. These changes compounded Yugoslavia's problems with regionalism, however, and reopened conflict between the so–called liberals and conservatives as well as between the wealthier and poorer republics. The less–developed republics, such as Serbia and Montenegro, argued that the changes benefited only the developed republics. Croatia and Slovenia, on the other hand, argued that the changes didn't go far enough and that they were still subsidizing the rest of the country.

One of the foremost opponents of the reforms was Alexander Rankovich, then Vice–President of Yugoslavia, strongman of the Serbian party organization, influential in the security police and once considered a likely successor to Tito. The decision to expel him from the Central Committee of the Party in 1966 was a decisive victory for the reformists, this time backed by Tito. Although the decision was a blow to Serb nationalists, it did not eliminate the basic anxiety of the remaining republics over Serbian domination of Yugoslavia. In order to give the individual republics a greater stake in the general af-

# Yugoslavia

fairs of the country, a group of amendments was adopted in 1967 giving a stronger voice to the Chamber of Nationalities and in general increasing the role of the individual republics in decision–making at the center.

There was another series of amendments in 1971 which, in addition to establishing a collective presidency to handle the matter of the succession after Tito, made a number of economic changes. Worker councils were given greater authority to determine how the surplus funds of their enterprises were to be allocated, and private individuals were guaranteed the right to work with their own "means of production" and to employ workers on a contractual basis.

In 1974, a new constitution introduced a system of elections to the various legislative assemblies based on delegations drawn from occupational and interest groups. It also provided that the federal legislature—the Assembly of the Socialist Federal Republic of Yugoslavia—be made up of an equal number of delegates from each of Yugoslavia's six republics. Elections to the federal legislature were indirect. Delegates to the assemblies of the individual republics, themselves representing local occupation and interest groups, selected delegates to the federal legislature.

One purpose of the new system was to give the League of Communists of Yugoslavia (LCY) greater control over the elected representatives. Under its self–managing socialism, Yugoslavia had created a degree of economic democracy; politically, however, the LCY retained its monopoly of power.

The period of the 1970's saw a number of purges within the party, the most prominent of which was the more or less mass purge of the Croatian wing of the LCY in 1971–72 because of alleged nationalistic deviations. Between 1972 and 1974, there were additional purges within the Serbian wing, this time because of an over–liberal attitude toward dissent within LCY ranks. Despite these purges, there remained a large core of veterans, both in the LCY and the government who had remained more or less continuously in office since 1945.

The core of the problem was that the LCY attempted to withdraw from direct control of the economy while retaining an overall political ascendancy. The economic reforms devolved considerable authority to the republic level, to regional banks and to individual enterprises and the result was to create a tremendous stake in control over local economic activity. This often encouraged local decisions which were at variance with national political policy, in particular the commitment at the national level to redistribute funds to poorer areas of the country for the purpose of financing industrialization. After

The May 5, 1980, edition of *Politika* announces Tito's death

Tito's death in 1980, it also acted to frustrate attempts of the new national leadership to control growing inflation through a national austerity program. What Yugoslavians discovered was that, control over the economy having been shifted to the Republic/Autonomous Province level, the federal government no longer had the tools to manipulate the economy. This chiefly explains the continued high inflation of the 1980s.

## The "Republic of Kosovo"
### (pronouced KO-sovo)

**Nationalism in the Autonomous Province of Kosovo**

The interest of the political leadership of the individual republics to retain the maximum amount of scarce investment funds for local use also led to grievances upon which local nationalism then fed. The autonomous region of Kosovo in the

Republic of Serbia is one area that became particularly disaffected. The homeland of almost all of Serbia's ethnic Albanians who constitute approximately 90 percent of the population of the province, it is primarily an agricultural area with little industry. It was always one of the poorest parts of Yugoslavia and its unemployment rate is also the highest in the nation. It also has an extremely high birthrate. In the 1970s, its per capita income actually dropped.

At the beginning of the 1980s, dissatisfaction with the local situation produced a wave of nationalist agitation. Riots began in Kosovo in March–April 1981, led by youths from the University of Pristina (in mid–1981 renamed "Kosovo University"). Eventually thousands of demonstrators joined in clashes with police and openly propounded nationalistic slogans. Originally limited to the city of Pristina, the demonstrations spread to other parts of Kosovo and then to the neighboring Republic of Macedonia (where another 374,000 ethnic Albanians live).

The University was closed on April 2, 1981, and the Yugoslav regime began a policy of "rooting out Albanian nationalism" and purging the local wing of the LCY of Albanian nationalist elements. The University had undoubtedly become a hotbed of Albanian nationalist sentiment, but the underlying cause of the agitation was almost certainly economic. While there were demands for creation of a separate Albanian Republic, there was no strong sentiment to merge the province with Albania. It is generally conceded that the standard of living of the people of Kosovo was higher than that of Albanians in Albania and they also had a freer life and were permitted to practice their religion. Only a tiny minority supported union with Albania at that time.

The abolition of Kosovo's autonomous status in early 1989 was followed by Serb attempts to stamp out all manifestations of Albanian nationalism. Among other things, the Serbs fired all Albanian teachers and issued new regulations requiring that all instruction be given only in the Serbian language. This policy extended also to Kosovo University.

Serbia's reestablishment of control over Kosovo left a sullen populace, but it also forced the main Albanian political party, the Democratic League of Kosovo, to respond in a more radical manner than it might otherwise have done. This was the declaration of the independent Republic of Kosovo in 1991, later confirmed by a popular referendum.

The Serbian Government's reaction was to carry out a massive purge throughout the province, dismissing Albanians from all important posts in the province. It also carried out arbitrary arrests, seized property, and tolerated, and possibly even encouraged, widespread police brutality. Although Serbs were only ten percent of the population, they now filled all governmental offices and all important positions in hospitals, universities, businesses, and schools.

The Republic of Kosovo has never received any international recognition, and a large number of Yugoslav army units stationed throughout the province act as a guarantee of continued Serbian control. Yet, in a real sense, the Republic of Kosovo exists, for the Albanians slowly constructed a parallel government and society over the next couple years. Unarmed and isolated, the Albanian political leadership opted for a program of passive resistance and non–cooperation. Perhaps they were lucky, for Ibrahim Rugova, the man they elected as President of their "Republic" in 1991, was firmly committed to a policy of non–violence, and he persuaded his people to go along with him. Rugova and his "government" collected their own taxes and used the monies to set up schools where the children could be educated in their own language and clinics where the people could receive medical assistance. Withdrawing into their own Albanian world, their only contact with Serbs was when they were stopped, and often harassed, by heavily armed Serbian police. Meanwhile, ordinary Serbs lived in their own villages, guarded by Serbian soldiers. Thus, even while a war went on for nearly three years in neighboring Bosnia, Kosovo remained quiet.

Yet younger, more radical Albanians became more and more frustrated by the failure of the passive resistance program to bring about any easing of the repression. In 1997, a new, more violent leadership arose to challenge the very idea of non–violence. This organization, calling itself the Kosovo Liberation Front (also known by its Albanian initials, U.C.K.), had actually been in existence since 1992, but played no significant role until it managed to obtain weapons from Albania during the collapse and civil war that raged for a time there in 1997. After that, it began launching guerrilla attacks against Serb military targets in Kosovo. Things came to a head in January 1998, when U.C.K. rebels killed two Serbian soldiers.

Responding to these attacks, the Serb Government dispatched combined police and paramilitary units from the Ministry of Interior to Kosovo "to restore order." The Serbs rounded up thousands of Albanians and questioned them, often under torture. Then, on March 6, they launched a series of "punitive raids" against Albanian villages. Armed with mortars, helicopter gunships, armored vehicles and heavy artillery, they shelled individual villages that had been identified as centers of rebel support. One such target was the Drenica region, where two days of heavy Serb assault resulted in the deaths of more than 80 villagers, including many women and children.

The killings led the United States, United Kingdom, Germany, France and Italy to agree to place an embargo on sales of arms to Yugoslavia, but demands that Serbia pull its special paramilitary forces out of Kosovo and open talks with the Albanian political leadership in Kosovo brought no reverse in Serbia's policy toward Kosovo. Still, continued pressure did bring a suggestion from the Serbian Government that it was willing to open talks with Kosovo that would address the issue of "self–rule" in Kosovo.

Amazingly, the Albanians managed to carry out new presidential and parliamentary elections on March 22, 1998, in the midst of the Serb occupation. Although the Serbs condemned the elections and attempted to prevent them, they were carried out with more than 80 percent of Albanian voters going to the polls. In fact, voting could not be carried out in several villages that were under tight Serb police control. But even as Rugova was overwhelmingly reelected President, young fighters of the Kosovo Liberation Army prepared for war with Serbia. It is anyone's guess what will happen next.

## Yugoslavia After Tito

Speculation about the internal and international outlook for Yugoslavia were understandably centered in recent years on the question of what would happen to the country if and when President Tito would disappear from the scene. The aging leader and his associates were certainly aware of the problem, and they decided to establish a system of post–Tito government hopefully designed to keep the country together in spite of deep–seated animosities kept alive among the various nationalities.

The Constitution of 1974, while making Tito president for life, provided for sever-

353

# Yugoslavia

**Branko Mikulic**

al collective bodies—including a rotating presidency of the supreme governing council—representative of the major national units. This body began to function when Tito, struggling for months against a terminal illness, gave up his position as chief of state.

The collective leadership thus gained experience in running the state without Tito at the helm. When the aged leader finally died in May 1980, his funeral became the occasion for a glittering assembly of heads of state and other dignitaries, ranging from kings to leaders of communist states.

The new leadership functioned with modest success until 1988, although it was unable to reverse growing economic difficulties. The government actually attempted to bring inflation under control, but soon found that the mandate of the 1974 constitution that all federal decisions of significance required the consensus of all six republics and two provinces meant it was powerless to do so. Unfortunately, there was no consensus and the result was a stalemate at the center. The government was thus reduced to the policy of muddling through.

By 1988, the annual rate of inflation was 200% and growing, and workers, worried about their dropping standard of living, launched a series of strikes. Intellectuals, losing confidence in the system, began to demand changes. In less–developed areas of the country, there was also growing dissatisfaction among individual ethnic groups who had come to believe that the system was treating them unfairly. Among the most disaffected were the ethnic Albanians of the autonomous province of Kosovo.

## Greater Serbian Domination Threatens the Union

Up to that moment, one might have described the situation as serious but not threatening. What turned it into a crisis was the emergence of a new Serbian leader, Slobodan Milosevic, who launched a broad movement to reassert Serbian leadership. Arguing that the promotion of regionalism was the root cause of Yugoslavia's problems, Milosevic demanded control over the police, judiciary and economy in the two autonomous provinces of the Voivodina and Kosovo. In addition, Milosevic demanded a radical increase in Serbia's power within the Yugoslav Federation.

To achieve these goals, Milosevic began mobilizing the Serbian masses. In the Voivodina, 100,000 Serbs besieged the provincial parliament in September 1988, forcing the resignation of the entire Voivodina leadership and their replacement by Milosevic loyalists. The same tactics were also tried against Kosovo, and demonstrations and counter–demonstrations continued over the next several months.

Meanwhile, inflation continued to grow and the worsening economic situation, coupled with the growing ethnic problems, led to a collapse of the Yugoslav Government on December 30, 1988. Branko Mikulic, President of the Federal Executive Council, submitted his resignation when he could not get his budget through the Yugoslav parliament. Yugoslavia remained without a government for almost three months before agreement was reached on a successor to Mikulic. Before agreement was reached, Stipe Suvar, the LCY Party President, also resigned his position and one–third of the membership of the party Central Committee was replaced. Ante Markovic was appointed President of the Federal Executive Council in March 1989. In May, Milan Pancevski was elected President of the *League of Communists*. Originally scheduled to serve only until a special party congress met, he was subsequently confirmed in that office.

The remainder of 1989 was characterized by a steadily worsening inflation and a seeming inability of anybody to do anything about it. Finally, it was Ante Markovic, President of the Federal Executive Council, who decided to take advantage of loopholes in the law and propose an economic stabilization program himself. Markovic's program, approved by the federal parliament on December 20, went into effect on January 1, 1990. The program consisted of making the Yugoslavian dinar convertible by pegging it to the West German Deutsche Mark, allowing interest to rise to market levels, and removing price–controls from most goods. Certain goods, including various raw materials and energy, were frozen. The program worked. By March, inflation had

sunk from over 2,000 percent to 8.4 percent. In addition, the government had managed to reduce the foreign debt by $3 billion and build up currency reserves of $7.5 billion. Unemployment was expected to rise and some state–subsidized businesses were expected to go bankrupt, but the government was determined to stick with its economic program.

This was the good news, however. Political developments continued to move in a direction that threatened the future of the united Yugoslav state. In January, an emergency congress of the *League of Communists* was held, among other things to discuss a move toward creation of a multiparty system. There was a serious split, on one side the hardliners, led by Slobodan Milosevic of Serbia, and on the other those pushing for a multiparty system, led by Ciril Ribicic of Slovenia. The Congress actually passed a resolution favoring creation of a multiparty system, but the Slovenian delegation walked out of the Congress, thus bringing it to a halt. They were particularly incensed about an economic boycott against Slovenia that Serbia had instituted at the end of November.

Thus, while in Serbia, Milosevic was threatening to colonize the province of Kosovo, Slovenia was moving toward creation of a multi–party democracy and suggesting that there was no future for Yugoslavia. In April elections, the people split their votes, electing Milan Kucan, candidate of the communists, as President while giving the *Demos*, a coalition of conservative political parties that had campaigned on a platform of independence within a year, control of the legislature. A month later, Croatia held its own multiparty elections, which were won by the *Croatian Democratic Union*, which campaigned on a platform of making a con-

**Slobodan Milosevic**

federation of sovereign states out of Yugoslavia.

Macedonia and Bosnia–Herzegovina held their own free, multiparty elections in November 1990. Montenegro and Serbia were scheduled to hold their own multiparty elections for December. In Serbia, Milosevic decided to further consolidate his control within Serbia by transforming the Serbian branch of the *League of Communists of Yugoslavia* into the *Serbian Socialist Party.* Thus the old *LCY*, already in a minority status in all the republics other than Montenegro and Serbia, lost out in its largest remaining base. Effectively it ceased to exist as a national party except in the Yugoslav army, where the leadership remained communist. This was a strange action by someone who claimed to stand for a strong, unified country. In fact, Milosevic is a Serbian nationalist who wanted to hold Yugoslavia together only if he could dominate it completely. Otherwise he would tear it apart and seize what other pieces of Yugoslavia he could.

A look at the policies he has pursued over the past few years bears that out. Appealing to Serbian nationalism, he demanded greater control in the two autonomous provinces of Kosovo and the Voivodina, eventually destroying their autonomy completely. In 1990, his agents began organizing Serbian nationals living in the other republics, fomenting them to demand secession of their areas from their republics and union with Serbia. He personally declared that he would demand a rectification of boundaries so as to reclaim Serbian lands if the federation broke up. The other republics had always reacted negatively to the idea of a Serbian–dominated Yugoslav government, for they were thereby reminded of the period after World War I when Serbs dominated the new Yugoslavia. Milosevic's Serbian chauvinism, and his destruction of the autonomy of Kosovo and the Voivodina, convinced many non–Serbs that he intended to once again assert Serbia's control over all of Yugoslavia. And at least three separate actions taken by Milosevic in 1990–91 contributed to that perception.

In December 1990, in the lead–up to Serbian elections, Milosevic undermined the financial stability of the national government by illegally siphoning off $1.5 billion from the Yugoslav National Bank. The money was taken in the form of a "loan" on the authority of a vote by the Serbian assembly. Both the Serbian assembly session and the removal of the money were kept secret from Yugoslavia's federal government. Milosevic then used the money to pay for pensions and salaries, which he had raised in the run–up to Serbian elections. The salary and pension increases were undoubtedly a factor in the elections, which Milosevic and his *Serbian Socialist Party* won handily. The other republics

were outraged when they learned of Milosevic's actions. Since the $1.5 billion was half of the new money the Yugoslav National Bank had assigned for circulation in 1991 in *all six republics*, Milosevic's action seriously undermined the federal government's economic stabilization program.

Milosevic's second action was to organize a boycott of Slovenian products and to begin levying a tariff on all items

**In economically-torn Montenegro, a youngster holds up a sign "We wait for you, Slo-vo" (Serbian leader Slobodan Milosevic) during an anti-government demonstration in Titograd**

# Yugoslavia

brought into Serbia from that republic, effectively negating the concept of a *united* Yugoslavia. Milosevic's third action in his program of rule or ruin was to block election of a new Federal President in May 1991. The outgoing President was Borisav Jovic, a Serb. Under Yugoslavia's system of rotating Presidencies, the incoming President was the man who had held the Vice–Presidency for the past year, Stipe Mesic, a Croat.

To be sure, Milosevic was not the sole offender in this regard. In 1990, when the leaders of Slovenia and Croatia began pushing for a change in the structure of the Yugoslav Federation to allow for greater autonomy for the individual republics, they passed laws declaring their laws to be superior to federal law and also created republic militias.

The sad thing is that this quarreling completely undermined the economic stabilization program of the federal government. Only the Yugoslav People's Army remained united at this point, though there were clear signs that this unity was very frail and depended in the army's not getting involved in the quarrels between the individual republics.

The army also had its own problems, the most important of which is that there was strong sentiment in the army to preserve a united Yugoslavia, even if it meant using force against a part of the Yugoslav people. A second problem was that 70% of the officers were Serbians and a good percentage of them were attracted to Milosevic's program. A third factor was that the army was the one remaining place where the *LCY* continued to exist. A final factor was that, while the officers were mainly Serbian, ordinary soldiers were conscripts who came from throughout Yugoslavia. Many feared, therefore, that the army would begin to disintegrate if it intervened against an individual republic and was perceived as doing so on behalf either of Serbia or the *LCY*.

## Yugoslavia Comes Apart

On May 19, 1991, the Croatian Government held a referendum on the question of independence for the republic. After a favorable vote, the Croatian Assembly adopted a declaration of independence on June 25. The Slovene Government adopted its own declaration on the same day. Both Governments did reiterate, however, that they remained willing to join a looser Yugoslav confederation in which the central government would handle foreign policy, defense and economic matters such as a common currency.

Meanwhile, the Yugoslav People's Army reacted to the declarations of independence by sending an invasion force into Slovenia. That republic was selected because it had moved to take control of its international border with Italy and Aus-

tria. The YPA was apparently not expecting much opposition, but the Slovenians fought back valiantly. Meanwhile, the rest of the world, which had encouraged the army action by asserting that they would not support a separate Slovenia or Croatia "under any circumstances," began calling for a ceasefire. At the same time, army desertions by non–Serbs began to be a problem. This led to an agreement with Slovenia that it could man the control posts if it would turn the revenues over to the central government. The YPA also agreed to return its forces to the barracks. Slovenia and Croatia also agreed to suspend their declarations of independence for three months. Serbia, in turn, agreed to allow Stipe Mesic to be elected President. The latter agreement was important in a military as well as a political sense because the President has also been the Commander–in–Chief of the Yugoslav People's Army.

The agreement brought peace to Slovenia, but not to Yugoslavia. One of the first actions of President Mesic was to arrange a cease–fire—the third—on July 2. That same day, General Blagoje Adzic, chief of the YPA General Staff, angrily repudiated the ceasefire—and thereby his own Commander–in–Chief—in an interview that appeared on Belgrade television and added that the army "accepted the challenge of total war that had been imposed on it" and would soon end it with a complete victory. The next day, an armored column left Belgrade for Croatia.

When Slovenia and Croatia began moving toward independence, President Milosevic called upon Serbs in other republics to remain loyal and not allow the Yugoslav union to be broken up. In Croatia, Serbs organized Serbian governments in two different parts of Croatia and declared these regions *independent* of Croatia. Hoping to conciliate the Serb leaders, the Croatian legislature passed a law guaranteeing protection for minority ethnic groups within the republic. Arguing that Serbs could secede from Croatia if Croatia could secede from Yugoslavia, Croatian Serbs held a referendum on July 7 affirming their intention to remain a part of the Socialist Federal Republic of Yugoslavia.

Meanwhile, President Milosevic of Serbia gave a speech on July 6 in which he told Serbs to be ready to defend themselves. He also gave Serb leaders in Croatia generous access to Serbian radio and television. The first fighting in Croatia began on July 7—the same day as the referendum—when Croatian Serbs attacked Croatian territorial defense forces near the town of Tenja.

As soon as fighting broke out, the Yugoslav People's Army sent in its own units "to keep the peace." It seemed, however, that its targets were always Croatian territorial units. There were, in fact, no reports

whatsoever of any Serbian territorial units being in conflict with YPA forces.

The fighting remained small–scale for some time, since President Tudjman had ordered Croatian units not to attack the Yugoslav People's Army. On its part, the YPA had received instructions from its Serb (but moderate) Defense Minister, General Veljko Kadijevic, that it should not initiate battles but only intervene when new fighting occurred. Gradually, however, the YPA's control of Croatian territory spread as Serb territorial forces launched new battles in area after area.

Croatia's Serbian problem existed because Serbs insisted on living in a state *controlled by Serbs*. But Croatians were not entirely free of this mentality of imperialism. The Republic of Bosnia–Herzegovina, which lies between Serbia and Croatia, has an extremely mixed population, with 31% Serbs and about 17% Croats. President Tudjman admitted in July that members of his government had held secret talks with Serbian leaders about carving up Bosnia between Serbia and Croatia, leaving a small Moslem rump that neither wanted. Word of these talks did not help Croatia internationally.

Croatia was "saved" by the fact that Serbia and the YPA were even more bloody–minded. In August, Milosevic revealed his plans for a reconstituted Yugoslavia which called for carving up Croatia and incorporating about a third of the territory into the new state, even though Serbs constituted only about 12 percent of Croatia's population at this time. Even more revealing, on August 20, Milosevic's chief ideologist praised the Moscow *coup* leaders as "tough men but not dogmatics" and accused Gorbachëv of pushing the Soviet Union toward a break–up by his attempt to create a union of sovereign states. Neither event made it easy for other countries to continue to defend the Serb side of the argument.

Meanwhile the YPA, which up to this time had contended that it was acting as a neutral buffer between the two sides, began bombarding Croatian cities with artillery and aircraft. In late August, much of the city of Vukovar was destroyed. By this time, perhaps twenty percent of the republic had fallen under YPA or Serb militia control. On September 18, Zagreb, the capital, came under fire from aircraft and artillery. At about the same time, the Yugoslav navy instituted a blockade of Croatia's Dalmatian ports. Soon it began attacking them, beginning with the city of Split. Up to this moment, the Croatian Government had been carrying out a "passive defense" and refusing to challenge the YPA directly. But it then cut oil lines across Croatia to Serbia and laid siege to Yugoslav army barracks in Croatia. The Yugoslav military retaliated by laying a naval siege around the Croatian city

**A scarecrow original.**                                    Photo by Prof. Janko Ravnik

of Dubrovnik and later bombarding it with artillery shells and missiles, leaving the city in ruins. The city was rebuilt with international assistance after the war ended.

Croatia got some indirect assistance from other republics when Bosnia–Herzegovina and Macedonia publicly declared the neutrality of their governments and ordered their citizens to ignore conscription notices from the YPA. The Serbian and Montenegrin political response was to order general mobilization in both those republics. Even in Serbia, however, many young men went into hiding rather than serve. The European Community had put itself forth as a peacemaker even before the war began, and subsequently negotiated cease–fire after cease–fire, only to see each new one broken.

They threatened Serbia with an economic embargo without effect. They arranged for a peace conference to begin at The Hague on September 7, 1991. This was also supposed to be accompanied by a cease–fire agreement, though that one fell through as well. The EC then appointed Lord Carrington as chairman of the European peace conference and sent him to Yugoslavia. He met with Presidents Milosevic and Tudjman plus Yugoslav Defense Minister Kadijevic. The three agreed that the YPA ought to return to its barracks, that the Croatian national guard should

be demobilized, and that all irregular militias should be disbanded. *Nothing actually happened, however, and the war went on.* Kadijevic had apparently been ignored by his chief of staff, the radical General Adzic.

Meanwhile the three–month moratorium on the independence declarations of Croatia and Slovenia—agreed to at Brioni—expired on October 7, 1991. Freed of that limitation, the Croatian and Slovenian governments severed all ties with the Socialist Federal Republic of Yugoslavia. By this time, approximately a third of Croatia was occupied by the YPA and Serb militias. The Yugoslav air force marked the day with an attack on the presidential palace in Zagreb at the very moment that President Tudjman was in conference with Stipe Mesic, the Federal President, and Ante Markovic, the Federal Prime Minister. As the *Economist* put it, "the attack put to rest any pretense that there is real life left in the Yugoslav federation."

Four days earlier, the Serbs had taken control of the Federal Presidency. On October 3, Branko Kostic, Montenegrin representative to the SFRY Presidency and Vice President, called a meeting of the Presidency and submitted a declaration of a state of emergency. With President Mesic absent and the Slovenian representative to the Presidency boycotting the meeting, the proposal was passed with Kostic's

own vote plus the three votes controlled by Serbia (plus its two formerly autonomous regions).

By this time, it had become clear to almost everyone just what Serbia was attempting to do. After the October 3, 1991 meeting of the Presidency, characterized by President Gligorov of Macedonia as "illegitimate and unconstitutional," both Macedonia and Bosnia–Herzegovina withdrew their representatives to the Presidency. Macedonia's representatives to the Federal legislature also withdrew from that body as well.

Up to this time, Montenegrin troops had not been directly involved in the war. Now, however, they entered Croatia from the south, conquering the area up to Dubrovnik and establishing a land siege around that city. They were joined by troops of the Yugoslav People's Army who had pushed their way down from the north.

As the siege continued, the EC drew up yet another plan for peace. Serbia was given until November 5 to accept a ceasefire and enter serious negotiations or face economic sanctions. In this new peace plan, the EC proposed that Yugoslavia become a loose association of sovereign republics with a currency union. Internal border changes would be by mutual consent only and disputed areas where minorities lived would be demilitarized under international peacekeepers. Kosovo and the Voivodina would also regain their autonomous status. Serbia, rejecting the plan, insisted that it could not abandon Serb minorities outside Serbia.

It would not agree to any plan that did not be permit minorities to switch the regions where they were in a majority from one republic to another. The exasperated EC instituted economic sanctions against Serbia and Montenegro after the deadline had expired. The United States Government, for its own reasons, instituted economic sanctions against all of Yugoslavia, including Croatia and Slovenia.

Serbia then took the EC proposal for an international force to police disputed areas where minorities lived and expanded it, suggesting that all areas occupied by the YPA should be so policed. Serbia still insisted that minorities be given the right to vote on whether to remain under Croatian jurisdiction, however.

Meanwhile, the last vestige of a united Yugoslavian Government disappeared in December 1991 when Ante Markovic, the prime minister, resigned. The Yugoslav legislature, dominated by Serbia after representatives of Slovenia, Croatia and Macedonia had withdrawn, had already expressed its lack of confidence in Markovic, a Croat from Bosnia–Herzegovina. However, the reason Markovic gave for his resignation was that 81% of the proposed

# Yugoslavia

budget for 1992 was earmarked for the army.

By this time, Germany and Austria had begun to make a public case for recognition of Slovenia and Croatia. Some of the other members of the EC, in particular France and Britain, continued to oppose recognition until Germany announced that it would proceed unilaterally if the EC took no action. Prime Minister Major of Britain then threw his support to Germany, and France grudgingly gave in. In December, the EC announced that its members would implement recognition of those Yugoslav republics that requested it and deserved it on January 15, 1992.

General Veljko Kadijevic, the Yugoslav Defense Minister, resigned on January 8, citing ill health. That gave Serb radicals control of the YPA, but Slobodan Milosevic, President of Serbia, had by this time switched positions somewhat and he and the EC had reached agreement on a new ceasefire and peacekeeping plan modeled on the suggestions he had put forth in November. Under the plan, the YPA would pull out of the three Serb enclaves in Croatia and be replaced by a peace force from the United Nations. The UN force would disarm local militias and organize a local police force. Croatia would not have control over the enclaves, but neither would Serbia. The future of the enclaves would

have to be determined at subsequent talks. The cease–fire—the fifteenth—went into effect on January 3. Five days later, the UN Security Council voted to send 50 UN observers to Croatia to report on the feasibility of the plan.

By January 15, 1992 four republics—Slovenia, Croatia, Macedonia and Bosnia–Herzegovina—had requested recognition by the EC. The EC actually recognized only the first two, largely out of political considerations. The various governments of the EC were worried that recognition of Bosnia–Herzegovina would cause the war to be expanded to that republic. The *Serbian Democratic Party*, the main spokesman for Serbs in Bosnia–Herzegovina, opposed separation of it from Yugoslavia and threatened to lead a secession of Serb–dominated areas. The Serbs formed their own "Serbian Republic of Bosnia–Herzegovina" and began arming themselves.

Because of this development, the EC advised the government of Bosnia–Herzegovina to hold a referendum on independence to establish that a majority actually wanted to break free from Yugoslavia. The referendum was held on March 1 and produced a two–thirds majority in favor of independence. Serbs, who had boycotted the referendum, threw up barricades throughout the capital city of Sarajevo that evening and it appeared that a major

civil war was ready to break out. President Alija Izetbegovic managed to get the leaders of the Serbs to meet with him and the major Croat leaders and thereby defused the situation. The Serbs agreed to dismantle their barricades and the other two political factions agreed to joint patrols by the Yugoslav People's Army and the Bosnian police.

On March 18, the leaders of the three communities agreed on a plan for restructuring the state, creating "three constituent units, based on national principles and taking into account economic, geographic and other criteria."

The plan would have created three autonomous units within the governmental structure, one for Moslems, one for Croats and one for Serbs. Control in each municipality would have been by that national group which was in an "absolute or relative majority." Since the three communities have always lived side by side and many families are mixed, the agreement would have been difficult to implement. In any case, it was never given a chance. The radical Serb leaders who wanted a single Greater Serbia forestalled that possibility by launching a war of conquest in April.

In essence, the Yugoslav army, overwhelmingly dominated by Serbs, split itself into two parts, those with any ties to Bosnia or other non–Serb lands remaining in Bosnia with the rest of the army removing itself to Serbia and Montenegro. Units left behind in Bosnia were provided with tanks, artillery and all the equipment of a modern army. General Ratko Mladic became the military commander of this force, while political leadership was exercised by Radovan Karadzic. The Yugoslav army has continued to provide support and resupply from Serbia, however. Thus the Yugoslav army, having learned from its involvement in Croatia that it could not afford to be seen as being present itself, created a proxy to continue its war for a Greater Serbia. Within three months, this Serbian army in Bosnia had managed to capture approximately 70 percent of the territory of Bosnia. They also laid siege to the capital, Sarajevo, in the process directing an unceasing bombardment into this once–beautiful medieval city in an effort to crush resistance. With the west continuing to enforce the arms embargo it had instituted at the beginning of the fighting, the lightly armed Bosnian army was no match for the tanks and artillery of the Serbs and the siege and the shelling went on, gradually reducing large parts of the city to ruins.

Meanwhile, Serbs used their control of the Yugoslav legislature to pass new laws establishing customs zones in Serb–inhabited areas of Croatia and parts of Bosnia–Herzegovina. In the case of Croatia, they also decreed that Yugoslav, not Croatian,

**A ploughman.**

Photo by Prof. Janko Ravnik

law would apply in Serb areas occupied by the UN peacekeeping force. In addition, the legislature passed a law on the new Yugoslavia which states that the "new community be made up nations and republics which want to remain in Yugoslavia." They implemented this by giving Serbs living outside Serbia representation in the Yugoslav legislature.

Montenegro held its own referendum in March and the people voted overwhelmingly to remain in a Yugoslav Federation. A union of two nations, one with a population of ten million and the other with only half a million, is rather odd, but that is what exists at the moment.

The claim that there is a "Federal Yugoslavia" which is superior to and exists separately from the Republic of Serbia ceased to have any validity on June 1, 1993 when Milosevic ousted Dobrica Cosic as President. He was replaced by Zoran Lilic, a puppet who lacked real standing either domestically or internationally. As Cosic said, after his dismissal,

> "The federal state, if it is a state at all, is practically under the protectorate of Slobodan Milosevic and the Serbian Government."

The embargo instituted against Serbia for its support of the war in Bosnia hurt the republic economically, but not to such an extent that it was willing to end its war of conquest for a Greater Serbia. Serbs actually gave President Milosevic's party an increased percentage of the vote in the December 1993 elections. With the government's almost total control over the news media, it was easy to convince Serbs that they were the aggrieved party, particularly since the leadership of the Serbian Orthodox Church supported the government on this issue.

The change came in August 1994 when the Yugoslav Government publicly withdrew support from Bosnia's Serbs after they had rejected a new UN peace plan that would have ceded them 49% of Bosnia. Serbia now announced that it had "sealed" its border with Bosnia and would not permit the export of anything except food, clothing and medicine. After much negotiation, the Serbian Government agreed to allow 135 civilian observers to monitor the 370–mile frontier with Bosnia. This brought an easing of sanctions against Serbia at the end of September.

In spite of widespread reports of violations on the part of Serbia, the UN continued to look to Milosevic as a possible negotiating partner. They next attempted to win Milosevic's cooperation by offering a further relaxation of sanctions in return for his recognition of Croatia and Bosnia. Milosevic made it clear, however, that he would not recognize the independence of either republic until an overall settlement was reached. In the interim, Serbia continued to provide at least some limited support to the Bosnian and Croatian Serbs.

Milosevic's position began to change in May 1995 when the Croatian army recaptured western Slavonia, an area held by Croatian Serbs since 1991. Three months later, as it became clear that the Croatian army intended to launch an invasion of the Krajina, the remaining Croatian Serb enclave in the center of Croatia, the Serbian Government not only did nothing, but there is some evidence that they let the Croatian Serbs know that they could expect no support from Serbia. As a result, when the invasion began, the Croatian Serb government of Milan Martic collapsed and nearly all Croatian Serbs fled eastward even before the arrival of Croatian troops.

Milosevic also stood by as a Croatian army entered Bosnia and then, in cooperation with the Bosnian army and the separate Bosnian Croat forces, gradually increased their control of Bosnian territory to just over 50%. It appears clear that the sanctions against Serbia were having their desired effect and that Milosevic concluded from this that his dream of a Greater Serbia could not be achieved under the current circumstances. Most of the Bosnian Serbs must have come to the same conclusion, for they now agreed to give Milosevic the power to negotiate on their behalf. This led to the Dayton peace talks which concluded successfully with a formal signing ceremony in December 1995. This brought a suspension of the economic sanctions against Serbia and a promise that they would be permanently removed if Serbia continued to support the peace process. The Serbian economy was operating at an extremely low level by this time, and the people, exhausted by the war, hoped that the peace agreement would lead to renewed growth. Outside economists suggested that Serbia should launch a major privatization program such as had already been carried out nearly everywhere else in Eastern Europe. Neither got their wish. The end of the economic sanctions brought few dividends and Milosevic actually revoked some privatization and free–market measures.

### Recent Political Developments in Yugoslavia

New elections to the Yugoslav legislature took place in November 1996. Because of the disarray of the opposition parties at this level, there was never any doubt that the parties of the government coalition would win a majority of the seats—and over two–thirds of the seats were indeed won by the two parties led by Milosevic and his wife.

Two weeks later, however, municipal elections took place throughout Serbia. In a surprise, the opposition won control over 32 municipalities, including Belgrade and industrial cities such as Kragujevac and Nis. Milosevic had always had strong support in these cities, but the dismal state of the economy, the high unemployment rate of almost 50 percent, and the fact that even those who were employed often had to wait months for their money, had turned the workers against Milosevic.

A week later, the situation had changed completely after the government moved to invalidate opposition victories in 14 of Serbia's 19 largest cities. Beginning on November 20, huge crowds of up to 100,000 demonstrators gathered daily in the middle of Belgrade to demand that the opposition be permitted to take their seats. Gradually, the demonstrations spread to other cities in Serbia.

Because the United States and several governments of the European Union had made it clear that they would support reimposing economic sanctions if Milosevic used force to suppress the opposition, the government tried to buy off the demonstrators by economic measures such as reducing the cost of electricity and promptly paying pensioners. None of this worked, however, and the demonstrations continued.

The government next tried to shut off all information about the demonstrations by closing down or seizing all private radio and television stations. Radio Free Europe countered this by picking up the broadcasts of the banned stations and broadcasting them over RFE frequencies. The demonstrations continued until February, when Milosevic finally gave in and agreed to honor the opposition victories. The confrontation lasted for 78 days.

The victories temporarily introduced a small amount of political pluralism into Serbian life, but it was not destined to survive very long. Within a few months, Zajedno, the opposition political coalition, collapsed when its two main leaders began quarreling over which of them would stand for the Serbian presidency in the approaching election. Taking advantage of the disarray, Milosevic was soon able to install his own man as Mayor of Belgrade and to reassert control over regional television.

Milosevic's second term as President of Serbia ran out in 1997 and he was forbidden by the constitution to stand for a third term. Milosevic therefore decided to move to the federal level and get himself elected as President of Yugoslavia. Since the president is elected by the Yugoslav legislature and Milosevic's party was in firm control there, it was not difficult for him to arrange for his election as President of Yugoslavia in July 1997. More difficult was to maintain his control of Serbia by having his own man elected President of

# Yugoslavia

**The rapids on the Kira River.**

Photo by Prof. Janko Ravnik

Serbia, since this required winning a majority in a popular vote. It took three elections, but Milosevic finally managed to have his own man, Milan Milutinovic, installed as President of Serbia in December 1997. Milutinovic, a loyal lieutenant of Milosevic's, had previously been foreign minister of Yugoslavia. It took another two months to form a government in Serbia, however, since Milosevic's Socialist Party had lost its majority in the legislature in the September 1997 elections. The new government, installed in March 1997, is a coalition.

Milosevic's most pressing challenge is probably what has been happening recently in Kosovo. (See pp. 352-353 for a discussion in greater depth of this situation.) After remaining quiet throughout the period of the Bosnian War, it now appears that Kosovo might explode. Since Serbian attempts to repress the Albanian majority through paramilitary units and national police have brought quick condemnations from a number of western powers, including the United States, it is not clear whether Milosevic will continue to use repression as his chosen tool. Certainly, continued use of military measures in Kosovo will destroy any chance that the remaining sanctions against Yugoslavia will be removed.

The other recent change came in Montenegro, the second republic that makes up Yugoslavia. Until 1997, Montenegro,

under the leadership of President Momir Bulatovic, was a loyal supporter of Milosevic's policies. But Bulatovic was challenged for the presidency by his prime minister, Milo Djukanovic, who accused him of being a puppet of Milosevic. Djukanovic won and has since taken an independent line vis-à-vis Milosevic. However, new parliamentary elections are scheduled for May 1998 and Djukanovic must win those if he is to retain control in Montenegro.

## Foreign Policy

Yugoslavia has been a "friend" of the West so long that it was always easy to forget that Yugoslav's leaders remained communists and that its relations with the West were the result of its having been expelled from the communist bloc by Stalin, not because they had ceased being communists. Nevertheless, this led Yugoslavia to sign a five-year Treaty of Friendship and Assistance with Turkey and Greece in 1953 which was subsequently known as the Balkan Pact. The following year, it was converted into a full defensive alliance. Yugoslavia also settled an outstanding issue with Italy that had been left over from World War II, the disposition of Trieste, by agreeing to divide the disputed land.

It also built up its international prestige by actively courting the non-aligned nations of Africa and Asia. These nations accepted Yugoslavian leadership in the

non-aligned movement because Tito had given Yugoslavia what they thought of as the best of all possible worlds—following a course of socialist development, though free of Soviet control, and receiving aid from the West, but without becoming an economic adjunct to capitalism. As communism–socialism has crumbled throughout the world, this dream has evaporated.

Yugoslavia thus positioned itself between the two blocs. It was never an ally of the United States and it welcomed the resumption of diplomatic relations with the Soviet Union in June 1953, after the death of Stalin. Thereafter, Yugoslav–Soviet relations alternated between periods of calm and storm, depending on the extent of control Moscow was attempting to exercise over Yugoslavia.

Bulganin and Khrushchëv of Russia visited Belgrade in 1955. Syrupy words flowed as the Soviets acknowledged that what the Yugoslavs were doing was their own business. In turn, Tito agreed to support Soviet policy on arms limitation, the division of Germany and the then Soviet cause of getting Red China admitted to the UN.

Following Khrushchëv's denunciations of Stalin in 1956, the dissolution of the *Cominform* in the same year, and the dismissal of Vyacheslav Molotov from the Soviet Foreign Ministry, there were further improvements in Yugoslav–Soviet relations. All of these moves indicated a Soviet acceptance of the possibility of different paths toward socialism. By June 1956 the two sides announced that they had achieved a "complete normalization" of relations on party and state levels.

But this was only a brief interlude. The actions of the Soviets and the apparent willingness to deal with Yugoslavia on an independent basis created false hopes of liberalization in Poland and Hungary. Hungary embarked upon a liberal and more independent course and the result was a harsh Soviet military invasion in the fall of 1956. Subsequent Soviet attacks on "revisionism" reopened the old conflict between Tito and Moscow. It was not until 1960–61 that a new attempt to smooth relations was made, probably to counteract the effect of increasing difficulties between the Soviet Union and China.

In 1968–69, Soviet–Yugoslav relations suffered once again under the impact of an international crisis. Tito had spoken out in favor of programs of liberalization that were taking place in Czechoslovakia; when the Soviet Union intervened militarily in that country, Tito voiced his condemnation of this move in the strongest terms. He rejected the *Brezhnev Doctrine*, the Soviet explanation for the move, as no more than an attempt to justify a violation of the sovereignty of a communist state by invoking the higher interests of socialism. Brezhnev paid a visit to Yugoslavia in

1971 for the first time since the invasion of Czechoslovakia. During the meeting with Tito, the Soviet leader disavowed the existence of any doctrine of limited sovereignty and, to Tito's satisfaction, endorsed the view that each country has the right to develop socialism according to its own experience. The reaffirmation of the 1955 Belgrade Declaration opened the door to better relations between the two countries.

One major issue between Yugoslavia and the Soviet Union in the 1970's was the latter's desire for a European Communist Conference. Yugoslavian participation in it was extremely important, for without it several of the Western European communist parties would probably have refused to attend.

Yugoslavia's price, exacted at a 1974 preparatory meeting in Warsaw, was that the meeting be open to the public, that it would not become a forum for attacking parties that had declined to attend, and that all decisions be by con census. Yugoslavia was supported in this stand by Romania and by the delegates representing the Italian, Spanish and French parties.

The conference finally took place in the summer of 1976 in Berlin. Although the meeting endorsed the main lines of Soviet foreign policy, the Soviets could not have been happy with other parts of the concluding document, which reiterated the Yugoslav–Romanian formula for interparty relations of "voluntary cooperation" based on the principles of equality, sovereignty, noninterference in internal affairs, and the respect for different roads to socialism.

Soviet–Yugoslav relations remained at about the same level until December 1979. Then the Yugoslavs condemned the Soviet invasion of Afghanistan and political relations turned cool. Yugoslavia did sign a ten–year economic agreement with the Soviet Union in 1980; however, the reasons were almost certainly economic. As a result of the second oil crisis in 1979, Yugoslavia was finding it harder and harder to compete in western markets. The economic agreement with the Soviet Union seemed to offer the promise of a long–term market for Yugoslav goods. The Soviets paid in convertible rubles, however. As the Yugoslav Government eventually learned, convertible rubles were of little value if the Soviet Union was not producing the things Yugoslavia was willing to import. Yugoslavia eventually built up a huge credit of several billion rubles which it was unable to use.

Yugoslav relations with the Soviet Union improved after Gorbachëv came to power in 1985. The Yugoslavian people welcomed him when he visited in March 1988. Gorbachëv traveled to various parts of the country, making speeches wherever he went. In retrospect, the visit took on a greater significance because of Gorba-

chëv's assertion, in the agreed joint statement at the conclusion of the visit, that every country had a right to pursue the variant of communism that it chose. This statement, which was essentially a repudiation of the Brezhnev Doctrine, paved the way for the 1989 revolutions in eastern Europe.

U.S.–Yugoslav relations were always based on the premise that Yugoslavia espoused a non–expansionist and therefore more benign form of communism and that it therefore offered an alternate pattern of development that might influence other communist countries in eastern Europe. Because of this strategic role assigned to it, the U.S. supported a unified, federal Yugoslavia.

The collapse of communism in eastern Europe in 1989 ended this strategic role for Yugoslavia and, in fact, exposed it as being a badly run communist state. Reformers in the western part of the country argued first for radical reforms, only to have their projects blocked by the Serb leadership. They then abandoned communism and carried out democratic elections. In Serbia, however, the communists changed the name of the party but managed to keep political control. Since they continued to obstruct real reform at the federal level, the democrats eventually opted for independence.

The U.S. Government never understood the dynamics of what was going on in Yugoslavia and continued to support a *unified* Yugoslavia even after it had become clear that such a Yugoslavia would be dominated by Serbia and neo–communist in its policies. In the summer of 1991, for example, even after President Milosevic of Serbia had destroyed the autonomy of

Kosovo and the Voivodina, had instituted a boycott of goods from Slovenia, had organized Serbs in other republics to oppose their republic's policies, and undermined the economic policy of the Yugoslav government at the national level, Secretary of State Baker announced that the United States would not support a break–up of Yugoslavia "under any circumstances."

Thus encouraged, Milosevic, supported by the Yugoslav People's Army—the last stronghold of communism at the national level—launched his war against Croatia and threatened one against Bosnia–Herzegovina. Even in November 1991, when Serbia's aims had become clear to the world and the EC had decided to institute economic sanctions against Serbia and Montenegro, the two aggressors, the U.S. decided to institute economic sanctions against both sides, *aggressors and victims*.

This was a classic case of a policy outliving its usefulness. The EC extended recognition to Slovenia and Croatia on January 15, 1992. The U.S. waited another three months before following suit. Ambassador Warren Zimmerman remained in Belgrade, however, and the U.S. Government continued to maintain good relations with the Serb–dominated Yugoslav Government. All of this ended when, with U.S. backing, the UN voted to impose economic sanctions against Serbia and Montenegro in late May 1992. The U.S. Government had begun to press Serbia on its treatment of Albanians in Kosovo, however. On March 23, Ambassador Zimmermann traveled to Pristina to open an exhibition organized to mark the 50th anniversary of the *Voice of America*. While there, he held talks with representatives of Albanian parties.

Photo by Prof. Janko Ravnik

# Yugoslavia

Even though the United States did not recognize the new "Yugoslav" Government, it continued to staff an embassy in Belgrade over the next several years, the stated purpose being to maintain contacts with the Serbian Government in order to try to persuade them to agree to a negotiated peace settlement in Bosnia. After the end of the Bosnian War, U.S.–Serbian relations improved because the U.S. Government was counting on Milosevic's continued support of the Dayton Accords to make them work. Gradually, many of the sanctions against Yugoslavia were removed and it appeared that Yugoslavia was about to lose its pariah status. That was put on hold in February 1998 after Serbia had launched a series of punitive attacks on Albanian villages in Kosovo. Now it appears that the U.S. Government will demand that Kosovo be given back its status as an autonomous province before it allows U.S.–Yugoslav relations to improve.

## Nature of the Regime

The collapse of Yugoslavia in 1991–92 as a result of the withdrawal of four of the six republics left behind a rump Yugoslavia composed of the two remaining republics of Serbia and Montenegro. When this occurred, Serbia organized Serbs outside of Serbia into a separate political force and arranged for their continued representation in the Yugoslav legislature. Serbia took control of the national institutions—the presidency, the legislature.

The Serbian enclaves in Croatia have all subsequently collapsed and the "Serbian Republic" in Bosnia–Herzegovina is slowly being reintegrated into Bosnia as the Dayton Accords are gradually implemented, so that leaves Serbia and its two formerly autonomous provinces of Voivodina and Kosovo, plus the Republic of Montenegro. Even though Serbia and Montenegro are, in theory, equal republics, Serbia has always dominated the federal institutions, partly because of its greater size and partly because it has three votes at the federal level because the two formerly autonomous provinces each have one vote, while Montenegro has one. Serbia's control became even more evident in 1997, when Milosevic, the longtime President of Serbia, had himself elected President of Yugoslavia.

The President of Yugoslavia was always a ceremonial position without a great deal of power, but Milosevic has already shown that he is not content to fill a ceremonial position. Thus far, he has managed to assert his political leadership indirectly by getting his own man elected President of Serbia, but many people think he will try to enhance the power of the President of Yugoslavia through a formal change in the constitution. Meanwhile, he continues to be the paramount power in Yugoslavia through his indirect control of Serbia.

There is a federal prime minister and cabinet, but these positions are filled by loyal lieutenants who take their orders from Milosevic. Milosevic's greatest political problem is that he lost control of Montenegro in 1997 when Momir Bulatovic, his loyal lieutenant there, was defeated for reelection as President. The new President of Montenegro is Milo Djukanovic, who blames Milosevic for the poor economic situation in the country. Still, Montenegro has only one–twentieth the population of Serbia, so that's probably not a great challenge.

## The Economy

Rump Yugoslavia or the "new" Yugoslavia which is supposed to emerge—in either case the two republics of Serbia and Montenegro—still has what must be called a socialist market economy. This means that it is neither a capitalist nor a totally government–directed economy. Although most industry is publicly owned, there is a significant private sector. In agriculture, 84% of the land is in private hands, the private purchase and sale of land is permitted, and there exists a free market in agricultural products. The government still encourages peasant work cooperatives and there still exist a few state farms. There is also a maximum limit of 10 hectares (about 25 acres) on the amount of land an individual peasant may own.

In the public sector, the government introduced the concept of worker self–management in 1952 and that system continues today. In each enterprise, a workers' council is elected by all the members of the facility; the management is then selected by the council and both take part in hiring a director.

Yugoslavia was a leader among the socialist states in economic decentralization, but it remained a *socialist* state. Fast economic growth in the period of the 1970's brought better living conditions, but a multitude of problems as well. Mounting inflation became more and more of a problem and the foreign trade deficit began to grow as well. Not wishing to put an end to the economic growth, the leadership rather reluctantly responded with things like import restrictions and a ceiling on wage increases. Eventually it was also forced to begin devaluating the currency as well. The great increase in energy prices in 1973–74 and again in 1979 eventually proved too much for the Yugoslav economy and it, like most of the world, slipped into recession.

While Yugoslavia's economy drifted during the 1980's, inflation grew year after year until, by the end of 1988, it had gotten out of control completely, soaring to an annual rate of 2,500%. The situation frightened the political leadership and in desperation they turned to Ante Markovic, an exponent of the free market. He was installed as President of the Federal Executive Council in March 1989.

Even then, there was stiff opposition to his stabilization program, but he managed to get it adopted after several months and it went into effect on January 1, 1990. Within three months, the dinar had been stabilized and inflation had been brought down to single digits. In addition, currency reserves were up and the foreign debt had been reduced to $16 billion. Foreign investment also began pouring into the country and several thousand privately–owned businesses were started by individual Yugoslavs.

Passersby in Belgrade look at the new technology

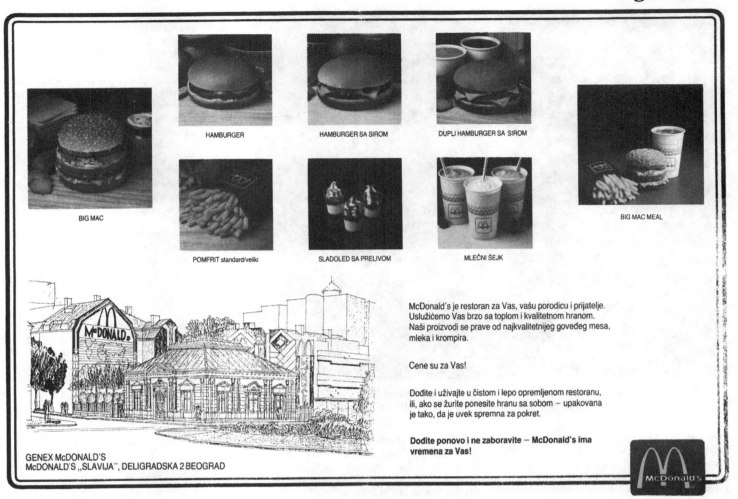

A *McDonald's* "tray-liner"—Belgrade, Yugoslavia

With the stabilization program so successful, politics reasserted itself. The second phase of Markovic's program called for beginning the privatization of state–owned industry, instituting radical changes in the federal tax structure and making banks more independent of the government, But elections were scheduled in the various republics, so the politicians demanded that the national wage freeze be lifted instead. It was Slobodan Milosevic, President of Serbia, who most strongly opposed the privatization policy. Lacking support in the republics, the national stabilization program was put on hold.

Meanwhile, free elections in Slovenia and Croatia brought a repudiation of the old communist leadership and their replacement by nationalist leaders who began talking of the need to replace the federation by a loose confederation of sovereign nations. Domestically, these new leaders adopted free market economic policies. This contrasted with the position of Slobodan Milosevic, the Serbian President and head of the Serbian branch of the League of Communists, who argued for a strong centralized Yugoslavia and against free market economic policies.

Caught between the two forces, the economic stabilization program of the Markovic government collapsed. By the beginning of 1991, inflation was again running at an annual rate of 120% and the dinar had to be devalued by 30%. In addition, internal convertibility was suspended when local banks were barred from access to hard currency. By April 1991, strikes were breaking out all over the country as thousands of enterprises were unable to meet their payrolls. Things were bad all over the country, but Serbian industry, the largest and most inefficient in the country, was worst off. Unemployment was at 15% percent and rising as industrial production continued to plummet. Thus an economic stabilization plan that had been working was completely destroyed by national and political rivalries.

The secession of Slovenia and Croatia in June 1991, followed by an attempt by the Serbs and the Yugoslav People's Army to keep the two republics in the federation *by force*, actually resulted in international recognition of those two republics and the withdrawal of two further republics, Macedonia and Bosnia–Herzegovina, from the federation. Since the war was fought al-

most exclusively on Croatian soil, Serbia and Montenegro, the two remaining republics in the SFRY, suffered no direct war damage. On the other hand, the EC eventually instituted an economic embargo against the two offending republics. In addition, the very existence of the war meant that the tourist industry, normally a large earner of foreign exchange, was dead.

None of this stopped Serbia from instigating a war in Bosnia in 1992, then continuing to support it fully until 1994 and fitfully until 1995. These actions had a terrible effect on the Serbian economy. The cost of Milosevic's financial support for the Bosnian and Croatian Serbs averaged, at least until 1994, an estimated 40% of Serbia's GDP. This produced a hyperinflation that effectively destroyed the Serbian currency by the end of 1993 and caused the GDP to drop by two–thirds or to about $10 billion. Milosevic did manage to pull off a coup when "Yugoslavia" issued a New Dinar tied to the German Mark in early 1994. This put an end to hyperinflation and brought a temporary lift to the economy, but it made it more difficult to provide significant assistance to the Bosnian Serbs and may have been the factor

# Yugoslavia

Passersby in Belgrade ponder the candidates of the two U.S. political parties in the 1988 elections.

"hegemonic" and "bullying." Montenegrins are usually described as "proudly independent" by admirers, "rural rustics" by detractors. Both Serbs and Montenegrins are also described as "fierce fighters." Such adjectives should not be taken too seriously, for they are more a reflection of Serbia's and Montenegro's relations with their neighbors than any underlying reality.

Serbs can be justly proud of the beautiful Serbian Orthodox churches and monasteries that date from that one great blossoming of culture during the middle ages. Modern Belgrade is in its own way a beautiful city, and an attractive city to visit because of its many sidewalk cafes, where one can order Turkish coffee and linger as long as one wants drinking it. Serbs are also, individually, a friendly people with a grace and charm all their own. Unfortunately, they can be easily stirred by appeals to Serbian nationalism, whereupon they lose their individual personalities and become, in effect, a mob. They have been badly misled by their government in recent years, but there are signs that they are beginning to wake up to reality. Let us all hope so, for the sake of Serbia itself as well as the rest of the Balkans.

## The Future

The Serb nationalistic binge that led to the collapse of the Socialist Federal Republic of Yugoslavia and a war that left large parts of Croatia and Bosnia–Herzegovina in ruins appears to have run its course and President Milosevic, giving up his dream of a "Greater Serbia" for now, has negotiated a peace agreement that has brought an end to the fighting in former Yugoslavia. But the peace may only be temporary. Serb leaders in Bosnia and Croatia are still not willing either to live under a government they do not control or to permit Croats and Muslims to live in areas that *they* control. Thus there have already been difficulties in implementing the new peace agreement. Thus far, however, President Milosevic has supported the peace agreement, and for that he has won the gratitude of the West.

The big question is whether he can succeed in getting the Bosnian Serbs to cooperate in implementing the terms of the peace. So far, he is succeeding. Moreover, his leverage is such that he will probably be successful, at least until the UN and NATO pull out their troops. In the meanwhile, peace has returned to the Balkans and economic activity is beginning to revive everywhere. It would be too much to say that the future is hopeful, but clearly the present is an improvement.

that caused Milosevic to throw his support to a Bosnian peace plan in 1994. He also reduced his military assistance to the Bosnian and Croatian Serbs at that time. However, this was not enough to persuade the west to lift the economic embargo against Serbia.

Milosevic further reduced his support for the Bosnian and Croatian Serbs in the summer of 1995 and even stood by when Croatia retook the Krajina in September. That apparently convinced the Bosnian Serbs that they could no longer count on support from Serbia. They then authorized Milosevic to negotiate on their behalf and that led to the Dayton peace negotiations, which produced an accord which was signed in December. The west then rewarded Milosevic by "suspending" the economic embargo against Serbia and promising to remove it entirely if the peace agreement held.

Serbs are now hopeful that they can get their economy back on track once again. Almost nothing has been done in the area of economic reform in Serbia, however, so the political leadership has to decide what it wants to do in that area as well.

## Culture

The withdrawal of Croatia, Slovenia, Bosnia–Herzegovina and Macedonia from the Socialist Federal Republic of Yugoslavia has left behind a rump Yugoslavia consisting of the republics of Serbia and Montenegro. That has not eliminated all of the differences in cultures which have fascinated foreign visitors, but it has reduced them considerably. Now what is left is essentially Serbian culture, characterized by the Serbian language, written in a 38–character Cyrillic alphabet, the Serbian Orthodox religion, and the remnants of a communist political–economic system which the current political leaders—all ex–communists—have thus far preserved. This "federation" still includes approximately half a million Montenegrins, but they speak a language that is almost identical to Serbian and they use the Cyrillic alphabet. They also are Orthodox Christians.

The Republic of Serbia does have two formerly autonomous provinces, the Voivodina and Kosovo, where Serbs are in a minority. Hungarians are the dominant group in the Voivodina, while Albanians make up approximately 90% of the population of Kosovo. Hungarians are usually Roman Catholic or Protestant. Most Albanians are Muslim, though there is a small minority that is Roman Catholic and even a few who are Orthodox.

We often attempt to characterize peoples by using adjectives. Words that have been used to describe Serbs include "emotional," "hot–tempered," and "proud." Their enemies tend to use words like

A young Serbian shopkeeper

# The Republic of Slovenia

**The island in Lake Bled with its ancient church.**

Photo by Prof. Janko Ravnik

**Area:** 7,819 square miles (20,251 sq. km.).

**Population:** 1,940,000 (estimated).

**Capital City:** Ljubljana (255,000, estimated. (Pronounced Lube–lee–anna).

**Climate:** Mediterranean west of Ljubljana; continental in the rest of the republic.

**Neighboring Countries:** Italy (west); Austria (north); Hungary (east); Croatia (south).

**Official Language:** Slovenian.

**Other Principal Tongue:** Serbo–Croatian.

**Ethnic Background:** South Slavic with strong Germanic influences.

**Principal Religion:** Roman Catholicism.

**Chief Commercial Products:** Agricultural products and processed foods, dairy products, metals, machinery.

**Currency:** Tolar (issued on October 8, 1991).

**Recent Political Status:** Part of the Austro–Hungarian Empire until 1919, part of Yugoslavia since 1929.

**Independence Day:** June 25, 1991.

**Chief of State:** Milan Kucan, President (pronounced *Cooch*–an). Reelected in November 1997.

**Head of Government:** Janez Drnovsek (pronounced Der–no–sheck), Prime Minister.

**National Flag:** Equal horizontal stripes of white, blue, and red, with the nation's coat–of–arms on the left over the white and blue stripes.

## The Land

The newly independent Republic of Slovenia was until 1991 known as the Socialist Republic of Slovenia and was part of the Socialist Federal Republic of Yugoslavia. It is located in the northwestern part of the Balkans.

The Julian Alps run along most of the border with Italy, while the Karavanke Mountains mark the border with Austria. Somewhat further south and southeast are the Kamnik Mountains. The Sava River forms a wide valley between the Julian Alps and the Karavanke Mountains, then flows across the republic in a southeastern direction. A second major river, the Drava, forms in Austria (where it is known as the Drau), then enters the republic north of the Kamnik Mountains. It then flows in a southeastern direction across the republic before crossing into Croatia. Except for the mountainous area, most of Slovenia is covered by often steep, heavily forested rolling hills, with the exception of the plateau area of gray karst limestone east of Trieste.

Slovenia also takes in the northeastern part of the Istrian Peninsula, which gives it a coastline on the Adriatic Sea. Its major port is, however, the one–time Italian city of Trieste.

## The People

The Republic of Slovenia has a population about 88% of whom belong to the majority ethnic group. Except for some Italians living in the western part of the republic, most of the "minorities" are people who came to the republic from other parts of former Yugoslavia in search of work. However, a flood of Moslems fleeing Bosnia–Herzegovina as a result of Serbian aggression, was entering Slovenia from mid–1992.

## History

The Slovenes migrated into the area of the western Balkans in the sixth century, the first of the Slavic peoples to enter the region. In 627, a Slavic kingdom came into existence in the Sava River Valley. It lasted for about 120 years, then was incorporated into the Carolingian Empire in 748. It was at this time that the Slovenians were converted to Roman Christianity.

In the ninth century, the Carolingian Empire was divided, and Slovenia passed to Germans; in the tenth century it became part of the Holy Roman Empire. This area remained within the Holy Roman Empire through several changes of rulers and eventually passed to the Hapsburgs, who established their capital at Vienna. Periodic attempts at Germanization shrunk the area of Slovenian culture, but not most of the Slovenian heartland, through the efforts of native Roman Catholic priests.

Slovenian peasants were eventually enserfed, along with the peasantry in other parts of the empire. This produced a number of uprisings in the fifteenth and sixteenth centuries, but things remained very much the same until the eighteenth century, when Maria Theresa and her son, Joseph II, attempted to ameliorate the lot of the people by granting them personal freedom.

After the collapse of the Austrian Empire in 1918, Slovenian leaders supported creation of the Kingdom of Serbs, Croats and Slovenes. This became the Kingdom of Yugoslavia in 1929. Slovenia was partitioned during World War I, with Italy taking the southwest, Hungary a small piece of land north of the Mura River called Prekomurje, and Germany took the northeast. This led to a Slovenian resistance movement, the most significant of which was the communist–led *Liberation Front*.

After the defeat of Germany in World War II, Slovenia became one of the constituent republics of the People's Republic of Yugoslavia. In 1947, the republic received some additional territory from Italy as part of the Paris Peace Treaty. In 1954, some of the former Free Territory of Trieste was transferred to Slovenia.

Slovenians are a hard–working people with a good republic leadership; they did well economically up through about 1980. Yugoslavia never recovered from the oil shock of 1979, however, and the wealthier parts of the country found themselves called upon to provide more assistance to badly run and failing large–scale industry in the eastern part of the country. By the middle of the 1980s, political leaders in Slovenia and Croatia were pushing for a change in the economic system, but they were opposed, particularly, by the leadership of Serbia; Slovenia and Croatia then proposed a loosened form of federation that would give them economic independence. This was unacceptable to Serbia.

Faced with this stalemate at the national level, Slovenia and Croatia began to push for internal changes. By the spring of 1990, Slovenia had ended the political monopoly formerly held by the *Slovenian Communist Party* and created a *de facto* pluralistic system. In April 1990, multi–party elections resulted in a legislature dominated by the six–party *Democratic United Opposition*, or *Demos*.

The *Demos*, a coalition of conservative

**President Milan Kucan**

political parties, had campaigned on a platform of independence within a year. At the same time, Milan Kucan, candidate of the communists, was elected President. Shortly thereafter, the communists became the *Party of Democratic Renewal* and endorsed independence as well.

On July 2, 1990, the Assembly adopted a "declaration of sovereignty" by an overwhelming 187 votes to 3. In September, the Assembly took control of the "territorial defense force." A referendum on independence was held on December 23, 1990. Of those voting, 88.5% opted for independence, "unless it proved possible to negotiate a looser Yugoslav confederation." The Assembly then adopted its own endorsement of the declaration on December 26. The Assembly voted in February 1991 that republic law would henceforth take precedence over laws of the Yugoslav Federation.

Meanwhile, all attempts to negotiate a new union proved unavailing, as Serbia stonewalled. After Slovenia has passed its legislation establishing the paramountcy of republic legislation, Serbia went further and instituted a boycott of goods from Slovenia. Then it took another step in May when it refused to accept the election of the Croatian Vice President to the Yugoslav Presidency. For two months, the office of President remained vacant. Finally, Slovenia and Croatia declared their independence on June 25, 1991.

On June 27, the Yugoslav People's Army moved against Slovenia, probably selecting Slovenia because the republic had taken charge of some border posts with Austria and Italy. The Slovenes fought back, however, and even managed to capture some tanks.

Meanwhile, the West, which had attempted to dissuade the Slovenians and

# Slovenia

Croatians by refusing, as Secretary of Baker put it, to recognize their independence "under any circumstances," was appalled by the bloodshed and began to offer mediating services.

Some of the European nations even began talking about extending recognition to Slovenia and Croatia. This led to a break in the stalemate at the center and the installation of Stipe Mesic as President. Finally, after two cease–fires had broken down, the third held. In a compromise imposed by negotiators from the EC, Slovene agents were authorized to collect federal customs duties at the disputed custom posts, while Slovenia agreed to suspend application of its declaration of independence for three months.

This brought an end to the war in Slovenia, but it actually only moved the venue of the war to Croatia. Three months later, the Yugoslavian People's Army was still trying to conquer Croatia and nothing had been settled. Slovenia thereupon activated its declaration of independence as of October 7.

By December, with the war in Croatia still going on, most European nations were fed up with Serbia and the leadership of the Yugoslav People's Army. Germany now pressed the EC to recognize the two republics and this was finally agreed to, effective as of January 15, 1992. Secretary of State Baker refused to follow suit, however, in effect continuing support for the hardline, Serbian nationalist and ex–communist leadership of Serbia and the Yugoslavia People's Army. Apparently anything was better to Secretary Baker than to see one more part of Europe falling apart. This changed only after the Yugoslav army began to spread its destruction throughout most of the rest of former Yugoslavia. The United States then changed its mind and sponsored UN economic sanctions against Serbia and Montenegro.

Slovenia held new parliamentary elections in December 1992 which essentially confirmed the previous political situation and Janez Drnovsek was reappointed Prime Minister in January. The government's program continued to be essentially what it had been three years earlier, prior to the country's independence. Although committed in theory to a large–scale privatization program, little was accomplished until 1994 because of disagreement among the coalition members concerning the speed of transition. The delay was further caused by the fact that most industry was not "state–owned" but "socially–owned," a result of Yugoslavia's "worker self–management" form of economic organization. As the head of Slovenia's Privatization Agency commented, "In effect, there are no owners," and the role of the Privatization Agency is "to advise and oversee the process. The rest is up to the company directors." Most Slovene enterprises that have been privatized have done so through management–employee internal share distribution programs; most larger Slovene enterprises have, however, opted for the alternative method of issuing public share offerings.

New elections in November 1996 brought a slight change in the government coalition, but the government was essentially returned to power. Prime Minister Drnovsek's party, the *Liberal Democrats*, came in first with 25 of the 90 seats. The *Liberal Democrats* are a left–center party, strongly committed to making Slovenia part of NATO and the European Union. The second party, the *Slovene People's Party*, won 19 seats. The *Slovene People's Party*, a center–right party, joined the government after the election, replacing the *Christian Democrats*. The third place winner in the elections was the *Social Democrats*, who won 16 seats. In spite of the name, the *Social Democrats* are a right–leaning party. The party leader is Janez Jansa, considered to be a rival to Prime Minister Drnovsek for power.

President Milan Kucan easily won re-election to a second five–year term in November 1997, winning 55 percent of the popular vote in a field of eight candidates. Parliamentary speaker Janez Podobnik came in second with 18 percent of the vote. One factor in President Kucans's unusually good showing may have been that he was a stronger supporter of Slovenia's entry into the European Union. Slovenia was one of five nations invited to join the European Union in 1997.

## Foreign Policy

The Slovenian Government very much wants to be part of the West and it is working hard to give that orientation a physical reality. It signed up for NATO's "Partnership for Peace" in February 1994 and has since been pushing for eventual full membership in NATO. It signed an association agreement with the European Union in June 1996 and expects to be ready for full membership by the year 2000. Already, 60% of its trade is with four EU members—Austria, Germany, France and Italy—and 90% of its foreign investment comes from these same four nations. It also signed a free trade agreement with the Czech Republic in 1994.

Its relations with the United States Government are "normal," but individual members of the Slovenian Government have much closer private ties. For example, Prime Minister Drnovsek travelled to the United States in 1994 to receive an honorary degree from Boston University. One irritant in U.S.–Slovenian relations in 1993–95 was that Prime Minister Drnovsek was a consistent critic of Western inaction in Bosnia in those years. U.S.–Slovenian relations have improved recently.

## Nature of the Regime

Slovenia has been a multiparty democracy since 1990, when a six–party *Democratic United Opposition*, also known as the

Slovenia's capital, Ljubljana, as seen from the Castle.

# Slovenia

Slovenia's Miro Cerar, world champion on parallels and horizontal bars, European gymnastics champion, prepares for the Olympics.

*Demos*, won 55% of the vote. The *Slovenian Communist Party*, which had changed its name to the *Party of Democratic Renewal*, won 18% of the vote, but the former communist leader, Milan Kucan, won the presidency with 52% of the vote. The old *Demos* coalition has since disintegrated, but most of the winning political parties in the November 1996 elections had been members of the old coalition. The largest party today is Prime Minister Drnovsek's *Liberal Democrats*.

A new constitution, adopted in 1991, established a presidential–parliamentary system. The role of the President is largely ceremonial, though President Kucan has carved out an important role for himself in the area of foreign affairs. He is a strong advocate of Slovenia's entry into NATO and the European Union.

The Prime Minister, the official head of government, presides over the cabinet and is responsible for government policy. He must be affirmed in office by a positive vote of the National Assembly and may be removed by a negative vote of confidence.

Slovenia has a bicameral legislature, referred to as the parliament, composed of two houses, the National Assembly, and the National Council. The National Assembly, composed of 90 members, is the "popular" house, equivalent to the British House of Commons.

## Culture

Slovenian culture reflects the fact that this is an overwhelmingly Roman Catholic country, but it differs from Croatia, which is also Roman Catholic, in that it is much more western in its orientation. Driving through the beautiful countryside, it is impossible to differentiate this area from those of Austria across the border. Towns and cities are clean and prosperous–looking and the people dress much as

they do elsewhere in Europe. Only the signs in Slovenian make it clear what country you are in.

There is not a great deal of literature in Slovenian and much of what exists is religious in nature. The Freising manuscripts, dating from about the year 1000, are the earliest works available. Slovenian came into wider use during the reformation, when Protestants translated the Bible and also produced some tracts in the language. The Slovenians eventually rejected Protestantism, however. In the eighteenth century, a Roman Catholic version of the Bible appeared in Slovenian and this was followed by grammars in the early nineteenth century. Slovenian came into common use only after the middle of the nineteenth century, however.

## Economy

Slovenia is still primarily agricultural, though the harvesting of forestry products provides an additional income for many rural inhabitants. Crops include wheat, corn, rye, oats, potatoes, rapeseed, sugar beets, and fruit. Livestock raising (cattle, sheep, pigs, poultry) is also carried on throughout the republic. Agriculture is highly mechanized and the standard of living in the countryside approximates that of its neighbor, Austria.

It has a significant steel industry that produces approximately three–quarters of a million tons of steel annually. It also manufactures trucks and automobiles. It produces its own coal and has some hydroelectric stations, but all other energy must be imported. Other industrial products include cement, sulphuric acid, cotton and woolen fabrics, plus processed agricultural products such as sugar.

The economic dislocations associated with its declaration of independence and the resulting loss of the "Yugoslav" mar-

ket led to a three year recession, but the economy began growing again in the last quarter of 1993. A three–year stalemate in the legislature over privatization was broken in early 1994 and the government then launched a large–scale privatization program using a system of vouchers.

This new process applied only to larger firms. Most Slovenian firms were small and they were "socially–owned," in line with Yugoslavia's system of worker self–management. Such firms were privatized through a form of internal share distribution, i.e., all shares were distributed to the employees and management. Larger firms, on the other hand, were privatized using public share offerings. In that case, 20% of the shares were transferred to the Slovene Development Fund, which sold the shares to authorized investment firms in which the public had invested their privatization vouchers.

The Slovene Development Fund also assumes outright ownership of firms in financial or organizational disorder. Such firms are reorganized and rehabilitated, then prepared for sale to the public. This is also the one group of firms where foreign direct investment is possible as a form of privatization.

Slovenia's per capita income is now over $9,000 and it boasts one of the most prosperous economies of Central and Eastern Europe. The structure of the economy has changed since 1991, however, with industry in relative decline while the service sector is growing. Annual inflation was down to 10.7% in 1996. The one weakness in the economy is in jobs; unemployment has remained fairly stable over the past several years at 14%.

## The Future

Slovenia represents one of the success stories of Eastern Europe. It has a stable, democratic political system and a vigorous economy. Slovenians worry about their Eastern neighbor, Croatia, however, and they are therefore eager to "join Europe" by becoming members of NATO and the European Union. They apparently have a fairly good chance of achieving membership in the EU, though immediate membership in NATO appears more doubtful.

369

# The Republic of Croatia

The picturesque medieval city of Dubrovnik on the Adriatic Coast before its bombardment by the Serbs

**Area:** 21,829 square miles (56,538 sq. km.).
**Population:** 4,760,344 (April 1991).
**Capital City:** Zagreb (765,000).
**Climate:** Mediterranean in the west; Mild continental east of Zagreb.
**Neighboring Countries:** Slovenia (north); Hungary (northeast); Serbia, SFRY (east); Bosnia (east and south); Montenegro (southwest).
**Official Language:** Croatian.
**Other Principal Tongues:** Serbo–Croatian.
**Ethnic Background:** South Slavic.
**Principal Religions:** Roman Catholicism, Serbian Orthodox.
**Chief Commercial Products:** Agricultural products, lumber, coal, steel, plastics, cement, cotton fabrics.
**Currency:** Kuna.
**Former Political Status:** Constituent republic of SFRY.
**National Day:** June 25, 1991.
**Head of State:** Franjo Tudjman, President (reelected for a third term in June 1997).
**Head of Government:** Zlatko Matesa, Prime Minister.
**National Flag:** Three horizontal stripes from the top—red, white, blue, with a checkered crest of the country imposed on the white stripe.

## The Land

The Republic of Croatia is the independent successor state to the *Socialist Republic of Croatia*, one of the six republics of the now defunct Socialist Federal Republic of Yugoslavia. Croatia declared its independence in June 1991. After a bitter six month war fought against it by Serbia and the Yugoslav People's Army, it received international recognition by the members of the European Community in January 1992.

Croatia, has a long coastline on the Adriatic Sea. In the north and east, the chief topographical features are the Sava and Drava River valleys, plus the Croatian–Slavonian Mountains, a mountainous ridge that separates the two river valleys. The Drava River forms the border with Hungary while the Sava forms the border with Bosnia–Herzegovina. Most of the rest of Croatia consists of either mountains or uplands.

The Great Kapela Chain crosses the republic in the northwest. Somewhat further south, the Velebit Range begins, followed by the Dinarian Alps, which run along the border with Bosnia–Herzegovina. The long Croatian coastline consists of the Dalmatian Islands plus a fairly narrow strip of the mainland reaching down as far as Montenegro. This is essentially a coastal plain backed by mountains. This, plus the Dalmatian Islands, became a major summer resort area for West Europeans.

This region was once the ancient Greek Kingdom of Dalmatia and includes such historic cities as Split, where the Emperor Diocletian lived after his retirement from 305 to 313. The nucleus of the town is actually the Palace of Diocletian. Another important city is Dubrovnik, a town founded in the seventh century and famous for its late–Renaissance buildings. The city's former picturesque streets, which are narrow and winding (and now in ruins) are closed to motor vehicles. Dubrovnik was badly damaged when it was shelled by the Yugoslav People's Army in the fall of 1991 and early 1992.

## The People

Prior to independence, Croats represented 77.9% of the population with Serbs, the largest minority, accounting for another for 12.2%. A further 2.2% listed themselves as Yugoslavs, and one 1% Moslems. The war resulted in a major shift in populations, however, with Croats being pushed out of areas controlled by Croatian Serbs and many Moslem refugees making their way into Croat–controled areas of the republic from Bosnia in 1991–1992. A further major change occurred in the summer of 1995 when at least 150,000 Serbs fled out of the Krajina as that area was being recaptured by Croatian soldiers. Today, Serbs are only found in significant numbers in the eastern part of Croatia, in the Serb–controlled area of East Slavonia. Since that area is scheduled to revert to Croat control in a year or so, it is likely that most of Croatia's remaining Serbs will make their way eastward into Serbia prior to that time. One can only speculate on how many Moslems will remain in Croatia if the current peace settlement holds and stability returns to Bosnia. The reason why they might stay is that many have no homes to return to, since the peace settlement left the areas they were expelled from under Serb control.

## History

The Croatians entered the Balkan Peninsula from the area of the western Carpathian Mountains in the 7th century. Even at this time they were separate from the Serbs, constituting, along with the Slavonians, the western division of the Serbo–Croatian migration, while the Serbs formed the eastern portion. At this time, the Croats were ruled by tribal institutions. While the Slovenians were being incorporated into the Carolingian Empire, however, the Croats fell under the domination of the Byzantine Empire beginning in 877.

Rebelling against this outside control,

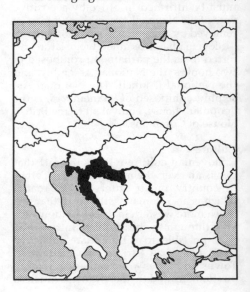

370

they formed the first united Croatian Kingdom in 910. The ruler of this first Croatian kingdom was Tomislav and the kingdom he founded lasted for about two centuries. During this time, Croatia waged war against Bulgaria and managed to extend its control over part of the Dalmatian coast. This period of history is, in fact, looked on by many Croatian nationalists as the golden age of their country. They did build up a large navy and for a time at the end of the tenth century even exacted tribute from Venice.

Croatia was included in the new Kingdom of Serbs, Croats and Slovenes which was formed on December 4, 1918. In 1921, a constitution was adopted which created a unitary central government. Since Serbs made up about 40% of the overall population, their party, the *Radical Party*, tended to dominate this new kingdom. When Stepjan Radic, leader of the *Croatian Peasant Party*, protested the Serbian domination, the government responded by arresting him and banning his party. The period from 1921 to 1928 was one of constant conflict over the issue of centralism versus federalism, with Croatian nationalists advocating creation of a federal state.

When Radic was assassinated within the parliament building by a Montenegrin in 1928, the Croatian deputies withdrew from the body, threatening not to return until a federal state had been created in which Croatians were not dominated by Serbs. King Alexander I (see Yugoslavia) opposed the idea of a federal state so, in 1929, he abolished the constitution and took power himself. After he had proclaimed his royal dictatorship, he changed the name of the country to Yugoslavia.

Alexander was assassinated in 1934 by a Macedonian associated with the Croatian dissidents. Since Alexander's son, Peter, was then only a child, Alexander's cousin, Prince Paul, was named regent; he ruled until 1941. In 1939, he attempted to solve the problem of nationalist dissent by creating an internally self–governing Croatia.

Paul was deposed in March 1941 after he allied Yugoslavia with Germany. The denunciation of the alliance brought a German invasion in April 1941 and German occupation of the country between 1941 and 1945. Hitler permitted an "independent" Croatia to be proclaimed in April 1941, however. The head of this entity was Ante Pavelic, head of a fascist organization called *Ustasha*. The Pavelic regime was characterized by brutality and violence, much of it targeted against local Serbs. One of the problems the Croatian Government has today with Serbs is that they remember the actions of a previous Croatian Government and are unwilling to trust the current one.

There were lots of Croats who opposed this Ustasha Government, however, one of

whom was Josef Broz Tito, leader of the *Partisan Forces* against the Germans. During the war, Tito and his Communist Partisans organized local committees throughout Croatia as they liberated individual areas from German or Ustasha control. Toward the end of the war, these local committees were organized into a council of national liberation and after Zagreb was liberated, this council proclaimed itself the People's Government of Croatia. When the country was reconstituted as the People's Republic of Yugoslavia in 1945, the People's Republic of Croatia joined as one of the six constituent republics.

The self–promoted Marshal Tito, who ruled Yugoslavia from 1945 to 1980, ruthlessly suppressed all nationalist agitation within the country. Franjo Tudjman, now President of the Republic of Croatia, was one of Tito's generals. In the early 1970s, he and Stipe Mesic, the last President of Yugoslavia, were among Croatian Communist leaders imprisoned on charges of nationalistic deviations.

Croatian nationalist groups began to reemerge in the late 1980s. Most of these eventually joined to form the *Croatian Democratic Union*. This political party won the republic elections in April 1990. Franjo Tudjman, leader of the party, was elected President at the same time. The political program of the movement only called for increased autonomy within a more confederal Yugoslavia.

It was Yugoslavia's tragedy that a Serbian dominist, Slobodan Milosevic, rose to power within the *League of Communists of Serbia* at this same time. Milosevic not only opposed all political concessions to Croatia, he also deliberately sabotaged economic reform as well. He therefore created a political stalemate which was also destroying the economy.

On May 19, 1991, the Croatian Government held a referendum on the question of independence for the republic. After a favorable vote, the Croatian Assembly adopted a declaration of independence on June 25. The Croatian Government did reiterate, however, that it was willing to continue discussions on a looser Yugoslav confederation, with the central government confined to foreign policy, defense and a common currency.

When the Government of Croatia began moving toward independence, the Serbs within the republic, egged on by Milosevic and a press dominated by Serbs, organized two autonomous regions. Despite a new law passed by the Croatian legislature guaranteeing protection for minority ethnic groups, the Croatian Serbs held their own referendum on July 7 reaffirming their loyalty to the Socialist Federal Republic of Yugoslavia.

Meanwhile, the Yugoslav People's Army (YPA) reacted to the declarations of independence by sending an invasion

force into Slovenia. That republic was selected instead of Croatia because it moved to take control of its international border with Italy and Austria. The YPA was apparently not expecting much opposition, but the Slovenians fought back valiantly.

Meanwhile, the rest of the world, which had encouraged the army action by asserting that they would not support a separate Slovenia or Croatia "under any circumstances," began calling for a cease–fire. At the same time, army desertions by non–Serbs began to be a problem. This led to an agreement with Slovenia that it could man the control posts if it would turn the revenues over to the central government. The YPA also agreed to return its forces to the barracks.

Slavonia and Croatia also agreed to suspend their declarations of independence for three months. Serbia, in turn, agreed to allow Stipe Mesic to be elected President. The latter agreement was important in a military as well as a political sense because the President was also the Commander–in–Chief of the Yugoslav People's Army.

The agreement brought peace to Slovenia, but not to Yugoslavia. One of the first actions of President Mesic was to arrange a ceasefire—the third—on July 2. That same day, General Blagoje Adzic, chief of the YPA General Staff, angrily repudiated the ceasefire—and thereby his own Commander–in–Chief—in an interview that appeared on Belgrade television and added that the army "accepted the challenge of total war that had been imposed on it" and would soon end it with a complete victory. The next day, an armored column left Belgrade for Croatia.

On July 6, 1991, Milosevic gave a speech in which he told Serbs to be ready to defend themselves. He also gave Serb leaders in Croatia generous access to Serbian radio and television. The first fighting in

**President Franjo Tudjman**

# Croatia

Croatia began on July 7 when Croatian Serbs allied with Milosevic attacked Croatian territorial defense forces near the town of Tenja. Once the fighting had begun, the Yugoslav People's Army intervened "to keep the peace," though its targets were always Croatian territorial units. Since President Tudjman ordered Croatian units not to attack the YPA, the fighting remained small scale for some time. In addition, the YPA did not initiate battles at this time and only advanced when new fighting would break out. Gradually, however, the YPA's control of Croatian territory spread as Serb territorial forces launched new battles in area after area.

The Serbian problem existed because Serbs insisted on living in a state controlled by Serbs. But the Croatians were not entirely free of this empire mentality themselves. The Republic of Bosnia–Herzegovina, which lies between Serbia and Croatia, has an extremely mixed population, with 33% Serbs and about 17% Croats. In July, President Tudjman admitted that members of his government had held secret talks with Serbian leaders about carving up Bosnia between the two, leaving a small Moslem rump that neither wanted. Word of these talks did not help Croatia internationally.

Croatia was "saved" by the fact that Serbia and the YPA were even more bloody–minded. In August, Milosevic revealed his plans for a reconstituted Yugoslavia which called for carving up Croatia and incorporating about a third of the territory into the new state, although Serbs constitute only 12% of Croatia's popula-

tion. Even more revealing, on August 20, Milosevic's chief ideologist praised the Moscow *coup* leaders as "tough men but not dogmatics" and accused Gorbachëv of pushing the Soviet Union toward a break–up by his attempt to create a union of sovereign states.

Meanwhile the YPA, which up to this time had contended that it was acting as a neutral buffer between the two sides, began bombarding Croatian cities with artillery and aircraft. In late August, much of the city of Vukovar was destroyed. By this time, perhaps twenty percent of the republic had fallen under YPA or Serb militia control.

On September 18, 1991, Zagreb, the capital, came under fire from aircraft and artillery. At about the same time, the Yugoslav navy instituted a blockade of Croatia's Dalmatian ports. Soon it began attacking them, beginning with the city of Split. Up to this moment, the Croatian Government had been carrying out a "passive defense" and refusing to challenge the YPA directly. Now it cut oil lines across Croatia to Serbia and laid siege to Yugoslav army barracks in Croatia. Croatia also began getting some indirect assistance from other republics when Bosnia–Herzegovina and Macedonia adopted a position of neutrality and ordered their citizens to ignore conscription notices from the YPA. Even in Serbia, however, many young men went into hiding rather than serve.

The three–month moratorium on Croatia and Slovenia's independence declarations—agreed to at Brioni—was set to ex-

pire on October 7. Freed of that limitation, the Croatian Assembly approved a resolution severing all ties with the Socialist Federal Republic of Yugoslavia. By this time, approximately a third of the country was occupied by the YPA and the Serbs. The Yugoslav air force marked the day with an attack on the presidential palace in Zagreb at the very moment that President Tudjman was in conference with Stipe Mesic, the Federal President, and Ante Markovic, the Federal Prime Minister. As the *Economist* put it, "the attack put to rest any pretense that there is real life left in the Yugoslav federation."

Four days earlier, the Serbs showed that they realized this when they instituted a maneuver to take control of the Federal Presidency. On October 3, Branko Kostic, Montenegrin representative to the SFRY Presidency and Vice President, called a meeting of the Presidency in President Mesic's absence and proposed declaring a state of emergency. The resolution was passed with the support of the three votes controlled by Serbia (Serbia plus its two formerly autonomous regions), plus Kostic's own vote.

By this time, it had become clear to almost everyone just what Serbia was attempting to do. But it took almost three months more before Britain and France could be persuaded to abandon the ideal of a united Yugoslavia. And even then, the American Government refused to abandon that ideal. But the European Community announced in December that they would recognize Slovenia and Croatia as of January 15. The fighting continued up to that date, but tapered off afterwards. Under the terms of the eventual ceasefire, a United Nations Protection Force (UN-PROFOR) was deployed in and along the boundaries of the three Serb controlled areas which called themselves the independent "Serbian Republic of the Krajina." The declaration of independence was only pro forma, however. The goal of the Serbians was to unite with Serbia and the Serb–occupied areas of Bosnia in a "Greater Serbia."

Croatia subsequently made three attempts to reintegrate the Serb–occupied territory into Croatia, twice in 1993 and once in March 1994. On each occasion, the Serbs launched artillery attacks on Zagreb and other Croatian towns. In addition, UNPROFOR opposed Croatian efforts to restore control over Serb–held areas.

In January 1995, with the Croatian Serbs still armed and in control of one–third of the country and continuing to act as a separate government attached to Yugoslavia, President Tudjman decided that the UN-PROFOR mission had failed and that it was time for them to leave. He then informed the United Nations that the UN-PROFOR mandate would not be renewed when it expired at the end of March. What

**The Tudjman family occupies the front pew in Zagreb Cathedral**

worried Tudjman is that the "Contact Group" (U.S. Russia, France, Great Britain and Germany), negotiating with the Bosnian Serbs had accepted their demand that they be permitted to confederate with Serbia. Tudjman expected that the Croatian Serbs would make the same demand and Krajina would be lost forever. Tudjman also recognized that, although the Croatian Serbs were heavily armed, their mini–state was economically inviable on its own and was only surviving because of continuing support from Serbia by means of a thin corridor several hundred miles long across the north part of Bosnia. Removal of the UNPROFOR troops would give Croatia the chance to cut that lifeline to Serbia.

Tudjman's decision actually constituted a great gamble, for it ignored the possibility that Serbia might reintervene directly if Tudjman moved against the Croatian Serbs and they started to lose. Certainly this is what bothered the "Contact Group," which put Tudjman under heavy pressure to reverse his decision. What finally occurred was a sort of compromise. Tudjman agreed that he would permit half of the 12,000 UNPROFOR troops to stay while the UN agreed to provide another 500 troops to police the border between Serb–held parts of Croatia and Bosnia and Serbia.

Two months later, Croatia sent its troops into the eastern section of Croatian Serb–held Krajina, known as western Slavonia, and managed to recapture the area in just 40 hours. Although the Croatian Serbs retaliated with rocket attacks against Zagreb and other Croatian towns, Croatia held onto the pocket. Several thousand Serbs fled out of the area, making their way either to the remaining part of Krajina or to Serb–held Bosnia. Approximately two months later, Croatian forces overran the remaining section of Serb Krajina in just four days, between on August 4 and 8. They met very little resistance; in fact, the Croatian Serb forces just seemed to melt away. As the Croatian forces entered from the west, as many as 150,000 Serbs fled eastward into Bosnia, many making their way across Bosnia into Serbia. The refugees included the 16,000 militiamen who had made up the Serb Krajina army.

### The Recovery of Eastern Slavonia

President Tudjman next set his sights on Eastern Slavonia, the remaining part of Croatia still held by Serbs. After shifting a significant part of his forces to the eastern part of the country, he made a public demand for the return of Eastern Slavonia. The purpose of these actions was undoubtedly to ensure that Eastern Slavonia was included on the agenda of the upcoming peace talks, but he also made it clear that he would use force if diplomacy

The rugged, mountainous Croatian terrain on the road to Karlovac

failed. "The world," Tudjman was quoted as saying, "should not deceive itself into thinking that Croatia will be prepared to postpone a settlement of this issue indefinitely."

In the end, no force was necessary. On November 12, the Croatian Serbs agreed during the Dayton peace talks to accept Croatian sovereignty over Eastern Slavonia after a transition period of one to two years. The transition period actually lasted for three years for Eastern Slavonia was not turned over to Croatian control until January 1998. During that interregnum, a transitional administration set up by the UN Security Council governed the territory. Some UN peacekeeping forces were already there from the previous UN mission to Croatia and others began arriving in January 1996. The United Nations hoped that, with a sufficiently long transition, the majority of Serbs living in the

area could become reconciled to living under Croatian control and remain. In that sense, the operation appears to have been a failure. Although Croatia requested that UN police remain in Eastern Slavonia after Croatia took official control on January 15, this did little to convince Serbs to remain. It now appears that at least 10,000 Serbs left the area in the month preceding the final transfer of authority. Most went to Serbia.

The Croatian Government must bear some of the responsibility for this outflow, for it made clear that Croats who had been expelled from the area during the war would be resettled with government assistance. At the same time, the 60,000 Serbs who had lived in other parts of Croatia before the war were refused permission to return to those areas. In addition, hard–line Croatian nationalists did their best to instill fear in the Serbs by dis-

# Croatia

Portion of the 16 lakes connected by 92 waterfalls in the Plitvice National Park

tributing pamphlets threatening to kill those Serbs who chose to remain.

The raising of the Croatian flag over the area does not, in fact, mean that the area has been reintegrated into Croatia. Thus far, for example, almost no Croats have returned to the area. The real test, therefore, will be in the future. As Croats begin to return in larger numbers, the likelihood of clashes between Serbs and Croats will increase. When that happens, and particularly if the government sides with the Croats, more Serbs will flee across the border into Serbia. In addition, increasing number of Serbs have begun applying for asylum in Western Europe. If the trend continues, it will eventually be mostly older Serbs that remain.

### President Tudjman and the Chances for Democracy in Croatia

President Tudjman took advantage of the euphoria that swept Croatia following the recovery of Krajina to call for national elections. These took place on October 29, 1995 and resulted in an absolute majority for Tudjman's party, the Croatian Democratic Union (HDZ). In a setback, however, a coalition of seven center–left opposition parties won a combined majority in the Zagreb regional assembly. Tudjman's authoritarianism now reasserted itself; personally intervening, he ordered the representatives of his HDZ to boycott the opening session of the regional assembly

in order to deny the opposition the quorum needed to organize the assembly. He then offered to allow the opposition a role in the regional government if it would permit the HDZ to name the mayor. The opposition refused and appealed the matter to the Constitutional Court. In the meanwhile, Tudjman rejected every candidate for mayor put forth by the opposition and the fourth candidate. Tudjman's own candidate for mayor, appointed in March, was thrown out of office by the city council in a vote of no–confidence.

This dispute over the Zagreb regional assembly highlights a problem which many in the West have had with the Tudjman regime—the recurrent lapses into authoritarianism and the occasional abuse of human rights. In March 1996, in fact, the Tudjman regime angered human rights activists even more when it sponsored two new laws whose effect would be to limit basic freedoms guaranteed in the constitution. Under the first law, anyone desiring to establish an organization to monitor the actions or to supplement the work of government ministries would need the permission of the government. The second law would make it a crime to insult "the dignity and authority of leading authorities."

Using these new laws, the government attempted to close down two of four remaining independent newspapers, the *Feral Tribune* and the *Novi List*, in May 1996. Partly in response, the Council of

Europe voted to postpose indefinitely Croatia's entry into that body. This led the Croatian Government to pass a new press law in October which set out certain press guarantees. Croatia was admitted to the Council of Europe shortly thereafter. Because President Tudjman underwent treatment for stomach cancer at the Walter Reed Army Hospital in Washington, D.C. in November 1996, there was a great deal of speculation in 1997 about a possible successor. Croatia has no Vice President; according to the terms of the constitution, the Speaker of the Parliament assumes the President's powers temporarily in case of the incapacity or death of the President. He then calls new elections 60 days after the President leaves office.

As for a permanent successor, the consensus was that Tudjman was most likely to be succeeded by a hard–line Croat nationalist, the dominant faction in Tudjman's ruling party, the Croatian Democratic Union. Opinion was divided about whether such a leader could win election on his own in Croatian national elections. As one European diplomat commented,

"Without Tudjman the ruling party could have a hard time holding on to power in free and fair elections. But we worry about the lack of commitment by many of the people around the President to democratic procedures."

It also appeared that the political opposition had been galvanized by anti–democratic governmental actions such as Tudjman's refusal to allow the opposition to name the mayor of Zagreb, even though they had won a majority on the City Council in the 1996 elections, the government's attempts to intimidate independent newspapers and radio, and the issue of Tudjman's failing health which, it was speculated, might prevent him from running for reelection. This turned out to be a misreading both of the state of Tudjman's health and of the electorate, for Tudjman stood for reelection as President in the June 1997 elections and won by a wide margin. His new mandate will allow him to serve until 2002 if he lives that long. Moreover, Tudjman's victory came after local elections held in April 1997, which resulted in Tudjman's party retaking control of the Zagreb City Council. Part of the reason for Tudjman's victory was the strong support he had among the 300,000 ethnic Croats of Bosnia–Herzegovina who voted in the elections. Another was that the opposition was unable to unite behind a single candidate. Although eight parties supported Vlado Gotovac, leader of the Liberals, the Social Democrats decided to run their own leader, Zdravko Tomac. The effect was to split the opposition vote and allow Tudjman to win in the first round of voting.

# Croatia

## Foreign Policy

Croatia likes to think of itself as a western nation and President Tudjman once argued to reporters that Croatia is not part of the Balkans. President Tudjman has not managed to bring Croatia into the European mainstream, however, partly because many Europeans are suspicious of his sometimes dictatorial ways and partly because of his occasional incursions into Byzantine diplomacy. On at least two occasions, for example, he held conversations with Belgrade on a possible division of the territories of the former Yugoslavia into a Greater Croatia and a Greater Serbia.

Tudjman's stance may have been based on his fear that the west's inaction was permitting Serbia to create a Greater Serbia on its own, leaving Croats squeezed into a small part of the western Balkans. That would explain why he intervened in Bosnia in 1993 in support of radical Bosnian Croat leaders who favored the partition of Bosnia between Croats and Serbs and later sent an army of up to 10,000 Croatian soldiers into Bosnia to assist the Bosnian Croats.

Tudjman then negotiated an agreement with Belgrade in January 1994 that was touted at the time as a first step toward normalizing relations. In actuality, it appears to have been a cynical agreement between Croatia and Serbia to cooperate in the division of Bosnia. But a carving of separate Serb and Croat territories out of Bosnia would have created a precedent for a partition of Croatia, as western diplomats carefully pointed out to President Tudjman. When the west produced its own ultimatum in February 1994 forcing the Serbs to withdraw their artillery from the environs of Sarajevo, Tudjman changed his position and threw his support behind a Croat–Muslim federation in Bosnia associated with Croatia.

President Tudjman has welcomed NATO's offer of a "Partnership for Peace" and would eventually like to establish ties with the European Union. Croatia received a $128 million World Bank loan in July 1994 and was in line for an IMF loan as well. The U.S. Government has signed several accords with Croatia dealing with trade, science and technology, education and nontechnical military assistance. It also furnished some funds for its democratization projects.

In spite of these things, however, Croatia's relations with the West have not been very good. The European Union has not yet negotiated any major accords, nor has any individual EU member. The problem is Croatia's human rights record. In the past, there had been numerous accusations of discrimination against Serbs living in Croatian–controlled parts of Croatia. Very few of those remain, but now President Tudjman stands accused of acting in an au-thoritarian manner toward the political opposition. The EU has called for more genuine political liberalization, particularly an end to extensive controls over the media, but it did agree to admit Croatia to the Council of Europe in October 1996.

## Nature of the Regime

The Republic of Croatia has a Presidential–Parliamentary system with the fulcrum of power resting with the President. President Tudjman was originally elected to that office by the Assembly in 1990, but he has been twice reelected since that time. Tudjman, born in August 1921, completely dominates Croatian political life. Since 1990, he has gone through numerous cabinet officers, including prime ministers. While there is a prime minister and a cabinet, critical decisions are made in the name of the National Security Council, which is presided over by the president.

Croatia has a multi–party system, but the *Croatian Democratic Union*, the party of President Tudjman, has dominated the Croatian Assembly since independence. It won a new majority in the October 1995 elections, called by Tudjman to take advantage of the national euphoria following the capture of Krajina a month earlier. Other parties include the *Social Liberal Party* and the *Croatian Peasant Party*. A seven–party coalition won control of the Za-greb regional assembly in October 1995, but Tudjman has systematically worked to frustrate its attempts to name the mayor.

## Culture

The Croatian people have a dominant Roman Catholic religious tradition which permeates and largely defines the culture. For example, it was Bishop Josip Juraj Strossmayer who carried out a reorganization of the University of Zagreb in 1874. A secular tradition tended to develop in the nineteenth century. One such cultural figure was Franjo Rachki, the Croatian historian.

Linguistically, Croatian does not differ greatly from Serbian, though borrowed–words in the vocabulary tend to come from German or Latin rather than from Greek or Turkish as in the case of Serbia. Another difference is that Croatian uses the Roman alphabet, while Serbian uses the Cyrillic alphabet. There are, of course, differences in pronunciation as well. As a result of the war, Serbs continue to live in significant numbers only in the area of eastern Slavonia.

## Economy

About half of Croatia's work force is engaged in industry, while the other half support themselves from agriculture. Croatia has a great deal of excellent farmland in the northeastern part of the coun-

**Pre–war beach scene near Dubrovnik**　　WORLD BANK

375

# Croatia

try, but farming is carried on throughout the republic. Corn is the chief grain crop, followed by wheat. Other commercial crops include plums, used in the production of *slivovitz* (a dry, usually colorless brandy), grapes, which are processed into wine and other brandies, sugar beets, flax, hemp, and fruits.

The raising of livestock also plays a significant role, with it about equally divided between cattle and sheep. Pigs and poultry are also important farm products. Croatia still has significant forest areas, so timber products provide employment to many rural inhabitants.

Manufacturing is better developed in Croatia than in any of the other republics. Most of this is light industry which concentrates on manufacturing goods for sale to consumers, though Croatia also produces extractive products such as petroleum, coal, and bauxite. Fishing is also a major industry for people along the Dalmatian coast. Perhaps the greatest money–maker of all used to be tourism, particularly along the Dalmatian coast, famous for its many resorts.

The war left a stagnant economy and thousands of refugees, particularly in the area of Zagreb. The demobilization that began with the end of the war also contributed to an already massive unemploy-ment. Unemployment still stood at about 15 percent at the end of 1997, but Croatia's economy is beginning to look much better in most other areas. The economy grew at a 4.2 percent rate in 1996 and continued to grow at about a 4 percent rate in 1997. A major factor has been the return of tourism as a major factor in the economy after the ending of the war. Tourist arrivals in the summer of 1997 were up by 34 percent over 1996. Inflation in 1997 was also a low 3.5 percent. One negative factor was the trade deficit, which grew from $3.3 billion in 1996 to $4.4 billion in 1997.

The government has been pursuing a policy of privatization for a number of years, but in many cases this has led to companies passing into the hands of enterprise managers or political cronies of the administration. Privatization did lead to a major bank restructuring, however, and most outside observers praise this outcome.

## The Future

Croatia has been at peace since the latter part of 1995 and the country has started to slowly recover economically. Tourism, a major earner of hard currency for the country, began to come back in 1996 but really flourished in 1997. As a result, the economy grew by 4 percent in 1997. In addition, Croatia got back Eastern Slavonia in January 1998, so the country is again reunited. That is the good news.

The bad news is that President Tudjman, whose democratic credentials were always suspect, has shown an authoritarian streak in the last couple years that bodes ill for the development of democracy in Croatia. Further, it is unlikely that Croatia will be welcome as a part of Europe until it does develop democratic credentials. Whether President Tudjman doesn't realize this or just doesn't care is the big question at the moment. However, Tudjman, who was reelected President in June 1997, will remain in charge until 2002, if he lives that long. Some people had hoped that he might be willing to retire after he had achieved his goal of a national, independent Croatia, but that no longer appears to be a possibility.

Moreover, President Tudjman has not yet come to terms with the idea of an independent Bosnia. Ethnic Croats living in Bosnia have been given Croatian citizenship and are permitted to vote in Croatian elections. It even appears that President Tudjman continues to harbor designs on the Herzegovina part of Bosnia. None of this gives much hope for political stability in the Balkans in the near future.

**The Opera House, Zagreb**

The Renaissance fountain called *Mala Cesma* and the baroque church of St. Blaise (1715) in Dubrovnik.

# The Republic of Bosnia–Herzegovina

(pronounced Hairs–eh–govena)

**A Bosnian Serb soldier holds a refugee child**

**Area:** 19,696 square miles (51,129 sq. km.); almost 3/4 of the territory is under Bosnian Serb control, militarily supported by Serbia.

**Population:** 4,364,574 (April 1991 census).

**Capital City:** Sarajevo (450,000).

**Ethnic Background:** South Slavic. Moslem (44%), Serb (33%), Croat (17%).

**Climate:** Continental in the north; Mediterranean in the southwest.

**Neighboring Countries:** Serbia, SFRY (east); Montenegro, SFRY (southeast); Croatia (west and north).

**Official Language:** Serbo–Croatian.

**Other Principal Tongues:** Albanian.

**Principal Religions:** Islam, Serbian Orthodox, Roman Catholicism.

**Chief Commercial Products:** Grains, potatoes, plums, livestock, timber, coal, iron ore, bauxite, cement, cotton fabrics, cars.

**Currency:** The Muslim, Croat and Serb sections all have their individual currencies. In Croatian–dominated areas, it is the Croatian *kuna*; in Muslim areas, it is the Bosnian *dinar*; and in Serb–controlled areas, it is the Yugoslavian *dinar*. In most areas, however, either the *Deutsche Mark* or the U.S. dollar tends to be the currency of choice.

**Former Political Status:** Constituent republic of SFRY.

**Chief of State:** Three–member presidency consisting of Alija Izetbegovic (Muslim) and Kresimir Zubak (Croat), elected from the Muslim–Croat Federation, plus Momcilo Krajisnik (Serb), representing the Bosnian Serb entity. Izetbegovic (pronounced Ease–*et*–beh*go*–vich) occupies the position of Chair, having won the largest amount of votes in the September 1996 elections.

**Head of Government:** Haris Silajdzic (Muslim) and Boro Bosic (Serb), Co–Chairmen of the Council of Ministers (appointed January 1997).

**National Flag:** A tricolor, white, blue, and yellow, with no national symbols. The design was selected in February 1998 by Carlos Westendorp, the High Representative of the international community, after the joint legislature was unable to agree on a common flag.

## The Land

The Republic of Bosnia–Herzegovina is the independent successor state to the Socialist Republic of Bosnia–Herzegovina which was until 1991 part of the Socialist Federal Republic of Yugoslavia. The republic is roughly triangular. It also has a tiny, 13 mile section of coastline on the Adriatic Sea, but no harbor. It has an area of 19,696 square miles (51,129 sq. km.), almost all of which is mountainous. Herzegovina, the name which applies to the southern part of the republic, is derived from *Herzog*, a Germanic title meaning duke taken by a local ruler in the fifteenth century. The name Bosnia is derived from the Bosna River, a tributary of the Sava River. The course of the 168–mile long river is almost entirely within the republic. It begins in Herzegovina in the south and then flows northeastward through Bosnia and enters the Sava River at the border. The Sava River, in turn, forms the western border with Croatia.

A second river, the Drina, forms a large part of the border with Serbia. The Drina is also a tributary of the Sava. Two further rivers flow from south to north across the republic, the Vrbas to the west of the Bosna and the Una in the extreme northwest part of the republic. The source of all of these rivers is the mountain chain known as the Dinarian Alps, which runs in a northwest–southeastern direction across the western part of the republic.

Individual peaks soar to over 7,500 feet, though wide valleys running in the same direction separate the ridges. The center of the republic is a piedmont region with an average height of 1500 feet, while the Sava and Drina River valleys produce lowlands in the east. About half the land of the republic is arable, with most of the remainder covered by forests of pine, beech and oak. The exception is the area of Herzegovina in the south. A native proverb says that "Bosnia begins with the forest, Herzegovina with the rock." The mountains of Herzegovina are of gray Karst limestone, filled with crevices, sinkholes and pits, and they overwhelm the viewer with their barren desolation. Most of this area has very little population. It is only possible to live in the fertile river valleys that cut through the mountains and in some upland hollows where there is arable soil. Bosnia's weather is generally mild with cold winters. In Herzegovina, on the other hand, summers are often oppressively hot.

## The People

The population of the Republic of Bosnia–Herzegovina is just under 4.4 million and it is the most diverse of the republics of the old Yugoslav Federation. No single group is in a majority, but Moslems have been the largest grouping with 44% percent of the population. Serbs account for 33% percent of the population, while Croats constitute a further 17% percent. The basis of the three "nations" of Bosnia–Herzegovina is religion, not language. The Moslems of Bosnia–Herzegovina are a Slavic people who converted to Islam and the language they speak is Serbo–Croatian. Serbs are adherents of the Serbian Orthodox Church, while Croats are Roman Catholics.

## History

Although the present–day area of Bosnia–Herzegovina was settled by Slavic–speaking peoples as early as the seventh century, it first emerged as a separate political entity toward the end of the twelfth century when a nobleman by the name of Kulin managed to gain control of most of the lands along the Bosna River, which became known as the Ban of Bosnia. Kulin's principality did not last long, but one of the things he did was to convert to Bogomilism and make it the state religion.

Bogomilism had originated two centuries earlier, further to the east in Bulgaria, but by the twelfth century it had become well established in Bosnia. Its distinguishing characteristic was it taught that the world was governed by two principles, good and evil, the first spiritual and the second material. The physical world, being material, is the realm of the devil. This Manichaean dualism was condemned as heretical by both the Roman Catholic and Greek Orthodox churches, so Bogomils found themselves rejected by both the west and the east.

Early in the thirteenth century, the Roman Catholic Church dispatched a papal legate to the area to institute a purge of the local clergy. Somewhat later, Dominican missionaries were sent in to fight the heresy. They came with military might provided by the Hungarian monarchy. These military forces brought Bosnia under Hungarian control. In 1299, The Hungarian king granted Bosnia as a fief to a Croatian aristocrat by the name of Paul Subic. After he took over, Subic brought in Franciscan missionaries to help stamp out the Bogomils.

Subic passed the principality on to his son, Mladen, but the latter was overthrown by the local nobility in 1322. He was replaced as *Ban* by Stephen Kotromanic, a native Bosnian. Kotromanic was succeeded by his nephew, Stephen Tvrtko, who expanded the principality greatly during his lifetime, annexing part of Dalmatia to the west and part of the area of modern–day Montenegro to the south. Tvrtko eventually took the title "Stephen I, King of Serbia, Bosnia, Dalmatia, Croatia, and the Primorje."

Tvrtko was succeeded by his younger brother, who was crowned as Stephen II in 1391. By the time of his death seven years later, the Turks had launched an invasion of Bosnia and the kingdom began to disintegrate. The kingdom soon broke down into several principalities, most of them paying a yearly tribute to the Turks. The ruler of one of these principalities opted to become a vassal of the Holy Roman Emperor instead, however, and for this had bestowed on him the title of *Herzog* (duke) of St. Sava. Over time, this title became attached to the land instead of the ruler, and in its modern form is Herzegovina.

After the fall of Constantinople in 1453, the Turks decided to take control of the Balkan Peninsula directly. The new invasion of Bosnia began in 1460. Some parts tried to hold out against the Turks, but many of the Bogomil leaders apparently saw the Moslem Turks as being preferable to the Hungarian Roman Catholics, still trying to stamp out Bogomilism, and allied themselves with the Turks. Afterwards, most of these Bogomils converted to Islam.

These new converts adopted the dress, titles, and etiquette of the Turkish court, while retaining their lands, their language, and most of their old customs. They also became the local military caste, which gave them a rank just below that the Turkish governor. They remained loyal to the Ottoman Empire and some of them even rose to the highest offices in the empire. One such was Ali Pasha, who became grand vizier in 1570. His successor, Mahomet Beg Sokolovic, also came from Bosnia. Meanwhile, most of the peasants remained Orthodox Christians.

Little changed until the seventeenth century, when the Austrian Empire, then still known as the Holy Roman Empire, began to push down into the Balkans. Prince Eugene of Savoy burned Sarajevo in 1697. Part of the sea coast area of Herzegovina plus a part of Bosnia that bordered on the Sava River passed to Austria in 1718. Turkey took the Bosnian territory back in 1739, but it passed back under Austrian control 1791.

In the first half of the nineteenth century, an estrangement began to grow between the Moslem aristocrats of Bosnia and the Ottoman government, primarily over the issue of traditional privileges. There were several revolts between 1820 and 1850 that led the regime to strip the aristocracy of most of its privileges. The peasantry were also growing dissatisfied as a result of increasing tax obligations and this led to other revolts.

Things came to a head in July 1875 when a revolt among Christian peasants soon spread throughout the country and turned into a war specifically against Turks. The revolt next spread to Herzegovina, then to Bulgaria. Serbia and Montenegro then declared war against the Ottoman Empire in July 1876. Russia entered the war in July 1877.

Russia and Austria–Hungary had been rivals in the Balkans throughout the nineteenth century, so Alexander II, the Russian Tsar, opened negotiations with the Austro–Hungarian Government immediately after Serbia entered the war against Turkey. The agreement the two sides signed at Reichstadt stipulated among other things that Austria–Hungary would receive territorial concessions in case of a change in the *status quo* in the Balkans.

After Russia had won its war against Turkey, the Austro–Hungarian regime was outraged when it learned of the terms of the treaty. The creation of a large Bulgarian state clearly constituted a change in the *status quo*, but the treaty made no mention of corresponding territorial concessions to Austria–Hungary. It then threatened Russia with war and Bismarck, the German Chancellor, had to step in to preserve the peace. He suggested a congress of European nations to meet at Berlin. A Congress, among other things, awarded Austria–Hungary administrative control of Bosnia–Herzegovina. The territory was not formally annexed at this time because the Austro–Hungarian Prime Minister, a Hungarian, did not want any more Slavs in the empire. This was a technicality, however. From this moment onward, Bosnia–Herzegovina became a part of the Austro–Hungarian Empire. And in 1908, after a successful revolt of the Young Turks against the Ottoman Empire, Austria–Hungary annexed Bosnia–Herzegovina formally.

Ten years later, the Austro–Hungarian Empire was in collapse as a result of its defeat in World War I. The Serbs, with Allied blessing, claimed all of the South Slavic lands for a new Kingdom of Serbs, Croats and Slovenes, which was proclaimed on December 4, 1918. In 1929, this new state changed its name to Yugoslavia. The area of Bosnia–Herzegovina was submerged within this centralized state of South Slavs. Bosnia–Herzegovina was at this time both poor and rural, with no strong local political leaders. Serbs tended to look to Serbia, while Croats looked to Croatian leaders outside of Bosnia.

Bosnia did produce one outstanding leader during this time, Josef Broz, better known by his revolutionary *nom de guerre*, Tito. But he was head of the *Communist Party of Yugoslavia*, and had to work underground, since the party was illegal during the interwar period. After World War II, however, Tito became the ruler of the reconstituted Yugoslavia and he saw to it that Bosnia–Herzegovina became one of the six constituent republics of the new state.

The people of the republic were satisfied to be part of the Socialist Federal Republic of Yugoslavia, even though the republic remained primarily rural where even today approximately two thirds of the people make their living from agriculture. It did develop its own republic leadership, however, and when things began falling apart in the late 1980s, the political leadership of Bosnia–Herzegovina had its own ideas about what should be done.

The political discussions remained within the *League of Communists of Bosnia–Herzegovina*—the monopoly party—until 1990, when new elections were set to occur. When the party authorized the formation of additional political parties, however, the old system collapsed. The November 1990 elections were won by three new parties, the Moslem *Party of*

# Bosnia–Herzegovina

Democratic Action, which gained 86 assembly seats, the Serbian Democratic Party, which won 70 seats, and the Croat Democratic Union, which got 45 seats. These three political parties subsequently formed a coalition and in December they elected Alija Izetbegovic, leader of the Party of Democratic Action, as President of the republic.

The political leadership of Bosnia–Herzegovina mainly stood aside as the quarrel between the Serbs on one side and the Croats and Slovenes on the other grew more heated in 1990–91. They favored continuation of a united Yugoslavia, but also wanted economic reforms, repudiation of the communist leaders, and a more decentralized political structure. When Croatia and Slovenia declared their independence on June 25, 1991, the political leaders of Bosnia–Herzegovina once again urged calm on both sides, but to no avail. After the Serbs and Yugoslav People's Army began their war against Croatia, however, the Bosnian leadership began to prepare for the break–up of the country. They wanted a united Yugoslavia, but were unwilling to remain in a truncated Yugoslavia—dominated by Serbia.

Bosnian representatives stopped participating in the institutions of the Yugoslav Federal Government on October 3, 1991 after Serbian and Montenegrin leaders pulled off a coup, and took control of the Yugoslav Presidency. On December 20, the Bosnian Government voted to ask the EC for recognition as an independent state. The Government split on the issue, with the Moslems and Croats voting for independence and the Serbs insisting that Bosnia–Herzegovina ought to remain part of the Federal State of Yugoslavia. The Serbs then threatened to form their own "Serbian Republic of Bosnia–Herzegovina" encompassing those territories where Serbs are in a majority.

On March 18, 1992 the leaders of the three communities agreed in principle to restructure the state, creating "three constituent units, based on national principles and taking into account economic, geographic and other criteria."

The effect would have been to create three autonomous units within the governmental structure, one for Moslems, one for Croats and one for Serbs. Control in each municipality would have been by that national group which was in a "absolute or relative majority." The agreement would have been extremely difficult to implement, since the three communities have always lived side by side and many families are mixed. Its main value, therefore, appeared to be more as a way to forestall a civil war rather than as a practical blueprint.

In early April, the European Community and the United States recognized the independence of Bosnia–Herzegovina. Although gratifying in the abstract, it had a negative side for the Serbian Democratic Party then withdrew from the coalition, its two Serbian members of the Presidency resigned, and Serb leaders announced the formation of a "Serbian Republic of Bosnia–Herzegovina" which intended to remain part of Yugoslavia. The Yugoslav Army was also still statioined in Bosnia at that time. It announced that it would withdraw, moving its forces to Serbia and Montenegro. In fact, it divided is forces, leaving in Bosnia all those who had any connection with Bosnia or other non–Serb states. These forces, provided with tanks, artillery and all the equipment needed to fight a modern war, became the army of the Bosnian Serbs.

With a UN arms embargo making it impossible for the Bosnian government to obtain any significamt weaponry, Bosnia found itself completely outclassed. Within three months, the Bosnian Serbs controlled 70% if the Bosnian territory (with the Bosnian Croats, who were receiving military assistance from Croatia controlling most of the rest); they surrounded the capital, Sarajevo, placing that city under siege. Accompanied by periodic diplomatic discussion in Geneva, the Serbs continued their shelling. Meanwhile, the west continued its arms embargo against Bosnia.

UN negotiators, convinced that Bosnia had lost the war, tried to get the leadership to agree to a partition which would have left the Serbs in control of half of the territory. But the Bosnian government refused to sign and the siege went on. Convinced that the west intended to allow Serbia to succeed in creating a "Greater Serbia," the Bosnian Croats, under encouragement from the Croation government, switched sides. Serbs, attempted to enlarge the area of Bosnia they controlled at the expense of the Bosnian government.

A change came in February 1994 when western public opinion, appalled by a particularly atrocious shelling of Sarajevo which killed 66 people and injured 200 others, caused western governments to take action. This produced a NATO ultimatum that the Serbs remove their heavy artillery pieces from a 12.5 mile zone around Sarajevo. The Serbs refused, whereupon the UN proposed a compromise: the Serb guns could remain where they were and the UN Protection Force (UNPROFOR) would dispatch peacekeepers to these locations, in theory to assure that the Serbs did not resume their bombardment of Sarajevo.

The Serbs agreed to accept UN peacekeepers at their artillery sites. Time would prove that this was a mistake, for the compromise placed the UN peacekeepers in a situation where they could become hostages, should a new war of wills erupt between the UN and the Serbs. The compromise did temporarily end the shelling, however, and an overland route to Sarajevo closed for two years was also reopened at this time. Sarajevo began to return to something approaching normality.

The NATO ultimatum to the Serbs paid yet another dividend for, in this new atmosphere, the Bosnian Croats were persuaded that they could hold more of Bosnia by joining a U.S.–sponsored Bosnian–Croat federation than by continuing on their own. A separate federation government was subsequently set up, and has continued to exist, but it must be added that Muslim–Croat cooperation has remained a sometime thing. The current president of the federation is Kresimir Zubak, a Bosnian Croat.

Yet these two successes, if they be successes, did not bring an end to the war. Forced to stop their artillery barrages of Sarajevo, the Serbs merely intensified their attacks against other besieged Bosnian Government enclaves, including the towns of Tuzla and Gorazde. The UN protested these new attacks, but the Serbs continued with the artillery barrages until NATO once again used force, shooting down four Serbian jets over Bosnia. These various actions reduced the level of fighting temporarily, though it did not really change the overall situation. Bosnian Serbs still controlled 70% of Bosnia and continued their pressure on the rest. There may have been a slight weakening in the general Bosnian Serb position over the next several months, however, as the Bosnian Government made use of the period of comparative quiet to build up its forces.

Meanwhile, the United Nations released a new peace plan in July 1994 which again proposed a division of the country giving the Bosnian Serbs 49% of Bosnia. President Milosevic of Serbia, reversing his earlier stance, endorsed the new peace plan, then broke publicly with the Bosnian Serb leadership and "sealed" the border between Serbia and Bosnia when they rejected it. He also agreed to allow the placement of 135 civilian monitors along the 370–mile border to verify that aid to the Bosnian Serbs had stopped. Although almost no one believes that Serbia really ended all support for the Bosnian Serbs at this time, the amount of assistance did diminish.

Reacting to this additional pressure, the Bosnian Serbs attempted to sabotage the peace plan by launching attacks on the UNPROFOR peacekeepers. By firing on planes attempting to land at Sarajevo airport, they managed to shut down the UN food airlift and end all commercial flights into Sarajevo. The first UN reaction was to do nothing, presumably because of a fear that any action against the Bosnian Serbs would bring Serbia formally back into the war. In fact, Sir Michael Rose, commander of UNPROFOR in Bosnia, threatened to call in air strikes against Bosnian Government forces at the beginning of August after the Bosnian army tried to drive back Bosnian Serb forces just north of the Sarajevo.

A disagreement between the U.S. and other members of the "Contact Group" also broke out in August when the U.S. Government began urging an end to the military embargo against the Bosnian Government. Great Britain, in particular, objected, but France was opposed as well. The U.S. Government stopped enforcing the embargo in November after the UN General Assembly adopted a resolution urging the Security Council to lift the arms embargo on Bosnia. This was the second such General Assembly resolution, an earlier one having been passed in 1993. Since France and Great Britain, both permanent members of the Security Council with the power of veto, opposed lifting the embargo, however, no action was taken.

In October 1994, the Bosnian army launched an attack against the Bihac pocket in northwestern Bosnia. The Bosnians managed to overrun the area, but could not hold it after a counter–attack by Serbs from across the border in Croatia. At the end of December, ex–President Jimmy Carter mediated a 4–month "cessation of hostilities" between the Bosnian Serbs and the Bosnian Government. The truce held for a while, but was mainly used by both sides to strengthen their forces. It came to an end at the beginning of April when the Bosnian Government struck pre–emptively in an attempt to disrupt Bosnian Serb communications facilities.

**President Alija Izetbegovic**

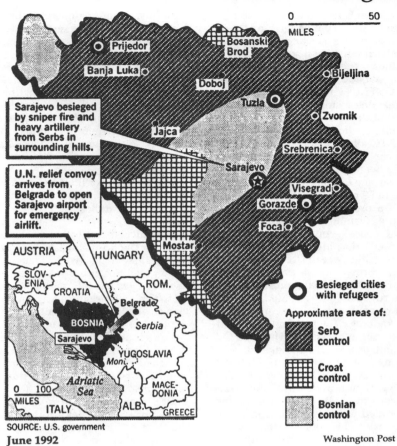

Sarajevo besieged by sniper fire and heavy artillery from Serbs in surrounding hills.

U.N. relief convoy arrives from Belgrade to open Sarajevo airport for emergency airlift.

Besieged cities with refugees

Approximate areas of:

Serb control

Croat control

Bosnian control

SOURCE: U.S. government

**June 1992**

Washington Post

**Agreed Zones of Control**
(Dayton Accord, December 1995)

Muslims / Croats — Muslim-Croat Federation

Serbs

Sector dividing lines

Cease-fire line

# Bosnia–Herzegovina

The Bosnian Serb response was to seize their heavy artillery pieces from UN–supervised storage areas and begin a new artillery barrage on Sarajevo. They also renewed their siege of the city, cutting it off from the outside world. General Rupert Smith, UNPROFOR commander in Bosnia, demanded a stop to the artillery barrage and a lifting of the siege. When the Bosnian Serbs did not respond, he called for a NATO air strike on an ammunition dump near Pale, the Bosnian Serb "capital." The Bosnian Serbs then launched a mortar barrage on the city of Tuzla which resulted in 70 civilian deaths. When General Smith ordered a second NATO air strike, the Bosnian Serbs took 350 UNPROFOR peacekeepers hostage. It was now the UN that blinked. General Bernard Janvier, the overall UN military commander in former Yugoslavia, and Yasushi Akashi, the UN's special representative in former Yugoslavia, overruled General Smith's recommendation to continue the NATO bombings, then took away his authority to call in air strikes. UNPROFOR, they announced, would not take sides.

Anxious to win release of the UNPROFOR hostages, the UN agreed to hand back several hundred tanks, howitzers and mortars to the Bosnian Serbs in June. The so–called weapons collection points ceased to exist. This got rid of the UN hostage situation, but the Serbs, with their heavy weapons back, began shelling Sarajevo again, killing nine civilians lining up for water on June 24. Meanwhile, the UN "safe–haven" cities of Zepa, Srebrenica and Gorazde were once more cut off by surrounding Serb forces and being slowly starved out. Even UN peacekeeper forces stationed in these cities could not be resupplied.

The governments of France and Great Britain, considering the situation on the ground in Bosnia to be unacceptable, now decided to up the ante. Recognizing that the lightly–armed UN peacekeeper force was incapable of defending itself, they decided to create a heavily–armed 12,500–man rapid reaction force separate from the UNPROFOR. These troops began arriving in Bosnia in July but the new force came too late to prevent the fall of Srebenica on July 11, then Zepa on July 22.

Women, children, and older men subsequently made their way from the fallen enclaves to Bosnian Government–controlled areas, but as many as 4,000 Bosnian men remained missing. Later, it would become clear that most of these men had been shot, their bodies dumped into mass graves, shortly after being taken prisoner by General Mladic's forces. General Mladic appears to bear a major responsibility for these deaths, since he was in charge of the sieges of both Srebenica and Zepa and personally toured Zepa on July 27.

In July, an international tribunal in The Hague indicted General Mladic and Radovan Karadzic as war criminals. The indictments were based, not on events in the fallen enclaves but on earlier actions of these two Bosnian Serb leaders. Yet the Bosnian Serb leaders, ignoring the indictments, appeared convinced that nothing could stop them. That same week, the weekly newspaper *Svet* published an interview with General Ratho Mladic in which he said,

> "By autumn we'll take Gorazde, Bihac and in the end Sarajevo, and we'll finish the war in Bosnia."

This turned out to be the high water mark for the Bosnian Serbs, however. The events associated with Srebenica and Zepa plus the continued shelling of Sarajevo appalled the international community, which now began calling for some decisive action. On August 30, NATO demanded that the Bosnian Serbs pull back their artillery from around Sarajevo. When General Mladic refused, NATO launched air strikes against Bosnian Serb command posts, ammunition dumps and radar sites. NATO continued its bombing until September 2, then gave the Bosnian Serbs until September 4 to begin removing their artillery. General Mladic again refused, whereupon the air strikes were resumed on September 6. The bombing continued for another two weeks before the Bosnia Serbs relented and began removing their heavy weapons from the vicinity of Sarajevo. Meanwhile, at least three brigades of Croatian army troops entered Bosnia in early September. Operating in conjunction with Bosnian Croat forces plus forces of the Bosnian army, they began an offensive that gradually reduced the amount of land held by Bosnian Serbs from 70% to about 50%.

Meanwhile, things were beginning to happen on the diplomatic front. The first breakthrough occurred on August 29 when Karadzic agreed that President Milosevic of Serbia was empowered to negotiate on behalf of the Bosnian Serbs. Next, the U. S. Government invited the foreign ministers of Serbia, Bosnia and Croatia to a meeting in Geneva and here, on September 8, the three foreign ministers signed off on a statement of principles for peace in Bosnia. This, in turn, paved the way for the Dayton peace talks, which resulted in a peace accord signed by the presidents of the three republics on November 21, 1995.

The agreement, which went into effect after being formally signed by the three presidents in Paris in mid–December, provided for the division of Bosnia between a Bosnian Serb entity and a Bosnian–Croat federation. The two sub entities were to have their own presidents and their own

legislatures, but there would still be a central government with a group presidency, a two–house legislature, a court and a central bank.

The agreement also called for a NATO force of 60,000 members to keep the peace and that force began arriving toward the end of December. The various opposing forces then withdrew to agreed positions and the situation began to stabilize. It was only a truce, not a reconciliation, however. When the Serb–occupied suburbs of Sarajevo were turned over to Bosnian Government control in March, almost all Serbs fled—but not before dismantling and taking along whatever was transportable and burning or dynamiting anything that remained, including houses, public buildings and factories.

This attitude persisted during the run up to internationally monitored elections that took place on September 14, 1996. The Dayton Accords had specified that individuals were to be permitted to return to their previous place of residence to vote. In fact, those—mostly Muslims—who tried to return to places where they had previously resided were turned back from both the Serb and Croat controlled areas. The elections also reflected this division, with people in each area permitted to vote only for candidates representing the dominant national grouping.

As it turned out, the same men whose followers had fought a bitter four–year war won the open positions on the three–person collective presidency. Thus the new collective presidency consists of Alija Izetbegovic, leader of the Muslim *Party of Democratic Action*; Kresimir Zubak, leader of the *Croat Democratic Community*; and Momcilo Krajisnik, head of the *Serbian Democratic Party*.

Creating the new national political institutions envisioned by the treaty has proved to be extremely challenging, and the Bosnian–Croat Federation, which is supposed to exercise primary governmental authority over 51% of the territory, appears to be little more than a fiction as well. In connection with this, the Croatian Republic of Herzeg–Bosna, supposedly dissolved into the Muslim–Croat Federation, is still very much alive. The people of Herzeg–Bosna have been effectively incorporated into the Croatian Republic, with Croatian flags, money, stamps, and vehicle license tags in use, and even a telephone area code tied to Croatia instead of Bosnia.

As for the newly created all–Bosnian institutions, the collective presidency held its first meeting on September 30, but the session had to be held in a hotel at the edge of Sarajevo because Krajisnik refused to meet in a government building downtown, citing security concerns. Krajisnik then did not show up to take a formal oath of office in October because he was unwilling to swear allegiance to a united

# Ljiljan

*nacionalni sedmični list*

SARAJEVO - LJUBLJANA. OD 24. DO 31. MAJA 1995. BROJ 123. GODINA IV. IZLAZI SRIJEDOM

CIJENA 100 BHD 7 K 160 SIT 3,90 DEM 29 ATS 4 CHF 3,5 AUD 80 FLUX 17,50 DKR 22 SKR 50000 TL 15 FRF 80 BFR 4,75 HFL 22,50 NKR 80 DEN

## Sarajevsko bojište
### RUSKI UNPROFORCI TRANSPORTERIMA IZVLAČILI POGINULE ČETNIKE

## Tuzlansko bojište
### KO POKUŠAVA UBITI GENERALA DELIĆA

### IMA JEDNA MORA S ONE STRANE KORIDORA

### Bender neće Republiku, a hoće hrvatsko Sarajevo

# BRITANSKI "PLAVCI" ĆE SE POVUĆI PREKO TUZLANSKOG AERODROMA

### Jozef Školč, predsjednik Parlamenta Slovenije
### RAT U BOSNI NIJE POČEO IZNUTRA I SAMO SE FORMALNO VODI SA PALA

### Ko sprječava povratak bosanskih prognanika iz Makedonije

### Ljiljan prvi prekida šutnju o stradanju Bošnjaka u Jasenovcu i Bleiburgu

The daily Sarajevo newspaper *Ljiljan* announces the withdrawal of British UN troops from the country via Tuzla airport

# Bosnia–Herzegovina

**A column of Bosnian policemen, Sarajevo.** AP/Wide World Photo

Bosnia. The newly elected national legislature, scheduled to meet for its first session in October, was postponed for the same reason. The legislature finally met in January 1997, after it was agreed to dispense with the oath. A new national government was then formed, consisting of a Council of Ministers presided over by co–chairs, Boro Bosic, representing the Serbs, and Haris Silajdzic, a Muslim. But the international community has found that, although it can create joint institutions, it cannot force cooperation among the still–quarreling factions, even with the offer of large amounts of foreign assistance. As a result, the six nations that oversee the Bosnian peace effort—the United States, France, Germany, Italy, Great Britain, and Russia—decided in December 1997 to authorize Carlos Westendorp, the High Representative, to make decisions on behalf of Bosnia whenever the factionized Bosnian Government was unable to do so. Since January 1998, therefore, Carlos Westendorp has stepped in to resolve issues such as media licensing, housing and tariff laws. When the joint legislature found itself deadlocked on issues such as common license plates, common passports, a common currency, a common flag, and a national emblem, Westendorp's office made the selections for the Bosnians.

And whenever Bosnian elected officials have attempted to obstruct the Dayton peace accords, Westendorp's office has not hesitated to dismiss them. There thus exists a sort of protectorate over Bosnia at the moment whose goal is to create a situation where the separatism and particularism will be harder and harder to maintain.

This will be an extremely difficult task, however. For example, during local elections that took place in September 1997, displaced persons were permitted to vote either where they were currently living or in the district from which they came. Many chose to cast their ballots in their home district and, as a result, each ethnic group managed to elect representatives to local councils in towns from which their group had been ethnically cleansed during the war. They have not been permitted to return, however, and only 45 out of 136 municipalities have respected the results of the vote.

The current goal, therefore, is to create the circumstances which will make it possible for some of the three million displaced persons and refugees to return to their former homes, as stipulated in the Dayton Accords. As a start, top officials in the Muslim and Croat federation agreed in December 1997 to allow 120,000 refugees to return to 156 villages in central

Bosnia under the control of the other nationality. This will be extremely difficult to accomplish, however, since opposition to a return of refugees exists everywhere at the local level.

There has been one hopeful development in the Bosnian Serb Republic in the past several months. Biljana Plavsic, who was elected president of Bosnian Serbia in 1996 after Radovan Karadzic was ruled ineligible for that office by international authorities, broke with the Serb hard–liners in the summer of 1997 after she had accused Karadzic and his allies of massive corruption. Expelled from the Serbian Democratic Party, she formed her own political party, the Serbian People's Union, then dissolved the Serb parliament and set new elections for October 1997. The hard–liners then attempted a coup against her government by seizing six police stations in Banja Luka. They were foiled when NATO forces intervened, took charge of the police stations, and turned them over to Plavsic supporters. From that time onward, Plavsic supporters controlled the northern part of Bosnian Serbia, with Banja Luka as its capital, while hard–liners continued to control the southern half, with Pale as its capital.

The parliamentary elections, which actually took place on November 22–23, were indecisive. The Karadzic–dominated Serbian Democratic Party lost its majority, dropping from 45 seats in the previous parliament to 24 seats in the current one. An ally, the Serbian Radical Party, won another 15 seats, but this still left the hard–liners 5 seats short of a majority. Plavsic's Serbian People's Union won 15 seats, while an ally won an additional two seats. Moslem and Croatian parties won 18 seats, while the remaining 9 seats were taken by the Socialists, a branch of President Milosevic's Serbian party of the same name.

The new parliament convened on December 27. Plavsic had the support of the Socialists, which gave her 26 seats, not enough to form a government. The stalemate was broken on January 17 when Muslim and Croatian deputies threw their support to Milorad Dodik, Plavsic's nominee for Prime Minister. Prime Minister Dodik promised the next day to respect the Dayton Accords and to cooperate with the international community. He also announced that the capital would be moved from Pale to Banja Luka. Since Dodik was a moderate who stood out by advocating a truce and negotiations during the war, international officials view his election as a hopeful sign. To indicate its support, the European Union approved a $6.5 million aid package at the end of January and an additional $8.5 in February. The World Bank signed an agreement with President Plavsic in January extending a $17 million credit to Bosnian Serbia, then agreed to a

$20 million loan in February during talks with Prime Minister Dodik during his visit to Washington in February 1998. Dodik also received a promise of up to $60 million in U.S. aid during the visit.

Hard–line Serbs first announced that they would not recognize any of the new government's decisions and talked about creating a separate parliament, but they soon backed down. Momcilo Krajisnik, the Serbian member of the Bosnian joint presidency and a leader of the Serbian Democratic Party, issued a statement on February 7 pledging to work with Prime Minister Dodik and President Plavsic "in the interests of the Bosnian Serb Republic."

### Nature of the Regime

The Government of Bosnia–Herzegovina was essentially remade as a part of the Dayton Accords, which called for the creation of a new Bosnian Government composed of two entities, a Bosnian–Croat Federation and a Republic of the Serbs. These two entities were to divide the territory of Bosnia on a 51%/49% basis and, together, they were supposed to elect a Bosnian Government with its own group presidency and two–house legislature. This new Bosnian Government was also given its own court and central bank.

Elections aimed at creating this new national entity, as well as separate elections in the three enclaves, took place on September 14, 1996 under the supervision of the Organization for Security and Cooperation in Europe (OSCE). The result was that the previous leadership was confirmed in all three enclaves. In addition, the respective Muslim, Serb and Croat leaders were elected to the new three–person presidency; meanwhile, their political parties took control of the new Bosnian legislature.

Although the OSCE managed to organize the elections and carry them out successfully, the new Bosnian Government is not given any great chance for success. The hatreds engendered by 3 1/2 years of war, plus the separatist ideologies of both the Serb and Croat leaders, will continue to make cooperation between Muslims, Serbs, and Croats difficult at best.

To make things worse, the Muslim–Croat Federation is still largely a fiction with power still concentrated in the two separate Croat and Muslim entities. In particular, Herzog–Bosna, the Croatian half of the federation—which according to the terms of the Dayton peace agreement was supposed to have been disbanded in January 1996—is still very much in existence, and operates in nearly every respect as an integral part of the Republic of Croatia. Croatian currency, stamps, uniforms, telephone area codes rates, and even customs levies are used throughout Herzog–Bosna.

Its connections with the other half of the so–called federation are minimal.

The three–member presidency formally took office in October but Momcilo Krajisnik, the Serbian member, boycotted the ceremony because he was unwilling to take an oath of allegiance to Bosnia. The two chamber legislature, also scheduled to meet in October, did not finally become organized until January 1997, again because of Serb objections to taking an oath of allegiance to Bosnia but also because they refused to meet in Sarajevo. The inaugural January session finally took place in the Serb–controlled town of Lukavica. Here a new council of ministers was named, along with Muslim and Serb co–chairs—Haris Silajdzic, representing the Muslim–Croat Federation, and Boro Bosic, representing the Republic of Serbia.

Haris Silajdzic characterized the creation of the joint institutions for Bosnia as being "the victory of democracy over dictatorship" and spoke optimistically of "the reintegration of Bosnia–Herzegovina with Europe." Others at the ceremonies were nearly as optimistic. Only time will tell whether the optimism was justified.

### The UN Tribunal for War Crimes

Another Serb policy, practiced from the beginning of the war, is "ethnic cleansing." In areas under their control, the Serbs have systematically destroyed mosques and, less systematically, Roman Catholic churches. They have also either destroyed or seized the homes of Moslems and Catholics, forcing them to flee these areas. Some 750,000 Moslems plus a smaller number of Catholic Croats were forced out of these areas. Large numbers of non–Serbs were also arrested and put in concentration camps. Moslem women were systematically raped, either in their homes or after they had been detained. Such atrocities occurred particularly during the first year of the war, while the Serbs were consolidating control over the 70% of the country that they eventually ended up controlling.

The reports of such atrocities were so wide–spread and so documented that the United Nations decided to set up a tribunal for war crimes in ex–Yugoslavia. The tribunal, established at The Hague, began operating in 1994 and has since been collecting information. Thus far, it has brought charges against 22 Serbs, for killing and rape at the Omarska concentration camp.

Of all the evidence collected by the tribunal, some of the most interesting came from a Serb defector, Cedomirt Mihailovic, a former member of the Serb secret police. The documents include a directive from Serbian state security services in Belgrade concerning the running of concentration camps in Bosnia, putting a

lie to Serbian Government assertions that it was not directly involved in the war. Another document, also from Serbian state security services, gives explicit instructions to the Serbian paramilitary commander known as Arkan and concerns the eviction and killing of Moslems in the Bosnian town of Bijeljina, which was cleansed of Moslems at the beginning of the war. In April 1995, Richard Goldstone, chief prosecutor for The Hague tribunal, named Radovan Karadzic, leader of the Bosnian Serbs, and Ratko Mladic, commander of the Bosnian Serb army, as suspected war criminals. Indictments were returned against them in July 1995. A number of other indictments have also been issued since that time.

Since July 1997, NATO–led troops in Bosnia have begun arresting indicted war criminals and escorting them to The Hague for trial. British commandos arrested Milan Kovacevic in July while another indicted Serb, Simo Drljaca, resisted arrest and was killed. In December, Dutch forces seized two Croats who were under indictment for war crimes. Although the numbers of those seized are still small, persons indicted for war crimes can no longer feel safe in Bosnia. It has even been reported that Radovan Karadzic has abandoned his home in Pale and is now in hiding.

### Culture

One of the more interesting cultural elements in Bosnia–Herzegovina is that approximately 44 percent of the population are Moslems. These Moslems speak Serbo–Croatian, however, and they are a Slavic people who converted to Islam.

In the tenth century, a new religious sect arose in Bulgaria under the leadership of an Orthodox monk called Bogomil. Bogomilism, as it came to be called, spread through various parts of the Balkans and by the twelfth century was well established in Bosnia. Then Kulin, the Bosnian leader, converted to Bogomilism and established it firmly throughout Bosnia, where it came to be known as the "Bosnian Church." Bogomilism shared many common characteristics with Catharism or Albigensianism—in particular a belief in a Manichaean dualism—and was eventually condemned as a heresy by both the Roman Catholic and Orthodox Churches.

Various attempts were made to stamp out this heresy beginning in the thirteen century, but the church still existed in the late fifteenth century when this area was overrun and incorporated into the Ottoman Empire. Most of the Bogomil aristocracy allied themselves with the Turks and assisted them in their conquest of the area. They then converted to Islam, impelled apparently by their hatred of the Roman Catholic Hungarians who had waged religious war against them for the

# Bosnia–Herzegovina

previous two centuries. Their descendants are the modern Bosnian Moslems now fighting for their existence against efforts by Serbia and Serbs in Bosnia to wipe them out through a process of ethnic cleansing.

## Economy

Four years of war have left Bosnia–Herzegovina and most cities in ruins and millions of land mines have rendered much of the countryside unusable. The 1995 Dayton Accords produced a truce, and a 60,000 NATO–led Implementation Force (IFOR) has, in the words of one commander, "created the conditions under which peace might develop." Technically, IFOR was phased out in December 1996, but a slightly smaller replacement force continues to guarantee the truce. The economy has begun to revive somewhat, but much of this is associated more with money coming into the economy because of the presence of 60,000 foreign troops plus international aid efforts rather than a domestic economic revival. As an example, a driver for the United Nations currently earns $600 a month; a doctor at Sarajevo's Kosovo hospital is paid $300. As a result, many professionals have abandoned their positions to take unrelated jobs that pay more money.

Officially, unemployment is 70% of the workforce, but that reflects only the current situation. Further implementation of the Dayton Accords will require the reintegration of 300,000 soldiers into the economy, not to mention the large quantities of refugees in Western Europe—320,000 in Germany alone.

The situation is exacerbated by the fact that a new national government was formed only in January 1997 and no one yet knows whether the three factions that make up the government will be able to work together or not. The largest problem is that Bosnia has not yet begun the transition from a centralized economy to a market–oriented one. All larger industry technically remains in state hands, though nearly all of it is closed and has been that way since the beginning of the war. Another unresolved problem is that most industry was integrated before the war on a Yugoslav–wide basis, with raw materials coming from other republics and finished products shipped to customers throughout the country. Now most of those links have disappeared.

In an even more disturbing development, economic links between the Muslim, Croatian and Serb parts of Bosnia have largely disappeared, replaced by an integration of the Croatian and Serbian sectors into the economies of Croatia and Serbia. Economically, therefore, Bosnia

has already ceased to exist; reversal of this situation will require a political will that currently does not exist.

What is it that the new national government has to work with? First of all, industry contributed over half the GDP prior to 1992, but Bosnia–Herzegovina is, in fact, still overwhelmingly agricultural. Herzegovina, with its warmer climate has traditionally specialized in semitropical crops like pomegranates, lemons, olives, rice and tobacco. Further north, the chief crops are cereal grains and soybeans, supplemented by potatoes, melons, grapes, plums, mulberries and figs. Cattle, sheep, pigs, and poultry are raised throughout the republic.

Before the war, Bosnia–Herzegovina was a major manufacturer of military equipment. It also manufactured Volkswagen automobiles and there was some textile manufacturing in the larger cities. The majority of its industry was extractive in nature, however. Bosnia was a major producer of coal, iron, copper, manganese, lead, mercury, bauxite and silver, as well as things like marble and building stone. Asphalt and lignite are found in the southern part of Herzegovina. Timber is another major industry.

## The Future

Does Bosnia–Herzegovina have a future? Although the Dayton Accords brought an end to the fighting, they did not reunite the country. New elections in September 1996 only confirmed that the leaders of the parties responsible for the war were still very much in charge in their respective enclaves. The Bosnian Serb leaders have been the most blatant in this respect. Not only have they refused to take an oath of allegiance to the new national government or to recognize the national flag, they have also refused to attend meetings of the presidency and sessions of the new legislature in Sarajevo. After a stalemate of three months, the legislature met,

in the Serb–held town of Lukavica on January 3, 1997. Here they managed to appoint a new Council of Ministers, presided over by Serb and Muslim co–chairs, but none of this leads one to be optimistic about the future.

Nor is that the only problem. The separate Croatian enclave of Herzog–Bosna continues to exist, though it was supposed to have been officially dissolved in 1996. Though theoretically part of the Muslim–Croat federation that supposedly shares power with the Bosnian Serbs, it continues to act as though it were a part

of Croatia, and has closed its borders to both Muslims and Serbs.

Finally, the Bosnian economy is almost totallly moribund with unemployment running at 70%. Some international assistance has begun to flow in, but there has been no revival of industry, since both Serbs and Croatians continue to oppose any reintegration of the three sectors. Millions of land mines scattered across the countryside have made it difficult to revive farming. It is difficult not to be pessimistic about Bosnia's future.

**The bridge at Zepa dating from the 16th century**

# The Republic of Macedonia

The covered marketplace and the Isac Mosque in Bitola, southern Macedonia

**Area:** 9,928 square miles (25,713 sq. km.).
**Population:** 1,936,377 (July 1994).
**Capital City:** Skopje, pronounced *Scope–yeh* (505,000).
**Climate:** Mediterranean in the south; mild, temperate elsewhere.
**Neighboring Countries:** Albania (west); Greece (south); Bulgaria (east); Serbia, (north).
**Official Language:** Macedonian.
**Other Principal Tongues:** Albanian, Turkic, Serbo–Croatian.
**Ethnic Background:** South Slavic.
**Principal Religions:** Orthodox Christianity; Islam.
**Chief Commercial Products:** Agricultural products, chemicals, steel, textiles.
**Currency:** Denar.
**Former Political Status:** Constituent Republic of SFRY.
**National Day:** August 2.
**Chief of State:** Kiro Gligorov, President.
**Head of Government:** Branko Crvenkovski, Prime Minister.
**National Flag:** A golden eight–ray sun is centered on a red field. The flag was slightly revised in 1995 so it no longer looks like the sixteeen–pointed Star of

Vergina associated with Alexander the Great.

## The Land

The Republic of Macedonia is the independent successor of the Socialist Republic of Macedonia, a constituent republic of the Socialist Federal Republic of Yugoslavia. It declared its independence in September 1991 after a referendum on independence had won the support of the Macedonian population.

Located in the area of the southwestern Balkans, Macedonia borders on Greece to the south, Albania to the west, Serbia, SFRY to the north and Bulgaria to the east. The center of the republic is dominated by the valley of the Vardar River, commonly referred to as the Vardar Plain. This lowland area is the only place in the Balkans where the mountains can be traversed both north–south and east–west.

The Vardar River begins in the northwestern part of the republic and flows north and east until it reaches Skopje, the capital. It continues southeastward down through the republic, hemmed in by mountains to the west and east, then

crosses into Greece. At the Greek border, it becomes the Axios River. Flowing down through Greek Macedonia, it empties into the Gulf of Salonica. This provides Macedonia with a natural outlet toward the

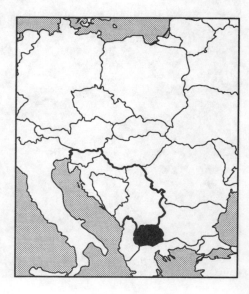

south, though this is dependent on the status of relations with the Government of Greece. This passage has been closed since February 1994, when Greece instituted an embargo against Macedonia in an attempt to force it to change its name.

The east–west route connects the Albanian port of Durres with Bulgaria in the east. Albania's long isolation means that the western route has been little used in recent times.

The chain of mountains, which dominates the western part of Macedonia, is a series of ridges that run in a southwest–northeast direction, and fairly wide valleys are to be found between the ridges. A second chain of mountains, the Sar, runs west–east along the border with Serbia. In the center, the Black Mountains reach down into Macedonia from Serbia, stopping just north of Skopje. Another mountain, the Osogovske Chain, marks most of the border with Bulgaria.

## The People

Macedonia's population as of the July 1994 census was 1,936,377; Macedonians represent 66.5 percent of this total. The language is closely related to other Slavic languages. Albanians, the largest minority, are 22.9 percent of the total. Albanians live mainly in the western part of the republic. Other minorities include Turks (4%), Romanies (Gypsies, 2.3%), and Serbs (2%). Almost all Serbs live in the northeastern part of Macedonia, near the city of Kumanovo and villages on Mount Skopska Crna Gora near the capital of Skopje.

## History

The name Macedonia is an ancient one, going back to the fourth century B.C. and earlier. Modern Macedonia has little, if anything, to do with that particular past, however.

There was also a larger Macedonia that was part of the Ottoman Empire from 1371 to 1912. It was probably always an area of mixed populations, but the Turks ruled non–Islamic peoples through their religious structures and most Macedonians are Orthodox Christians. Thus the Turks made no differentiation beyond this point.

In 1913, this historic Macedonia was divided up by Greece, Bulgaria and Serbia after they had wrestled it from the Ottoman Empire in the First Balkan War. Greece carried out a Hellenization of the territories it obtained, so today Macedonian speakers are only found in the northern part of the province. Bulgaria always treated Macedonians as Bulgarians and so they tended to become amalgamated to the larger Bulgarian population, though Macedonia continues to be spoken in western Bulgaria. Serbia treated the Macedonians as Serbs until World War II. During the war, Macedonians fought along

with the *Partisan Movement* of the communist leader, Marshal Tito. After the war, he turned Yugoslavia into a Federal Republic and the Socialist Republic of Macedonia became one of the six constituent republics.

Macedonians were not unhappy as part of a federal Yugoslavia, but the failure of the *Communist Party of Yugoslavia* to solve the country's economic problems led to a slow disintegration. Macedonians never took the lead in this process but they, like the Slovenians and Croatians, supported abandonment of communist economic policies. In 1990, the legislature passed legislation asserting Macedonia's sovereignty and new elections resulted in the first non–communist government.

By the beginning of 1991, they supported a major reformation of the SFRY, though they continued to favor some continued form of union. When Serbia and Montenegro kept their communist leaders in their own republic elections, the stage was set for a confrontation. It was the new Slovenian and Croatian leaders who made the strongest case for change, but it was the Serbian stonewalling that eventually convinced Macedonians that they could not remain part of a Yugoslavia dominated by Serbia. In September 1991, therefore, Macedonians followed the lead of Slovenia and Croatia and voted in a referendum for a "sovereign and independent" republic.

On October 3, Branko Kostic, Montenegrin representative to the SFRY Presidency, called a meeting of the Presidency in his role as Vice President and proposed declaring a state of emergency in the country. Since the president, Stipe Mesic, was not present and the Slovenian delegate was boycotting the meeting, Kostic got his resolution passed with the support of the three votes controlled by Serbia (Serbia plus its two formerly autonomous regions). As a result, the Macedonian delegate to the Presidency withdrew from subsequent meetings of the Presidency and the Macedonian Assembly condemned Kostic's actions as unconstitutional and invalid. The Macedonian Government then condemned the war against Croatia, declared its neutrality, called upon Macedonian soldiers to return to Macedonia, and requested the Yugoslavia People's Army to withdraw its local forces. The YPA, apparently not wanting to drive Macedonia into an alliance with Croatia, agreed to have all of its troops out of Macedonia by April 15. The Macedonian delegates to the SFRY legislature also stopped attending the sessions of the legislature in November.

In January 1992, the Macedonian Assembly passed two amendments to the constitution demanded by the EC as a price for recognition. The first amendment stated that Macedonia does not

have any territorial claims toward its neighbors. The second amendment states that Macedonia will not interfere in the internal affairs of the neighboring sovereign countries. Other related actions by the Assembly included repealing the two sections of the constitution that provided for participation in federal organs, terminating the term of the representative to the Presidency, and recalling all Macedonians in the diplomatic staff. In addition, the Assembly approved the formation of a Macedonian national army of 25,000–30,000 troops.

Since that time, peace has continued in Macedonia. International diplomatic recognition was slow in coming, but that, too, is now an accomplished fact. There have always been serious concerns about a possible political destabilization caused by one or more of Macedonia's neighbors trying to interfere in domestic politics, and an attempt on President Gligorov's life in October 1995 brought those fears once more to the fore. What happened is that a car bomb was exploded at the side of the road as President Gligorov's official limousine passed enroute to his office. The president's driver was killed and several bystanders were injured. The president himself was hit in the head by shrapnel and had to be hospitalized. No group took credit for the attempt on the president's life, but one possibility is that it might have been the work of Bulgarian extremists. Another possibility is that it was the work of Macedonian nationalists who objected to concessions that President Gligorov made to Greece relating to the flag and constitution. (See Foreign Relations, below, for more details.) Stojan Andov, the Speaker of Parliament, was named interim president until President Gligorov resumed his office.

Over the past year or so, a growing do-

**President Kiro Gligorov**

# Macedonia

mestic problem has been the increasing demands by nationalist Albanians for greater political and cultural autonomy. One issue has been the display of the Albanian flag, particularly on government buildings where ethnic Albanians are in the majority. In July 1997, there were riots in the city of Gostivar after the mayor, an ethnic Albanian, insisted to flying the Albanian flag over city hall and police forces were dispatched to Gostivar to take down the flag. The resulting clashes between ethnic Albanians and police left three dead and at least 50 persons injured. In addition, approximately 320 persons were arrested.

Another issue is the lack of possibilities for higher education in the Albanian language. The authorities have granted the Albanians the right to use Albanian at the pedagogic faculty at Skopje University but this has not satisfied them. Albanians founded an unauthorized university at Tetovo in 1995, but the government has refused to give it official authorization to operate on the grounds that an Albanian language university would stoke nationalist sentiments among ethnic Albanians. Although ethnic Albanians hold five ministries in the government, President Gligorov has been unwilling to make ad-

ditional concessions to Albanian nationalism. Recent events in Kosovo have also played a role in increasing the militancy among ethnic Albanians.

## Foreign Relations

Although Macedonia opted for independence because it believed that Serbia would dominate any federation with Croatia and Slovenia gone, it wants to maintain good economic relations with Serbia and all other neighboring countries. It also favors a common market among the former republics, although that appears unlikely at the moment. Macedonia has good relations with Bulgaria and Turkey and fairly good relations with Albania.

The EU did not extend recognition to Macedonia at the time it recognized Slovenia and Bosnia–Herzegovina because Greece, a European Union member and Macedonia's most important neighbor from an economic point of view, objected to its use of the name Macedonia and the sixteen pointed star that it had on its flag.

It insisted that Macedonia had to change its name before it could be recognized, apparently fearing that an independent Macedonia could exert some influence on its own Macedonian–speaking

citizens in *Greek* Macedonia. Greece finally dropped its objections to Macedonia's admission to the United Nations in April 1993, provided it would agree to use the name "Former Yugoslav Republic of Macedonia." On that basis, Macedonia received general recognition and was admitted to the United Nations. It was also understood that Macedonia's flag would not be flown at the United Nations.

Greece continued to insist that the name Macedonia was properly applied only to a part of northern Greece, however, and managed to keep the European Union from extending diplomatic recognition to Macedonia until December 1993. The United States, which had sent 500 American troops to Macedonia in July 1993 as part of a 1000–troop United Nations presence, had refrained from recognizing Macedonia for the same reason. The EU move allowed the United States to reverse itself and extend diplomatic recognition to Macedonia in February 1994. Greece's reaction was to announce an embargo on all imports and exports to Macedonia, other than food and medicine. The EU attempted to get the trade blockade removed and when the Greek Government refused, brought Greece before the European Court of Justice in April. The embargo continued until October 1995. Greece then agreed to lift the embargo after the Macedonian parliament gave into Greek demands and voted to change the flag and constitution. The new flag consists of an eight–ray golden sun on a red background. Although the Greek Government has continued to assert that the name Macedonia applies only to its own northern region and that the former Yugoslav republic must find another name for itself, Greek–Macedonian relations appear to have improved in the last year. In particular, normal transportation, economic and diplomatic communication have been established.

Macedonia has applied for associate membership in the European Union and has stated that it eventually wants full membership. It signed a trade and cooperation treaty with the European Union in June 1996. It is actively taking part in the Partnership for Peace program, and eventually wishes to become a full member of NATO also. This recent nation is already a member of the Council of Europe and the OSCE.

## Nature of the Regime

The President of Macedonia is Kiro Gligorov. In elections held during October–November 1994, he was reelected to office for five years with 53% of the votes. The government is a coalition of the *Social Democratic Alliance* and several smaller parties. The second largest political party is the *Internal Macedonian Revolutionary Organization–Democratic Party for Macedon-*

**On the way to a marketplace**

*ian Unity*, usually identified by its Macedonian initials, *VMRO*.

The strongest party in the republic is the *Social Democratic Alliance of Macedonia*, successor of the former communist party. It supports Macedonian independence. When Branko Kostic, the Yugoslav Vice President and the Montenegrin representative to the Presidency, began calling meetings of the presidency and making decisions in the name of the presidency with only four individuals present, the *Social Democratic Alliance* accused the Yugoslav People's Army of having carried out a *coup*. It also accurately accused the Serbian authorities of having ideas of a "Greater Serbia and Serbian hegemony, directly threatening its neighbors, primarily Macedonia."

The third largest of the political parties represented in the Assembly is the *Party for Democratic Prosperity*, which held its first congress in February 1992. This is essentially an Albanian party. The chairman of the party is Nevzat Halili. The main plank of the party is a demand for political and territorial autonomy for Albanians in Macedonia. Another is that the party recognizes the Republic of Kosovo. Albanians make up some twenty percent of the republic's population. There is also a second "Albanian" political party, the *National Democratic Party*. It also supports demands for political and territorial autonomy.

## Culture

There is a separate Macedonian culture, but it is very similar to that of Bulgaria and Serbia. The chief element that defines the culture is that most people live in villages in the countryside and make their living from agriculture. There also is a more middle class and cosmopolitan culture associated with the city of Skopje.

Religion is the second defining influence. Most Macedonians are Orthodox Christians. The Church was part of the Serbian Orthodox Church until 1967, when it broke away and formed the Macedonian Orthodox Church. The Serbian Orthodox Church has never accepted the split, however, and does not recognize the Macedonian Church. Approximately 21% of the population is Muslim. Most of these speak Albanian as their first language.

## Economy

Macedonia is overwhelmingly an agricultural area, with most people living in the Vardar River Valley or the valleys interspersed between ridges in the west. Because of the limited farmland available, many young workers live and work in other Western countries. The per capita income of Macedonia trails that of Serbia.

The chief crops are wheat, barley, corn, tobacco, cotton, rice, sunflowers and sugar beets. Cattle raising is also important.

**View of Skopje**

Almost all industry is concentrated in the Skopje area. Heavy industry consists of steel and chemicals. Light industry includes textiles, furniture, porcelain, and chinaware. The Macedonian Government reported in 1996 that 750 companies, accounting for 40% of GNP, had been privatized, with another 250 scheduled to be privatized by the end of 1996. Another 200 companies were listed for privatization in 1997 or later. Economic growth in 1996 was 1.6 percent for the year, the first time that growth had been positive since independence. Growth increased to 2.4 percent for the first six months of 1997. On the other hand, Macedonia had a current account deficit of $345 million in 1996 and unemployment was 27 percent in 1997. A major problem appears to be that wages and prices in Macedonia are relatively high, which cuts the country's competitiveness.

## The Future

Macedonia has always worried about an internal destabilization as individual factions disagreed on a proper reaction to, say, some Serb action in Kosovo. Now that Serbian police and paramilitary units have been sent into Kosovo, that fear is even greater. Thus far, Serb actions in Kosovo have probably contributed to increasing ethnic Albanian demands for greater autonomy, but the fighting has not yet spilled over the border. The presence of ethnic Albanians in the government has probably been the most important reason why Macedonia has remained quiet thus far.

The recession that set in after independence finally came to an end in 1997, but Macedonia is still a poor land and economic progress is likely to be slow. Still, Macedonians can now be somewhat more hopeful as they look to the future, even as they realize that they can expect several difficult years before they can see significant improvements.

# BIBLIOGRAPHY OF KEY
# ENGLISH LANGUAGE BOOKS

## RUSSIA
### GENERAL

Bermeo, Nancy (ed.). *Liberalization and Democratization: Change in the Soviet Union and Eastern Europe*. Baltimore: Johns Hopkins University Press, 1992; 200 p. (pb).

Blum, Douglas W. (ed.). *Russia's Future: Consolidation or Disintegration?*. Boulder, CO: Westview Press, 1994; 173 p. (pb).

Kaiser, Robert G. *Russia: The People and the Power*. New York: Pocket Books, 1974; 557 p. (pb).

Lapidus, Gail W. (ed.). *The New Russia*. Boulder, CO: Westview Press, 1994; 280 p. (pb).

Remnik, David. *Lenin's Tomb: The Last Days of the Soviet Empire*. New York: Vintage, 1992; 608 p. (pb).

Rozman, Gilbert (ed.). *Dismantling Communism: Common Causes and Regional Variations*. Baltimore: Johns Hopkins University Press, 1992; 304 p. (pb).

Smith, Hedrick. *The New Russians*. New York: Avon Books, 1991; 734 p. (pb)

### HISTORY

Chamberlin, William Henry. *The Russian Revolution*. 2 vols., New York: Macmillan, 1952.

Daniels, Robert V. *The Conscience of the Revolution: Communist Opposition in Soviet Russia*. Cambridge: Harvard U. Press, 1960; 524 p.

Dmytryshyn, Basil. *A History of Russia* Englewood Cliffs, N.J.: Prentice Hall, 1977; 648. p.

Dmytryshyn, Basil. *U.S.S.R.: A Concise History*. New York: Charles Scribner's Sons, 1978; 620 p.

Florinsky, Michael T. *Russia: A History and an Interpretation*. 2 vols, New York: Macmillan, 1954.

Pipes, Richard. *Russia Under the Old Regime*. New York: Charles Scribner's Sons, 1974; 361 p.

Riasanovsky, Nicholas. *A History of Russia*. New York. Oxford University Press, 1993; 768 p.

Thompson, John M. *Russia and the Soviet Union*. (3rd ed); Boulder, CO: Westview Press, 1994; 320 p. (pb).

Treadgold, Donald W. *Twentieth Century Russia*. (8th ed); Boulder, CO: Westview Press, 1994; 498 p.

Wren, Melvin C. *The Course of Russian History*. Prospect Heights, IL: Waveland Press, 1994; 617 p. (pb).

### THE COMMUNIST ERA

Arbatov, Georgi. *The System: An Insider's Life in Soviet Politics*. New York: Times Books, 1993; 380 p. (pb).

Bailer, Seweryn. *Stalin's Successors: Leadership, Stability, and Change in the Soviet Union*. Cambridge, Eng.: Cambridge University Press, 1980; 312 p. (pb).

Bailes, Kendall E. *Technology and Society under Lenin and Stalin: Origins of the Soviet Technical Intelligentsia*. Princeton: Princeton Univ. Press, 1978; 472 p.

Breslauer, George W. *Khrushchëv and Brezhnev as Leaders: Building Authority in Soviet Politics*. London: Allen Unwin, 1982; 318 p. (pb).

Daniels, Robert V. *Trotsky, Stalin and Socialism*. Boulder, CO: Westview Press, 1991; 208 p.

Daniels, Robert Vincent. *Stalin Revolution: Foundations of Soviet Totalitarianism*. (2nd ed.) Boston: Heath, 1973; 106 p.

Djilas, Milovan. *Conversations with Stalin*. New York: Harcourt Brace World, 1962; 211 p.

Goldgeier, James M. *Leadership Style and Soviet Foreign Policy: Stalin, Khrushchev, Brezhnev, Gorbachëv*. Baltimore: Johns Hopkins University Press, 1994; 192 p.

Gorbachëv, Mikhail. *Memoirs*. New York: Doubleday, 1996; 800 p.

Karcz, Jerzy F. *The Economics of Communist Agriculture: Selected Papers*. Bloomington, Ind.: International Development Institute, 1979; 494 p.

Ligachëv, Yegor. *Inside Gorbachëv's Kremlin*. trans. Catherine A Fitzpatrick, Michele A Berdy, and Dobrochna Dyrcz–Freeman. New York: Pantheon Books, 1993; 369 p.

Linden, Carl. *Khrushchëv and the Soviet Leadership: With an Epilogue on Gorbachëv*. Baltimore: Johns Hopkins University Press, 1990; 304 p. (pb).

Radzinsky, Edward. *Stalin*. New York: Doubleday, 1996; 560 p.

Ulam, Adam B. *The Bolsheviks: The Intellectual and Political History of the Triumph of Communism in Russia.* New York: Macmillan, 1965; 598 p.

Yakovlev, Alexander. *The Fate of Marxism in Russia.* Trans. Catherine A. Fitzpatrick. New Haven: Yale University Press, 1993; 256 p.

## SOVIET/RUSSIAN FOREIGN POLICY

Aron, Leon and Kenneth M. Jensen (eds.). *The Emergence of Russian Foreign Policy.* Herndon, Va.: United States Institute of Peace Press, 1994; 221 p. (pb)

Beschloss, Michael R. and Strobe Talbott. *At the Highest Levels: The Inside Story of the End of the Cold War.* Boston: Little, Brown, 1993; 498 p.

Bialer, Seweryn. *The Soviet Paradox–External Expansion, Internal Decline.* New York: Alfred Knopf, 1986; 391 p.

Fischer, Louis. *Russia's Road from Peace to War.* New York: Harper Rowe, 1969; 499 p.

Harriman, W. Averill. *Special Envoy to Churchill and Stalin, 1941–1946.* New York: Random House, 1975; 595 p.

Kennan, George F. *Russia and the West under Lenin and Stalin.* Boston: Little, Brown, 1961; 411 p.

Shearman, Peter (ed.). *Russian Foreign Policy Since 1990.* Boulder,CO: Westview Press, 1995; 320 p. (pb).

Ulam, Adam B. *Expansion and Coexistence.* New York: Praeger, 1968; 797 p.

Ulam, Adam B. *The Rivals: America and Russia Since World War II.* New York: Viking Press, 1971; 405 p.

Wettig, Gerhard. *Changes in Soviet Policy Toward the West.* Boulder, CO: Westview Press, 1991; 193 p.

## COLLAPSE OF COMMUNISM

Balzer, Harley D.(ed.). *Five Years That Shook the World: Gorbachëv's Unfinished Revolution.* Boulder, CO: Westview Press, 1991; 267 p. (pb).

Dallin, Alexander and Gail W. Lapidus (eds.). *The Soviet System: From Crisis to Collapse.* Boulder, CO: Westview Press, 1994; 725 p. (pb).

Goldman, Marshal I. *USSR in Crisis: the Failure of an Economic System.* New York: W.W. Norton, 1983; 210 p. (pb).

Goldman, Marshall I. *What Went Wrong with Perestroika?.* New York: Norton, 1991.

Gorbachëv, Mikhail. *The August Coup: The Truth and the Lessons.* New York: Harper-Collins, 1991; 127 p.

Jones, Anthony, Walter D. Conner and David E. Powell (eds.). *Soviet Social Problems.* Boulder, CO: Westview Press, 1991; 337 p. (pb).

Kaiser, Robert. *Why Gorbachëv Happened: His Triumphs and His Failures.* New York: Simon Schuster, 1991; 476 p.

Kotkin, Stephen. *Steeltown, USSR: Soviet Society in the Gorbachëv Era.* Berkeley: University of California Press, 1991; 269 p.

Kull, Steven. *Burying Lenin: The Revolution in Soviet Ideology and Foreign Policy.* Boulder, CO: Westview Press, 1992; 219 p. (pb).

Shane, Scott. *Dismantling Utopia: How Information Ended the Soviet Union.* Chicago: Ivan R. Dee, Inc. Publisher, 1995; 336 p.

Sharlet, Robert. *Soviet Constitutional Crisis: From De–Stalinization to Disintegration.* Armonk, NY: M. E. Sharpe, 1992; 204 p. (pb).

Solomon, Andrew. *The Irony Tower: Soviet Artists in a Time of Glasnost.* New York: Knopf, 1991; 170 p.

Nahaylo, B. and V. Svoboda. *Soviet Disunion.* New York: Free Press, 1990.

White, Stephen. *Gorbachëv and After.* New York, Cambridge University Press, 1992; 327 p. (pb).

Zaslavskaya, Tatyana. *The Second Socialist Revolution: An Alternative Soviet Strategy.* Bloomington, IN: Indiana University Press, 1990; 241 p. (pb).

## POLITICS

Barry, Donald D. (ed.). Towards the Rule of Law in Russia: Political and Legal Reform in the Transition Period. Armonk, NY: Sharpe, 1992.

Blum, Douglas W. (ed.). Russia's Future: Consolidation or Disintegration. Boulder, CO: Westview Press, 1994; 192 p. (pb).

Feltbrugge, F.J.M. Russian Law: The end of the Soviet System and the Role of Law. Dordrecht: Martinus Nijhoff, 1993.

Fish, Steven. *Democracy from Scratch.* Princeton: Princeton University Press, 1996; 312 p. (pb)

Friedgut, Theodore H. and Jeffrey W. Hahn (eds.). Local Power and Post–Soviet Politics. Armonk, NY: M. E. Sharpe, 1994; 320 p. (pb).

Medish, Vadim (ed.). *My Russia: The Political Autobiography of Gennady Zyuganov.* Armonk, NY: M. E. Sharpe, 1997; 224 p.

Lapidus, Gail W. (ed.). The New Russia: Troubled Transformation. Boulder, CO: Westview Press, 1994; 320 p. (pb).

Saivetz, Carol R. and Anthony Jones. *In Search of Pluralism: Soviet and Post–Soviet Politics*. Boulder, CO: Westview Press, 1994; 174 p. (pb).

Smith, Gordon B. (ed.). *State–Building in Russia: The Yeltsin Legacy and the Challenge of the Future*. Armonk, NY: M. E. Sharpe, 1998; 224 p.

Waller, J. Michael. *Secret Empire: The KBG in Russia Today*. Boulder, CO: Westview Press, 1994; 375 p. (pb).

Yeltsin, Boris. *The Struggle for Russia*. New York: Times Books, 1995; 336 p.

## ECONOMY

Aslund, Anders and Richard Layard (eds.). *Changing the Economic System in Russia*. London: Pinter, 1993.

Boeva, Irina and Viacheslav Shironin. *Russians Between State and Market*. Glasgow: University of Strathclyde Centre for the Study of Public Policy, SPP 205, 1992.

Ellman, Michael and Vladimir Kontorovich (eds.). *The Disintegration of the Soviet Economic System*. New York: Routledge, 1994; 281 p. (pb).

McKinnon, Ronald. *The Order of Economic Liberalization: Financial Control in the Transition to a Market Economy*. Baltimore: Johns Hopkins University Press, 1993; 224 p. (pb).

Keren, Michael and Gur Ofer (eds.). *Trials of Transition: Economic Reform in the Former Communist Bloc*. Boulder, CO: Westview Press, 1992; 308 p. (pb).

Nelson, Lynn D. and Irina Y. Kuzes. *Property to the People: The Struggle for Radical Economic Reform in Russia*. Armonk, NY: M./ E. Sharpe, 1994; 280 p. (pb).

## CULTURAL

Buckley, Mary. *Redefining Russian Society and Polity*. Boulder, CO: Westview Press, 1993; 346 p. (pb).

Davis, Nathaniel. *A Long Walk to Church: A Contemporary History*. Boulder, CO: Westview Press, 1994; 381 p. (pb) Hilton, Alison. *Russian Folk Art*. Bloomington: Indiana University Press, 1995; 320 p.

Goscilo, Helena. *Dehexing Sex: Russian Womanhood During and After Glasnost*. Ann Arbor, MI: University of Michigan Press, 1996; 192 p. (pb).

Hosking, Geoffrey A. *Beyond Socialist Realism: Soviet Fiction Since Ivan Denisovich*. New York: Holmes Meier Publishers, 1980; 260 p.

Jones, Anthony (ed.). *Education and Society in the New Russia*. Armonk, NY: M. E. Sharpe, 1994; 360 p. (pb).

Orlov, Yuri. *Dangerous Thoughts*. New York: Morrow, 1991; 339 p.

Ramet, Sabrina P. *Rocking the State: Rock Music and Politics in Eastern Europe and Russia*. Boulder, CO: Westview Press, 1994; 317 p. (pb).

Rand, Robert. *Comrade Lawyer: Inside Soviet Justice in an Era of Reform*. Boulder, Westview Press, 1991; 166 p. (pb).

Scanlan, James P. (ed.). *Russian Thought After Communism*. Armonk, NY: M. E. Sharpe, 1994; 256 p. (pb).

Segal, Harold B. *Twentieth–century Russian Drama: From Gorky to the Present*. New York: Columbia Univ. Press, 1979; 502 p.

Shlapentikh, Vladimir. *Soviet Intellectuals and Political Power*. Princeton, NJ: Princeton University Press, 1991; 321 p.

Shneidman, N.N. *Soviet Literature in the 1970's: Artistic Diversity and Ideological Conformity*. Toronto: University of Toronto Press, 1979; 128 p.

Smith, Gerald S. (ed. and trans.). *Contemporary Russian Poetry*. Bloomington: Indiana University Press, 1993; 390 p.

Solzhenitsyn, Alexander *et al*. *From Under the Rubble*. trans. A.M. Brock. Boston: Little, Brown, 1975; 308 p.

Solzhenitsyn, Alexander. *The Gulag Archipelago: 1918–1956*. trans. Thomas R. Whitney. New York: Harper Row, 1974; 640 p. (pb).

Terras, Victor. *A History of Russian Literature*. New Haven: Yale University Press, 1992; 672 p. (pb).

## COMMONWEALTH OF INDEPENDENT STATES

Akiner, Shirin. *Islamic Peoples of the Soviet Union*. New York: Routledge Kegan Paul, 1986; 462 p.

Banuazizi, Ali and Myron Weiner (eds.). *New Geopolitics of Central Asia*. Bloomington, IN: Indiana University Press, 1994; 288 p. (pb).

Bremmer, Ian and Ray Taras (eds.). *Nations and Politics in the Soviet Successor States*. New York: Cambridge University Press, 1993; 577 p. (pb).

Brzezinski, Zbigniew and Paige Sullivan. *Russia and the Commonwealth of Independent States: A Historical and Geopolitical Evolution*. Armonk, NY: M. E. Sharpe, 1996.

Chahin, M. *The Kingdom of Armenia*. New York: Dorset Press, 1987; 332 p.

Coulton, Timothy J. and Robert C. Tucker (eds). *Patterns of Post–Soviet Leadership*. Boulder, CO: Westview Press, 1995; 256 p. (pb).

Denber, Rachel (ed.). *The Soviet Nationality Reader: The Disintegration in Context*. Boulder, CO: Westview Press, 1992; 635 p. (pb).

d'Encausse, Helen Careere. *Decline of an Empire: The Soviet Socialist Republics in Revolt*. trans. by Martin Sokolinsky and Henry A. La Farge. New York: Newsweek Books, 1978; 304 p.

Enders, Wimbush S. *Soviet Nationalities in Strategic Perspective*. New York: St. Martin's Press, 1985; 253 p.

Frydman, Roman *et al*. *The Privatization Process in Russia, Ukraine and the Baltic States*. Budapest: Central European University Press, 1993.

Gitelman, Zvi (ed.). *The Politics of Nationality and the Erosion of the USSR*. London: Macmillan, 1992.

Hajda, L and M. Beissinger (eds.). *The Nationalities Factor in Soviet Politics and Society*. Boulder: Westview Press, 1990.

Hosking, Geoffrey *et al*. The Road to Post–Communism: Independent Political Movements in the Soviet Union 1985–1991. London: Pinter, 1992.

Hunter, Shireen. *Central Asia Since Independence*. New York: Praeger, 1996; 220 p. (pb).

Hunter, Shireen. *The Transcaucasus in Transition: Nation–Building and Conflict*. New York: Praeger, 1994; 240 p. (pb)

Kuzio, Taras (ed.). *Contemporary Ukraine: Dynamics of Post–Soviet Transformation*. Armonk, NY: M. E. Sharpe, 1998; 272 p. (pb)

Lentini, Peter. *Political Parties and Movements in the Commonwealth of Independent States*. Manchester: Lorton House, 1992.

Mandelbaum, Michael (ed.). *The Rise of Nations in the Soviet Union: American Foreign Policy and the Disintegration of the USSR*. New York: Council on Foreign Relations, 1991; 104 p. (pb).

Motyl, Alexander J. $Dilemmas of Independence: Ukraine after Totalitarianism. New York: Council on Foreign Relations, 1993.

Nahaylo, B. and V. Svoboda. *Soviet Disunion*. New York: Free Press, 1990.

Olcott, Martha Brill. *Central Asia's New States: Independence, Foreign Policy, and Regional Security*. Herndon, Va.: United States Institute of Peace Press, 1966; 256 p. (pb)

Paksoy, H. B. (ed.). *Central Asian Reader: The Rediscovery of History*. Armonk, NY: M. E. Sharpe, 1994; 216 p. (pb).

Peterson, D. J. *Troubled Lands: The Legacy of Soviet Environmental Destruction*. Boulder, CO: Westview Press, 1993; 276 p. (pb).

Remington, Thomas F. (ed.). *Parliaments in Transition: The New Legislative Politics in the Former USSR and Eastern Europe*. Boulder, CO: Westview Press, 1994; 246 p. (pb).

Rumer, Boris Z. *Soviet Central Asia: A Tragic Experiment*. Boston: Unwin Hyman, 1989; 204 p. (pb).

Rywkin, Michael. *Moscow's Muslim Challenge: Soviet Central Asia*. Armonk, NY: M. E. Sharpe, 1990; 181 p.

Rywkin, Michael. *Moscow's Lost Empire*. NY: M.E. Sharpe, 1994; 230 p. (pb).

Shlapentokh, Vladimir and Munir Sendich (eds.). *The New Russian Diaspora: Russian Minorities in the Former Soviet Republics*. Armonk, NY: M. E. Sharpe, 1994; 248 p. (pb).

Suny, Ronald Grigor. *Looking Toward Ararat: Armenia in Modern History*. Bloomington: Indiana University Press, 1993; 304 p. (pb).

Suny, Ronald Grigor. *The Making of the Georgian Nation*. Bloomington: Indiana University Press, 1994; 448 p. (pb).

Walker, Christopher J. *Armenia: The Survival of a Nation*. New York: St Martin's Press, 1990; 476 p.

Zaprudnik, Jan. *Belarus: At a Crossroads in History*. Boulder, CO: Westview Press, 1993; 278 p. (pb).

## EASTERN EUROPE
## HISTORY GENERAL

Palmer, Alan. *The Lands Between: A History of East–Central Europe Since the Congress of Vienna*. New York: Macmillan, 1970; 405 p.

Wolff, Robert Lee. *The Balkans in Our Time*. New York: W.W. Norton, 1967; 618 p. (pb).

## THE COMMUNIST ERA

Fischer–Galati, Stephen (ed). *Eastern Europe in the 1980s*. Boulder, CO: Westview Press, 1981; 291 p. (pb).

McInnes, Simon *et al* (eds.). *The Soviet Union and East Europe in the 1980s*. Oakville, On.: Mosaic Press, 1978; 340 p.

Schnitzer, Martin. *U.S. Business Involvement in Eastern Europe: Case Studies of Hungary, Poland and Romania.* New York: Praeger, 1981; 155 p.

Triska, Jan F. and Charles Gati (eds.). *Blue Collar Workers in Eastern Europe.* Winchester, Mass: Allen and Unwin, 1981; 320 p. (pb).

Volgyes, Ivan. *Politics in Eastern Europe.* Chicago: The Dorsey Press, 1986, 368 p. (pb).

## POST–COMMUNIST EASTERN EUROPE

Barany, Zoltan and Ivan Volgyes (eds.). *Legacies of Communism in Eastern Europe.* Baltimore: The Johns Hopkins University Press, 1995, 272 p.

Brown, J. F. *Surge to Freedom: The End of Communist Rule in Eastern Europe.* Durham, NC: Duke University Press, 1991; 338 p. (pb).

Bugajski, Janusz. *Nations in Turmoil: Conflict and Cooperation in Eastern Europe.* (2nd ed); Boulder, CO: Westview Press, 1995; 252 p. (pb).

DeBardeleben, Joan and John Hannigan (eds.). *Environmental Security and Quality After Communism.* Boulder, CO: Westview Press, 1994; 188 p. (pb).

Graubard, Stephen R. (ed.). *Eastern Europe . . . Central Europe . . . Europe.* Boulder, CO: Westview Press, 1991; 350 p. (pb).

Heller, Agnes and Ferenc Feher. *From Yalta to Glasnost: The Dismantling of Stalin's Empire.* Cambridge, England: Basil Blackwell, 1990; 288 p.

Einhorn, Barbara. *Cinderella Goes to Market: Citizenship, Gender, and Women's Movements in East Central Europe.* London: Verso, 1993.

Kovrig, Bennett. *Of Walls and Bridges: The United States and Eastern Europe.* New York: New York University Press, 1991; 425 p. (pb).

Lampe, John R. (ed.). *Creating Capital Markets in Eastern Europe.* Baltimore: The Johns Hopkins University Press, 1992, 128 p.

Marer, Paul and Andras Köves (eds.). *Foreign Economic Liberalization: Transformations in Socialist and Market Economies.* Boulder, CO: Westview Press, 1991; 260 p. (pb).

Mason, David S. *Revolution in East–Central Europe: The Rise and Fall of Communism.* Boulder, CO: Westview Press, 1992; 216 p. (pb).

Ramet, Sabrina Petra (ed.). *Rocking the State: Rock Music and Politics in Eastern Europe and Russia.* Boulder, CO: Westview Press, 1994; 317 p. (pb).

Rothschild, Joseph. *Return to Diversity: A Political History of East Central Europe Since World War II.* New York: Oxford University Press, 1993; 320 p. (pb).

Rueschemeyer, Marlyn (ed.). *Women in the Politics of Postcommunist Eastern Europe.* Armonk, NY: M. E. Sharpe, 1998; 320 p. (pb)

Stokes, Gale. *The Walls Came Tumbling Down: The Collapse of Communism in Eastern Europe.* New York: Oxford University Press, 1993; 336 p. (pb).

Toman, Michael A. (ed.). *Pollution Abatement Strategies in Central and Eastern Europe.* Baltimore: The Johns Hopkins University Press, 1994, 100 p.

Weigel, George. *The Final Revolution: The Resistance Church and the Collapse of Communism.* New York: Oxford University Press, 1992; 288 p.

## ALBANIA

Hamm, Harry. *Albania: China's Beachhead in Europe.* London: Victor Gollancz, 1977; 230 p.

Marmullaku, Ramadan. *Albania and the Albanians.* London: Hurst, 1975; 178 p.

Prifti, Peter R. *Albania Since 1944.* Cambridge: MIT Press, 1978; 311 p.

## BALTIC REPUBLICS

Clemens, Walter C., Jr. *Baltic Independence and Russian Empire.* New York: St. Martin's Press, 1991; 346 p. (pb)

Daumantas, Juozas. *Fighters for Freedom: Lithuanian Partisans versus the USSR.* New York: Manyland Books, 1975; 275 p.

Kaslas, Bronis S. *The Baltic Nations: The Quest for Regional Integration and Political Liberty.* Pittston, PA: Euramerica Press, 1976; 319 p.

Lieven, Anatol. *The Baltic Revolution: Estonia, Latvia, Lithuania and the Path to Independence.* New Haven: Yale University Press, 1993; 478 p. (pb).

Manning, Clarence. *The Forgotten Republics.* New York: Philosophical Library, 1952; 264 p.

Rubulis, Aleksis. *Baltic Literature.* Notre–Dame, IN: University of Notre Dame Press, 1970; 215 p.

Trapans, Jan Arveds (ed.). *Toward Independence: The Baltic Popular Movements.* Boulder, CO: Westview Press, 1991; 166 p.

Taagepera, Rein. *Estonia: Return to Independence.* Boulder, CO: Westview Press, 1993; 268 p. (pb).

Vardys, V. Stanley and Judith B. Sedaitis. *Lithuania: The Rebel Nation.* Boulder, CO: Westview Press, 1995; 240 p. (pb).

## BULGARIA

Dellin, L.A.D. (ed.). *Bulgaria*. New York: Praeger, 1957.

Feiwel, George R. *Growth and Reforms in Centrally Planned Economies: The Lessons of the Bulgarian Experience*. New York: Praeger, 1977; 345 p.

Zhivkov, Todor. *Modern Bulgaria: Problems and Tasks in Building an Advanced Socialist Society*. New York, International Publishers, 1974; 238 p. (pb).

## THE CZECH REPUBLIC AND SLOVAKIA

Benes, Edward. *Memoirs of Dr. Edward Benes*. London: Allen Unwin, 1954; 364 p.

El Mallakh, Dorothea H. *The Slovak Autonomy Movement, 1935–1939: A Study in Unrelenting Nationalism*. (Boulder: East European Quarterly, 1979); 260 p.

Fogel, Daniel S. *Managing in Emerging Market Economies: Cases from the Czech and Slovak Republics*. Boulder, CO: Westview Press, 1994; 237 p. (pb).

Golan, Galia. *Reform Rule in Czechoslovakia: The Dubcek Era, 1968–1969*. Cambridge, Eng.: Cambridge U. Press, 1975; 349 p.

Kusin, Vladimir V. *From Dubcek to Charter 77*. New York: St. Martin's Press, 1978; 353 p.

Journalist M. *A Year is Eight Months*. Garden City, N.Y.: Doubleday Co., 1971; 260 p.

Littell, Robert (ed.). *The Czech Black Book*. New York: Praeger, 1969; 303 p.

Mikus, Joseph A, J.D. *Slovakia, A Political History: 1918–1950*. Milwaukee: The Marquette University Press, 1963; 392 p.

Paul, David W. *Czechoslovakia: Profile of a Socialist Republic at the Crossroads of Europe*. Boulder, CO: Westview Press, 1981; 196 p.

Wheaton, Bernard and Zdenek Kavan. *The Velvet Revolution: Czechoslovakia, 1988–1991*. Boulder, CO: Westview Press, 1992; 255 p. (pb).

Steiner, Eugen. *The Slovak Dilemma*. (Cambridge: Cambridge University Press, 1973); 229 p.

## HUNGARY

Ferge, Zsursa. *A Society in the Making: Hungarian Social and Societal Polities, 1945–75*. White Plains, N.Y.: E.M. Sharpe, 1980; 288 p.

Hare, Paul *et al* (eds.). *Hungary: A Decade of Economic Reform*. Winchester, Mass: Allen Unwin, 1981; 257 p.

Held, Joseph (ed.). *The Modernization of Agriculture: Rural Transformation in Hungary*. New York: Columbia Univ. Press, 1980; 508 p.

Kerály, Béla K. (Ed.). *Lawful Revolution in Hungary, 1989–1994*. New York: Columbia University Press, 1996; 300 p.

Kourig, Bennett. *Communism in Hungary: From Kun to Kadar*. Stanford: Hoover Institution Press, 1979; 525 p.

Kun, Joseph C. *Hungarian Foreign Policy: The Experience of a New Democracy*. New York: Praeger, 1993; 168 p. (pb)

Sugar, Peter F. (ed.). *A History of Hungary*. Bloomington: Indiana University Press, 1994; 448 p. (pb).

Toth, Zoltan (ed). *Some Issues of the Political System in Hungary*. Budapest: Institute of the Social Sciences, 1979; 179 p.

## POLAND

Bethell, Nicholas. *Gomulka, His Poland and His Communism*. Harmondsworth, Eng.: Penguin Books, 1972; 307 p. (pb).

Brumberg, Abraham (ed). *Poland, Genesis of a Revolution*. New York: Random House, 1983; 322 p.

Glazyca, George and Ryszard Rapacki. *Poland into the 1990s: Economy and Society in Transition*. New York: St. Martin's, 1991; 148 p.

Halecki, O. *A History of Poland*. New York: Dorset Press, 1992; 472 p.

Karpinski, Jakub. *Countdown: The Polish Upheavals of 1956, 1970, 1976, 1980*. trans. by Olaga Amsterdamska Gene M. Moore. New York: Karz–Cohl, 1982; 214 p.

Kurski, Jaroslaw. *Lech Walesa: Democrat or Dictator?*. Boulder, CO: Westview Press, 1993; 178 p (pb).

Nagengast, Carole. *Reluctant Socialists, Rural Entrepreneurs: Class, Culture, and the Polish State*. Boulder, CO: Westview Press, 1993; 239 p. (pb).

## ROMANIA

Braun, Aurel. *Romanian Foreign Policy Since 1965*. New York: Praeger, 1978; 218 p.

Graham, Lawrence S. *Romania: A Developing Socialist State*. Boulder, Colo.: Westview Press, 1982; 136 p.

King, Robert R. *History of the Romanian Communist Party*. Stanford, Cal.: Hoover Institution Press, 1980; 190 p.

Nelson, Daniel N. (ed.). *Romania in the 1980s*. Boul 313 p.

Tsantis, Andreas C. and Roy Pepper. *Romania, the Industrialization of an Agrarian Economy Under Socialist Planning*. Washington, D.C.: World Bank, 1979; 707 p.

## EX–YUGOSLAVIA

Borowiec, Andrew. *Yugoslavia After Tito*. New York: Praeger, 1977; 177 p.

Dunn, William N. Josip Obradovic. *Workers' Self–Management and Organizational Power in Yugoslavia*. Pittsburgh: Univ. of Pittsburgh Press, 1978; 448 p.

Cohen, Lenard J. *Broken Bonds: The Disintegration of Yugoslavia*. (2nd ed); Boulder, CO: Westview Press, 1995; 440 p. (pb).

Friedman, Francine. *The Bosnian Muslims*. Boulder, CO: Westview Press, 1995; 400 p. (pb).

Glenny, Misha. *The Fall of Yugoslavia: The Third Balkan War*. New York: Penguin Books USA, Inc., 1992; 194 p. (pb).

Poulton, Hugh. *Who are the Macedonians?*. Bloomington: Indiana University Press, 1994; 256 p.

Ramet, Sabrina P. *Nationalism and Federalism in Yugoslavia, 1962–1991*. Bloomington: Indiana University Press, 1992; 368 p. (pb).

Shrenk, Martin *et al*. *Yugoslavia: Self Management Socialism and the Challenges of Development*. Baltimore: Johns Hopkins University Press, 1979; 329 p.

Sher, Gerson S. *Praxis: Marxism Criticism and Dissent in Socialist Yugoslavia*. Bloomington, Ind.: Indiana Univ. Press, 1977; 360 p.

Sirc, Ljubo. *The Yugoslav Economy Under Self–Management*. New York: St. Martin's Press, 1979; 270 p.

Stankovic, Slobodan. *The End of the Tito Era*. Stanford: Hoover Institution Press, 1981; 168p.